Perspectives on American Government
2nd Edition

The second edition of this much-admired book offers an accessible and coherent selection of readings illustrating for students the depth and contours of how American politics has developed over time. Grounded in foundational debates, classic political science scholarship, and the best contemporary analysis of American political development, this reader invites students to probe the historical dynamics that brought the United States to where it is today and how those dynamics are likely to affect its future course. The second edition features almost three dozen new or replaced readings, revised introductions to the selections, and an expanded section on civil rights and liberties.

Jillson and Robertson have carefully edited each selection to ensure readability and fidelity to the original arguments. Their insightful editorial introductions frame the context in which these topics are studied and understood. Several key pedagogical tools help students along the way:

- An introductory essay on American political development
- Chapter introductions to provide necessary context
- Head notes introducing each reading
- Questions for Discussion and Further Reading lists at the end of each chapter.

Cal Jillson is Professor of Political Science at Southern Methodist University. He is a frequent commentator on domestic and international politics for local, national, and international media.

David Brian Robertson is Professor of Political Science and Fellow in the Public Policy Research Center at the University of Missouri–St. Louis. He is Associate Editor of the *Journal of Policy History* and he edits *CLIO*, the newsletter of the Politics and History section of the American Political Science Association. Robertson has received numerous awards for Teaching Excellence.

Perspectives on American Government

Readings in Political Development and Institutional Change

2ND EDITION

EDITED BY Cal Jillson and David Brian Robertson

Routledge
Taylor & Francis Group

NEW YORK AND LONDON

This edition published 2014
by Routledge
711 Third Avenue, New York, NY 10017

and by Routledge
2 Park Square, Milton Park, Abingdon, Oxon OX14 4RN

Routledge is an imprint of the Taylor & Francis Group, an informa business

First edition published 2009 by Routledge

Library of Congress Cataloging in Publication Data
Perspectives on American government: readings in political development and institutional change
/ edited by Cal Jillson and David Brian Robertson.
— Second edition.
    pages cm
  1. United States—Politics and government.   I. Jillson, Calvin c., 1949-
  II. Robertson, David.
  JK21. P474 2013
  320. 973—dc23

                   2013033003

ISBN: 978–0–415–73522–3 (pbk)

Typeset in Minion by
Swales & Willis Ltd, Exeter, Devon, UK

Printed and bound in the United States of America by Sheridan Books, Inc. (a Sheridan Group Company).

To our teachers and our students

"We must not always exhaust a subject, so as to leave no work at all for the reader. My business is not to make people read, but to make them think."

Montesquieu, *The Spirit of the Laws*, 1748, Bk XI: 20

Brief Contents

Full Contents

15   *Government, the Economy, and Domestic Policy*   492

16   *America's Place in a Dangerous World*   524

Acknowledgments

One of the great joys near the end of a book project is thinking back on all of the people who helped, in their various ways, to move the project along. But producing a "reader" is a special kind of book project and the list of persons deserving gratitude and thanks extends broadly. The selections in a reader are explicitly meant to be the best of their kind, in this case, the most formative and insightful writings that exist on American political development. Making these selections gave us an opportunity to reassess and more fully appreciate the writing that has shaped all our work and thinking for more than thirty years. We also come away from this work impressed with the creativity and insight of our colleagues and confident in the health and vibrancy of our field—the study of American politics and American Political Development (APD).

More practically, the Routledge team has been ever faithful to this project. Michael Kerns saw the opportunity for a reader with an APD focus and brought us together around the idea. Darcy Bullock has been the editorial assistant responsible to see that the project remains on track. Her gentle insistence has kept two easily distracted academics on task and on time.

Our families deserve and have our gratitude for their patience and support. Time spent here came at the sacrifice of other opportunities, some of which were ranked higher by other principals. We also want to thank colleagues, faculty and staff, at Southern Methodist University and the University of Missouri, St Louis, for their advice and support. At SMU, Dennis Ippolito, Dennis Simon, Joe Kobylka, Matt Wilson, Jimmeca Dorsey and Chris Carberry deserve particular thanks. At the UMSL, we thank Ray Deppen, Ben Chambers, David Kimball, Bryan Fogarty, Lana Vierdag, Raphael Hopkins and the Faculty Resource Center staff.

Several of our colleagues reviewed the proposal and an earlier draft of the selection of readings. For their constructive and helpful suggestions, we would like to thank: Michael K. Baranowski, Northern Kentucky University; Kimberley S. Johnson, Barnard College; Joel Lefkowitz, State University of New York at New Paltz; Justin Phillips, Columbia University; David W. Rohde, Duke University; Ronald P. Seyb, Skidmore College; Christopher M. Stadler, Wheeling Jesuit University; Richard Valelly, Swarthmore College; and McGee Young, Marquette University.

Introduction

How does American government work, and why does it work the way it does? By understanding the way people have answered these questions in the past and present, we can better understand the enduring puzzles of the American political system—and we can use it more effectively in the future. More than ever, we need to step back and understand how our government and politics have developed over time, to help us make sense of the dramatic political, economic, and social changes that now are challenging American democracy. Americans count on their national government to keep the nation prosperous, to protect it against enemies, to ensure their freedoms, to guarantee that they are treated fairly, and to make sure that they have access to roads, parks, education, and other important public services. Government touches our lives in many more ways than we think. Yet American government often seems mysterious and distant.

Citizens, leaders, scholars, and thoughtful observers have studied the puzzles of American government for over two centuries because they have dealt with many of the problems that we face today. By drawing on the lessons they draw from the past, we can better appreciate the way the president, federalism, the two-party system, and other institutions affect our lives now. More important, with historical perspective we can better understand those features of our government that are evolving, such as civil liberties and rights, the impact of the media, economic management, and foreign policy. It is impossible to appreciate these features merely by taking a snapshot of current elections, institutions or public policies. American government is best understood as a "movie" still in progress, rather than a snapshot frozen in time. To truly understand current trends, we must understand the way earlier scenes in the movie of American government helped set up the scenes we see today, and are likely to see tomorrow. We must understand the development of American government over long periods of time.

For over three decades, scholars in the field of American Political Development, or APD, have studied the evolution of American government to find better answers to these enduring questions. These scholars focus on the ways that political culture, ideology, governing bodies, and institutions that link citizens and government (such as political parties, interest groups, and the media) have shaped political conflict and government action over decades. American Political Development emphasizes that the decisions of the past laid down paths that led us to the political choices we face today. Understanding these paths helps us approach the puzzles of government with more knowledge and wisdom.

The field of American Political Development is rooted in a very broad and realistic view of government as it evolves over time. Often, the APD approach begins by asking, what has American government had in common with other governments, in other places and times? How and why does American government differ from these other governments? Most APD scholars begin with the medieval idea of "the state" rather than "government" to broaden their grasp of the problems and basic tasks that all governments confront. The word "state" refers to an organization that tries to control a territory and a people.[1] The definition of the state includes "continuous administrative, legal, bureaucratic and coercive systems," that is, offices and legal procedures that last beyond one or two national leaders.[2] Like every other government in history, American government tries to keep order within the nation, and to defend its citizens from foreign threats. To accomplish this task, American government has developed such enduring institutions as an army and navy, the U.S. Department of Justice, the Border Patrol, the Internal Revenue Service, state and local police forces, an extensive system of courts, and a network of prisons. Like other governments, American government tries to maintain the loyalty of its citizens and its legitimacy, that is, the willingness of powerful groups and the population as a whole to obey its rules. To accomplish this task, American government enables citizens to influence government officials (most notably, through elections) and provides public policies that serve many interests. Examples of such policies include public education, highways, the national parks, small business loans, the Social Security program, and the National Weather Service.

By starting with the state, APD scholars can pose important questions about American government that often are overlooked by those who focus only on current political events. Instead of analyzing the most recent election, APD scholars examine the way elections have evolved up to now, and how the recent presidential elections resemble and differ from other elections in American history. Understanding these similarities and differences helps us see more clearly whether or not the last election marks a fundamental turning point in American politics. Instead of asking why Congress passed a recent law, APD scholars ask how the new policy continues and breaks with the policy traditions of the past, and what these patterns are likely to produce in the future.

These questions of political continuity and change are at the heart of the concept of "political development," a term defined by political scientists Karen Orren and Stephen Skowronek as "a durable shift in governing authority." These authors define "governing authority," in turn, as "the exercise of control over persons or things that is designated and enforceable by the state."[3] Political development, then, examines the use and control of government authority. This approach frames the key questions for understanding American government: How has the state exercised control in the past, and how does it exercise control now? How has the state enforced its will in the past, and how does it enforce it now? How has the American state changed over time, and what features of the state have stayed the same? These questions invite the study of "state-building," or the growth and decline of state powers, such as the power to tax and to redistribute resources, or the power to police and regulate behavior.

The APD approach offers three clear advantages to anyone who wants to understand American politics. First, APD examines the changing capacity of the state to accomplish tasks, the limits on its powers to succeed, and the reasons for those limits. For example, every government must find a way to levy and collect taxes without inciting citizens to revolt or to evade taxes on a massive scale. In 1787, the American national government had almost no capacity to collect the revenues it needed to pay its debts, provide for national security, and promote the nation's growth. Massachusetts faced an armed revolt sparked, in part, by its tax policies. Since the Founding, the United States has developed an extraordinarily efficient system of levying and collecting taxes. In 2014, the federal government alone is expected to collect over three trillion dollars in revenue. In its taxes, as in its military power, economic management, social welfare programs, and environmental management, the capacity of American government is continuing to develop, even while this evolving capacity triggers new political controversies.

Second, APD examines changes within government, such as the evolution of the powers of individual political institutions, the evolution of public policy, and the development of political influence. The Constitution's framers insisted on dividing the three basic powers of government—to make laws (the legislative power), to enforce laws (the executive power), and to settle disputes about laws (the judicial power)—by delegating legislation to the Congress, the executive power to the president and administrators, and judicial responsibility to the courts. Because the framers meant these institutions to be durable, they made the Constitution difficult to change. The U.S. Congress, for example, still remains divided into a House of Representatives in which each state is represented according to its population size, and a Senate in which each state has two members regardless of the state's size. But ever since the nation's founding, national government institutions have battled each other for power, so that the balance of power in American government is constantly evolving. Congress dominated national policy making for most of the nineteenth century, for example, but presidential power has grown substantially over the last hundred years. The Supreme Court's influence has grown because it has enlarged its power to invalidate laws. This ebb and flow of institutional power affects the ability of government to accomplish its tasks as well as the outcomes of political struggles.

A third advantage of APD is its attention to the state's evolving effect on American society, especially on the distribution of power and wealth, two vital political battlegrounds in every nation. For example, the U.S. government initially protected slave owners' rights. Although the United States banned slavery in the 1860s, it permitted southern states to enforce laws segregating the races and allowing the economic exploitation of African Americans. When the national government eliminated legal segregation by protecting civil rights and voting rights in the 1960s, it set in motion a series of revolutionary changes in American society that continue to echo through the nation. The impact of this history has profound consequences now. Blocked from building savings and property ownership over generations, most African Americans found it much more difficult to build the wealth that white families could build; today, the median wealth of white families is twenty times larger than the median wealth of African American families.[4] Women initially were excluded from voting and many other legal privileges, but women successfully struggled to eliminate these inequities over the course of the twentieth century.[5] Still, women lag men in filling important public offices; women constituted fewer than one in five legislators in the 113th U.S. Congress (2013–2014). The struggle for women's rights, in turn, helped place many new issues on the government agenda. One of these issues, the legal right to abortion, became a bitterly divisive issue in American politics. Another issue, the debate over expanding civil rights protections to homosexuals, will generate strong passions long into the future.

Government institutions, rules, and policies, then, can give some people advantages or disadvantages that last for generations. We can only appreciate these effects fully by looking at them over time. In the nineteenth century, the U.S. government nurtured capitalism and helped the nation grow into an industrial powerhouse by assisting the expansion of railroads and protecting manufacturers from foreign competition. Industrial growth helped create the nation's great cities, like New York, Chicago, and Los Angeles. Government policies beginning in the 1930s favored the highways and home ownership policies that have expanded American suburbs, which now house half of the American people. The American state, then, has deeply changed American society and profoundly affected every person's prospects in life.

Because government institutions resist change and people adapt to them over time, the longer these institutions are in place, the more they shape the development of government, politics, and public policy. Political scientist Paul Pierson describes this process as "path dependence," a tendency for an established way of doing things to become self-reinforcing for most people.[6] The tendency for a technique to become accepted routine is common in everyday life, such as computer technology. For example, QWERTY keyboards (laid out with the "Q" key as the upper left hand letter, "W" as the next letter, and so on) are familiar in every office and at every college library terminal. Though the QWERTY computer keyboard was invented for typewriters in the 1870s, it is still widely used for two reasons. First, most people have come to expect these keyboards and have learned to use them. Most computer users would rather continue using these keyboards than learn new ones, even if the new systems are potentially more efficient, because it takes so much time and effort to relearn typing. Second, because so many people use these systems, it is easy to use them in any office, and would be very difficult to coordinate activity if offices used different keyboards. For similar reasons, Microsoft Windows applications dominate computer software because so many people have become accustomed to these programs. These examples demonstrate that techniques, once put in place, often become taken for granted because they provide many advantages that reinforce themselves over time, and because it would be much more costly to change than to stay the same. Staying the same is the path of least resistance.

Government laws and institutions, like these technologies, become self-reinforcing because the more people become accustomed to them, the more people are likely to resist major changes in them. Washington, D.C. may not be the ideal location for the nation's capital, but because it was located on the Potomac two centuries ago, and so much has been invested in building the government at that location, it would be far too costly to relocate it anywhere else. Members of Congress have learned to win reelection under current rules, by delivering services to constituents, advertising themselves, taking positions that appeal to their constituents, and using congressional committees and staff to position themselves favorably with the voters. Naturally, members of Congress would prefer to continue enjoying these advantages, so they resist reforms that would undermine them. Interest groups have laboriously built mechanisms to influence the current policy process, such as hiring influential former members of Congress, setting up special political action committees, and developing the ability to mobilize hundreds of constituents of any member of Congress. Lawyers have become accustomed to dealing with the routines of courts. Regulatory agencies and businesses have become accustomed to current economic regulations. Food stamp recipients, grocery stores, and social welfare administrators have become accustomed to arrangements for food stamps (now known as the Supplemental Nutrition Assistance Program). Developers, builders, county land use authorities, sewer districts, and others have become accustomed to state and local rules for building suburban developments.

All of these individuals and groups have a reason to oppose changes in existing arrangements, because changes would force them to invest time and money into learning a different system, and they could not be sure that a different set of rules would be as advantageous as the current set. Those who are comfortable with existing laws usually will fight against changes in lobbying or campaign finance laws. This resistance, in turn, continues to make it very difficult to implement far-reaching political reforms or policy changes. For example, the institutions that deliver American health care—insurance companies, doctors and specialists, Health Maintenance Organizations, hospitals, pharmaceutical firms, and private companies that depend on the current system—consistently have tried to obstruct changes in the health care system that threaten to raise their costs and create more uncertainty for them.[7]

Even when a large majority of Americans demand change, government usually responds slowly because it is designed to resist big, rapid changes. Government institutions are built to be stable despite many intense but momentary political controversies, and laws are written to bind current citizens and future citizens. Nothing better illustrates the impact of change-resistant institutions and rules than the U.S. Constitution. The Constitution's framers intentionally made it difficult to change the Constitution in the future. An amendment can only receive formal consideration if it receives support from an extraordinarily large majority of two-thirds of each house of Congress, or two-thirds of the states. Furthermore, no amendment can go into effect unless it has support of an even larger majority of three-quarters of the states. It is no wonder that the nation has enacted only twenty-seven Constitutional amendments since 1789, even though more than 10,000 constitutional amendments have been introduced in Congress. The Electoral College has been a particularly controversial provision of the Constitution. Majorities of Democrats, Republicans, and independents express support for electing the president by direct popular vote, rather than through the Electoral College.[8] Since the Constitution took effect, there have been over 700 proposals made to abolish or change the Electoral College, more than any other reform.[9] Yet only two constitutional amendments directly have touched on the Electoral College process, and neither altered the procedure for choosing the president. The Twelfth Amendment (1804) dealt only with the procedure for choosing the vice-president, and the Twenty-Third Amendment (1961) allowed the District of Columbia to cast at least three electoral votes.

Despite the built-in resistance to change in American institutions, change occurs regularly. Most changes come in small increments, often unnoticed by the general public, because such small changes are easier to achieve than massive ones. Due to path dependence, these incremental changes can gradually build up over time and become a major part of American life. In the decades after 1935, when the Social Security Act initially was adopted, Congress and the president slowly added coverage and benefits, including insurance for disability and a health care program for the elderly (Medicare).[10] Other changes come in fits and starts. The American military has tended to grow during urgent national security crises, and retract somewhat afterwards. Some institutions can just evolve out of existence, such as the Whig Party or several of the anti-Depression programs of the 1930s. Others may evolve and adapt to new circumstances. After achieving its goal of landing a man on the moon, the National Aeronautics and Space Agency developed a new space shuttle mission. In many cases, new tasks are layered on top of older ones. Reforms of the military and railroad regulation in the twentieth century patched over institutions built over the previous hundred years.[11] Even though the use of combat airplanes in World War II produced a new government institution, the U.S. Air Force, the U.S. Army, Navy, and Marines successfully insisted that they, too, required their own air combat units, and they have these units today.

More spectacular and far-reaching changes in American politics are uncommon, but when they happen, these critical moments change the course of American history. The civil rights revolution shows how a critical crossroads can change American life. For many decades after the 1870s, legal segregation of the races was deeply entrenched in the southern states. But new circumstances gradually built an irresistible force against these "Jim Crow" laws and voting restrictions. New ideas about American democracy and justice, articulated by leaders like Martin Luther King, Jr, helped convince many Americans that the nation's status as the world's leading democracy required it to ensure that African Americans enjoyed the full freedom that other Americans took for granted. Through highly publicized marches, boycotts, sit-ins, and "freedom rides" on segregated buses, the civil rights movement brought many Americans into the battle against segregation, and many more to the realization that segregation had to end. Evolving ideas among political party leaders, key members of Congress, in the federal courts and in the White House brought the battle to end segregation to the national government's agenda and then paved the way for its success.[12]

Some of the most fascinating large-scale developments in American politics involve changes in the balance of power between the major political parties and emergence of a new "party era." These durable, far-reaching shifts seem to occur every few decades in American history. A new party era is marked by growing difficulties for whichever political party tends to dominate elections, followed by an election that sweeps a new president and new members of Congress into office, and by major changes in national policy shifts in the party loyalty of groups of voters.[13] For over fifty years, political scientists have identified the presidential elections of 1800, 1828, 1860, 1896, and 1932 as key moments that have shifted the course of American politics.

The Civil War, for example, reshaped American politics. In the 1860 presidential election, the Democratic Party shattered over the intractable issue of slavery, and the new Republican Party squeezed out a victory for its presidential candidate, Abraham Lincoln. The 1860 election gave the Republicans control of Congress as well as the White House, and when the Southern states seceded, even more Democrats left Congress and the Republican majority strengthened further. Empowered by their dominance of national government, the Republicans conducted a war against the Confederate states, pressed for popular laws such as the Homestead Act, the construction of a transcontinental railroad, and support for public higher education in the states. As Richard Bensel shows, the Republican Congresses after the Civil War created a set of policies that helped build the nation's economy, including a tariff that generated enormous money for the federal treasury and a large, politically popular program of pensions for veterans of the Union Army. Republican presidents (along with the only Democrat elected president in these years, Grover Cleveland) managed the nation's money supply conservatively to attract foreign investment, and federal courts gradually issued rulings that imposed national rules beneficial to the national expansion of the capitalist economy. These years laid the foundation for American industrialization, but they also produced new political conflicts between American regions, between rural and urban residents, and between workers and employers.[14] By the end of the nineteenth century, these growing conflicts helped bring about a new party era. Similarly, the bitter partisan polarization of our own time can only be understood as the product of decades of change in the coalitions supporting the Republican and Democratic parties.

Health care and immigration, two contentious issues in today's highly polarized politics, show how APD helps us better understand change and continuity in politics. A long chain of events that developed over many decades shaped the 2010 Affordable Care Act ("Obamacare") and its impact on Americans. As early as the 1910s, efforts to establish public health insurance in a few American states faltered when the American Medical Association (AMA) emerged as a strong interest group to help defeat them. Strong opposition from the AMA and other groups persuaded federal policy makers to drop public health insurance from the Social Security Act of 1935 and sank mandatory national health insurance proposals in the late 1940s. Meanwhile, new organizations filled the American political system with a wide variety of potent organizations interested in health care. For example, a change in federal income tax laws in the 1950s promoted the growth of employer-provided health insurance and fostered a thriving private health insurance industry that strengthened opposition to public health insurance. In 1965, public health insurance was enacted, but only for groups who were not in the workforce: elderly retirees (who received Medicare) and the poor (who received Medicaid). By the 1970s, a huge constellation of powerful public and private interests—including private employers, health insurers, hospitals, pharmaceutical and health supply companies, doctors, state and local officials, and an array of federal bureaus— created a political minefield for proposals to expand public health insurance beyond the elderly and the poor. From the 1970s through the 1990s, repeated efforts to expand public health insurance to the millions of Americans who lacked health security foundered when they ran up against the politically potent network of private health insurance interests. By 2010, one out of six Americans—just under fifty million in all—lacked health insurance, and only about 55 percent of employers offered health insurance to their employees. Yet health care costs in the

United States were much higher than those in comparable nations. The Obama administration, determined to expand coverage and reduce costs and working with Democratic majorities in Congress, helped construct a reform plan that carefully enlisted or worked around many of the powerful institutions with a stake in health care. The Affordable Care Act expanded the number of Americans with access to health insurance by enlarging state-run Medicaid eligibility, by providing subsidies to employers and citizens to meet mandates for purchasing private insurance, and by creating health insurance exchanges that would allow private insurance companies to compete to provide insurance to the uninsured.

Immigration helps define what it means to be an American. Today, Americans inherit a long history of conflict over what kinds of people immigrate into the United States and layers of policies that answered that question in different ways. The United States welcomed immigrants during its first century because it had more land than people to work it. The Constitution's Fourteenth Amendment (1868) made the lasting promise that a child born in the United States, even to immigrant parents, would be an American citizen. But as the sources of immigration changed, U.S. policies limited immigration. Congress began to restrict Chinese immigration in 1882. After hundreds of thousands of immigrants from Southern and Eastern Europe poured into the country around the turn of the century, the government further tightened immigration. From the 1920s to the 1960s, the United States set quotas on immigrants from individual nations (these rules favored northern European nations and barred immigrants from Asia).

By the late 1940s, new conditions produced new demands to ban Communist immigrants and to permit more political refugees, foreign relatives of American citizens, and skilled workers to enter the country. A 1952 law layered on top of the existing immigration laws lifted quotas for immigrants with needed skills and relatives of U.S. citizens, but banned political subversives (Communists), criminals, and those perceived as immoral. In 1965, Congress abolished country quotas (replacing them with caps on overall immigration from a nation) and established preferences for refugees, family members, and those with needed skills. These changes allowed more Africans, Asians, and Latin Americans to immigrate. As more workers without documents came into the country, a 1986 law strengthened the enforcement of immigration laws and allowed those who had established long-term residency in the country to become citizens. But a historic tide of immigration from Mexico and parts of Central and South America swelled both the legal and the undocumented immigration population in the 1990s and early 2000s. Debates about immigration in 2014 are the legacy of these layered policies. The flashpoints of policy today are familiar in American immigration history: border enforcement, the status and educational opportunities of children of immigrant families, the need for workers, justice toward immigrants—and, above all, the identity of the American nation.

Like other policy areas, health care and immigration policy build on a foundation of institutions and layered changes that collide with the controversies of the moment. Path dependence shapes our efforts to change the nation's course. We know this fact instinctively because our own lives, and those of everyone we know, are path dependent. After all, to better understand our friends, we learn about the way they grew up, the places they have lived, and the experiences that shaped their lives. Similarly, APD examines the way American government has grown and the experiences that made it what it is today. Understanding a subject as broad as American government requires us to understand how it has come to work the way it does; only then can we see how it is adapting in the present and will adapt in the future. We cannot appreciate Barack Obama's speeches and his achievement without understanding the history of race relations and the civil rights movement in the United States. We cannot appreciate the emergence of the Tea Party without understanding the qualities of a past America that its adherents want to restore.

The American Political Development approach, then, allows us to frame better questions and develop better answers to the mysteries of American government and politics. The enduring questions about government remain. Who should be included in American society? What does it mean to be an American? How do we ensure that a democracy produces good public policy? How do you balance economic growth with democracy? How much should we respect the original ideas behind the Constitution, and how much do we need to adapt constitutional principles to the needs of the twenty-first century? How much should we defer to experts and scientists in making public policy and public decisions? How do we ensure justice without restricting freedom? How do we ensure as much freedom as possible without endangering our security? How large a military can our democracy and our national budget bear?

Three central questions guide our selection of readings to help explain the development of American politics and government.

1. Why do Americans have the governing **institutions and public policies** they have? What problems did these institutions aim to address, and how did these institutions address them?
2. What durable **changes** have occurred in these governing institutions and public policies? What kinds of things cause major changes in the American political system?
3. How do these changes in durable government institutions and policies affect American politics **today**?

To begin to answer such questions, this book presents readings that trace the development of American politics over time. We chose these readings because they help understand how political ideas, political institutions, and public policy have developed over time. In this book, each chapter includes important readings from original sources (such as the Constitutional Convention of 1787, the *Federalist*, George Washington's Farewell Address, and Abraham Lincoln's writings), from classic writings of past observers of American politics (such as Alexis de Tocqueville, V.O. Key, and E.E. Schattschneider), and contemporary analysis from APD scholars and others.

The first three chapters explore the basic principles of American politics, the impact of these principles in the American Revolution and the Constitution, and the impact of the Constitution, particularly federalism, on the development of American government and politics. The five following chapters deal with the way Americans think about their government and the way those opinions are formed, the way the mass media has developed and interacted with government, the development of organizations of citizens through social movements and interest groups, the formation of political parties devoted to contesting elections and winning public offices, and the evolving processes of voting, campaigns, and elections. The next four chapters discuss the development of the four principal institutions of national government: Congress, the Presidency, the bureaucracy, and the courts. The final four chapters deal with the development of government action and public policy: civil rights; civil liberties; economic and social welfare management; and foreign and defense policy.

The past is ever present in our politics. Our national buildings intentionally remind us of America's debt to the Greek and Roman republics. British and Latin words abound in our laws and public institutions. Monuments to past wars are common in cities and small towns, where silent cannons often are displayed on courthouse lawns. Moreover, the past matters to us now. As President Barack Obama said when speaking to Congress about the nation's economic problems in the first month of his presidency, he explained that "it is only by understanding how we arrived at this moment that we'll be able to lift ourselves out of this predicament."[15]

Notes

1. Theda Skocpol, *States and Social Revolutions: A Comparative Analysis of France, Russia and China* (Cambridge and New York, 1979), 31.
2. Alfred Stepan quoted in Theda Skocpol, "Bringing the State Back In," in Peter Evans, Theda Skocpol, and Dietrich Rueschemeyer, eds., *Bringing the State Back In* (Cambridge and New York: Cambridge University Press, 1985), 7.
3. Karen Orren and Stephen Skowronek, *The Search for American Political Development* (Cambridge and New York: Cambridge University Press, 2004), 123.
4. Rakesh Kochhar, Richard Fry and Paul Taylor, "Twenty-to-One: Wealth Gaps Rise to Record Highs Between Whites, Blacks and Hispanics," Pew Research Center, July 26, 2011, http://www.pewsocialtrends.org/files/2011/07/SDT-Wealth-Report_7-26-11_FINAL.pdf (accessed April 23, 2013).
5. Gretchen Ritter, *The Constitution as Social Design: Gender and Civic Membership in the American Constitutional Order* (Stanford, CA: Stanford University Press, 2006); Paula Baker, "The Domestication of Politics: Women and American Political Society, 1780–1920," *American Historical Review* 89 (1984), 620–664; Jane Mansbridge, *Why We Lost the ERA* (Chicago: University of Chicago Press, 1985).
6. Paul Pierson, *Politics in Time: History, Institutions, and Social Analysis* (Princeton, NJ: Princeton University Press, 2004), 17–53.
7. Jacob S. Hacker, *The Road to Nowhere: The Genesis of President Clinton's Plan for Health Security* (Princeton, NJ: Princeton University Press, 1997).
8. National Popular Vote, "The Washington Post-Kaiser Family Foundation-Harvard University: Survey of Political Independents," http://www.nationalpopularvote.com/resources/Wash-Post-Kaiser-Harvard-June-2007.pdf (accessed December 22, 2008).
9. U.S. National Archives, "Frequently Asked Questions" about the Electoral College, http://www.archives.gov/federal-register/electoral-college/faq.html#reforms (accessed November 26, 2013).
10. Martha Derthick, *Policymaking for Social Security* (Washington, DC: Brookings Institution, 1979).

11. Stephen Skowronek, *Building a New American State: The Expansion of National Administrative Capacities, 1877–1920* (Cambridge and New York: Cambridge University Press, 1982).

12. Robert C. Lieberman, "Ideas, Institutions, and Political Order: Explaining Political Change," *American Political Science Review* 96 (2002), 697–712.

13. V.O. Key, Jr, "A Theory of Critical Elections," *Journal of Politics* 17 (1955), 3–18; Walter Dean Burnham, *Critical Elections and the Mainsprings of American Politics* (New York: W.W. Norton, 1970); David Brady, *Critical Elections and Congressional Policy Making* (Stanford, CA: Stanford University Press, 1988); David R. Mayhew, *Electoral Realignments: A Critique of an American Genre* (New Haven, CT: Yale University Press, 2002).

14. Richard Franklin Bensel, *The Political Economy of American Industrialization, 1877–1900* (Cambridge and New York: Cambridge University Press, 2000).

15. "Remarks of President Barack Obama—As Prepared for Delivery Address to Joint Session of Congress," Tuesday, February 24th, 2009, http://www.whitehouse.gov/the_press_office/Remarks-of-President-Barack-Obama-Address-to-Joint-Session-of-Congress/ (accessed February 26, 2009).

1

The Origins of American Political Principles

Introduction

American Political Development (APD) is the study of how American political ideas, institutions, and processes have changed over time. APD also asks what forces and dynamics have driven these changes and what impact they have had on the pattern and substance of life in America. In Chapter 1, we ask what ideas lay at the foundation of American public life? What ideas did the first generations of Americans draw upon as they thought about how to organize political, economic, and social life in the new world? What ideas were most influential during the colonial generations and as the Founding generation chose revolution and then moved to build and rebuild institutions for a newly free nation? And how have these ideas influenced later generations of Americans as they thought about the meaning of their country and its place in the world.

These are not easy questions to answer either for students or their teachers. But one of the first lessons taught to students of APD is to treat history with care and respect. In the readings in this and later chapters it will become evident that words we think we know, liberal and republican, for example, did not mean the same thing in the seventeenth and eighteenth centuries as they do today. In these readings, if you take the time to figure out what earlier generations meant by the word liberal, for example, you will not only avoid drawing the wrong lessons from what they said but will improve your chances of drawing useful lessons from them.

Most colonial Americans, though not black slaves, were Europeans. They left European societies that were hierarchical in every respect. They were governed by monarchs and landed nobles. Monarchs determined the religion of their subjects and whether and how much religious space was available to dissidents. Oftentimes, university admissions, professional status, and political office depended upon one's class and religious background.

Colonists brought to America both the social, political, and economic assumptions of their native countries and grievances about how those societies worked. Especially in the early days, immigrants adopted structures with which they were comfortable, adjusted to resolve the complaints they had had at home. Our first selection, John Winthrop's "A Model of Christian Charity," is a wonderful example of early colonists trying to balance their traditional hierarchical assumptions with their dissident religious, political, and social ideas and their new wilderness surroundings.

Large numbers of English Puritans began arriving in the Massachusetts Bay colony in 1630. John Winthrop, the Puritan's political leader, delivered a speech, actually a lay-sermon, before the Puritans even stepped ashore. Winthrop reminded his co-religionists and fellow immigrants that to survive as individuals and thrive as a colony they would have to set aside their individual goals and interests and put the goals and interests of the community first. Winthrop sought to use their strong religious beliefs, the covenant they had made with God—bring us safely across the sea and we will live in the light of your word—to bind them together in communal brotherhood. But as the Puritan community grew, became more secure, and ultimately thrived, community ties loosened in favor of the individual goals, interests, and aspirations of each member of the community. Every society, new and old, must balance the needs of the community and the interests of its individual members.

Over the course of the 1600s, both in England and in her American colonies, the forces of individualism pulled at the ties of centralization and community. John Locke's famous *Second Treatise of Government* (1690) highlights the rise of individualist or liberal ideas. John Locke's social contract theory, presented in our second selection, is a philosophical or rationalist description of how free men might leave the dangers and uncertainties of the state of nature by adopting limited government. Individuals would, by their own consent, give up some of their natural rights and liberties to better secure the rest. Government would provide sensible laws, executive enforcement, and judicial resolution of disputes.

The principles of Lockean liberalism deeply influenced the Founding generation, but they were also impressed by a secularized version of Winthrop's communitarian principles. Charles Secondat, the Baron de Montesquieu, wrote *The Spirit of the Laws* (1748) to argue that constitutions and laws had to fit the people they were to govern. Like Locke, Montesquieu began from the premise that God provided a Law of Nature to guide human societies. Both argued that men were not close students of the natural law and that individual self-interest led to clashes between men in the absence of government. Locke reasoned philosophically from individual rights to limited government by consent of the governed. Montesquieu followed the path of comparative sociology by asking what nature and principles produced the world's governments. He concluded that the world's governments were republican, monarchical, or despotic. Republics, which he favored, were based on the consent and suffrage of some (aristocratic republics) or all (democratic republics) of the people. These ideals, tracing their roots back to the republicanism of ancient Rome, the civic republicanism of the Italian Renaissance, and the "country party" ideology of the English Civil Wars, focused on virtuous, patriotic citizens willing to set aside self-interest to serve the public interest and the common good.

The Founding generation was particularly attracted to Montesquieu's argument that republics, unlike monarchies and despotisms, were dependent on the virtues of the citizenry. By virtue, especially republican virtue, Montesquieu and the

Founders did not mean the polite virtues. Rather, they meant the knowledge, strength, and public-spiritedness to love and serve the broad and permanent interests of the nation, the community, and its laws. But the Founders were sobered by Montesquieu's claim that equality and frugality were necessary for a stable republic and these were only possible in a "small republic," meaning a limited geographical territory.

Alexis de Tocqueville, a minor French aristocrat, but an important scholar and social observer, visited America in the 1830s and published *Democracy in America* (1835). Tocqueville is commonly called the most astute foreign observer and social analyst of American society ever. Tocqueville wrote almost six decades after the American Revolution and 50 years after the adoption of the Constitution, so he could look back on the ideas that had shaped the new nation. Tocqueville's description of what America had become highlights the importance of religious, political, and social ideas first pointed to by Winthrop, Locke, and Montesquieu. Tocqueville was confident of the nation's future because, he contended, it had combined religion and liberty, communitarian and individualist principles, better than any previous nation in history.

But if two sets of related, but distinct, ideals—Lockean individualism and the communitarian ideals of civic republicanism—were simultaneously present, which was dominant, how did they interact, and has their relationship and interaction changed over time? Contemporary scholars have sought to answer these questions by offering numerous "conflicting" or "multiple" traditions accounts. Two of the best conclude the readings for Chapter 1.

Conflicting traditions accounts tend to see Lockean liberalism, with its focus on individualism, competition, and self-interest, as the ideology of normal American politics. This normal focus on self-interest and competition tends to devolve into corruption and, over time, a too stark differentiation of winners and losers. Then normal politics is disrupted by a spasm of revolutionary or reform politics that focus on honesty, equality, and the public good. When reform ebbs, normal politics returns. In our fifth selection, James Morone describes the impact of democratic spasms as decidedly mixed and often illusory.

Our highlight piece is Rogers Smith's modern classic, "Beyond Tocqueville, Myrdal, and Hartz: The Multiple Traditions in America." Rogers Smith adds interesting complexity to the debate over the American political culture by highlighting traditions of ascriptive hierarchy—meaning racial, ethnic, and gender discrimination—to the influences of liberalism and republicanism. Smith argues that neither liberalism nor republicanism explain the prevalence and tenacity, now more than two centuries into our national history, of white male privilege, particularly at the top of our economic and social hierarchies. American history cannot be well understood unless hierarchical assumptions, including racism and sexism, are seen as just as formative and influential as liberalism and republicanism.

1.1 John Winthrop, "A Model of Christian Charity" (1630)

John Winthrop led about 1,000 religious dissenters, called Puritans, out of England to the Massachusetts-Bay colony in 1630. Earlier dissenters had preceded them, beginning with 100 Pilgrims in 1620, but Massachusetts was still very much a wilderness in 1630. As the Puritan flotilla approached Massachusetts, Governor Winthrop wrote and delivered a lay-sermon intended to prepare his followers for the challenges they were about to face. The Puritans fled England to escape intrusive political and religious authorities, so there was a clear streak of individualism in their thinking. But they faced dangers that they could only confront together.

Winthrop sought to use the deep religious convictions of the Puritans to deliver a strong communitarian message—not only are we all in this together, we have formed a covenant with our God for this enterprise, he has fulfilled his part by bringing us here safely and now we must join together to fulfill our side of the agreement. He argued that both an explicit recognition of the merits of hierarchy and of the importance of Christian charity, assisting fellows in need, were required to assure the community's survival. Of the 1,000 who landed with or soon after Winthrop, 200 died during the first winter and another 200 returned to England in the spring, but the colony held together and, eventually, thrived.

GOD ALMIGHTY in His most holy and wise providence, hath so disposed of the condition of mankind, as in all times some must be rich, some poor, some high and eminent in power and dignity; others mean and in submission.

The Reason hereof:

1st Reason. First to hold conformity with the rest of His world, being delighted to show forth the glory of his wisdom in the variety and difference of the creatures, and the glory of His power in ordering all these differences for the preservation and good of the whole, and the glory of His greatness, that as it is the glory of princes to have many officers, so this great king will have many stewards, counting himself more honored in dispensing his gifts to man by man, than if he did it by his own immediate hands.

2nd Reason. Secondly, that He might have the more occasion to manifest the work of his Spirit: first upon the wicked in moderating and restraining them, so that the rich and mighty should not eat up the poor, nor the poor and despised rise up against and shake off their yoke. Secondly, in the regenerate, in exercising His graces in them, as in the great ones, their love, mercy, gentleness, temperance etc., and in the poor and inferior sort, their faith, patience, obedience etc.

3rd Reason. Thirdly, that every man might have need of others, and from hence they might be all knit more nearly together in the bonds of brotherly affection. From hence it appears plainly that no man is made more honorable than another or more wealthy etc., out of any particular and singular respect to himself, but for the glory of his Creator and the common good of the creature, man. Therefore God still reserves the property of these gifts to Himself as Ezek. 16:17, He there calls wealth, His gold and His silver, and Prov. 3:9, He claims their service as His due, "Honor the Lord with thy riches," etc.—All men being thus (by divine providence) ranked into two sorts, rich and poor; under the first are comprehended all such as are able to live comfortably by their own means duly improved; and all others are poor according to the former distribution.

There are two rules whereby we are to walk one towards another: Justice and Mercy. These are always distinguished in their act and in their object, yet may they both concur in the same subject in each respect; as sometimes there may be an occasion of showing mercy to a rich man in some sudden danger or distress, and also doing of mere justice to a poor man in regard of some particular contract, etc. . . .

Thirdly, the Law of Nature would give no rules for dealing with enemies, for all are to be considered as friends in the state of innocence, but the Gospel commands love to an enemy. Proof: If thine enemy hunger, feed him; "Love your enemies . . . Do good to them that hate you" (Matt. 5:44).

This law of the Gospel propounds likewise a difference of seasons and occasions. There is a time when a Christian must sell all and give to the poor, as they did in the Apostles' times. There is a time also when Christians (though they give not all yet) must give beyond their ability, as they of Macedonia (2 Cor. 8). Likewise, community of perils calls for extraordinary liberality, and so doth community in some special service for the church.

Lastly, when there is no other means whereby our Christian brother may be relieved in his distress, we must help him beyond our ability rather than tempt God in putting him upon help by miraculous or extraordinary means. This duty of mercy is exercised in the kinds: giving, lending and forgiving (*of a debt*).

Question: What rule shall a man observe in giving in respect of the measure?

Answer: If the time and occasion be ordinary he is to give out of his abundance. Let him lay aside as God hath blessed him. If the time and occasion be extraordinary, he must be ruled by them; taking this withal, that then a man cannot likely do too much, especially if he may leave himself and his family under probable means of comfortable subsistence. . . .

Objection: "The wise man's eyes are in his head," saith Solomon, "and foreseeth the plague;" therefore he must forecast and lay up against evil times when he or his may stand in need of all he can gather.

Answer: This very Argument Solomon useth to persuade to liberality (Eccle. 11), "Cast thy bread upon the waters . . . for thou knowest not what evil may come upon the land." Luke 16:9, "Make you friends of the riches of iniquity . . ." You will ask how this shall be? Very well. For first he that gives to the poor, lends to the Lord and He will repay him even in this life an hundredfold to him or his. The righteous is ever merciful and lendeth, and his seed enjoyeth the blessing; and besides we know what advantage it will be to us in the day of account when many such witnesses shall stand forth for us to witness the improvement of our talent. And I would know of those who plead so much for laying up for time to come, whether they hold that to be Gospel Matthew 6:19, "Lay not up for yourselves treasures upon earth," etc. If they acknowledge it, what extent will they allow it? If only to those primitive times, let them consider the reason whereupon our Savior grounds it. The first is that they are subject to the moth, the rust, the thief. Secondly, they will steal away the heart: "where the treasure is there will your heart be also." . . .

Question: What rule must we observe in lending?

Answer: Thou must observe whether thy brother hath present or probable or possible means of repaying thee, if there be none of those, thou must give him according to his necessity, rather then lend him as he requires (*requests*). If he hath present means of repaying thee, thou art to look at him not as an act of mercy, but by way of commerce, wherein thou art to walk by the rule of justice; but if his means of repaying thee be only probable or possible, then he is an object of thy mercy, thou must lend him, though there be danger of losing it. (Deut. 15:7–8): "If any of thy brethren be poor . . . thou shalt lend him sufficient." That men might not shift off this duty by the apparent hazard, He tells them that though the year of Jubilee were at hand (when he must remit it, if he were not able to repay it before), yet he must lend him, and that cheerfully. It may not grieve thee to give him, saith He. And because some might object, why so I should soon impoverish myself and my family, he adds, with all thy work, etc., for our Savior said (Matt. 5:42), "From him that would borrow of thee turn not away."

Question: What rule must we observe in forgiving (*a debt*)?

Answer: Whether thou didst lend by way of commerce or in mercy, if he hath nothing to pay thee, thou must forgive, (except in cause where thou hast a surety or a lawful pledge). Deut. 15:1–2—Every seventh year the creditor was to quit that which he lent to his brother if he were poor, as appears in verse 4. "Save when there shall be no poor with thee." In all these and like cases, Christ gives a general rule (Matt. 7:12), "Whatsoever ye would that men should do to you, do ye the same to them."

Question: What rule must we observe and walk by in cause of community of peril?

Answer: The same as before, but with more enlargement towards others and less respect towards ourselves and our own right. Hence it was that in the primitive Church they sold all, had all things in common, neither did any man say that which he possessed was his own. . . . "If thou pour out thy soul to the hungry, then shall thy light spring out in darkness, and the Lord shall guide thee continually, and satisfy thy soul in draught, and make fat thy bones, thou shalt be like a watered garden, and they shalt be of thee that shall build the old waste places," etc. On the contrary most heavy curses are laid upon such as are straightened towards the Lord and his people (Judg. 5:23), "Curse ye Meroshe . . . because they came not to help the Lord." He who shutteth his ears from hearing the cry of the poor, he shall cry and shall not be heard." (Matt. 25) "Go ye cursed into everlasting fire," etc. "I was hungry and ye fed me not." (2 Cor. 9:6) "He that soweth sparingly shall reap sparingly." . . .

From hence we may frame these conclusions:

First of all, true Christians are of one body in Christ (1 Cor. 12). Ye are the body of Christ and members of their part. All the parts of this body being thus united are made so contiguous in a special relation as they must needs partake of each other's strength and infirmity; joy and sorrow, weal and woe. If one member suffers, all suffer with it, if one be in honor, all rejoice with it.

Secondly, the ligaments of this body which knit together are love.

Thirdly, no body can be perfect which wants its proper ligament.

Fourthly, All the parts of this body being thus united are made so contiguous in a special relation as they must needs partake of each other's strength and infirmity, joy and sorrow, weal and woe. (1 Cor. 12:26) If one member suffers, all suffer with it; if one be in honor, all rejoice with it.

Fifthly, this sensitivity and sympathy of each other's conditions will necessarily infuse into each part a native desire and endeavor, to strengthen, defend, preserve and comfort the other. To insist a little on this conclusion being the product of all the former, the truth hereof will appear both by precept and pattern. 1 John 3:16, "We ought to lay down our lives for the brethren." Gal. 6:2, "Bear ye one another's burden's and so fulfill the law of Christ." . . .

The next consideration is how this love comes to be wrought. Adam in his first estate was a perfect model of mankind in all their generations, and in him this love was perfected in regard of the habit. But Adam, himself rent from his Creator, rent all his posterity also one from another; whence it comes that every man is born with this principle in him to love and seek himself only, and thus a man continueth till Christ comes and takes possession of the soul and infuseth another principle, love to God and our brother, and this latter having continual supply from Christ, as the head and root by which he is united, gets predominant in the soul, so by little and little expels the former. 1 John 4:7—Love cometh of God and every one that loveth is born of God, so that this love is the fruit of the new birth, and none can have it but the new creature. Now when this quality is thus formed in the souls of men, it works like the Spirit upon the dry bones. Ezek. 37:7—"Bone came to bone." It gathers together the scattered bones, or perfect old man Adam, and knits them into one body again in Christ, whereby a man is become again a living soul.

The third consideration is concerning the exercise of this love, which is twofold, inward or outward. The outward hath been handled in the former preface of this discourse. From unfolding the other we must take in our way that maxim of philosophy, "simile simili gaudet," or like will to like; for as of things which are turned with disaffection to each other, the ground of it is from a dissimilitude or arising from the contrary or different nature of the things themselves; for the ground of love is an apprehension of some resemblance in the things loved to that which affects it. This is the cause why the Lord loves the creature, so far as it hath any of his Image in it; He loves his elect because they are like Himself, He beholds them in His beloved son. . . .

It rests now to make some application of this discourse, by the present design, which gave the occasion of writing of it. Herein are four things to be propounded; first the persons, secondly, the work, thirdly the end, fourthly the means.

First, for the persons. We are a company professing ourselves fellow members of Christ, in which respect only, though we were absent from each other many miles, and had our employments as far distant, yet we ought to account ourselves knit together by this bond of love and live in the exercise of it, if we would have comfort of our being in

Christ. This was notorious in the practice of the Christians in former times; as is testified of the Waldenses, from the mouth of one of the adversaries Aeneas Sylvius "mutuo ament pene antequam norunt"—they use to love any of their own religion even before they were acquainted with them.

Secondly for the work we have in hand. It is by a mutual consent, through a special overvaluing providence and a more than an ordinary approbation of the churches of Christ, to seek out a place of cohabitation and consortship under a due form of government both civil and ecclesiastical. In such cases as this, the care of the public must oversway all private respects, by which, not only conscience, but mere civil policy, doth bind us. For it is a true rule that particular estates cannot subsist in the ruin of the public.

Thirdly, the end is to improve our lives to do more service to the Lord; the comfort and increase of the body of Christ, whereof we are members, that ourselves and posterity may be the better preserved from the common corruptions of this evil world, to serve the Lord and work out our salvation under the power and purity of his holy ordinances.

Fourthly, for the means whereby this must be effected. They are twofold, a conformity with the work and end we aim at. These we see are extraordinary, therefore we must not content ourselves with usual ordinary means. Whatsoever we did, or ought to have done, when we lived in England, the same must we do, and more also, where we go. That which the most in their churches maintain as truth in profession only, we must bring into familiar and constant practice; as in this duty of love, we must love brotherly without dissimulation, we must love one another with a pure heart fervently. We must bear one another's burdens. We must not look only on our own things, but also on the things of our brethren. . . .

Thus stands the cause between God and us. We are entered into covenant with Him for this work. We have taken out a commission. The Lord hath given us leave to draw our own articles. We have professed to enterprise these and those accounts, upon these and those ends. We have hereupon besought Him of favor and blessing. Now if the Lord shall please to hear us, and bring us in peace to the place we desire, then hath He ratified this covenant and sealed our commission, and will expect a strict performance of the articles contained in it; but if we shall neglect the observation of these articles which are the ends we have propounded, and, dissembling with our God, shall fall to embrace this present world and prosecute our carnal intentions, seeking great things for ourselves and our posterity, the Lord will surely break out in wrath against us, and be revenged of such a people, and make us know the price of the breach of such a covenant.

Now the only way to avoid this shipwreck, and to provide for our posterity, is to follow the counsel of Micah, to do justly, to love mercy, to walk humbly with our God. For this end, we must be knit together, in this work, as one man. We must entertain each other in brotherly affection. We must be willing to abridge ourselves of our superfluities, for the supply of others' necessities. We must uphold a familiar commerce together in all meekness, gentleness, patience and liberality. We must delight in each other; make others' conditions our own; rejoice together, mourn together, labor and suffer together, always having before our eyes our commission and community in the work, as members of the same body. So shall we keep the unity of the spirit in the bond of peace. The Lord will be our God, and delight to dwell among us, as His own people, and will command a blessing upon us in all our ways, so that we shall see much more of His wisdom, power, goodness and truth, than formerly we have been acquainted with. We shall find that the God of Israel is among us, when ten of us shall be able to resist a thousand of our enemies; when

He shall make us a praise and glory that men shall say of succeeding plantations, "may the Lord make it like that of New England." **For we must consider that we shall be as a city upon a hill. The eyes of all people are upon us. So that if we shall deal falsely with our God in this work we have undertaken, and so cause Him to withdraw His present help from us, we shall be made a story and a by-word through the world.** We shall open the mouths of enemies to speak evil of the ways of God, and all professors for God's sake. We shall shame the faces of many of God's worthy servants, and cause their prayers to be turned into curses upon us till we be consumed out of the good land whither we are going.

And to shut this discourse with that exhortation of Moses, that faithful servant of the Lord, in his last farewell to Israel, Deut. 30. "Beloved, there is now set before us life and death, good and evil," in that we are commanded this day to love the Lord our God, and to love one another, to walk in his ways and to keep his Commandments and his ordinance and his laws, and the articles of our Covenant with Him, that we may live and be multiplied, and that the Lord our God may bless us in the land whither we go to possess it. **But if our hearts shall turn away, so that we will not obey, but shall be seduced, and worship other Gods, our pleasure and profits, and serve them; it is propounded unto us this day, we shall surely perish out of the good land whither we pass over this vast sea to possess it.**

> **Therefore let us choose life,**
> **that we and our seed may live,**
> **by obeying His voice and cleaving to Him,**
> **for He is our life and our prosperity.**

1.2 John Locke, "Of the Beginnings of Political Societies" (1690)

John Locke (1632–1704) was an English philosopher whose work had a formative influence on the American Founders. The selections offered here are from Locke's *Second Treatise on Government* (1690), specifically chapters viii and ix. In these passages, Locke lays out an argument for the origins and purposes of free and legitimate government. This argument is generally called social contract theory. He posits that men (people today), prior to government, were free, equal, and rational. This assumption is called individualism. Locke asks why free men would create government and what kind of government they would create. He argues that they would create government to protect their persons and property. They would create limited government to provide laws, impartial judges, and dependable enforcement. Thomas Jefferson drew heavily on Lockean principles in writing the U.S. Declaration of Independence. Locke's broad political philosophy struck the Founding generation as commonsensical.

Chapter VIII

Of the Beginning of Political Societies

§ 95. Men being, as has been said, by nature all free, equal, and independent, no one can be put out of this estate, and subjected to the political power of another, without his own consent. The only way whereby any one divests himself of his natural liberty, and puts on the bonds of civil society, is by agreeing with other men to join and unite into a community, for their comfortable, safe, and peaceable living one amongst another, in a secure enjoyment of their properties, and a greater security against any that are not of it. This any number of men may do, because it injures not the freedom of the rest; they are left as they were in the liberty of the state of nature. When any number of men have so consented to make one community or government, they are thereby presently incorporated, and make one body politic, wherein the majority have a right to act and conclude the rest.

§ 96. For when any number of men have, by the consent of every individual, made a community, they have thereby made that community one body, with a power to act as one body, which is only by the will and determination of the majority; for that which acts any community being only the consent of the individuals of it, and it being necessary to that which is one body to move one way; it is necessary the body should move that way whither the greater force carries it, which is the consent of the majority: or else it is impossible it should act or continue one body, one community, which the consent of every individual that united into it agreed that it should; and so every one is bound by that consent to be concluded by the majority....

§ 119. Every man being, as has been showed, naturally free, and nothing being able to put him into subjection to any earthly power, but only his own consent; it is to be considered, what shall be understood to be a sufficient declaration of a man's consent, to make him subject to the laws of any government. There is a common distinction of an express and a tacit consent, which will concern our present case. Nobody doubts but an express consent of any man entering into any society, makes him a perfect member of that society, a subject of that government. The difficulty is, what ought to be looked upon as a tacit consent, and how far it binds, *i.e.* how far any one shall be looked on to have consented, and thereby submitted to any government, where he has made no expressions of it at all. And to this I say, that every man, that hath any possessions, or enjoyment of any part of the dominions of any government, doth thereby give his tacit consent, and is as far forth obliged to obedience to the laws of that government, during such enjoyment, as any one under it; whether this his possession be of land, to him and his heirs for ever, or a lodging only for a week; or whether it be barely travelling freely on the highway; and, in effect, it reaches as far as the very being of any one within the territories of that government....

§ 122. But submitting to the laws of any country, living quietly, and enjoying privileges and protection under them, makes not a man a member of that society: this is only a local protection and homage due to and from all those, who, not being in a state of war, come within the territories belonging to any government, to all parts whereof the force of its laws extends. But this no more makes a man a member of that society, a perpetual subject of that commonwealth, than it would make a man a subject to another, in whose family he found it convenient to abide for some time; though, whilst he continued in it, he were obliged to comply with the laws, and submit to the government he found there. And thus we see, that foreigners, by living all their lives under another government, and enjoying the privileges and protection of it, though they are bound, even in conscience, to submit to its administration, as far forth as any denison; yet do not thereby come to be subjects or members of that commonwealth. Nothing can make any man so, but his actually entering into it by positive engagement, and express promise and compact. This is that which I think concerning the beginning of political societies, and that consent which makes any one a member of any commonwealth.

Chapter IX

Of the Ends of Political Society and Government

§ 123. If man in the state of nature be so free as has been said; if he be absolute lord of his own person and possessions, equal to the greatest, and subject to nobody, why will he part with his freedom, why will he give up this empire, and subject himself to the dominion and control of any other power? To which it is obvious to answer, that though in the state of nature he hath such a right, yet the enjoyment of it is very uncertain, and constantly exposed to the invasion of others; for all being kings as much as he, every man his equal, and the greater part no strict observers of equity and justice, the enjoyment of the property he has in this state is very unsafe, very unsecure. This makes him willing to quit a condition, which, however free, is full of fears and continual dangers: and it is not without reason that he seeks out, and is willing to join in society with others, who are already united, or have a mind to unite, for the mutual preservation of their lives, liberties, and estates, which I call by the general name property.

§ 124. The great and chief end, therefore, of men's uniting into commonwealths, and putting themselves under government, is the preservation of their property. To which in the state of nature there are many things wanting.

First, There wants an established, settled, known law, received and allowed by common consent to be the standard of right and wrong, and the common measure to decide all controversies between them: for though the law of nature be plain and intelligible to all rational creatures; yet men being biassed by their interest, as well as ignorant for want of studying it, are not apt to allow of it as a law binding to them in the application of it to their particular cases.

§ 125. Secondly, In the state of nature there wants a known and indifferent judge, with authority to determine all differences according to the established law: for every one in that state being both judge and executioner of the law of nature, men being partial to themselves, passion and revenge is very apt to carry them too far, and with too much heat, in their own cases; as well as negligence and unconcernedness, to make them too remiss in other men's.

§ 126. Thirdly, In the state of nature there often wants power to back and support the sentence when right, and to give it due execution. They who by any injustice offend, will seldom fail, where they are able, by force to make good their injustice; such resistance many times makes the punishment dangerous, and frequently destructive to those who attempt it.

§ 127. Thus mankind, notwithstanding all the privileges of the state of nature, being but in an ill condition, while they remain in it, are quickly driven into society. Hence it comes to pass, that we seldom find any number of men live any time together in this state. The inconveniencies that they are therein exposed to, by the irregular and uncertain exercise of the power every man has of punishing the transgressions of others, make them take sanctuary under the established laws of government, and therein seek the preservation of their property. It is this makes them so willingly give up every one his single power of punishing, to be exercised by such alone as shall be appointed to it amongst them; and by such rules as the community, or those authorized by them to that purpose, shall agree on. And in this we have the original right of both the legislative and executive power, as well as of the governments and societies themselves.

§ 128. For in the state of nature, to omit the liberty he has of innocent delights, a man has two powers.

The first is to do whatsoever he thinks fit for the preservation of himself and others within the permission of the law of nature: by which law, common to them all, he and all the rest of mankind are one community, make up one society, distinct from all other creatures. And, were it not for the corruption and viciousness of degenerate men, there would be no need of any other; no necessity that men should separate from this great and natural community, and by positive agreements combine into smaller and divided associations.

The other power a man has in the state of nature, is the power to punish the crimes committed against that law. Both these he gives up when he joins in a private, if I may so call it, or particular politic society, and incorporates into any commonwealth, separate from the rest of mankind.

§ 129. The first power, viz. "of doing whatsoever he thought fit for the preservation of himself" and the rest of mankind, he gives up to be regulated by laws made by the society, so far forth as the preservation of himself and the rest of that society shall require; which laws of the society in many things confine the liberty he had by the law of nature.

§ 130. Secondly, The power of punishing he wholly gives up, and engages his natural force (which he might before employ in the execution of the law of nature, by his own single authority, as he thought fit), to assist the executive power of the society, as the law thereof shall require: for being now in a new state, wherein he is to enjoy many conveniencies, from the labour, assistance, and society of others in the same community, as well as protection from its whole strength; he is to part also with as much of his natural liberty, in providing for himself, as the good, prosperity, and safety of the society shall require; which is not only necessary, but just, since the other members of the society do the like.

§ 131. But though men, when they enter into society, give up the equality, liberty, and executive power they had in the state of nature, into the hands of the society, to be so far disposed of by the legislative as the good of the society shall require; yet it being only with an intention in every one the better to preserve himself, his liberty and property (for no rational creature can be supposed to change his condition with an intention to be worse); the power of the society, or legislative constituted by them, can never be supposed to extend farther than the common good; but is obliged to secure every one's property, by providing against those three defects above-mentioned, that made the state of nature so unsafe and uneasy. And so whoever has the legislative or supreme power of any commonwealth, is bound to govern by established standing laws, promulgated and known to the people, and not by extemporary decrees; by indifferent and upright judges, who are to decide controversies by those laws; and to employ the force of the community at home, only in the execution of such laws; or abroad to prevent or redress foreign injuries, and secure the community from inroads and invasion. And all this to be directed to no other end but the peace, safety, and public good of the people.

1.3 Montesquieu, *The Spirit of the Laws* (1748)

Charles Secondat, Baron de Montesquieu (1689–1755), a French philosopher and sociologist, rivaled John Locke as an influence on the political thinking of the American Founders. Like Locke, Montesquieu operated in the social contract theory tradition. But unlike Locke, Montesquieu hurried through the discussion of man in the state of nature and the origins of civil society to discuss at length the real world impact of culture, climate, and geography on how societies were governed. Montesquieu explored the social and cultural bases of limited government and individual liberty just as such a society was emerging in North America. The American Founders knew well Montesquieu's *The Spirit of the Laws*, with its claim that liberty thrived best in moderate commercial republics. But they worried about his claim that only "small republics" could foster equality, frugality, and civic virtue while "large republics" inevitably fell to inequality and centralized power. The Founders wondered which kind of republic they were.

Book I. Of Laws in General

1. Of the Relation of Laws to Different Beings

Laws, in their most general signification, are the necessary relations arising from the nature of things. In this sense all beings have their laws: the Deity His laws, the material world its laws, the intelligences superior to man their laws, the beasts their laws, man his laws.

They who assert that a blind fatality produced the various effects we behold in this world talk very absurdly; for can anything be more unreasonable than to pretend that a blind fatality could be productive of intelligent beings?

There is, then, a prime reason; and laws are the relations subsisting between it and different beings, and the relations of these to one another.

God is related to the universe, as Creator and Preserver; the laws by which He created all things are those by which He preserves them. He acts according to these rules, because He knows them; He knows them, because He made them; and He made them, because they are in relation to His wisdom and power....

But the intelligent world is far from being so well governed as the physical. For though the former has also its laws, which of their own nature are invariable, it does not conform to them so exactly as the physical world. This is because, on the one hand, particular intelligent beings are of a finite nature, and consequently liable to error; and on the other, their nature requires them to be free agents. Hence they do not steadily conform to their primitive laws; and even those of their own instituting they frequently infringe....

Man, as a physical being, is like other bodies governed by invariable laws. As an intelligent being, he incessantly transgresses the laws established by God, and changes those of his own instituting. He is left to his private direction, though a limited being, and subject, like all finite intelligences, to ignorance and error: even his imperfect knowledge he loses; and as a sensible creature, he is hurried away by a thousand impetuous passions. Such a being might every instant forget his Creator; God has therefore reminded him of his duty by the laws of religion. Such a being is liable every moment to forget himself; philosophy has provided against this by the laws of morality. Formed to live in society, he might forget his fellow-creatures; legislators have therefore by political and civil laws confined him to his duty.....

Book II. Of Laws Directly Derived from the Nature of Government

1. Of the Nature of the three different Governments

There are three species of government: republican, monarchical, and despotic. In order to discover their nature, it is sufficient to recollect the common notion, which supposes three definitions, or rather three facts: that a republican government is that in which the body, or only a part of the people, is possessed of the supreme power; monarchy, that in which a single person governs by fixed and established laws; a despotic government, that in which a single person directs everything by his own will and caprice.

This is what I call the nature of each government; we must now inquire into those laws which directly conform to this nature, and consequently are the fundamental institutions.

2. Of the Republican Government, and the Laws in
relation to Democracy

When the body off the people is possessed of the supreme power, it is called a democracy. When the supreme power is lodged in the hands of a part of the people, it is then an aristocracy.

In a democracy the people are in some respects the sovereign, and in others the subject.

There can be no exercise of sovereignty but by their suffrages, which are their own will; now the sovereign's will is the sovereign himself. The laws therefore which establish the right of suffrage are fundamental to this government. And indeed it is as important to regulate in a republic, in what manner, by whom, to whom, and concerning what, suffrages are to be given, as it is in a monarchy to know who is the prince, and after what manner he ought to govern.....

The people, in whom the supreme power resides, ought to have the management of everything within their reach: that which exceeds their abilities must be conducted by their ministers.

But they cannot properly be said to have their ministers, without the power of nominating them: it is, therefore, a fundamental maxim in this government, that the people should choose their ministers—that is, their magistrates.....

The people are extremely well qualified for choosing those whom they are to entrust with part of their authority. They have only to be determined by things to which they cannot be strangers, and by facts that are obvious to sense. They can tell when a person has fought many battles, and been crowned with success; they are, therefore, capable of electing a general.... These are facts of which they can have better information in a public forum than a monarch in his palace. But are they capable of conducting an intricate affair, of seizing and improving the opportunity and critical moment of action? No; this surpasses their abilities.....

Book III. Of the Principles of the Three Kinds of Government

1. Difference between the Nature and Principle of Government

Having examined the laws in relation to the nature of each government, we must investigate those which relate to its principle.

There is this difference between the nature and principle of government, that the former is that by which it is constituted, the latter that by which it is made to act. One is its particular structure, and the other the human passions which set it in motion.

Now, laws ought no less to relate to the principle than to the nature of each government. We must, therefore, inquire into this principle, which shall be the subject of this third book.

2. Of the Principle of different Governments

I have already observed that it is the nature of a republican government that either the collective body of the people, or particular families, should be possessed of the supreme power; of a monarchy, that the prince should have this power, but in the execution of it should be directed by established laws; of a despotic government, that a single person should rule according to his own will and caprice. This enables me to discover their three principles; which are thence naturally derived. I shall begin with a republican government, and in particular with that of democracy.

3. Of the Principle of Democracy

There is no great share of probity necessary to support a monarchical or despotic government. The force of laws in one, and the prince's arm in the other, are sufficient to direct and maintain the whole. But in a popular state, one spring more is necessary, namely, virtue. . . .

Book IV. That the Laws of Education Ought to be in Relation to the Principles of Government

5. Of Education in a Republican Government

It is in a republican government that the whole power of education is required. The fear of despotic governments naturally arises of itself amidst threats and punishments; the honour of monarchies is favoured by the passions, and favours them in its turn; but virtue is a self-renunciation, which is ever arduous and painful.

This virtue may be defined as the love of the laws and of our country. As such love requires a constant preference of public to private interest, it is the source of all private virtues; for they are nothing more than this very preference itself.

This love is peculiar to democracies. In these alone the government is entrusted to private citizens. Now a government is like everything else: to preserve it we must love it.

Has it ever been known that kings were not fond of monarchy, or that despotic princes hated arbitrary power?

Everything therefore depends on establishing this love in a republic; and to inspire it ought to be the principal business of education: . . .

Book V. That the Laws Given by the Legislator Ought to Be in Relation to the Principle of Government

1. Idea of this Book

That the laws of education should relate to the principle of each government has been shown in the preceding book. Now the same may be said of those which the legislator gives to the whole society. The relation of laws to this principle strengthens the several springs of government; and this principle derives thence, in its turn, a new degree of vigour. And thus it is in mechanics, that action is always followed by reaction.

Our design is, to examine this relation in each government, beginning with the republican state, the principle of which is virtue.

2. What is meant by Virtue in a political State

Virtue in a republic is a most simple thing: it is a love of the republic; it is a sensation, and not a consequence of acquired knowledge: a sensation that may be felt by the meanest as well as by the highest person in the state. When the common people adopt good maxims, they adhere to them more steadily than those whom we call gentlemen. It is very rarely that corruption commences with the former: nay, they frequently derive from their imperfect light a stronger attachment to the established laws and customs.

The love of our country is conducive to a purity of morals, and the latter is again conducive to the former. The less we are able to satisfy our private passions, the more we abandon ourselves to those of a general nature. . . .

3. What is meant by a Love of the Republic in a Democracy

A love of the republic in a democracy is a love of the democracy; as the latter is that of equality.

A love of the democracy is likewise that of frugality. Since every individual ought here to enjoy the same happiness and the same advantages, they should consequently taste the same pleasures and form the same hopes, which cannot be expected but from a general frugality.

The love of equality in a democracy limits ambition to the sole desire, to the sole happiness, of doing greater services to our country than the rest of our fellow-citizens. They cannot all render her equal services, but they all ought to serve her with equal alacrity. At our coming into the world, we contract an immense debt to our country, which we can never discharge.

Hence distinctions here arise from the principle of equality, even when it seems to be removed by signal services or superior abilities.

The love of frugality limits the desire of having to the study of procuring necessaries to our family, and superfluities to our country. Riches give a power which a citizen cannot use for himself, for then he would be no longer equal. They likewise procure pleasures which he ought not to enjoy, because these would be also repugnant to the equality.

The good sense and happiness of individuals depend greatly upon the mediocrity of their abilities and fortunes. Therefore, as a republic, where the laws have placed many in a middling station, is composed of wise men, it will be wisely governed; as it is composed of happy men, it will be extremely happy. . . .

16. Distinctive Properties of a Republic

It is natural for a republic to have only a small territory; otherwise it cannot long subsist. In an extensive republic there are men of large fortunes, and consequently of less moderation; there are trusts too considerable to be placed in any single subject; he has interests of his own; he soon begins to think that he may be happy and glorious, by oppressing his fellow-citizens; and that he may raise himself to grandeur on the ruins of his country.

In an extensive republic the public good is sacrificed to a thousand private views; it is subordinate to exceptions, and depends on accidents. In a small one, the interest of the public is more obvious, better understood, and more within the reach of every citizen; abuses have less extent, and of course are less protected. . . .

17. Distinctive Properties of a Monarchy
A monarchical state ought to be of moderate extent. Were it small, it would form itself into a republic; were it very large, the nobility, possessed of great estates, far from the eye of the prince, with a private court of their own, and secure, moreover, from sudden executions by the laws and manners of the country—such a nobility, I say, might throw off their allegiance, having nothing to fear from too slow and too distant a punishment. . . .

19. Distinctive Properties of a despotic Government
A large empire supposes a despotic authority in the person who governs. It is necessary that the quickness of the prince's resolutions should supply the distance of the places they are sent to; that fear should prevent the remissness of the distant governor or magistrate; that the law should be derived from a single person, and should shift continually, according to the accidents which necessarily multiply in a state in proportion to its extent.

20. Consequence of the preceding Chapters
If it be, therefore, the natural property of small states to be governed as a republic, of middling ones to be subject to a monarch, and of large empires to be swayed by a despotic prince; the consequence is, that in order to preserve the principles of the established government, the state must be supported in the extent it has acquired, and that the spirit of this state will alter in proportion as it contracts or extends its limits.

1.4 Alexis de Tocqueville, "Origin of the Anglo-Americans" (1835)

Alexis de Tocqueville (1805–1859) is almost universally regarded as the most astute foreign observer ever to visit and to write at length about the United States. His visit, ostensibly to study American prisons, commenced in New York in May 1831 and ended there in February 1832. He visited most of the then 24 states, took copious notes, and interviewed Americans of every class, including President Andrew Jackson. Just 25 when he commenced his tour, he was just 29 when his celebrated *Democracy in America* was published in Paris.

The selection published here is from Book 1, Chapter 2, entitled "Origin of the Anglo-Americans, and Importance of This Origin in Relation to Their Future Condition." Tocqueville argues that the future of America can best be understood through a close study of its origins and development—a classic American Political Development (APD) view. He contends that the Puritan immigrants to New

England brought with them two ideas, "the spirit of religion and the spirit of liberty," that had conflicted elsewhere, but that checked, moderated, and supported each other in America. As you will see, Tocqueville, like Montesquieu, thought that only those who understand history have a chance to shape it.

A MAN has come into the world; his early years are spent without notice in the pleasures and activities of childhood. As he grows up, the world receives him when his manhood begins, and he enters into contact with his fellows. He is then studied for the first time, and it is imagined that the germ of the vices and the virtues of his maturer years is then formed.

This, if I am not mistaken, is a great error. We must begin higher up; we must watch the infant in his mother's arms; we must see the first images which the external world casts upon the dark mirror of his mind, the first occurrences that he witnesses, we must hear the first words which awaken the sleeping powers of thought, and stand by his earliest efforts if we would understand the prejudices, the habits, and the passions which will rule his life. The entire man is, so to speak, to be seen in the cradle of the child.

The growth of nations presents something analogous to this; they all bear some marks of their origin. The circumstances that accompanied their birth and contributed to their development affected the whole term of their being. . . .

America is the only country in which it has been possible to witness the natural and tranquil growth of society, and where the influence exercised on the future condition of states by their origin is clearly distinguishable.

At the period when the peoples of Europe landed in the New World, their national characteristics were already completely formed; each of them had a physiognomy of its own; and as they had already attained that stage of civilization at which men are led to study themselves, they have transmitted to us a faithful picture of their opinions, their manners, and their laws. The men of the sixteenth century are almost as well known to us as our contemporaries. America, consequently, exhibits in the broad light of day the phenomena which the ignorance or rudeness of earlier ages conceals from our researches. The men of our day seem destined to see further than their predecessors into human events; they are close enough to the founding of the American settlements to know in detail their elements, and far enough away from that time already to be able to judge what these beginnings have produced. Providence has given us a torch which our forefathers did not possess, and has allowed us to discern fundamental causes in the history of the world which the obscurity of the past concealed from them. If we carefully examine the social and political state of America, after having studied its history, we shall remain perfectly convinced that not an opinion, not a custom, not a law, I may even say not an event is upon record which the origin of that people will not explain. The readers of this book will find in the present chapter the germ of all that is to follow and the key to almost the whole work.

The emigrants who came at different periods to occupy the territory now covered by the American Union differed from each other in many respects; their aim was not the same, and they governed themselves on different principles.

These men had, however, certain features in common, and they were all placed in an analogous situation. The tie of language is, perhaps, the strongest and the most durable that can unite mankind. All the emigrants spoke the same language; they were all children of the same people. Born in a country which had been agitated for centuries by the struggles of faction, and in which all parties had been obliged in their turn to place themselves under the protection of the laws, their political education had been perfected in this rude school; and they were more conversant with the notions of right and the principles of true freedom than the greater part of their European contemporaries. At the period of the first emigrations the township system, that fruitful germ of free institutions, was deeply rooted in the habits of the English; and with it the doctrine of the sovereignty of the people had been introduced into the very bosom of the monarchy of the house of Tudor.

The religious quarrels which have agitated the Christian world were then rife. England had plunged into the new order of things with headlong vehemence. The character of its inhabitants, which had always been sedate and reflective, became argumentative and austere. General information had been increased by intellectual contests, and the mind had received in them a deeper cultivation. While religion was the topic of discussion, the morals of the people became more pure. All these national features are more or less discoverable in the physiognomy of those Englishmen who came to seek a new home on the opposite shores of the Atlantic.

Another observation, moreover, to which we shall have occasion to return later, is applicable not only to the English, but to the French, the Spaniards, and all the Europeans who successively established themselves in the New World. All these European colonies contained the elements, if not the development, of a complete democracy. Two causes led to this result. It may be said that on leaving the mother country the emigrants had, in general, no notion of superiority one over another. The happy and the powerful do not go into exile, and there are no surer guarantees of equality among men than poverty and misfortune. It happened, however, on several occasions, that persons of rank were driven to America by political and religious quarrels. Laws were made to establish a gradation of ranks; but it was soon found that the soil of America was opposed to a territorial aristocracy. It was realized that in order to clear this land, nothing less than the constant and self-interested efforts of the owner himself was essential; the ground prepared, it became evident that its produce was not sufficient to enrich at the same time both an owner and a farmer. The land was then naturally broken up into small portions, which the proprietor cultivated for himself. Land is the basis of an aristocracy, which clings to the soil that supports it; for it is not by privileges alone, nor by birth, but by landed property handed down from generation to generation that an aristocracy is constituted. A nation may present immense fortunes and extreme wretchedness; but unless those fortunes are territorial, there is no true aristocracy, but simply the class of the rich and that of the poor.

All the British colonies had striking similarities at the time of their origin. All of them, from their beginning, seemed destined to witness the growth, not of the aristocratic liberty of their mother country, but of that freedom of the middle and lower orders of which the history of the world had as yet furnished no complete example. In this general uniformity, however, several marked divergences could be observed, which it is necessary to point out. Two branches may be distinguished in the great Anglo-American family, which have hitherto grown up without entirely commingling; the one in the South, the other in the North.

Virginia received the first English colony; the immigrants took possession of it in 1607. The idea that mines of gold and silver are the sources of national wealth was at that time singularly prevalent in Europe; a fatal delusion, which has done more to impoverish the European nations who adopted it, and has cost more lives in America, than the united influence of war and bad laws. The men sent to Virginia[1] were seekers of gold, adventurers without resources and without character, whose turbulent and restless spirit endangered the infant colony[2] and rendered its progress uncertain. Artisans and agriculturists arrived afterwards; and, although they were a more moral and orderly race of men, they were hardly in any respect above the level of the inferior classes in England.[3] No lofty views, no spiritual conception, presided over the foundation of these new settlements. The colony was scarcely established when slavery was introduced;[4] this was the capital fact which was to exercise an immense influence on the character, the laws, and the whole future of the South. Slavery, as I shall afterwards show, dishonors labor; it introduces idleness into society, and with idleness, ignorance and pride, luxury and distress. It enervates the powers of the mind and benumbs the activity of man. The influence of slavery, united to the English character, explains the manners and the social condition of the Southern states.

On this same English foundation there developed in the North very different characteristics. Here I may be allowed to enter into some details.

In the English colonies of the North, more generally known as the New England states,[5] the two or three main ideas that now constitute the basis of the social theory of the United States were first combined. The principles of New England spread at first to the neighboring states; they then passed successively to the more distant ones; and at last, if I may so speak, they interpenetrated the whole confederation. They now extend their influence beyond its limits, over the whole American world. The civilization of New England has been like a beacon lit upon a hill, which, after it has diffused its warmth immediately around it, also tinges the distant horizon with its glow.

The foundation of New England was a novel spectacle, and all the circumstances attending it were singular and original. Nearly all colonies have been first inhabited either by men without education and without resources, driven by their poverty and their misconduct from the land which gave them birth, or by speculators and adventurers greedy of gain. Some settlements cannot even boast so honorable an origin; Santo Domingo was founded by buccaneers; and at the present day the criminal courts of England supply the population of Australia.

The settlers who established themselves on the shores of New England all belonged to the more independent classes of their native country. Their union on the soil of America at once presented the singular phenomenon of a society containing neither lords nor common people, and we may almost say neither rich nor poor. These men possessed, in proportion to their number, a greater mass of intelligence than is to be found in any European nation of our own time. All, perhaps without a single exception, had received a good education, and many of them were known in Europe for their talents and their acquirements. The other colonies had been founded by adventurers without families; the immigrants of New England brought with them the best elements of order and morality; they landed on the desert coast accompanied by their wives and children. But what especially distinguished them from all others was the aim of their undertaking. They had not been obliged by necessity to leave their country; the social position they abandoned was one to be regretted, and their means of subsistence were certain. Nor did they cross the Atlantic to improve their situation or to increase their wealth; it was a purely intellectual craving that called them from the comforts of their former homes; and in facing the inevitable sufferings of exile their object was the triumph of an idea.

The immigrants, or, as they deservedly styled themselves, the Pilgrims, belonged to that English sect the austerity of whose principles had acquired for them the name of Puritans. Puritanism was not merely a religious doctrine, but corresponded in many points with the most absolute democratic and republican theories. It was this tendency that had aroused its most dangerous adversaries. Persecuted by the government of the mother country, and disgusted by the habits of a society which the rigor of their own principles condemned, the Puritans went forth to seek some rude and unfrequented part of the world where they could live according to their own opinions and worship God in freedom....

It must not be imagined that the piety of the Puritans was merely speculative, or that it took no cognizance of the course of worldly affairs. Puritanism, as I have already remarked, was almost as much a political theory as a religious doctrine. No sooner had the immigrants landed on the barren coast ... than it was their first care to constitute a society, by subscribing the following Act:[6] IN THE NAME OF GOD AMEN. We, whose names are underwritten, the loyal subjects of our dread Sovereign Lord King James, &c. &c., Having undertaken for the glory of God, and advancement of the Christian Faith, and the honour of our King and country, a voyage to plant the first colony in the northern parts of Virginia; Do by these presents solemnly and mutually, in the presence of God and one another, covenant and combine ourselves together into a civil body politick, for our better ordering and preservation, and furtherance of the ends aforesaid: and by virtue hereof do enact, constitute, and frame such just and equal laws, ordinances, acts, constitutions, and offices, from time to time, as shall be thought most meet and convenient for the general good of the Colony: unto which we promise all due submission and obedience," etc.

This happened in 1620, and from that time forwards the emigration went on. The religious and political passion which ravaged the British Empire during the whole reign of Charles I drove fresh crowds of sectarians every year to the shores of America. In England the stronghold of Puritanism continued to be in the middle classes; and it was from the middle classes that most of the emigrants came. The population of New England increased rapidly; and while the hierarchy of rank despotically classed the inhabitants of the mother country, the colony approximated more and more the novel spectacle of a community homogeneous in all its parts. A democracy more perfect than antiquity had dared to dream of started in full size and panoply from the midst of an ancient feudal society.

The English government was not dissatisfied with a large emigration which removed the elements of fresh discord and further revolutions. On the contrary, it did everything to encourage it and seemed to have no anxiety about the destiny of those who sought a shelter from the rigor of their laws on the soil of America. It appeared as if New England was a region given up to the dreams of fancy and the unrestrained experiments of innovators....

I have said enough to put the character of Anglo-American civilization in its true light. It is the result (and this should be constantly kept in mind) of two distinct elements, which in other places have been in frequent disagreement, but which the Americans have succeeded in incorporating to some extent one with the other and combining admirably. I allude to the spirit of religion and the spirit of liberty.

The settlers of New England were at the same time ardent sectarians and daring innovators. Narrow as the limits of some of their religious opinions were, they were free from all political prejudices.

Hence arose two tendencies, distinct but not opposite, which are everywhere discernible in the manners as well as the laws of the country.

Men sacrifice for a religious opinion their friends, their family, and their country; one can consider them devoted to the pursuit of intellectual goals which they came to purchase at so high a price. One sees them, however, seeking with almost equal eagerness material wealth and moral satisfaction; heaven in the world beyond, and well-being and liberty in this one.

Under their hand, political principles, laws, and human institutions seem malleable, capable of being shaped and combined at will. As they go forward, the barriers which imprisoned society and behind which they were born are lowered; old opinions, which for centuries had been controlling the world, vanish; a course almost without limits, a field without horizon, is revealed: the human spirit rushes forward and traverses them in every direction. But having reached the limits of the political world, the human spirit stops of itself; in fear it relinquishes the need of exploration; it even abstains from lifting the veil of the sanctuary; it bows with respect before truths which it accepts without discussion.

Thus in the moral world everything is classified, systematized, foreseen, and decided beforehand; in the political world everything is agitated, disputed, and uncertain. In the one is a passive though a voluntary obedience; in the other, an independence scornful of experience, and jealous of all authority. These two tendencies, apparently so discrepant, are far from conflicting; they advance together and support each other.

Religion perceives that civil liberty affords a noble exercise to the faculties of man and that the political world is a field prepared by the Creator for the efforts of mind. Free and powerful in its own sphere, satisfied with the place reserved for it, religion never more surely establishes its empire than when it reigns in the hearts of men unsupported by aught beside its native strength.

Liberty regards religion as its companion in all its battles and its triumphs, as the cradle of its infancy and the divine source of its claims. It considers religion as the safeguard of morality, and morality as the best security of law and the surest pledge of the duration of freedom.

NOTES

1. The charter granted by the crown of England in 1609 stipulated, among other conditions that the adventurers should pay to the crown a fifth of the produce of all gold and silver mines. See Life of Washington, by Marshall Vol. I, pp. 18–66.

2. A large portion of the adventurers, says Stith (History of Virginia), were unprincipled young men of family, whom their parents were glad to ship off in order to save them from an ignominious fate, discharged servants, fraudulent bankrupts, debauchees, and others of the same class, people more apt to pillage and destroy than to promote the welfare of the settlement. Seditious leaders easily enticed this band into every kind of extravagance and excess. See for the history of Virginia the following works: History of Virginia, from the First Settlements in the Year 1624, by Smith; History of Virginia, by William Stith; History of Virginia, from the Earliest Period by Beverley, translated into French in 1807.

3. It was not till some time later that a certain number of rich English landholders came to establish themselves in the colony.

4. Slavery was introduced about the year 1620, by a Dutch vessel, which landed twenty Negroes on the banks of the James River. See Chalmer.

5. The New England states are those situated to the east of the Hudson. They are now six in number: (1) Connecticut, (2) Rhode Island, (3) Massachussetts, (4) New Hampshire, (5) Vermont, (6) Maine.

6. The emigrants who founded the state of Rhode Island in 1638, those who landed at New Haven in 1637, the first settlers in Connecticut in 1639, and the founders of Providence in 1640 began in like manner by drawing up a social contract, which was acceded to by all the interested parties. See Pitkin's History, pp. 42 and 47.

It is impossible to read this opening paragraph without an involuntary feeling of religious awe; it breathes the very savor of Gospel antiquity. The sincerity of the author heightens his power of language. In our eyes, a well as in his own, it was not a mere party of adventurers gone forth to seek their fortune beyond seas, but the germ of a great nation wafted by Providence to a predestined shore.

1.5 James Morone, "The Democratic Wish" (1998)

James Morone asks how the competing ideas and ideals of the Founding period—individualism and the consequent fear of concentrated power vs. a commitment to community and democratic action—create the pattern of American politics and public life. The liberal perspective focuses on the pursuit of self-interest while the republican perspective focuses on the collective life of the community, especially the community right to rise up and slap down the elites and the monied interests when their greed threatens to become destructive.

Morone argues that "the periodicity of American democratic reform is hard to miss." He sees normal politics as reflecting the general pursuit of economic self-interest, punctuated by a recurrent compulsion to communitarian reform. Morone argues that the American Creed of a people capable of governing themselves in the broad public interest is a myth—long standing and influential—but a myth nonetheless. While the democratic myth can be and has been avidly pursued, as a myth, it cannot be obtained or realized, and, hence, is a source of endless frustration.

At the heart of American politics lies a dread and a yearning. The dread is notorious. Americans fear public power as a threat to liberty. Their government is weak and fragmented, designed to prevent action more easily than to produce it. The yearning is an alternative faith in direct, communal democracy. Even after the loose collection of agrarian colonies had evolved into a dense industrial society, the urge remained: the people would, somehow, put aside their government and rule themselves directly.

The story I tell is how Americans master their antistatist trepidations by pursuing their democratic wish. In the recurring quest for the people, Americans redesign political institutions and rewrite political rules. The direct results have been uneven; some efforts enhance popular control, some attenuate it, some seem to manage both. Paradoxically, the unanticipated consequences are more constant. The institutions designed to enhance democracy expand the scope and authority of the state, especially its administrative capacity. A great irony propels American political development: the search for more direct democracy builds up the bureaucracy.[1] ...

Rival Views of American Political Development

Social scientists tell the story of American political development in different ways, engaging in spirited controversies about the underlying dynamics. Were early Americans liberal individualists or republican communitarians? Is the nation's progress marked more fundamentally by shared values or by economic fights? How, more generally, should we characterize growth and change in American public administration? The pattern of dread and yearning offers a perspective on each of these familiar debates.

The Soul of American Politics: Liberal or Republican?

The dread of government, described earlier, rests on a reading of America as a liberal polity. In this view, Americans designed their regime to protect private rights from public meddling. Rejecting classical notions of public good, the Founders left individuals to define and pursue their own self-interest.

Accordingly, government is carefully limited; it is organized to protect private rights and promote fair interplay among self-interested individuals. The liberal vision seems a distinctly modern one, calculated to work harmoniously, even among citizens who are less than virtuous (or men who are not angels, as Madison had it).[2] Indirect elections are designed to set the people at a distance from their limited state which is, itself, constituted with checks and balances so that ambitions for power offset one another.

There are multiple variations of the liberal paradigm. Some emphasize idealistic social obligations; all give primacy to liberty. However, the dominant interpretation of liberal America focuses on the pursuit of self-interest. From this perspective, it is easy to see why Americans took readily to commerce and capitalism. Indeed, scholars in this tradition often lament the depth and power of the liberal ideology in American culture. Liberalism is not, in their view, merely a set of institutional arrangements. It is a mind-set so pervasive as to eclipse every alternative; it impoverishes American politics by truncating the range of possibilities Americans find in their social world.[3]

The liberal orthodoxy has recently been challenged by an interpretation known as classical republicanism. Rather than a polity founded on modern liberalism, these revisionists see a backward-looking ideal drawn from classical antiquity. To them, the spirit of Machiavelli runs as deep in Americans as that of John Locke.

In the republican view, the colonial and Revolutionary ideal lay, not in the pursuit of private matters, but in the shared public life of civic duty, in the subordination of individual interests to the *res publica*. Citizens were defined and fufilled by participation in political community. To the first American generation, the political community was a single organic whole, binding each of its members into a civic body of shared interests that transcended individual concerns. Natural leaders were expected to rise up among the people; others would acknowledge their place within the natural order and contribute their own talents to the common good.

Rather than institutions framed to harness self-interest, the revisionists see a social vision that demanded (and fostered) virtue in its citizens. Rather than holding people at a distance from their government, republican America expected them to participate directly. Instead of a nation primed for commerce, the new view finds one clinging to small homogeneous communities and the yeoman self-reliance of agriculture. Here, then, is an image of a virtuous, united people, bound together by a shared public good, active in civic affairs, and populating rural communities outside historical time. Americans, conclude the proponents of this analytic perspective, were not liberals but republicans, not individualists but communitarians, no longer celebrants of self but participants in a shared public life.[4]

Though the debate is lively, the issue at stake has grown murky. Proponents of the republican interpretation began with an important but limited claim. This world view, argued Bernard Bailyn, informed the colonists as the English began to meddle in New World politics; the imperial menace to republican ideals helps explain why the settlers moved so swiftly to revolution. The next step was Gordon Wood's powerful exposition of how the classical images of communal republic shaped the first American decade until they were swamped by factional conflicts and displaced by the Constitution. Most political scientists emphatically concur, at least regarding the factionalism of the 1780s. It is difficult to find aspirations of community or public-interested consensus on either side of the ratification debate. Citing the *Federalist* papers, the Antifederalists, the Constitution itself, many political scientists conclude that, whatever the colonial experience, the new order introduced a profoundly liberal set of rules.[5]

And yet, by the early nineteenth century, other scholars find a vibrant republicanism. The paradigm has proved a powerful heuristic, organizing new interpretations of working-class formation, the role of women in the cities, models of public school education, debates over the national bank, the organization of political parties, and a host of other topics.[6]

In its most sweeping form, articulated by J. G. A. Pocock, the republican view would displace the liberal interpretation of America. For Pocock and the scholars who follow him, the republican paradigm is an analytic key to American history and culture. From the other side, social scientists who see a liberal nation have been long and loud in their critique.

What are we to make of this passionate intellectual debate? The democratic wish suggests one way the two paradigms might fit into a single conceptual story. The civic republicanism of the 1770s is, I argue, the first manifestation of the recurring American ideology of revolution and reform. . . .

The March of Democracy: Consensus or Conflict?

The periodicity of American democratic reform is hard to miss. But where do the great outbursts come from? What are they really about? What do they accomplish? The answers divide theories of American democracy—crudely speaking—into two schools: class conflict and ideological consensus. The debate has been long and lively, for the two schools see the same phenomena in almost precisely opposite ways. In one view, a profound agreement about democratic principles has led to the steady expansion of citizen rights; in the other, powerful economic conflicts often (but not always) preserved the status quo. Americans either concur about democracy or clash over class. Consider each in turn.

The consensus argument rests, of course, on the liberal tradition. Samuel Huntington has articulated the most forceful recent version. Ideas matter, argued Huntington. Ideas like equality, freedom (Americans, uniquely, believe in both simultaneously), inalienable rights, and the consent of the governed from a powerful "American Creed." When political reality diverges too widely from these ideals, Americans rebel. (They have done so four times.) The reformers win, more or less, because the reforms they seek accord with what Americans believe. However, democratic triumphs never fully achieve democratic ambitions; when they fall short, they establish the conditions of the next outburst.[7]

Before Huntington's contribution, political scientists who saw an American consensus appeared to have written their theory into a historical dead end, with no places for large-scale change. Americans, they said, agreed on the big matters; American politics were the petty adjustments of incremental pluralism. While Huntington gave pluralists a consensus theory with historical dimensions, historians had long been employing the consensus approach. Consider, for example, what they made of two great American reformations undertaken two centuries apart.[8]

While political science was rediscovering consensus in the American present, scholars like Edmund and Helen Morgan were finding it in the past. Never mind class conflict, wrote the Morgans. When Americans demanded rights and representation from George III, that is precisely what they wanted. Americans united in a "glorious cause" dominated by such bold new ideas as popular sovereignty. Though their first efforts at self-government may have been excessive in populism (and deficient in administrative "energy"), the new nation checked its "drift toward anarchy" with the Constitution of 1789. (This story may sound like the one normally put out for popular consumption, but it was distinctly out of favor with historians till the consensualists restored it in the 1950s.)[9]

Or take the civil rights movement in the 1960s. The condition of American black people violated the American creed. Despite agonizingly slow progress against an implacable white minority, civil rights protesters eventually won both legislation and voting rights because they articulated ideas that Americans believe in and, generally, agree on.

The consensus approach finds similar cases throughout American history. Universal male suffrage (in the Jacksonian era), Emancipation, the Fourteenth and Fifteenth Amendments (after the Civil War), the extension of the franchise to women (the Progressive era), or the legitimation of labor (1930s) all illustrate the steady progress of citizenship rights.[10]

The alternative tradition was originally formulated by the Progressive historians and is now carried on by social scientists loosely identified as New Left. In their view, class conflict has propelled social and democratic progress in America. The Progressives put it starkly. The movements celebrated by the liberals as a kind of unfolding of the American idea were, in reality, fights about economic interest. Ideas counted for little, they were obfuscations or propaganda. Consensus, where it appeared at all, was illusory.[11]

The perspective has grown increasingly sophisticated in the hands of such diverse authors as Lawrence Goodwin, Gary Nash, Edward Pessen, Eric Foner, Sean Wilentz, and Gordon Wood. They have updated the Progressive interpretation. They replace the brute class categories with a more dynamic view. Class continues to matter, but it is embedded in social and political relationships that go far beyond simple economic categories. Still, the American political development remains a series of struggles between haves and have-nots. In this view, clashes prompted by democratic reform movements reflect the working out of socio-economic tensions in the structure of society. As the nation evolved, these underlying tensions repeatedly drove reform to the surface of American political life. There, ideas may have played a role; but each case was profoundly shaped by underlying social and economic imperatives. . . .

The same pattern, say the New Left scholars, was repeated in each step of the "march of democracy." The celebrated rise of the common man during the age of Jackson meant subordination to party hierarchy, to new forms of labor organization, and to new accumulations of capital (with little of the economic mobility long celebrated in American myth). Reconstruction ended cruelly when the American majority tossed aside their "creed" and permitted the reassertion of white supremacy. Progressive reforms enfeebled political parties and urban immigrants while empowering economically based interest groups. Though judgments about winners and losers vary among proponents of the conflict tradition, the process invariably involves entrenched élites struggling to maintain (or extend) their privileges from the challenge of the have-nots.[12]

The two traditions are almost exact opposites. They examine the same political episodes and see different causes (democratic ideas or economic differences) and different political processes (consensus or conflict). Recent work also differs about the outcomes. Consensualists look at the progress of formerly suppressed interests and celebrate the American promise; the New Left weighs the same promise by the economic progress of the have-nots and declares it a fraud (or, in more moderate hands, an exaggeration).

Once again, an argument debated as long as this one is likely to have insight on each side. In this case, each view concedes merit to the other.[13] There is evidence of both conflict and consensus, of both material forces and ideas that matter. The question (besides which matters more fundamentally) is, once again, how the evidence on each side can be pieced together. The politics of the democratic wish offers the following perspective.

The American democratic ideology fosters a consensus that permits new conflicts. The ideology is not propaganda (as the Progressives had it); nor is it an idea with the reforming power that consensualists ascribe to democracy. Rather, it is myth. The people that American reformers pursue is a chimera. However, it is a most significant illusion precisely because it conjures up the consensus that liberals ascribe to the "American creed." . . .

The democratic ideals that inspire reformers are, like any myth, unattainable. Judged by the hope of restoring the people, the movements—from the Founding to the civil rights crusade—all failed. Moreover, as I suggested in the preceding section, the reforms simultaneously introduce and limit political change. The former enable optimistic conclusions; consensus theorists can measure the political progress of previously shunned groups and celebrate the American process. On the other hand, the limits generate conclusions of co-optation and defeat. Neo-Progressives can measure the same events by social and economic indicators and judge them failures. . . .

NOTES

1. On ironic state building, see Michael Nelson's wonderful "A Short Ironic History of American Bureaucracy," paper prepared for the annual meetings of the American Political Science Association, New York, 3–6 September 1981.

2. *Federalist*, No. 51.

3. On idealism and liberalism, see Nancy Rosenblum, ed., *Liberalism and Moral Life* (Cambridge, Mass.: Harvard University Press, 1989), introduction. On pessimistic liberalism, see Hartz, *Liberal Tradition*; and John Diggins, *The Lost Soul of American Politics* (New York: Basic Books, 1984).

4. The most often cited works of the republican revisionism are Bernard Bailyn, *The Ideological Origins of the American Revolution* (Cambridge, Mass.: Harvard University Press, 1967); Wood, *Creation of the American Republic*; J. G. A. Pocock, *The Machiavellian Moment: Florentine Political Thought and the Atlantic Republican Tradition* (Princeton, N.J.: Princeton University Press, 1975).

   Important additional work includes Drew McCoy, *The Elusive Republic: Political Economy in Jeffersonian America* (New York: W. W. Norton, 1980); Lance Banning, *The Jeffersonian Persuasion: Evolution of a Party Ideology* (Ithaca, N.Y.: Cornell University Press, 1978); Gerald Stourzh, *Alexander Hamilton and the Idea of Republican Government* (Palo Alto, Calif.: Stanford University Press, 1970).

   Among the many works seeking to reconcile the traditions are Jean Yarborough, "Republicanism Reconsidered: Some Thoughts on the Foundation and Preservation of the American Republic," *Review of Politics* 41 (January 1979): 61–65; Joyce Appleby, *Capitalism and the New Social Order: The Republican Vision of the 1790s* (New York: New York University Press, 1984); Charles Taylor, "Cross Purposes: The Liberal-Communitarian Debate," in Rosenblum, *Liberalism and Moral Life*, 159–82.

5. On the critique of republicanism, see Issac Kramnick, "Republican Revisionism Revisited," *American Historical Review* 83 (June 1982): 629–64. The most agitated statement is surely Diggins, *The Lost Soul of American Politics*. Thomas Pangle, *The Spirit of Modern Republicanism* (Chicago: University of Chicago Press, 1988), would seize republicanism away from Bailyn, Wood, and Pocock and fit it into the rubric established by Leo Strauss. See also Steven Dworetz, "The Rise of 'Cato' and the Decline of Locke," paper prepared for the annual meetings of the American Political Science Association, Washington, D.C., 1 September 1988.

   The reviews in this area are great fun. See Gordon Wood on Diggins ("Hellfire Politics") and on the students of Leo Strauss ("Fundamentalists and the Constitution"), *New York Review of Books*, 28 February 1985, pp. 29–32, and 18 February 1988, pp. 33–40, respectively; Pocock on Wood and Stourzh, "Virtue and Commerce in the Eighteenth Century," *Journal of Interdisciplinary History* 3 (1972): 199–234.

6. Among the works in the nineteenth-century republican studies, see Sean Wilentz, *Chants Democratic* (New York: Oxford University Press, 1984); Christine Stansell, *City of Women* (Chicago: University of Illinois Press, 1987); Thomas James, "Rights of Conscience and State School Systems in Nineteenth-Century America," in Paul Tinkelman and Stephen Gottlieb, eds., *In Search of a Usable Past: The Origins and Implications of State Protections of Liberty* (Athens: University of Georgia Press, 1990); Jean Baker, *Affairs of Party: The Political Culture of Northern Democrats in Mid-Nineteenth Century* (Ithaca, N.Y.: Cornell University Press, 1983).

7. Samuel P. Huntington, *American Politics and the Promise of Disharmony* (Cambridge, Mass.: Harvard University Press, 1981), 24, 17, and passim.

8. Hartz, *Liberal Tradition*, is generally credited with articulating the most sweeping account of the consensus tradition and its roots. See generally the works of Daniel Bell, Seymor Martin Lipset, and David Potter for examples of the consensualist vision.

   The pluralist argument was articulated in 1908 by Arthur Bentley, *The Process of Government* (Cambridge, Mass.: Harvard University Press, 1966). It was developed by David Truman, *The Governmental Process*—the title a conscious homage to Bentley—(New York: Alfred A. Knopf, 1951); Robert Dahl, *A Preface to Democratic Theory* (Chicago: University of Chicago Press, 1956); and Robert Dahl, *Who Governs?* (New Haven: Yale University Press, 1961).

   For an outstanding analysis of the tradition, see J. David Greenstone, "Group Theory," in Fred Greenstein and Nelson Polsby, eds., *The Handbook of Political Science*, vol. II (Boston:

Addison Wesley, 1975). See also Mark Kesselman, "The Conflictual Evolution of American Political Science: From Apologetic Pluralism to Trilateralism and Marxism," in J. David Greenstone, ed., *Public Values and Private Powers in American Politics* (Chicago: University of Chicago Press, 1982), 34–67.

The more critical neopluralists include Grant McConnell, *Private Power and American Democracy*; and Theodore Lowi, *The End of Liberalism* (New York: W. W. Norton, 1969).

9. Edmund and Helen Morgan, *The Stamp Act Crisis: Prologue to Revolution* (Chapel Hill: University of North Carolina Press, 1953). See also Edmund Morgan, "Conflict and Consensus in the American Revolution," in Stephen Kurtz and James Hutson, eds., *Essays on the American Revolution* (Chapel Hill: University of North Carolina Press, 1973). For a useful review of the early literature on conflict and consensus, see Jack Greene, "The Reappraisal of the American Revolution in Recent Historical Literature," in Jack Greene, ed., *The Reinterpretation of the American Revolution* (New York: Harper & Row, 1968). For a synthesis less hostile to the Progressives, see Gordon Wood, "Rhetoric and Reality in the American Revolution," *William and Mary Quarterly* 23 (January 1966): 3–32.

10. On the Jacksonians, see Marvin Myers, *The Jacksonian Persuasion* (New York: Vintage Books, 1960). On the Progressive era and the New Deal, see Richard Hofstadler, *The Age of Reform* (New York: Alfred A. Knopf, 1956).

11. The outstanding figure of Progressive historiography is Charles Beard. See, for example, *An Economic Interpretation of the Constitution* (New York: Macmillan, 1913). Compare the later Charles and Mary Beard, *The Rise of the American Civilization* (New York: Macmillan, 1927) and *American at Midpassage* (New York: Macmillan, 1939).

See also Vernon Parrington, *Main Currents in American Thought*, 3 vols. (New York: Harcourt, Brace & World, 1927, 1930); and John Simpson Penman, *The Irresistible Movement of Democracy* (New York: Macmillan, 1923).

See the contrast of consensualist and conflictualist historians laid out in David Noble, *The End of American History* (Minneapolis: University of Minnesota Press, 1985).

12. See Edward Pessen, *Riches, Class and Power Before the Civil War* (Lexington, Mass.: D. C. Heath, 1973), on the Jacksonians; Eric Foner, *Reconstruction* (New York: Harper & Row, 1988); Walter Dean Burnham, *Critical Elections and the Mainsprings of American Democracy* (New York: W. W. Norton, 1970).

13. See Wood, "Rhetoric and Reality," 3–31.

1.6 Rogers M. Smith, "The Multiple Traditions in America" (1993)

Rogers Smith's "multiple traditions" interpretation of American politics is a modern classic. As with much of the best work in APD (including Morone above), Smith identified conflicting streams in American intellectual life and describes how their interplay structures and gives characteristic shape to American political history. Like many others, he identified Lockean liberalism and civic republicanism as formidable influences on American political culture and development.

But two things have made this article particularly influential. First, it identifies a third stream of thought in American public life. Many others had noted it, but almost always as an aberration, either overcome or in the inevitable process of being overcome. This third strain is racism and its progeny, which Smith describes as "inegalitarian ideologies and institutions of ascriptive hierarchy." Second, Smith argues that better appreciating the strength of ascriptive privileges and hierarchical structures in American public life explains why "changes have come only through difficult struggles and then have often not been sustained." Keeping this ongoing clash between liberal, republican, and ascriptive influences front of mind discourages both complacency and despair in favor of vigilance and struggle.

Analysts of American politics since Tocqueville have seen the nation as a paradigmatic "liberal democratic" society, shaped most by the comparatively free and equal conditions and the Enlightenment ideals said to have prevailed at its founding. These accounts must be severely revised to recognize the inegalitarian ideologies and institutions of ascriptive hierarchy that defined the political status of racial and ethnic minorities and women through most of U.S. history. . . . American political culture is better understood as the often conflictual and contradictory product of multiple political traditions, than as the expression of hegemonic liberal or democratic political traditions.

Since the nation's inception, analysts have described American political culture as the preeminent example of modern liberal democracy, of government by popular consent with respect for the equal rights of all. They have portrayed American political development as the working out of liberal democratic or republican principles, via both "liberalizing" and "democratizing" socioeconomic changes and political efforts to cope with tensions inherent in these principles. Illiberal, undemocratic beliefs and practices have usually been seen only as expressions of ignorance and prejudice, destined to marginality by their lack of rational defenses. A distinguished line of writers, from Hector St. John Crevecoeur in the eighteenth century and Harriet Martineau and Lord Bryce in the nineteenth century to Gunnar Myrdal and Louis Hartz in the twentieth century serves as authority for this view. Today, leading social scientists such as Samuel P. Huntington, Walter Dean Burnham, and Ira Katznelson, legal scholars, historians, and cultural analysts such as Kenneth Karst, John Diggins, and Sacvan Bercovitch, and many others still structure their accounts on these premises. Virtually all appeal to the classic analysis of American politics, Tocqueville's *Democracy in America*.

Tocqueville's thesis—that America has been most shaped by the unusually free and egalitarian ideas and material conditions that prevailed at its founding—captures important truths. Nonetheless, the purpose of this essay is to challenge that thesis by showing that its adherents fail to give due weight to inegalitarian ideologies and conditions that have shaped the participants and the substance of American politics just as deeply. For over 80% of U.S. history, its laws declared most of the world's population to be ineligible for full American citizenship solely because of their race, original nationality, or gender. For at least two-thirds of American history, the majority of the domestic adult population was also ineligible for full citizenship for the same reasons. Contrary to Tocquevillian views of American civic identity, it did not matter how "liberal," "democratic," or "republican" those persons' beliefs were.[1]

The Tocquevillian story is thus deceptive because it is too narrow. It is centered on relationships among a minority of Americans (white men, largely of northern European ancestry) analyzed via reference to categories derived from the hierarchy of political and economic statuses men have held in Europe: monarchs and aristocrats, commercial burghers, farmers, industrial and rural laborers, and indigents. Because most European observers and British American men have regarded these categories as politically fundamental, it is understandable that they have always found the most striking fact about the new nation to be its lack of one type of ascriptive hierarchy. There was no hereditary monarchy or nobility native to British America, and the revolutionaries rejected both the authority of the British king and aristocracy and the creation of any new American substitutes. Those features of American political life made the United States appear remarkably egalitarian by comparison with Europe.

But the comparative moral, material, and political egalitarianism that prevailed at the founding among moderately propertied white men was surrounded by an array of other fixed, ascriptive systems of unequal status, all largely unchallenged by the American revolutionaries.[2] Men were thought naturally suited to rule over women, within both the family and the polity. White northern Europeans were thought superior culturally—and probably biologically—to black Africans, bronze Native Americans, and indeed all other races and civilizations. Many British Americans also treated religion as an inherited condition and regarded Protestants as created by God to be morally and politically, as well as theologically, superior to Catholics, Jews, Muslims, and others.

These beliefs were not merely emotional prejudices or "attitudes." Over time, American intellectual and political elites elaborated distinctive justifications for these ascriptive systems, including inegalitarian scriptural readings, the scientific racism of the "American school" of ethnology, racial and sexual Darwinism, and the romantic cult of Anglo–Saxonism in American historiography. All these discourses identified the true meaning of *Americanism* with particular forms of cultural, religious, ethnic, and especially racial and gender hierarchies.[3] Many adherents of ascriptive Americanist outlooks insisted that the nation's political and economic structures should formally reflect natural and cultural inequalities, even at the cost of violating doctrines of universal rights. Although these views never entirely prevailed, their impact has been wide and deep.

Thus to approach a truer picture of America's political culture and its characteristic conflicts, we must consider more than the familiar categories of (absent) feudalism and socialism and (pervasive) bourgeois liberalism and republicanism. The nation has also been deeply constituted by the ideologies and practices that defined the relationships of the white male minority with subordinate groups, and the relationships of these groups with each other. When these elements are kept in view, the flat plain of American egalitarianism mapped by Tocqueville and others suddenly looks quite different. We instead perceive America's initial conditions as exhibiting only a rather small, recently leveled valley of relative equality nestled amid steep mountains of hierarchy. And though we can see forces working to erode those mountains over time, broadening the valley, many of the peaks also prove to be volcanic, frequently responding to seismic pressures with outbursts that harden into substantial peaks once again.

To be sure, America's ascriptive, unequal statuses, and the ideologies by which they have been defended have always been heavily conditioned and constrained by the presence of liberal democratic values and institutions. The reverse, however, is also true. Although liberal democratic ideas and practices have been more potent in America than elsewhere, American politics is best seen as expressing the interaction of multiple political traditions, including *liberalism, republicanism,* and *ascriptive forms of Americanism,* which have collectively comprised American political culture, without any constituting it as a whole.[4] Though Americans have often struggled over contradictions among these traditions, almost all have tried to embrace what they saw as the best features of each.

Ascriptive outlooks have had such a hold in America because they have provided something that neither liberalism nor republicanism has done so well. They have offered creditable intellectual and psychological reasons for many Americans to believe that their social roles and personal characteristics express an identity that has inherent and transcendant worth, thanks to nature, history, and God. Those rationales have obviously aided those who sat atop the nation's political, economic, and social hierarchies. But many Americans besides elites have felt that they have gained meaning, as well as material and political benefits, from their nation's traditional structures of ascribed places and destinies.

Conventional narratives, preoccupied with the absence of aristocracy and socialism, usually stress the liberal and democratic elements in the rhetoric of even America's dissenters (Hartog 1987). These accounts fail to explain how and why liberalizing efforts have frequently lost to forces favoring new forms of racial and gender hierarchy. Those forces have sometimes negated major liberal victories, especially in the half-century following Reconstruction; and the fate of that era may be finding echoes today.

My chief aim here is to persuade readers that many leading accounts of American political culture are inadequate. I will also suggest briefly how analyses with greater descriptive and explanatory power can be achieved by replacing the Tocquevillian thesis with a *multiple-traditions* view of America. This argument is relevant to contemporary politics in two ways. First, it raises the possibility that novel intellectual, political, and legal systems reinforcing racial, ethnic, and gender inequalities might be rebuilt in America in the years ahead. That prospect does not seem plausible if the United States has always been essentially liberal democratic, with all exceptions marginal and steadily eliminated. It seems quite real, however, if liberal democratic traditions have been but contested parts of American culture, with inegalitarian ideologies and practices often resurging even after major enhancements of liberal democracy. Second, the political implications of the view that America has never been completely liberal, and that changes have come only through difficult struggles and then have often not been sustained, are very different from the complacency—sometimes despair—engendered by beliefs that liberal democracy has always been hegemonic. . . .

The Multiple-Traditions Thesis of American Civic Identity

It seems prudent to stress what is not proposed here. This is not a call for analysts to minimize the significance of white male political actors or their conflicts with each other. Neither is it a call for accounts that assail "Eurocentric" white male oppressors on behalf of diverse but always heroic subjugated groups. The multiple-traditions thesis holds that Americans share a *common* culture but one more complexly and multiply constituted than is usually acknowledged. Most members of all groups have shared and often helped to shape all the ideologies and institutions that have structured American life, including ascriptive ones. A few have done so while resisting all subjugating practices. But members of every group have sometimes embraced "essentialist" ideologies valorizing their own ascriptive traits and denigrating those of others, to bleak effect. Cherokees enslaved blacks, (Perdue, 1979), champions of women's rights disparaged blacks and immigrants,

(DuBois 1978); and blacks have often been hostile toward Hispanics and other new immigrants (Daniels 1990, 323, 376). White men, in turn, have been prominent among those combating invidious exclusions, as well as those imposing them.

Above all, recognition of the strong attractions of restrictive Americanist ideas does not imply any denial that America's liberal and democratic traditions have had great normative and political potency, even if they have not been so hegemonic as some claim.[5] Instead, it sheds a new—and, in some respects, more flattering—light on the constitutive role of liberal democratic values in American life. Although some Americans have been willing to repudiate notions of democracy and universal rights, most have not; and though many have tried to blend those commitments with exclusionary ascriptive views, the illogic of these mixes has repeatedly proven a major resource for successful reformers. But we obscure the difficulty of those reforms (and thereby diminish their significance) if we slight the ideological and political appeal of contrary ascriptive traditions by portraying them as merely the shadowy side of a hegemonic liberal republicanism.

At its heart, the multiple-traditions thesis holds that the definitive feature of American political culture has been not its liberal, republican, or "ascriptive Americanist" elements but, rather, this more complex pattern of apparently inconsistent combinations of the traditions, accompanied by recurring conflicts. Because standard accounts neglect this pattern, they do not explore how and why Americans have tried to uphold aspects of all three of these heterogeneous traditions in combinations that are longer on political and psychological appeal than on intellectual coherency.

A focus on these questions generates an understanding of American politics that differs from Tocquevillian ones in four major respects. First, on this view, purely liberal and republican conceptions of civic identity are seen as frequently unsatisfying to many Americans, because they contain elements that threaten, rather than affirm, sincere, reputable beliefs in the propriety of the privileged positions that whites, Christianity, Anglo–Saxon traditions, and patriarchy have had in the United States. At the same time, even Americans deeply attached to those inegalitarian arrangements have also had liberal democratic values. Second, it has therefore been typical, not aberrational, for Americans to embody strikingly opposed beliefs in their institutions, such as doctrines that blacks should and should not be full and equal citizens. But though American efforts to blend aspects of opposing views have often been remarkably stable, the resulting tensions have still been important sources of change. Third, when older types of ascriptive inequality, such as slavery, have been rejected as unduly illiberal, it has been normal, not anomalous, for many Americans to embrace new doctrines and institutions that reinvigorate the hierarchies they esteem in modified form. Changes toward greater inequality and exclusion, as well as toward greater equality and inclusiveness, thus can and do occur. Finally, the dynamics of American development cannot simply be seen as a rising tide of liberalizing forces progressively submerging contrary beliefs and practices. The national course has been more serpentine. The economic, political, and moral forces propelling the United States toward liberal democracy have often been heeded by American leaders, especially since World War II. But the currents pulling toward fuller expression of alleged natural and cultural inequalities have also always won victories. In some eras they have predominated, appearing to define not only the path of safety but that of progress. In all eras, including our own, many Americans have combined their allegiance to liberal democracy with beliefs that the presence of certain groups favored by history, nature, and God has made Americans an intrinsically "special" people. Their adherents have usually regarded such beliefs as benign and intellectually well founded; yet they also have always had more or less harsh discriminatory corollaries....

In sum, if we accept that ideologies and institutions of ascriptive hierarchy have shaped America in interaction with its liberal and democratic features, we can make more sense of a wide range of inegalitarian policies newly contrived after 1870 and perpetuated through much of the twentieth century. Those policies were dismantled only through great struggles, aided by international pressures during World War II and the Cold War; and it is not clear that these struggles have ended. The novelties in the policies and scientific doctrines of the Gilded Age and Progressive Era should alert us to the possibility that new intellectual systems and political forces defending racial and gender inequalities may yet gain increased power in our own time.

The achievements of Americans in building a more inclusive democracy certainly provide reasons to believe that illiberal forces will not prevail. But just as we can better explain the nation's past by recognizing how and why liberal democratic principles have been contested with frequent success, we will better understand the present and future of American politics if we do not presume they are rooted in essentially liberal or democratic values and conditions. Instead, we must analyze America as the ongoing product of often conflicting multiple traditions.

NOTES

1. The percentage varies according to whether one dates the United States from 1776, the Declaration of Independence, or 1789, the ratified Constitution. State policies prior to 1789 on the whole made nonwhites and women ineligible for full citizenship. Women could always formally be U.S. citizens, but they were almost universally denied the vote until 1920, making them clearly second-class citizens. Other overt legal discriminations on their political and economic rights continued through the 1960s. Naturalization was confined to whites from 1790 through 1868 and closed to most Asian nationals until 1952. By then, the national origins quota system of immigration restrictions, enacted in the 1920s, prevented most Asians and many southern Europeans from coming to the United States and becoming permanent residents or citizens, explicitly because of their original nationality or ethnicity. That system was not repealed until 1965. Despite formal constitutional guarantees enacted in the mid-1860s, blacks were also widely denied basic rights of citizenship until the 1964 Civil Rights Act and the 1965 Voting Rights Act (Higham 1975, 29–66; Kettner 1978, 287–322; Smith 1989). Thus, though the specifics changed, denials of access to full citizenship based explicitly on race, ethnicity, or gender always denied large majorities of the world's population any opportunity for U.S. citizenship up to 1965. That represents about 83% of the nation's history since the Constitution, 88% since the Declaration of Independence. If, controversially, one assumes that women became full citizens with the vote in 1920, then a majority of the domestic adult population became legally eligible for full citizenship then. This still means that a majority of domestic adults were ineligible for full citizenship on racial, ethnic, or gender grounds for about two-thirds of U.S. history (from either starting point).
2. Orren (1991), a major alternative critique of Tocquevillian accounts, shows ascriptive inegalitarian labor systems long prevailed even among white men.
3. From early on, many American intellectuals and politicians believed that "like the Chain of Being, the races of man consisted of an ordered hierarchy" (Haller 1971, 11; Russett 1989, 201–3). Some believed in a natural order of rank among the races, some that cultures fell into a higher and lower levels of civilization. Most thought race and culture linked. Scholars disagreed about the relative ranks of Asiatics, blacks, Native Americans, and other races and

cultures, but these gradations mattered less than the supremacy of whites over nonwhites. Mulattoes, for example, were legally treated as an intermediate racial group in antebellum America, but by the 1850s whites began to reduce their status to that of "pure" blacks (Williamson 1980).

4. A tradition here is comprised by (1) a worldview or ideology that defines basic political and economic institutions, the persons eligible to participate in them, and the roles or rights to which they are entitled and (2) institutions and practices embodying and reproducing those precepts. Hence traditions are not *merely* sets of ideas. The liberal tradition involves limited government, the rule of law protecting individual rights, and a market economy, all officially open to all minimally rational adults. The republican tradition is grounded on popular sovereignty exercised via institutions of mass self-governance. It includes an ethos of civic virtue and economic regulation for the public good. Adherents of what I term ascriptive Americanist traditions believe true Americans are in some way "chosen" by God, history, or nature to possess superior moral and intellectual traits, often associated with race and gender. Hence many Americanists believe that nonwhites and women should be governed as subjects or second-class citizens, denied full market rights, and sometimes excluded from the nation altogether. My thesis—that an evolving mix of these traditions is visible in America's political culture, institutions, and the outlooks of Americans of *all* backgrounds—is indebted to Orren and Skowronek 1993.

5. I also agree that tensions between liberal and democratic ideas and institutions have been vital factors in American history, visible, for example, in the great struggles between the defenders of property rights and populist and labor movements. Those conflicts have, however, also always involved battles over the nation's racial, ethnic, and gender ordering.

REFERENCES

Daniels, Roger. 1990. *Coming to America: A History of Immigration and Ethnicity in American Life*. New York: Harper Collins.

DuBois Ellen, Carol. 1978. *Feminism and Suffrage: The Emergence of an Independent Women's Movement in America, 1848–1869*. Ithaca: Cornell University Press.

Epstein, Richard A. 1985. *Takings: Private Property and the Power of Eminent Domain*. Cambridge: Harvard University Press.

Epstein Richard, A. 1992. *Forbidden Grounds: The Case Against Employment Discrimination Laws*. Cambridge: Harvard University Press.

Fairchild, Halford H. 1991. "Scientific Racism: The Cloak of Objectivity." *Journal of Social Issues* 47: 101–115.

Fuchs, Lawrence H. 1990. *The American Kaleidoscope: Race, Ethnicity, and the Civic Culture*. Hanover, NH: University Press of New England.

Haller, John S. Jr. 1971. *Outcasts from Evolution: Scientific Attitudes of Racial Inferiority, 1859–1900*. Urbana: University of Illinois Press.

Hartog, Hendrik. 1987. "The Constitution of Aspiration and 'The Rights that Belong to Us All.'" In *The Constitution and American Life*, ed. David Thelen. Ithaca: Cornell University Press.

Higham, John. 1975. *Send These to Me*. New York: Atheneum Press.

Kettner, James. 1978. *The Development of American Citizenship, 1608–1870*. Chapel Hill: University of North Carolina Press.

Orren, Karen. 1991. *Belated Feudalism: Labor, the Law, and Liberal Development in the United States*. New York: Cambridge University Press.

Orren, Karen, and Skowronek, Stephen. 1993. "Beyond the Iconography of Order: Notes for a 'New Institutionalism.'" In *The Dynamics of American Politics: Approaches and Interpretations*, ed. Lawrence C. Dodd and Calvin Jillson. Boulder: Westview Press.

Perdue, Theda. 1979. *Slavery and the Evolution of Cherokee Society, 1540–1866*. Knoxville: University of Tennessee Press.

Russett, Cynthia Eagle. 1989. *Sexual Science: The Victorian Construction of Womanhood*. Cambridge: Harvard University Press.

Smith, Rogers M. 1989. "'One United People' Second-Class Female Citizenship and the American Quest for
    Community." *Yale Journal of Law and the Humanities* 1: 229–293.
Williamson, Joel. 1980. *New People: Miscegenation and Mulattoes in the United States.* New York: Free Press.

Discussion Questions

1. What does the word liberal mean in regard to John Locke's social contract theory
   and how does that differ from what we commonly mean by liberal today?
2. What does Montesquieu mean by "republicanism" or republican political thought
   and how do these words and phrases differ from what we commonly mean by
   similar words and phrases today?
3. James Morone argues that American political development has been characterized
   by surges in democratic commitment followed by a waning of those commitments
   and disappointment in the achievements of democratic reform. Do you agree or
   disagree with his description of why reform frequently is disappointing?
4. Is contemporary America as sensitive to the ascriptive characteristics of individuals
   in determining their appropriate social roles as the society was 100 years ago or 50
   years ago? What evidence do you see that supports your view?
5. In light of Barack Obama's re-election as president, how should we think about
   Rogers Smith's multiple traditions thesis? Does Obama's re-election put the thesis
   in a broader context or does it seem to argue for or against the thesis?

Suggested Additional Reading

Francis D. Adams and Barry Sanders, *Alienable Rights: The Exclusion of African-Americans
   in a White Man's Land, 1619–2000* (New York: Harper Collins, 2003).
Cal Jillson, *Pursuing the American Dream: Opportunity and Exclusion Over Four
   Centuries* (Lawrence, KS: University of Kansas Press, 2004).
Joseph Lowndes, Julie Novkov, and Dorian T. Warren (eds.) *Race and American Political
   Development* (New York: Routledge, 2008).
Karen Orren and Stephen Skowronek, *The Search for American Political Development*
   (New York: Cambridge University Press, 2004).
Fareed Zakaria, *The Future of Freedom: Illiberal Democracy at Home and Abroad* (New
   York: W.W. Norton, 2003).

2

The Revolution and the Constitution

Introduction

How can a government be powerful enough to battle for the nation's interests, and yet limited enough to prevent its leaders from abusing their powers for their own selfish gain? Governments have the legitimate right to use the military and police to keep order. What prevents leaders from using these tools to prevent their removal from office, to jail political opponents, or to exploit citizens for personal enrichment? If the military and police are too limited, a nation risks invasion, terrorism, and social disorder. The central question of designing government, as James Madison put it in *Federalist* 51, is that "You must first enable the government to controul the governed; and in the next place, oblige it to controul itself."[1]

The difficult problems of constructing a good government were even more complicated when the United States formally divorced itself from Britain in 1776. The first reading in this section comes from *Common Sense*, Thomas Paine's call for American political separation from Britain months before the publication of the Declaration of Independence. Paine encouraged the nation to strike out on its own, insisting that the nation *could* govern itself and *should* do so. When the United States declared independence, the colonies renamed themselves "states," and governed as if they were small, independent republics. The people were the ultimate source of authority in these republics. Voters elected all the most important policy-makers. These states adopted written, republican constitutions that strictly limited and separated governing institutions. The states established state militias (and some created navies), taxes, regulations, and other laws that governed the territory they controlled. What little national governing existed was conducted by a "Congress" (a word that suggests a gathering of representatives of independent nations). This Continental Congress had no executive, no courts, and no reliable source of revenue. During the Revolution, it barely sustained a Continental Army to fight the British. After the war it became harder and harder for Congress to maintain itself or the nation. It was a crisis of national government that compelled twelve of the thirteen states to send delegates to Philadelphia to reform the national government in May, 1787.

Building a new American state in the 1780s was easier said than done, then, because the state governments already had built resilient and durable institutions.

The Constitution created a national government layered on top of these state governments. As David Robertson pointed out in the second reading, politics and path dependence dominated the process of designing the Constitution. The state politicians who wrote the Constitution not only wanted to prevent the national government from abusing its power, but also wanted to ensure that the interests of their state would be furthered, and not wrecked, by the new government. Each major decision in the Convention affected the ensuing decisions at the Convention. For example, the failure of Virginia's plan for a Congress in which seats in both houses would be proportionate to population made delegates from the slave states unwilling to add extensive, open-ended authority to the U.S. government.

The Constitution is, above all, a product of political pragmatism applied to practical problems and inherited institutions. In the third reading, Benjamin Franklin, speaking in the privacy of the Constitutional Convention on its final day, attested to the imperfections of the Constitution. Franklin, the oldest statesman at the meeting, explained that although he did not approve of "several parts" of the Constitution, he did not think the Convention could design a better one because of the diverse politics and personalities of the delegates. Moreover, he promised he would not criticize the Constitution in public. In a public letter to Congress that accompanied their Constitution (the companion excerpt), the Convention delegates reminded us of how difficult it was to design a government that would be neither too strong nor too weak, and that only political compromise made the document possible at all.

As the delegates anticipated, specific provisions of the Constitution immediately generated opposition. Because the Constitution's adoption depended on ratification in each state, the Constitution's opponents—labeled "anti-federalists"—attacked specific provisions as risky or inconsistent with the political values that all Americans shared. These attacks cast doubt on the entire document. Their opposition differed somewhat in different states, but there were some general lines of anti-federalist attack. In the fourth reading, Herbert Storing pulled together these lines of attack to explain what the Anti-Federalists sought as an alternative to the Constitution. The fifth reading provides James Madison's response to one of the serious objections to the Constitution. In *Federalist* 47 and 48, Madison defended the Constitution against the anti-federalist claim that the plan violated republican doctrine by failing to separate government powers adequately.

Our highlight piece in Chapter 2 is by Akhil Reed Amar, who took a broader perspective on the American Constitution's solution to the dilemma of state-building and its consequences. Amar emphasized how path-breaking the Constitution was at the time. The Constitution begins with a preamble that insists on rule by the people, and the document "infuses democracy into each of its seven main Articles." The Constitution also established the enduring institutions of American government—a Congress with two houses, a president chosen by the Electoral College, an independent judiciary, and a collection of states that share sovereignty with the national government.

This framework has structured American political development for two centuries, and everyone who advocates major political change has had to confront the Constitution. In 1933, President Franklin Roosevelt said in his first inaugural address that "Our Constitution is so simple, so practical that it is possible always to meet extraordinary needs by changes in emphasis and arrangement without loss of essential form. That is why our constitutional system has proved itself the most superbly enduring political mechanism the modern world has ever seen."[2] Yet Roosevelt himself found that Congress, the courts, and the states placed substantial obstacles in the way of his plans for change. For all our expectation that a new leader will bring change to American politics, then, they must deal with the institutions the Constitution gives us, as these institutions have been developing over the course of American history.

Notes

1. *Federalist* 51, in Jacob E. Cooke, ed., *The Federalist* (Hanover, NH: Wesleyan University Press, 1961), 349.
2. First Inaugural Address of President Franklin D. Roosevelt, March 4, 1933 (http://avalon.law.yale.edu/20th_century/froos1.asp, accessed May 4, 2013).

2.1 Thomas Paine, "Common Sense" (1776)

In January of 1776, Thomas Paine's new pamphlet, *Common Sense*, electrified American readers. The British-born Paine had only arrived in the United States in October, 1774, but in that time the first battles of American Revolution were fought at Lexington and Concord, Massachusetts, on April 19, 1775. Before the appearance of *Common Sense*, many American leaders were very reluctant to make the final break with Britain. In his pamphlet, Paine argued that all the Americans' grievances were part of a broader pattern of British corruption and abuse of power. He held that governments should be based on rule by the people. Americans, he argued, should show the world they could govern themselves: "The cause of America is, in great measure, the cause of all mankind."[1] Paine pressed Americans to publish a manifesto laying out their grievances with the British government and declaring their colonies independent. *Common Sense* sold over 100,000 copies in the early months of 1776, and by mid-summer, the Continental Congress had published the manifesto Paine urged: the Declaration of Independence.

Some writers have so confounded society with government as to leave little or no distinction between them; whereas they are not only different, but have different origins. Society is produced by our wants and government by our wickedness; the former promotes our happiness *positively* by uniting our affections, the latter *negatively* by restraining our vices. The one encourages intercourse, the other creates distinctions. The first is a patron, the last a punisher.

Society in every state is a blessing, but government, even in its best state, is but a necessary evil; in its worst state an intolerable one; for when we suffer or are exposed to the same miseries *by a government*, which we might expect in a country *without government*, our calamity is heightened by reflecting that we furnish the means by which we suffer. Government, like dress, is the badge of lost innocence; the palaces of kings are built upon the ruins of the bowers of paradise. For were the impulses of conscience clear, uniform, and irresistibly obeyed, man would need no other lawgiver; but that not being the case, he finds it necessary to surrender up a part of his property to furnish means for the protection of the rest; and this he is induced to do by the same prudence which in every other case advises him out of two evils to choose the least. *Wherefore*, security being the true design and end of government, it unanswerably follows that whatever *form* thereof appears most likely to ensure it to us, with the least expense and greatest benefit, is preferable to all others.

... In the following pages I offer nothing more than simple facts, plain arguments, and common sense....

Volumes have been written on the subject of the struggle between England and America. Men of all ranks have embarked in the controversy, from different motives, and with various designs; but all have been ineffectual, and the period of debate is closed. Arms as the last resource decide the contest; the appeal was the choice of the king, and the continent has accepted the challenge.

... The sun never shined on a cause of greater worth. 'Tis not the affair of a city, a county, a province, or a kingdom; but of a continent—of at least one-eighth part of the habitable globe. 'Tis not the concern of a day, a year, or an age; posterity are virtually involved in the contest, and will be more or less affected even to the end of time by the proceedings now. Now is the seedtime of continental union, faith, and honor. The least fracture now will be like a name engraved with the point of a pin on the tender rind of a young oak; the wound would enlarge with the tree, and posterity read it in full grown characters.

By referring the matter from argument to arms, a new era for politics is struck—a new method of thinking has arisen. All plans, proposals, &c. prior to the nineteenth of April, i.e. to the commencement of hostilities, are like the almanacks of the last year; which though proper then, are superseded and useless now. Whatever was advanced by the advocates on either side of the question then, terminated in one and the same point, viz. a union with Great Britain; the only difference between the parties was the method of effecting it; the one proposing force, the other friendship; but it has so far happened that the first has failed, and the second has withdrawn her influence.

As much has been said of the advantages of reconciliation, which, like an agreeable dream, has passed away and left us as we were, it is but right that we should examine the contrary side of the argument, and inquire into some of the many material injuries which these colonies sustain, and always will sustain, by being connected with and dependent on Great Britain. To examine that connection and dependence on the principles of nature and common sense; to see what we have to trust to, if separated, and what we are to expect, if dependent.

I have heard it asserted by some, that as America has flourished under her former connection with Great Britain, the same connection is necessary towards her future happiness, and will always have the same effect. Nothing can be more fallacious than this kind of argument. We may as well assert that because a child has thrived upon milk, that it is never to have meat, or that the first twenty years of our lives is to become a precedent for the next twenty. But even this is admitting more than is true; for I answer roundly that America would have flourished as much, and probably much more, had no European power taken any notice of her. The commerce by which she hath enriched herself are the necessaries of life, and will always have a market while eating is the custom of Europe.

But she has protected us, say some. That she hath engrossed us is true, and defended the continent at our expense as well as her own is admitted; and she would have defended Turkey from the same motive, viz., for the sake of trade and dominion.

Alas! we have been long led away by ancient prejudices and made large sacrifices to superstition. We have boasted the protection of Great Britain without considering that her motive was *interest*, not *attachment*; and that she did not protect us from *our enemies* on *our account*, but from her enemies on her own account, from those who had no quarrel with us on any *other account*, and who will always be our enemies on the *same account*.

. . . But where, say some, is the king of America? I'll tell you, friend, he reigns above, and doth not make havoc of mankind like the Royal Brute of Great Britain. Yet that we may not appear to be defective even in earthly honors, let a day be solemnly set apart for proclaiming the charter; let it be brought forth placed on the divine law, the Word of God; let a crown be placed thereon, by which the world may know, that so far as we approve of monarchy, that in America THE LAW IS KING. For as in absolute governments the king is law, so in free countries the law *ought* to BE king, and there ought to be no other. But lest any ill use should afterwards arise, let the crown at the conclusion of the ceremony be demolished, and scattered among the people whose right it is.

A government of our own is our natural right; and when a man seriously reflects on the precariousness of human affairs, he will become convinced, that it is infinitely wiser and safer to form a constitution of our own in a cool deliberate manner, while we have it in our power, than to trust such an interesting event to time and chance.

. . . I have never met a man either in England or America who hath not confessed his opinion that a separation between the countries would take place, one time or other. And there is no instance in which we have shown less judgment than in endeavoring to describe what we call the ripeness or fitness of the continent for independence.

As all men allow the measure, and vary only in their opinion of the time, let us, in order to remove mistakes, take a general survey of things, and endeavor if possible to find out the very time. But I need not go far, the inquiry ceases at once, for the *time hath found us*. The general concurrence, the glorious union of all things, proves the fact.

It is not in numbers but in unity that our great strength lies; yet our present numbers are sufficient to repel the force of all the world. The continent has at this time the largest body of armed and disciplined men of any power under heaven; and is just arrived at that pitch of strength, in which no single colony is able to support itself, and the whole, when united, is able to do anything. Our land force is more than sufficient, and as to naval affairs, we cannot be insensible that Britain would never suffer an American man of war to be built while the continent remained in her hands. Wherefore, we should be no forwarder a hundred years hence in that branch than we are now; but the truth is, we should be less so, because the timber of the country is every day diminishing.

. . . Another reason why the present time is preferable to all others is that the fewer our numbers are, the more land there is yet unoccupied which, instead of being lavished by the king on his worthless dependents, may be hereafter supplied not only to the discharge of the present debt but to the constant support of government. No nation under heaven hath such an advantage as this.

The infant state of the colonies, as it is called, so far from being against, is an argument in favor of independence. We are sufficiently numerous, and were we more so we might be less united. It is a matter worthy of observation that the more a country is peopled the smaller their armies are. In military numbers, the ancients far exceeded the moderns; and the reason is evident, for trade being the consequence of population men became too much absorbed thereby to attend to anything else. Commerce diminishes the spirit both of patriotism and military defense. And history sufficiently informs us that the bravest achievements were always accomplished in the nonage of a nation. With the increase of commerce England hath lost its spirit. The city of London, notwithstanding its numbers, submits to continued insults with the patience of a coward. The more men have to lose, the less willing are they to venture. The rich are in general slaves to fear, and submit to courtly power with the trembling duplicity of a spaniel.

Youth is the seedtime of good habits, as well in nations as in individuals. It might be difficult, if not impossible, to form the continent into one government half a century hence. The vast variety of interests, occasioned by an increase of trade and population, would create confusion. Colony would be against colony. Each, being able, would scorn each other's assistance; and while the proud and foolish gloried in their little distinctions, the wise would lament that the union had not been formed before. Wherefore the present time is the true time for establishing it. The intimacy which is contracted in infancy and the friendship which is formed in misfortune are of all others the most lasting and unalterable. Our present union is marked with both these characters; we are young, and we have been distressed; but our concord hath withstood our troubles, and fixes a memorable era for posterity to glory in.

The present time, likewise, is that peculiar time which never happens to a nation but once, viz. the time of forming itself into a government. Most nations have let slip the opportunity, and by that means have been compelled to receive laws from their conquerors instead of making laws for themselves. First they had a king, and then a form of government; whereas the articles or charter of government should be formed first, and men delegated to execute them afterwards: but from the errors of other nations let us learn wisdom and lay hold of the present opportunity—*to begin government at the right end.*

... TO CONCLUDE. However strange it may appear to some, or however unwilling they may be to think so, matters not, but many strong and striking reasons may be given to show that nothing can settle our affairs so expeditiously as an open and determined DECLARATION FOR INDEPENDENCE. Some of which are:

First. It is the custom of nations, when any two are at war, for some other powers not engaged in the quarrel to step in as mediators, and bring about the preliminaries of a peace; but while America calls herself the Subject of Great Britain, no power, however well disposed she may be, can offer her mediation. Wherefore, in our present state we may quarrel on forever.

Secondly. It is unreasonable to suppose that France or Spain will give us any kind of assistance if we mean only to make use of that assistance for the purpose of repairing the breach and strengthening the connection between Britain and America; because those powers would be sufferers by the consequences.

Thirdly. While we profess ourselves the subjects of Britain, we must, in the eyes of foreign nations, be considered as rebels. The precedent is somewhat dangerous to *their peace,* for men to be in arms under the name of subjects: we, on the spot, can solve the paradox; but to unite resistance and subjection requires an idea much too refined for common understanding.

Fourthly. Were a manifesto to be published and despatched to foreign courts, setting forth the miseries we have endured and the peaceful methods which we have ineffectually used for redress; declaring at the same time that, not being able any longer to live happily or safely under the cruel disposition of the British court, we have been driven to the necessity of breaking off all connections with her; at the same time assuring all such courts of our peaceable disposition towards them, and of our desire of entering into trade with them: such a memorial would produce more good effects to this continent, than if a ship were freighted with petitions to Britain.

Under our present denomination of British subjects, we can neither be received nor heard abroad: the custom of all courts is against us, and will be so until by an independence we take rank with other nations.

These proceedings may at first seem strange and difficult, but like all other steps which we have already passed over, will in a little time become familiar and agreeable; and until an Independence is declared, the continent will feel itself like a man who continues putting off some unpleasant business from day to day, yet knows it must be done, hates to set about it, wishes it over, and is continually haunted with the thoughts of its necessity.

NOTE

1. Thomas Paine, "Common Sense," in Bruce Kuklick, ed., *Political Writings/Thomas Paine* (Cambridge and New York: Cambridge University Press, 1989), 2.

2.2 David Brian Robertson, "Madison's Opponents and Constitutional Design" (2005)

Political scientist David Robertson reminded us that the framers of the Constitution could not and did not design American government from scratch. First, as political leaders sent as representatives of their respective states, each brought different preferences and interests to the Constitutional Convention in Philadelphia in the summer of 1787. Second, they inherited a set of problems and institutions that inevitably narrowed the options they could consider. As a result, the Constitution was built provision by provision, choice by choice. The delegates' initial decisions affected their decisions about other provisions days or weeks later. Robertson focused on the conflicts that arose again and again between the ambitions of the young James Madison and the elder statesman, Roger Sherman. Madison was determined to build a strong national government, while Sherman was just as determined to protect accomplishments of the states. The Constitution, born of political conflict, has not only set the basic framework for the path of American political development, but set the basic rules of American political conflict as well. The Constitution is a weapon used by both sides in battles over federalism, congressional power, presidential power, judicial authority, civil rights and liberties, and domestic and foreign policy.

... The delegates' central political dilemma ... was to reconstitute the national government so it could provide the national public goods they believed necessary, without endangering the vital interests of their constituents and the polities they had built. Each state legislature charged its delegates to render the national government "adequate to the Exigencies of the Union." There was widespread agreement that the national government needed a steady stream of income and some specific additional powers to deal with national security, civil unrest, commerce, and currency problems. Because the states had different economic assets (McCusker and Menard 1985), cultures, histories, policy commitments, and political equilibria, however, each delegation specifically defined "adequate" in a different way. Delegates from New Jersey and Connecticut advocated the nationalization of tariffs and currency while they defended other state prerogatives (RFC [*The Records of the Federal Convention of 1787*] August 16, II, 309; August 28, II, 439). Several delegates, including William Paterson, George Mason, and John Dickinson, hoped to ban the slave trade (RFC June 9, I, 561; August 22, II, 370, 372). While Luther Martin fiercely resisted the expansion of many national powers at the Convention, he also insisted on nationalized control over public lands (RFC August 30, II, 464). Each delegate made his own evaluation about the benefits and risks of any *specific* national power for his own state and the nation (see also McGuire 2003 and Siemers 2002) ...

James Madison's Agenda for Constitutional Design

The delegates' anxiety about the nation's future, combined with the hazy status of specific solutions, opened a window of political opportunity for James Madison. He prepared for the Convention more thoroughly than any other delegate (Banning 1995; Rakove 1996, 46–56, 59; Robertson 2003). As a member of the Confederation Congress, Madison had supported stronger national revenue and commercial powers. He approached the Convention with a much bolder agenda for reform and a strategy for getting the Convention to adopt it.

Madison sought three kinds of far-reaching changes in national government design. First, Madison sought to transfer to the national government the complete authority over taxes, commerce, and other basic tools of economic policy. Madison had become convinced that the states had too much authority over economic policy, and their abuse of that authority was harming the nation's interests and its republican experiment. Much like Adam Smith, Madison believed that government had an important but limited role, primarily facilitating trade and market-driven economic development (Fleischacker 2002; Matthews 1995, 314). The states' debt, currency, and trade policies were inhibiting free markets and the nation's prosperity. In letters to George Washington,

Thomas Jefferson, and Virginia Governor Edmund Randolph, Madison insisted on the establishment of a fully sovereign national government, "armed," he told Randolph, "with a positive & compleat authority in all cases where uniform measures are necessary" (PJM [*The Papers of James Madison*] 9: 370; 317–22, 382–87). The delegates took it for granted, he claimed, that the U.S. national government should "have powers far beyond those exercised by the British Parliament when the States were part of the British Empire" (RFC June 29, I, 464). National officials' ambitions should be driven by a material concern for national advantage and nothing else. Madison reasoned by analogy that, if state policy authority resulted in the incentive to pursue parochial interests, expanded national authority could give national government officials the incentive to pursue purely national interests. To the end of the Convention he argued that complete authority over the nation's commerce, including intrastate commerce, was indispensable (RFC August 28, II, 442; September 15, II, 625). Madison also believed that taxation should be nationalized, on the grounds that a "compleat power of taxation" was "the highest prerogative of supremacy" (RFC June 28, I, 447) and "no line could be drawn between authority to regulate trade and authority to levy taxes" (RFC August 13, II, 276). Madison also sought broad national authority to govern the militias, to charter corporations, to develop canals and other infrastructure projects, to found a national university, and to establish patents and copyrights (RFC August 18, II, 324–25, 332; August 23, II 332; September 14, II, 615). To anchor this broad national authority, Madison proposed the extraordinary national power to veto *state* legislation at will, asserting at the Convention that "an indefinite power to negative legislative acts of the States" was "absolutely neces-sary to a perfect system" (Hobson 1979; PJM 9: 383–84; RFC June 8, I, 164–68, 171–72; June 19, I, 319; July 17, I, 28).

Second, Madison's basic plan aimed to minimize the state governments' role in choosing national policy-makers. Madison believed it essential to avoid "too great an agency of the State Governments in the General one . . ." (RFC June 6, I, 134). The Virginia Plan proposed that the voters directly choose the members of the House of Representatives, the foundation of the national policy-making system. The House then would elect the Senate from slates proposed by the states, and the national legislature would choose the national executive and judiciary. Madison described this scheme as a "policy of refining the popular appointments by successive filtrations" (RFC May 31, I, 49–50), and it would disconnect national policy making from the states, stabilize popular control of government, and deliver better policy outcomes for the nation. The third basic element of Madison's plan was tactical as well as substantive: The Convention would have to establish what he termed "proportional representation" (that is, apportioning seats in the national legislature according to population size) as the first order of business. Proportional representation in both houses of Congress would further nationalize policy, by reducing the influence of state governments as units of representation, and it would substantially increase the influence of Madison's own constituents by giving Virginia the largest delegation in Congress.

Tactically, Madison depended on a swift victory for proportional representation to bind together a winning Convention coalition of six states. The three largest states, Massachusetts, Pennsylvania, and Virginia, would gain from proportional representation in the short run. Georgia and the Carolinas would gain in the foreseeable future as their rapidly growing populations eclipsed the eastern states (PJM 9: 318–19, 369–70, 383). The success of this strategy depended on winning early agreement for proportional representation in both chambers of the new legislature (Jillson 1988, 47) and on delaying debate on the substance of national authority, particularly the divisive issues of tariffs, trade, and public lands. Once the Convention adopted proportional representation in the new national legislature, this coalition would gel and sweep his remaining agenda through the Convention. He wrote hopefully to Jefferson that "if a majority of the larger States concur, the fewer and smaller States must finally bend to them. This point being gained, many of the objections now urged in the leading States ag[ain]st renunciations of power will vanish" (PJM 9:319; see also Lee and Oppenheimer 1999, 36–37). Virginia's delegates gambled that smaller states could be prevailed upon "in the course of the deliberations, to give up their equality for the sake of an effective Government" (RFC May 28, I, 10–11, note)....

The Pivotal Role of Connecticut and Roger Sherman

Connecticut's delegates led the opposition, relentlessly disputing Madison's most important Convention proposals. Connecticut also became the pivotal delegation by taking a key role in framing and then defeating the New Jersey Plan, pressing for the "Connecticut" compromise on House and Senate apportionment, providing northern support for protecting the slave trade, and injecting state agency into presidential selection ...

Roger Sherman led an unusually cohesive and pragmatic three-man Connecticut delegation (Rakove 1996, 86). At the Convention, Sherman was the most active spokesman among the Virginia Plan's opponents. Madison and Sherman took positions explicitly opposed to one another on 39 occasions. Sherman spoke, made motions, or seconded motions 160 times, much more often than John Dickinson or Maryland's Luther Martin and 10 times more often than any delegate from New Jersey. Madison himself spoke, made motions, or seconded motions 177 times. Sherman's talented younger colleague, Oliver Ellsworth, greatly admired Sherman and looked to him as his model. Sherman and his protégé Ellsworth rarely expressed differences (though when they did, Ellsworth was willing to provide marginally more power to the national government than was Sherman; RFC August 9, II, 232; August 23, II, 385). William Samuel Johnson, who was somewhat more open to national authority than Sherman, had been Sherman's legal mentor (Collier 1971, 234). Thirty years older than Madison, Sherman came to the Convention with a formidable political reputation as a leading American statesman. He had served on the congressional committees that wrote the Resolves of 1774, the Declaration of Independence, and the Articles of Confederation. Only Sherman signed all three of these documents and the Constitution. In the mid-1780s Sherman was serving—simultaneously—as mayor of New Haven, a member of the Connecticut's Council of Assistants (which functioned as the state senate), a judge on the Connecticut Superior Court, and a delegate to the Confederation Congress.

Sherman had strong intellectual differences with Madison and aimed to achieve a much narrower agenda of reform. He advocated as much direct, equal-state agency in national policy-making as feasible, as little nationalization of public goods as necessary, and as much state control of everyday economic management as possible. While he also supported certain stronger national powers, Sherman preferred that the scope of national authority should be expanded in a much more limited and specific ways. No one argued earlier and more forcefully against the conventional wisdom that sovereignty could not be divided. Instead, he argued for the idea of dual sovereignty, insisting that the state and national governments should have discrete areas of policy responsibility (RFC May 30, I, 34–35; June 6, I, 133; June 7, I, 150). He conceded that the Confederation government required additional powers, "particularly that of raising money" and the national management of currency and interstate commerce, both pressing interests for a state squeezed by Rhode Island's paper currency and New York's tariffs. Circumstantial evidence indicates that he supported national authority to assume the states' debts (Currie 1997, 77; RFC August 18, II, 326–68, August 21, II, 355–56). States should be prohibited from issuing currency or interfering with contractual obligations. But Sherman insisted from the start that states should retain control of "matters of internal police ... wherein the general welfare of the United States is not affected" (Collier 1971, 230–33; RFC May 30, I, 34). While Madison believed that the burden of proof for retaining economic policy authority rested on the states, for Sherman, the burden for absorbing such authority rested on the national government. Sherman argued, for example, that states should retain even the power to embargo goods. A plan he wrote early in the Convention would have retained the Confederation system of requisitions, which allowed the states to fund the national government through revenues of their choosing. Congress should be the agent of the states, he believed, with national policy-makers ultimately selected and paid by the state governments (Collier 1973, 10, 47, 61, 68, 71–73; RFC II, 439–40; III, 615–16). Madison ally Rufus King thought Sherman favored "a sort of collateral Government" (RFC June 6, I, 142–43).

Roger Sherman's direct confrontations with James Madison demonstrate Sherman's influence on the Constitution's design. Madison lost many battles at the Convention. By Forrest McDonald's (1985) count, "Of seventy-one specific proposals that Madison moved, seconded, or spoke unequivocally in regard to, he was on the losing side forty times" (208–9). On 39 occasions Sherman and Madison took explicitly conflicting positions at the Convention. Three of these disagreements involved differences of interpretation that did not bear on a specific issue under consideration. Seven resulted in compromises between their positions. Of the remaining 29 disputes, the Convention ultimately adopted Sherman's position 19 times and Madison's position 10. Conspicuously, the Convention chose Sherman's position over Madison's more frequently as the Convention wore on. After a Committee of Detail produced a draft Constitution on August 6, the Convention took Sherman's position 13 times and Madison's only twice.

A close reading of Madison's own Convention notes shows how Sherman put his formidable political skills to work for his agenda. Fellow politicians considered Sherman shrewd and "cunning as the devil" (RFC III, 88–89; Rossiter 1966, 91). They credited him with such political coups as the acquisition of Connecticut's Western Reserve in Ohio, an area physically the size of Connecticut itself (Boardman 1938, 160; Collier 1971, 15, 146–48; PJM 9, 61). Sherman was the first delegate to inject concerns about political feasibility into the debates, warning the Convention against making "too great inroads on the existing system ... by inserting such as would not be agreed to by the States" (RFC May 30, I, 34–35). On some of the most critical Convention issues—representation in the Congress and presidential power and selection—Sherman skillfully declared an impasse, urged that the issue be delegated to a committee, and then served on the committee and shaped its solution (RFC July 2, I, 511; July 9, I, 560; August 31, II, 481). These *ad hoc* committees took up the Convention's most divisive design issues, forged a coalition of committee members (generally one from each state delegation) around mutually dependent design agreements, and reported a plan that structured the subsequent voting agenda on these issues. In all, Sherman managed to serve on five key Convention committees that played a large role in settling many of the Convention's most fundamental and sensitive political issues: congressional representation, the apportionment of House seats, the national assumption of state debts, the regulation of tariffs and ports, and presidential selection and powers (RFC July 5, I, 526; July 9, I, 652; August 18, II, 322; August 25, II, 418; August 31, II, 481). For the most part, the reports of these five committees became incorporated into the final Constitution.

Sherman skillfully used rhetoric, timing, and, compromise to manipulate the design agenda and alternatives (Riker 1996 termed these skills "heresthetics"). Sherman slashed at Madison's abstractions with Ockham's Razor, incisively questioning the need for such proposals as the national veto, proportional representation in both houses of Congress, and special ratifying conventions for the new Constitution. Sherman used his adversaries' own claims to frame issues in a way that weakened their resolve and united Madison's opponents. By comparing states to individuals, for example, Sherman drew on the emotionally powerful and widely shared narrative of republicanism itself to defend equal state influence (RFC June 28, I, 450). While Madison reasoned that "extending the sphere" of government would strengthen the national government by helping control factions, Sherman reversed Madison's logic with the pithy equation that "[t]he small States have more vigor in their Gov[ernmen]ts than the large ones, the more influence therefore the large ones have, the weaker will be the Gov[ernmen]t" (RFC July 7, I, 550). Sherman displayed a keen sense of political timing, injecting a telling point or exploiting his opponents' concessions at opportune moments. Most notably, Sherman proposed a bicameral compromise on representation at the start of the week's business on Monday morning, June 11, an optimal moment for undercutting the Virginia Plan with an alternative agenda. He staked out positions diametrically opposed to Madison and then expressed a readiness to compromise on a middle ground, drawing the delegates to his apparently moderate position while making Madison's position seem unwarranted or extreme (Collier 1971, 147; RFC June 21, I, 359; June 28, I, 450; July 7, I, 550). Like Madison, Sherman pressed his agenda when he perceived an advantage and tacked toward conciliation when the political winds were less favorable (Collier 1971, 177; 1973, 10, 47, 61, 68, 71–73; Rossiter 1966, 91).

Madison's Convention opponents changed his proposed design for the Constitution by derailing his political strategy for the Convention and then altering his substantive plans for national authority and policy making. As a result, Constitutional design emerged more as a by-product of many specific design choices than as a deliberate choice of one plan instead of another. The Convention's choices were path-dependent, made in a sequence in which choices reflected political calculations set in motion by earlier choices and then affected subsequent political calculations (on path dependence, see Pierson 2000). . . .

The Influence of Madison's Convention Opponents

James Madison played a principal role in bringing the U.S. Constitution into existence. Without his pre-Convention efforts to build an agenda, a supportive coalition, and Convention legitimacy, it is hard to imagine how the delegates would have produced a document endorsed by political leaders from every state but Rhode Island. His Convention notes remain the most definitive record of its proceedings. His tactic for popularly elected state ratifying conventions (which succeeded despite Sherman's opposition) and his vigorous advocacy of the Constitution in New York and Virginia probably were necessary for the Constitution's adoption. Perhaps the most important proponent of religious freedom in the United States (Wills 2002), Madison shepherded the Bill of Rights through the first Congress. As a leader in the House of Representatives, President George Washington's sometime ghostwriter, founder of the Democratic Republican party, Secretary of State, President, and esteemed elder statesman, Madison subsequently exercised a singular influence in Constitutional development.

Bringing the Constitution into existence was very different from designing its provisions, however. Madison failed to persuade the delegates to include the three most significant features of his spring, 1787 plan for reconstituting government. First, he sought very broad national authority to regulate commerce, levy taxes, guide economic development, and veto state laws. Instead, the Convention produced a national government with comparatively narrow, specified authority. The original Constitution underwrote the state governments' authority to govern routine activities of most Americans, and it made national preemption of state authority much more difficult than Madison hoped. Second, Madison sought to eliminate state agency in national policy-making entirely. Instead, the Convention thrust into the middle of the national policy process an assembly of state agents, a Senate that would represent each state government on an equal basis. The Constitution gave to this Senate the special privileges of consenting to treaties, approving presidential appointees, and potentially convicting the president of impeachable offenses. Third, Madison sought to establish relative population or wealth as the basis for apportioning seats in both the House and Senate, and he needed to achieve this goal very soon after the start of Convention deliberations. Instead, the Convention compelled him to accept an unwanted compromise on this central goal. Roger Sherman, John Dickinson, and other delegates from the economically disadvantaged states defeated Madison's aspiration for a relatively brief meeting driven by a swift agreement on proportional representation in both houses of Congress. Instead, they changed the Convention's dynamics, forcing a three and a half-month political struggle largely defined by Madison's aspirations for the nation's political future and Sherman's defense of the nation's political present.

Endorsements by Roger Sherman and his Connecticut colleagues legitimized several other Constitutional provisions, thus facilitating their inclusion: a bicameral legislature, an independently selected president checked by the Senate, temporary tolerance of the slave trade, and an independent judiciary with the power of judicial review of state laws. Sherman also legitimized a host of less important provisions, such as the designation of the Vice President as President of the Senate and of the House of Representatives as the final arbiter of presidential selection (RFC September 6, II, 527; September 7, II, 537).

Evidently, the states outside of Madison's coalition considered the Constitution a success for their interests. They had reduced the two main threats posed by the Virginia Plan by retaining control over their internal policy and by making it hard to use the national government to harm their constituents and their economic assets. They achieved their three main objectives. The Constitution nationalized specific public goods, established strong defenses for their existing advantages, and allowed for the nationalization of further public goods only if proponents could meet the high transaction costs required for making public policy in the new national system. Soon after the signing of the Constitution, Roger Sherman and Oliver Ellsworth declared victory in a letter to their governor. The Convention "endeavoured to provide for the energy of government on the one hand, and suitable checks on the other hand, to secure the rights of the particular states, and the liberties and properties of the citizens." Just as in the Confederation Congress, Connecticut would continue to enjoy a one-thirteenth share in selecting important national policy-makers: Connecticut would fill one-thirteenth of the seats in the new U.S. House of Representatives and Senate and cast one-thirteenth of the votes in the Electoral College. Connecticut's delegates had secured a satisfactory distribution of national and state public goods. "Some additional powers are vested in congress, which was a principal object that the states had in view in appointing the convention. Those powers extend only to matters respecting the common interests of the union, and are specially defined, so that the particular states retain their sovereignty in all other matters" (RFC III, 99–100). Madison would not have been able to disagree with this assessment.

Madison's Convention Opponents and American Politics

The original Constitution's design is not the product of a systematic philosophical plan, but the by-product of a path-dependent sequence of political compromises largely forced on Madison and his allies by their Convention opponents. No one in May 1787 anticipated the final product. No delegate told the Convention that the result was philosophically superior to any other theoretical plan. Instead of fully solving their central political dilemma—getting better national public policy from a republican national government that would not itself threaten vital interests—the framers narrowed the scope of the problem, allocating some authority clearly while delegating to the political process the divisive issues that remained too intractable in the summer of 1787. Constitutional rules about policy agency and policy-making set constraints on this political process. For 39 signers, the document met the criteria for republican government and seemed likely to produce better policy outcomes than the status quo. Subsequently, constructing the Constitution essentially has been a political task (Whittington 1999).

The political accommodations on which Madison's Convention opponents insisted have had an enduring impact on American political development. Federalism illustrates this impact as well as any Constitutional feature ... Federalism in the Constitution emerged from a long series of interdependent, issue-by-issue compromises, guided by the ongoing clash between the Madison and the Sherman positions on *which* level of government would control *which* tools of public policy and how each level would use those tools to govern politics. Sherman and his allies got a limited nationalization of public goods, a list of enumerated national powers, state control of residual policy authority, and some defensive tools that states could use to fight the aggregation of power by the national government ... Madison and his allies got a sort of ersatz national veto vested in the federal courts through the supremacy clause and some Constitutional language that could be used to press for the expansion of national power on a case-by-case basis.

The delegates artfully blurred many politically portentous terms and boundaries between state and national authority and then handed the ensuing boundary issues over to the politicians who would contest them according to the newly established policy-making rules. They neither defined this boundary clearly nor provided definitive guidelines for resolving these future conflicts (see also Rakove 1996, 201) ...

Conclusion

The Convention delegates who opposed James Madison's Virginia Plan have had a far greater impact on American politics than most Americans appreciate. Opponents of the Virginia Plan aimed to add a few carefully chosen powers and offices to the national government while, at the same time, protecting most of the states' policy prerogatives and ensuring that the state governments would influence the way the national government used its powers. Undeniably, Madison's opponents achieved much of what they sought. Led by Roger Sherman and the Connecticut delegation, they spoiled Madison's strategy for the Convention. They altered key features of his Constitutional plan and engineered substitute provisions better suited to their states' political interests. Because of Sherman and his Convention allies, the Constitution established a national government with less authority and less independence of the states than Madison initially wanted. Madison's Convention opponents, then, made the basic, enduring rules of American politics much more protective of the states, and more resistant to geographical redistribution, than the rules Madison set out to put in place.

Because American politicians have had to play by these basic rules since 1789, Sherman and his allies have had a cumulative and lasting effect on the way American politics has evolved. Madison's Convention opponents helped produce government that is more complicated and harder to use than any delegate expected (Robertson 2005). Their influence endures in Constitutional provisions that protect the states' policy authority, that safeguard equal state influence in national policy-making through the Senate, and that provide for a state-based system for selecting the president. If Madison had had his way, for example, the national government would have enjoyed unambiguous authority to control *intra*state commerce. If the national government exercised this uncontested commercial authority from the beginning, America's most explosive policy conflicts, including slavery, trade unions, and civil rights, would have played out differently, changing Americans' political inheritance in fundamental ways.

Yet if either Madison or his main opponents had walked away from the Constitutional Convention, it is difficult to imagine how the meeting would have produced a comparable political success. The political synergy between Madison and Sherman, then, very well may have been necessary for the Constitution's adoption. Ironically, his opponents' achievements also became indispensable for the success of Madison's own subsequent political career. During the Convention, Madison concentrated on strengthening political institutions to pursue national interests and ignored the possibility that national interest could be pursued in ways antagonistic to his own vision for the nation's future. But their inherently incompatible visions of national interest opened a political chasm between U.S. Representative Madison and Treasury Secretary Alexander Hamilton in the early 1790s. During the Convention, Sherman concentrated on defending the political economies of the states and ignored the difficulties of drawing a clear distinction between state and national authority. It was Madison, not Sherman, who was among the first American politicians to seize on this distinction. Madison, defending "state's rights," used Constitutional guarantees of state policy authority to build a national coalition of diverse interests opposed to Hamilton's program for national economic direction. Madison's political career after 1787, like America's political development, owes a considerable—if unappreciated—debt to his opponents' influence on the Constitution's design.

REFERENCES

Banning, Lance. 1995. *The Sacred Fire of Liberty: James Madison and the Founding of the Federal Republic.* Ithaca, NY: Cornell University Press.

Boardman, Roger Sherman. 1938. *Roger Sherman: Signer and Statesman.* Philadelphia: University of Pennsylvania Press.

Collier, Christopher. 1971. *Roger Sherman's Connecticut: Yankee Politics and the American Revolution.* Middletown, CT: Wesleyan University Press.

Collier, Christopher. 1973. *Connecticut in the Continental Congress.* Chester, CT: Pequot Press

Currie, David P. 1997. *The Constitution in Congress: The Federalist Period, 1789-1801.* Chicago: University of Chicago Press.

Fleischacker, Samuel. 2002. "Adam Smith's Reception among the American Founders, 1776-1790." *William and Mary Quarterly* (3rd ser.) 59 (October): 897–924.

Hobson, Charles F. 1979. "The Negative on State Laws: James Madison, the Constitution and the Crisis of Republican Government." *William and Mary Quarterly* (3rd ser.) 36 (April): 215–35.

Jillson, Calvin C. 1988. *Constitution Making: Conflict and Consensus in the Federal Convention of 1787.* New York: Agathon Press.

Lee, Frances E., and Oppenheimer, Bruce I. 1999. *Sizing Up the Senate: The Unequal Consequences of Equal Representation.* Chicago: University of Chicago Press.

Matthews, Richard K. 1995. *If Men Were Angels: James Madison and the Heartless Empire of Reason.* Lawrence: University Press of Kansas.

McCusker, John J., and Menard, Russell. 1985. *The Economy of British America, 1607-1789.* Chapel Hill: University of North Carolina Press.

McDonald, Forrest. 1985. *Novus Ordo Seculorum: The Intellectual Origins of the Constitution.* Lawrence: University Press of Kansas.

McGuire, Robert A. 2003. *To Form a More Perfect Union: A New Economic Interpretation of the United States Constitution.* New York: Oxford University Press.

Pierson, Paul. 2000. "Increasing Returns, Path Dependence, and the Study of Politics." *American Political Science Review* 94 (June): 251–67.

PJM [*The Papers of James Madison*]. 1962-1991. ed. William T. Hutchinson et al. 17 vols. Chicago: University of Chicago Press/Charlottesville: University of Virginia Press.

Rakove, Jack N. 1996. *Original Meanings: Politics and Ideas in the Making of the Constitution.* New York: Alfred A. Knopf.

RFC [*The Records of the Federal Convention of 1787*]. 1937. ed. Max Farrand. 4 vols. New Haven, CT: Yale University Press.

Riker, William H. 1996. *The Strategy of Rhetoric: Campaigning for the American Constitution.* New Haven, CT: Yale University Press.

Robertson, David Brian. 2003. "Constituting a National Interest: Madison Against the States' Autonomy." In *James Madison: The Theory and Practice of Republican Government*, ed. Samuel Kernell. Stanford, CA: Stanford University Press, 184–216.

Robertson, David Brian. 2005. *The Constitution and America's Destiny.* New York: Cambridge University Press.

Rossiter, Clinton. 1966. *1787: The Grand Convention.* New York: Macmillan.

Siemers, David J. 2002. *Ratifying the Republic: Antifederalists and Federalists in Constitutional Time.* Stanford, CA: Stanford University Press.

Whittington, Keith E. 1999. *Constitutional Construction: Divided Powers and Constitutional Meaning.* Cambridge, MA: Harvard University Press.

Wills, Garry. 2002. *James Madison.* New York: Times Books.

2.3 The Conclusion of the Constitutional Convention (1787)

Benjamin Franklin's Comments on Signing the Constitution

Eighty-one-year-old Benjamin Franklin was the senior delegate at the Constitutional Convention. An active participant, Franklin proposed several provisions that the delegates ultimately rejected. On the day the delegates signed the final document and prepared to make it public, Franklin conceded that he thought the document was imperfect. In this speech, Franklin admitted that the document was a political compromise. He expected "no better" Constitution than the one he would sign. Franklin called upon his fellow delegates to keep their doubts about the Constitution to themselves, as he would do, and fight wholeheartedly for the Constitution's ratification. Three delegates had promised that they would not sign the Constitution because of its faults. As a final act of political pragmatism, Franklin suggested that the Constitution end with a statement that its signers merely "witnessed" that the states in convention agreed to the plan—not that they personally supported it in its entirety. Franklin hoped this language would nudge the dissenters to sign the document. Unconvinced, the trio refused to sign the Constitution.

Mr. President

I confess that there are several parts of this constitution which I do not at present approve, but I am not sure I shall never approve them: For having lived long, I have experienced many instances of being obliged by better information or fuller consideration, to change opinions even on important subjects, which I once thought right, but found to be otherwise. It is therefore that the older I grow, the more apt I am to doubt my own judgment, and to pay more respect to the judgment of others. Most men indeed as well as most sects in Religion, think themselves in possession of all truth, and that where ever others differ from them it is so far error. Steele, a Protestant in a Dedication tells the Pope, that the only difference between our Churches in their opinions of the certainty of their doctrines is, the Church of Rome is infallible and the Church of England is never in the wrong. But though many private persons think almost as highly of their own infallibility as of that of their sect, few express it so naturally as a certain French lady, who in a dispute with her sister, said "I don't know how it happens, Sister but I meet with no body but myself, that's always in the right ...".

In these sentiments, Sir, I agree to this Constitution with all its faults, if they are such; because I think a general Government necessary for us, and there is no form of Government but what may be a blessing to the people if well administered, and believe farther that this is likely to be well administered for a course of years, and can only end in Despotism, as other forms have done before it, when the people shall become so corrupted as to need despotic Government, being incapable of any other. I doubt too whether any other Convention we can obtain may be able to make a better Constitution. For when you assemble a number of men to have the advantage of their joint wisdom, you inevitably assemble with those men, all their prejudices, their passions, their errors of opinion, their local interests, and their selfish views. From such an Assembly can a perfect production be expected? It therefore astonishes me, Sir, to find this system approaching so near to perfection as it does; and I think it will astonish our enemies, who are waiting with confidence to hear that our councils are confounded like those of the Builders of Babel; and that our States are on the point of separation, only to meet hereafter for the purpose of cutting one another's throats. Thus I consent, Sir, to this Constitution because I expect no better, and because I am not sure, that it is not the best. The opinions I have had of its errors, I sacrifice to the public good—I have never whispered a syllable of them abroad—Within these walls they were born, and here they shall die—If every one of us in returning to our Constituents were to report the objections he has had to it, and endeavor to gain partizans in support of them, we might prevent its being generally received, and thereby lose all the salutary effects & great advantages resulting naturally in our favor among foreign Nations as well as among ourselves, from our real or apparent unanimity. Much of the strength & efficiency of any Government in procuring and securing happiness to the people, depends on opinion, on the general opinion of the goodness of the Government, as well as of the wisdom and integrity of its Governors. I hope therefore that for our own sakes as a part of the people, and for the sake of posterity, we shall act heartily and unanimously in recommending this Constitution (if approved by Congress & confirmed by the Conventions) wherever our influence may extend, and turn our future thoughts & endeavors to the means of having it well administered.

On the whole, Sir, I cannot help expressing a wish that every member of the Convention who may still have objections to it, would with me, on this occasion doubt a little of his own infallibility—and to make manifest our unanimity, put his name to this instrument."—He then moved that the Constitution be signed by the members and offered the following as a convenient form [as follows:] "Done in Convention, by the unanimous consent of the States present the 17th. of Sepr. &c—In Witness whereof we have hereunto subscribed our names."

Letter to Congress to Accompany the Constitution

When the Constitutional Convention finished its work, it added a letter to the Congress and the American people. This letter was the first public defense of the Constitution. Echoing Benjamin Franklin, the letter emphasized the diverse interests of the delegates. The Constitution, it conceded, was the product of political give and take, and, finally, political compromise (or, as the authors deftly write, of "mutual deference and concession").

In Convention, September 17, 1787

Sir,

WE have now the honor to submit to the consideration of the United States in Congress assembled, that Constitution which has appeared to us the most adviseable.

The friends of our country have long seen and desired, that the power of making war, peace and treaties, that of levying money and regulating commerce, and the correspondent executive and judicial authorities should be fully and effectually vested in the general government of the Union: but the impropriety of delegating such extensive trust to one body of men is evident—Hence results the necessity of a different organization.

It is obviously impracticable in the fœderal government of these States, to secure all rights of independent sovereignty to each, and yet provide for the interest and safety of all—Individuals entering into society, must give up a share of liberty to preserve the rest. The magnitude of the sacrifice must depend as well on situation and circumstance, as on the object to be obtained. It is at all times difficult to draw with precision the line between those rights which must be surrendered, and those which may be reserved; and on the present occasion this difficulty was increased by a difference among the several States as to their situation, extent, habits, and particular interests.

In all our deliberations on this subject we kept steadily in our view, that which appears to us the greatest interest of every true American, the consolidation of our Union, in which is involved our prosperity, felicity, safety, perhaps our national existence. This important consideration, seriously and deeply impressed on our minds, led each State in the Convention to be less rigid on points of inferior magnitude, than might have been otherwise expected; and thus the Constitution, which we now present, is the result of a spirit of amity, and of that mutual deference and concession which the peculiarity of our political situation rendered indispensable.

That it will meet the full and entire approbation of every State is not perhaps to be expected; but each will doubtless consider, that had her interest alone been consulted, the consequences might have been particularly disagreeable or injurious to others; that it is liable to as few exceptions as could reasonably have been expected, we hope and believe; that it may promote the lasting welfare of that country so dear to us all, and secure her freedom and happiness, is our most ardent wish.

> With great respect,
> We have the honor to be.
>> SIR,
>> Your Excellency's most
>>> Obedient and humble Servants,
>>> GEORGE WASHINGTON, PRESIDENT.

By unanimous Order of the Convention.
HIS EXCELLENCY

The President of Congress.

2.4 Herbert Storing, "What the Anti-Federalists Were *For*" (1981)

Despite the signers' unwavering support for the Constitution, many Americans strongly objected to the plan and strongly opposed its ratification. Political scientist

Herbert Storing, a foremost expert on the Constitution's opponents, collected and explained the chief arguments of the Constitution's many critics. In these selections, Storing explained what these "anti-federalists" were *for*. The Anti-Federalists believed that the Constitution marked a step in the wrong direction, away from republican values and toward a centralized government that the people would not control. These constitutional critics sought to preserve more of the state governments' power than the document allowed. They believed that only in governments of small territories, like the present state governments, could the people truly maintain control over their rulers. They objected to the consolidation of power in a central government, the complexity built into that central government to keep it under control, and the complicated mixture of government powers. They also insisted that the document include a bill of rights, a statement that would specify ways in which the national government was required to protect freedom and fairness in its dealings with its citizens. When the Constitution was ratified, the new U.S. Congress tried to address the Anti-Federalists' remaining concerns by proposing ten amendments that would add these protections. These amendments—the Bill of Rights—became part of the Constitution in 1791. (Opposition to government "consolidation" would run through battles over federalism for decades; see Chapter 3).

Far from straying from the principles of the American Revolution, as some of the Federalists accused them of doing,[1] the Anti-Federalists saw themselves as the true defenders of those principles. "I am fearful," said Patrick Henry, "I have lived long enough to become an old fashioned fellow: Perhaps an invincible attachment to the dearest rights of man, may, in these refined enlightened days, be deemed *old fashioned*: If so, I am contented to be so: I say, the time has been, when every pore of my heart beat for American liberty, and which, I believe, had a counterpart in the breast of every true American."[2] The Anti-Federalists argued, as some historians have argued since, that the Articles of Confederation were the constitutional embodiment of the principles on which the Revolution was based:

> Sir, I venerate the spirit with which everything was done at the trying time in which the Confederation was formed. America had then a sufficiency of this virtue to resolve to resist perhaps the first nation in the universe, even unto bloodshed. What was her aim? Equal liberty and safety. What ideas had she of this equal liberty? Read them in her Articles of Confederation.[3]

The innovators were impatient to change this "most excellent constitution," which was "sent like a blessing from heaven," for a constitution "essentially differing from the principles of the revolution, and from freedom," and thus destructive of the whole basis of the American community. "Instead of repairing the old and venerable fabrick, which sheltered the United States, from the dreadful and cruel storms of a tyrannical British ministry, they built a stately palace after their own fancies. . . ."[4]

The principal characteristic of that "venerable fabrick" was its federalism: the Articles of Confederation established a league of sovereign and independent states whose representatives met in congress to deal with a limited range of common concerns in a system that relied heavily on voluntary cooperation. Federalism means that the states are primary, that they are equal, and that they possess the main weight of political power. The defense of the federal character of the American union was the most prominent article of Anti-Federalist conservative doctrine ...

The Anti-Federalists stood, then, for federalism in opposition to what they called the consolidating tendency and intention of the Constitution—the tendency to establish one complete national government, which would destroy or undermine the states.[5] They feared the implications of language like Washington's reference, in transmitting the Constitution to Congress, to the need for "the consolidation of our Union."[6] They saw ominous intentions in Publius' opinion that "a NATION, without a NATIONAL GOVERNMENT, is, in my view, an awful spectacle."[7] They resented and denied suggestions that "we must forget our local habits and attachments" and "be reduced to one faith and one govern-ment."[8] They saw in the new Constitution a government with authority extending "to every case that is of the least importance"[9] and capable of acting (preeminently in the crucial case of taxation) at discretion and independently of any agency but its own. Instead of thus destroying the federal character of the Union, "the leading feature of every amendment" of the Articles of Confederation ought to be, as Yates and Lansing expressed it, "the preservation of the individual states, in their uncontrouled constitu-tional rights, and ... in reserving these, a mode might have been devised of granting to the confederacy, the monies arising from a general system of revenue; the power of regu-lating commerce, and enforcing the observance of foreign treaties, and other necessary matters of less moment."[10]

The Small Republic

... The Anti-Federalists' defense of federalism and of the primacy of the states rested on their belief that there was an inherent connection between the states and the preserva-tion of individual liberty, which is the end of any legitimate government. Robert Whitehill of Pennsylvania, for example, feared that the proposed Constitution would be "the means of annihilating the constitutions of the several States, and consequently the liberties of the people ...."[11] "We are come hither," Patrick Henry urged his fellow Virginians, "to preserve the poor Commonwealth of Virginia, if it can be possibly done; Something must be done to preserve your liberty and mine."[12] The states have to be preserved because they are the natural homes of individual liberty ...

Why must the essential business of government be done by governmental units like the states? Primarily this was, in the Anti-Federalist view, a question of size. It was thought to have been demonstrated, historically and theoretically, that free, republican governments could extend only over a relatively small territory with a homogeneous population.[13] Even among the states this rule was evident, for "the largest States are the Worst Governed."[14] One problem is that in large, diverse states many significant differ-ences in condition, interest, and habit have to be ignored for the sake of uniform admin-istration. Yet no genuine equality of government is possible in such a large state. The capital city, to take the prime example, will be close to some parts of the large state, but it will be remote, in every relevant sense, from the extremities.[15] A national government would be compelled to impose a crude uniform rule on American diversity, which would in fact result in hardship and inequity for many parts of the country.

Behind the administrative defects of a large republic lie three fundamental considerations, bearing on the kind of government needed in a free society. Only a small republic
can enjoy a voluntary attachment of the people to the government and a voluntary
obedience to the laws. Only a small republic can secure a genuine responsibility of the
government to the people. Only a small republic can form the kind of citizens who
will maintain republican government. These claims are central to the Anti-Federalist
position.[16] . . .

An efficient federal government need not, however, imply one so powerful as that
proposed in the Constitution. The broad grants of power, taken together with the
"supremacy" and the "necessary and proper" clauses, amounted, the Anti-Federalists
contended, to an unlimited grant of power to the general government to do whatever it
might choose to do. In the provision (Art. I, sec. 4) granting Congress the power to alter
state regulations, or make its own, regarding the times, places, and manner of electing
senators and representatives, for example, the Anti-Federalists saw endless possibility of
usurpation and tyranny.[17] Could any possible good compensate for the dangers of such
a provision? Moreover, the Anti-Federalists insisted, in contradiction to their opponents,
that the powers of the proposed government, not its organization, was the central question.[18] All of the arguments of the Federalists that this new government was better
constructed than the old one fell before the massive fact that the old government was
weak and this one would be strong. "The old Confederation is so defective in point of
power," William Grayson plaintively explained to the Virginia convention, "that no
danger can result from creating offices under it; because those who hold them cannot be
paid. . . . Why not make this system as secure as that, in this respect?"[19] Not many Anti-
Federalists were quite so transparent, but their opponents were quick to insist that
Grayson's position was precisely the ridiculous conclusion to which the Anti-Federalist
argument led: without the power to do good, a government can do no harm. But a
government must have the capacity to accomplish its ends, otherwise liberty itself is in
danger: "there is no way more likely to lose ones liberty in the end than being too
niggardly of it in the beginning. . . ."[20] The means, the Federalists argued again and again,
must be proportioned to the end, and the end in the case of the general government is
not capable of being limited in advance. As bounds cannot be set to a nation's wants, so
bounds ought not to be set to its resources. "The contingencies of society are not
reducible to calculations. They cannot be fixed or bounded, even in imagination." . . .[21]

[According to an author known as "a Farmer"]; Prudence dictates granting too few
powers rather than too many; rulers will always exercise their full legal powers, and it is
easier to increase power than to lessen it. Nor is it sufficient to say that the exigencies
facing the general government are in principle illimitable. Reasonable estimates can in
practice be made and acted upon: ". . . every nation may form a rational judgment, what
force will be competent to protect and defend it, against any enemy with which it is probable it may have to contend."[22] It is far more prudent to act upon such judgments than to
rush to provide the government at once with all the power it may conceivably need. The
maxim that unlimited means are necessary to meet unlimited ends is balanced by the
maxim, which applies to all forms of power, "that all governments find a use for as much
money as they can raise."[23] Extraordinary needs can be met as they arise. If a national
credit and a national treasury are needed in time of war, let them be provided in time of
war, Patrick Henry said; republics always put forth their utmost resources when
required.[24]

Complex Government

John Adams [a Federalist], directly and explicitly rejects the idea of simple government. Centinel, on the other hand, advocates simple government, and most of the Anti-Federalists were at least inclined in that direction, despite all their participation in the discussion about balances. Centinel contends that a system such as Adams' is beyond the wisdom of man to establish and maintain and that it would in any case not accomplish its objectives. "If the administrators of every government are actuated by views of private interest and ambition, how is the welfare and happiness of the community to be the result of such jarring adverse interests?" The true principle—or perhaps it would be better to say the pure or primary principle—of free government is not balance but responsibility. "I believe it will be found that the form of government, which holds those entrusted with power, in the greatest responsibility to their constituents, the best calculated for freemen." A republican or free government can only exist where the people are virtuous and property evenly distributed; "in such a government the people are the sovereign and their sense or opinion is the criterion of every public measure; for when this ceases to be the case, the nature of government is changed, and an aristocracy, monarchy or despotism will rise on its ruin."[25] This is of course a version of the argument for the small republic that we have considered above. Responsibility is best attained in a government of simple structure, under which the people can quickly and easily identify the source of abuse. Complex governments, A [Maryland] Farmer argued, "seem to bid defiance to all responsibility, (the only true test of good government) as it can never be discovered where the fault lies...."[26]

Bill of Rights

While the Federalists gave us the Constitution, then, the legacy of the Anti-Federalists was the Bill of Rights. But it is an ambiguous legacy, as can be seen by studying the debate. Indeed, in one sense, the success of the Bill of Rights reflects the failure of the Anti-Federalists. The whole emphasis on reservations of rights of individuals implied a fundamental acceptance of the "consolidated" character of the new government. A truly federal government needs no bill of rights. Indeed, there were some Federalists who tried to use the Anti-Federalists' federalism to destroy the Anti-Federalists' argument for a bill of rights (incidentally undermining their own position). One Alfredus contended, for example, that a bill of rights was not necessary because the Constitution was a compact not between individuals but between sovereign and independent societies.[27] This argument is easy enough to answer, and the Anti-Federalists often answered it: the government under the Constitution was not a mere compact of sovereign states—at least not in its operation—and it was not exempt from the need for a bill of rights on that account. But in making this reply the Anti-Federalists decisively abandoned the doctrine of strict federalism....

Despite all their rhetorical emphasis on a bill of rights, however, the Anti-Federalists were typically quite doubtful about the practical utility of this kind of provision in the new Constitution. Thus Samuel Chase wrote to John Lamb, "A declaration of rights alone will be of no essential service. Some of the powers must be abridged, or public liberties will be endangered, and, in time, destroyed."[28] Of far more practical importance than bills of rights were the powers and structure of the general government—the unlimited power to tax, for example, and the inadequate representation in the federal legislature. A bill of rights, without more, would make little difference. Why, then, did the Anti-Federalists emphasize a bill of rights as much as they did? Why did they invite the brilliantly successful Federalist tactic of first standing fast on all points, then opening the door to a bill of rights and watching the Anti-Federalists stumble through it to a strong national government? In some cases they doubted that they could win on the greater questions. In many cases they must have been influenced by the rhetorical attractiveness of arguments for bills of rights compared to arguments about state prerogatives and federal powers. But there were also deeper reasons. The debate over the bill of rights was an extension of the general debate over the nature of limited government, and at this level the Anti-Federalists can perhaps claim a substantial, though not unmitigated, accomplishment ...

... [S]ome of the Anti-Federalists argued that one of the functions of a bill of rights in a republican government is to serve as a check against majority faction. To the question, whom does a bill of rights protect in a popular government? Agrippa answered: "such a government is indeed a government by ourselves; but as a just government protects all alike, it is necessary that the sober and industrious part of the community should be defended from the rapacity and violence of the vicious and idle. A bill of rights therefore ought to set forth the purposes for which the compact is made, and serves to secure the minority against the usurpation and tyranny of the majority."[29]

Moreover, the Anti-Federalists contended that *this* constitution was not an adequate bill of rights. If ever there was a case for an explicit reservation of individual rights, the proposed constitution provided one, with its very extensive powers, its shadow of genuine representation, and its weak and dubious checks on the encroachments of the few. Identical considerations apply to the Federalist argument that the states would serve as powerful checks on the general government.[30] If the general government lays excessive taxes, "the constitution will provide ... no remedy for the people or the states—the people must bear them, or have recourse, not to any constitutional checks or remedies, but to that resistance which is the last resort, and founded in self-defence."[31] The state legislatures can only check the general legislators "by exciting the people to resist constitutional laws."[32] The best of the Federalists understood the validity of this point. Although they judged the states' intrinsic advantages to be weightier, longer-lasting, and more dangerous than did the Anti-Federalists, they saw that the Constitution placed the weight of legality on the side of the federal government. The ultimate check is, indeed, the revolutionary one, made more significant, however, by the support and coherence that the state governments will lend the populace in case of such an ultimate resort. After all, Publius emphasized, along with many defenders of the Constitution, the ultimate security of the people rests in their understanding of their rights and their willingness to defend them.[33]

NOTES

1. *The Federalist* no. 78, 527. For an unusually radical Federalist statement of the right of the people to change their governments, see Conciliator to the Honest American, Philadelphia *Independent Gazetteer* 15 January 1788.
2. Henry 5.16.1.
3. G. Livingston, Elliot II, 287. Cf. Jensen, *The Articles of Confederation* ch. 1; Jensen, *New Nation*, conclusion; Vernon Parrington, *Main Currents in American Thought* (New York 1927–30) I, chs. 1, 2; III, pp. 410–11.

4. Lowndes 5.12.1; Philadelphiensis XI, 3.9.89; Denatus 5.18.14. See also Old Whig I, 3.3.3; Tredwell, Elliot II, 401.

5. Albany Anti-Federal Committee 6.10.2; Pennsylvania Convention Minority 3.11.16–20; Smith 6.12.5; Plebeian 6.11.13; Warren 6.14.49; Philadelphiensis IX, 3.6.60; Gerry 2.1.4–5; Officer of the Late Continental Army 3.8.3; Agrippa III, 4.6.13; X, 4.6.43; [Pennsylvania] Farmer 3.14.18–21; Symmes 4.5.2; Brutus I, 2.9.5; Mason, Virginia ratifying convention, Elliot III, 29; Georgian 5.9.2–3; Martin 2.4 passim.

6. Farrand II, 667. See Republican Federalist 4.13.10; see extract of letter from William Pierce to St. George Tucker, 28 September 1787, *Gazette of the State of Georgia* 20 March 1788: "The great object of this new government is to consolidate the Union, and to give us the appearance and power of a nation."

7. *The Federalist* no. 85, 594. Cf. King, Elliot II, 55; Charles Pinckney, Elliot IV, 255–56.

8. James Wilson, Farrand I, 413 (25 June); Demosthenes Minor, *Gazette of the State of Georgia* 15 November 1787.

9. Brutus I, 2.9.5.

10. Yates and Lansing 2.3.6.

11. McMaster and Stone 287.

12. Henry 5.16.2.

13. Hamilton himself confessed that "the extent of the Country to be governed, discouraged him." Farrand I, 287 (18 June); see also Wilson's account, McMaster and Stone 220ff. For arguments in defense of the small republic, this volume 16–21; Yates and Lansing 2.3.7; Brutus I, 2.9.11; Federal Farmer I, 2.8.14; IV, 2.8.75; XVII, 2.8.208; Sidney 6.8.1–2; Cato Uticensis 5.7.6; [Maryland] Farmer III, 5.1.52–53; Pennsylvania Convention Minority 3.11.16; Old Whig IV, 3.3.20; Monroe 5.21.13; Cato III, 2.6.12–13; Agrippa XII, 4.6.48; Albany Anti-Federal Committee 6.10.2; Centinel I, 2.7.19; V, 2.7.94; Martin 2.4.44; [Pennsylvania] Farmer 3.14.7, 9; Columbian Patriot 4.28.4; Warren 6.14.5; Smith 6.12.19–20; Henry 5.16.2; Clinton 6.13.13; etc.

14. Ellsworth, Farrand I, 406 (25 June); see Martin, Farrand II, 4 (14 July).

15. Federal Farmer II, 2.8.17; XII, 2.8.158; Cato III, 2.6.16; Impartial Examiner 5.14.6.

16. In Gordon Wood's view, the Anti-Federalists became fervent defenders "of the traditional assumption that the state was a cohesive organic entity with a single homogeneous interest at the very time they were denying the consequences of this assumption." Wood understands this traditional view, the "republicanism" of the Revolution, to be a secularized Puritanism aimed at securing a sacrifice of individual interest to the common good. *Creation* 499, 418, and ch. 2.

17. See this volume 111–12, references at Art. I, sec. 4.

18. See this volume 67–68.

19. Elliot III, 375.

20. State Soldier, *Virginia Independent Chronicle* 16 January 1788.

21. Hamilton, Elliot II, 351; Iredell, Elliot IV, 95; see also Gore, Elliot II, 66; Sedgwick, ibid. 96.

22. Brutus VII, 2.9.90; cf. Federal Farmer XVIII, 2.8.215ff.

23. Smith 6.12.37; Plebeian 6.11.2; Cornelius 4.10.3; Old Whig IV, 3.3.38; Symmes 4.5.2.

24. Henry 5.16.23.

25. Centinel I, 2.7.8–9. For a fuller and better argument in favor of simple government, see [anon.] *Four Letters on Interesting Subjects* (Pennsylvania 1776) (Evans, *Early American Imprints* no. 14759).

26. [Maryland] Farmer II, 5.1.34.

27. New Hampshire *Freeman's Oracle* 18 January 1788; Luther Martin, Ford, *Essays* 364–65; cf. James Wilson's federal liberty argument, this volume 11. See Remarker, *Boston Independent Chronicle* 22 December 1787.

28. Samuel Chase, letter to John Lamb, 13 June 1788, in Leake, *Memoir of the Life and Times of General John Lamb* 310; see Philadelphiensis 3.9.43.

29. Agrippa XVI, 4.6.73; see this volume 40.
30. Hamilton, Elliot II, 239; see Smith 6.12.20 n. 21, and Elliot II, 354–55.
31. Federal Farmer IX, 2.8.121. Agrippa XV, 4.6.71: "But for want of a bill of rights the resistance is always by the principles of their government, a rebellion which nothing but success can justify."
32. Brutus X, 2.9.128; see VI, 2.9.69. Luther Martin contended that a man might find himself compelled to be guilty of treason against the general government or against his state, when the latter is resisting the arbitrary encroachments of the former. Martin 2.4.96.
33. *The Federalist* no. 28, 179. It is striking that Publius' references to checks by the states on the general government are usually connected with some reference to the ultimate defense by the people of their rights. See *The Federalist* no. 26, 169; no. 46, 321–22; no. 60, 404.

REFERENCES

References to volume 1 of Herbert Storing's *The Complete Anti-Federalist* (Chicago: University of Chicago Press, 1981) are indicated as "this volume." References to other volumes are indicated by a three digit number (for example, "Lowndes 5.12.1" is located in volume 5 of *The Complete Anti-Federalist*).

Jonathan Elliot, The Debates of the State Conventions on the Adoption of the Constitution, as Recommended by the General Convention at Philadelphia in 1787, 2nd ed., ed. Jonathan Elliot (Philadelphia 1866).

The Federalist, ed. Jacob E. Cooke (Middletown, CT, 1961).

Merrill Jensen, *The New Nation* (New York, 1950).

Gordon S. Wood, *The Creation of the American Republic* (Chapel Hill, 1969).

2.5 *Federalist Papers* 47 and 48 (1788)

Although five states ratified the Constitution by January, 1788, the vigorous anti-federalist criticisms were raising concerns about whether vital states like New York or Virginia would reject it. James Madison, Alexander Hamilton, and John Jay, writing under the pseudonym "Publius," published a series of articles defending the Constitution in New York newspapers that was later collected into a volume titled the *Federalist*. In these selections from the *Federalist*, Madison directly confronted the Anti-Federalists' charge that the new government was insufficiently republican. The Anti-Federalists argued that the plan violated the principle of separation of government powers laid down by Montesquieu, the French political philosopher whom republicans admired (see Chapters 1 and 13). Madison argued that the sharing of some institutional powers in the Constitution is consistent with both Montesquieu's theories and existing state government practices. He also insisted that the people can be protected only in a government in which these institutional powers are blended. These papers set the stage for *Federalist* 51, in which he argued that "the great security against a gradual concentration of the several powers in the same department, consists in giving to those who administer each department the necessary constitutional means and personal motives to resist encroachments of the others."

The Federalist No. 47

James Madison

January 30, 1788

To the People of the State of New York.

... I proceed to examine the particular structure of this government, and the distribution of this mass of power among its constituent parts.

One of the principal objections inculcated by the more respectable adversaries to the constitution, is its supposed violation of the political maxim, that the legislative, executive and judiciary departments ought to be separate and distinct. In the structure of the federal government, no regard, it is said, seems to have been paid to this essential precaution in favor of liberty. The several departments of power are distributed and blended in such a manner, as at once to destroy all symmetry and beauty of form; and to expose some of the essential parts of the edifice to the danger of being crushed by the disproportionate weight of other parts ...

The oracle who is always consulted and cited on this subject, is the celebrated Montesquieu ... From these facts by which Montesquieu was guided it may clearly be inferred, that in saying "there can be no liberty where the legislative and executive powers are united in the same person, or body of magistrates," or "if the power of judging be not separated from the legislative and executive powers," he did not mean that these departments ought to have no *partial agency* in, or no *controul* over the acts of each other. His meaning, as his own words import, and still more conclusively as illustrated by the example in his eye, can amount to no more than this, that where the *whole* power of one department is exercised by the same hands which possess the *whole* power of another department, the fundamental principles of a free constitution, are subverted. This would have been the case in the constitution examined by him, if the King who is the sole executive magistrate, had possessed also the compleat legislative power, or the supreme administration of justice; or if the entire legislative body, had possessed the supreme judiciary, or the supreme executive authority. This however is not among the vices of that constitution. The magistrate in whom the whole executive power resides cannot of himself make a law, though he can put a negative on every law, nor administer justice in person, though he has the appointment of those who do administer it. The judges can exercise no executive prerogative, though they are shoots from the executive stock, nor any legislative function, though they may be advised with by the legislative councils. The entire legislature, can perform no judiciary act, though by the joint act of two of its branches, the judges may be removed from their offices; and though one of its branches is possessed of the judicial power in the last resort. The entire legislature again can exercise no executive prerogative, though one of its branches constitutes the supreme executive magistracy; and another, on the empeachment of a third, can try and condemn all the subordinate officers in the executive department.

The reasons on which Montesquieu grounds his maxim are a further demonstration of his meaning. "When the legislative and executive powers are united in the same person or body" says he, "there can be no liberty, because apprehensions may arise lest *the same* monarch or senate should *enact* tyrannical laws, to *execute* them in a tyrannical manner." Again "Were the power of judging joined with the legislative, the life and liberty of the subject would be exposed to arbitrary controul, for *the judge* would then be *the legislator*.

Were it joined to the executive power, *the judge* might behave with all the violence of *an oppressor.*" Some of these reasons are more fully explained in other passages; but briefly stated as they are here, they sufficiently establish the meaning which we have put on this celebrated maxim of this celebrated author.

If we look into the constitutions of the several states we find that notwithstanding the emphatical, and in some instances, the unqualified terms in which this axiom has been laid down, there is not a single instance in which the several departments of power have been kept absolutely separate and distinct. . . .

. . . The constitution of Massachusetts . . . declares "that the legislative department shall never exercise the executive and judicial powers, or either of them: the executive shall never exercise the legislative and judicial powers, or either of them: the judicial shall never exercise the legislative and executive powers, or either of them." This declaration corresponds precisely with the doctrine of Montesquieu, as it has been explained, and is not in a single point violated by the plan of the convention. It goes no farther than to prohibit any one of the entire departments from exercising the powers of another department. In the very Constitution to which it is prefixed, a partial mixture of powers has been admitted. The Executive Magistrate has a qualified negative on the Legislative body; and the Senate, which is a part of the legislature, is a court of impeachment for members both of the executive and judiciary departments. The members of the judiciary department, again, are appointable by the executive department, and removable by the same authority on the address of the two legislative branches. Lastly, a number of the officers of government are annually appointed by the legislative department. As the appointment to offices, particularly executive offices, is in its nature an executive function, the compilers of the Constitution have, in this last point at least, violated the rule established by themselves. . . .

The constitution of New York contains no declaration on this subject; but appears very clearly to have been framed with an eye to the danger of improperly blending the different departments. It gives, nevertheless, to the executive magistrate, a partial controul over the legislative department; and, what is more, gives a like control to the judiciary department; and even blends the executive and judiciary departments in the exercise of this controul. In its council of appointment members of the legislative are associated with the executive authority, in the appointment of officers, both executive and judiciary. And its court for the trial of impeachments and correction of errors is to consist of one branch of the legislature and the principal members of the judiciary department. . . .

PUBLIUS.

The Federalist No. 48

James Madison

February 1, 1788

To the People of the State of New York.
It was shewn in the last paper, that the political apothegm there examined, does not require that the legislative, executive and judiciary departments should be wholly unconnected with each other. I shall undertake in the next place, to shew that unless these departments be so far connected and blended, as to give to each a constitutional control over the others, the degree of separation which the maxim requires as essential to a free government, can never in practice, be duly maintained.

It is agreed on all sides, that the powers properly belonging to one of the departments, ought not to be directly and compleatly administered by either of the other departments. It is equally evident, that neither of them ought to possess directly or indirectly, an over-ruling influence over the others in the administration of their respective powers. It will not be denied, that power is of an encroaching nature, and that it ought to be effectually restrained from passing the limits assigned to it. After discriminating therefore in theory, the several classes of power, as they may in their nature be legislative, executive, or judi-ciary; the next and most difficult task, is to provide some practical security for each against the invasion of the others. What this security ought to be, is the great problem to be solved.

Will it be sufficient to mark with precision the boundaries of these departments in the Constitution of the government, and to trust to these parchment barriers against the encroaching spirit of power? This is the security which appears to have been principally relied on by the compilers of most of the American Constitutions. But experience assures us, that the efficacy of the provision has been greatly over-rated; and that some more adequate defence is indispensibly necessary for the more feeble, against the more powerful members of the government. The legislative department is every where extending the sphere of its activity, and drawing all power into its impetuous vortex.

... in a representative republic, where the executive magistracy is carefully limited both in the extent and the duration of its power; and where the legislative power is exercised by an assembly, which is inspired by a supposed influence over the people with an intrepid confidence in its own strength; which is sufficiently numerous to feel all the passions which actuate a multitude; yet not so numerous as to be incapable of pursuing the objects of its passions, by means which reason prescribes; it is against the enter-prising ambition of this department, that the people ought to indulge all their jealousy and exhaust all their precautions.

The legislative department derives a superiority in our governments from other circumstances. Its constitutional powers being at once more extensive and less suscep-tible of precise limits, it can with the greater facility, mask under complicated and indirect measures, the encroachments which it makes on the co-ordinate departments. It is not unfrequently a question of real-nicety in legislative bodies, whether the operation of a particular measure, will, or will not extend beyond the legislative sphere. On the other side, the executive power being restrained within a narrower compass, and being more simple in its nature; and the judiciary being described by land marks, still less uncertain, projects of usurpation by either of these departments, would immediately betray and defeat themselves. Nor is this all: As the legislative department alone has access to the pockets of the people, and has in some Constitutions full discretion, and in all, a prevailing influence over the pecuniary rewards of those who fill the other depart-ments, a dependence is thus created in the latter, which gives still greater facility to encroachments of the former ...

The conclusion which I am warranted in drawing from these observations is, that a mere demarckation on parchment of the constitutional limits of the several depart-ments, is not a sufficient guard against those encroachments which lead to a tyrannical concentration of all the powers of government in the same hands.

PUBLIUS.

2.6 Akhil Reed Amar, "America's Constitution" (2005)

Akhil Reed Amar, a professor of Constitutional law, reviewed the meaning of the Constitution's ratification for government in the United States and the world. "In 1787," Amar wrote, "democratic self-government existed almost nowhere on earth." The preamble to the Constitution firmly established that "the people" were the foundation of the new government. The ratification process implemented that principle, and the document implied that the people could change the Constitution as they willed. Amar showed how the Constitution's promise of self-government itself set the United States on a path to expand democracy, however slowly, to all adult white men, and eventually to women and racial minorities. The Constitution proved Thomas Paine right: the American cause of self-government became a cause throughout the world, and many nations deliberately have drawn lessons from the American constitutional experience. For Americans, though, implementing and maintaining the American Constitution has required hard work. This constitution had to be adapted to the rapid growth, wrenching changes, and unexpected challenges that have confronted the United States since 1789.

IT STARTED WITH A BANG. Ordinary citizens would govern themselves across a continent and over the centuries, under rules that the populace would ratify and could revise. By uniting previously independent states into a vast and indivisible nation, New World republicans would keep Old World monarchs at a distance and thus make democracy work on a scale never before dreamed possible.

"We . . . do"

With simple words placed in the document's most prominent location, the Preamble laid the foundation for all that followed. "We the People of the United States, ... do ordain and establish this Constitution ..."

These words did more than promise popular self-government. They also embodied and enacted it. Like the phrases "I do" in an exchange of wedding vows and "I accept" in a contract, the Preamble's words actually performed the very thing they described. Thus the Founders' "Constitution" was not merely a text but a deed—a *constituting*. We the People *do* ordain. In the late 1780s, this was the most democratic deed the world had ever seen.

Behind this act of ordainment and establishment stood countless ordinary American voters who gave their consent to the Constitution via specially elected ratifying conventions held in the thirteen states beginning in late 1787. Until these ratifications took place, the Constitution's words were a mere proposal—the text of a contract yet to be accepted, the script of a wedding still to be performed.

In the end, the federal Constitution proposed by Washington and company would barely squeak through. By its own terms, the document would go into effect only if ratified by specially elected conventions in at least nine states, and even then only states that said yes would be bound. In late 1787 and early 1788, supporters of the Constitution won relatively easy ratifications in Delaware, Pennsylvania, New Jersey, Georgia, and Connecticut. Massachusetts joined their ranks in February 1788, saying "we do" only after weeks of debate and by a close vote, 187 to 168. Then came lopsided yes votes in Maryland and South Carolina, bringing the total to eight ratifications, one shy of the mark. Even so, in mid-June 1788, a full nine months after the publication of the Philadelphia proposal, the Constitution was still struggling to be born, and its fate remained uncertain. Organized opposition ran strong in all the places that had yet to say yes, which included three of America's largest and most influential states. At last, on June 21, tiny New Hampshire became the decisive ninth state by the margin of 57 to 47. A few days later, before news from the North had arrived, Virginia voted her approval, 89 to 79.

All eyes then turned to New York, where Anti-Federalists initially held a commanding lead inside the convention. Without the acquiescence of this key state, could the new Constitution really work as planned? On the other hand, was New York truly willing to say no and go it alone now that her neighbors had agreed to form a new, more perfect union among themselves? In late July, the state ultimately said yes by a vote of 30 to 27.

A switch of only a couple of votes would have reversed the outcome. Meanwhile, the last two states, North Carolina and Rhode Island, refused to ratify in 1788. They would ultimately join the new union in late 1789 and mid-1790, respectively—well after George Washington took office as president of the new (eleven!) United States.

Although the ratification votes in the several states did not occur by direct statewide referenda, the various ratifying conventions did aim to represent "the People" in a particularly emphatic way—more directly than ordinary legislatures. Taking their cue from the Preamble's bold "We the People" language, several states waived standard voting restrictions and allowed a uniquely broad class of citizens to vote for ratification-convention delegates. For instance, New York temporarily set aside its usual property qualifications and, for the first time in its history, invited all free adult male citizens to vote.[1] Also, states generally allowed an especially broad group of Americans to serve as ratifying-convention delegates. Among the many states that ordinarily required upper-house lawmakers to meet higher property qualifications than lower-house members, none held convention delegates to the higher standard, and most exempted delegates even from the lower. All told, eight states elected convention delegates under special rules that were more populist and less property-focused than normal, and two others followed standing rules that let virtually all taxpaying adult male citizens vote. No state employed special election rules that were more property-based or less populist than normal....

All this was breathtakingly novel. In 1787, democratic self-government existed almost nowhere on earth. Kings, emperors, czars, princes, sultans, moguls, feudal lords, and tribal chiefs held sway across the globe. Even England featured a limited monarchy and an entrenched aristocracy alongside a House of Commons that rested on a restricted and uneven electoral base. The vaunted English Constitution that American colonists had grown up admiring prior to the struggle for independence was an imprecise hodgepodge of institutions, enactments, cases, usages, maxims, procedures, and principles that had accreted and evolved over many centuries. This Constitution had never been reduced to a single composite writing and voted on by the British people or even by Parliament.

The ancient world had seen small-scale democracies in various Greek city-states and pre-imperial Rome, but none of these had been founded in fully democratic fashion. In the most famous cases, one man—a celebrated lawgiver such as Athens's Solon or Sparta's

Lycurgus—had unilaterally ordained his countrymen's constitution. Before the American Revolution, no people had ever explicitly voted on their own written constitution.[2] . . .

FROM ANOTHER ANGLE, the drama was just beginning. Preamble-style popular sovereignty was an ongoing principle. No liberty was more central than the people's liberty to govern themselves under rules of their own choice,[3] and the Preamble promised to secure this and other "Blessings of Liberty" not just to the Founding generation, but also, emphatically, to "our Posterity."

As Wilson explained in Pennsylvania's ratification debates, the people's right to "ordain and establish" logically implied their equal right "to repeal and annul." The people "retain the right of recalling what they part with. . . . WE [the people] reserve the right to do what we please." Leading Federalists in sister states echoed this exposition. North Carolina's James Iredell, who would one day sit on the Supreme Court alongside Wilson, reminded his listeners that in America "our governments have been clearly created by the people themselves. The same authority that created can destroy; and the people may undoubtedly change the government." Not content to leave the matter implicit, Virginia ratified the Constitution on the express understanding that "the powers granted under the Constitution, being derived from the people of the United States, may be resumed by them, whensoever the same shall be perverted to their injury or oppression."[4]

Similar ideas surfaced in New York. Writing as Publius in *The Federalist* No. 84, Alexander Hamilton explained that "here, in strictness, the people . . . retain everything [and] have no need of particular reservations. 'WE THE PEOPLE . . ., to secure the blessings of liberty to ourselves and our posterity, do *ordain* and *establish* this Constitution. . . .' Here is a [clear] recognition of popular rights." By "popular rights" Publius meant rights of the people qua sovereign, including their right to revise what they had created. Following Virginia's lead, New York used its ratification instrument to underscore its understanding of the Preamble's principles: "All power is originally vested in, and consequently derived from the people. . . . The powers of government may be reassumed by the people whensoever it shall become necessary to their happiness."[5]

These assorted speeches, essays, and ratification texts emphasizing the "popular rights" that "the people" "retain" and "reserve" and may "resume" and "reassume" exemplified what the First Congress had centrally in mind in 1789 when it proposed certain amendments as part of a general bill of rights. With its last three words proudly paralleling the Preamble's first three, the sentence that eventually became the Ninth Amendment declared rights implicitly "retained by the people," such as their right to alter what they had ordained. Similarly, the Tenth Amendment declared powers "reserved . . . to the people," and the First Amendment guaranteed "the right of the people peaceably to assemble" in constitutional conventions and elsewhere. In all these places, the phrase "the people" gestured back to the Constitution's first and most prominent use of these words in the Preamble.[6]

In the First Congress, lawmakers pointed not just to the Preamble's words but also to its more immediate "practical" effect concerning the right to amend.[7] By ordaining the federal Constitution, Americans had in practice altered their state constitutions and abolished the Articles of Confederation. For example, most state constitutions in place before 1787 had given state legislatures power to issue paper money and emit bills of credit.[8] The federal Constitution abrogated these and other powers by fastening a new regulatory framework upon state governments.[9] In deed as well as word, the Preamble stood for ongoing popular sovereignty—the people's right to change their mind as events unfolded.

Even more dramatically, the Preamble by its very deed implicitly affirmed that the people's right to amend ultimately required only a simple majority vote, at least within a state. In Massachusetts, a two-thirds vote of the electorate had been required to launch the 1780 state constitution; and the document had provided for an amendment process to begin in 1795 if endorsed by "two-thirds of the qualified voters . . . who shall assemble and vote." Yet the federal Constitution drafted at Philadelphia proposed to modify this state constitution well before 1795, and to do so by a mere majority of a specially elected Massachusetts convention, which in the end voted 187 to 168 for the new legal order—far short of two-thirds, and not by a direct tally of all the qualified voters. Even so, once this vote occurred, Massachusetts Anti-Federalists immediately acquiesced, acknowledging that the people had truly spoken, albeit not in the precise manner that had been set out in 1780. In essence, Bay Staters in 1788 reconceptualized their earlier amendment clause as merely one way, rather than the only way, by which the sovereign people might alter their government.[10] Ratification of the federal Constitution broke similar new ground in several of Massachusetts's sister states, where analogous state constitutional issues arose.

Preamble-style ratification also broke new ground by establishing that the people's right to alter government did not require proof of past tyranny. When the Declaration of Independence trumpeted "the Right of the People to alter or abolish" governments, it had limited this right (as had the influential English philosopher John Locke)[11] to situations in which governments had grossly abused their powers—"whenever any Form of Government bec[ame] destructive" of its legitimate ends. The longest section of the Declaration aimed precisely to detail the insufferable "Evils," the "long Train of Abuses and Usurpations, pursuing invariably the same Object, evinc[ing] a design to reduce [Americans] under absolute Despotism." Such a clear pattern of "repeated Injuries and Usurpations, all having in direct Object the Establishment of an absolute Tyranny" justified a people in exercising their right to change government, even if the consequence would be all-out war against the king.

By the late 1780s, Americans had toppled the old order of George III, and the right to alter could now operate far more freely. Unlike the Declaration, the Constitution did not purport to show—because it did not *need* to show—that the regime it was amending was tyrannical. The people could properly amend whenever they deemed the status quo outdated or imperfect. If reformers proposed a change, ballots rather than bullets would decide the contest. In contrast to Old World monarchs, New World public servants would accept the people's constitutional verdict without waging war on them.

Americans understood this transformation even as they were doing the transforming and marveling at their own handiwork. "The people may change the constitutions whenever and however they please," explained Wilson. "It is a power paramount to every constitution, inalienable in its nature."[12] By their very act of assembling in ratifying conventions to debate the Philadelphia plan, the people were making these words flesh. "Under the practical influence of this great truth, we are now sitting and deliberating, and under its operation, we can sit as calmly and deliberate as coolly, in order to change a constitution, as a legislature can sit and deliberate under the power of a constitution, in order to alter or amend a law."[13]

AMERICA'S FOUNDING GAVE the world more democracy than the planet had thus far witnessed. Yet many modern Americans, both lawyers and laity, have missed this basic fact. Some mock the Founding Fathers as rich white men who staged a reactionary coup, while others laud the framers as dedicated traditionalists rather than democratic revolutionaries. A prominent modern canard is that the very word "democracy" was anathema to the Founding generation.[14] When today's scholars quote the framers on how America's Constitution broke with ancient Greek practices, the standard quotation comes not from Wilson's July 4 oration or Madison's similar *Federalist* No. 38, but rather from a passage in Madison's *Federalist* No. 63 that is brandished to prove that the framers were *less* democratic than the ancients, and proudly so: "The true distinction between [ancient democracies] and the American governments, lies *in the total exclusion of the people, in their collective capacity,* from any share in the *latter.* . . . The distinction . . . must be admitted to leave a most advantageous superiority in favor of the United States."

This conventional account misreads both Madison and the Constitution. True, Madison did harbor strong anxieties about the ability of a large mass of people to meet together to legislate. . . . However, Madison was not an antidemocrat scoffing at the limited capacities of ordinary folk, but rather a republican proceduralist pondering how best to structure lawmaking institutions. Even if every citizen *were* a philosopher king, how could a legislature function if composed of "six or seven thousand" (Madison's hypothetical) all clamoring to be heard? . . .

In fact, the Constitution infused some form of democracy into each of its seven main Articles. Echoing the Preamble's first three words, Article I promised that all members of the new House of Representatives would be elected directly "by the People." No constitutional property qualifications would limit eligibility to vote for or serve in Congress; nor could Congress add any qualifications by statute. Also, Article I prohibited both state and federal governments from creating hereditary government positions via titles of nobility. Under Articles II and III, the presidency and federal judgeships would be open to men of merit regardless of wealth or lineage. Government servants in all three branches would receive government salaries, lest the right to hold office or public trust be restricted to the independently wealthy. Military hierarchies would answer to democratically elected leaders, not vice versa. Juries of ordinary people would counterbalance professional judges in the judicial branch, as militias of ordinary people would check professional armies in the executive branch. Article IV guaranteed every state a "Republican Form of Government"—that is, a government ultimately derived from the people, as opposed to an aristocracy or monarchy. (The word "republican" came from the same etymological roots—*publica, poplicus*—as the pivotal Preamble word "people," whose Greek counterpart, *demos,* in turn underlay the word "democracy.") If ordinary legislatures clogged necessary reforms, Article V enabled Americans to bypass these legislatures with specially elected conventions to propose and ratify new constitutional rules. Article VI banned Old World religious hierarchies from formally entrenching themselves in the federal government or excluding adherents of competitor religions from federal service. Finally, Article VII specified how the Preamble's ordainment and establishment would take place.

The Federalist reflected these populist themes from start to finish. The first paragraph of Publius's first essay reminded ordinary citizens that "you are called upon to deliberate on a new Constitution" and by an "election" set a new example in world history. The last paragraph of his last essay reiterated the point. "The establishment of a Constitution, in time of profound peace, by the voluntary consent of a whole people, is a prodigy." Between these bookend paragraphs, Publius repeatedly extolled and elaborated the Preamble's enactment of popular sovereignty.[15] Indeed, in *The Federalist* No. 39, Madison/ Publius wrote that the "first question" to be asked about the Constitution as a whole was whether "the government be strictly republican"—essentially, "a government which derives all its powers directly or indirectly from the great body of the people," as opposed to an aristocracy or monarchy. Why was *this* the first question? Because "no other form would be reconcilable with the genius of the people of America [and] the fundamental principles of the Revolution." Throughout the rest of *The Federalist*, Publius linked this idea of republicanism to the Constitution's defining characteristics—its extensive geographic and demographic reach; the interior design of each of its three main branches; its limits on state governments; and so on.[16] Similarly, in both his opening and concluding speeches before the Pennsylvania ratifying convention, Wilson pronounced the Constitution "purely democratical," and in yet another speech he boasted that "the DEMOCRATIC principle is carried into every part of the government."[17]

Although some modern readers have tried to stress property protection rather than popular sovereignty as the Constitution's bedrock idea, the words "private property" did not appear in the Preamble, or anywhere in the document for that matter. The word "property" itself surfaced only once, and this in an Article IV clause referring to *government* property. Above and beyond the Constitution's plain text, its clear commitment to people over property shone through in its direct act: As we have seen, the Founders generally set aside ordinary property qualifications in administering the special elections for ratification-convention delegates. . . .

From a twenty-first-century perspective, the idea that the Constitution was truly established by "the People" might seem a bad joke. What about slaves and freeborn women?

The question is particularly pointed in modern America because it reflects more than some purely subjective or theoretical definition of democracy. Rather, the sensibility underlying the question is itself a constitutional sensibility, informed by the very vision of democracy embodied in the United States Constitution. The Constitution *as amended*, that is. Later generations of the American people have surged through the Preamble's portal and widened its gate. Like constitutions, amendments are not just words but deeds—flesh-and-blood struggles to redeem America's promise while making amends for some of the sins of our fathers.

In both word and deed, America's amendments have included many of the groups initially excluded at the Founding. In the wake of the Civil War, We the People abolished slavery in the Thirteenth Amendment, promised equal citizenship to all Americans in the Fourteenth Amendment, and extended the vote to black men in the Fifteenth Amendment. A half-century later, We guaranteed the right of woman suffrage in the Nineteenth Amendment, and during a still later civil-rights movement, We freed the federal election process from poll taxes and secured the vote for young adults in the Twenty-fourth and Twenty-sixth Amendments, respectively. No amendment has ever cut back on prior voting rights or rights of equal inclusion. (If this be Whiggism, Americans should make the most of it.)

Previously excluded groups have played leading roles in the amendment process itself, even as amendments have promised these groups additional political rights. Black voters, already enfranchised in many states, propelled the federal Fifteenth Amendment forward; women voters helped birth the Nineteenth; and the poor and the young spearheaded movements to secure their own constitutionally protected suffrage. Through these dramatic acts and texts of amendment, We the People of later eras have breathed new life into the Preamble's old prose.

NOTES

1. Ten of the thirteen states used broader suffrage rules for the convention and/or used broader delegate-qualification rules or simply had an especially expansive franchise to begin with. The three states outside this general pattern were Rhode Island, Delaware, and Virginia.
2. For a powerful discussion, see Jed Rubenfeld, *Freedom and Time* (2001), 13, 163–68.
3. See Del. Const. (1776), Declaration of Rights, sec. 6 ("the right in the people to participate in the Legislature, is the foundation of liberty and of all free government"); Md. Const. (1776), Declaration of Rights, art. V (similar); Wood, *Creation*, 24–25, 60–61, 362; Gordon S. Wood, *The Radicalism of the American Revolution* (1991), 104.
4. For Wilson, see *Elliot's Debates*, 2:434–35, 437. Wilson reiterated the point in his later lectures. Wilson, *Works*, 1:304. For Iredell, see *Elliot's Debates*, 4:230. For the Virginia convention, see ibid., 1:327.
5. *Elliot's Debates*, 1:327.
6. In Virginia, Edmund Pendleton had specifically linked the right of popular amendment to the people's right to "assemble." Ibid., 3:37. For more discussion of the interlinkages between the Preamble, the First Amendment right of "the people" to assemble, and the rights and powers of "the people" guaranteed by the Ninth and Tenth Amendments, see Akhil Reed Amar, *The Bill of Rights: Creation and Reconstruction* (1998), 26–32, 119–22.
7. In response to a proposal to add language to the Preamble expressly declaring, à la Virginia and New York, that "the people have an indubitable, unalienable and indefeasible right to reform or change their Government," Representative James Jackson of Georgia argued that the Preamble's "words, as they now stand, speak as much as it is possible to speak; it is a practical recognition of the right of the people to ordain and establish Governments, and is more expressive than any other more paper declaration." *Annals* [of Congress] 1:451 (June 8, 1789), 741 (Aug. 13). Connecticut's Roger Sherman agreed: "If this right is indefeasible, and the people have recognised it in practice, the truth is better asserted than it can be by any words whatever. The words 'We the people' in the original constitution, are as copious and expressive as possible; any addition will only drag out the sentence without illuminating it." Ibid., 746 (Aug. 14). For earlier language from Wilson stressing the Preamble's "practical" import, see p. 13; *Elliot's Debates*, 2:434.
8. Both the Massachusetts and New Hampshire Constitutions, which had been ordained by the voters themselves, contained specific clauses contemplating bills of credit. See Mass. Const. (1780), pt. II, ch. II, sec. I, art. XI; N.H. Const. (1784), pt. II (unnumbered para. beginning "No monies shall be issued ...").
9. See, e.g., U.S. Const., art. I, sec. 10, para. 1 ("No state shall ... coin Money; emit Bills of Credit; make any Thing but gold and silver Coin a Tender in Payment of Debts"). For a candid acknowledgment of the fact that the federal Constitution would effect amendments of existing state constitutions, see *Federalist* No. 44. For more discussion, see James Madison to George Washington, April 16, 1787, in Madison, *Papers*, 9:385; *Farrand's Records*, 1:317 (Madison), 2:88, 92–93 (Mason, Rufus King, and Madison), 3:229 (Luther Martin's "Genuine Information").
10. Mass. Const. (1780), pt. II, ch. VI, art. X; *DHRC*, 14:220 (diary of John Quincy Adams) ("I think it my duty to submit. ... In our Government, opposition to the acts of a majority of the people is rebellion to all intents and purposes"). Cf. *Elliot's Debates*, 2:157 (Ames: "such a [constitution] as the majority of the people approve *must* be submitted to by this state; for what right have an eighth or tenth part of the people to dictate a government for the whole?"). For discussion of the possible implications of this principle for federal constitutional amendment under (or outside) Article V, see Chapter 8.
11. See John Locke, *The Second Treatise of Government* (1690), secs. 221, 243.

12. *Elliot's Debates*, 2:432; *DHRC*, 2:348–49. For later statements from Wilson to the same effect, see Wilson, *Works*, 1:77–79, 317.

13. *Elliot's Debates*, 2:458. See also ibid., 432–33.

14. For a detailed refutation of this canard, see John Adams, *FAC*, 96–114. Adams demonstrates that "democracy" and "republic" were broadly synonymous from 1776 to 1787, and that, although some Federalists, such as Madison, tried to contradistinguish the two words, other leading Federalists continued to use them synonymously. Adams dismisses as "pseudo-learned" the notion "that the Founding Fathers intended the United States to be a republic but not a democracy."

15. See, e.g., *Federalist* No. 14 ("the structure of the Union . . . has been new modelled by the act of your [Philadelphia] convention, and it is that act on which you are now to deliberate and to decide"); No. 22 ("The fabric of American empire ought to rest on the solid basis of THE CONSENT OF THE PEOPLE. The streams of national power ought to flow immediately from that pure, original fountain of all legitimate authority"); No. 39 ("the Constitution is to be founded on the assent and ratification of the people of America, given by deputies elected for the special purpose"); No. 40 (proposed Constitution is "submitted TO THE PEOPLE THEMSELVES"—the "supreme authority"); No. 43 ("The express authority of the people alone could give due validity to the Constitution"); No. 46 ("ultimate authority, wherever the derivative may be found, resides in the people alone"); No. 49 ("the people are the only legitimate fountain of power, and it is from them that the constitutional charter, under which the several branches of government hold their power, is derived"); No. 53 ("The important distinction so well understood in America, between a Constitution established by the people and unalterable by the government, and a law established by the government and alterable by the government, seems to have been little understood and less observed in any other country"); No. 78 (Constitution declares will of "the people" and a "fundamental principle of republican government . . . admits the right of the people to alter or abolish their established Constitution"); No. 84 ("Here, in strictness, the people surrender nothing; and as they retain every thing, they have no need of particular reservations. 'WE, THE PEOPLE of the United States, to secure the blessings of liberty to ourselves and our posterity, do ORDAIN and ESTABLISH this Constitution for the United States of America.' Here is a [clear] recognition of popular rights").

16. In *Federalist* No. 10, Madison/Publius elaborated on how congressional representation in a large and diverse country would afford "a republican remedy for the diseases most incident to republican government"—an argument that Madison at Philadelphia had labeled "the only defence agst. the inconveniences of democracy consistent with the democratic form of Govt." *Farrand's Records*, 1:134–35.

17. *Elliot's Debates*, 2:434, 482, 523 (emphasis deleted).

Discussion Questions

1. Why did Thomas Paine believe that the American Revolution required the colonies to form their own government?

2. How did politics shape the Constitution, according to David Robertson, Benjamin Franklin and the Constitutional Convention delegates' letter to Congress? In what ways did political bargaining improve the Constitution? In what ways did political bargaining make it worse?

3. What kind of Constitution would the Anti-Federalists have written? How would it have been different from the Constitution they opposed? Would their Constitution have worked better than the Constitution that was adopted?

4. Akhil Reed Amar makes a strong case that the Constitution was a very democratic document. Is it democratic enough for the 21st century? What parts need to be rewritten to make it democratic enough for the present?
5. What difference does the Constitution make in Americans' lives today? Give specific examples.

Suggested Additional Reading

Richard Beeman, *Plain, Honest Men: The Making of the American Constitution* (New York: Random House, 2009).

Max M. Edling, *A Revolution in Favor of Government: Origins of the U.S. Constitution and the Making of the American State* (Oxford and New York: Oxford University Press, 2003).

David Hume, "The Idea of a Perfect Commonwealth" (1777), from *Essays, Moral, Political, and Literary* (Indianapolis, IN: Liberty Fund, 1985).

James Madison, "Vices of the Political System of the United States," 1787 (http://press-pubs.uchicago.edu/founders/documents/v1ch5s16.html).

Pauline Meier, *Ratification: The People Debate the Constitution, 1787–1788* (New York: Simon and Schuster, 2010).

Jack N. Rakove, *Original Meanings: Politics and Ideas in the Making of the Constitution* (New York: Alfred A. Knopf, 1996).

David J. Siemers, *Ratifying the Republic: Antifederalists and Federalists in Constitutional Time* (Stanford, CA: Stanford University Press, 2002).

3

Federalism and the American Political System

Introduction

Federalism has affected every aspect of American political development since 1787. In a federal political system, regional governments (called "states" in the U.S., Australia, and Brazil, "provinces" in Canada and "Länder" in Germany) share with the national government the sovereign power to make public policy. State government power was an important feature of the U.S. Constitution; James Madison explained that the Constitution was "partly national" and "partly federal." The states used their power to do most of the nation's domestic governing, and still do so today. States tax sales, income and property, and they regulate property, estates, corporations, labor, the insurance industry, the professions, health and safety, environmental quality, marriage, divorce, abortion and the relationship rights of gay couples. States provide highways, universities, state parks and historic sites, workers' compensation and welfare. States control elementary and secondary education. States are free to use their powers in different ways, as the case of capital punishment shows. Thirty-six states use the death penalty in the most serious criminal cases; fourteen states do not provide for capital punishment. Some states use the death penalty infrequently, others much more often. Colorado has executed only one person since 1976, while Texas has executed over 500 people in that time.[1]

Federalism has played a vital role in the political conflicts that drive American political development. The first reading, from the *Federalist*, shows how the battle over the ratification of the Constitution forced James Madison to emphasize the decisive role the states would continue to play in the proposed political system (and that the new system would not establish a "consolidated" national government, as Anti-Federalists feared). In the first decade of the new American government, James Madison and Thomas Jefferson used states' rights to fight Alexander Hamilton, who proposed that the national government absorb the states' debts, aid the growth of manufactures, and create a national bank.

Early nineteenth-century American leaders employed federalism as a weapon in their major battles over the size of national tariffs, the use of federal government land, and the protection of slavery. In the second reading, U.S. Senator Robert Hayne from South Carolina debated with Senator Daniel Webster from Massachusetts over the meaning of the union in a famous 1830 dispute (in which fear of "consolidation" still played a central role). Thirty years later, Americans were driven to Civil War over the right of states to leave the union. The Civil War settled the question of secession, but left countless issues about the relative powers of the state and national government open to passionate debate.

American federalism underwent a major, durable shift during the first half of the twentieth century, as legal scholar Edwin Corwin argues in reading three, his classic article, "The Passing of Dual Federalism." Corwin argues that the pressures of the New Deal and World War II—with the sanction of the Supreme Court— shifted away from the system of "dual" federalism that marked the rivalry, conflict and limited national power of the American system in the nineteenth century. Now, federalism was "cooperative": the national, state and local governments collaborated to ensure that the economic and other priorities of the national government were implemented across the nation.

Margaret Weir emphasized the political consequences of developments in federalism (reading four). Weir argued that federalism shaped the development of national policy and politics in this period by limiting the reach of New Deal liberal reform in all the states. Until the 1960s, rural areas in the states were allowed to have more representation in state legislatures than cities. As American urban areas grew, state laws concerning land use in urban areas encouraged the growth of independent suburbs. The fragmentation of metropolitan areas, in turn, fragmented and weakened the constituency for government activism, and fostered the emergence of support for free-market conservatism in the 1980s.

While Weir pointed out the impact of federalism on the development of American *politics*, Suzanne Mettler (reading five) highlighted the way federalism affected national *policy* by delegating the income security of men and women to different levels of government. The Social Security Act's provisions established a fully national program of old-age insurance for male wage-earners, but gave responsibility to the states to manage income assistance for widows and single mothers. This "partly national," "partly federal" program divided the citizenship rights of men and women. The state responsibility for the program produced very unequal policy results across the states, and far less economic security for women than men nationwide.

The highlight piece in this chapter is a selection from David Robertson's *Federalism and the Making of America*. This book critically examined the role of federalism from the perspective of American political development. Today, federalism shapes political battles ranging from abortion and gay rights to health care, economic development, climate change, criminal law, trade union organizing and college tuition. He found that federalism has had a profound and enduring effect on such political struggles principally because opponents used it as a political weapon for all the important past and present conflicts in American politics. Federalism shaped the sequence, substance and strategies of American political reform over the decades, and it still does so today. For example, conservative reformers in recent decades used federalism as a tactic to achieve some of their goals. They did not hesitate to increase national power at the expense of the states when they felt it necessary to accomplish more essential goals.

Note

1. Death Penalty Information Center (http://www.deathpenaltyinfo.org/number-executions-state-and-region-1976; accessed November 26, 2013).

3.1 *Federalist Papers* 39 and 45 (1788)

At the Constitutional Convention, Oliver Ellsworth of Connecticut argued that Americans "were partly national; partly federal."[1] Madison objected to this formulation in Philadelphia, but, in these selections from the *Federalist*, he uses the formulation enthusiastically to reassure New York voters that the Constitution would protect the states' interests and not produce the "consolidation," or centralization, of all government power in the national government (a fear stoked by the use of this word in the letter the Constitutional Convention sent to Congress along with the document; reading 2.3). He carefully laid out the ways in which states remain sovereign, and assured readers that the national government would be dependent on the states. Further, he made the pragmatic argument that federal officials would find it politically expedient to defend state interests. Note that, when Madison argued that the system mixes national and state power, he played into the hands of another anti-federalist criticism of the Constitution: that the plan is dangerously complex. Madison's essay did not provide much clear guidance about the precise boundary between state and national authority. That ambiguity has made federalism a flashpoint of American political conflict to this day.

Note

1. Oliver Ellsworth in Max Farrand, ed., *The Records of the Federal Convention of 1787*, vol. I, 468.

The Federalist No. 39

James Madison

January 16, 1788

To the People of the State of New York.

... It was not sufficient, say the adversaries of the proposed Constitution, for the Convention to adhere to the republican form. They ought, with equal care, to have preserved the *federal* form, which regards the union as a *confederacy* of sovereign States; instead of which, they have framed a *national* government, which regards the union as a *consolidation* of the States. And it is asked by what authority this bold and radical innovation was undertaken. The handle which has been made of this objection requires, that it should be examined with some precision.

...In order to ascertain the real character of the government it may be considered in relation to the foundation on which it is to be established; to the sources from which its ordinary powers are to be drawn; to the operation of those powers; to the extent of them; and to the authority by which future changes in the government are to be introduced.

On examining the first relation, it appears on one hand that the Constitution is to be founded on the assent and ratification of the people of America, given by deputies elected for the special purpose; but on the other, that this assent and ratification is to be given by the people, not as individuals composing one entire nation; but as composing the distinct and independent States to which they respectively belong. It is to be the assent and ratification of the several States, derived from the supreme authority in each State, the authority of the people themselves. The act therefore establishing the Constitution, will not be a *national* but a *federal* act.

That it will be a federal and not a national act, as these terms are understood by the objectors, the act of the people as forming so many independent States, not as forming one aggregate nation, is obvious from this single consideration that it is to result neither from the decision of a *majority* of the people of the Union, nor from that of a *majority* of the States. It must result from the *unanimous* assent of the several States that are parties to it, differing no other wise from their ordinary assent than in its being expressed, not by the legislative authority, but by that of the people themselves. Were the people regarded in this transaction as forming one nation, the will of the majority of the whole people of the United States, would bind the minority; in the same manner as the majority in each State must bind the minority; and the will of the majority must be determined either by a comparison of the individual votes; or by considering the will of a majority of the States, as evidence of the will of a majority of the people of the United States. Neither of these rules has been adopted. Each State in ratifying the Constitution, is considered as a sovereign body independent of all others, and only to be bound by its own voluntary act. In this relation then the new Constitution will, if established, be a *federal* and not a *national* Constitution.

The next relation is to the sources from which the ordinary powers of government are to be derived. The house of representatives will derive its powers from the people of America, and the people will be represented in the same proportion, and on the same principle, as they are in the Legislature of a particular State. So far the Government is *national* not *federal*. The Senate on the other hand will derive its powers from the States, as political and co-equal societies; and these will be represented on the principle of equality in the Senate, as they now are in the existing Congress. So far the government is *federal*, not *national*. The executive power will be derived from a very compound source. The immediate election of the President is to be made by the States in their political characters. The votes allotted to them, are in a compound ratio, which considers them partly as distinct and co-equal societies; partly as unequal members of the same society. The eventual election, again is to be made by that branch of the Legislature which consists of the national representatives; but in this particular act, they are to be thrown into the form of individual delegations from so many distinct and co-equal bodies politic. From this aspect of the Government, it appears to be of a mixed character presenting at least as many *federal* as *national* features.

The difference between a federal and national Government as it relates to the *operation of the Government* is supposed to consist in this, that in the former, the powers operate on the political bodies composing the confederacy, in their political capacities: In the latter, on the individual citizens, composing the nation, in their individual capacities. On trying the Constitution by this criterion, it falls under the *national*, not the *federal* character; though perhaps not so compleatly, as has been understood. In several cases and particularly in the trial of controversies to which States may be parties, they must be viewed and proceeded against in their collective and political capacities only. So far the national countenance of the Government on this side seems to be disfigured by a few federal features. But this blemish is perhaps unavoidable in any plan; and the operation of the Government on the people in their individual capacities, in its ordinary and most essential proceedings, may on the whole designate it in this relation a *national* Government.

But if the Government be national with regard to the *operation* of its powers, it changes its aspect again when we contemplate it in relation to the *extent* of its powers. The idea of a national Government involves in it, not only an authority over the individual citizens; but an indefinite supremacy over all persons and things, so far as they are objects of lawful Government. Among a people consolidated into one nation, this supremacy is compleatly vested in the national Legislature. Among communities united for particular purposes, it is vested partly in the general, and partly in the municipal Legislatures. In the former case, all local authorities are subordinate to the supreme; and may be controuled, directed or abolished by it at pleasure. In the latter the local or municipal authorities form distinct and independent portions of the supremacy, no more subject within their respective spheres to the general authority, than the general authority is subject to them, within its own sphere. In this relation then the proposed Government cannot be deemed a *national* one; since its jurisdiction extends to certain enumerated objects only, and leaves to the several States a residuary and inviolable sovereignty over all other objects. It is true that in controversies relating to the boundary between the two jurisdictions, the tribunal which is ultimately to decide, is to be established under the general Government. But this does not change the principle of the case. The decision is to be impartially made, according to the rules of the Constitution; and all the usual and most effectual precautions are taken to secure this impartiality. Some such tribunal is clearly essential to prevent an appeal to the sword, and a dissolution of the compact; and that it ought to be established under the general, rather than under the local Governments; or to speak more properly, that it could be safely established under the first alone, is a position not likely to be combated.

If we try the Constitution by its last relation, to the authority by which amendments are to be made, we find it neither wholly *national*, nor wholly *federal*. Were it wholly national, the supreme and ultimate authority would reside in the *majority* of the people of the Union; and this authority would be competent at all times, like that of a majority of every national society, to alter or abolish its established Government. Were it wholly federal on the other hand, the concurrence of each State in the Union would be essential to every alteration that would be binding on all. The mode provided by the plan of the Convention is not founded on either of these principles. In requiring more than a majority, and particularly, in computing the proportion by *States*, not by *citizens*, it departs from the *national*, and advances towards the *federal* character: In rendering the concurrence of less than the whole number of States sufficient, it loses again the *federal*, and partakes of the *national* character.

The proposed Constitution therefore is in strictness neither a national nor a federal constitution; but a composition of both. In its foundation, it is federal, not national; in the sources from which the ordinary powers of the Government are drawn, it is partly federal, and partly national: in the operation of these powers, it is national, not federal: In the extent of them again, it is federal, not national: And finally, in the authoritative mode of introducing amendments, it is neither wholly federal, nor wholly national.

PUBLIUS.

The Federalist No. 46

James Madison

January 29, 1788

To the People of the State of New York.

It has been already proved, that the members of the fœderal will be more dependent on the members of the State governments, than the latter will be on the former. It has appeared also, that the prepossessions of the people on whom both will depend, will be more on the side of the State governments, than of the Fœderal Government. So far as the disposition of each, towards the other, may be influenced by these causes, the State governments must clearly have the advantage. But in a distinct and very important point of view, the advantage will lie on the same side. The prepossessions which the members themselves will carry into the Fœderal Government, will generally be favorable to the States; whilst it will rarely happen, that the members of the State governments will carry into the public councils, a bias in favor of the general government. A local spirit will infallibly prevail much more in the members of the Congress, than a national spirit will prevail in the Legislatures of the particular States. Every one knows that a great proportion of the errors committed by the State Legislatures proceeds from the disposition of the members to sacrifice the comprehensive and permanent interest of the State, to the particular and separate views of the counties or districts in which they reside. And if they do not sufficiently enlarge their policy to embrace the collective welfare of their particular State, how can it be imagined, that they will make the aggregate prosperity of the Union, and the dignity and respectability of its government, the objects of their affections and consultations? For the same reason, that the members of the State Legislatures, will be unlikely to attach themselves sufficiently to national objects, the members of the Fœderal Legislature will be likely to attach themselves too much to local objects. The States will be to the latter, what counties and towns are to the former. Measures will too often be decided according to their probable effect, not on the national prosperity and happiness, but on the prejudices, interests and pursuits of the governments and people of the individual States. What is the spirit that has in general characterized the proceedings of Congress? A perusal of their journals as well as the candid acknowledgments of such as have had a seat in that assembly, will inform us, that the members have but too frequently displayed the character, rather of partizans of their respective States, than of impartial guardians of a common interest; that whereon one occasion improper sacrifices have been made of local considerations to the aggrandizement of the Fœderal Government; the great interests of the nation have suffered on an hundred, from an undue attention to the local prejudices, interests and views of the particular States. I mean not by these reflections to insinuate, that the new Fœderal Government will not embrace a more enlarged plan of policy than the existing government may have pursued, much less that its views will be as confined as those of the State Legislatures; but only that it will partake sufficiently of the spirit of both, to be disinclined to invade the rights of the individual States, or the prerogatives of their governments. The motives on the part of the State governments, to augment their prerogatives by defalcations from the Fœderal Government, will be overruled by no reciprocal predispositions in the members.

PUBLIUS.

3.2 The Webster-Hayne Debates (1830)

Within a few years of the Founding, American leaders found themselves deeply divided by disagreements over the precise boundary between national and state government power. Slavery elevated states' rights into a central battleground for American politics. A U.S. Senate discussion of public land policy in January, 1830, grew into momentous debate over the idea of the union and national power. Robert Y. Hayne, a Senator from the slave state of South Carolina, insisted that national power was limited, that the Constitution did not "consolidate" all government power in the national government, and that states have the authority to limit the scope of national power. Hayne believed in "nullification," the doctrine that a state could invalidate a national law if it believed the national law to be unconstitutional. Senator Daniel Webster of Massachusetts challenged Hayne's view, arguing that states could not control national laws and must submit to them. Both Senators appealed to what they believed to be the original meaning of the Constitution to advance their arguments. This conflict over the Constitution's meaning shows how the Constitution in general, and federalism in particular, have served as major political battlegrounds throughout the political development of the United States.

Senator Robert Y. Hayne:

I distrust therefore sir, the policy of creating a great permanent *national treasury*, whether, to be derived from public lands or from any source. If I had, sir, the powers of a magician, and could, by a wave of my hand, convert this capitol into gold for such a purpose, I would not do it. If I could, by a mere act of my will, put at the disposal of the federal government any amount of treasure which I might think proper to name, I should limit the amount to the means necessary for the legitimate purposes of the government. Sir, an immense national treasury would be a *fund for corruption*. It would enable congress and the executive to exercise a control over states, as well as over great interests in the country—nay, even over corporations and individuals, utterly destructive of the purity, and fatal to the duration of our institutions. It would be equally fatal to the sovereignty and independence of the states.

Sir, I am one of those who believe that the very life of our system is the independence of the states; and that there is no evil more to be deprecated than the *consolidation of* this government. It is only by a strict adherence to the limitations imposed by the constitution on the federal government, that this system works well, and can answer the great ends for which it was instituted. I am opposed, therefore, in any shape, to all unnecessary extension of the powers or the influence of the legislature or executive of the union of the states; and, most of all, I am opposed to those partial distributions of favors whether by *legislation* or *appropriation*, which has a direct and powerful tendency to spread corruption through the land—to create an abject spirit of dependence—to sow the seeds of dissolution—to produce jealousy among the different portions of the union, and, finally, to sap the very foundations of the government itself.

Senator Daniel Webster:

I am aware that these, and similar opinions, are espoused by certain persons out of the capitol, and out of this government, but I did not expect so soon to find them here. Consolidation!—that perpetual cry both of terror and delusion—consolidation! Sir, when gentlemen speak of the effects of a common fund, belonging to all the states, as having a tendency to consolidation, what do they mean? Do they mean, or can they mean any thing more than that the union of the states will be strengthened, by whatever continues or furnishes inducements to the people of the states to hold together? If they mean merely this, then no doubt, the public lands, as well as every thing else in which we have a common interest, tends to consolidation and to this species of consolidation every true American ought to be attached; it is neither more nor less than strengthening the union itself. This is the sense in which the framers of the Constitution use the word consolidation and in which sense I adopt and cherish it. They tell us, in the letter submitting the constitution to the consideration of the country, that "In all our deliberations on this subject, we kept steadily in our view that which appears to us the greatest interest of every true American, the consolidation of our union, in which is involved our prosperity, felicity, safety, perhaps our national existence. This important consideration, seriously and deeply impressed on our minds led each state in the convention to be less rigid on points of inferior magnitude, than might have been otherwise expected."

This, sir, is general Washington's consolidation. This is the true constitutional consolidation. I wish to see no new powers drawn to the general government; but I confess I rejoice in whatever tends to strengthen the bond that unites us; and encourages the hope that our union may be perpetual. And, therefore, I cannot but feel regret at the expression of such opinions as the gentleman has avowed; because I think their obvious tendency is to weaken the bond of our connexion.

... Sir, I deprecate and deplore this tone of thought and feeling. I deem far otherwise of the union of the states, and so did the framers of the constitution themselves. What they said I believe; fully and sincerely believe, that the union of the states is essential to the prosperity and safety of the states. I am a unionist, and in this sense, a national republican. I would strengthen the ties that hold us together. Far, indeed, in my wishes, very far distant be the day, when our associated and fraternal stripes shall be severed asunder, and when that happy constellation under which we have risen to so much renown, shall be broken up and be seen sinking star after star, into obscurity and night!

Senator Hayne:

In the course of my former remarks, Mr. President, I took occasion to deprecate, as one of the greatest evils, the consolidation of this government. The gentleman takes alarm at the sound. "Consolidation," like the tariff grates upon his ear. He tells us, "we have heard much of late about consolidation; that it is the rallying word of all who are endeavoring to weaken the Union, by adding to the power of the states." But consolidation (says the gentleman) was the very object for which the Union was formed; and, in support of that opinion, he read a passage from the address of the president of the convention to Congress, which he assumes to be authority on his side of the question. But, sir, the gentleman is mistaken. The object of the framers of the constitution, as disclosed in that address, was not the consolidation of the government, but "the consolidation of the Union." It was not to draw power from the states, in order to transfer it to a great national government, but, in the language of the constitution itself, "to form a more perfect Union;"—and by what means? By "establishing justice, promoting domestic tranquillity, and securing the blessings of liberty to ourselves and our posterity." This is the true reading of the Constitution. But, according to the gentleman's reading, the object of the constitution was, to consolidate the government, and the means would seem to be, the promotion of injustice, causing domestic discord, and depriving the states and the people "of the blessings of liberty" forever.

. . . Who, then, Mr. President, are the true friends of the Union? Those who would confine the federal government strictly within the limits prescribed by the constitution; who would preserve to the states and the people all powers not expressly delegated; who would make this a federal and not a national Union, and who, administering the government in spirit of equal justice, would make it a blessing, and not a curse. And who are its enemies? Those who are in favor of consolidation; who are constantly stealing power from the states, and adding strength to the Federal government; who, assuming an unwarrantable Jurisdiction over the states and the people, undertake to regulate the whole industry and capital of the country. But, sir, of all descriptions of men, I consider those as the worst enemies of the Union, who sacrifice the equal rights which belong to every member of the confederacy to combinations of interested majorities, for personal or political objects. But the gentleman apprehends no evil from the dependence of the states on the federal government; he can see no danger of corruption from the influence of money or of patronage . . .

. . . Sir, as to the doctrine that the federal government is the exclusive judge of the extent as well as the limitations of its powers, it seems to me to be utterly subversive of the sovereignty and independence of the states. It makes but little difference, in my estimation, whether Congress or Supreme Court are invested with this power. If the federal government, in all, or any, of its departments, is to prescribe the limits of its own authority and the states are bound to submit to the decision, and are not to be allowed to examine and decide for themselves, when the barriers of the constitution shall be overleaped, this is "practically government without limitation of powers." The states are at once reduced to mere petty corporations and the people are entirely at your mercy.

Senator Webster:

I understand the honorable gentleman from South Carolina to maintain, that it is a right of the State legislatures to interfere, whenever, in their judgment, this government transcends its constitutional limits, and to arrest the operation of its laws.

... I understand him to maintain an authority, on the part of the States, thus to interfere, for the purpose of correcting the exercise of power by the general government, of checking it, and of compelling it to conform to their opinion of the extent of its powers.

I understand him to maintain, that the ultimate power of judging of the constitutional extent of its own authority is not lodged exclusively in the general government, or any branch of it; but that, on the contrary, the States may lawfully decide for themselves, and each State for itself, whether, in a given case, the act of the general government transcends its power.

... This leads us to inquire into the origin of this government and the source of its power. Whose agent is it? Is it the creature of the State legislatures, or the creature of the people? If the government of the United States be the agent of the State governments, then they may control it, provided they can agree in the manner of controlling it; if it be the agent of the people, then the people alone can control it, restrain it, modify, or reform it ....

It is, Sir, the people's Constitution, the people's government, made for the people, made by the people, and answerable to the people. The people of the United States have declared that this Constitution shall be the supreme law. We must either admit the proposition, or dispute their authority. The States are, unquestionably, sovereign, so far as their sovereignty is not affected by this supreme law. But the State legislatures, as political bodies, however sovereign, are yet not sovereign over the people. So far as the people have given power to the general government, so far the grant is unquestionably good, and the government holds of the people, and not of the State governments. We are all agents of the same supreme power, the people. The general government and the State governments derive their authority from the same source.

... One of two things is true; either the laws of the Union are beyond the discretion and beyond the control of the States; or else we have no constitution of general government, and are thrust back again to the days of the Confederation.

... I have not allowed myself, Sir, to look beyond the Union, to see what might lie hidden in the dark recess behind. I have not coolly weighed the chances of preserving liberty when the bonds that unite us together shall be broken asunder. I have not accustomed myself to hang over the precipice of disunion, to see whether, with my short sight, I can fathom the depth of the abyss below; nor could I regard him as a safe counsellor in the affairs of this government, whose thoughts should be mainly bent on considering, not how the Union may be best preserved, but how tolerable might be the condition of the people when it should be broken up and destroyed. While the Union lasts, we have high, exciting, gratifying prospects spread out before us, for us and our children. Beyond that I seek not to penetrate the veil. God grant that, in my day, at least, that curtain may not rise! God grant that on my vision never may be opened what lies behind! When my eyes shall be turned to behold for the last time the sun in heaven, may I not see him shining on the broken and dishonored fragments of a once glorious Union; on States dissevered, discordant, belligerent; on a land rent with civil feuds, or drenched, it may be, in fraternal blood! Let their last feeble and lingering glance rather behold the gorgeous ensign of the republic, now known and honored throughout the earth, still full high advanced, its arms and trophies streaming in their original lustre, not a stripe erased or polluted, nor a single Star obscured, bearing for its motto, no such miserable interrogatory as "What is all this worth?" nor those other words of delusion and folly, "Liberty first and Union afterwards"; but everywhere, spread all over in characters of living light, blazing on all its ample folds, as they float over the sea and over the land, and in every wind under the whole heavens, that other sentiment, dear to every true American heart—Liberty and Union, now and for ever, one and inseparable!

3.3 Edwin S. Corwin, "The Passing of Dual Federalism" (1950)

Edwin Corwin was among the leading Constitutional scholars of the twentieth century (his Constitutional text is still used in college classes across the country). For most of American history, he argued in this piece, U.S. federalism was defined by limited federal government powers, substantial state powers, and tension between the two levels of government. The growth of federal grants and the Supreme Court's acceptance of broad federal powers have left the old federalism all but dead. In this shift toward "consolidation" of government powers, the federal government has established cooperative relationships with the state governments to achieve policy goals. He observed that national government priorities inevitably dominate in this new kind of federalism. Corwin saw danger in this expansion of national power and warned about the potential threat of the passing of dual federalism for American democracy itself.

Within the generation now drawing to a close ... [w]e have fought two world wars, the second of which answered every definition of "total war", and have submitted to the regimentation which these great national efforts entailed. We have passed through an economic crisis which was described by the late President [Franklin Roosevelt] as "a crisis greater than war". We have become the exclusive custodian of technology's crowning gift to civilization [the atomic bomb], an invention capable of blowing it to smithereens, and we greatly hope to retain that honorable trusteeship throughout an indefinite future. Meantime we have elected ourselves the head and forefront of one of two combinations of nations which together embrace a great part of the Western World and in this capacity are at present involved in a "cold war" with the head of the opposing combination; and as one phase of this curious and baffling struggle we find ourselves driven to combat at obvious risk to certain heretofore cherished constitutional values, the menace of a hidden propaganda which is intended by its agents to work impairment of the national fiber against the time when the "cold war" may eventuate in a "shooting war". Lastly, though by no means least, the most wide-spread and powerfully organized political interest in the country, that of organized labor, has come to accept unreservedly a new and revolutionary conception of the role of government. Formerly we generally thought of government as primarily a policeman, with an amiable penchant for being especially helpful to those who knew how to help themselves. By the ideological revolution just alluded to, which stems from the Great Depression and the New Deal, it becomes the duty of government to guarantee economic security to all as the indispensable foundation of constitutional liberty.

Naturally, the stresses and strains to which the nation has been subjected by these pressures has not left our Constitutional Law unaffected. In general terms, our system has lost resiliency and what was once vaunted as a Constitution of Rights, both State and private, has been replaced by a Constitution of Powers. More specifically, the Federal System has shifted base in the direction of a consolidated national power, while within the National Government itself an increased flow of power in the direction of the President has ensued . . . .

In just what fashion then has the shift . . . of our Federal System toward consolidation registered itself in our Constitutional Law in response to the requirements of war, economic crisis, and a fundamentally altered outlook upon the purpose of government? The solution of the conundrum is to be sought in the changed attitude of the [U.S. Supreme] Court toward certain postulates or axioms of constitutional interpretation closely touching the Federal System, and which in their totality comprised what I mean by Dual Federalism. These postulates are the following: 1. The national government is one of enumerated powers only; 2. Also the purposes which it may constitutionally promote are few; 3. Within their respective spheres the two centers of government are "sovereign" and hence "equal"; 4. The relation of the two centers with each other is one of tension rather than collaboration.

. . . It was early in this period [the Supreme Court under Chief Justice Roger Taney, 1836–1864] that the concept of the Police Power emerged. This, broadly considered, was simply what Taney termed "the power to govern men and things" defined from the point of view of the duty of the State to "promote the happiness and prosperity of the community"; more narrowly, it was a certain central core of this power, namely the power of the States to "provide for the public health, safety, and good order". Within this latter field at least, the powers reserved to the States by the Tenth Amendment were "sovereign" powers, "complete, unqualified, and exclusive". Yet this did not signify that the States, acting through either their legislatures or their courts, were the final judge of the scope of these "sovereign" powers. This was the function of the Supreme Court of the United States, which for this purpose was regarded by the Constitution as standing outside of and over both the National Government and the States, and vested with authority to apportion impartially to each center its proper powers in accordance with the Constitution's intention. And the primary test whether this intention was fulfilled was whether conflict between the two centers was avoided.[1]

. . . Thus the principle of national supremacy came to be superseded by an unlimited discretion in the Supreme Court to designate this or that State power as comprising an independent limitation on national power. In only one area was the earlier principle recognized as still operative, and that was the field of interstate commercial regulation. This field, indeed, was not properly speaking a part of the "reserved powers" of the States at all; it belonged to Congress's enumerated powers.

. . . While, as we have seen, the Police Power was defined in the first instance with the end in view of securing to the States a near monopoly of the right to realize the main objectives of government, the concept came later to embrace the further idea that certain subject-matters were also segregated to the States and hence could not be reached by any valid exercise of national power. That production, and hence mining, agriculture, and manufacturing, and the employer-employee relationship in connection with these were among such subject-matters was indeed one of the basic postulates of the Court's system of Constitutional Law in the era of *laissez faire*.[2]

... This entire system of constitutional interpretation touching the Federal System is today in ruins. It toppled in the Social Security Act cases and in *N.L.R.B.* v. *Jones & Laughlin Steel Corporation*, in which the Wagner Labor Act was sustained.[3] This was in 1937 while the "Old Court" was still in power. In 1941 in *United States* v. *Darby*,[4] the "New Court" merely performed a mopping-up operation. The Act of Congress involved was the Fair Labor Standards Act of 1938, which not only bans interstate commerce in goods produced under sub-standard conditions but makes their production a penal offense against the United States if they are "intended" for interstate or foreign commerce. Speaking for the unanimous Court, Chief Justice [Harlan] Stone went straight back to Marshall's opinions in *McCulloch* v. *Maryland* and *Gibbons* v. *Ogden*, extracting from the former his latitudinarian construction of the "necessary and proper" clause and from both cases his uncompromising application of the "supremacy" clause.[5]

Today neither the State Police Power nor the concept of Federal Equilibrium is any "ingredient of national legislative power", whether as respects subject-matter to be governed, or the choice of objectives or of means for its exercise.

Lastly, we come to the question whether the two centers of government ought to be regarded as standing in a competitive or co-operative relation to each other.

... The competitive theory of Federalism ... is today largely moribund in consequence of the emergence of the *cooperative* conception. According to this conception, the National Government and the States are mutually complementary parts of a single governmental mechanism all of whose powers are intended to realize the current purposes of government according to their applicability to the problem in hand. It is thus closely intertwined with the multiple-purpose conception of national power and with recent enlarged theories of the function of government generally. Here we are principally interested in two forms of joint action by the National Government and the States which have developed within recent years, primarily through the *legislative* powers of the two centers.

Thus in the first place the National Government has brought its augmented powers over interstate commerce and communications to the support of local policies of the States in the exercise of their reserved powers. By the doctrine that Congress's power to regulate "commerce among the States" is "exclusive", a State is frequently unable to stop the flow of commerce from sister States even when it threatens to undermine local legislation. In consequence Congress has within recent years come to the assistance of the police powers of the States by making certain crimes against them, like theft, racketeering, kidnapping, crimes also against the National Government whenever the offender extends his activities beyond state boundary lines.[6]

Justifying such legislation, the Court has said

> Our dual form of government has its perplexities, state and Nation having different spheres of jurisdiction ... but it must be kept in mind that we are one people; and the powers reserved to the states and those conferred on the nations are adapted to be exercised, whether independently or concurrently, to promote the general welfare, material and moral.[7] ...

Secondly, the National Government has held out inducements, primarily of a pecuniary kind, to the States—the so-called "grants-in-aid"—to use their reserved powers to support certain objectives of national policy in the field of expenditure. In other words, the greater financial strength of the National Government is joined to the wider coercive powers of the States. Thus since 1911, Congress has voted money to subsidize forest-protection, education in agricultural and industrial subjects and in home economics, vocational rehabilitation and education, the maintenance of nautical schools, experimentation in reforestation and highway construction in the States; in return for which cooperating States have appropriated equal sums for the same purposes, and have brought their further powers to the support thereof along lines laid down by Congress.[8]

The culmination of this type of National-State cooperation to date, however, is reached in The Social Security Act of August 14, 1935. The Act brings the national tax-spending power to the support of such States as desire to cooperate in the maintenance of old-age pensions, unemployment insurance, maternal welfare work, vocational rehabilitation, and public health work, and in financial assistance to impoverished old age, dependent children, and the blind. Such legislation is, as we have seen, within the national taxing-spending power. What, however, of the objection that it "coerced" complying States into "abdicating" their powers? Speaking to this point in the *Social Security Act* cases, the Court has said: "The ... contention confuses motive with coercion.... To hold that motive or temptation is equivalent to coercion is to plunge the law in endless difficulties."[9] And again: "The United States and the state of Alabama are not alien governments. They co-exist within the same territory. Unemployment is their common concern. Together the two statutes before us [the Act of Congress and the Alabama Act] embody a cooperative legislative effort by state and national governments, for carrying out a public purpose common to both, which neither could fully achieve without the cooperation of the other. The Constitution does not prohibit such cooperation."[10]

It has been argued, to be sure, that the cooperative conception of the federal relationship, especially as it is realized in the policy of the "grants-in-aid", tends to break down State initiative and to devitalize State policies. Actually, its effect has often been the contrary, and for the reason pointed out by Justice Cardozo in *Helvering* v. *Davis*,[11] also decided in 1937; namely, that the States, competing as they do with one another to attract investors, have not been able to embark separately upon expensive programs of relief and social insurance.

The other great objection to Cooperative Federalism is more difficult to meet, if indeed it can be met. This is, that "Cooperative Federalism" spells further aggrandizement of national power. Unquestionably it does, for when two cooperate it is the stronger member of the combination who calls the tunes. Resting as it does primarily on the superior fiscal resources of the National Government, Cooperative Federalism has been, to date, a short expression for a constantly increasing concentration of power at Washington in the instigation and supervision of local policies.

...Federalism's first achievement was to enable the American people to secure the benefits of national union without imperilling their republican institutions.... In fact, the founders of the American Federal System for the first time in history ranged the power of a potentially great state on the side of institutions which had hitherto been confined to small states. Even the republicanism of Rome had stopped at the Eternal City's walls.

Then in the century following, American federalism served the great enterprise of appropriating the North American continent to western civilization. For one of the greatest lures to the westward movement of population was the possibility which federalism held out to the advancing settlers of establishing their own undictated political institutions, and endowing them with generous powers of government for local use. Federalism thus became the instrument of a new, a *democratic, imperialism*, one extending over an "Empire of liberty," in Jefferson's striking phrase.

Then, about 1890, just as the frontier was disappearing from the map, federalism became, through judicial review, an instrument of the current *laissez faire* conception of the function of government and a force promoting the rise of Big Business. Adopting the theory that the reason why Congress had been given the power to regulate "commerce among the several states" was to prevent the states from doing so, rather than to enable the National Government to pursue social policies of its own through exerting a positive control over commerce, the Court at one time created a realm of no-power, "a twilight zone","a no-man's land" in which corporate enterprise was free to roam largely unchecked. While the economic unification of the nation was undoubtedly aided by this type of Constitutional Law, the benefit was handsomely paid for in the social detriments which attended it, as became clear when the Great Depression descended on the country.

Finally . . . American federalism has been converted into an instrument for the achievement of peace abroad and economic security for "the common man" at home. In the process of remolding the Federal System for these purposes, however, the instrument has been overwhelmed and submerged in the objectives sought, so that today the question faces us whether the constituent States of the System can be saved for any useful purpose, and thereby saved as the vital cells that they have been heretofore of democratic sentiment, impulse, and action.

And it was probably with some such doubt in mind that Justice Frankfurter wrote a few years ago, in an opinion for the Court:

> The interpenetrations of modern society have not wiped out state lines. It is not for us to make inroads upon our federal system either by indifference to its maintenance or excessive regard for the unifying forces of modern technology. Scholastic reasoning may prove that no activity is isolated within the boundaries of a single State, but that cannot justify absorption of legislative power by the United States over every activity.[12]

These be brave words. Are they likely to determine the course of future history any more than Madison's similar utterance 130 years ago has done to date?

NOTES

1. On this system of constitutional interpretation, see especially New York v. Miln, 11 Pet. 102, 9 L. Ed. 648 (U.S. 1837); see also License Cases, 5 How. 504, 527–37, 573–74, 588, 613, 12 L. Ed. 256, 266–71, 287–88, 294, 305 (U.S. 1847) *passim*.
2. See CORWIN, COMMERCE POWER VERSUS STATES RIGHTS 175–209 (1936).
3. 301 U.S. 1, 57 Sup. Ct. 615, 81 L. Ed. 893 (1937).
4. 312 U.S. 100, 61 Sup. Ct. 451, 85 L. Ed. 609 (1941).
5. Ibid. See also United States v. Carolene Products Co., 304 U.S. 144, 58 Sup. Ct. 778, 82 L. Ed. 1234 (1938); Mulford v. Smith, 307 U.S. 38, 59 Sup. Ct. 648, 83 L. Ed. 1092 (1939).
6. For references, see CORWIN, COURT OVER CONSTITUTION 148–50 and notes (1938).
7. Hoke v. United States, 227 U.S. 308, 322, 33 Sup. Ct. 281, 284, 57 L. Ed. 523, 527 (1913).
8. CORWIN, *op. cit. supra* note 6, at 157–63.
9. Steward Machine Co. v. Davis, 301 U.S. 548, 589, 57 Sup. Ct. 883, 892, 81 L. Ed. 1279, 1292 (1937).

10. Carmichael v. Southern Coal & Coke Co., 301 U.S. 495, 526, 57 Sup. Ct. 868, 880, 81 L. Ed. 1245, 1262 (1937).
11. 301 U.S. 619, 57 Sup. Ct. 904, 81 L. Ed. 1307 (1937).
12. Polish National Alliance v. NLRB, 322 U.S. 643, 6.

3.4 Margaret Weir, "States, Race, and the Decline of New Deal Liberalism" (2005)

In her wide-ranging analysis of the political impact of the New Deal of the 1930s, political scientist Margaret Weir argues that federalism helped make it difficult to sustain its liberal impulses after the 1930s. The New Deal of the 1930s did not reverse the disproportionate influence of rural areas in state government, and, because it failed to establish national party control over state political parties, national and state party politics diverged. The spread of suburbia after World War II worsened the fragmentation of urban areas and allowed rural interests to continue to dominate the states. Suburbanites in the 1970s and 1980s drifted toward conservative agendas that promised to seal them off from the problems of the central cities. Weir's analysis shows that federalism can explain a great deal about the way politics and political institutions have evolved together over the decades and have shaped the political landscape today.

There is no escaping the New Deal's pivotal place in studies of twentieth-century American politics. Social scientists have vigorously debated the causes of the New Deal's distinctive features and continue to argue about its consequences for subsequent American political development.

... The notion of a "New Deal order" implies a relatively coherent political configuration in which the development of national political processes and politics form the main focus of inquiry.[1] Subnational political processes and policies enter this literature in two ways: through references to urban liberalism and, most importantly, to the role of the South. Southern defense of a regional racial caste system and low-wage economy made the South the major deviation from the emerging liberal political order. The South was also the main factor checking the development of New Deal liberalism, as southern members of Congress used their disproportionate power to limit the scope of legislation and eventually to block new initiatives altogether.

This article argues that the national focus of the New Deal narrative neglects crucial aspects of state politics and policy that limited liberalism and ultimately contributed to its political failure. Indeed, states occupy a peculiar place in the history of twentieth century state-building and political reform. Although states were an important target for the early twentieth-century Progressive reformers, they largely drop out of accounts that track the development of activist government for the next half-century, apart from occasional references to them as political backwaters. How did states go from being at the forefront of reform to being a drag on the development of active government, and how did their development affect the trajectory of activist government in the United States? ...

The Limited Impact of the New Deal on the States

The political impact of the New Deal was so sweeping that it is presumed to have rocked all of American politics. Yet, the effect of the New Deal on the states was surprisingly small. Not only did states themselves initiate few significant institutional or policy changes in response to the Great Depression, they resisted federal efforts to build state capacities. In contrast to the picture of dramatic change at the federal level during the 1930s, the story in the states was much more one of continuity.[2]

Political Divergence: States and the Federal Government during the New Deal

James T. Patterson's analysis of the New Deal highlights the striking contrast between the ongoing conservatism in the states and the liberalism developing in the federal government.[3] On the spending side, states did not imitate the rapid federal growth in spending. State spending increased far less in the 1930s than it had in the preceding decades, and states were especially reluctant to spend on relief. Moreover, a combination of ineptness and outright corruption tarnished relief efforts across the states. State tax systems actually became more regressive in the 1930s as state after state enacted sales taxes to shore up their faltering budgets. Nor did labor fare well in the states as most states were reluctant to enact progressive labor laws. In contrast Congress, where urban liberals sought to give labor new voice, state legislatures remained dominated by business and rural interests that had little sympathy for organized labor.

In a handful of states, "little New Deals" explicitly sought to mimic the liberal impulses of the federal government. In some of the most successful, such as New York and Massachusetts (which was receptive to much of the New Deal even though it was controlled by Republicans), enduring changes in the administration of relief and in labor laws were enacted. But in most states where New Deal liberalism made an appearance, it arrived late and left early. For example, Democrats controlled both houses of the Pennsylvania legislature and the governorship only between 1936 and 1938. When Republicans reassumed power in 1938, they began to roll back Democratic measures, targeting labor laws in particular.[4] In other states, such as Michigan and Georgia, little New Deals left even more meager legacies as they were quickly swept out of office.[5]

The transience of Democratic power in the states is striking. At the federal level, Democrats won control of both Houses of Congress in 1932 and held onto them—with only a brief interlude of Republican rule in the 1950s and early 1980s—for fifty years. Although these Democratic majorities would never be as liberal as those at the height of the New Deal, they were able to strike compromises that allowed many of the key social policy achievements of the New Deal to endure. And even when legislative progress stalled in the 1940s and 1950s, liberal Democrats could use congressional committees and administrative agencies to develop their policy agenda.

In the states, the rhythm of reform differed. In even the most liberal states, the New Deal did not influence state politics until 1936, leaving the wave of reform momentum at the national level little time to build in the states. Even in the states with the strongest support for the New Deal nationally, Democrats only briefly rode Roosevelt's coattails to power in the mid–1930s. By 1938, most of their majorities had evaporated. An examination of the thirty-five nonsouthern state legislatures shows that during the 1930s, only 40 percent were controlled by Democrats; 40 percent had divided legislatures, and 20 percent had Republican legislatures. In the 1940s, the picture for Democrats darkened considerably: Democrats controlled only 23 percent of nonsouthern state legislatures during that decade, Republicans 63 percent; 14 percent of the legislatures experienced divided control.[6] With limited control over state legislatures, which in any case lacked the capabilities to press forward on policy, liberal Democrats made little headway in the states during the 1940s and 1950s. It was not until 1959 that Democratic strength in state legislatures outside the South exceeded that of Republicans.

Three major obstacles kept New Deal Democrats from replicating their national success in the politics of nonsouthern states, where they might have been expected to thrive. First, legislative malapportionment limited the legislative power of Democrats in many states. Malapportionment certainly muted the impact of labor's growing political strength in the states. The overrepresentation of rural areas and the chronic underrepresentation of metropolitan areas in state legislatures worsened between 1910 and 1960.[7] In Michigan, for example, where 21.2 percent of the nonfarm workforce was unionized in 1939 and 44.6 percent was unionized in 1953, Democrats only fully controlled the state legislature from 1932 to 1934.[8] Democrats split control with Republicans from 1934 to 1938; however, after 1940, both houses of the legislature were controlled by Republicans until 1958. The combination of state constitutional provisions and the failure of the state to reapportion according to population led to substantial underrepresentation of the Democratic vote. For example, heavily Democratic Detroit comprised 43.5 percent of the population in 1930 but only 25 percent of the state Senate and 24 percent of the House in 1937.[9] Not until 1964, did Democrats win both houses of the Michigan legislature. In Pennsylvania, where organized labor made a major effort to build political strength in the 1930s, Democrats only controlled the state legislature from 1936 to 1938, splitting control with Republicans in 1934 to 1936 and 1942 to 1944.[10] Liberal Democratic governors were elected in both states between 1936 and 1960, but with little ability to control the legislature, their accomplishments were sharply limited.

In other states, the disjuncture between state and national party control was reinforced by weak state parties, a legacy of Progressive reform. In their study of California voting patterns, Michael Rogin and John Shrover, for example, demonstrate a persistently weak correlation between the vote for president and the vote for governor in the 1930s and 1940s. The practice of cross-filing, the off-cycle scheduling of gubernatorial elections combined with the weakness of parties and the importance of the press to hinder the growth of the Democratic party at the state level.[11] Democrats did not win control of the state legislature in California until 1958.[12]

Finally, issue-oriented liberal Democrats were outnumbered in most states by traditional organization Democrats, who were themselves often arrayed into warring factions. As a result, even when Democrats were victorious in state politics, their victories did not mean the same thing as at the federal level. Most northern industrial states, where much of the strength of organized labor was concentrated, were dominated by what Mayhew called typical party organizations or they suffered from persistent factionalism.[13]

Accounts of state politics in the 1930s emphasize the factionalism among Democrats as patronage-oriented politicians vied with a new breed of liberal and labor-oriented Democrats.[14] In Michigan, for example, the state Democratic Party was controlled by patronage politicians who had little interest in New Deal-style liberal government. Ironically, as labor's political power was growing in national politics, the United Auto Workers (UAW) did little to engage Michigan politics until 1948. In Michigan's case, a very limited supply of patronage (due to civil service reform) and an unusually strong labor presence allowed labor to take over the Democratic Party.[15] In other states, such as Illinois, however, patronage politics fueled factionalism and a fierce defense of party organization by traditional politicians. In this context, labor organizations tended to fit into the predominant style of issueless patronage politics, rather than to challenge it. Even in states where labor was strong, Democratic politics often had little to do with activist liberal government. The myriad divisions and struggles for power among Democrats undermined their appeal to voters and provided political opportunities that Republican challengers quickly seized.

. . . Despite the greatly enhanced power of the federal government during the 1930s, the New Deal did not transform the bottom-up character of American political parties nor did it alter the internal workings of state politics that made states such inhospitable terrain for advancing the liberal goals of activist government. As Patterson notes, "Problems presented by state courts, unfair apportionment, and state constitutions were soluble by state action alone."[16] In fact, in the decades after the New Deal, the federal government through requirements about social policy implementation and landmark decisions such as U.S. Supreme Court's 1962 "one man one vote" decision in *Baker v. Carr*, did begin to alter state politics. Even with federal prodding, however, state action proceeded at a slow pace, trailing the federal government by some four decades.

For the twenty-five years following the New Deal, the distinct reform trajectories in states and in the federal government were evident in the continued appetite for policy innovation in Washington compared with the listless activity in most states. Even though the political mobilization and reform energies of the New Deal had ebbed, supporters of a more active federal role worked from within the federal bureaucracy to expand public powers and to develop ideas for new initiatives that would be ready when the national political tides turned.[17] And, despite the political setbacks that Democrats experienced during these decades, they continued to control Congress for most of this time. Although liberal congressional Democrats were not strong enough to enact major policy innovations, they used their power to convene hearings and commission studies that would prepare the way for future initiatives.

In the states, the situation was quite different. For the most part, states lacked the executive capacity to generate and promote new policy ideas. State bureaucracies did not draw the kind of educated policy experts that staffed the federal government; instead poorly-funded state agencies typically attracted patronage and other types of political appointees with little interest in promoting policy changes. State legislatures were more likely to be controlled by politicians with little interest in policy innovation, and, because most met biennially and for only part of the year at that, they were poor settings in which to lay the groundwork for future initiatives. Together, these features meant that state-level politics continued to provide an open political arena for antireform forces long after they had been forced to vie for power at the federal level.

States and the Political Geography of Exit

If New Deal reforms had completely displaced the states as significant policy makers, the slow pace of change in the states would have mattered little for the later development of liberal policy and politics. In fact, because states retained important powers, the divergence in the trajectories of state and federal political change had far reaching consequences. Scholars have just begun to explore the repercussions of these different time lines for the development of liberalism in the United States.[18]

In this section, I illustrate one of the most significant consequences of federal/state divergence—the persistence of the racially divided metropolis. The federal role in creating the divided metropolis—especially through housing and transportation policies—has been well documented, but the critical significance of the states has been largely unexplored.[19] The key domains of land development, local jurisdictional status and land use were all governed by state rules that bore the decentralized stamp of their Progressive Era origins. By permitting businesses to spearhead the creation of new low-tax jurisdictions, these rules allowed racial prejudices to take on a specific new institutional form in postwar America, symbolized in the political geography of the black urban ghetto and the white homogeneous suburb.[20] "American Apartheid," as sociologists Douglas Massey and Nancy Denton called it, became the dominant feature of postwar social, political, and economic life.[21] Since separate political jurisdictions provided a key instrument by which wealthier residents and businesses shielded themselves from the costs of the less well off, they played a critical role in driving the growing spatial inequality that would be a hallmark of metropolitan areas from the 1950s forward.[22]

By inscribing racial inequalities into political boundaries, the new metropolitan political geography made inequalities more enduring and more difficult to remedy. Moreover, geographically-reinforced inequalities blocked economic opportunity for African Americans and limited their incorporation into the growing middle class just as the federal government was dismantling the edifice of southern segregation. Starting in the mid-1960s, federal efforts to promote opportunity for African Americans in housing, education, and employment each foundered when confronted with the legal force of local autonomy.[23]

As the 1960s drew to a close, several high profile federal commissions surveyed the condition of urban America, seeking to explain the civil disorders and to propose remedies. One of the central problems they identified was the sharp racial division between city and suburb. The National Commission on Urban Problems noted that the federal government had begun to reverse the policies that had promoted racial segregation, and it urged the states to reassert their control over land use as one of the most important ways to loosen "the white suburban noose around the inner city."[24]

As Desmond King and Rogers Smith note, just as the federal government was at last embracing a transformative racial order, local political boundaries were giving new life to a segregationist order that most politicians and citizens were now overtly repudiating.[25]

The divided metropolis not only exacerbated the enormous barriers to promoting racial equality, it also helped to undermine labor's organizational strength in politics. The great victory of organized labor in national politics in the 1930s was not matched by broad success in the states. Scholars have examined the failures to organize the South and the resultant regional imbalance in labor strength.[26] The impact of the new metropolitan political geography on labor's organizational power in the places where it was strongest is less well documented. It is clear, however, that the flight of the white working class from cities undermined labor's ability to reach its members politically.

After the New Deal, organized labor relied heavily on city-based Central Labor Councils to carry out its nationally devised political goals.[27] As white workers escaped the cities, these organizations grew less and less able to educate and mobilize union workers. This fact was brought home painfully to AFL-CIO [American Federation of Labor-Congress of Industrial Organizations] leaders in the aftermath of the 1966 elections, when the Congress most sympathetic to labor goals in twenty years was voted out of office. Astounded by the outcome, labor leaders in Washington sought to understand why union members had displayed such apathy during the election. A poll of union members conducted in 1967 revealed that the growing ranks of labor—younger white suburban homeowners—did not share the same political concerns as the Washington-based leadership. Instead these workers listed "fair tax assessment, crime, zoning laws, and street and sewer repair" as the most important political issues they faced.

... By the 1980s, a distinctive suburban pattern of political behavior and preferences had emerged.[28] As Juliet Gainsborough has shown, beginning in the 1980s, suburbanites were more likely to vote for Republican presidential and congressional candidates and less likely to support increases in federal government spending (with the exception of Social Security) than their urban counterparts. Moreover, these differences were sharpest in metropolitan areas where the economic fortunes of the main city and surrounding suburbs diverged the most.[29] The desire for protection from urban decline, rising crime rates, and the national economic downturn gave the ideas of localism and antigovernmentalism broad appeal.

The political geography of postwar metropolitan America helps explain why conservative alternatives to activist government resonated so widely across the country. The expanding scope of liberal national government after the 1930s coincided in time with the unfolding of a very different set of ideas about the role of government in metropolitan areas across the country. When the New Deal's style of activist government confronted sharp economic challenges in the 1970s, the antitax, small government ideology that had flourished in the hothouse environment of white suburbia was already waiting in the wings.

The state-generated exit options that had helped to create the divided metropolis sapped liberalism's political strength by shaping new interests and ideologies from the bottom up. Local political boundaries provided culturally-resonant mechanisms for limiting the reach of redistributive government. In an era when formal racial barriers were falling and open defense of racial segregation was become increasingly unacceptable, the new political geography shaped the terms on which race would become politicized over the following decades.

NOTES

1. See, for example, The *Rise and Fall of the New Deal Order, 1930–1980*, ed. Steve Fraser and Gary Gerstle (Princeton, NJ: Princeton University Press, 1989).

2. James T. Patterson, *The New Deal and the States: Federalism in Transition* (Princeton, NJ: Princeton University Press, 1968).

3. Ibid. Edwin Amenta, focusing on the implementation of social policy, presents a somewhat more positive picture of the impact of the New Deal on the states. His account is focused, however, on state implementation of nationally developed programs, and he notes the many factors that kept many nonsouthern as well as southern states from building on the activist government of the New Deal (Amenta, *Bold Relief: Institutional Politics and the Origins of Modern American Social Policy* [Princeton, NJ: Princeton University Press, 1998], chap. 5).

4. Richard C. Keller, "Pennsylvania's Little New Deal," in *The New Deal: The State and Local Levels* ed. John Braeman, Robert H. Bremner and David Brody (Columbus: Ohio State University Press, 1975), 72.

5. See Patterson, *New Deal and The States*, 144–53; Amenta, *Bold Relief*.

6. Data compiled from the *Book of the States* (Lexington, KY: Council of State Governments, various years).

7. Paul T. David and Ralph Eisenberg, *Devaluation of the Urban and Suburban Vote: A Statistical Investigation of Long-Term Trends in State Legislative Representation* (Charlottesville, VA: Bureau of Public Administration University of Virginia, 1961), 10.

8. For unionization rates, see Leo Troy, *Distribution of Union Membership among the States, 1939 and 1953* (New York: National Bureau of Economic Research, 1957).

9. David O. Walter, "Representation of Metropolitan Districts," *National Municipal Review* 27 (1938): 129–37.

10. On labor's political activities in Pennsylvania, see Thomas T. Spencer, "'Labor is with Roosevelt': The Pennsylvania Labor Non-Partisan League and the Election of 1936," *Pennsylvania History* 39 (1979): 3–16.

11. Michael P. Rogin and John L. Shrover, *Political Change in California: Critical Elections and Social Movements, 1890–1966* (Westport, CT: Greenwood Publishing Corporation, 1969), 139–47.

12. Rogin and Shrover's *Political Change in California* shows that malapportionment was not the only force at work in California.

13. David R. Mayhew, *Placing Parties in American Politics* (Princeton, NJ: Princeton University Press, 1986), 17–103, 196, 200.

14. See John Braeman, Robert H. Bremner and David Brody, eds., *The New Deal: The State and Local Levels* (Columbus: Ohio State University Press, 1975); Mayhew, *Placing Parties*; Pegram, *Partisans and Progressives*.

15. John H. Fenton, *Midwest Politics* (New York: Holt, Rinehart and Winston, 1966), 28–34; Dudley Buffa, *Union Power and American Democracy: The UAW and the Democratic Party* (Ann Arbor: University of Michigan Press, 1984). However, even with control of the Democratic Party and a popular liberal governor, the liberal/labor coalition could not control state politics because legislative malapportionment meant that Democrats did not win majorities in either House from 1938 to 1958.

16. Patterson, "New Deal and the States," 81.

17. See James L. Sundquist, *Politics and Policy: The Eisenhower, Kennedy and Johnson Years* (Washington, DC: Brookings Institution, 1968).

18. See, for example, Anthony Chen, "From Fair Employment to Equal Employment Opportunity and Beyond: Affirmative Action and the Politics of Civil Rights in the New Deal Order, 1941–1972" (Ph.D. diss., University of California, Berkeley, 2003); Isaac Martin, "The Roots of Retrenchment: Tax Revolts and Policy Change in the United States and Denmark, 1945–1990" (Ph.D. diss., University of California, Berkeley, 2004).

19. On the federal government and race, see Desmond S. King, *Separate and Unequal: Black Americans and the U.S. Federal Government* (New York: Oxford University Press, 1995); Jackson, *Crabgrass Frontier*; Robert C. Lieberman, *Shifting the Color Line: Race and the American Welfare State* (Cambridge, MA: Harvard University Press, 1998); Jill Quadagno, *The*

Color of Welfare: How Racism Undermined the War on Poverty (New York: Oxford University Press, 1994).

20. On the roles of business and race in forming new local governments, see Nancy Burns, *The Formation of American Local Governments: Private Values in Public Institutions* (New York: Oxford University Press, 1994), 83–95.

21. Douglas S. Massey and Nancy A. Denton, *American Apartheid: Segregation and the Making of the Underclass* (Cambridge, MA: Harvard University Press, 1993).

22. See Richard Briffault, "Our Localism: Part I—The Structure of Local Government Law," and "Our Localism: Part II—Localism and Legal Theory," *Columbia Law Review* 90 (1990) 1–115, 346–454; Gregory R. Weiher, "Public Policy and Patterns of Residential Segregation," *Western Political Quarterly* 42 (1989), 651–77.

23. On the impact of local boundaries on remedies for racial discrimination and disadvantage, see Briffault, *Our Localism Part I, Part II.*

24. *Building the New American City: Report of the National Commission on Urban Problems to the Congress and to the President of the United States* (Washington DC: U.S. Government Printing Office, 1968).

25. Desmond S. King and Rogers M. Smith, "Racial Orders in American Political Development," *American Political Science Review* 99 (2005): 75–92.

26. Michael Honey, "Operation Dixie: Labor and Civil-rights in the Postwar South", *Mississippi Quarterly* 45 1992): 439–52; Barbara S. Griffith, *The Crisis of American Labor: Operation Dixie and the Defeat of the CIO* (Philadelphia: Temple University Press, 1988).

27. Alan Draper, *A Rope of Sand: The AFL-CIO Committee on Political Education, 1955–1967* (New York: Praeger Publishers, 1989), 50–51; J. David Greenstone, *Labor in American Politics* (Chicago: University of Chicago Press, 1969).

28. Juliet F. Gainsborough, *Fenced Off: The Suburbanization of American Politics* (Washington DC: Georgetown University Press, 2001), chap. 5.

29. Ibid., 95.

3.5 Suzanne Mettler, "Gender and Federalism in New Deal Public Policy" (1998)

As federalism affects politics, it also shapes the design of national programs and the impact of these programs on different groups of citizens. In her study of the Social Security Act, political scientist Suzanne Mettler reminded us that the states remain "separate and distinct political communities" that do things differently. States often have used their discretion to provide less inclusive rights for some citizens, such as women as well as minorities. New Deal policies, such as the Social Security Act, compounded some of these differences in citizenship. Keen on building support among male bread-winners, Democrats designed the Social Security system around male workers in cities; the relatively steady incomes of these men would provide a reliable revenue stream for Social Security old-age and unemployment insurance. Relatively few women or minorities, though, were part of this workforce. Their needs were met instead by programs like Aid to Dependent Children, which required often humiliating assessments of personal income and very low benefits for those who were judged deserving of welfare. These dynamics, Mettler concludes, "institutionalized gender inequalities and built political barriers against further social change."

During the century and a half preceding the New Deal, under the unique system of federalism hammered out at the Constitutional Convention of 1787, the actual content of American citizenship was defined primarily by the individual states rather than by national government. State governments determined the rights and privileges and the duties and obligations of those living within their borders by enacting the vast majority of policy decisions that affected their residents' daily lives. They legislated on subjects as diverse as property, family, morality, education, commerce and labor, banking and criminal procedure. The national government was restricted from interfering in such activities because its powers were understood to be relatively limited, extending primarily to the promotion of commercial activity through such means as subsidies and tariffs.[1] As a patchwork of laws developed, the character of American citizenship evolved in a manner inextricably bound to the political geography of this variegated system of federalism . . . .

Citizenship and American Federalism

The arrangements of American federalism, according to many scholars, enhance the participatory dimensions of citizenship. Federalism provides multiple loci for political mobilization and participation and can thus foster policy development in a uniquely decentralized fashion. Theda Skocpol, for example, has detailed in *Protecting Soldiers and Mothers* how "widespread federated interests" in the United States have worked precisely through the federal structure to promote the development of social policies, especially mothers' pensions and protective labor legislation, across the individual states.[2] Richard Valelly has shown how federalism, at least into the 1930s, provided a ripe climate for state-level radicalism by third parties, and such parties helped spur the development and implementation of public policies.[3] From the Progressive Era to the present, many have lauded the states as "laboratories of democracy" that permit policy experimentation as well as the adaptation of nationally planned programs to local purposes.

But although decentralized governing arrangements may provide multiple points of access for the participatory dimensions of citizenship, the incorporation of citizens in the context of American federalism has tended to undercut possibilities for full inclusion, in turn curtailing more complete opportunities for participation in public life. This becomes evident when policy analysis turns from the deliberative and formative stages of policy-making amid state-level governance to policy outcomes. For example, though the movement for mothers' pensions studied by Skocpol did indeed spread "like wildfire," the implementation of such laws proved much less auspicious. Although forty-five states had enacted mothers' pensions laws by 1934, fewer than half of the local units empowered to administer the statutes actually had programs in operation.[4] Those programs that were in effect made assistance conditional on the willingness of recipients, often immigrant women, to adapt to restrictive cultural norms of child rearing and housekeeping that were measured through "fit-mother" and "suitable-home" criteria.[5]

The particular manner in which these state-level programs extended social citizenship to women, then, failed to provide them with a sufficient means to inclusion in public life, and it constrained beneficiaries to a role in the polity that was attached to their ascribed status as mothers.

Social citizenship determined by the states, judging by its ability to incorporate citizens on a broad and equal basis, has generally tended to be interior to social citizenship with national standards for eligibility and administration. If political parties or associations are well organized and active at the state level, as in the case of the Townsend movement in western states and the labor movement in various states in the late 1930s and 1940s, they may be able to promote successful policy development and implementation.[6] More typically, however, when social and labor policies have been left in the hands of states and localities, standards have been lowered or neglected in more areas than not. Other nations characterized by federalism have also developed social programs later, more slowly, and less completely than nations with more centralized governing arrangements, but particular aspects of U.S. federalism have served to accentuate those tendencies.[7]

Political-institutional factors explain some of the differences in national and state-level citizenship in the United States. Contrary to the pervasive assumption that decentralized governance is more democratic than centralized governance, the states in the U.S. system, well into the twentieth century, often fostered domination of the political process by narrow interests. At the national level, by contrast, such factions were, at least on occasion, countered and diffused. E. E. Schattschneider and Grant McConnell suggested a connection between, on the one hand, the relatively small size of the constituency and scope of conflict in the American states and, on the other hand, limitations on the expansion of democracy in the context of U.S. federalism.[8] But McConnell and Schattschneider neglected to identify a significant institutional feature primarily at the disposal of the states in that era, which combined with their narrow political scope to give state governance an inherently inegalitarian character: the police power.

The U.S. constitutional system traditionally endowed the states with the police power, a governing capacity with communitarian roots that predate liberal conceptions of the rule of law. "Policing" in the eighteenth century meant promoting the public good or the life of the community as opposed to the modern emphasis on maintaining order and preserving security.[9] Defined by the mid-nineteenth-century Taney Court as the power to "provide for the public health, safety, and good order" of the community, the police power was interpreted broadly as a "sovereign power" reserved to the states by the Tenth Amendment.[10] Acting on the police power, state legislatures proceeded to define the rights and obligations of those citizens living within their boundaries by creating a broad and eclectic patchwork of laws.[11] But as neither the Bill of Rights nor the Fourteenth Amendment was understood as applying to the states except in the most narrow circumstances, states were relatively unrestrained in their application of the police power.[12] Without liberal guarantees of rights, the potentially communitarian character of life in the states easily dissolved into arrangements that more closely resembled feudalism.

By exercising the police power within a narrow scope of conflict, states tended to become separate and distinct political communities that functioned to preserve the social order—in a multitude of ways—rather than to promote equality. The police power was used effectively and with the approval of the Supreme Court to uphold the dominant social system and political-economic relations within individual states. Maintaining racial segregation under the Jim Crow laws, for example, was justified as an appropriate exercise of the police power.[13] In keeping with the police power, state legislation designed to address the social and economic situation of women tended to be designed in a paternalistic manner. Thus though laws such as Married Women's Property Acts and protective labor legislation were created to improve women's individual lives, they served to institutionalize women's marginal status in society and politics.[14] The states retained their capacity to exercise the police power in a fairly autonomous fashion until the late 1950s and 1960s, when they were restrained by various reforms and court decisions at the national level.

Besides the political-institutional factors, the willingness of the states to enact and carry out broad and inclusive social and labor policies has been and continues to be restrained by the political-economic features of U.S. federalism. As observed by David B. Robertson and Dennis R. Judd, the Constitution created "the world's largest 'free trade' zone," inasmuch as the individual states lack the power either to prevent businesses from entering and leaving their borders or, unlike the national government, to protect businesses within their borders.[15] Rather, states must compete with one another to establish a favorable "business climate" in order to attract and retain businesses. Thus, even in celebrated periods of social reform at the state level, most notably the Progressive Era, the majority of states have been reluctant to implement policies that may act or be perceived as acting to increase the cost of doing business within their boundaries.[16] As Paul Peterson has shown, when states administer redistributive policies, they tend to neglect standards as they engage in a "race to the bottom," competing to make benefits less generous in amount and more punitive in form. They fear becoming "welfare magnets," or being considered as such by businesses. National government, in contrast, does not have to be as concerned about the outward flow of capital, and it has a greater taxing power than the states. National government is thus far better positioned than state or municipal governments to administer redistributive policies.[17]

In sum, the states have, historically, tended to incorporate citizens in a manner inferior to that of national government. Governance left to the states has been particularly disadvantageous for groups that are relatively lacking in political power. Without the requirements of national standards for eligibility and administration, state-level policies have often institutionalized social and economic inequalities. And when some citizens have been incorporated as national citizens and others as state-level citizens, fragmentation has been inscribed in the heart of the American polity. Such were the implications of the New Deal in terms of gender.

Dividing Citizens in the New Deal

...In fact, the politics of New Deal policymaking had less to do with gendered battles over policy priorities than with seemingly "gender-neutral" debates over the shape of policy design and the institutional framework for American politics, namely, federalism. Yet, nonetheless, the welfare state that emerged was inherently gendered. This demonstrates that, although some aspects of policy outcomes can be traced directly to the ideas and intentions of policymakers, policies are also affected by critical political and institutional factors in the policymaking context, by particular features of policy design, and by the institutional context of the implementation process. Thus, political debates and institutional dynamics that might appear to have little to do with gender can still affect state development and policy outcomes in "gendered" ways, albeit indirectly and unintentionally.[18]

Political and institutional analysis is particularly necessary for understanding how New Deal policies shaped citizenship in terms of gender. First, whereas earlier in the century male and female social reformers and policy officials had worked quite separately from one another, the divide between maternalists and paternalists had blurred significantly by the 1930s. Franklin D. Roosevelt appointed an unprecedented number of women to key posts in his administration. For example, Frances Perkins,[19] who as secretary of labor was the first woman cabinet member in U.S. history, spearheaded the formation of all the critical New Deal social and labor policies examined in this book. Besides the fact that women played a critical role in shaping public assistance-type programs in the New Deal, continuing the Progressive Era maternalist tradition, social insurance plans were also engineered by a woman, Barbara Nachtrieb Armstrong. Second, unlike Progressive Era policies, which tended to be very rigidly gender-identified, New Deal policies were characterized for the most part by gender-neutral language and somewhat less definitive ideas about men's and women's proper roles in society. Earlier in the century, the Supreme Court had defined male workers as "independent" and able to take care of themselves in market society; the "protection" of women through protective labor legislation had, in contrast, been construed as a worthy government interest.[20] Social policies geared toward women and children succeeded in the form of mothers' pensions and the Sheppard-Towner Maternity and Infancy Protection Act, but comparable policies aimed toward men as breadwinners failed.[21] In the New Deal, policy officials, the Supreme Court, and the public all recognized a governmental responsibility to provide for the welfare of both men and women. But despite these changes, still the outcome was that citizens became divided by gender between two different forms of governance . . . .

The first of the core arguments of this book is that New Deal policy officials did shape policies in some directly gender-specific ways. In some regards, these actions by policy-makers were conscious and intentional. Most policymakers in the Roosevelt administration, for example, were sympathetic to the "family wage" ideal, the notion that men's work in the market economy should enable them to serve as "breadwinners" for their families, so that women could attend to unpaid domestic work and refrain from taking jobs that could otherwise belong to men. Almost reflexively, then, they drew on policy alternatives from the Progressive Era inscribed with assumptions about distinct gender roles.

But not all the direct gendering of policies during the New Deal was, as others have implied, intentional or conscious. Policymakers in the 1930s were not rigidly bound to preexisting policy traditions and ideologies, nor were they guided by an ideological agenda aiming to preserve ascribed gender roles. Rather, they were enmeshed by the politics of the New Deal and preoccupied with serving key constituencies and interests. These political forces coalesced in a manner that confirmed officials' preexisting inclinations to channel men and women into separate and distinct types of policies. As Schattschneider observed, "Organization is itself a mobilization of bias in preparation for action. . . . Some issues are organized into politics while others are organized out."

. . . The Democratic Party's political-economic agenda combined the interests of labor unions, whose ranks were predominantly male, with the demands of urban interests in the North and agricultural interests in the impoverished South, both eager to draw on the largesse of the federal government. Southern members of Congress also insisted, however, on administrative arrangements that would preserve "states' rights" and local autonomy. They had the necessary leverage to accomplish their goals: the unchallenged one-party rule in the prereapportionment, Jim Crow South combined with seniority rules in Congress gave them institutional advantages in securing key committee assignments and chairmanships.[22]

These political forces produced New Deal policies that placed priority on the concerns of men, especially white men.

...The second core argument posited here is that in the New Deal, policy officials made public policy by reshaping the contours of federalism, enlarging the authority and scope of national government in the system of dual sovereignty while at the same time retaining and even bolstering the power of the individual states. The particular rearrangements of federalism facilitated a gendered division of Americans as social citizens, as programs geared toward men became nationally administered programs and those aimed toward women retained state-level authority.

...The shape of New Deal federalism resulted in part from efforts by members of Congress to preserve "states' rights" and local autonomy in public policy. Southern and western senators and representatives, dominating critical committees and leadership positions, purposefully excluded various categories of workers, including domestic and agricultural workers, from programs to be administered from national government. They also altered programs that administration officials had already planned to be administered primarily at the state level, so as further to restrain national bureaucrats from intervening in policy implementation and to guarantee that state and local officials would instead retain a high degree of discretionary authority. Scholars have noted that Congress thus excluded most African Americans from nationally administered programs and vested local officials with authority that was subsequently used in many southern and western states to omit nonwhite applicants from coverage in public assistance programs.[23] This analysis will show that efforts to preserve state and local authority had important gender effects as well. Several of the occupational groups that congressional committees dropped from coverage in the national program were disproportionately female. Congressmen also altered the public assistance programs on which women would most rely in ways that rendered them far more subject to provincial rule than they would otherwise have been.

...The unintended consequences of policy implementation accentuated divided citizenship. After policy formation is completed, policies are shaped anew through the politics and institutional context surrounding their implementation. Political agendas of bureaucrats may be distinct from those of policymakers, particularly as they attempt to institutionalize the power and authority of their agencies. Such dynamics drove the early implementation of old age insurance and unemployment insurance in the hands of the Social Security Board. Implementation, furthermore, is enormously complicated by federalism. Theodore Lowi and Benjamin Ginsberg have shown that in policies decided by the national government all but handed over to state and local officials for implementation, such as the grant-in-aid public assistance programs of the New Deal, the multiplication of layers of responsibility makes for a proliferation of "access points and opportunities for influence."[24] Indeed, during the decades after the New Deal, state and local officials shaped programs in their jurisdiction to reflect cultural norms and local political-economic priorities rather than the goals of national policymakers. Such dynamics further intensified the distinctions between national and state-level citizenship for men and women.

In sum, a combination of deliberate choices and indirect decisions led New Deal policymakers to consolidate the new power of national government by incorporating mostly male wage earners under its jurisdiction, and to leave substantial authority to the states to provide for the welfare and security of most women. Through the subsequent politics of policy implementation, the separateness and gender-specific character of two forms of citizenship, national and state-level, institutionalized gender inequalities and built political barriers against further social change.

NOTES

1. Edward S. Corwin, "The Passing of Dual Federalism," *Virginia Law Review* 36 (February 1965): 1–24; Theodore J. Lowi, *The Personal President* (Ithaca: Cornell University Press, 1985), p. 24; see also Harry N. Scheiber, "The Conditions of American Federalism: An Historian's View," in *American Intergovernmental Relations*, ed. Laurence J. O'Toole, Jr. (Washington DC: Congressional Quarterly, 1993), pp. 67–74.

2. Theda Skocpol, *Protecting Soldiers and Mothers: The Political Origins of Social Welfare Policy in the U.S.* (Cambridge, MA: Harvard University Press, 1992) pp. 54–57; see also Samuel H. Beer, "The Modernization of American Federalism," *Publius* 3 (fall 1973): 49–95, and "Federalism, Nationalism, and Democracy in America," *American Political Science Review* 72 (1978): 9–21; and Jack L. Walker, "The Diffusion of Innovations among the American States," ibid. 63 (1969): 880–99.

3. Richard M. Valelly, *Radicalism in the States: The Minnesota Farmer-Labor Party and the American Political Economy* (Chicago: University of Chicago Press, 1989).

4. See Eveline Burns, *Toward Social Security* (New York: McGraw-Hill, 1936), pp. 111–12.

5. Gwendolyn Mink, *The Wages of Motherhood: Inequality in the Welfare State, 1917–1942* (Ithaca: Cornell University Press, 1995).

6. This theme emerges in Chapters 4 and 6. See also Valelly, *Radicalism in the States*, and Edwin Amenta et al., "The Political Origins of Unemployment Insurance in Five American States," *Studies in American Political Development* 2 (1987): 137–82.

7. Robert T. Kudrle and Theodore R. Marmor, "The Development of Welfare States in North America," in *The Development of Welfare States in Europe and America*, ed. Peter Flora and Arnold J. Heidenheimer (New Brunswick: Transaction Books, 1982), pp. 81–121.

8. E. E. Schattschneider, *The Semisovereign People* (New York: Holt, Rinehart and Winston, 1960), pp. 1–19; Grant McConnell, *Private Power and American Democracy* (New York: Knopf, 1966), esp. pp. 3–8, 91–118, 166–95.

9. Christopher L. Tomlins, "Law, Police, and the Pursuit of Happiness in the New American Republic," *Studies in American Political Development* 4 (1990): 3–34; William J. Novak, *Intellectual Origins of the State Police Power: The Common Law Vision of a Well-Regulated Society*, Legal History Program, Working Papers, ser. 3 (Madison: University of Wisconsin, Institute for Legal Studies, 1989).

10. David B. Walker, *The Rebirth of Federalism* (Chatham, NJ: Chatham House, 1995), p. 69.

11. Corwin, "Passing of Dual Federalism"; Scheiber, "Conditions of American Federalism."

12. Under the traditional system of dual federalism, Americans were formerly considered dual citizens: citizens of both national and state governments, as established by *Barron v. Baltimore*, 7 Peters 243 (1833). The decision was interpreted to mean that the Bill of Rights did not apply to state or local governments. On the limited interpretation of the Fourteenth Amendment before the 1950s, see Kelly, Harbison and Belz, *American Constitution*, 2:355–61, 689–90.

13. *Plessy v. Ferguson*, 163 U.S. 537 (1896); C. Vann Woodward, *The Strange Career of Jim Crow*, 3rd rev. ed. (New York: Oxford University Press, 1974), pp. 97–102.

14. Joan Hoff, *Law, Gender, and Injustice* (New York: New York University Press, 1991), pp. 127–31; Smith, " 'One United People,' " pp. 249, 253; *Muller v. Oregon*, 208 U.S. 412 (1908); Alice Kessler-Harris, *Out to Work* (New York: Oxford University Press, 1982), pp. 194, 205–14.

15. David B. Robertson and Dennis R. Judd, *The Development of American Public Policy: The Structure of Policy Restraint* (Glenview, IL: Scott, Foresman, 1989), p. 31.

16. David Brian Robertson, "The Bias of American Federalism: The Limits of Welfare-State Development in the Progressive Era," *Journal of Policy History* 1 (1989): 261–91; William Graebner, "Federalism in the Progressive Era: A Structural Interpretation of Reform," *Journal of American History* 54 (1977): 331–57.

17. Paul E. Peterson, "Who Should Do What? Divided Responsibility in the Federal System," *Brookings Review* (spring 1995): 6–11, and *City Limits* (Chicago: University of Chicago Press, 1981).

18. Only a few examples in the literature on gender and public policy illustrate this perspective, namely, Vivien Hart, *Bound by Our Constitution: Women, Workers, and the Minimum Wage* (Princeton: Princeton University Press, 1994); Theda Skocpol and Gretchen Ritter, "Gender and the Origins of Modern Social Policies in Britain and the United States," *Studies in American Political Development* 5 (1991): 36–93; Skocpol, *Protecting Soldiers and Mothers*; and Barbara J. Nelson, "The Origins of the Two-Channel Welfare State: Workmen's Compensation and Mothers' Aid," in *Women, the State, and Welfare*, ed. Linda Gordon (Madison: University of Wisconsin Press, 1990), pp. 123–51.

19. Susan Ware, *Beyond Suffrage: Women in the New Deal* (Cambridge: Harvard University Press, 1981).

20. *Lochner v. New York*, 198 U.S. 45 (1905); *Muller v. Oregon*, 208 U.S. 412 (1908).

21. Skocpol, *Protecting Soldiers and Mothers*.

22. Frank Freidel, *F.D.R. and the South* (Baton Rouge: Louisiana State University Press, 1965). On the political economy of the South in the 1930s and the implications of New Deal policies for the region, see Arthur F. Raper, *Preface to Peasantry* (New York: Atheneum, 1968); and David Eugene Conrad, *The Forgotten Farmers: The Story of Sharecroppers in the New Deal* (Urbana: University of Illinois Press, 1965).

23. Robert C. Lieberman, "Race and the Development of the American Welfare State from the New Deal to the Great Society" (Ph.D. diss., Harvard University, 1994); Jill Quadagno, "From Old-Age Assistance to Supplemental Security Income: The Political Economy of Relief in the South, 1935–1972," in *Politics of Social Policy*, ed. Weir, Orloff and Skocpol, pp. 235–64; Phyllis Palmer, "Outside the Law: Agricultural and Domestic Workers under the Fair Labor Standards Act," *Journal of Policy History* 7 (1995): 416–40.

24. Theodore J. Lowi et al., *Poliscide* (Lanham, MD: University Press of America, 1990), pp. 27–28; see also Jeffrey L. Pressman and Aaron Wildavsky, *Implementation* (Berkeley: University of California Press, 1973).

3.6 David Brian Robertson, "Federalism and the Making of America" (2011)

Despite dynamic change over two centuries, American federalism remains resilient. In his book, *Federalism and the Making of America*, political scientist David Robertson argued that American politics was built on the foundation of federalism, and that the use of federalism in American politics has been pragmatic and driven by larger political objectives. Federalism provides a clear example of the importance of path dependence and the sequence of change, as discussed in the introduction to this book. Most notably, the fact that the national government had the power to raise and spend money long before it had the power to regulate the economy helps explain why "cooperative" federalism grew so extensively, and why the federal grants system is so complex today. For contemporary Republicans and Democrats, federalism remains a vigorously contested battleground that powerfully affects the political future of the U.S.

Federalism shapes Americans' lives because it has shaped the past and present of their nation. Federalism—the division of government authority between the national government and the states—affects the prosperity, security, and many everyday choices of each person living in the United States.... Because federalism's impact is so broad and so deep, political rivals have battled over federalism since the nation's founding. Federalism has influenced all the important political battles in American history. The United States, its government, and its public policy are a still-evolving legacy of choices powerfully influenced by federalism over time.

This book argues that federalism has played a pivotal part in the making of America because it has been a principal battlefield of political conflict. Political opponents have fought about federalism to advance or to stop government actions. Over time these political conflicts helped construct the unique path that the development of American government, politics and public policy has followed.

Federalism has shaped American life most powerfully by converting many political conflicts over whether government should act into conflicts over which level of government—the U.S. national government or the states—should exercise power to resolve the conflict. The most bitter and spectacular political conflicts in American history have been fought on the battlefield of federalism, including states' rights to leave the union, and government power to regulate business, to institute political reform, and to respond to problems of race, poverty, pollution, abortion and many more. The consequences of these choices played out over time and cumulatively have altered American political development. Federalism helped fragment American politics, encourage policy innovation and diversity, foster the American market economy, and place hurdles in the way of efforts to mitigate the consequences of economic change ....

Federalism and Politics

...From the start, political opponents have fought about federalism because it affects who wins and who loses a particular fight. The states produce different policy results than the national government. These different levels of government face different opportunities, constraints and circumstances. Some of the state governments almost always have responded to public problems rapidly, and often act before the national government deals with an issue. State policy experiments often influence national policies. None of the states have as many policy tools as the national government, however. State officials must be very cautious about enacting pathbreaking innovations in public policy because they are keenly aware of intense competition for business investment from states with lower taxes, fewer regulations on business, and less generous social benefits.

...Opponents have used federalism as a strategic weapon, either as a shield against change, or as a sword to bring change about. Public debates may evoke highly principled arguments for or against federalism or national power, but these philosophical assertions usually cloak the real purpose behind the struggle over state versus national power: to get government to do something that they want it to do, or to prevent government from doing something they want to prevent. In many ways, federalism resembles a "common carrier" like a railroad, but one that is used to transport a wide variety of political pressures instead of cars full of freight. Both liberals and conservatives, and both Democrats and Republicans, have used federalism as an expedient political weapon to deal with controversial issues such as labor, the environment, education, abortion, and gay rights. Their support for federalism is almost invariably contingent on their calculations about the different results that the states or the national government are likely to produce. Virtually no conservatives or liberals hesitate to jettison federalism when it interferes with more substantive political priorities. Efforts to treat federalism as an abstract philosophical question divorced from political reality, or as a purely administrative issue without political implications, are misguided and misleading ....

Federalism and Path Dependence

...To better understand the United States, it is essential to understand the way federalism has influenced politics and policy in American history. Federalism has worked gradually, rewarding the interests of individuals, political parties, pressure groups, government officials, and others who learn how to use it effectively. Once its framers fixed federalism in the U.S. Constitution, for example, Americans got used to its role in the new government and built it into their expectations and use of American government. Federalism also affected the new institutions, such as political parties and interest groups, that began to emerge soon after the new government started operating in 1789. Once established, such new institutions and policies created new reasons to defend federalism and states' prerogatives.

...The United States, its government, and its public policy are a legacy of choices strongly influenced by federalism. Federalism helps explain why American public policy has been more fragmented, uneven and often limited than policy and politics in comparable nations.[1] American political parties and powerful interest groups, such as business and labor, also are more fragmented than those abroad because they have learned to adjust to American federalism. Together, the cumulative impacts of federalism help explain some of the most important features of the United States, most notably conflict over racial policy, economic development driven by free markets, and the prominent role of the states in national reform movements.

Federalism and the Sequence of Change

...[E]xpanding government activism was constructed atop the foundation of federalism, resulting in a durable, thriving intergovernmental system today. State and local governments have remained active, influential, innovative, and indispensable. Federalism offered a bundle of strategic possibilities for anyone who wanted to bring about policy change. Many new initiatives—including alcohol prohibition, business regulation, social welfare programs, and environmental protection—were established in some of the states before they became Federal policy.

Federalism, then, played a crucial role in the *sequence* of events in the growth of American government activism since the late nineteenth century.[2] It is particularly important that the Federal government enjoyed broad authority to raise money long *before* the surge in government activism, but was conceded the authority to police domestic affairs only *after* the growth of government activism was well underway. The Constitution clearly gave the U.S. national government the legitimate power to impose import and other taxes. The Constitutional authority to levy a Federal income tax in the early twentieth century expanded Federal revenue capacity. But Federal court decisions continued to set strict limits on Federal regulatory authority into 1937. This sequence had two important consequences when industrialization increased demands for more active government in the late nineteenth century. First, the states took the lead in instituting regulations to control business and social policies to mitigate the effects of industrialization. Second, the Federal government adapted creatively to its powers and their limits. It provided grants-in-aid to states to carry out purposes such as highway construction and vocational education. By the time the Supreme Court in the late 1930s allowed more Federal regulation of the domestic economy, Federal-state grants were becoming a wider and more deeply embedded part of American government activism.

In a sequence of events that drove American political development along a path that could not be predicted in advance, prior arrangements shaped major policy change by shaping the subsequent strategic opportunities and constraints of the advocates of government activism.

(1) Progressive era reformers inherited a system of broad state authority and [constrained] national authority, and changed the federal system to increase the engagement and professionalization of governments at all levels.
(2) The New Deal inherited a system of governments that were more active than they had been in the nineteenth century, and changed the federal system to establish Federal leadership in actively mitigating the problems that resulted from market-driven economic growth.
(3) Post-World War II liberals inherited a New Deal system of intergovernmental activism, and changed the federal system to expand rights, equalize opportunity and reduce risk nationally.
(4) Conservatives in the 1980s inherited a very active Federal-state system of regulations and social welfare benefits, and used the federal system to promote market-driven economic growth and traditional social values.

Federalism and Strategies for Reform

In each of these periods, reformers employed three strategies to overcome the hurdles that federalism placed in their path. While these strategies often limited the range of the states' actions, each strategy also reinforced the intergovernmental system and the strength of the states in some way.[3]

First, advocates of policy change battled for *partial national rules* to set legal limitations on some of the actions of all the states, often to place a uniform limit on the uses of state authority. These rules have taken the form of Constitutional amendments (such as the Eighteenth Amendment that prohibited the manufacture and sale of intoxicating liquors in all the states, or the Twenty-Fourth Amendment that banned states from imposing poll taxes), Congressional laws (such as rules banning legal segregation based on race or that limit automobile exhausts), or Federal court rulings (setting basic national rules for state capital punishment or for abortion regulation). The Federal government subtly reinforces state authority even when it constrains it, because Federal rules generally allow and expect the states to exercise residual policy discretion, and the states' exercise of this discretion often has politically significant consequences for Americans. For example, the diverse state laws enacted since the 1973 Supreme Court abortion decision, *Roe* v. *Wade*, make access to abortion uneven across the states.

Second, reformers employ *layering*, a tactic of placing new responsibilities on the states to produce desired outcomes, usually in return for a conditional grant of money or some other benefit. Layering is the most common approach to expanding government activism, because it provides the least disruption of existing arrangements, the least threat to diverse centers of power, and often generates less conflict than national rules. For example, when the Morrill Act of 1862 authorized Federal land grants to the states to provide higher education in science, engineering, and agriculture, the law supplemented existing state colleges and did not replace them. Many of the reforms of the Progressive era, the New Deal, and the Great Society typically were layered on top of deeply rooted older institutions. To motivate state action, the Federal government has initiated grants in every area of state responsibility from highways and policing to health, education and welfare. The history of public policy toward medical care is a history of layer after layer of supplemental policy, from Federal grants for maternal and infant child care in the Progressive era, to tax breaks for business health insurance after World War II, to grants for medical care to the poor during the 1960s, and finally the effort to create an overarching framework for the many healthcare institutions in the Patient Protection and Affordable Health Care Act of 2010.

Third, reformers who confront obstacles at the state level sometimes try to *bypass* existing state government and political institutions by energizing new institutions that are more likely to produce the outcomes they seek. During Reconstruction, the Federal Freedmen's Bureau attempted bypass southern governments to help newly freed slaves become self-sufficient and acquire lands in the former Confederacy. In the 1930s, the New Deal attempted to bypass state governments by creating grants programs that encouraged states to establish new agencies with professionals in highway construction, welfare services, and other areas who would share the mind-set of national professional leaders and Federal administrators. In the 1960s War on Poverty, the Federal government bypassed state and local governments and funded new Community Action Agencies, which were created by local residents, provided services in poor areas, and helped mobilize the poor politically . . . .

Federalism and the Reagan Administration

. . . [President Ronald] Reagan's administration used federalism to pull the national government back from liberal policies. The Reagan administration sought to convert categorical grants to block grants and cut funding for them. Federal tax cuts and the initially deep cuts in Federal domestic spending (the Omnibus Budget Reconciliation Act, or OBRA, of 1981) aimed to cut the Federal government's ability to fund domestic programs, including all grants-in-aid. Ultimately, OBRA eliminated 140 grants programs and reduced Federal spending on grants by six billion dollars from the previous budget.... During Reagan's presidency, Federal grant-in-aid spending dropped for the first time since World War II. Federal spending on grants, adjusting for inflation, remained below the levels of the Carter administration . . . [4]

Conservative Nationalism

Conservative presidents since 1980 decentralized power *when and if* decentralization was likely to produce conservative results, but they expanded Federal power where state and local discretion would undercut their more important priorities, such as reducing business regulation. For example, the Reagan administration allowed the states more power to implement clean air laws in the hope the states would relax enforcement, while it favored total Federal preemption of state laws to free the transportation, communications, and banking industries from state interference.[5] . . .

During Reagan's presidency alone, the Federal government preempted state authority in ten civil rights laws, thirty-one commercial and business laws, seventeen environmental laws, four financial laws, eleven health laws, two immigration laws, and seventeen safety laws. Reagan vetoed only two of these laws . . . [6]

. . . The administration of George W. Bush further nationalized public policy to achieve conservative ends. According to federalism scholars Timothy Conlan and John Dinan, Bush lacked "any philosophical commitment to federalism."[7] The No Child Left Behind Act imposed more Federal control over elementary and secondary education. The Help America Vote Act of 2002 placed new requirements on state election procedures. The Real ID Act of 2005 required state-issued drivers' licenses and other identification documents to meet Federal standards.[8] . . .

The Resurgence of the States

. . . The Federal retreat energized many states to take a more direct role in solving their problems.[9] Like their Progressive-era predecessors, liberal reformers who served as governors and state legislators in this period advanced innovative policies and resisted the conservative turn in national policy.... By the end of the Reagan administration, policy activists again were touting the states as "laboratories of democracy."[10]

State innovations have thrived since the 1980s. Some states addressed climate change, raised the minimum wage, strengthened anti-discrimination laws, and provided access to higher education for undocumented residents.[11] . . . Richard Nathan used the phrase "the paradox of devolution" to describe the way the conservative ascendance in Federal policy has sparked so much state activism.[12] In his view,

> In periods when support for governmental activism was on the wane in Washington and in the country as a whole, the existence of a state-level counterforce kept the pressure on for public sector growth. Innovations, particularly those of progressive states, have been tested, refined, debugged, and often diffused across the country. In some cases, they have been morphed into national policies and programs ... In liberal periods, liberal activists are likely to view the center as their best bet for getting things done—as do conservative groups in conservative time. It is not federalism that these coalitions care about. It is advancing their interests.[13]

Conservatives, of course, also have used state innovations to advance their agenda. . . . In the twenty-first century, social conservatives have successfully advanced stricter criminal sentences, restrictions on abortion, bans on affirmative action and on gay marriage in a number of states.

NOTES

1. John Kingdon, *America the Unusual* (New York: St. Martin's, 1999), 7–22; Graham K. Wilson, *Only in America? The Politics of the United States in Comparative Perspective* (Chatham House, 1998), 5–8; Sven Steinmo and Jon Watts, "It's the Institutions, Stupid! Why Comprehensive National Health Insurance Always Fails in America," *Journal of Health Politics, Policy and Law* 20:2 (Summer 1995): 329–372.

2. On the importance of sequence, see Paul Pierson, "Not Just What, but *When*: Timing and Sequence in Political Processes," *Studies in American Political Development* 14:1 (Spring 2000), 72–92; and the responses to Pierson by Robert Jervis, "Timing and Interaction in Politics: A Comment on Pierson;" Kathleen Thelen, "Timing and Temporality in the Analysis of Institutional Change;" and Amy Bridges, "Path Dependence, Sequence, History, Theory," *Studies in American Political Development* 14:1 (Spring, 2000), 93–112.

3. On institutional change in American Political Development research, see Kathleen Thelen, *How Institutions Evolve: The Political Economy of Skills in Germany, Britain, the United States and Japan* (Cambridge and New York: Cambridge University Press, 2004); Eric Schickler, *Disjointed Pluralism: Institutional Innovation and the Development of the U.S. Congress* (Princeton, NJ: Princeton University Press, 2001); Margaret Weir, "When Does Policy Change? The Organizational Politics of Change," in *Rethinking Political Institutions: The Art of the State*, ed. Ian Shapiro, Stephen Skowronek and Daniel Galvin (New York: New York University Press, 2006); and James Mahoney and Kathleen Thelen, eds. *Explaining Institutional Change: Ambiguity, Agency, and Power* (Cambridge and New York: Cambridge University Press, 2009).

4. David B. Walker, *The Rebirth of Federalism: Slouching toward Washington*, 2nd ed. (Chatham, NJ: Chatham House, 1999), 147; Ben Canada, "Federal Grants to State and Local Governments: A Brief History," Congressional Research Service Report RL30705 (Washington: Congressional Research Service, February 19, 2003), 10, http://usinfo.org/enus/government/statelocal/docs/fedgrants.pdf (accessed October 15, 2013).

5. Joseph F. Zimmerman, "Federal Preemption under Reagan's New Federalism," *Publius*, 21:1 (Winter, 1991), 7–28.

6. Ibid.

7. Timothy J. Conlan and John Dinan, "Federalism, the Bush Administration, and the Transformation of American Conservatism," *Publius* 37:3 (Summer 2007), 279.

8. Paul L. Posner, "Mandates: The Politics of Coercive Federalism," in *Intergovernmental Management for the 21st Century*, ed. Timothy J. Conlan and Paul L. Posner (Washington, DC: Brookings Institution, 2008), 286–309; National Association of State Budget Officers, Issue Brief: The REAL ID Act, March 23, 2006, http://www.nasbo.org/sites/default/files/The%20REAL%20ID%20Act.pdf (accessed October 15, 2013); Jim VandeHei, "Blueprint Calls for Bigger, More Powerful Government," *Washington Post*, February 9, 2005, 1; http://www.washingtonpost.com/wp-dyn/articles/A9307-2005Feb8.html (accessed January 2, 2011).

9. Walker, *The Rebirth of Federalism*, 150.

10. David Osborne, *Laboratories of Democracy* (Boston, MA: Harvard Business School Press, 1988).

11. Dale Krane, "The Middle Tier in American Federalism: State Government Policy Activism during the Bush Presidency" *Publius* 37:3 (Summer 2007), 453–77; Richard Thompson Ford, "The New Blue Federalists: The Case for Liberal," *Slate*, January 6, 2005, http://www.slate.com/

id/2111942/ (accessed July 1, 2010). In 2010, nine states provided in-state tuition for undocumented students; Dream Act Portal, http://dreamact.info/students/in-state (accessed January 3, 2011).

12. Richard P. Nathan, "Federalism: The Great 'Composition,'" in *The New American Political System*, ed. Anthony King (Washington, DC: American Enterprise Institute, 1990), 233.
13. Richard P. Nathan, "Updating Theories of Federalism," in *Intergovernmental Management for the Twenty-First Century*, ed. Timothy J. Conlan and Paul L. Posner (Washington, DC: Brookings Institution, 2008), 16, 21.

Discussion Questions

1. Do you agree with James Madison that the Constitution gave the states enough influence to protect their powers?
2. Senator Robert Hayne opposed "all unnecessary extension of the powers" of the national government. How can you tell if any particular extension of federal power is necessary or not?
3. Why does Corwin fear that the U.S. national government has acquired enough power to place democracy in danger? Do you agree?
4. How do Corwin, Weir and Mettler differ in their views about grants programs? If the states manage a policy such as health care for the poor, what national rules (if any) should limit the way they manage it?
5. What specific rights should be guaranteed by the national government to all citizens? What rights should the states protect, if any?
6. How is federalism shaping the path of political development during the Obama administration? How will it affect the Republican or Democratic administration that follows Obama?

Suggested Additional Reading

Martha Derthick, *Keeping the Compound Republic: Essays on American Federalism* (Washington, DC: Brookings Institution, 2001).

Kimberley S. Johnson, *Governing the American State: Congress and the New Federalism, 1877–1929* (Princeton, NJ: Princeton University Press, 2007).

Alison LaCroix, *The Ideological Origins of American Federalism* (Cambridge, MA: Harvard University Press, 2010).

Forrest McDonald, *States' Rights and the Union: Imperium in Imperio, 1776–1876* (Lawrence, Kansas: University Press of Kansas, 2000).

John D. Nugent, *Safeguarding Federalism: How States Protect Their Interests in National Policymaking* (Norman, OK: University of Oklahoma Press, 2009).

Jonathan A. Rodden, *Hamilton's Paradox: The Promise and Peril of Fiscal Federalism* (Cambridge and New York: Cambridge University Press, 2006).

Harry N. Scheiber, "American Federalism and the Diffusion of Power: Historical and Contemporary Perspectives," *University of Toledo Law Review* 9 (1975), 619–680.

Aaron Wildavsky, "Federalism is About Inequality," in *The Costs of Federalism*, ed. Robert T. Golembiewski and Aaron Wildavsky (New Brunswick, NJ: Transaction Books, 1984), 55–72.

4

Political Socialization and Public Opinion

Introduction

Political socialization is the study of how citizens come to adopt and share the broad commitments of their political culture. In the United States these are widely shared commitments to ideas like democracy, majority rule, equal rights, and capitalism. Public opinion is the distribution of opinion on politically relevant issues of the day—issues like war, taxes, and abortion. Political socialization involves the broad background commitments of society's members and public opinion involves their more changeable foreground opinions on the issues of the day. APD scholars study both, because both change, though background commitments and convictions change more slowly than foreground impressions and opinions.

American commitments to democracy and equality have been in place since the nation's earliest days, but to whom they apply and how best to secure them has changed over time. Consider, for example, political socialization about gender and race in eighteenth- and nineteenth-century America. American men fought a revolution for freedom and liberty, generally without believing that that meant that slaves and women had to be, even could be, treated as equals. But ideas, even fundamental ideas like freedom and liberty, do change and APD traces those changes in ways that respect the historical integrity of earlier times and informs our understanding of the prospects and mechanisms of change in our day.

The first selection below presents a famous exchange between John and Abigail Adams, just weeks before the Declaration of Independence was adopted in Congress, about the appropriate role of women in the new nation. Be alert to the tone of this exchange. Abigail calls on John to challenge the existing political culture and to think about women in a new way. But she is not wagging her finger under his nose, because she knows that it is asking a great deal for John to think beyond the accepted wisdom of his day. John, just a bit nervous, hides behind humor, but does so in a way that makes clear that he knows that women, like slaves, do not have the freedom that men enjoy. It is an important exchange, but almost a century and a half would pass before women got the vote. Big changes often come slowly.

Our second selection, by the prominent contemporary historian Gordon Wood, makes the point that the revolution did bring some important changes to the American political culture. Prior to the revolution, though the colonies were more open and egalitarian than Europe, local and state elites still believed that their superior education, social standing, and wealth entitled them to social and political leadership. Wood explains that during the last quarter of the eighteenth century and first years of the nineteenth century, debates about who had the right to speak and be listened to in public debate created modern "public opinion." As the American political culture evolved to accept all white men in the public arena, public opinion as the right of all white men, elite or not, informed or not, to be heard and considered came into view for the first time.

The American political culture of the nineteenth century was deeply committed, perhaps to deeply committed, Alexis de Tocqueville thought, to liberty, equality, democracy, and majority rule for white men. In our third selection, Tocqueville worries about the "Unlimited Power of the Majority in the United States." He argues that the commitment to equality makes white Americans believe that the majority is always right and makes men who hold a minority opinion unwilling to voice it publicly. Despite his reservations, Tocqueville was generally effusive about equality, majority rule, and democracy in America.

Gunnar Myrdal, a Nobel prize-winning Swedish economist and social scientist, wrote his path-breaking, even myth-shattering, book, *The American Dilemma: The Negro Problem and American Democracy* (1944), more than a century after Tocqueville. In our fourth selection, entitled "American Ideals and the American Conscience," Myrdal both lauds the American political culture's commitment to equality and democracy and dispassionately, though bluntly, highlights its on-going denial to black Americans. Just as bluntly, Myrdal argues that the solution to the "Negro dilemma" lay in opening the heart of white America. The themes articulated in *The American Dilemma* played a powerful role in the civil rights revolution of the 1950s and 1960s.

In our fifth selection and the focus piece for this chapter, the prominent political scientist Sidney Verba explores the strengths and weaknesses of survey research for the richness and integrity of our democracy. Verba's key point is that many aspects of democratic politics, including voting, volunteering, contributing to campaigns, contacting public officials, and standing for office skew toward elites—the well-educated, secure, and comfortable. Survey research, on the other hand, treats every respondent alike; each is weighted as one and only one in the poll results. Verba is, of course, aware that surveys can be well or poorly done, their findings dependable or not. But a well-done survey offers citizens and public officials alike a clear view of what people think on the issue or issues in focus.

Cass Sunstein, in our sixth selection, shares similar concerns. Sunstein (2007) worries that the prevalence of misinformation and ill-formed opinions are aggravated and magnified by modern communication systems, especially the Internet. The Internet promotes social fragmentation and radicalization by making it so easy for like-minded people, perhaps scattered around the country and beyond, to find each other and, speaking only among themselves, to reinforce their views and demonize those who do not share them. Sunstein hopes, though does not seem to expect, that the Internet also allows good information to wrestle with and hopefully displace bad information.

A question that runs throughout the readings in Chapter 4 and that remains open at the end—and perhaps must remain perpetually open—is how public opinion should relate to public policymaking in a democratic society. Should public opinion drive policymaking, or should we be concerned, with Tocqueville, Sunstein, and many more, that stereotypes, misinformation, and ignorance require checks, filters, and brakes on public opinion?

4.1 John and Abigail Adams, "Women in the New Nation" (1776) ·

In the early spring of 1776 Abigail Adams was at home in Braintree, Massachusetts, while her husband, John Adams, was attending the Continental Congress in Philadelphia. The battles of Lexington and Concord had happened nearly a year earlier and Congress's adoption of the Declaration of Independence was still a month away, but Abigail knew that independence would bring many changes and she had a point that she wanted to make. The lifelong correspondence between John and Abigail Adams, who were often apart, is one of the great treasures of American literature.

In this exchange, Abigail opens with some questions about the preparations for war and some news of home before getting to her main point—the place of women in the new republic. She calls upon John to revise the laws to place women beyond the too ready tyranny of men permitted by the current law. John's response is to deflect her request by making light of it. Little change in women's place in American society came with independence, but the topic had been raised. Change in public opinion would not begin in earnest for half a century and is incomplete today.

Abigail Adams

Braintree, 31 March 1776

I wish you would ever write me a letter half as long as I write you, and tell me, if you may, where your fleet are gone; what sort of defense Virginia can make against our common enemy; whether it is so situated as to make an able defense. Are not the gentry lords, and the common people vassals? Are they not like the uncivilized vassals Britain represents us to be? I hope their riflemen, who have shown themselves very savage and even bloodthirsty, are not a specimen of the generality of the people. I am willing to allow the colony great merit for having produced a Washington; but they have been shamefully duped by a Dunmore.

I have sometimes been ready to think that the passion for liberty cannot be equally strong in the breasts of those who have been accustomed to deprive their fellow-creatures of theirs. Of this I am certain, that it is not founded upon that generous and Christian principle of doing to others as we would that others should do unto us.

Do not you want to see Boston? I am fearful of the small-pox, or I should have been in before this time. I got Mr. Crane to go to our house and see what state it was in. I find it has been occupied by one of the doctors of a regiment; very dirty, but no other damage has been done to it. The few things which were left in it are all gone. Cranch has the key, which he never delivered up. I have wrote to him for it and am determined to get it cleaned as soon as possible and shut it up. I look upon it as a new acquisition of property—a property which one month ago I did not value at a single shilling, and would with pleasure have seen it in flames.

The town in general is left in a better state than we expected; more owing to a precipitate flight than any regard to the inhabitants; though some individuals discovered a sense of honor and justice, and have left the rent of the houses in which they were, for the owners, and the furniture unhurt, or, if damaged, sufficient to make it good . . . .

I long to hear that you have declared an independency. And, by the way, in the new code of laws which I suppose it will be necessary for you to make, I desire you would remember the ladies and be more generous and favorable to them than your ancestors. Do not put such unlimited power into the hands of the husbands. Remember, all men would be tyrants if they could. If particular care and attention is not paid to the ladies, we are determined to foment a rebellion, and will not hold ourselves bound by any laws in which we have no voice or representation.

That your sex are naturally tyrannical is a truth so thoroughly established as to admit of no dispute; but such of you as wish to be happy willingly give up the harsh title of master for the more tender and endearing one of friend. Why, then, not put it out of the power of the vicious and the lawless to use us with cruelty and indignity with impunity? Men of sense in all ages abhor those customs which treat us only as the vassals of your sex; regard us then as beings placed by Providence under your protection, and in imitation of the Supreme Being make use of that power only for our happiness.

John Adams

14 April

You justly complain of my short letters, but the critical state of things and the multiplicity of avocations must plead my excuse. You ask where the fleet is? The inclosed papers will inform you. You ask what sort of defense Virginia can make? I believe they will make an able defense. Their militia and minute-men have been some time employed in training themselves, and they have nine battalions of regulars, as they call them, maintained among them, under good officers, at the Continental expense. They have set up a number of manufactories of fire-arms, which are busily employed. They are tolerably supplied with powder, and are successful and assiduous in making saltpetre. Their neighboring sister, or rather daughter colony of North Carolina, which is a warlike colony, and has several battalions at the Continental expense, as well as a pretty good militia, are ready to assist them, and they are in very good spirits and seem determined to make a brave resistance. The gentry are very rich, and the common people very poor. This inequality of property gives an aristocratical turn to all their proceedings, and occasions a strong aversion in their patricians to "Common Sense." But the spirit of these Barons is coming down, and it must submit . . . .

As to declarations of independency, be patient. Read our privateering laws and our commercial laws. What signifies a word?

As to your extraordinary code of laws, I cannot but laugh. We have been told that our struggle has loosened the bands of government everywhere; that children and apprentices were disobedient; that schools and colleges were grown turbulent; that Indians slighted their guardians, and negroes grew insolent to their masters. But your letter was the first intimation that another tribe, more numerous and powerful than all the rest, were grown discontented. This is rather too coarse a compliment, but you are so saucy, I won't blot it out. Depend upon it, we know better than to repeal our masculine systems. Although they are in full force, you know they are little more than theory. We dare not exert our power in its full latitude. We are obliged to go fair and softly, and, in practice, you know we are the subjects. We have only the name of masters, and rather than give up this, which would completely subject us to the despotism of the petticoat, I hope General Washington and all our brave heroes would fight; I am sure every good politician would plot, as long as he would against despotism, empire, monarchy, aristocracy, oligarchy, or ochlocracy. A fine story, indeed! I begin to think the ministry as deep as they are wicked. After stirring up Tories, land-jobbers, trimmers, bigots, Canadians, Indians, negroes, Hanoverians, Hessians, Russians, Irish Roman Catholics, Scotch renegadoes, at last they have stimulated the—to demand new privileges and threaten to rebel.

4.2 Gordon Wood, "The Founders and the Creation of Modern Public Opinion" (2006)

Gordon Wood, one of the leading American historians of the last half century, describes the evolution of the American political culture of the Founding period as new men forced their way into the public sphere. The issue, then as now, is who is entitled to speak, to have an opinion, with an expectation of being listened to? As Wood explains, in colonial times, as in Europe at the time, only a narrow social and political elite were assumed to have the right to personal opinions, so they spoke and wrote mostly to each other. But as the revolution brought widespread social change, new voices, still those of white men, but sometimes of lower-class white men, demanded to be heard respectfully. Moreover, the apparent unwillingness of Federalists to heed the opinions of lower-class white men opened the door to their Jeffersonian Republican opponents. The Jeffersonians, tentatively at first and never without reservation, were carried to political dominance on the shoulders of these new men.

BECAUSE THE revolutionary leaders were cultivated gentlemen with special privileges and responsibilities, tied to the people through lines of personal and social authority, they believed that their speeches and writings did not have to influence directly and simultaneously all the people but only those who were rational and enlightened, who in turn would bring the rest of the populace with them through the force of deferential respect. The politically minded public in eighteenth-century America may have been large compared with contemporary England, but most of the political literature of the period, unlike much of the religious literature, showed little evidence of a broad reading public.[1] The revolutionary leaders for the most part wrote as if they were dealing with reasonable and cultivated readers like themselves. Of course, by publishing their writings, they realized they were exposing their ideas to the vulgar, and therefore often resorted to pseudonyms, but before the Revolution they made very few concessions to this wider public. They were aware of the term *public opinion*, which had first arisen in the English-speaking world in the early 1700s, but they conceived of the public as a very limited sphere.[2] . . .

Because politics was still very personal, the honor and reputation of the political leaders seemed essential to social order and stability. It was difficult in this early modern world for men to conceive of anyone's becoming a political leader who did not already have an established social and moral superiority. Today a politician's reputation and social status are often a consequence of his political office; in the eighteenth century the process was reversed: An individual's social position and reputation were thought to be the necessary prerequisites to political officeholding. In other words, important offices of government were supposed to be held only by those who had already established their social and moral superiority. They at least ought to be "gentlemen," and preferably gentlemen of talent, education, and character.

The reasons seemed obvious to many American leaders of the time, both Federalists and Republicans. Since early modern governments lacked most of the coercive powers of a modern state—a few constables and sheriffs scarcely constituted a police force—officeholders had to rely on their social respectability and their reputation for character to compel the obedience of ordinary people and maintain public order. It is not surprising therefore that public officials should have been acutely sensitive to criticism of their character. "Whatever tends to create in the minds of the people, a contempt of the persons who hold the highest offices in the state," declared the conventional eighteenth-century wisdom, whatever convinces people that "subordination is not necessary, and is no essential part of government, tends directly to destroy it."[3] . . .

The debate over the Sedition Act marked the crucial turning point in the democratization of American intellectual life. It fundamentally altered America's understanding not only of its intellectual leadership but of its conception of public truth. The debate, which spilled over into the early years of the nineteenth century, drew out and articulated the logic of America's intellectual experience since the Revolution, and in the process it undermined the foundations of the elitist eighteenth-century classical world on which the founders stood.

Americans believed in freedom of the press and had written it into their Bill of Rights. But they believed in it as Englishmen did. The English had celebrated freedom of the press since the seventeenth century but had meant by it, in contrast with the French, no prior restraint or censorship of what was published. Under English law people were nevertheless held responsible for what they published. If a person's publications were slanderous and calumnious enough to bring public officials into disrespect, then under the common law the publisher could be prosecuted for seditious libel. The truth of what was published was no defense; indeed, it even aggravated the offense. Furthermore, under the common law, judges, not juries, had the responsibility to decide whether or not a publication was seditious. Although this common law view of seditious libel had been challenged by the Zenger trial in New York in 1735, it had never been fully eradicated from American thinking or practice in the state courts.

The Federalists in their Sedition Act of 1798 thought they were being generous by changing the common law conception of seditious libel and enacting the Zenger defense into law. They not only allowed juries to determine what was seditious but made truth a defense, stating that only those statements that were "false, scandalous, and malicious" would be punished. But the Republican polemicists would have no part of this generosity. In the debate over the sedition law the Republican libertarian theorists rejected both the old common law restrictions on the liberty of the press and the new legal recognition of the distinction between truth and falsity of opinion that the Federalists had incorporated into the Sedition Act. While the Federalists clung to the eighteenth century's conception that "truths" were constant and universal and capable of being discovered by enlightened and reasonable men, the Republicans argued that opinions about government and governors were many and diverse an their truth could not be determined simply by individual judges and juries, no matter how reasonable such men were. Hence they concluded that all political opinions—that is, words as distinct from overt acts—even those opinions that were "false, scandalous, and malicious," ought to be allowed, as Jefferson put it, to "stand undisturbed as monuments of the safety with which error of opinion may be tolerated where reason is left free to combat it."[4]

The Federalists were incredulous. "How … could the rights of the people require a liberty to utter falsehood?" they asked. "How could it be right to do wrong?"[5] It was not an easy question to answer, as we continue to discover even in our own time. The Republicans thought they could not deny outright the possibility of truth and falsity in political beliefs and thus fell back on a tenuous distinction, developed by Jefferson in his first inaugural address, between principles and opinions. Principles, it seemed, were hard and fixed, while opinions were soft and fluctuating; therefore, said Jefferson, "every difference of opinion is not a difference of principle." The implication was, as Benjamin Rush suggested, that individual opinions did not count as much as they had in the past, and for that reason such individual opinions could be permitted the freest possible expression.[6]

What ultimately made such distinctions and arguments comprehensible was the Republicans' assumption that opinions about politics were no longer the monopoly of the educated and aristocratic few. Not only were true and false opinions equally to be tolerated, but everyone and anyone in the society should be equally able to express them. Sincerity and honesty, the Republican polemicists argued, were far more important in the articulation of ultimate political truth than learning and fancy words that had often been used to deceive and dissimulate. Truth was actually the creation of many voices and many minds, no one of which was more important than another and each of which made its own separate and equally significant contribution. Solitary individual opinions may thus have counted for less, but in their numerous collectivity they now added up to something far more significant than had ever existed before. Mingled together, they resulted into what was called *public opinion*. But this public opinion was no longer the small intimate entity it had been for the revolutionary leaders; it was huge and impersonal, modern and democratic, and it included everyone's opinion. This new expanded idea of public opinion soon came to dominate all of American intellectual life.[7]

Public opinion is so much a part of our politics that it is surprising that we have not incorporated it into the Constitution. We constantly use the term, seek to measure whatever it is and to influence it, and worry about who else is influencing it. Public opinion exists in any nation, but in our democracy it has a special power. The Revolution in America transformed it and gave it its modern significance. By the early years of the nineteenth century Americans had come to realize that public opinion, "that invisible guardian of honour—that eagle eyed spy on human actions—that inexorable judge of men and manners—that arbiter, whom tears cannot appease, nor ingenuity soften and from whose terrible decisions there is no appeal," had become "the vital principle" underlying American government, society, and culture.[8] It became the resolving force not only of political truth but of all truth, from disputes among religious denominations to controversies over artistic taste. Nothing was more important in explaining and clarifying the democratization of American culture than this new conception of public opinion. In the end it became America's nineteenth-century popular substitute for the elitist intellectual leadership of the revolutionary generation. . . .

It was not a world the founders wanted or expected; indeed, those who lived long enough into the nineteenth century to experience its full democratic force were deeply disillusioned by what they had wrought. Still, they had helped create this popular world, for it was rooted in the vital principle that none of them, Federalists included, ever could deny: the people. In the end nothing illustrates better the transforming power of the American Revolution than the way its intellectual and political leaders, that remarkable group of men, contributed to their own demise.

NOTES

This is a revised and expanded version of my article "The Democratization of Mind in the American Revolution," in Library of Congress Symposia on the American Revolution, 3d, 1974, *Leadership in the American Revolution* (Washington: Library of Congress, 1974), 63–89.

1. David D. Hall has contended that eighteenth-century evangelical religious writing was already popular and designed to reach a wide readership. No doubt he is correct about the early trans-formation of evangelical writing, but most of the political literature remained part of the cosmopolitan "system" that "presumed hierarchy and privilege." David D. Hall, *Cultures of Print: Essays in the History of the Book* (Amherst, MA: University of Massachusetts Press, 1996), 152.
2. For the intimate nature of the networks of communication in the eighteenth century see Richard D. Brown, *Knowledge Is Power: The Diffusion of Information in Early America*, 1700–1865 (New York: Oxford University Press, 1989), 89–90, 271, 278. This public sphere is essen-tially the polite and clubby world David S. Shields has reconstructed so brilliantly in his *Civil Tongues & Polite Letters in British America* (Chapel Hill: University of North Carolina Press, 1997). Although Shields emphasizes the ways the "discursive manners" of this world crossed social ranks and spread throughout American society, it seems evident that in comparison to what followed in the nineteenth century the eighteenth-century world he describes was still at heart an aristocratic one.
3. Wood, *Radicalism*, 86
4. [George Hay], *An Essay on the Liberty of the Press* . . . (Philadelphia: Printed at the Aurora office, 1799), 40; TJ, Inaugural Address, March 4, 1801, *Jefferson: Writings*, 493.
5. Samuel Dana, debates in Congress, January 1801, quoted in Buel, *Securing the Revolution*, 252.

6. Jefferson, Inaugural Address, March 4, 1801, *Jefferson: Writings*, 493; Benjamin Rush to TJ, March 12,1801, Lyman H. Butterfield, ed., 2 vols., in *Letters of Benjamin Rush* (Princeton: Princeton University Press, 1951), 2: 831.

7. Tunis Wortman, *A Treatise Concerning Political Enquiry, and the Liberty of the Press* (New York: Printed by G. Forman for the author, 1800), 118–23, 155–57.

8. William Crafts, Jr., *An Oration on the Influence of Moral Causes on National Character, Delivered Before the Phi Beta Kappa Society, on Their Anniversary, 28 August, 1817* (Cambridge: Hilliard and Metcalf, 1817), 5–6; Wortman, *Treatise*, 180.

4.3 Alexis de Tocqueville, "Unlimited Power of the Majority in the United States" (1835)

Alexis de Tocqueville's 1835 classic, *Democracy In America*, is widely seen as the most insightful analysis of the fundamental nature and dynamics of the new American democracy. Tocqueville, a French nobleman notionally touring America to study its prison system, produced a wide-ranging study of the American people and the effects that democratic politics and institutions had on them. Tocqueville believed that democracy was the wave of the future. Since democracy had come to America first, he believed that Europe could produce a superior democracy if it studied the American experience closely.

In this selection, Tocqueville is concerned about majority rule and its potential abuse. America, he believed, was settled by persons broadly equal who saw majority rule as natural and restraints on it as unnecessary. Because Americans think of themselves as equal to their fellow citizens, no better and no worse, they find it difficult to stand against public opinion. Europe, with its social classes, its titled nobility, its educated elites, and its religious diversity, breeds independent minds. A nobleman, finding that he held opinions that differed from the general public, would swell with pride rather than be quieted. Tocqueville worried that the tyranny of the majority threatened real freedom of mind, real independence, in America.

Chapter XV

Unlimited Power of the Majority in the United States, and its Consequences

The very essence of democratic government consists in the absolute sovereignty of the majority; for there is nothing in democratic states that is capable of resisting it. Most of the American constitutions have sought to increase this natural strength of the majority by artificial means.

Of all political institutions, the legislature is the one that is most easily swayed by the will of the majority. The Americans determined that the members of the legislature should be elected by the people *directly*, and for a *very brief term*, in order to subject them, not only to the general convictions, but even to the daily passions, of their constituents. The members of both houses are taken from the same classes in society and nominated in the same manner; so that the movements of the legislative bodies are almost as rapid, and quite as irresistible, as those of a single assembly. It is to a legislature thus constituted that almost all the authority of the government has been entrusted.

At the same time that the law increased the strength of those authorities which of themselves were strong, it enfeebled more and more those which were naturally weak. It deprived the representatives of the executive power of all stability and independence; and by subjecting them completely to the caprices of the legislature, it robbed them of the slender influence that the nature of a democratic government might have allowed them to exercise. In several states the judicial power was also submitted to the election of the majority; and in all of them its existence was made to depend on the pleasure of the legislative authority, since the representatives were empowered annually to regulate the stipend of the judges.

Custom has done even more than law. A proceeding is becoming more and more general in the United States which will, in the end, do away with the guarantees of representative government: it frequently happens that the voters, in electing a delegate, point out a certain line of conduct to him and impose upon him certain positive obligations that he is pledged to fulfill. With the exception of the tumult, this comes to the same thing as if the majority itself held its deliberations in the market-place.

Several particular circumstances combine to render the power of the majority in America not only preponderant, but irresistible. The moral authority of the majority is partly based upon the notion that there is more intelligence and wisdom in a number of men united than in a single individual, and that the number of the legislators is more important than their quality. The theory of equality is thus applied to the intellects of men; and human pride is thus assailed in its last retreat by a doctrine which the minority hesitate to admit, and to which they will but slowly assent. Like all other powers, and perhaps more than any other, the authority of the many requires the sanction of time in order to appear legitimate. At first it enforces obedience by constraint; and its laws are not *respected* until they have been long maintained.

The right of governing society, which the majority supposes itself to derive from its superior intelligence, was introduced into the United States by the first settlers; and this idea, which of itself would be sufficient to create a free nation, has now been amalgamated with the customs of the people and the minor incidents of social life.

The French under the old monarchy held it for a maxim that the king could do no wrong; and if he did do wrong, the blame was imputed to his advisers. This notion made obedience very easy; it enabled the subject to complain of the law without ceasing to love and honor the lawgiver. The Americans entertain the same opinion with respect to the majority.

The moral power of the majority is founded upon yet another principle, which is that the interests of the many are to be preferred to those of the few. It will readily be perceived that the respect here professed for the rights of the greater number must naturally increase or diminish according to the state of parties. When a nation is divided into several great irreconcilable interests, the privilege of the majority is often overlooked, because it is intolerable to comply with its demands.

If there existed in America a class of citizens whom the legislating majority sought to deprive of exclusive privileges which they had possessed for ages and to bring down from an elevated station to the level of the multitude, it is probable that the minority would be less ready to submit to its laws. But as the United States was colonized by men holding equal rank, there is as yet no natural or permanent disagreement between the interests of its different inhabitants.

There are communities in which the members of the minority can never hope to draw the majority over to their side, because they must then give up the very point that is at issue between them. Thus an aristocracy can never become a majority while it retains its exclusive privileges, and it cannot cede its privileges without ceasing to be an aristocracy.

In the United States, political questions cannot be taken up in so general and absolute a manner; and all parties are willing to recognize the rights of the majority, because they all hope at some time to be able to exercise them to their own advantage. The majority in that country, therefore, exercise a prodigious actual authority, and a power of opinion which is nearly as great; no obstacles exist which can impede or even retard its progress, so as to make it heed the complaints of those whom it crushes upon its path. This state of things is harmful in itself and dangerous for the future.

Tyranny of the Majority

In my opinion, the main evil of the present democratic institutions of the United States does not arise, as is often asserted in Europe, from their weakness, but from their irresistible strength. I am not so much alarmed at the excessive liberty which reigns in that country as at the inadequate securities which one finds there against tyranny.

When an individual or a party is wronged in the United States, to whom can he apply for redress? If to public opinion, public opinion constitutes the majority; if to the legislature, it represents the majority and implicitly obeys it; if to the executive power, it is appointed by the majority and serves as a passive tool in its hands. The public force consists of the majority under arms; the jury is the majority invested with the right of hearing judicial cases; and in certain states even the judges are elected by the majority. However iniquitous or absurd the measure of which you complain, you must submit to it as well as you can.[1] ...

Power Exercised by the Majority in America Upon Opinion

It is in the examination of the exercise of thought in the United States that we clearly perceive how far the power of the majority surpasses all the powers with which we are acquainted in Europe....

The authority of a king is physical and controls the actions of men without subduing their will. But the majority possesses a power that is physical and moral at the same time, which acts upon the will as much as upon the actions and represses not only all contest, but all controversy.

I know of no country in which there is so little independence of mind and real freedom of discussion as in America. In any constitutional state in Europe every sort of religious and political theory may be freely preached and disseminated; for there is no country in Europe so subdued by any single authority as not to protect the man who raises his voice in the cause of truth from the consequences of his hardihood. If he is unfortunate enough to live under an absolute government, the people are often on his side; if he inhabits a free country, he can, if necessary, find a shelter behind the throne. The aristocratic part of society supports him in some countries, and the democracy in others. But in a nation where democratic institutions exist, organized like those of the United States, there is but one authority, one element of strength and success, with nothing beyond it.

In America the majority raises formidable barriers around the liberty of opinion; within these barriers an author may write what he pleases, but woe to him if he goes beyond them. Not that he is in danger of an auto-da-fé, but he is exposed to continued obloquy and persecution. His political career is closed forever, since he has offended the only authority that is able to open it. Every sort of compensation, even that of celebrity, is refused to him. Before making public his opinions he thought he had sympathizers; now it seems to him that he has none any more since he has revealed himself to everyone; then those who blame him criticize loudly and those who think as he does keep quiet and move away without courage. He yields at length, overcome by the daily effort which he has to make, and subsides into silence, as if he felt remorse for having spoken the truth . . . .

Absolute monarchies had dishonored despotism; let us beware lest democratic republics should reinstate it and render it less odious and degrading in the eyes of the many by making it still more onerous to the few . . . .

Effect of the Tyranny of the Majority upon the National Character of the Americans—the Courtier Spirit in the United States

Democratic republics extend the practice of currying favor with the many and introduce it into all classes at once; this is the most serious reproach that can be addressed to them. This is especially true in democratic states organized like the American republics, where the power of the majority is so absolute and irresistible that one must give up one's rights as a citizen and almost abjure one's qualities as a man if one intends to stray from the track which it prescribes.

In that immense crowd which throngs the avenues to power in the United States, I found very few men who displayed that manly candor and masculine independence of opinion which frequently distinguished the Americans in former times, and which constitutes the leading feature in distinguished characters wherever they may be found. It seems at first sight as if all the minds of the Americans were formed upon one model, so accurately do they follow the same route. A stranger does, indeed, sometimes meet with Americans who dissent from the rigor of these formulas, with men who deplore the defects of the laws, the mutability and the ignorance of democracy, who even go so far as to observe the evil tendencies that impair the national character, and to point out such remedies as it might be possible to apply; but no one is there to hear them except yourself, and you, to whom these secret reflections are confided, are a stranger and a bird of passage. They are very ready to communicate truths which are useless to you, but they hold a different language in public . . . .

NOTE

1. A striking instance of the excesses that may be occasioned by the despotism of the majority occurred at Baltimore during the War of 1812. At that time the war was very popular in

Baltimore. A newspaper that had taken the other side excited, by its opposition, the indignation of the inhabitants. The mob assembled, broke the printing-presses, and attacked the house of the editors. The militia was called out, but did not obey the call; and the only means of saving the wretches who were threatened by the frenzy of the mob was to throw them into prison as common malefactors. But even this precaution was ineffectual; the mob collected again during the night; the magistrates again made a vain attempt to call out the militia; the prison was forced, one of the newspaper editors was killed upon the spot, and the others were left for dead. The guilty parties, when they were brought to trial, were acquitted by the jury.

4.4 Gunnar Myrdal, "American Ideals and the American Conscience" (1944)

One of the great classics of American social inquiry is Gunnar Myrdal's *An American Dilemma: The Negro Problem and American Democracy* (1944). Like Montesquieu and Tocqueville, Gunnar Myrdal, a Swedish economist and sociologist, looked deeply into the American political culture, but from outside. Americans, socialized from childhood into the myths and truths of their society, are trained both in what to see, the American Creed, and in what not to see, the racial discrimination in their society. Myrdal's research project, funded by the Carnegie Foundation, was to evaluate American political and social ideals in light of the place of blacks in mid-twentieth-century America. In two volumes and nearly 1,500 pages of scrupulous social science research, Myrdal and his team laid bare the deep gulf between the American Creed, with its professed values of liberty, equality, and opportunity, and the real prospects facing black Americans. Often compared in its social impact to Harriett Beecher Stowe's pre-Civil War classic, *Uncle Tom's Cabin, An American Dilemma* changed how people thought about meaning of the American Creed for blacks and, soon, for other non-whites and women.

---

1. Unity of Ideals and Diversity of Culture

It is a commonplace to point out the heterogeneity of the American nation and the swift succession of all sorts of changes in all its component parts and, as it often seems, in every conceivable direction. America is truly a shock to the stranger. The bewildering impression it gives of dissimilarity throughout and of chaotic unrest is indicated by the fact that few outside observers—and, indeed, few native Americans—have been able to avoid the intellectual escape of speaking about America as "paradoxical."

Still there is evidently a strong unity in this nation and a basic homogeneity and stability in its valuations. Americans of all national origins, classes, regions, creeds, and colors, have something in common: a social *ethos*, a political creed. It is difficult to avoid the judgment that this "American Creed" is the cement in the structure of this great and disparate nation.

When the American Creed is once detected, the cacophony becomes a melody. The further observation then becomes apparent: that America, compared to every other country in Western civilization, large or small, has the *most explicitly expressed* system of general ideals in reference to human interrelations. This body of ideals is more widely understood and appreciated than similar ideals are anywhere else. The American Creed is not merely—as in some other countries—the implicit background of the nation's political and judicial order as it functions. To be sure, the political creed of America is not very satisfactorily effectuated in actual social life. But as principles which *ought* to rule, the Creed has been made conscious to everyone in American society.

Sometimes one even gets the impression that there is a relation between the intense apprehension of high and uncompromising ideals and the spotty reality. One feels that it is, perhaps, the difficulty of giving reality to the *ethos* in this young and still somewhat unorganized nation—that it is the prevalence of "wrongs" in America, "wrongs" judged by the high standards of the national Creed—which helps make the ideals stand out so clearly. America is continuously struggling for its soul. These principles of social ethics have been hammered into easily remembered formulas. All means of intellectual communication are utilized to stamp them into everybody's mind. The schools teach them, the churches preach them. The courts pronounce their judicial decisions in their terms. They permeate editorials with a pattern of idealism so ingrained that the writers could scarcely free themselves from it even if they tried. They have fixed a custom of indulging in high-sounding generalities in all written or spoken addresses to the American public, otherwise so splendidly gifted for the matter-of-fact approach to things and problems. Even the stranger, when he has to appear before an American audience, feels this, if he is sensitive at all, and finds himself espousing the national Creed, as this is the only means by which a speaker can obtain human response from the people to whom he talks.

The Negro people in America are no exception to the national pattern. "It was a revelation to me to hear Negroes sometimes indulge in a glorification of American democracy in the same uncritical way as unsophisticated whites often do," relates the Dutch observer, Bertram Schrieke. A Negro political scientist, Ralph Bunche, observes:

> Every man in the street, white, black, red or yellow, knows that this is "the land of the free," the "land of opportunity," the "cradle of liberty," the "home of democracy," that the American flag symbolizes the "equality of all men" and guarantees to us all "the protection of life, liberty and property," freedom of speech, freedom of religion and racial tolerance.

The present writer has made the same observation. The American Negroes know that they are a subordinated group experiencing, more than anybody else in the nation, the consequences of the fact that the Creed is not lived up to in America. Yet their faith in the Creed is not simply a means of pleading their unfulfilled rights. They, like the whites, are under the spell of the great national suggestion. With one part of themselves they actually believe, as do the whites, that the Creed is ruling America.

These ideals of the essential dignity of the individual human being, of the fundamental equality of all men, and of certain inalienable rights to freedom, justice, and a fair opportunity represent to the American people the essential meaning of the nation's early struggle for independence. In the clarity and intellectual boldness of the Enlightenment period these tenets were written into the Declaration of Independence, the Preamble of the Constitution, the Bill of Rights and into the constitutions of the several states. The ideals of the American Creed have thus become the highest law of the land. The Supreme Court pays its reverence to these general principles when it declares what is constitutional and what is not. They have been elaborated upon by all national leaders, thinkers and statesmen. America has had, throughout its history, a continuous discussion of the principles and implications of democracy, a discussion which, in every epoch, measured by any standard, remained high, not only quantitatively but also qualitatively . . . .

Introduction

1. The Negro Problem as a Moral Issue

There is a "Negro problem" in the United States and most Americans are aware of it, although it assumes varying forms and intensity in different regions of the country and among diverse groups of the American people. Americans have to react to it, politically as citizens and, where there are Negroes present in the community, privately as neighbors.

To the great majority of white Americans the Negro problem has distinctly negative connotations. It suggests something difficult to settle and equally difficult to leave alone. It is embarrassing. It makes for moral uneasiness. The very presence of the Negro in America[1]; his fate in this country through slavery, Civil War and Reconstruction; his recent career and his present status; his accommodation; his protest and his aspiration; in fact his entire biological, historical and social existence as a participant American represent to the ordinary white man in the North as well as in the South an anomaly in the very structure of American society. To many, this takes on the proportion of a menace—biological, economic, social, cultural, and, at times, political. This anxiety may be mingled with a feeling of individual and collective guilt. A few see the problem as a challenge to statesmanship. To all it is a trouble.

These and many other mutually inconsistent attitudes are blended into none too logical a scheme which, in turn, may be quite inconsistent with the wider personal, moral, religious, and civic sentiments and ideas of the Americans. Now and then, even the least sophisticated individual becomes aware of his own confusion and the contradiction in his attitudes. Occasionally he may recognize, even if only for a moment, the incongruence of his state of mind and find it so intolerable that the whole organization of his moral precepts is shaken. But most people, most of the time, suppress such threats to their moral integrity together with all of the confusion, the ambiguity, and inconsistency which lurks in the basement of man's soul. This, however, is rarely accomplished without mental strain. Out of the strain comes a sense of uneasiness and awkwardness which always seems attached to the Negro problem.

The strain is increased in democratic America by the freedom left open—even in the South,[2] to a considerable extent—for the advocates of the Negro, his rights and welfare. All "pro-Negro" forces in American society, whether organized or not, and irrespective of their wide differences in both strategy and tactics, sense that this is the situation. They all work on the national conscience. They all seek to fix everybody's attention on the suppressed moral conflict. No wonder that they are often regarded as public nuisances, or worse—even when they succeed in getting grudging concessions to Negro rights and welfare.

At this point it must be observed that America, relative to all the other branches of Western civilization, is moralistic and "moral-conscious." The ordinary American is the opposite of a cynic. He is on the average more of a believer and a defender of the faith in humanity than the rest of the Occidentals. It is a relatively important matter to him to be true to his own ideals and to carry them out in actual life. We recognize the American, wherever we meet him, as a practical idealist. Compared with members of other nations of Western civilization, the ordinary American is a rationalistic being, and there are close relations between his moralism and his rationalism.... This man is a rationalist; he wants intellectual order in his moral set-up; he wants to pursue his own inclinations into their hidden haunts; and he is likely to expose himself and his kind in a most undiplomatic manner.

In hasty strokes we are now depicting the essentials of the American *ethos*. This moralism and rationalism are to many of us—among them the author of this book—the glory of the nation, its youthful strength, perhaps the salvation of mankind. The analysis of this "American Creed" and its implications have an important place in our inquiry. While on the one hand, to such a moralistic and rationalistic being as the ordinary American, the Negro problem and his own confused and contradictory attitudes toward it must be disturbing; on the other hand, the very mass of unsettled problems in his heterogeneous and changing culture, and the inherited liberalistic trust that things will ultimately take care of themselves and get settled in one way or another, enable the ordinary American to live on happily, with recognized contradictions around him and within him, in a kind of bright fatalism which is unmatched in the rest of the Western world. This fatalism also belongs to the national *ethos*.

The American Negro problem is a problem in the heart of the American. It is there that the interracial tension has its focus. It is there that the decisive struggle goes on. This is the central viewpoint of this treatise. Though our study includes economic, social, and political race relations, at bottom our problem is the moral dilemma of the American—the conflict between his moral valuations on various levels of consciousness and generality. The "American Dilemma," referred to in the title of this book, is the ever-raging conflict between, on the one hand, the valuations preserved on the general plane which we shall call the "American Creed," where the American thinks, talks, and acts under the influence of high national and Christian precepts, and, on the other hand, the valuations on specific planes of individual and group living, where personal and local interests; economic, social, and sexual jealousies; considerations of community prestige and conformity; group prejudice against particular persons or types of people; and all sorts of miscellaneous wants, impulses, and habits dominate his outlook ....

2. Valuations and Beliefs

The Negro problem in America would be of a different nature, and, indeed, would be simpler to handle scientifically, if the moral conflict raged only between valuations held by different persons and groups of persons. The essence of the moral situation is, however, that the conflicting valuations are also held by the same person. *The moral struggle goes on within people and not only between them. As people's valuations are conflicting, behavior normally becomes a moral compromise. There are no homogeneous "attitudes" behind human behavior but a mesh of struggling inclinations, interests, and ideals, some held conscious and some suppressed for long intervals but all active in bending behavior in their direction.*

The unity of a culture consists in the fact that all valuations are mutually shared in some degree. We shall find that even a poor and uneducated white person in some isolated and backward rural region in the Deep South, who is violently prejudiced against the Negro and intent upon depriving him of civic rights and human independence, has also a whole compartment in his valuation sphere housing the entire American Creed of liberty, equality, justice, and fair opportunity for everybody. He is actually also a good Christian and honestly devoted to the ideals of human brotherhood and the Golden Rule. And these more general valuations—more general in the sense that they refer to all human beings—are, to some extent, effective in shaping his behavior. Indeed, it would be impossible to understand why the Negro does not fare worse in some regions of America if it were not constantly kept in mind that behavior is the outcome of a compromise between valuations, among which the equalitarian ideal is one. At the other end, there are few liberals, even in New England, who have not a well-furnished compartment of race prejudice, even if it is usually suppressed from conscious attention. Even the American Negroes share in this community of valuations: they have eagerly imbibed the American Creed and the revolutionary Christian teaching of common brotherhood; under closer study, they usually reveal also that they hold something of the majority prejudice against their own kind and its characteristics.

The intensities and proportions in which these conflicting valuations are present vary considerably from one American to another, and within the same individual, from one situation to another. The cultural unity of the nation consists, however, in the fact that *most Americans have most valuations in common* though they are arranged differently in the sphere of valuations of different individuals and groups and bear different intensity coefficients. This cultural unity is the indispensable basis for discussion between persons and groups. It is the floor upon which the democratic process goes on.

In America as everywhere else people agree, as an abstract proposition, that *the more general valuations—those which refer to man as such and not to any particular group or temporary situation—are morally higher.* These valuations are also given the sanction of religion and national legislation. They are incorporated into the American Creed. The other valuations—which refer to various smaller groups of mankind or to particular occasions—are commonly referred to as "irrational" or "prejudiced," sometimes even by people who express and stress them. They are defended in terms of tradition, expediency or utility . . . .

3. A White Man's Problem

Although the Negro problem is a moral issue both to Negroes and to whites in America, we shall in this book have to give *primary* attention to what goes on in the minds of white Americans . . . practically all the economic, social, and political power is held by whites. The Negroes do not by far have anything approaching a tenth of the things worth having in America.

It is thus the white majority group that naturally determines the Negro's "place." All our attempts to reach scientific explanations of why the Negroes are what they are and why they live as they do have regularly led to determinants on the white side of the race line. In the practical and political struggles of effecting changes, the views and attitudes of the white Americans are likewise strategic. The Negro's entire life, and, consequently, also his opinions on the Negro problem, are, in the main, to be considered as secondary reactions to more primary pressures from the side of the dominant white majority.

The Negro was brought to America for the sake of the white man's profits. He was kept in slavery for generations in the same interest. A civil war was fought between two regional groups of white Americans. For two years no one wanted Negroes involved in the fighting. Later on some two hundred thousand Negro soldiers fought in the Northern army, in addition to all the Negro laborers, servants, spies, and helpers in both armies. But it was not the Negroes' war. As a result of the war, which took a toll of some half million killed and many more wounded, the four million Negro slaves were liberated. Since then the Negro's "place" in American society has been precarious, uncertain and changing; he was no longer so necessary and profitable to the white man as in slavery before the Civil War. In the main, however, the conflicting and vacillating valuations of the white majority have been decisive, whether the issue was segregation in the schools, discrimination with reference to public facilities, equal justice and protection under the laws, enjoyment of the franchise, or the freedom to enter a vocation and earn an honest living. The Negro, as a minority, and a poor and suppressed minority at that, in the final analysis, has had little other strategy open *to him* than *to* play on the conflicting values held in the white majority group. In so doing, he has been able to identify his cause with broader issues in American politics and social life and with moral principles held dear by the white Americans. This is the situation even today and will remain so in the foreseeable future. In that sense, "this is a white man's country." . . .

4. Not an Isolated Problem

Closely related to the thesis that the Negro problem is predominantly a white man's problem is another conclusion . . . *The Negro problem is an integral part of, or a special phase of, the whole complex of problems in the larger American civilization. It cannot be treated in isolation.* There is no single side of the Negro problem—whether it be the Negro's political status, the education he gets, his place in the labor market, his cultural and personality traits, or anything else—which is not predominantly determined by its total American setting. We shall, therefore, constantly be studying the American civilization in its entirety, though viewed in its implications for the most disadvantaged population group . . . .

The relationship between American society and the Negro problem is not one-sided. The entire structure of American society is itself greatly conditioned by the presence of the thirteen million Negro citizens. American politics, the labor market, education, religious life, civic ideals, art, and recreation are as they are partly because of the important conditioning factor working throughout the history of the nation. New impulses from the Negro people are constantly affecting the American way of life, bending in some degree all American institutions and bringing changes in every aspect of the American's complex world view. While primary attention will be focused on the Negro people and on the influences *from* the larger society working on them, their influence *back on* white society will not be ignored.

NOTES

1. The word *America* will be used in this book as a synonym for continental United States.
2. The more precise meaning of the words, *South, North,* and other terms for regions in America will be explained in Appendix 4.

4.5 Sidney Verba, "The Citizen as Respondent: Sample Surveys and American Democracy" (1995)

Sidney Verba's 1995 presidential address to the American Political Science Association's annual meeting is our focus piece in this chapter. Verba explored the potential of survey research for improving and enriching the American democracy. Verba's thesis is that while most forms of political participation, including contacting officials, contributing to campaigns, and voting are skewed toward the well-educated and wealthy, well-designed surveys elicit responses from everyone. An unbiased poll, based on a well-drawn random sample, treats every respondent, rich and poor, male and female, equally. However, Verba is also quite aware that surveys have limitations. Surveys set the agenda by selecting some topics and not others, they shape the questions asked, and, in many cases, the answers permitted. Nonetheless, given that inequality of wealth, social status, and access are built into our society, the political equality—every respondent opinion counting the same—built into a well-constructed survey is a benefit to our democracy.

Citizen participation is the main way in which the public communicates its needs and preferences to the government and induces the government to be responsive. Since participation depends on resources and resources are unequally distributed, the resulting communication is a biased representation of the public. Thus, the democratic ideal of equal consideration is violated. Sample surveys provide the closest approximation to an unbiased representation of the public because participation in a survey requires no resources and because surveys eliminate the selection bias inherent in the fact that participants in politics are self-selected. The contrast between the participatory process and the sample survey is used to highlight the nature of the bias in the former. Surveys, however, are not seen as a practical way of providing more equal representation.

The study of political participation and the sample survey are closely linked. The latter is the main method by which the former has been studied (Barnes and Kaase 1979; Rosenstone and Hansen 1993; Verba and Nie 1972; Verba, Nie, and Kim 1979; Verba, Schlozman, and Brady 1995). There is a good reason for that connection, since surveys give the researcher access to the "public," an otherwise broad, amorphous, and hard-to-deal-with phenomenon. Surveys tell us what the public does and provide data for analyses of why they do it.

Surveys are especially useful for dealing with issues of democratic representation. Participation is a mechanism for representation, a means by which governing officials are informed of the preferences and needs of the public and are induced to respond to those preferences and needs. It is crucial, therefore, to know how well or how badly the participatory system represents the public to those leaders. But how do we know what the "real" picture is, the interests, preferences, and needs of the public? The sample survey is key to answering this question. In the work on participation by Verba, Schlozman, and Brady

(1995), the representative sample survey was used to provide baseline information on the state of the public—its needs and preferences—in order to ascertain the extent to which the messages communicated by the active citizens distort the situation of the public as a whole.

There is a close connection between subject and method in this research, between citizen participation and representative democracy, on the one hand, and survey research, on the other. The sample survey is a major social science tool. In addition, it is a technology with an important influence on representative democracy. The nature of the technology, particularly the use of random sampling, has an intimate connection with issues of representation. Social science technology, the political theory of representation, and some real issues in contemporary American politics all come together in relation to political surveys.

Surveys create information that would not otherwise exist. What would our democracy be like if no one had invented them? In particular, I want to consider the social survey as a means of political participation. Citizens participate as voters, protesters, letter writers, campaign contributors, and in many other ways. That participation is one of the major means by which governing officials learn about the needs and preferences of the public. It is not the only means, of course; interest groups and the media also provide input. But citizen activity is perhaps the major way the public's needs and preferences are communicated to governing elites. When citizens participate as respondents, what is added to that flow of information by surveys? In trying to answer this question, I hope to address not only the role of surveys but also some more general questions about the nature of democratic representation.

Political Equality

The problem in representation with which I wish to deal is as follows: Democracy implies responsiveness by governing elites to the needs and preferences of the citizenry. More than that, it implies equal responsiveness; in the democratic ideal, elected officials should give equal consideration to the needs and preferences of all citizens. This equal consideration is embodied most clearly in the principle of one person, one vote.

Equality, as we all know, is one of the more complex and multidimensioned concepts we have, given the variety of factors on which it can be based and the fundamental heterogeneity of human beings. Let me briefly indicate what I have in mind. I am not concerned with the extent to which the government in fact treats all citizens equally in the policies it produces; what that would mean and whether it is possible is beyond me. I want to deal with a narrower but still basic issue. Rather than looking at the results of the policy process, I want to focus on the extent to which governing officials have the capacity to provide equal consideration, in particular, whether they have equal information about the needs and preferences of all citizens. If some citizens are invisible, one cannot respond to them.

This means, in turn, that citizens have to supply that information. Thus, if the government is to have the capability of giving equal consideration to the needs and preferences of all citizens, the public must be equally capable of providing that information. They must provide information about themselves—who they are, what they want, what they need. If citizen activity is the main way in which that is done, then democratic responsiveness depends on citizen participation, and equal responsiveness depends on equal participation.

Of course, things do not work out that way. Citizen voices are very unequal. Not everyone votes. More important, there are many more ways in which citizens can be active, and here, of course, voices are more unequal. Only small proportions of the citizenry work in campaigns or make contributions. There may be a flood of letters to Washington and, more recently, a flood of faxes and e-mail. But only a small proportion of the public uses these means, and that minority is not a random sample of the population; it comes disproportionately from the more advantaged members of society (Verba and Nie 1972; Verba, Schlozman, and Brady 1995).

All this means that governing officials receive more information about needs and preferences from some parts of the public than from others. If we believe that each individual is the best judge of his or her needs and preferences, then the differential expression of these needs and preferences through differential activity levels means that officials receive a biased view of the public.

In a market—in an economic system—such differential engagement is expected and poses no problem. Customer voices, as revealed by their consumer behavior, are not equal. People have different preferences and different budget constraints. No one expects equality in a market-based economy with differential income and wealth.

What about politics? Here, too, preferences vary; some people want things from the government, others do not; and those who want things want different things. Budget constraints also differ. Some people have more resources than others—money, time, skills, connections—and these enable them to act and act effectively. This is what explains differential political activity and the resulting bias in information received by the government.

That some are active and some quiescent is inevitable. But it makes a big difference whether the quiescence is due to preference or resources—to not wanting to act or to being unable to act. If people are not active because they have nothing they want from the government or because they choose to allocate their time to other activities, this poses little challenge to the notion of equal consideration of the needs and preferences of all. But if they are not active because they do not have the resources to be active, that is more of a challenge.

In his recent book, *Inequality Reexamined* (1992), Amartya Sen argues for an approach to equality based on the equal capability to achieve one's goals. It is an attractive notion in relation to political equality. It is something less than equality of outcome—policies that treat everyone equally. But it is something more than the usual notion of equality of opportunity, which ordinarily refers to the absence of barriers to accomplishment. In Sen's approach, equal capability includes the absence of barriers and the presence of the means or the resources needed to accomplish one's objectives. The participatory system in the United States today provides equality of opportunity in that there are few if any legal impediments to political activity. But it is a system based on unequal resources and, therefore, unequal capabilities.

Surveys in American Political Life

This is the background to my concern with surveys. Citizens also participate as respondents. The sample survey is a special source of information about the public because the citizen voice expressed does not, as does the participatory voice, depend on having resources or—and this adds an important complexity—on being motivated to participate. This makes the survey a special kind of voice of the people, with some interesting advantages and disadvantages.

The pioneers of political surveys, Gallup, Crossley, and Roper, were optimistic about this new technique. Surveys, they predicted, would be widely used, would bring science and precision into an area where there had previously just been speculation, and would create a new and more responsive democracy (Converse 1987, Gallup and Rae 1940).

They were right about how much surveys would be used. Public opinion polls have become ubiquitous in politics. No political campaign can be conducted without them. Polls provide information that did not previously exist. They allow adjustments of campaign strategies to the winds of opinion, something impossible before polling, when a campaign strategy would be set at the beginning of a campaign and basically adhered to. Anthony Downs predicts that campaign managers will steer their parties and candidates toward the middle of the distribution of opinions. That may be the approach dictated by the logic of vote maximization, but one can only steer in that direction if one knows where the median voter is located. Now, surveys give both parties information on this and may indeed allow campaigners to follow the dictates of theory (Geer 1991).

Polls are closely watched between elections. A presidential administration without a pollster is as unlikely as one without a national security advisor. From the President of the United States on down, elected officials monitor presidential popularity and the response of the public to policy initiatives. The presidential approval questions—one of the longest series of replicated questions—are a running retrospective evaluation of the chief executive's performance. The evidence seems fairly clear that they affect the ability of the president to be effective in Washington (Brody 1991, Edwards 1980, Rivers and Rose 1985). In addition, polls give some content to the level of public support by dealing with the reactions of the public to particular policies. Polls on every issue, large and small, appear in the media. Indeed, virtually every report on a current issue—from Medicare to Bosnia to the O.J. Simpson trial—contains information on what the public thinks. The range is very wide. Surveys hold, as it were, the mirror up to the nation.

Surveys are, I have always believed, a peculiarly U.S. product. The survey industry is now worldwide, but there are good reasons why it developed in and diffused from the United States as an academic research tool, as an instrument in politics, and as a technique for commerce. It fits the consumer-oriented U.S. economy. It fits U.S. culture, where individuals are supposed to have ideas and express them, and where people are accustomed to listening and talking to strangers. And it fits the U.S. polity, where institutions are weak, and therefore the views and attitudes of citizens—as autonomous individuals—make more of a difference in their political behavior than is the case where a person's party, religion, or ethnicity is more predictive,

Surveys as Science, Surveys as Representation

Two main features of the sample survey make it particularly attractive in the U.S. context: its "scientificness" and representativeness (Herbst 1993). Our society vacillates between a belief in science and the expert and a belief in populism and the wisdom of the ordinary citizen. Surveys satisfy both. They give us a scientific measure of the people's will. It is no wonder that surveys play such a major role in the market, in politics, and in academic research.

Surveys produce just what democracy is supposed to produce—equal representation of all citizens. The sample survey is rigorously egalitarian; it is designed so that each citizen has an equal chance to participate and an equal voice when participating. Here is where science and political representation meet. In the social sciences one of the great threats to valid inference, perhaps the most common, is selection bias (King, Keohane, and Verba 1994). Researchers go to great lengths to avoid it. The random sample is a method for eliminating bias. Survey design eliminates bias in two ways: The respondent does not self-select to enter the survey (that is why we reject mail-in polls using forms clipped out of magazines), and the interviewers are given careful instructions as to whom they should select (that is why we reject quota sampling).

Surveys are by no means perfectly random. Poll respondents are not perfectly representative. Some are hard to find; increasingly, many refuse to participate. Pollsters seek out the respondents, but many cannot be reached, a problem especially severe for telephone surveys. Nor are those who cannot be reached a random group. They tend to be like those uncounted by the census—people with no stable dwelling place, people who are missed by society in general. Once contacted, people may refuse to take part, a growing problem in recent years. In the early days of the NES, refusal rates were below 10%. In recent years, surveys such as NES or the General Social Survey (GSS) of the National Opinion Research Center have been experiencing refusal rates in the 25–30% range.[1]

Surveys are not perfectly representative but offer, nevertheless, a better cross-section of the public than do almost any other means, and certainly they are more representative than any of the modes of citizen activity. Surveys provide us with a relatively unbiased view of the public by combining science and representativeness, indeed, by achieving representativeness through science. They are very like elections in which each individual has an equal voice only better. They get better turnout, since good surveys seek out the participants and do not passively wait for them to come to the polls. They get richer information. The vote says little about the preferences of voters except in the narrow sense of their choice of candidate. Surveys can probe preferences on many issues. Indeed, one of the uses to which surveys are put is the reduction in mandate uncertainty after an election. And surveys are more continuous; they monitor the public between elections.

Random and Biased Selection: Social Surveys and the Real World of Politics

The essence of the science of surveys and the essence of the representativeness of surveys are both found in the random processes by which participants are selected. But this also makes surveys very unreal. The processes by which participants are selected are fundamentally different in the controlled world of the social survey and the real world of political participation. Politics may be studied with techniques that try to eliminate selection bias—that is what our profession is all about—but real life is dominated by selection bias. We select the circumstances that then affect our social and economic life. We choose schools, jobs, spouses, locations. We choose within constraints to be sure, but the constraints are by no means constant or random across individuals. The constraints are biased as well.

The same happens in political life. The recent analysis by Verba, Schlozman, and Brady (1995) of the processes by which citizens come to be active is, in fact, a study of selection bias in the real world. Citizens differ in motivation and resources; thus, they self-select to take part in politics because of this differential motivation and because they are differentially constrained by resources. This biased selection process produces a biased participatory population. The voices of the well educated and the well heeled sound more loudly.

Each method of selection—unbiased survey sampling and the socially structured real world processes of selection—produces a different result. Random sample surveys are statistically sound, and they treat each individual qua individual the same. Polls provide information about the public as a whole, motivated or unmotivated, resource rich or resource poor, rather than about those who make their presence known through their political participation. Polls are thus an important tool for equal representation. This also means that polls take no account of race or ethnicity, wealth or education, passion or political commitment. In short, they ignore the mainsprings of political life, and this makes them very artificial.

Of what use are such artificial measures of the public? Here is where surveys intersect with one of the basic issues of citizen representation: the meaning of quiescence. Ordinary modes of citizen activity—voting, writing letters, going to a protest, taking part in a campaign or a community project—allow quiescence; they are voluntary, and no one has to take part and express preferences. Surveys do not let people be quiescent; they chase them down and ask them questions. If people are hard to find, the good survey looks for them, calling again and again. And random-digit dialing rather than phone book listings are used in order to catch those would-be shirkers who get unlisted numbers so they can avoid their civic obligation to take phone calls during dinner....

Motivation and the Politics of Abortion

Consider motivation or the lack of it. Much activity derives from the greater intensity of preferences among the activists. The examples of the intensely concerned minority are legion; indeed, they are the basis for much of the political action in the United States. I will choose one example from our research, the politics of abortion (Verba, Schlozman, and Brady 1995, chapter 14). The public at large—as revealed by surveys—is divided on abortion rights. Exactly how they divide depends on the questions asked. Most citizens are not pro or anti; they are pro under some circumstances and anti under others. On balance, however, the public tilts in a pro-choice direction. Twice as many respondents in our survey are in the farthest pro-choice position as are in the farthest pro-life position. In addition, those with the strongest pro-choice views have more participatory resources than do those with the strongest pro-life views. They are three times as likely to have a college education and substantially more likely to belong to an organization. They are the kinds of people you would expect to be more active in politics, and they are. That activity, however, is spread across all sorts of issues. Those who take the more extreme pro-life positions are not particularly well endowed with participatory resources, tending on average to be less affluent and less skilled. They are, however, very motivated—intense in their views, concentrated on that particular issue, and likely to act on that issue. Thus, they provide much more of the action, especially the heated action like protesting, on abortion.

The concentration of activity among the pro-life respondents in our study is striking. We asked them about the subject of their activity, whether some issue motivated their letter to a representative, or the protest in which they took part, or their activity in a campaign, and so on. We can then see how much of an individual's activity—across various acts—is focused on the same subject. Eleven percent of the activity of the pro-choice respondents concerns abortion; they are very active but are active about many things. The pro-life respondents, 58% of whose activity concerns abortion, are much more single-minded.

If elected officials heed the voices of the active citizens, they will give greater attention to the pro-life group than its proportion of the population warrants. That does not seem inappropriate, even in the face of the notion that each person's preferences should be given equal weight. There are preferences and preferences, and those strongly held ought to weigh more.

In such a situation, polls do not and should not eliminate the special consideration likely to be given to the intense minority. Rather, they mitigate it somewhat by providing information about preferences in the public at large. Officials can know, at least, that the activists do not represent the population as a whole. And the existence of a gap between the public as a whole and the activists can be used as part of the debate about the proper policy to follow. The quiescence of inactive citizens when they could be active if they cared more justifies paying less attention to them, but knowing their views adds an important ingredient to the political debate. . . .

Survey Democracy?

I am certainly not recommending a government by survey. Gallup referred to the survey as a "sampling referendum," but even he did not think of it as a means of legislating. Rather, I am arguing that one has to view surveys in the context of the participatory process, which exists with or without surveys. Some argue that surveys create a leadership which follows the polls rather than leading. But surveys per se do not make some leaders abandon leadership to follow public whim. In the absence of surveys, such leaders would still sway with the wind of opinion. The wind would just blow from different quarters, more likely from the better parts of town.

Polls are thus a way to give everyone a voice, but they do not reflect the strongest of voices. The information polls communicate may be equal, but it is also limited. And the limitation derives from the strongest feature of polls, the fact that they represent all citizens equally. What message is sent by a method that gives voice to all citizens, with little regard for their level of information or their motivation to participate, and one whose messages are all *in response* to questions selected by and posed by strangers at the door? Certainly, the messages are not the clearest.

One limitation on the role of surveys relates to agendas. First, because the initiative is taken by the surveyor rather than the surveyed, the agenda reflects the interests of the poll taker. It gives the inarticulate a chance to express their views and their concerns, but only on the issues that the surveyor thinks are important. Second, since surveyors have their own agenda—to increase readership, or find information to help a particular candidate, or test a pet academic theory—the set of issues covered may be very different from that which is on the mind of the respondents.

Another limitation has to do with the questions asked: The answers received depend on them. The voice of the citizenry, especially the otherwise quiescent who are of special interest here, can sound very different depending on what is asked.

There is another qualification on the ability of surveys to equalize the voice of the resource poor. Few resources may be needed to respond to a survey, but real resources are required to conduct a survey. Although the selection of respondents may not be biased, the selection of when to have a survey and what to ask (and how to interpret the data) certainly are. This gives a louder voice to the more affluent in several ways. Well-heeled campaigners and wealthy interests can afford to take their own polls. They can then use them as they want, including selective reporting. On top of that, to do a poll one needs to hire professionals, which takes money, and campaigns thus value contributions of money rather than time. Money is, in turn, much more stratified than time; the affluent have money (of course), but time is more equally available to both the advantaged and the disadvantaged (Verba, Schlozman, and Brady 1995, chapter 10). Thus, the survey process reintroduces some of the socioeconomic stratification found in political activity through decisions as to when, what, and whom to survey.

Another qualification is that what people answer—what they think is important, how they evaluate policies and politicians—is in good part a reaction to what they hear from the media or from governing officials. Thus, the questions asked and the answers given do not come from a separate autonomous public but are affected by the processes of politics and policy that they may, in turn, influence. As in so many other areas of politics and political analysis, there is a serious problem of endogeneity.

Finally, polls provide low-grade information. Answers to closed questions do not capture the richness of individuals' views. And the views, themselves, are often ill-formed. Indeed, it is commonplace to note that the opinions are often nonexistent until the question is asked and the respondent is faced with the necessity to answer.

This last point, about the quality of information in polls, needs qualification. We have all been trained to be suspicious of survey results on issues far from the consciousness of respondents, when they are asked for opinions on some policy matter. But surveys can give better information than that. It all depends on the subject of the questions. Some information about the public is fairly solid—its positions on issues, its social circumstances, its needs; people know the answers, and the answers are stable. In some of the examples I gave above, questions were asked about whether the respondents participated in Social Security or in AFDC and whether they had faced serious problems paying for necessities in the past year. These are important questions about citizen need, and the individual citizen—of whatever level of sophistication—knows the answers better than anyone. Citizens know their own life circumstances. They also know their own values, and although their values may be in conflict one with another (whose values are not?), they are likely to be fairly stable.[2]

Can the Quiescent Gain a Voice?

This brings me back to my concern with the politically quiescent. How can constraints be broken to achieve the democratic ideal of equal voice? Surveys break the constraints by seeking out those who would otherwise be inactive, but the voice is not very strong or clear. Another means of bringing in the quiescent is political mobilization. Resource poor and apathetic citizens can be brought out to vote or take other actions by social movements or political organizations. There are many historical examples, the civil rights movement being one of the most important. Our research shows, however, that for most activity, the forces of mobilization bring in the same people who would be active spontaneously. There is a vast network of what one might call day-today political recruiters, people who call for campaign contributions, get people out to a community meeting, or mobilize citizens to write their representative. These recruiters seek those with motivation and resources. The recruitment process largely reinforces the other biased processes that lead to political activity (Brady, Schloz-man, and Verba 1995).

Political inequality is, thus, embedded deeply in American society. Can the ideal of political equality be achieved? More modestly, can we move closer to that ideal? It is hard to see how. The constraint on political participation from unequal resources derives from the basic institutions in society, from differential education and differential economic position. Mobilization breaks the pattern from time to time, but the system of mobilization is also embedded in the same set of institutions, and mobilization generally reinforces the inequality of political voice. Surveys, if done well and used honestly (two significant qualifications), may help, but they can hardly change things. Greater equality in our basic institutions—greater income equality and, more important perhaps, greater educational equality—would certainly help equalize political resources. That is a tall order, and I certainly have no scheme to achieve it nor any expectation that others do either.

NOTES

Sidney Verba is the Carl H. Pforzheimer University Professor and Director, Harvard University Library, Harvard University, Cambridge, MA 02138.

The data for this paper come largely from the Citizen Participation Study, a large-scale survey of activism in U.S. political life supported by the National Science Foundation as well as the Ford, Hewlett, and Spencer foundations. The main analysis of these data can be found in Verba, Schlozman, and Brady (1995). I am grateful to Kay L. Schlozman and Henry E. Brady for helpful comments and the collaboration out of which much of this paper grew.

1. The nonparticipants in surveys are analyzed by Brehm (1993, chapter 2), who calls them phantom respondents. They differ from the public as a whole but in somewhat surprising ways. Respondents overrepresent the elderly and women, which is not a surprise. According to Brehm's analysis, however, the underrepresentation of the poor and minorities that we might have expected does not appear in the data. The patterns are somewhat varied across survey organizations, but it appears as if the NES and the GSS both overrepresent African Americans and underrepresent the rich. Education is the best single predictor of political activity. NES telephone interviews are consistent with this, as they underestimate the proportion in the population with less than a high school education. Yet, the face-to-face interviews of NES and GSS overrepresent those with lower education levels. Academic surveys, although not perfect, have better response rates than media polls, many of which have rates that call the accuracy of the survey into question (Brady and Orren 1992).

2. Attitudes on complex public policies may be ill-informed and changeable. But as John Zaller (1993) has argued, the "on-the-fly" answers that polls elicit have a certain logic to them. They often reflect a balancing, not a careful balancing but a balancing nevertheless, of alternative values. They are a form of quick-and-dirty reasoning.

REFERENCES

Barnes, Samuel I., and Max Kaase. 1979. *Political Action: Mass Participation in Five Western Democracies.* Beverly Hills, CA: Sage Publications.

Brady, Henry E., and Gary Orren. 1992. "Polling Pitfalls: Sources of Error in Media Surveys." In *Media Polls and American Democracy*, ed. Thomas E. Mann and Gary R. Orren. Washington, D.C.: Brookings.

Brady, Henry E., Kay L. Schlozman, and Sidney Verba. 1995. "Prospecting for Participants: A Rational Expectations Approach to Mobilizing Activists." Presented at the Annual Meeting of the American Political Science Association, Chicago.

Brehm, John. 1993. *The Phantom Respondents: Opinion Surveys and Political Representation*. Ann Arbor: University of Michigan Press.

Brody, Richard. 1991. *Assessing the President*. Stanford: Stanford University Press.

Converse, Jean. 1987. *Survey Research in the United States*. Berkeley: University of California Press.

Downs, Anthony. 1957. *The Economic Theory of Democracy*. New York: Harper and Row.

Edwards, George C., III. 1980. *Presidential Influence on Congress*. San Francisco: W.H. Freeman.

Gallup, George, Jr., and Saul Rae. 1940. *The Pulse of Democracy*. New York: Simon.

Geer, John C. 1991. "Critical Alignment and the Public Opinion Poll." *Journal of Politics* 53:435–53.

Herbst, Susan. 1993. *Numbered Voices: How Opinion Polling Has Shaped American Politics*. Chicago: University of Chicago Press.

King, Gary, Robert O. Keohane, and Sidney Verba. 1994. *Designing Social Inquiry: Scientific Inference in Qualitative Research*. Princeton: Princeton University Press.

Rivers, Douglas, and Nancy Rose. 1985. "Passing the President's Program: Public Opinion and Presidential Power in Congress." *American Journal of Political Science* 29:183–96.

Rosenstone, Steven J., and John Mark Hansen. 1993. *Mobilization, Participation, and Democracy in America*. New York: Macmillan.

Sen, Amartya. 1992. *Inequality Reexamined*. Cambridge: Harvard University Press.

Wolfinger, Raymond E., and Steven J. Rosenstone. 1980. *Who Votes?* New Haven: Yale University Press.

Verba, Sidney, Kay Lehman Schlozman, and Henry E. Brady. 1995. *Voice and Equality: Civic Voluntarism in American Democracy*. Cambridge: Harvard University Press.

Verba, Sidney, and Norman H. Nie. 1972. *Participation in America: Political Democracy and Social Equality*. New York: Harper and Row. (Reprinted by University of Chicago Press, 1987.)

Verba, Sidney, Norman H. Nie, and Jae-on Kim. 1979. *Participation and Political Equality: A Seven Nation Comparison*. New York: Cambridge University Press, 1978. (Reprinted by University of Chicago Press, 1987.)

Zaller, John. 1993. *The Nature and Origins of Mass Opinions*. Cambridge and New York: the University Press.

4.6 Cass Sunstein, "Polarization and Cybercascades" (2007)

Tocqueville's concern that a too uniform public opinion constrained freedom of thought and diversity of opinion in America has, for Cass Sunstein, given way to concern that the Internet creates group polarization and a high degree of fragmentation in public opinion. The Internet makes it easy for like-minded people to find each other and reinforce each others' views, perhaps making them more extreme, without coming in contact with the moderating influence of other views.

Sunstein is concerned that modern technology encourages people to accept unreliable information about issues they do not personally know much about. In informational and reputational "cascades," individuals accept information or refuse to challenge information they doubt so as not to seem out of step with others. Examples include information as wildfire and the phenomenon of information tipping points. The phrase "going viral" suggests the nature of Sunstein's concerns.

Group Polarization and the Internet

Group polarization is unquestionably occurring on the Internet. It seems plain that the Internet is serving, for many, as a breeding group for extremism, precisely because like-minded people are deliberating with greater ease and frequency with one another, and often without hearing contrary views. Repeated exposure to an extreme position, with the suggestion that many people hold that position, will predictably move those exposed, and likely predisposed, to believe in it. One consequence can be a high degree of frag-mentation, as diverse people, not originally fixed in their views and perhaps not so far apart, end up in extremely different places, simply because of what they are reading and viewing. Another consequence can be a high degree of error and confusion. YouTube is a lot of fun, and in a way it is a genuine democratizing force; but there is a risk that isolated clips, taken out of context, will lead like-minded people to end up with a distorted understanding of some issue, person, or practice . . . .

Cascades

The phenomenon of group polarization is closely related to the widespread phenom-enon of "social cascades." No discussion of social fragmentation and emerging commu-nications technologies would be complete without an understanding of cascades—above all because they become more likely when information, including false information, can be spread to hundreds, thousands, or even millions by the simple press of a button.

It is obvious that many social groups, both large and small, move rapidly and dramatically in the direction of one or another set of beliefs or actions.[1] These sorts of "cascades" typically involve the spread of information; in fact they are usually driven by information. Most of us lack direct or entirely reliable information about many matters of importance—whether global warming is a serious problem, whether there is a risk of war in India, whether al Qaeda is very dangerous, whether a lot of sugar is actu-ally bad for you, whether Mars really exists, whether Pluto is a planet. If you lack a great deal of private information, you might well rely on the statements or actions of others.

To understand the dynamics here, we need to distinguish between two kinds of cascades: informational and reputational. In an informational cascade, people cease relying, at a certain point, on their private information or opinions. They decide instead on the basis of the signals conveyed by others. It follows that the behavior of the first few people can, in theory, produce similar behavior from countless followers. A stylized example: Suppose that Joan is unsure whether hybrid vehicles are in fact good for the environment; she may be moved in the direction of enthusiasm if Mary thinks that hybrid vehicles are good for the environment. If Joan and Mary are both favorably disposed toward hybrid vehicles, Carl may end up agreeing with them, at least if he lacks reliable independent information to the contrary. If Joan, Mary, and Carl believe that hybrid vehicles have large benefits, Don will have to have a good deal of confidence to reject their shared conclusion. And if Joan, Mary, Carl, and Don present a united front on the issue, others may well go along . . . .

We can imagine the possibility of *reputational cascades*, parallel to their informational siblings.[2] In a reputational cascade, people think that they know what is right, or what is likely to be right, but they nonetheless go along with the crowd in order to maintain the good opinion of others. Even the most confident people sometimes fall prey to this pressure, silencing themselves in the process. Fearing the wrath of others, people might not publicly contest practices and values that they privately abhor. The social practice of sexual harassment long predated the legal notion of "sexual harassment," and the innumerable women who were subject to harassment did not like it. But mostly they were silent, simply because they feared the consequences of public complaint. It is interesting to wonder how many current practices fall in the same general category: they produce harm, and are known to produce harm, but they persist because most of those who are harmed believe that they will suffer if they object in public.

To see how a reputational cascade might work, suppose that Albert suggests that global warming is a serious problem, and that Barbara concurs with Albert, not because she actually thinks that Albert is right, but because she does not wish to seem, to Albert, to be ignorant or indifferent to environmental protection. If Albert and Barbara seem to agree that global warming is a serious problem, Cynthia might not contradict them publicly and might even appear to share their judgment, not because she believes that judgment to be correct, but because she does not want to face their hostility or lose their good opinion. It is easy to see how this process might generate a reputational cascade. Once Albert, Barbara, and Cynthia offer a united front on the issue, their friend David might be most reluctant to contradict them even if he thinks that they are wrong. The apparent views of Albert, Barbara, and Cynthia carry information; that apparent view might be right. But even if David thinks that they are wrong and has information supporting that conclusion, he might be most reluctant to take them on publicly.

Cybercascades: Information as Wildfire and Tipping Points

The Internet greatly increases the likelihood of diverse but inconsistent cascades. Cybercascades occur every day. Here is some fun and illuminating evidence from the domain of music.[3] Experimenters created an artificial music market, including 14,341 participants. The participants were given a list of previously unknown songs from unknown bands; they were asked to listen to a brief selection of any songs that interested them, to decide what songs (if any) to download, and to assign a rating to the songs they chose. About half of the participants were asked to make their decisions independently, based on the names of the bands and the songs and their own judgment about the quality of the music. About half of the participants could see how many times each song had been downloaded by other participants. These participants were also randomly assigned to one or another of eight possible "worlds," with each evolving on its own; those in any particular world could see only the downloads in their own world. A key question was whether people would be affected by the choices of others—and whether different music would become popular in the different "worlds."

Did social influences matter? Did cascades develop? There is not the slightest doubt. In all eight worlds, individuals are more likely to download songs that had been previously downloaded in significant numbers, and less likely to download songs that had not been so popular. Most strikingly, the success of songs is unpredictable; most songs can become very popular or very unpopular, with much depending on the choices of the first downloaders. The identical song can be a hit or a failure, simply because other people, at the start, were seen to choose to download it or not. To be sure, there is some relationship between quality and success. "In general, the 'best' songs never do very badly, and the 'worst' songs never do extremely well, but almost any other result is possible." And in terms of their market shares, the best songs turn out to be the most unpredictable of all! They can do exceptionally well and also pretty badly, depending on whether social influences—the previous choices of others—suggest that they are worth downloading . . . .

And if this is true for music, it is likely to be true for many other things as well, including movies, books, political candidates, and even ideas. ("Everyone is flocking to candidate X" or "idea Y is really catching on.") Candidates and ideas may enjoy stunning success (or failure), simply because social dynamics give them an early boost (or not). Here we can see a large effect from collaborative filtering, which may help create, and not merely reflect, individual preferences.

On the Internet, rumors often spread rapidly, and sometimes cascades are involved. . . . In the 1990s, many thousands of hours of Internet time were spent on elaborating paranoid claims about alleged nefarious activities, including murder, on the part of President Bill Clinton. A number of sites and discussion groups spread rumors and conspiracy theories of various sorts. . . . Both terrorism and voting behavior have been prime areas for false rumors and occasional cascade effects. In 2002, a widely circulated email said that the Pentagon had not, in fact, been hit by a Boeing aircraft on September 11. In 2004, many people were duly informed that electronic voting machines had been hacked, producing massive fraud. (If you're interested in more examples, you might consult http://snopes.com, a website dedicated to widely disseminated falsehoods, many of them spread via the Internet.) . . .

With respect to information in general, there is even a "tipping point" phenomenon, creating a potential for dramatic shifts in opinion. After being presented with new information, people typically have different "thresholds" for choosing to believe or do something new or different. As the more likely believers—that is, people with low thresholds—come to a certain belief or action, people with somewhat higher thresholds then join them, soon producing a significant group in favor of the view in question. At that point, those with still higher thresholds may join, possibly to a point where a critical mass is reached, making large groups, societies, or even nations "tip."[4] The result of this process can be to produce snowball or cascade effects, as large groups of people end up believing something—whether or not that something is true or false—simply because other people in the relevant community seem to believe that it is true.

There is a great deal of experimental evidence of informational cascades, which are easy to induce in the laboratory,[5] real-world phenomena also have a great deal to do with cascade effects. Consider, for example, going to college, smoking, participating in political protests, voting for third-party candidates, striking, recycling, filing lawsuits, using birth control, rioting, even leaving bad dinner parties.[6] In all of these cases, people are greatly influenced by what others do. Often a tipping point will be reached. Sometimes we give an aura of inevitability to social developments, with the thought that deep cultural forces have led to (for example) an increase in smoking or protesting or a candidate's success, when in fact social influences have produces an outcome that could easily have been avoided. The Internet is an obvious breeding ground for cascades, and as a result, thousands or even millions of people who consult sources of a particular kind will move in one or another direction or even believe something that is quite false.

The good news is that the Internet is easily enlisted to debunk false rumors as well as to start them. For this reason, most such rumors do no harm. But it remains true that the opportunity to spread apparently credible information to so many people can induce fear, error, and confusion in a way that threatens many social goals, including democratic ones. As we have seen, this danger takes on a particular form in a balkanized speech market, as local cascades lead people in dramatically different directions. When this happens, correctives, even via the Internet, may work too slowly or not at all, simply because people are not listening to one another.

NOTES

1. See, e.g., Sushil Bikhchandani et al., "Learning from the Behavior of Others," *J. Ecom. Persp.*, Summer 1998, 151; Andrew Daughety and Jennifer Reinganum, "Stampede to Judgment," *Am. L. & Ec. Rev.* 1 (1999): 158.
2. See Kuran, *Private Truths, Public Lies.*
3. See Matthew J. Salganik et al., "Experimental Study of Inequality and Unpredictability in an Artificial Cultural Market," *Science* 311 (2006): 854.
4. See Mark Granovetter, "Threshold Models of Collective Behavior," *Am. J. Sociology* 83 (1978): 1420; for a vivid popular treatment, see Malcolm Gladwell, *The Tipping Point* (Boston: Little, Brown, 2000).
5. See Lisa Anderson and Charles Holt, "Information Cascades in the Laboratory," *Am Econ Rev* 87 (1997): 847.
6. Several of these examples are discussed in ibid. and in Granovetter, "Threshold Models," 1422–24.

Discussion Questions

1. How would you describe the tone of the exchange between Abigail and John Adams over women's legal rights? Describe how the political culture of the day defined the relationship between men and women, especially husbands and wives, and then try to put this exchange of letters within the broader context of that relationship.
2. Do you share Tocqueville's concern with the "tyranny of the majority" in American life?
3. Do the readings in this chapter suggest that public opinion shapes government policy or that government policy shapes public opinion or some complex mix of the two? Which authors seem to take which view and what arguments do they offer for their view?
4. Though almost two centuries apart, Alexis de Toqueville and Cass Sunstein both are concerned about peer pressure, about how what those around you think impacts and structures what you think. How are their concerns similar and different and what are the main messages we should take from them?
5. Sidney Verba argues that survey research or polling has the potential to deepen and enrich our democracy. What evidence do you see that he is either right or wrong?

Suggested Additional Reading

Robert S. Erikson and Kent L. Tedin, *American Public Opinion: Its Origins, Content, and Impact*, Updated, 7th ed. (New York: Pearson/Longman, 2007).

Sara Evans, *Born For Liberty: A History of Women in America* (New York: Free Press, 1997).

Samuel P. Huntington, *Who Are We: The Challenges of American National Identity* (New York: Simon and Schuster, 2005).

Douglas Sosnick, et. al., *Applebee's America: How Successful Political, Business, and Religious Leaders Connect with the New American Community* (New York: Simon and Schuster, 2007).

James A. Stimson, *Tides of Consent: How Public Opinion Shapes American Politics* (Cambridge and New York: Cambridge University Press, 2004).

5

The Mass Media and the Political Agenda

Introduction

Throughout American history, politicians and the public have had a love/hate relationship with the media. While the shape and breadth of the media have changed over the course of our history, basic attitudes toward the media have not changed that much. Politicians and the public have always understood that the people must be well and accurately informed if they are to play their proper role in democracy. Yet both have been wary of the media. The public knows that the media act as a filter, selecting some information to present to citizens, from some perspective, while ignoring other information and other perspectives. Politicians love the visibility that the media offers them but they hate public criticism and try to suppress it when they can. The media know that while they perform a critical public service, they are a profit-making business that must attract subsidies, advertising, and subscriptions to keep the lights on.

Thomas Jefferson (1743–1826) was famously ambivalent about the press. In the first selection below (a 1787 letter to Colonel Edward House), Jefferson memorably declared that "were it left to me to decide whether we should have a government without newspapers, or newspapers without a government, I should not hesitate a moment to prefer the latter." After nearly two terms in the White House, where he constantly felt himself the victim of false and malicious reports, Jefferson wrote to John Norvell (1807) that "Nothing can now be believed which is seen in a newspaper. Truth itself becomes suspicious by being put into that polluted vehicle." In calmer moments, Jefferson was the champion of a free press, though often with clenched fists. All politicians and many citizens since Jefferson have shared his ambivalence toward the press.

The famous, many would say infamous, H.L. Mencken (1880–1956) explains why. Mencken, longtime columnist for the *Baltimore Sun*, was the most prominent social critic and political curmudgeon of the first third of the twentieth century. Americans read Mencken's slashing social and political commentary with glee. As the Roaring 20s gave way to the Great Depression, Mencken's star went into decline. The public abandoned him when he spat his venom at Franklin Roosevelt, the New Deal, and U.S. participation in WW II. In the selection below, Mencken explains, only somewhat tongue in check, that newspaper writing is a blood sport.

In *New York Times v. United States* (1971), the Supreme Court supports the good Jefferson's view that the press should operate freely to hold government accountable. Late in the Vietnam War, one Daniel Ellsberg purloined a secret Pentagon history of the war and gave it to the *Washington Post* and the *New York Times.* The Nixon administration sued, claiming that the Pentagon Papers, as they had come to be known, were both stolen and fraught with national secrets. A deeply divided court narrowly found for the newspapers. Associate Justice Hugo Black, writing for the majority, declared that "The Government's power to censor the press was abolished so that the press would remain forever free to censure the Government. The press was protected so that it could bare the secrets of government and inform the people."

In a classic APD piece and the highlight of Chapter 5, Samuel Kernell asks about the mix of national, state, and local news in the nineteenth century. One important historian, Robert Wiebe in a book entitled *The Opening of American Society* (1984), described the early nineteenth-century social landscape as composed of small, autonomous, homogenous "island communities." Kernell collected data about every story published in the Cleveland papers between 1818 and 1876. The data showed a surprising focus on national stories from the earliest days. One of the goals of APD is to confront rich description with relevant data and see if they match up.

Finally, Gadi Wolfsfeld and Diana Owen analyze the rise of "new" media, including the Internet, YouTube, Twitter, and the like, and how they have impacted "old" media and the way we communicate, get our news, and campaign for political office. In our fifth selection, Gadi Wolfsfeld analyzes the power/influence relationship between politicians and journalists and how they have changed with the evolving media landscape. He finds that the more prominent the politician the more likely he or she is to be able to command media attention and shape the content of the coverage—at least until crisis or scandal strikes and then all bets are off. He also finds, as others have, that old media do most of the original reporting and new media mostly re-report, repackage, and comment on old media content.

Diana Owen asks how the expansion of new media have changed political campaigns. Little more than two decades ago, old media, including the mail, radio, and television, were the primary means by which political campaigns communicated with potential voters. The rise and diffusion of new media, including email, blogs, campaign websites, and the Internet in general, have made campaign contacts both more personal and more interactive. The trick for campaigns, of course, is to meld the new media with the old to meet voters where they are and where they are most comfortable. Old media still predominate, especially in television advertising, but young voters are leading the way to the web.

Politicians from Jefferson's day to our own have known that they need the media to get their message out. In normal times, leading politicians can usually control the messages that the media carry about them. But when a crisis strikes or a scandal arises, politicians are rudely reminded that the media is for them a double-edged sword.

5.1 Thomas Jefferson, "Newspapers and Democracy" (1787)

Political instability, particularly Shays Rebellion, a series of assaults on local government authorities by debtor farmers in backcountry Massachusetts, spurred conservatives to call for a more powerful central government capable of putting down such challenges. Their call was answered when Congress called for a Constitutional Convention to meet in Philadelphia in May 1787. As many called for a more powerful central government, Jefferson called for calm and for a realization that popular protest had a legitimate role in democratic government. He called for more education and information so the people could judge correctly and would not feel that rebellion was their only course. Jefferson argued that democracy is best served when the people have "full information of their affairs through the channel of the public papers."

To Colonel Edward Carrington[1]

Paris, January 16, 1787

...The tumults in America I expected would have produced in Europe an unfavorable opinion of our political state. But it has not. On the contrary, the small effect of these tumults seems to have given more confidence in the firmness of our governments. The interposition of the people themselves on the side of government has had a great effect on the opinion here. I am persuaded myself that the good sense of the people will always, be found to be the best army. They may be led astray for a moment, but will soon correct themselves. The people are the only censors of their governors; and even their errors will tend to keep these to the true principles of their institution. To punish these errors too severely would be to suppress the only safeguard of the public liberty. The way to prevent these irregular interpositions of the people, is to give them full information of their affairs through the channel of the public papers, and to contrive that those papers should penetrate the whole mass of the people. The basis of our governments being the opinion of the people, the very first object should be to keep that right; and were it left to me to decide whether we should have a government without newspapers, or newspapers without a government, I should not hesitate a moment to prefer the latter. But I should mean that every man should receive those papers, and be capable of reading them. I am convinced that those societies (as the Indians) which live without government, enjoy in their general mass an infinitely greater degree of happiness than those who live under the European governments. Among the former public opinion is in the place of law, and restrains morals as powerfully as laws ever did anywhere. Among the latter, under pretence of governing, they have divided their nations into two classes, wolves and sheep. I do not exaggerate. This is a true picture of Europe. Cherish, therefore, the spirit of our people, and keep alive their attention. Do not be too severe upon their errors, but reclaim them by enlightening them. If once they become inattentive to the public affairs, you and I, and Congress and Assemblies, Judges and Governors, shall all become wolves. It seems to be the law of our general nature, in spite of individual exceptions; and experience declares that man is the only animal which devours his own kind; for I can apply no milder term to the governments of Europe, and to the general prey of the rich on the poor....

NOTE

1. Carrington was a member of a prominent Virginia family who served in the Revolution and was a member of the Continental Congress.

5.2 H.L. Mencken, "Newspaper Morals" (1914)

H.L. Mencken (1880–1956) was one of the most widely read and incisive social critics, political analysts, and newspapermen of the first third of the twentieth century. He was best known for an acerbic biting wit, which is clearly on display in the selection below. Mencken claims that the secret of newspaper writing is to tell a good story—but in personal and emotional rather than moral and intellectual terms.

With the touch of a sledge hammer social critic, here directed at his own profession of journalism, Mencken argued that the intelligent and educated few do not take their views from newspapers. Hence, newspapers address their real audience, the ignorant and unreflective, whipping them into emotional frenzies against specific persons representing some broader evil. Mencken concluded that newspaper morals cannot be loftier than popular morals and that this is no cause for shame among newspapermen. One wonders whether Jefferson would still have placed his hope in newspapers if he had read Mencken.

I know of no subject, save perhaps baseball, on which the average American newspaper, even in the larger cities, discourses with unfailing sense and understanding

'...I took counsel with an ancient whose service went back to the days of Our American Cousin [a prominent play of the 1850s], asking him what qualities were chiefly demanded by the craft.

'The main idea,' he told me frankly, 'is to be interesting, to write a good story. All else is dross. Of course, I am not against accuracy, fairness, information, learning ... But ... the only way to make them read you is to give them something exciting.'

'You suggest, then,' I ventured, 'a certain—ferocity?'

'I do,' replied my venerable friend. [...] You must give a good show to get a crowd, and a good show means one with slaughter in it.'

[...T]he advice of my ancient counselor kept turning over and over in my memory, and as chance offered I began to act upon it, and whenever I acted upon it I found that it worked. What is more, I found that other newspaper men acted upon it too, some of them quite consciously and frankly, and others through a veil of self-deception, more or less diaphanous. The primary aim of all of them ... was to please the crowd, to give a good show; and the way they set about giving that good show was by first selecting a deserving victim, and then putting him magnificently to the torture. This was their method when they were performing for their own profit only, when their one motive was to make the public read their paper; but it was still their method when they were battling bravely and unselfishly for the public good, and so discharging the highest duty of their profession. They lightened the dull days of midsummer by pursuing recreant aldermen with bloodhounds and artillery, by muckraking unsanitary milk-dealers, or by denouncing Sunday liquor-selling in suburban parks—and they fought constructive campaigns for good government in exactly the same gothic, melodramatic way. Always their first aim was to find a concrete target, to visualize their cause in some definite and defiant opponent. And always their second aim was to shell that opponent until he dropped his arms and took to ignominious flight. It was not enough to maintain and to prove; it was necessary also to pursue and overcome, to lay a specific somebody low, to give the good show aforesaid.

Does this confession of newspaper practice involve a libel upon the American people? Perhaps it does—on the theory, let us say, that the greater the truth, the greater the libel. But I doubt if any reflective newspaper man, however lofty his professional ideals, will ever deny any essential part of that truth. He knows very well that a definite limit is set, not only upon the people's capacity for grasping intellectual concepts, but also upon their capacity for grasping moral concepts. He knows that it is necessary, if he would catch and inflame them, to state his ethical syllogism in the homely terms of their habitual ethical thinking. And he knows that this is best done by dramatizing and vulgarizing it, by filling it with dynamic and emotional significance, by translating all argument for a principle into rage against a man.

In brief, he knows that it is hard for the plain people to *think* about a thing, but easy for them to *feel*. Error, to hold their attention, must be visualized as a villain, and the villain must proceed swiftly to his inevitable retribution. They can understand that process; it is simple, usual, satisfying; it squares with their primitive conception of justice as a form of revenge....

I assume here, as an axiom too obvious to be argued, that the chief appeal of a newspaper, in all such holy causes, is not at all to the educated and reflective minority of citizens, but frankly to the ignorant and unreflective majority. The truth is that it would usually get a newspaper nowhere to address its exhortations to the former, for in the first place they are too few in number to make their support of much value in general engagements, and in the second place it is almost always impossible to convert them into disciplined and useful soldiers. They are too cantankerous for that, too ready with embarrassing strategy of their own. One of the principal marks of an educated man, indeed, is the fact that he does *not* take his opinions from newspapers—not, at any rate, from the militant, crusading newspapers. On the contrary, his attitude toward them is almost always one of frank cynicism, with indifference as its mildest form and contempt as its commonest. He knows that they are constantly falling into false reasoning about the things within his personal knowledge,—that is, within the narrow circle of his special education,—and so he assumes that they make the same, or even worse errors about other things, whether intellectual or moral. This assumption, it may be said at once, is quite justified by the facts....

[The common man] is not interested in anything that does not stir him, and he is not stirred by anything that fails to impinge upon his small stock of customary appetites and attitudes. His daily acts are ordered, not by any complex process of reasoning, but by a continuous process of very elemental feeling. He is not at all responsive to purely intellectual argument, even when its theme is his own ultimate benefit, for such argument quickly gets beyond his immediate interest and experience. But he *is* very responsive to emotional suggestion, particularly when it is crudely and violently made, and it is to this weakness that the newspapers must ever address their endeavors. In brief, they must try to arouse his horror, or indignation, or pity, or simply his lust for slaughter. Once they have done that, they have him safely by the nose. He will follow blindly until his emotion wears out. He will be ready to believe anything, however absurd, so long as he is in his state of psychic tumescence.

In the reform campaigns which periodically rock our large cities,—and our small ones, too,—the newspapers habitually make use of this fact. Such campaigns are not intellectual wars upon erroneous principles, but emotional wars upon errant men: they always revolve around the pursuit of some definite, concrete, fugitive malefactor, or group of malefactors. That is to say, they belong to popular sport rather than to the science of government; the impulse behind them is always far more orgiastic than reflective. For good government in the abstract, the people of the United States seem to have no liking, or, at all events, no passion. It is impossible to get them stirred up over it, or even to make them give serious thought to it. They seem to assume that it is a mere phantasm of theorists, a political will-o'-the-wisp, a utopian dream—wholly uninteresting, and probably full of dangers and tricks. The very discussion of it bores them unspeakably, and those papers which habitually discuss it logically and unemotionally—for example, the New York *Evening Post*—are diligently avoided by the mob. What the mob thirsts for is not good government in itself, but the merry chase of a definite exponent of bad government. The newspaper that discovers such an exponent—or, more accurately, the newspaper that discovers dramatic and overwhelming evidence against him—has all the material necessary for a reform wave of the highest emotional intensity. All that it need do is to goad the victim into a fight. Once he has formally joined the issue, the people will do the rest. They are always ready for a man-hunt, and their favorite quarry is the man of politics. If no such prey is at hand, they will turn to wealthy debauchees, to fallen Sunday-school superintendents, to money barons, to white-slave traders, to unsedulous chiefs of police. But their first choice is the boss.

In assaulting bosses, however, a newspaper must look carefully to its ammunition, and to the order and interrelation of its salvos. There is such a thing, at the start, as overshooting the mark, and the danger thereof is very serious. The people must be aroused by degrees, gently at first, and then with more and more ferocity. They are not capable of reaching the maximum of indignation at one leap: even on the side of pure emotion they have their rigid limitations. And this, of course, is because even emotion must have a quasi-intellectual basis, because even indignation must arise out of facts. One fact at a time! If a newspaper printed the whole story of a political boss's misdeeds in a single article, that article would have scarcely any effect whatever, for it would be far too long for the average reader to read and absorb. He would never get to the end of it, and the part he actually traversed would remain muddled and distasteful in his memory. Far from arousing an emotion in him, it would arouse only ennui, which is the very antithesis of emotion. He cannot read more than three columns of any one subject without tiring: 6,000 words, I should say, is the extreme limit of his appetite. And the nearer he is pushed to that limit, the greater the strain upon his psychic digestion. He can absorb a single capital fact, leaping from a headline, at one colossal gulp; but he could not down a dissertation in twenty. And the first desideratum in a headline is that it deal with a single and capital fact. It must be 'McGinnis Steals $1,257,867.25,' not 'McGinnis Lacks Ethical Sense.'

Moreover, a newspaper article which presumed to tell the whole of a thrilling story in one gargantuan installment would lack the dynamic element, the quality of mystery and suspense. Even if it should achieve the miracle of arousing the reader to a high pitch of excitement, it would let him drop again next day. If he is to be kept in his frenzy long enough for it to be dangerous to the common foe, he must be led into it gradually. The newspaper in charge of the business must harrow him, tease him, promise him, hold him. It is thus that his indignation is transformed from a state of being into a state of gradual and cumulative becoming; it is thus that reform takes on the character of a hotly contested game, with the issue agreeably in doubt. And it is always as a game, of course, that the man in the street views moral endeavor. Whether its proposed victim be a political boss, a police captain, a gambler, a fugitive murderer, or a disgraced clergyman, his interest in it is almost purely a sporting interest. And the intensity of that interest, of course, depends upon the fierceness of the clash. . . .

The end of my space is near, and I find that I have written of popular morality very copiously, and of newspaper morality very little. But, as I have said before, the one is the other. The newspaper must adapt its pleading to its clients' moral limitations, just as the trial lawyer must adapt *his* pleading to the jury's limitations. Neither may like the job, but both must face it to gain a larger end. And that end, I believe, is a worthy one in the newspaper's case quite as often as in the lawyer's, and perhaps far oftener. The art of leading the vulgar, in itself, does no discredit to its practitioner. Lincoln practiced it unashamed, and so did Webster, Clay, and Henry. What is more, these men practiced it with frank allowance for the naïveté of the people they presumed to lead. It was Lincoln's chief source of strength, indeed, that he had a homely way with him, that he could reduce complex problems to the simple terms of popular theory and emotion, that he did not ask little fishes to think and act like whales. This is the manner in which the newspapers do their work, and in the long run, I am convinced, they accomplish far more good than harm thereby. . . .

5.3 *New York Times v. United States* (1971)

Freedom of the press is protected by the First Amendment, but U.S. courts long struggled to answer two broad questions. The first question was whether government can, under any circumstances, stop publication that it thinks will be harmful. The second question was whether and under what circumstances publication can be punished after the fact. National security issues are the best example of the first set of cases and libel issues are a good example of the second set. This famous case, also known as the Pentagon Papers case, was brought by the United States to stop publication of illegally obtained information contained in Pentagon documents concerning the origins and conduct of the Vietnam War.

The majority opinion in *New York Times v. United States* was written by Justice Hugo Black and two important dissents were written by Chief Justice Warren Burger and Justice Harry Blackmun. Justice Black contended that "Both the history and language of the First Amendment support the view that the press must be left free to publish news, whatever the source, without censorship, injunctions, or prior restraints." Chief Justice Burger argued that more time and respect should have been given to seeking a balance between the executive branch's national security claims and the newspapers' right to publish the news. Justice Blackmun made the related but stronger point that "The First Amendment, after all, is only one part of the entire Constitution" and other provisions, including the Article II powers of the president in national security affairs, deserve their due weight.

No. 1873

SUPREME COURT OF THE UNITED STATES

403 U.S. 713

Argued June 26, 1971

Decided June 30, 1971

Together with No. 1885, *United States v. Washington Post Co. et al.*, on certiorari to the United States Court of Appeals for the District of Columbia Circuit.

Syllabus

The United States, which brought these actions to enjoin publication in the New York Times and in the Washington Post of certain classified material, has not met the "heavy burden of showing justification for the enforcement of such a [prior] restraint."

No. 1873, 444 F.2d 544, reversed and remanded; No. 1885, U. S. App. D. C., 446 F.2d 1327, affirmed.

PER CURIAM We granted certiorari in these cases in which the United States seeks to enjoin the New York Times and the Washington Post from publishing the contents of a classified study entitled "History of U.S. Decision-Making Process on Viet Nam Policy." Post, pp. 942, 943.

"Any system of prior restraints of expression comes to this Court bearing a heavy presumption against its constitutional validity." *Bantam Books, Inc. v. Sullivan*, 372 U.S. 58, 70 (1963); see also *Near v. Minnesota*, 283 U.S. 697 (1931). The Government "thus carries a heavy burden of showing justification for the imposition of such a restraint." *Organization for a Better Austin v. Keefe*, 402 U.S. 415, 419 (1971). The District Court for the Southern District of New York in the New York Times case and the District Court for the District of Columbia and the Court of Appeals for the District of Columbia Circuit in the Washington Post case held that the Government had not met that burden. We agree.

The judgment of the Court of Appeals for the District of Columbia Circuit is therefore affirmed. The order of the Court of Appeals for the Second Circuit is reversed and the case is remanded with directions to enter a judgment affirming the judgment of the District Court for the Southern District of New York. The stays entered June 25, 1971, by the Court are vacated. The judgments shall issue forthwith.

So ordered.

MR. JUSTICE BLACK, with whom MR. JUSTICE DOUGLAS joins, concurring.

I adhere to the view that the Government's case against the Washington Post should have been dismissed and that the injunction against the New York Times should have been vacated without oral argument when the cases were first presented to this Court. I believe that every moment's continuance of the injunctions against these newspapers amounts to a flagrant, indefensible, and continuing violation of the First Amendment.... In my view it is unfortunate that some of my Brethren are apparently willing to hold that the publication of news may sometimes be enjoined. Such a holding would make a shambles of the First Amendment.

Our Government was launched in 1789 with the adoption of the Constitution. The Bill of Rights, including the First Amendment, followed in 1791. Now, for the first time in the 182 years since the founding of the Republic, the federal courts are asked to hold that the First Amendment does not mean what it says, but rather means that the Government can halt the publication of current news of vital importance to the people of this country.

In seeking injunctions against these newspapers and in its presentation to the Court, the Executive Branch seems to have forgotten the essential purpose and history of the First Amendment. When the Constitution was adopted, many people strongly opposed it because the document contained no Bill of Rights to safeguard certain basic freedoms.[1] They especially feared that the new powers granted to a central government might be interpreted to permit the government to curtail freedom of religion, press, assembly, and speech. In response to an overwhelming public clamor, James Madison offered a series of amendments to satisfy citizens that these great liberties would remain safe and beyond the power of government to abridge.... The amendments were offered to curtail and restrict the general powers granted to the Executive, Legislative, and Judicial Branches two years before in the original Constitution. The Bill of Rights changed the original Constitution into a new charter under which no branch of government could abridge the people's freedoms of press, speech, religion, and assembly. Yet the Solicitor General argues and some members of the Court appear to agree that the general powers of the Government adopted in the original Constitution should be interpreted to limit and restrict the specific and emphatic guarantees of the Bill of

Rights adopted later. I can imagine no greater perversion of history. Madison and the other Framers of the First Amendment, able men that they were, wrote in language they earnestly believed could never be misunderstood: "Congress shall make no law … abridging the freedom … of the press.…" Both the history and language of the First Amendment support the view that the press must be left free to publish news, whatever the source, without censorship, injunctions, or prior restraints.

In the First Amendment the Founding Fathers gave the free press the protection it must have to fulfill its essential role in our democracy. The press was to serve the governed, not the governors. The Government's power to censor the press was abolished so that the press would remain forever free to censure the Government. The press was protected so that it could bare the secrets of government and inform the people. Only a free and unrestrained press can effectively expose deception in government. And paramount among the responsibilities of a free press is the duty to prevent any part of the government from deceiving the people and sending them off to distant lands to die of foreign fevers and foreign shot and shell. In my view, far from deserving condemnation for their courageous reporting, the New York Times, the Washington Post, and other newspapers should be commended for serving the purpose that the Founding Fathers saw so clearly. In revealing the workings of government that led to the Vietnam war, the newspapers nobly did precisely that which the Founders hoped and trusted they would do.…

The Government argues in its brief that in spite of the First Amendment, "the authority of the Executive Department to protect the nation against publication of information whose disclosure would endanger the national security stems from two interrelated sources: the constitutional power of the President over the conduct of foreign affairs and his authority as Commander-in-Chief.[2]

In other words, we are asked to hold that despite the First Amendment's emphatic command, the Executive Branch, the Congress, and the Judiciary can make laws enjoining publication of current news and abridging freedom of the press in the name of "national security." The Government does not even attempt to rely on any act of Congress. Instead it makes the bold and dangerously far-reaching contention that the courts should take it upon themselves to "make" a law abridging freedom of the press in the name of equity, presidential power and national security, even when the representatives of the people in Congress have adhered to the command of the First Amendment and refused to make such a law.[3] See concurring opinion of MR. JUSTICE DOUGLAS, post, at 721–722. To find that the President has "inherent power" to halt the publication of news by resort to the courts would wipe out the First Amendment and destroy the fundamental liberty and security of the very people the Government hopes to make "secure." No one can read the history of the adoption of the First Amendment without being convinced beyond any doubt that it was injunctions like those sought here that Madison and his collaborators intended to outlaw in this Nation for all time.

The word "security" is a broad, vague generality whose contours should not be invoked to abrogate the fundamental law embodied in the First Amendment. The guarding of military and diplomatic secrets at the expense of informed representative government provides no real security for our Republic.… This thought was eloquently expressed in 1937 by Mr. Chief Justice Hughes—great man and great Chief Justice that he was—when the Court held a man could not be punished for attending a meeting run by Communists.

"The greater the importance of safeguarding the community from incitements to the overthrow of our institutions by force and violence, the more imperative is the need to preserve inviolate the constitutional rights of free speech, free press and free assembly in order to maintain the opportunity for free political discussion, to the end that government may be responsive to the will of the people and that changes, if desired, may be obtained by peaceful means. Therein lies the security of the Republic, the very foundation of constitutional government...."[4]

MR. CHIEF JUSTICE BURGER, dissenting.

So clear are the constitutional limitations on prior restraint against expression, that from the time of *Near v. Minnesota*, 283 U.S. 697 (1931) ... we have had little occasion to be concerned with cases involving prior restraints against news reporting on matters of public interest ... In these cases, the imperative of a free and unfettered press comes into collision with another imperative, the effective functioning of a complex modern government and specifically the effective exercise of certain constitutional powers of the Executive. Only those who view the First Amendment as an absolute in all circumstances—a view I respect, but reject—can find such cases as these to be simple or easy....

The newspapers make a derivative claim under the First Amendment; they denominate this right as the public "right to know"; by implication, the Times asserts a sole trusteeship of that right by virtue of its journalistic "scoop."...

It is not disputed that the Times has had unauthorized possession of the documents for three to four months, during which it has had its expert analysts studying them, presumably digesting them and preparing the material for publication. During all of this time, the Times, presumably in its capacity as trustee of the public's "right to know," has held up publication for purposes it considered proper and thus public knowledge was delayed. No doubt this was for a good reason; the analysis of 7,000 pages of complex material drawn from a vastly greater volume of material would inevitably take time and the writing of good news stories takes time.... After these months of deferral, the alleged "right to know" has somehow and suddenly become a right that must be vindicated instanter.

Would it have been unreasonable, since the newspaper could anticipate the Government's objections to release of secret material, to give the Government an opportunity to review the entire collection and determine whether agreement could be reached on publication? Stolen or not, if security was not in fact jeopardized, much of the material could no doubt have been declassified, since it spans a period ending in 1968. With such an approach—one that great newspapers have in the past practiced and stated editorially to be the duty of an honorable press—the newspapers and Government might well have narrowed the area of disagreement as to what was and was not publishable, leaving the remainder to be resolved in orderly litigation, if necessary....

Our grant of the writ of certiorari before final judgment in the Times case aborted the trial in the District Court before it had made a complete record pursuant to the mandate of the Court of Appeals for the Second Circuit....

I would affirm the Court of Appeals for the Second Circuit and allow the District Court to complete the trial aborted by our grant of certiorari, meanwhile preserving the status quo in the Post case. I would direct that the District Court on remand give priority to the Times case to the exclusion of all other business of that court but I would not set arbitrary deadlines....

MR. JUSTICE BLACKMUN, dissenting.

I join MR. JUSTICE HARLAN in his dissent. . . . The First Amendment, after all, is only one part of an entire Constitution. Article II of the great document vests in the Executive Branch primary power over the conduct of foreign affairs and places in that branch the responsibility for the Nation's safety. Each provision of the Constitution is important, and I cannot subscribe to a doctrine of unlimited absolutism for the First Amendment at the cost of downgrading other provisions. First Amendment absolutism has never commanded a majority of this Court. See, for example, *Near v. Minnesota*, 283 U.S. 697, 708 (1931), and *Schenck v. United States*, 249 U.S. 47, 52 (1919). What is needed here is a weighing, upon properly developed standards, of the broad right of the press to print and of the very narrow right of the Government to prevent. Such standards are not yet developed. The parties here are in disagreement as to what those standards should be. But even the newspapers concede that there are situations where restraint is in order and is constitutional. Mr. Justice Holmes gave us a suggestion when he said in Schenck,

"It is a question of proximity and degree. When a nation is at war many things that might be said in time of peace are such a hindrance to its effort that their utterance will not be endured so long as men fight and that no Court could regard them as protected by any constitutional right." 249 U.S., at 52.

I therefore would remand these cases to be developed expeditiously, of course, but on a schedule permitting the orderly presentation of evidence from both sides, with the use of discovery, if necessary, as authorized by the rules, and with the preparation of briefs, oral argument, and court opinions of a quality better than has been seen to this point. In making this last statement, I criticize no lawyer or judge. I know from past personal experience the agony of time pressure in the preparation of litigation. But these cases and the issues involved and the courts, including this one, deserve better than has been produced thus far.

It may well be that if these cases were allowed to develop as they should be developed, and to be tried as lawyers should try them and as courts should hear them, free of pressure and panic and sensationalism, other light would be shed on the situation and contrary considerations, for me, might prevail. But that is not the present posture of the litigation.

The Court, however, decides the cases today the other way. I therefore add one final comment.

I strongly urge, and sincerely hope, that these two newspapers will be fully aware of their ultimate responsibilities to the United States of America. Judge Wilkey, dissenting in the District of Columbia case, after a review of only the affidavits before his court (the basic papers had not then been made available by either party), concluded that there were a number of examples of documents that, if in the possession of the Post, and if published, "could clearly result in great harm to the nation," and he defined "harm" to mean "the death of soldiers, the destruction of alliances, the greatly increased difficulty of negotiation with our enemies, the inability of our diplomats to negotiate. . . ." I, for one, have now been able to give at least some cursory study not only to the affidavits, but to the material itself. I regret to say that from this examination I fear that Judge Wilkey's statements have possible foundation. I therefore share his concern. I hope that damage has not already been done. If, however, damage has been done, and if, with the Court's action today, these newspapers proceed to publish the critical documents and there results therefrom "the death of soldiers, the destruction of alliances, the greatly increased difficulty of negotiation with our enemies, the inability of our diplomats to negotiate," to which list I might add the factors of prolongation of the war and of further delay in the freeing of United States prisoners, then the Nation's people will know where the responsibility for these sad consequences rests.

NOTES

1. In introducing the Bill of Rights in the House of Representatives, Madison said: "But I believe that the great mass of the people who opposed [the Constitution], disliked it because it did not contain effectual provisions against the encroachments on particular rights...." 1 Annals of Cong. 433. Congressman Goodhue added: "It is the wish of many of our constituents, that something should be added to the Constitution, to secure in a stronger manner their liberties from the inroads of power." Id., at 426.
2. Brief for the United States 13–14.
3. Compare the views of the Solicitor General with those of James Madison, the author of the First Amendment. When speaking of the Bill of Rights in the House of Representatives, Madison said: "If they [the first ten amendments] are incorporated into the Constitution, independent tribunals of justice will consider themselves in a peculiar manner the guardians of those rights; they will be an impenetrable bulwark against every assumption of power in the Legislative or Executive; they will be naturally led to resist every encroachment upon rights expressly stipulated for in the Constitution by the declaration of rights." 1 Annals of Cong. 439.
4. *De Jonge v. Oregon*, 299 U.S. 353, 365.

5.4 Samuel Kernell, "The Early Nationalization of Political News in America" (1986)

Both nineteenth-century observers and modern scholars have described nineteenth-century America as dominated by isolated rural hamlets and small towns. Most Americans lived on the land or in small, generally insular and autonomous, villages and towns. Cities were few and communication was slow, particularly early in the nineteenth century. Samuel Kernell asks whether evidence from the newspapers of the day, specifically Cleveland newspapers between 1818 and 1876, reflected a local focus and how that focus changed as the nineteenth century wore on.

In fact, Kernell found that "Even as early as the 1830s when Cleveland was little more than an outlying hamlet of a thousand inhabitants, national politics occupied a sizeable share of political news." The slavery debate was overwhelmingly the dominant national issue, though when it waned other national issues, such as land policy, railroad and transportation policy, as well as national security issues, filled the space. Kernell concluded that nineteenth-century communities were self-reliant but by no means insular. They were never cut off from national news, though the proportion of local, state, and national news varied over time as the importance of particular issues rose and fell over time.

When Alexis de Tocqueville toured America in the 1830s, he found Washington occupying a lowly position in the political life of the country. In a footnote, *Democracy in America* informs the European reader, "America has no great capital city where direct or indirect influence is felt over the whole extent of the country."[1] Throughout the book, he expands on the effects of this decentralization. And we may fairly suspect that as much as any other, this observation led de Tocqueville to concentrate his inquiry on the performance of democracy in communities across the country.

De Tocqueville's antebellum report on the state of public life in America stands in stark contrast to that portrayed in a quite different book, a novel similarly entitled *Democracy*, written anonymously by Henry Adams half a century later. Describing a primal urge that prompts his heroine to abandon the fashionable but dull New York society in favor of the federal city, Adams writes: "What she wished to see, she thought, was the clash of interests, the interests of forty millions of people and a whole continent, centering at Washington; guided, restrained, controlled, or unrestrained and uncontrollable, by men of ordinary mould; the tremendous forces of government, and the machinery of society at work. What she wanted was Power."[2] Clearly, between de Tocqueville's and Adams's *Democracy*, Washington's status had undergone a profound improvement. The city, so desolate early on that one 1820s politician described life there as "splendid torment," was by the century's end fast becoming the political center of the nation.[3]

Recently historians and other students of America's political development have turned their attention to the emergence of a national political community during the late 19th century. . . .

Consider the stark backdrop of American society at midcentury depicted by Robert H. Wiebe as the country enters the 1880s.

> Small-town life was America's norm in the mid-seventies. . . . However much they actually relied upon the outside world, they still managed to retain the sense of living largely to themselves. With farms generally fanning around them, these communities moved by the rhythms of agriculture: the pace of the sun's day, the working and watching of the crop months, the cycle of the seasons. Relatively few families lived so far from town that they did not gravitate to some degree into its circle, and there people at least thought they knew all about each other after crossing and recrossing paths over the years. Usually homogeneous, usually Protestant, they enjoyed an inner stability that the coming and going of members seldom shook.[4]

National affairs, this imagery suggests, failed to engage members of these "island" communities, except perhaps as a periodic form of entertainment. . . .

In this article, we shall examine evidence that, in fact, raises serious questions about the insularity of America's hinterland communities at midcentury. After examining the growth in the volume of national news during the "premodern" era, I shall suggest how the finding of the early nationalization of the news can be squared with the "island" image of American society. . . .

Data and Method

Assessing the relative volume of national, state, and local politics in newspapers during the middle decades of the nineteenth century poses formidable problems for content analysis. Unlike most other research topics that involve examination of newspapers, it does not suffice here to inspect just headlines or even first-page stories. In an era in which the format of the paper as much as its content might vary greatly from one editor to the next, we cannot assume that the front page will adequately reveal the content of the paper. Clearly, in analyzing the distribution of political news across levels of government, we must assess the entire paper. . . .

Thanks to a remarkable resource, the *Annals of Cleveland*, the data reported below satisfy the criteria of exhaustively representing the day's news.[5] The *Annals* is a multivolume collection of newspaper synopses published by the Works Progress Administration in the 1930s. . . . In addition to a detailed summary of each news story, editorial, advertisement, and announcement, the *Annals* classifies each article by type (for example, advertisement) and identifies its location in the paper and length in column inches. . . .

The Findings

According to the thesis of late development, political coverage during the "premodern" era of 1820 to 1876 should have heavily favored local over state and national affairs. In figure 1, however, we find little evidence of this. Even as early as the 1830s when Cleveland was little more than an outlying hamlet of a thousand inhabitants, national politics occupied a sizable share of political news reported in the leading local paper.[6]

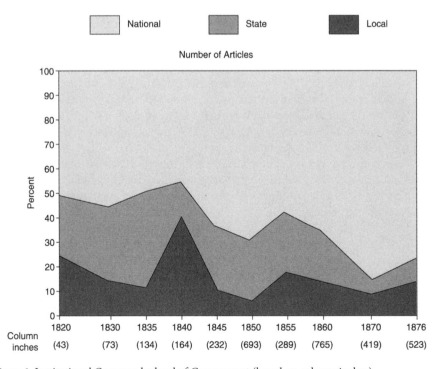

Figure 1 Institutional Coverage by level of Government (based on column inches)

Whether measured by the number of articles or by column inches, national stories began to dominate Cleveland's political news in 1860. By 1870, four of every five stories concerned national politics.

From these figures we can also discern which level—state or local—suffered the greatest relative losses in coverage with the growth of national news. Except for 1840, for reasons noted below, local news experienced greater displacement prior to 1855, at which time state news began to diminish sharply relative to national and even local news. By the 1870s, state politics in Ohio was consuming barely 10 percent of all political coverage. . . .

How does one reconcile the clear dominance of national news with the earlier stated view that "interest dwindled rapidly" as the political process moved beyond the community? . . .

Political Issues

To assess more precisely the issue content of political news across levels of government, each article was scored by the policy issue, if any were mentioned, receiving the greatest attention. . . .

To identify the national topics that attracted press attention, these issues have been further classified in table 1 into six broad areas of policy. No one who has perused antebellum newspapers could fail to be impressed by the passion slavery ignited whenever it became an issue. With the exception of the years 1830 and 1840, each of which represented a temporary hiatus in the slavery debate at the national level, Cleveland's papers were clearly preoccupied with this matter. Slavery in this stronghold of abolitionism was tinged with partisanship, with the prewar papers ardently supporting the antislavery platforms of the Free Soil and later the Republican parties.

What is more relevant to us here is the fact that the volume of articles on slavery closely followed the national disposition of the issue. The Compromise of 1850 was a difficult, time-consuming, and, ultimately, temporary resolution of a crisis. Accordingly, slavery dominated the papers that year. For the next decade, politicians' careers would be made and unmade according to their posturing on slavery and the Compromise. In 1855, this subject captured 80 percent of the "issue" reporting in the Cleveland *Leader*. During Reconstruction slavery became the "bloody shirt," and continued in this vein to be a prominent topic in this Republican paper.

The life cycle of slavery as a national issue is fully traced in its news coverage in table 1. Its episodic crises early in the century, its heightened politicization and regional polarization during the decade leading up to the Civil War, and afterward, its status as an issue with which the Republican party maintained hegemony are all present. By the admittedly crude indicator of column inches, appearance of the slavery issue in the Cleveland press closely follows its status as a national political issue. Events of the day account for the volume of news.

Next to slavery, other national issues pale in significance. When compared with coverage of state and local issues, however, they appear to have been quite prominent. A western state, Ohio turned early to the federal government for internal improvements. Land needed to be distributed to a growing population, postal and military roads opened, waterways improved. According to one historian, these considerations were of such moment, they contributed to the Ohio congressional delegation's decision, along with delegations from other western states, to support John Adams for president in 1824

Table 1 National Political Issues

	1820		1830		1835		1840		1845		1850		1855		1860		1870		1876	
	A	L	A	L	A	L	A	L	A	L	A	L	A	L	A	L	A	L	A	L
Slavery	56%	72%	5%	2%	52%	61%	0%	0%	30%	46%	90%	94%	76%	80%	64%	69%	14%	10%	12%	14%
Tariff	11	5	5	2	0	0	0	0	10	9	1	1	1	0	2	1	10	10	6	3
Defense/ foreign affairs	11	14	0	0	4	6	7	9	30	20	1	5	16	13	9	9	23	23	7	8
Govt. services/ patronage	17	6	71	71	39	32	44	42	22	16	6	3	5	2	11	10	12	9	10	6
Scandal	0	0	10	20	0	1	4	4	1	4	2	2	1	1	11	8	7	8	37	35
Rights	6	3	0	0	0	0	0	0	4	1	0	0	1	1	3	2	15	23	6	6
National affairs	0	0	10	5	0	0	44	45	0	3	0	0	0	1	1	1	19	17	23	28
N =	(18)	(64)	(21)	(85)	(23)	(186)	(27)	(139)	(142)	(1,155)	(451)	(5,812)	(178)	(1,940)	(301)	(2,249)	(419)	(1,708)	(178)	(1,244)

Note: A = Articles; L = Length (column inches). Slavery includes related issues such as Kansas and California admission; government services includes rivers and harbors, public lands, postal services, homesteading, veterans' benefits, roads, and general patronage. Among the prominent rights issues were polygamy, naturalization, and suffrage. Finance is the largest component of national affairs; this category also includes pardons, territories, Indian relations, and capital administration.

rather than the far more popular Andrew Jackson.[7] Appropriately, in table 1 we see that early in the century federal land disposal, contracts, and jobs were highly newsworthy topics.[8] By the end of our series many of these same issues—especially when they did not favor local interests—were being reported as scandal.

Other national issue categories in table 1 that came close to matching, if they did not in fact do so, the total space given to state and local issues are national affairs in 1840 and 1876, national defense and rights in 1870, and scandal in 1876. Thus, even when the slavery debate was quiescent, the issue agenda remained national. A clear instance of this occurs in 1840 when there were remarkably few slavery articles, and yet national issues still occupied more than twice the space given to state and local issues.

Despite the fact that communication and transportation between Cleveland and Washington at midcentury were measured by days rather than hours or minutes, one would be hard put to maintain in the face of these findings that Clevelanders were much insulated from even the routine affairs of the national government. Rather, measured by the availability of news, the "political distance" was greater to Columbus, or even to city hall. More direct evidence on this score can be seen in the reporting of day-to-day institutional activities across these different governmental levels. . . .

Conclusion: National News and the Island Community

How does one reconcile the notion of an island, or segmented, community with the finding that its sole means of mass communication was as nationally oriented as we have found the Cleveland press to be? The answer depends largely upon what one ascribes to the notion of the island community. One comprehensive meaning of this concept is that of a self-centered society, internally integrated and externally insulated against encroachment from the larger society. Indeed, America in this view may be regarded as little more than an archipelago of island communities.

A careful reading of Wiebe and others finds them frequently adopting what I shall call the bastion view of island communities.[9] . . .

The presence of a nationally oriented local press poses some serious problems to the bastion point of view. . . .

There is, however, one other conceptualization of America's island community for which the findings presented here are less threatening. Consider the concept to refer simply to a self-reliant social unit that represents an efficient, and hence highly legitimated, adaptation to a spacious and sparsely populated, preindustrial America. Gone are the internal mechanisms of conformity and barriers to the outside world. Localism becomes a culture bred not so much from organic parochialism but from an enveloping national political and economic order. Rather than bastions, island communities would be understood as the subunits of a national response to a particular environment. As conditions changed, so too did communities. This does not mean that the transition came smoothly. Undoubtedly, for many the loss of local identities was a shattering experience. What it does imply, however, is that one should view these islands not just as resisting change but, when profitable, as taking advantage of the new opportunities created as national society changed. So viewed, the early arrival of national news into America's otherwise isolated communities helped them prepare for and adapt to the subsequent emergence of a more national social and political order. . . .

NOTES

The research reported here was presented in part in papers delivered at the 1983 Annual Meeting of the Social Science History Association and at the 1984 Annual Meeting of the American Political Science Association. Some of the findings were also presented to fellow members of the History of Congress Seminar in 1983. Consequently, I have benefited from more than the usual complement of advice. Much of it I have heeded. I wish especially to thank the following people who helped me improve upon the earlier efforts: Ballard Campbell, whose incisive remarks prompted me to return to the *Annals of Cleveland* to add to my data three years without national elections, 1835, 1845, and 1855; Nelson W. Polsby, who advised me to back up the Cleveland findings with a sample of stories from the *Hartford Daily Courant*; Del Powell, who coded the data with unfailing diligence and care; and Anita Schiller, who discovered and pointed me to the *Annals* and thereby made a systematic study of fifty years of nineteenth-century news reporting a feasible enterprise. I also wish to thank Gary C. Jacobson and Michael Robinson for helpful comments on an earlier version of this paper.

1. Alexis de Tocqueville, *Democracy in America*, vol. 1, ed. T. P. Mayer (Garden City: Anchor Books, 1969), 278.
2. Henry Adams, *Democracy, An American Novel* (New York: Harmony Books, 1981), 10.
3. James Sterling Young, *The Washington Community: 1800–1828* (New York: Columbia University Press, 1966), chap. 3, esp. 49–64.
4. Ibid., pp. 27–28. For an endorsement of this view see Richard L. McCormick, "The Party Period and Public Policy: An Exploratory Hypothesis," *Journal of American History* 66 (September 1979): 293.
5. Works Progress Administration of Ohio, *Annals of Cleveland, 1818–[1876]* (Cleveland: WPA of Ohio, District Four, 1936–39).
6. Over the time frame of this study Cleveland grew from a town of 150 individuals to a leading industrial center of 140,000. The following decennial population estimates are taken from Edmund H. Chapman, *Cleveland: Village to Metropolis* (Cleveland: Western Reserve University, 1964): *1820*, 150; *1830*, 1,075; *1840*, 6,071; *1850*, 17,034; *1860*, 43,417; *1870*, 92,829; *1880*, 140,000.
7. Stevens, *The Early Jackson Party*.
8. Harry N. Scheiber has documented well how Ohio was exceptional in initiating many local improvements on its own—the most prominent being the Ohio canal. See his *Ohio Canal Era* (Athens: Ohio University Press, 1966). Nonetheless, federal public works remained a vital concern in Ohio as in the other western states. Francis P. Weisenburger related the story of how both John Adams's and Andrew Jackson's forces in Congress in 1827 sought to woo Ohio's support in the next election with internal improvements: "Each group attempted, through its representatives in Congress, to secure a liberal grant to aid Ohio in its canal program. Apparently the Jackson members succeeded in launching their bill first and insuring it prior consideration by the committee. But John Woods, an Administration congressman from Ohio and a member of the House Committee on Roads and Canals, was able to report the Administration measure, providing for a grant of 500,000 acres, first. When the measure was passed the Jackson measure seemed unnecessary. In the Senate, however, the Jacksonians secured the incorporation of their bill as an amendment to the Administration measure, and in this form it became a law. Thus, Ohio received a double grant of public lands, each party claiming the credit." In *The Passing of the Frontier, 1825–1850* (Columbus: Ohio State Archaeological and Historical Society, 1941), 230.
9. In addition to his *Search for Order*, Robert H. Wiebe elaborates this theme in *Segmented Society: An Introduction to the Meaning of America* (New York: Oxford University Press). Samuel P. Hays

offers a similar if somewhat more abstracted version of political transformation. Borrowing from Tonnies the concepts of community and society, he assigns them as endpoints on a continuum, which he then describes America as traversing during the late nineteenth century. See his "Political Parties and the Community-Society Continuum," in *American Party Systems*, ed. Chambers and Burnham, 152–81.

5.5 Gadi Wolfsfeld, "Political Power and Power Over the Media" (2011)

Gadi Wolfsfeld, a professor of political science and communications at Hebrew University in Jerusalem, is a close student of the evolving relationship between the media and political power. Wolfsfeld notes, as many have before him, that there is an "exchange relationship," which he calls a "competitive symbiosis," between politicians and journalists. Each needs the other; politicians need the media to get their messages out, and the media need the politicians to give them access and to help them tell their stories. Wolfsfeld argues that the more prominent the politician the more media access they have and the more favorable the coverage of them tends to be.

Some have argued that the new media landscape, especially the Internet, has evened the playing field, allowing many more people to get their opinions out and to discover what other people think. Wolfsfeld is skeptical, arguing that while the new media do offer more people a chance to express their opinions, the competition for attention, for "eyeballs" in Internet terms, is so intense that few people actually see or hear most messages. Generally, the old media still reigns. Stunningly, just 3.5 percent of news stories originate in the blogosphere and gravitate to the old media, while the rest, 96.5 percent, start in the old media and gravitate to the new media.

Power has made Reality its Bitch

—*Mark Danner*[1]

Think about two political actors, each trying to get into the news. For now let's talk only about the traditional news media (the new media will come into play a bit later). Assume, for the sake of argument that both are from the same political party, both have similar political views, and both look equally good in front of the camera. But there's one small difference between them: one is the president of the United States and the other is a new congressman from North Dakota. Presidents have a huge number of journalists assigned to them and can appear in the news any time they want. The congressman, on the other hand, has to compete with a horde of other politicians and convince reporters that he has something newsworthy to say. The president never has any problem getting into the national news, while the new congressman will be lucky if he gets covered in the local news.

Other powerful people in the government, whether it be the U.S. secretary of state, the secretary of defense, or the Speaker of the House also have little trouble getting into the news. If we were to build a ladder of influence from the most powerful people in Washington to the least important, we would have a pretty accurate measure of their chance of getting into the national news. Here's a good illustration of how political power leads to power over the media. Anybody who is reading this book probably knows the name of the secretary of state. Now try to name the secretary of Veterans Affairs. Unless you have some reason to be concerned with veteran issues, chances are you have no idea.

The reason, of course, is that the secretary of Veterans Affairs is simply not considered newsworthy, unless (s)he gets in trouble. A good rule of thumb is that journalists run after the politically powerful and politically weak run after journalists. . . .

One reason journalists consider the powerful more newsworthy is that these are the people who are most likely to have an impact on the country and the world. The president, after all, can go to war. The chance that an individual member of Congress can have a major impact on the political process is slim unless they are the deciding vote in an important piece of legislation. Even then, their fame is likely to be brief and they will quickly return to obscurity.

Here's another way to think of this idea. The relationship between journalists and political leaders can be considered a *competitive symbiosis*. It is a symbiotic relationship because each depends on the other in order to achieve their goals. Leaders want publicity and the journalists want interesting information they can turn into news. The reason the relationship is also competitive is that each wants to get the most from the other while "paying" as little as possible. Leaders want to get lots of publicity without having to reveal too much and reporters want to get the juiciest information without having to give a free ride to the politician. The more powerful leaders have the best information to "sell" and that's why journalists compete for the privilege of getting it, especially if they can get first crack at the story. . . .

Not Just More Coverage But Usually More Positive

Does the fact that powerful elites get covered *more* mean that they get covered more positively? The answer, for the most part, is yes. There are basically two doors for getting into the news. The front door is reserved for VIPs: the people with political power. When these people enter, they are usually treated with respect. They are covered because of who they are as much as for what they are doing or saying. Here is a typical front door story from the *New York Times* that appeared in September 2009.

White House Scraps Bush's Approach to Missile Shield

WASHINGTON—President Obama scrapped his predecessor's proposed antiballistic missile shield in Eastern Europe on Thursday and ordered instead the development of a reconfigured system designed to shoot down short- and medium-range Iranian missiles. In one of the biggest national security reversals of his young presidency, Mr. Obama canceled former President George W. Bush's plan to station a radar facility in the Czech Republic and 10 ground-based interceptors in Poland. Instead, he plans to deploy smaller SM-3 interceptors by 2011, first aboard ships and later in Europe, possibly even in Poland or the

Czech Republic. Mr. Obama said that the new system "will provide stronger, smarter and swifter defenses of American forces and America's allies" to meet a changing threat from Iran.[2]

In these types of stories political leaders are basically using the press as an electronic bulletin board. They announce what they are going to do and provide carefully prepared explanations about why they are doing it. Now this doesn't mean that every new organ will be equally accommodating. Thus the Fox News story for the same day covered the announcement much more negatively.[3] Generally, however, unless there is major controversy about what is being said, heads of state are given much more latitude to pass their messages to the public. As noted, the opposition is usually given a chance to respond but being able to respond to an event is very different than being able to initiate it. One has to add to all this the ability to produce endless amounts of soft stories such as the media frenzy that accompanied the debate about which dog would be lucky enough to be adopted by the Obamas. Dominating the headlines is one of the important advantages that come with political power....

What About the New Media?

Some readers probably think that everything said to this point is simply out of date. They would argue that in the age of cell phones with cameras, YouTube, and the Blogosphere political power becomes less important. Today, even the weakest groups can get their message out to everyone through the Internet and social networking platforms. All it takes is for one good political story to go viral and everyone—including the mainstream media—is paying attention.

The new technology does make a difference, sometimes even a huge difference. But in addition to the new opportunities that have become available because of the new media, there are also some important limitations. The new advantages and the limitations of this new technology can be understood by looking at the type of challenger that could most benefit from these changes: political movements.

Political Movements and the New Media

Most political movements are the classic "back door" challengers. Even the largest movements are usually not considered inherently newsworthy. They still must do something dramatic if they hope to get covered by the traditional media and, as said, this more often than not translates into negative coverage. The question that needs to be asked is how much the new communication technology changes the ability of these movements to become more powerful, to get their message out to supporters and the general public, and to bring about political change.

There are four major goals political movements attempt to achieve where the new Internet media could be useful. The first, and most obvious, is that it should help movements in their efforts to mobilize supporters to their cause. The second goal is to have their messages and news stories appear in the traditional media which will allow them to reach a much wider audience. Related to that amplification effect, the third goal is to have an influence on public opinion so the wider audience becomes more sympathetic with the movement. And ultimately, the fourth is to have an impact on politics. These four goals can be seen as four stations that movements have to pass in their attempts to climb an extremely steep mountain whose peak is called political success. It turns out that not only does it become increasingly difficult to pass each station, but one finds that the new technology becomes less and less helpful as one gets closer to the top.

The first station movements need to pass has to do with their ability to mobilize supporters and other resources in order to become more powerful. Here is where political movements receive their greatest boost from the new media technology. Here, the changes that have taken place with the advent of the new media are nothing short of revolutionary. The Internet ... provides movements with the potential to communicate instantly with millions of people around the world. Compare the cost and effectiveness of mailing leaflets to supporters as opposed to sending out emails that include both a video presentation and the opportunity to respond to what they've received. Think about the ability to remind people continually of a protest taking place, of being able to ask people to electronically sign a petition and pass it on to their friends, of allowing people to make a donation using a credit card while sitting in their pajamas in front of the computer, or of sending an inspiring speech by your leader to people living in thirty different countries. Now let's supercharge all of this by allowing every movement to put links on its web site that allows it to communicate and build coalitions with other similar movements around the country and the world. When you put all of these assets together you begin to understand the potential the new media represent for mobilizing people and groups for the cause.

The major thing to remember is that all of this revolutionary technology provides movements with the *potential* to exponentially increase their membership and resources. Whether it actually does depends, among many other things, on how much the movement's messages and leaders resonate with a large segment of the public. Here too it's a question of political context. There are tens of thousands of movements demanding our attention. The amount of time and attention any of us can or will devote to any one movement is still extremely limited. Thus, even if a movement has the best technology available it will remain small and obscure unless it appeals to a relatively large number of people who are willing to devote time and money to the cause. Even in the digital age, it is hard to get Americans excited about the preservation of historical sites in Albania.

Movement leaders also find that the fact that people are willing to sign an electronic petition about something does not mean they will either give money or come to a demonstration. In fact, because electronic participation is so easy it may give some people a sense that "they've done their part" and thus even lower the number of people who are willing to get out of their pajamas and do something active for the movement. Perhaps it is no coincidence that in May 2009 one of the oldest American social activists, Ralph Nader, made an extremely aggressive attack on Internet activism. He called the Internet "a huge waste of trivial time." He asked his audience of college students to consider what they were going to tell their grandchildren:

> You know. The world is melting down. They're nine years old. They're sitting on your lap. They've just become aware of things that are wrong in the world: starvation, poverty, whatever. And they ask you, what were you doing when all this was happening: Grandma? Grandpa? That you were too busy updating your profile on Facebook?[4]

A similar point was made by Evgeny Morozov who coined an extremely useful term for this: *slacktivism*.[5] Slacktivism is a combination of the word slacker and activism.

The idea is that there are quite a number of digital activities people can carry out that make them feel good about themselves but have absolutely no impact on either society or politics. One of the examples he gives is a Facebook group called "Saving the Children of Africa." Morozov points out that at first glance the organization looks very impressive because it has over 1.2 million members. At the time he wrote however, the organization had raised a paltry $6,000 (about a half a penny a person). As he puts it: "The problem, however, is that the granularity of contemporary digital activism provides too many easy way-outs: too many people decide to donate a penny where they may otherwise want to donate a dollar."[6]

As we move up the mountain of political success, the air gets increasingly thin and the new technology becomes much less helpful. The reason can be summed up in one word: *competition*. Consider attempting to just get past the second station of trying to get favorable coverage of your group in the traditional media. Generating buzz on the Internet about your cause can certainly make a difference, but it is no substitute for generating an investigative report on *CBS Evening News* or *Sixty Minutes*. There are tens of thousands of politicians, organizations, movements, companies, and (let us not forget) celebrities all competing to make it into these news and current events programs. All of these competitors use Twitter and many of them can use the new technology to produce newsworthy events. But the traditional media still have only so much space and time to allocate, even if their web sites provide more space than in the past. Younger journalists probably spend more time actively searching political blogs and Internet sites but they too only have so much time and energy to look. And guess what? They will be especially interested in spending time trying to find stories about the politically powerful.

It also turns out that only a small fraction of major news stories come from the blogosphere. Researchers Jute Leskovec, Lars Backstrom, and Jon Kleinberg employed a powerful computer program to search the web over a fairly large period of time to study the rise and fall of the biggest news stories.[7] They tracked an amazingly large 1.6 million mainstream media sites and blogs. The finding that is most relevant to this discussion was that a mere 3.5 percent of all major news cycles were initiated in the blogosphere and then moved to the other media. The vast majority of news stories ran in the opposite direction: the blogs and alternative news sites were following stories that first appeared in the traditional news media. This should tell you something important about how difficult it is for all political actors to use the new media as a means of breaking into the mainstream media. It should also tell you that traditional media remains the best tool for generating political waves about an issue.

The competition becomes even fiercer when an organization attempts to move beyond gaining news coverage and attempts to interest the broad public or to get policy makers to actually make changes. Starting with having an impact on public opinion, it is almost impossible for a small group to be heard above the crowd. There are, of course, people—you know who you are—who spend hours every day reading political blogs. But even they have no choice but to confine themselves to those issues that interest them. In that case, we are moving from the age of broadcasting to what many have called *narrowcasting*. . . .

Perhaps a metaphor would be helpful. Your organization has just purchased a megaphone so your leaders will be especially loud. The problem is that every group has a megaphone. To make things worse, those with political power not only have more megaphones, they also have sophisticated sound systems so their speeches are heard all over the country.

Despite all these limitations, there are two very different types of movements who seem to have benefited the most from the emergence of the Internet. The first are what are known as Transnational Advocacy Networks (TANs). Groups dealing with climate change, the dangers of globalization, nuclear proliferation, cruelty to animals, and human rights are all examples of movements who have far more power and influence now than in the past because of their ability to mobilize supporters and resources from around the world. Researchers, governments, and international companies have all begun to think about how these groups' increasing power is having an impact on the world. In fact researchers Sean Aday and Steve Livingston even go so far as to claim that in some cases the impact of these movements can be compared to that of countries.[8]

The second type of group that has seen a major change in their fortunes due to the Internet is terrorist organizations. The Internet provides these groups with a number of important advantages.[9] Terrorist organizations can instantly exchange information—including technical information about weapons—from and to any place on the planet. They can also distribute inspirational material and videos to supporters and potential supporters. The videos can include inspiring speeches from their leaders, threats to carry out terrorist attacks, and actual footage from the attacks they have carried out. Because such videos are considered newsworthy many Western journalists end up showing them to the broader public and in doing so unintentionally help the terrorists spread fear.

The Internet can also be used by terrorists to coordinate tactics and strategy. One of the most important traits of the Internet is that individuals around the world can create *communities* that give them a sense of belonging. While this can, in most cases, be seen as a positive development there are some communities the world could live without. The reason why terrorist groups are especially likely to be empowered by the new media is because mobilization—especially international mobilization—is such a central element in their overall strategy. Unlike more conventional movements, they are not usually attempting to convince the broad public or Western leaders about the legitimacy of their cause. Their goals are to intimidate their opponents. Terrorist groups don't enter the news media through the back door they simply blow it open.

The Internet also provides terrorists with an extremely effective and anonymous method for doing strategic research before an attack. A good example of this new found power can be seen in the report about the planning of the 9/11 attack that was published by the National Commission on Terrorist Attacks Upon the United States.[10] The leaders of Al-Qaeda were able to use the Internet to find flight schools that might accept them and to find routes and flight paths of various airlines and of course to communicate with each other. In fact, learning how to use the Internet was an important part of their terrorist training.

So in some ways the new media have radically changed the relationship between political and media power. But due to the rules of political competition, these cases remain the exception rather than the rule. When it comes to the ability of movements and other challengers to organize and mobilize it is certainly a new age. On the other hand, the new technologies appears to be less revolutionary when it comes to getting a message to the broad public or bringing about real change. Equally important, the ability of political actors to successfully exploit the new media depends first and foremost on who they represent, their goals, and the political environment in which they are operating. The powerful, it turns out, still have the upper hand.

NOTES

1. Mark Danner in a commencement address at the University of California at Berkeley, May 10, 2007, offering his own summary of comments made by a top Bush administration official concerning how they deal with the press. Mark Danner, "Words in a Time of War: On Rhetoric, Truth and Power," Mark Danner.com, http://www.markdanner.com/articles/show/136.
2. Peter Baker, "White House Scraps Bush's Approach to Missile Shield," *New York Times*, http://www.nytimes.com/2009/09/18/world/europe/18shield.html.
3. Fox News, "Intel Used by Obama Found Iran Long-Range Missile Capacity Would Take 3–5 Years Longer," http://www.foxnews.com/politics/2009/09/18/intel-used-obama-iran-long-range-missile-capacity-years-longe.
4. Mathew Laser, "Ralph Nader: Internet Not So Hot At "Motivating Action"," http://arstechnica.com/web/news/2009/05/ralph-nader-internet-not-so-hot-at-motivating-action.ars.
5. Evgeny Morozov, "From Slacktivism to Activism," *Foreign Policy*, http://neteffect.foreignpolicy.com/posts/2009/09/05/from_slacktivism_to_activism.
6. Ibid.
7. J. Leskovec, L. Backstrom, and J. Kleinberg, "Meme-Tracking and the Dynamics of the News Cycle" (2009).
8. S. Aday and S. Livingston, "Taking the State out of State—Media Relations Theory: How Transnational Advocacy Networks Are Changing the Press—State Dynamic," *Media, War & Conflict* 1, no. 1 (2008).
9. For a excellent survey of all the different ways in which terrorist organizations can use the Internet see: Gabriel Weinmann, *Terror on the Internet: The New Arena, the New Challenges*, Washington, D.C.: The United States Institute of Peace (2006).
10. National Commission on Terrorist Attacks Upon the United States, "AI Qaeda Aims at the American Homeland," U.S. Government Printing Office. http://gov-info.library.unt.edu/911/report/911Report_Ch5.pdf.

5.6 Diana Owen, "Media: The Complex Interplay of Old and New Forms" (2011)

The evolution of the media has affected few aspects of politics more than political campaigns. At each stage of political history, established forces usually have the resources to command traditional media and to move toward new media as their political potential becomes clear. However, the emergence of new media do give outsiders a chance to capitalize on the potential of new media before established forces, used to winning through the old media, become fully aware that a new door has opened.

Diana Owen highlights the interplay in political campaigns between old media—television, newspapers, opinion magazines—and new media—email, blogs, cell phones, and the Internet in general. Though most voters still get most of their political news from the old media, especially television, since 1992 the Internet has been a growing force in political news and campaigns. By 2008, almost as many people visited newspaper websites as read the physical paper to get their political news. While young people are still most comfortable getting the bulk of their news on the Internet, all age groups are increasingly comfortable there.

The election media environment now comprises a complex amalgamation of traditional and new media, and the interplay among them. Mainstream media, including television news, newspapers, and news magazines, maintain an important place in elections, while new media, especially online and digital communication platforms, have become more influential. Modern forms of campaign reporting, such as a citizen journalism and blogs, have emerged that complement and compete with the work of professional news organizations.

These developments in the campaign context reflect larger trends in the political media system which is in the midst of a fundamental restructuring that exhibits elements of both consolidation and fragmentation. Media institutions have become increasingly consolidated within a small number of large corporations. Message content is highly redundant across channels, even as the outlets for disseminating information have proliferated. At the same time, the media system has become highly fragmented. The number of available media options offering specialized content directed at specific audiences has multiplied. Micro-targeting, where political messages are tailored for particular segments of the media market, has become standard practice, including during campaigns (Howard 2006; Hillygus and Shields 2008)....

The Evolution of Campaign Communication

The media system undergoes periodic transformations in response to technological, economic, social, and political developments that can directly influence elections. Advances in print technology, lower paper production and distribution costs, and increased education and higher literacy rates gave rise to the penny press in the 1830s which made news readily available to the mass public. Newspapers contributed to a growth in associational life, including vigorous mass-based political parties that organized behind particular candidates in elections (Schudson 1998). Candidates were evaluated on their ability to deliver oratorical masterpieces that were printed verbatim in the press (Jamieson 1988). Broadcast technology and the availability of radio changed the way in which people experienced politics, as they could now listen to events, like the national nominating conventions, unfold in real time. News magazines referred to 1924 as "the radio year," and predicted that candidates would do much of their campaigning over the airwaves. Radio changed the tone and content of campaign discourse, as candidates adopted a more personal, straightforward style, shortened their speeches, and tailored their messages to reach a broad audience (Clark 1962).

Television gave rise to the modern mass-media campaign, fundamentally altering the dynamics of elections. By 1980, campaigns had become candidate-centric, especially at the presidential level. Post-Watergate reforms of the presidential nominating process diminished the role of party elites and opened up the process to greater participation by the mass electorate. Contenders used television to take their messages directly to the public, circumventing political party control. Campaigns employed media management strategies to generate coverage and staged pseudo events that produced dramatic visuals that conformed to the character of the medium. Televised ads that emulated commercials for consumer products sold candidates using short, simple, direct messages. Broadcast debates, where voters could compare candidates' performances on the same stage, eventually became a staple of campaigns. Candidates abbreviated their speech-making even further, as seconds-long sound bites were more conducive to television coverage than detailed addresses (Patterson 1980; Owen 1991; Hart 1999).

Recent developments in campaign communication coincide with transformations that have been underway for about a quarter of a century. The twenty-first-century media system departs fundamentally from that of earlier eras, and is marked by contradictions: consolidation and fragmentation, broadcasting and narrowcasting, stability and innovation. Traditional mass media affiliated with large conglomerates, such as television nightly news, newspapers, and news magazines, continue to form the backbone of the media system, despite being faced with financial and structural challenges. However, the number and variety of platforms accommodating political content have expanded exponentially. New political media, ranging from old mediums that have assumed new political roles to cutting-edge technologies that facilitate genuine innovations in political communication, have become an integral part of the electoral process.

The broadcast model of communication, which is predicated upon mass media widely disseminating messages of general societal interest, is associated with traditional media, especially television and radio. Historically, this model was predicated upon delivery systems that involve public ownership of scarce resources, especially the radio and television spectrum. These media were subject to regulation and oversight, which included the requirement that programming fulfill a public service imperative (McQuail 2000). The broadcast model is still very much in evidence, as corporate media organizations continue to thrive. Collectively, new media have precipitated movement away from the broadcast model of communication to a narrowcasting model. Many forms of new media disseminate specialized messages aimed at particular individuals or groups. From a business perspective, the term was initially associated with media that were made available to customers by subscription. Narrowcasting has become more broadly construed, and refers to media whose content is selectively directed toward specialized audiences (Mendelsohn and Nadeau 1996). Some election media exhibit characteristics of both broadcasting and narrowcasting models, especially hybrid forms. News websites, for example, make generalized information available to visitors while at the same time limiting specific content to subscribers.

The Era of New Media

The new media era may be viewed in terms of three overlapping phases of development. During the first period, which began in the late 1980s and early 1990s, well-established entertainment media formats supported by old-style communications technologies became more prominent in the political realm. These new media lacked a public service imperative, and their development was motivated heavily by profits. The second phase, initiated in the mid-1990s, was marked by the arrival of novel political platforms made possible by technological innovations, especially computer networks such as the Internet and World Wide Web, and e-mail. These new media were distinguished by their ability to subvert the top-down structure of traditional communication, and the interactivity between users that they made possible. The third phase in the evolution of political media witnessed an expansion of the ways in which technological tools are used for communication. These applications, labeled Web 2.0 when technologists first drew attention to them in 2004, are marked by higher levels of interactive information sharing, engagement, networking, collaboration, and community building than in the past. While audience members could comment on stories written by journalists in the Web 1.0 era, communities of users can now use wikis and social networking sites to collaboratively generate their own content. This phase of media evolution is closely associated with the twenty-first-century media campaign, as the 2008 presidential election stimulated and made visible these innovations in political communication.

Old Media, New Politics

Talk radio is perhaps most emblematic of the first generation of new media. A moribund medium by the 1970s, call-in talk radio was revitalized as a political forum as the First Gulf War and a spate of high-profile legal cases, including the 1991 sexual assault trial of William Kennedy Smith and the 1995 O.J. Simpson murder trial, stimulated public discussion (Davis and Owen 1999). As Baby Boomers' preferences moved from music to talk and their interests shifted from local to national concerns, the medium developed a steady following. Developments in satellite technology made it easy and cost-effective to broadcast talk programs nationally. The new talk radio was nascent in the 1988 presidential contest; four years later it had become a vigorous political force. Talk show hosts, such as popular conservative Rush Limbaugh, continue to use their platform to influence like-minded voters (Barker 2002; Jamieson 2008). Candidates on both sides of the aisle employ talk radio to recruit supporters and energize their base (Owen 1997).

Entertainment media, such as television talk shows and news magazine programs, print tabloids, and music television (MTV), also incorporated more political content into their offerings. Cable television and the proliferation of channels made numerous news and entertainment options available during election campaigns at both local and national levels. These new political media, with their infotainment focus, were able to reach voters who typically did not pay attention to hard news. Some candidates, such as Republican presidential contender George H.W. Bush in 1992, were reluctant to court new media outlets, worrying that they undermined the dignity of the office. Others, such as Bush's opponent Bill Clinton, embraced new media as a mechanism for subverting traditional media gatekeeping that limited candidates' ability to speak for themselves and control their campaign messaging strategies (Patterson 1993, 2002). Clinton donning shades and playing "Heartbreak Hotel" on the sax on the *Arsenio Hall Show* has become a symbol of this early aspect of new media. Trailing in the polls, Clinton used the appearance to appeal to young people and minority voters. During that same election, Ross Perot went on *Larry King Live* and told voters he would run for president if they would organize on his behalf, igniting his Reform Party candidacy. Candidates' talk show appearances have become a campaign staple. David Letterman quipped, "The road to the White House runs through me," as candidates made over 110 appearances on late-night television during the 2008 presidential election (Center for Media and Public Affairs 2008: 1).

The Net Campaign Takes Shape

The Internet has been present in presidential elections since 1992, and is the hallmark of the second phase of new media development. The Clinton campaign established a rudimentary website that functioned primarily as brochure-ware, providing textual information that resembled the candidate's promotional literature, including biographical material and position papers. The site received few visits from voters or journalists. The Bush campaign did not have a web presence (Davis 1999; Bimber and Davis 2003). Clinton's organization also made limited use of the Internet and e-mail to facilitate discussion among elite supporters (Foot and Schneider 2006). The Internet's role in campaigns has grown incrementally since that time, as existing platforms have become more sophisticated and new applications have been developed. By the 2000 election, all of the major candidates and many minor contenders had websites that primarily featured transcripts of speeches and issue statements (Owen and Davis 2008; Foot and Schneider 2006). Platforms that allowed voters to express their views and debate the merits of candidates, issues, and the campaign, including blogs and discussion boards, had become commonplace by the 2004 election (Lawson-Borders and Kirk 2005). Citizens took on roles similar to reporters by providing information and commentary. Still, the vast majority of campaign news stories, especially those that reached sizable audiences, was produced and distributed by mainstream media organizations (Owen and Davis 2008).

Prior to 2008, only a small proportion of the electorate accessed online campaign media. News sites received limited traffic (Scheufele and Nisbet 2002; Bimber and Davis 2003; Foot and Schneider 2006), and few people took advantage of blogging and online discussion functions during campaigns (Owen and Davis 2008). The percentage of voters who relied on the Internet to learn about the election was 9 percent in 2000 and 13 percent in 2004 (Pew Research Center 2008b). Evidence that exposure to online campaign communication translated into increased interest, knowledge, engagement, or likelihood of voting was mixed. Bimber (2003) found scant support for the contention that online news exposure contributed to political participation, civic engagement, or information seeking (Bimber 2003; Weaver and Drew 2001). Voters tended to access election websites in order to reinforce their political predispositions rather than to learn anything new (Mutz and Martin 2001; Park and Perry 2008). However, Internet news users can exhibit increased levels of political efficacy and participation (Johnson and Kaye 2003; Lupia and Philpot 2005), as well as a greater tendency to vote (Tolbert and McNeal 2003).

The Twenty-First Century Media Campaign

The 2008 presidential contest ushered in a new era in campaigning that coincides with the third phase of the new media's evolution. The communication environment encompassed an elaborate assortment of traditional mass media and new media, and showcased a range of innovations. The campaign marked another step in the development of an election media system where traditional and new sources coexist, complement, compete, and conflict with one another. Election media both drove and were influenced by dramatic advancements in candidates' campaign strategies, which have become more decentralized and specialized (Vaccari 2008). Candidates were able to bypass media gatekeepers and get their message out to voters directly via an assortment of alternative digital platforms, including their own highly sophisticated web presences. They also benefitted from and were targeted by messages generated by organizations and voters independent of candidate committees and political parties. The opportunities for people to follow the campaign and become informed were nearly boundless. The mechanisms for citizen interaction and direct campaign involvement via media were unprecedented.

Traditional Election Media Endure

It is premature to declare the "end of mass media" that some scholars have predicted (Bennett 2005; Miller 2008). Mainstream press coverage remains a fixture of campaigns, especially as the majority of original reporting still emanates from professional journalists. The audience for traditional media continues to outnumber that for new media, as the majority of people rely on mainstream news at least some of the time. Television news remains the public's main source of election information, although the percentage of loyal viewers has dropped as users move to online sources. Sixty-eight percent of voters named television as their primary source in 2008 compared to 76 percent in 2004 (Pew Research Center 2008b). More people still read print newspapers than their online counterparts, although the number of print subscribers has plummeted. In 2010, print papers were read by nearly 100 million adults per day compared to the 74 million unique visitors drawn to newspaper websites per month (Vanacore 2010). A growing audience segment relies on a combination of old and online media (Pew Research Center 2008a).

It is important to recognize developments that influence campaign coverage by the mainstream press that have consequences for new media as well. The 2008 presidential election brought the challenges facing the traditional news industry into full view. Presidential campaigns have become protracted affairs that effectively begin years before the first candidates officially declare their intentions to run. Media coverage is an essential element of the meta-campaign where candidates test their viability, raise funds, recruit key supporters, and attempt to generate awareness among voters. Maintaining interest in an election that may be years in the making is a difficult and resource-intensive task that can tax professional news operations. Financial cutbacks, the result of dropping advertising revenues and declining audiences (Plambeck 2010), coupled with the increased costs associated with newsgathering have caused media organizations to downsize their reporting staffs and limit the number of professional journalists on the campaign trail. Print news reporters who witness events first hand traditionally have been the source of original, in-depth stories that are frequently repurposed by other outlets and can set the agenda for the campaign (Roberts 2008). In 2008, only about two dozen print news organizations assigned journalists to travel "on the bus" with candidates, reducing the amount of fresh eyewitness copy that was produced by professionals. The perspectives of journalists working for a small number of major publications, including the *New York Times*, the *Wall Street Journal*, the *Washington post*, the *Los Angeles Times*, the *Chicago Tribune*, and *Newsweek*, were over-represented (Steinberg 2008; Owen 2009).

Established media organizations have been forced to adapt to the shifting communication environment to remain competitive. Traditional media have incorporated elements of both the broadcasting and narrowcasting models into their product, resulting in the development of hybrid media forms. The online counterparts of print newspapers and television news programs have incorporated new media innovations, including blogs and discussion boards, video sharing, and social networking features, into their election reporting. Professional media platforms have included the work of amateurs through eyewitness reporting, commentary, and photo and video postings. Amateur accounts of campaign events, in some instances, became primary source material for professional journalists, who did much of their reporting from the newsroom rather than on the campaign trail.

The Net Campaign Arrives

For years, scholars, political operatives, and journalists have harkened the advent of a new era in political campaigns, prematurely labeling recent presidential elections as "The Internet Election," "Campaign 2.0," and "The Digital Election" (Vaccari 2008). There is substantial evidence to suggest that the "net campaign" had finally arrived in 2008. As Gulati observes, "Not only did the Internet become fully institutionalized as a media platform, but also the range of online applications expanded" (2009: 187). The amount of campaign content populating the Internet increased exponentially in volume and diversity, and the audience grew significantly in size, dedication, and activation.

Perhaps the most significant development of the campaign online in 2008 was the increase in the amount and diversity of user-created content online. Non-professionals made use of the easily accessible tools afforded by the Internet and other digital technologies to generate news and information for public dissemination. Campaign blogs proliferated, running the gamut from rudimentary personal journals to professional quality platforms that resemble online newspapers, such as *Talking Points Memo and Huffington Post*. *Scoop08* was an online paper compiled entirely by junior high, high school, and college students with the assistance of an impressive editorial board of experienced journalists. This paper was so successful during the campaign that it was reincarnated after the election as *Scoop44*, a youth-run platform covering the Obama administration. Voters also made path-breaking use of video sharing sites, posting on the spot video reports and vlogs, creating original video ads and content streams, and generating sophisticated mash-ups mixing old and new content. These efforts were recognized and appropriated by candidates, campaign organizations, political parties, and journalists, which especially enhanced young voters' role in the electoral process (Owen 2008).

Another indication that 2008 was a landmark campaign for media is the size of the new media audience. While in past campaigns new media served as a supplement to traditional sources, especially television news and newspapers (Owen and Davis 2007), 36 percent of the public regularly depended on online news in 2008 (Pew Research Center 2008a). A majority of voters—nearly 60 percent—consulted the Internet at some point during the campaign, especially to find out information about candidates, issues, and the electoral process. Young people were especially inclined to use digital election media. Twenty-five percent of 18- to 24-year-olds stated that they got their news primarily online versus 7 percent of those over age 45. An expanding cohort of older voters used online sources for election information. In fact, citizens over age 60 were more inclined to read campaign blogs regularly than were younger people (Harris Interactive 2008). The Internet's ability to convey fast-breaking news throughout the campaign contributed to its popularity (Pew Research Center 2008; Gulati 2009; Owen 2009).

There is reason to temper somewhat the enthusiasm about 2008 as a game-changing election. While there were many new opportunities for individuals to take advantage of the Internet's participatory functions, many users treated the online information environment primarily as an extension of traditional media. Voters were far less inclined to engage the interactive features of online communication, even when they were literally right at their fingertips. The public's use of the interactive features of the Internet, including e-mail, text messaging, and social networking sites, in 2008 far exceeded that of previous elections. Still, the number of people who regularly engaged in these forms of interactive communication was relatively small. Only 7 percent of the public communicated with others daily about the campaign through e-mail, text messaging, or social networking sites, with an additional 14 percent doing so once a week. Only 5 percent of the population posted to a blog, discussion board/listserv, Facebook or MySpace page, or any other online platform (Pew Research Center 2008b). Furthermore, the excitement over the novel digital applications that emerged during the nominating campaign waned significantly during the general election, where the old-style, television-dominated mass-media campaign predominated (Owen 2009). Still, the landmark developments of the 2008 presidential contest have carried over to the 2010 midterm elections, and they are likely to take hold more fervently in the 2012 presidential contest.

BIBLIOGRAPHY

Barker, David C. 2002. *Rushed to Judgment*. New York: Columbia University Press.
Bennett, W. Lance. 2005. "The Twilight of Mass Media News." In *Freeing the Presses*, ed. Timothy E. Cook. Baton Rouge: Louisiana State University Press.
Bimber, Bruce. 2003. *Information and American Democracy: Technology in the Evolution of Political Power*. New York: Cambridge University Press.
Bimber, Bruce and Richard Davis. 2003. *Campaigning Online: The Internet in U.S. Elections*. New York: Oxford University Press.
Center for Media and Public Affairs. 2008. *Late-Nite Talk Shows Were Road to White House*. Research Report, Washington, DC: Center for Media and Public Affairs.
Clark, David G. 1962. "Radio in Presidential Campaigns: The Early Years (1924–1932)." *Journal of Broadcasting* 6(3): 229–338.
Davis, Richard and Diana Owen. 1999. *New Media and American Politics*. New York: Oxford University Press.
Foot, Kirsten A. and Steven M. Schneider. 2006. *Web Campaigning*. Cambridge, MA: MIT Press.
Gulati, Garish J. 2009. "No Laughing Matter: The Role of New Media in the 2008 Election," in *The Year of Obama*, ed. Larry J. Sabato. New York: Longman.
Harris Interactive. 2008. "More Than Half of Americans Never Read Political Blogs." March 10, Available at *harrisinteractive.com*., www.harrisinteractive.com/harris_poll/index.asp?PID=879 (accessed August 14, 2009).
Hart, Roderick P. 1999. *Seducing America*. Thousand Oaks, CA: Sage.
Hillygus, D. Sunshine and Todd G. Shields. 2008. *The Persuadable Voter: Wedge Issues in Presidential Campaigns*. Princeton, NJ: Princeton University Press.
Howard, Philip N. 2006. *New Media Campaigns and the Managed Citizen*. New York: Cambridge University Press.
Jamieson, Kathleen Hall. 1988. *Eloquence in the Electronic Age*. New York: Oxford University Press.
Jamieson, Kathleen Hall and Joseph N. Cappella. 2008. *Echo Chamber*. New York: Oxford University Press.
Johnson, Thomas J. and Barbara K. Kaye. 2003. "A Boost or Bust for Democracy? How the Web Influenced Political Attitudes and Behaviors in the 1996 and 2000 Presidential Elections." *Harvard International Journal of Press/Politics* 8:9–34.
Lawson-Borders, Gracie and Rita Kirk. 2005. "Blogs in Campaign Communication." *American Behavioral Scientist* 49(4): 548–59.
Lupia, Arthur and Tasha S. Philpot. 2005. "Views from Inside the Net: How Websites Affect Young Adults' Political Interest." *Journal of Politics* 67(4): 1122–42.
McQuail, Denis. 2000. *McQuail's Mass Communication Theory*, 4th Edition. London: Sage.

Mendelsohn, Matthew and Richard Nadeau. 1996. "The Magnification and Minimization of Social Cleavages by the Broadcast and Narrowcast News Media." *International Journal of Public Opinion Research* 8(4): 374–89.

Miller, Mark. 2008. "The End of Mass Media: Aging and the US Newspaper Industry," in *The Silver Market Phenomenon*, eds. Florian Kohlbacher and Cornelius Herstatt. Berlin: Springer Berlin Heidelberg.

Owen, Diana. 1991. *Media Messages in American Presidential Elections*. Westport, CT: Greenwood Press.

Owen, Diana. 1997. "Talk Radio and Evaluations of President Clinton." *Communication Research* 14: 333–53.

Owen, Diana. 2009. "The Campaign and the Media," in *The American Elections of 2008*, eds. Janet M. Box-Steffensmeier and Steven E. Schier. New York: Rowman & Littlefield.

Owen, Diana and Richard Davis. 2008. "United States: Internet and Elections," in *Making a Difference: A Comparative View of the Role of the Internet in Election Politics*, eds. Stephen Ward, Diana Owen, Richard Davis, and David Taras. Lanham, MD: Lexington Books.

Park, Hun Myoung, and James L. Perry. 2008. "Do Campaign Web Sites Really Matter in Electoral Civic Engagement? Empirical Evidence From the 2004 Post-Election Internet Tracking Survey." *Social Science Computer Review* 26 (2): 1902–12.

Patterson, Thomas E. 1980. *The Mass Media Election*. New York: Praeger.

Patterson, Thomas. 1993. *Out of Order*. New York: Alfred A. Knopf.

Patterson, Thomas. 2002. *The Vanishing Voter: Public Involvement in an Age of Uncertainty*. New York: Knopf.

Pew Research Center for the People and the Press 2008a. "Internet's Broader Role in Campaign 2008." *people-press.org*, January 11. Available at http://people-press.org/report/384/internets-broader-role-in-campaign-2008 (accessed November 20, 2008).

Pew Research Center for the People and the Press. 2008b. "High Marks for Campaign; High Bar for Obama." *pewresearch.org*, November 13. Available at http://people-press.org/report/?pageid=1429 (accessed November 20, 2008).

Plambeck, Joseph. 2010. "Newspaper Circulation Falls Nearly 9%." *New York Times*, April 26; B2.

Scheufele, Dietram A. and Matthew C. Nisbet. 2002. "Being a Citizen Online: New Opportunities and Dead Ends." *Harvard International Journal of Press/Politics* 7: 55–75.

Schudson, Michael. 1998. *The Good Citizen*. New York: The Free Press.

Steinberg, Jacques. 2008. "The Buzz on the Bus: Pinched, Press Steps Off." *nytimes. com*, March 26. Available at www.nytimes.com/2008/03/26/us/politics/26bus.html?hp (accessed November 1, 2008).

Tolbert, Caroline J. and Ramona S. McNeal. 2003. "Unraveling the Effects of the Internet on Political Participation." *Political Research Quarterly* 56(2): 175–85.

Vaccari, Cristian. 2008. "From the Air to the Ground: the Internet in the 2004 US Presidential Campaign." *New Media & Society* 10(4): 647–65.

Vanacore, Andrew. 2010. "US Newspaper Circulation Falls 8.7 Percent." *washingtonpost.com*, April 26. Available at www.washingtonpost.com/wp-dyn/content/article/2010/04/26/AR2010042601659.html (accessed April 26, 2010).

Weaver, David and Dan Drew. 2001. "Voter Learning and Interest in the 2000 Presidential Election: Did the Media Matter?" *Journalism and Mass Communication Quarterly* 78(Winter): 787–99.

Discussion Questions

1. Jefferson depends upon schools and newspapers to prepare citizens to play a responsible role in democratic politics. Mencken argues that newspapers necessarily play to the baser emotions of their general readership, but he concludes that newspapers are still of good service to their communities. Analyze these arguments and decide what you think.

2. Consider the arguments made in *New York Times v. United States*. Should newspapers have a near absolute right to publish what they wish or is there a balance that must be sought between the interests of national security and the rights of a free press?

3. Gadi Wolfsfeld argues that political power translates into power over the media. Is this inevitable, or what reforms can you think of to balance access to the media?

4. Are citizens and voters likely to get the news they need from old media, new media, or some combination of the two? What kind of information are they most likely to get from each?

5. Does the Web make you feel comfortable that free expression is safe today or do you worry that an unregulated Web invites proliferation of lies and misinformation that is often hard to tell from the truth?

Suggested Additional Reading

James I. Aucoin, *The Evolution of American Investigative Journalism* (Columbia, MO: University of Missouri Press, 2005).

Edward J. Bliss, Jr., *Now the News: The Story of Broadcast Journalism* (New York: Columbia University Press, 1992).

Timothy E. Cook, *Governing With the News: The News Media as a Political Institution* (Chicago: University of Chicago Press, 1998).

Henry Jenkins, *Convergence Culture: Where Old and New Media Collide*, revised edition (New York: New York University Press, 2008).

Lucas A. Powe, Jr., *The Fourth Estate and the Constitution: Freedom of the Press in America* (Berkeley, CA: University of California Press, 1991).

6

Interest Groups

Introduction

What the Founding generation called "factions" and what today we often call "special interests" have always been a concern to students of American politics. The reason is simple—to the extent that there is a public interest or common good that we want politics to serve, special interests seeking their own advantage may interfere. Initially, the Founders hoped that given the new nation's size and diversity, elections would place a natural elite of accomplished men in government who would be guided by the common good. These hopes did not last long. Conflict in the first Washington administration, generally arraying the urban commercial interests behind Alexander Hamilton against the rural agrarian interests behind Thomas Jefferson, suggested that clashing interests would always be present. Eventually, students of American politics came to believe that the clash of interests might, in fact, be positive. How would you expect the public interest to be discovered, they asked, except through open discussion, debate, and contestation in the arena of democratic politics. In this sense, the First Amendment rights to freedom of speech, association, and petition, protect the rights of individuals to form groups and to try to influence government. Interest groups, then, are central to democratic politics. Hence, the question of which interests form most fully and which form less fully or not at all is important.

James Madison and Alexis de Tocqueville, perhaps the two most widely respected theorists or interpreters of American political life in the nineteenth century (maybe ever), both worried that factions or interest groups posed a danger to democratic politics. Both believed that self-interest was an ineradicable element of human nature and so needed to be constrained if it could not be eliminated. In our first selection, Madison argues that the sheer size of the new nation guaranteed that so many interests would be present that none could reasonably threaten to win and hold control of the national government. In the second, Tocqueville agreed that factionalism posed a danger to democracy, but he contended that in the American case these dangers are mitigated by a free press and universal suffrage. Neither Madison nor Tocqueville envisioned a time when travel and communication technology would permit national interest groups.

If interest groups are inevitable in a democratic society, what do we know about how groups form and what impact they have on democracy and its policymaking process. Three selections, those by E.E. Schattschneider, Charles Lindblom, and Daniel Tichenor and Richard Harris, explore these critical questions. Into the mid-twentieth century and beyond, pluralist theory assumed that interest groups formed naturally and more or less fully. If there was an interest, especially if it came under pressure from competing interests, a group would form to defend it. On this reassuring view, democratic politics and public policy would be a fair reflection of the balance in the interest group system. Unfortunately, research painted a less reassuring picture. Schattschneider's pioneering study from 1960 found that some interests, particularly business and corporate interests, were much more energetically protected than others. In his famous formulation, "the flaw in the pluralist heaven is that the heavenly chorus sings with a strong upper class accent."

In our fourth selection, Charles E. Lindblom, a leading figure in both political science and economics, sets the relationship between democratic politics and capitalist economics in historical and theoretical perspective. He points out that democratic governments cannot simply order private businesses to speed up production, hire more workers, and pay higher salaries. Democratic governments must listen to business interests, respond to their policy and regulatory needs, and even cajole them with tax breaks, subsidies, tariff protections, regulatory forbearance, and other benefits to stimulate private sector growth. Hence, Lindblom concludes, business interests enjoy a "privileged position" that other interests can only envy.

In the highlight piece of Chapter 6, Daniel Tichenor and Richard Harris extend the temporal range of interest group studies back through the nineteenth century and ask whether the mix of interest groups and the pattern of their interaction has changed over time. They found that while business and corporate interests had always dominated the interest group system, the growth of the system had occurred earlier than previously understood. Previous studies assumed that the rapid growth of the interest group system had occurred after and in response to the policy changes of the New Deal and the Great Society. Tichenor and Harris showed that a previous surge in interest group organization and activity had occurred in the Progressive Era.

Finally, Elisabeth Clemens traced the evolution of women's groups between 1890 and 1925. She found that prior to women's suffrage, while women were outside the party system, they developed organizational forms that began as distinctively female forms and evolved in the direction of business and educational forms. These forms allowed women to work closely with government agencies dealing with children's health and educational issues. These patterns were disrupted after women won the vote and entered into more traditional forms of partisan politics.

The First Amendment freedoms of speech, press, assembly, and petition mean that interest groups have a right to form and express themselves. But the fact that half a century worth of studies show that the interest group system is tilted in favor of business and corporate interests gives many pause. Should we use law and policy, in areas such as taxation and campaign finance regulations, to check the role of interest groups and perhaps to balance the playing field a bit?

6.1 Debates at the Constitutional Convention, "Popular Participation, Factions, and Democratic Politics" (1787)

The United States was the world's first democracy on a national scale. Not surprisingly, the Founders were concerned to avoid or limit as many of the traditional weaknesses and foibles of popular government as possible. Hence, they spent a great deal of time in the Constitutional Convention discussing who could safely be permitted to vote and how the instability potential in interest groups—which they called factions—could be limited.

James Madison famously asked in *Federalist* 10 how to check the impact of factions on democratic politics. Because *Federalist* 10 is reprinted in every American Government text, we provide a different view of Madison's argument in our first selection. Madison had road-tested his *Federalist* 10 argument in the Constitutional Convention on June 6. Madison argued that the common wisdom of the time, that factions are most easily controlled in small and homogeneous communities, is wrong. In fact, he argued, large states are more stable because they encompass many factions, no one of which can gain control and all of which serve to check and balance one another.

On August 7 the delegates challenged another common assumption of their time to make room for democracy. Conservatives, led by Gouverneur Morris, sought to set aside state suffrage laws to put in place a national freehold requirement. The freehold—usually ownership of 50 acres—was the traditional British requirement for suffrage. It was meant to deny non-property owners the ballot. Progressives, led by Oliver Ellsworth and George Mason, advocated the looser requirement of a demonstrated attachment to the interests of the community. In the end, states were allowed to maintain their existing requirements and change came slowly over several decades.

The Records of the Federal Convention of 1787
[Farrand's Records, Volume 1]

MADISON Wednesday June 6th. In Committee of the whole

Mr. Pinkney according to previous notice & rule obtained, moved "that the first branch of the national Legislature be elected by the State Legislatures, and not by the people". contending that the people were less fit Judges <in such a case,> and that the Legislatures would be less likely to promote the adoption of the new Government, if they were to be excluded from all share in it . . . .

Mr. Sherman. If it were in view to abolish the State Govts. the elections ought to be by the people. If the State Govts. are to be continued, it is necessary in order to preserve harmony between the national & State Govts. that the elections to the former shd. be made by the latter. The right of participating in the National Govt. would be sufficiently secured to the people by their election of the State Legislatures. The objects of the Union, he thought were few. 1. defence agst. foreign danger. 2. agst. internal disputes & a resort to force. 3. Treaties with foreign nations 4 regulating foreign commerce, & drawing revenue from it. These & perhaps a few lesser objects alone rendered a Confederation of the States necessary. All other matters civil & criminal would be much better in the hands of the States. The people are more happy in small than large States. States may indeed be too small as Rhode Island, & thereby be too subject to faction. Some others were perhaps too large, the powers of Govt not being able to pervade them. He was for giving the General Govt. power to legislate and execute within a defined province.

Col. Mason. Under the existing Confederacy, Congs. represent the States not the people of the States: their acts operate on the States not on the individuals. The case will be changed in the new plan of Govt. The people will be represented; they ought therefore to choose the Representatives. The requisites in actual representation are that the Reps. should sympathize with their constituents; shd. think as they think, & feel as they feel; and that for these purposes shd. even be residents among them. Much he sd. had been alledged agst. democratic elections. He admitted that much might be said; but it was to be considered that no Govt. was free from imperfections & evils; and that improper elections in many instances, were inseparable from Republican Govts. But compare these with the advantage of this Form in favor of the rights of the people, in favor of human nature .…

Mr. Madison considered an election of one branch at least of the Legislature by the people immediately, as a clear principle of free Govt. and that this mode under proper regulations had the additional advantage of securing better representatives, as well as of avoiding too great an agency of the State Governments in the General one.—He differed from the member from Connecticut (Mr. Sherman) in thinking the objects mentioned to be all the principal ones that required a National Govt. Those were certainly important and necessary objects; but he combined with them the necessity, of providing more effectually for the security of private rights, and the steady dispensation of Justice. Interferences with these were evils which had more perhaps than any thing else, produced this convention. Was it to be supposed that republican liberty could long exist under the abuses of it practiced in <some of> the States. The gentleman (Mr. Sherman) had admitted that in a very small State, faction & oppression wd. prevail. It was to be inferred then that wherever these prevailed the State was too small. Had they not prevailed in the largest as well as the smallest tho' less than in the smallest; and were we not thence admonished to enlarge the sphere as far as the nature of the Govt. would admit. This was the only defence agst. the inconveniences of democracy consistent with the democratic form of Govt. All civilized Societies would be divided into different Sects, Factions, & interests, as they happened to consist of rich & poor, debtors & creditors, the landed the manufacturing, the commercial interests, the inhabitants of this district, or that district, the followers of this political leader or that political leader, the disciples of this religious sect or that religious sect. In all cases where a majority are united by a common interest or passion, the rights of the minority are in danger. What motives are to restrain them? A prudent regard to the maxim that honesty is the best policy is found by experience to be as little regarded by bodies of men as by individuals. Respect for character is always diminished in proportion to the number among whom the blame or praise is to be divided. Conscience, the only remaining tie is known to be inadequate in individuals: In large numbers, little is to be expected from it. Besides, Religion itself may become a motive to persecution & oppression.—These observations are verified by the Histories of every Country ancient & modern. In Greece & Rome the rich & poor, the creditors &

debtors, as well as the patricians & plebeians alternately oppressed each other with equal unmercifulness. What a source of oppression was the relation between the parent Cities of Rome, Athens & Carthage, & their respective provinces: the former possessing the power & the latter being sufficiently distinguished to be separate objects of it? Why was America so justly apprehensive of Parliamentary injustice? Because G. Britain had a separate interest real or supposed, & if her authority had been admitted, could have pursued that interest at our expense. We have seen the mere distinction of colour made in the most enlightened period of time, a ground of the most oppressive dominion ever exercised by man over man. What has been the source of those unjust laws complained of among ourselves? Has it not been the real or supposed interest of the major number? Debtors have defrauded their creditors. The landed interest has borne hard on the mercantile interest. The Holders of one species of property have thrown a disproportion of taxes on the holders of another species. The lesson we are to draw from the whole is that where a majority are united by a common sentiment and have an opportunity, the rights of the minor party become insecure. In a Republican Govt. the Majority if united have always an opportunity. The only remedy is to enlarge the sphere, & thereby divide the community into so great a number of interests & parties, that in the 1st. place a majority will not be likely at the same moment to have a common interest separate from that of the whole or of the minority; and in the 2d. place, that in case they shd. have such an interest, they may not be apt to unite in the pursuit of it. It was incumbent on us then to try this remedy, and with that view to frame a republican system on such a scale & in such a form as will controul all the evils wch. have been experienced . . . .

MADISON Tuesday August 7th. In Convention

Mr. Elseworth. thought the qualifications of the electors stood on the most proper footing. The right of suffrage was a tender point, and strongly guarded by most of the <State> Constitutions. The people will not readily subscribe to the Natl. Constitution, if it should subject them to be disfranchised. The States are the best Judges of the circumstances and temper of their own people . . . .

Mr. Dickenson. had a very different idea of the tendency of vesting the right of suffrage in the freeholders of the Country. He considered them as the best guardians of liberty; And the restriction of the right to them as a necessary defence agst. the dangerous influence of those multitudes without property & without principle, with which our Country like all others, will in time abound. As to the unpopularity of the innovation it was in his opinion chemirical. The great mass of our Citizens is composed at this time of freeholders, and will be pleased with it.

Mr Elseworth. How shall the freehold be defined? Ought not every man who pays a tax to vote for the representative who is to levy & dispose of his money? Shall the wealthy merchants and manufacturers, who will bear a full share of the public burdens be not allowed a voice in the imposition of them—<taxation and representation ought to go together.>

Mr. Govr. Morris. He had long learned not to be the dupe of words. The sound of Aristocracy therefore, had no effect on him. It was the thing, not the name, to which he was opposed, and one of his principal objections to the Constitution as it is now before us, is that it threatens this Country with an Aristocracy. The aristocracy will grow out of the House of Representatives. Give the votes to people who have no property, and they will sell them to the rich who will be able to buy them. We should not confine our attention to the present moment. The time is not distant when this Country will abound with mechanics & manufacturers who will receive their bread from their employers. Will such men be the secure & faithful Guardians of liberty? Will they be the impregnable barrier agst. aristocracy?—He was as little duped by the association of the words, "taxation & Representation"—The man who does not give his vote freely is not represented. It is the man who dictates the vote. Children do not vote. Why? because they want prudence. because they have no will of their own. The ignorant & the dependent can be as little trusted with the public interest. He did not conceive the difficulty of defining "freeholders" to be insuperable. Still less that the restriction could be unpopular. 9/10 of the people are at present freeholders and these will certainly be pleased with it. As to Merchts. &c. if they have wealth & value the right they can acquire it. If not they don't deserve it.

Col. Mason. We all feel too strongly the remains of antient prejudices, and view things too much through a British Medium. A Freehold is the qualification in England, & hence it is imagined to be the only proper one. The true idea in his opinion was that every man having evidence of attachment to & permanent common interest with the Society ought to share in all its rights & privileges. Was this qualification restrained to freeholders? Does no other kind of property but land evidence a common interest in the proprietor? does nothing besides property mark a permanent attachment. Ought the merchant, the monied man, the parent of a number of children whose fortunes are to be pursued in their own <Country>, to be viewed as suspicious characters, and unworthy to be trusted with the common rights of their fellow Citizens

Mr. <Madison.> the right of suffrage is certainly one of the fundamental articles of republican Government, and ought not to be left to be regulated by the Legislature. A gradual abridgment of this right has been the mode in which Aristocracies have been built on the ruins of popular forms. Whether the Constitutional qualification ought to be a freehold, would with him depend much on the probable reception such a change would meet with in States where the right was now exercised by every description of people. In several of the States a freehold was now the qualification. Viewing the subject in its merits alone, the freeholders of the Country would be the safest depositories of Republican liberty. In future times a great majority of the people will not only be without landed, but any other sort of, property. These will either combine under the influence of their common situation; in which case, the rights of property & the public liberty, <will not be secure in their hands:> or which is more probable, they will become the tools of opulence & ambition, in which case there will be equal danger on another side . . . .

Docr. Franklin. It is of great consequence that we shd. not depress the virtue & public spirit of our common people; of which they displayed a great deal during the war, and which contributed principally to the favorable issue of it . . . .

He did not think that the elected had any right in any case to narrow the privileges of the electors. He quoted as arbitrary the British Statute setting forth the danger of tumultuous meetings, and under that pretext, narrowing the right of suffrage to persons having freeholds of a certain value; observing that this Statute was soon followed by another under the succeeding Parliamt. subjecting the people who had no votes to peculiar labors & hardships. He was persuaded also that such a restriction as was proposed would give great uneasiness in the populous States. The sons of a substantial farmer, not being themselves freeholders, would not be pleased at being disfranchised, and there are a great many persons of that description.

On the question for striking out as moved by Mr. Govr. Morris, from the word "qualifications" to the end of the III article N. H. no. Mas. no. Ct. no. Pa. no. Del. ay. Md. divd. Va. no. N. C. no. S. C. no. Geo. not prest. [Ayes—1; noes—7; divided—1; absent—1.]
Adjourned

6.2 Alexis de Tocqueville, "Political Association in the United States" (1835)

In this fascinating selection Tocqueville declares that "the principle of association" has been more successfully and more broadly applied in the United States than in any other nation. Americans, he declared, are far more likely to form an association among interested and effected parties to solve a problem that confronts them than to look to government. Americans trust groups that they form with their fellow citizens while they mistrust the standing authority of government.

Just as interesting, however, Tocqueville weighed the strengths and weaknesses of freedom of the press and freedom of association in nations generally and in the United States specifically. He argued that freedom of the press is broadly beneficial while freedom of association poses both promise and risk. Where passions are violent or parties are too evenly balanced, minorities may chafe under their lack of influence. In such instances, "a nation may confine it (the right of association) within certain limits." Nonetheless, Tocqueville argued that the United States is protected against the worst evils of factionalism by the fact that partisan differences are "mere differences of hue" and universal suffrage gives elected majorities a moral authority that minorities must acknowledge.

Daily use *which the Anglo-Americans make of the right of association—Three kinds of political associations—How the Americans apply the representative system to associations—Dangers resulting to the state—Why the unlimited exercise of the right of association is less dangerous in the United States than elsewhere—Why it may be looked upon as necessary—Utility of associations among a democratic people.*

In no country in the world has the principle of association been more successfully used or applied to a greater multitude of objects than in America. Besides the permanent associations which are established by law under the names of townships, cities, and counties, a vast number of others are formed and maintained by the agency of private individuals.

The citizen of the United States is taught from infancy to rely upon his own exertions in order to resist the evils and the difficulties of life; he looks upon the social authority with an eye of mistrust and anxiety, and he claims its assistance only when he is unable to do without it. This habit may be traced even in the schools, where the children in their games are wont to submit to rules which they have themselves established, and to punish misdemeanors which they have themselves defined. The same spirit pervades every act of social life. If a stoppage occurs in a thoroughfare and the circulation of vehicles is hindered, the neighbors immediately form themselves into a deliberative body; and this extemporaneous assembly gives rise to an executive power which remedies the inconvenience before anybody has thought of recurring to a pre-existing authority superior to that of the persons immediately concerned. If some public pleasure is concerned, an association is formed to give more splendor and regularity to the entertainment. Societies are formed to resist evils that are exclusively of a moral nature, as to diminish the vice of intemperance. In the United States associations are established to promote the public safety, commerce, industry, morality, and religion. There is no end which the human will despairs of attaining through the combined power of individuals united into a society . . . .

An association consists simply in the public assent which a number of individuals give to certain doctrines and in the engagement which they contract to promote in a certain manner the spread of those doctrines. The right of associating in this fashion almost merges with freedom of the press, but societies thus formed possess more authority than the press. When an opinion is represented by a society, it necessarily assumes a more exact and explicit form. It numbers its partisans and engages them in its cause; they, on the other hand, become acquainted with one another, and their zeal is increased by their number. An association unites into one channel the efforts of divergent minds and urges them vigorously towards the one end which it clearly points out.

The second degree in the exercise of the right of association is the power of meeting. When an association is allowed to establish centers of action at certain important points in the country, its activity is increased and its influence extended. Men have the opportunity of seeing one another; means of execution are combined; and opinions are maintained with a warmth and energy that written language can never attain.

Lastly, in the exercise of the right of political association there is a third degree: the partisans of an opinion may unite in electoral bodies and choose delegates to represent them in a central assembly. This is, properly speaking, the application of the representative system to a party.

Thus, in the first instance, a society is formed between individuals professing the same opinion, and the tie that keeps it together is of a purely intellectual nature. In the second case, small assemblies are formed, which represent only a fraction of the party. Lastly, in the third case, they constitute, as it were, a separate nation in the midst of the nation, a government within the government. Their delegates, like the real delegates of the majority, represent the whole collective force of their party, and like them, also, have an appearance of nationality and all the moral power that results from it. It is true that they have not the right, like the others, of making the laws; but they have the power of attacking those which are in force and of drawing up beforehand those which ought to be enacted.

If, among a people who are imperfectly accustomed to the exercise of freedom, or are exposed to violent political passions, by the side of the majority which makes the laws is placed a minority which only deliberates and gets laws ready for adoption, I cannot but believe that public tranquillity would there incur very great risks. There is doubtless a wide difference between proving that one law is in itself better than another and proving that the former ought to be substituted for the latter. But the imagination of the multitude is very apt to overlook this difference, which is so apparent to the minds of thinking men. It sometimes happens that a nation is divided into two nearly equal parties, each of which affects to represent the majority. If, near the directing power, another power is established which exercises almost as much moral authority as the former, we are not to believe that it will long be content to speak without acting; or that it will always be restrained by the abstract consideration that associations are meant to direct opinions, but not to enforce them, to suggest but not to make the laws.

The more I consider the independence of the press in its principal consequences, the more am I convinced that in the modern world it is the chief and, so to speak, the constitutive element of liberty. A nation that is determined to remain free is therefore right in demanding, at any price, the exercise of this independence. But the *unlimited* liberty of political association cannot be entirely assimilated to the liberty of the press. The one is at the same time less necessary and more dangerous than the other. A nation may confine it within certain limits without forfeiting any part of its self-directing power; and it may sometimes be obliged to do so in order to maintain its own authority.

In America the liberty of association for political purposes is unlimited ....

The omnipotence of the majority appears to me to be so full of peril to the American republics that the dangerous means used to bridle it seem to be more advantageous than prejudicial.... There are no countries in which associations are more needed to prevent the despotism of faction or the arbitrary power of a prince than those which are democratically constituted. In aristocratic nations the body of the nobles and the wealthy are in themselves natural associations which check the abuses of power. In countries where such associations do not exist, if private individuals cannot create an artificial and temporary substitute for them I can see no permanent protection against the most galling tyranny; and a great people may be oppressed with impunity by a small faction or by a single individual ....

Different ways *in which the right of association is understood in Europe and in the United States—Different use which is made of it.*

The most natural privilege of man, next to the right of acting for himself, is that of combining his exertions with those of his fellow creatures and of acting in common with them. The right of association therefore appears to me almost as inalienable in its nature as the right of personal liberty. No legislator can attack it without impairing the foundations of society. Nevertheless, if the liberty of association is only a source of advantage and prosperity to some nations, it may be perverted or carried to excess by others, and from an element of life may be changed into a cause of destruction. A comparison of the different methods that associations pursue in those countries in which liberty is well understood and in those where liberty degenerates into license may be useful both to governments and to parties ....

In America the citizens who form the minority associate in order, first, to show their numerical strength and so to diminish the moral power of the majority; and, secondly, to stimulate competition and thus to discover those arguments that are most fitted to act upon the majority; for they always entertain hopes of drawing over the majority to their own side, and then controlling the supreme power in its name. Political associations in the United States are therefore peaceable in their intentions and strictly legal in the means which they employ; and they assert with perfect truth that they aim at success only by lawful expedients . . . .

In America the individuals who hold opinions much opposed to those of the majority can do nothing against it, and all other parties hope to win it over to their own principles. The exercise of the right of association becomes dangerous, then, in proportion as great parties find themselves wholly unable to acquire the majority. In a country like the United States, in which the differences of opinion are mere differences of hue, the right of association may remain unrestrained without evil consequences . . . .

But perhaps the most powerful of the causes that tend to mitigate the violence of political associations in the United States is universal suffrage. In countries in which universal suffrage exists, the majority is never doubtful, because neither party can reasonably pretend to represent that portion of the community which has not voted. The associations know as well as the nation at large that they do not represent the majority. This results, indeed, from the very fact of their existence; for if they did represent the preponderating power, they would change the law instead of soliciting its reform. The consequence of this is that the moral influence of the government which they attack is much increased, and their own power is much enfeebled . . . .

The Americans have also established a government in their associations, but it is invariably borrowed from the forms of the civil administration. The independence of each individual is recognized; as in society, all the members advance at the same time towards the same end, but they are not all obliged to follow the same track. No one abjures the exercise of his reason and free will, but everyone exerts that reason and will to promote a common undertaking.

6.3 E.E. Schattschneider, "The Scope and Bias of the Pressure System" (1960)

The role of factions or associations, later called interest groups, was clearly understood from the nation's earliest days. In the first decades of the twentieth century, Edward F. Bentley's *The Process of Government* (1908) argued that a theory of interest groups could explain all of politics. By mid-century, David B. Truman, in *The Governmental Process* (1951), had extended Bentley's argument by highlighting the intimate involvement of interest groups in every facet of governmental operations. These pluralist arguments assumed that if all interests were represented, then the struggle to shape policy was inherently democratic.

E.E. Schattschneider's *Semi-Sovereign People* (1960) brought a coolly analytical eye to the role of interest groups in American politics. In this selection, Schattschneider asks, what is the scope and bias of the pressure system? How encompassing is the interest group system, and, if it is not all-encompassing, which groups are represented and which are not? Schattschneider distinguished between public interest (broad or inclusive) groups and special (narrow and exclusive) and between organized (active) and unorganized (latent) groups. He concluded that the pressure system—the system of organized special interest groups that interact frequently with government—has a conservative, business-oriented bias. His famous formulation of this point is that "the flaw in the pluralist heaven is that the heavenly chorus sings with a strong upper class accent."

The scope of conflict is an aspect of the scale of political organization and the extent of political competition. The size of the constituencies being mobilized, the inclusiveness or exclusiveness of the conflicts people expect to develop have a bearing on all theories about how politics is or should be organized. In other words, nearly all theories about politics have something to do with the question of who can get into the fight and who is to be excluded.

Every regime is a testing ground for theories of this sort. More than any other system American politics provides the raw materials for testing the organizational assumptions of two contrasting kinds of politics, *pressure politics* and *party politics*.[1] The concepts that underlie these forms of politics constitute the raw stuff of a general theory of political action. The basic issue between the two patterns of organization is one of size and scope of conflict; pressure groups are small-scale organizations while political parties are very large-scale organizations. One need not be surprised, therefore, that the partisans of large-scale and small-scale organizations differ passionately, because the outcome of the political game depends on the scale on which it is played.

To understand the controversy about the scale of political organization it is necessary first to take a look at some theories about interest-group politics. Pressure groups have played a remarkable role in American politics, but they have played an even more remarkable role in American political theory. Considering the political condition of the country in the first third of the twentieth century, it was probably inevitable that the discussion of special-interest pressure groups should lead to development of "group" theories of politics in which an attempt is made to explain everything in terms of group activity, i.e., an attempt to formulate a universal group theory. Since one of the best ways to test an idea is to ride it into the ground, political theory has unquestionably been improved by the heroic attempt to create a political universe revolving about the group. Now that we have a number of drastic statements of the group theory of politics pushed to a great extreme, we ought to be able to see what the limitations of the idea are . . . .

One difficulty running through the literature of the subject results from the attempt to explain *everything* in terms of the group theory.[2] On general grounds it would be remarkable indeed if a single hypothesis explained everything about so complex a subject as American politics. Other difficulties have grown out of the fact that group concepts have been stated in terms so universal that the subject seems to have no shape or form.

The question is: Are pressure groups the universal basic ingredient of all political situations, and do they explain everything? To answer this question it is necessary to review a bit of rudimentary political theory.

Two modest reservations might be made merely to test the group dogma. We might clarify our ideas if (1) we explore more fully the possibility of making a distinction between public-interest groups and special-interest groups and (2) if we distinguished between organized and unorganized groups. These reservations do not disturb the main body of group theory, but they may be useful when we attempt to define general propositions more precisely. If both of these distinctions can be validated, we may get hold of something that has scope and limits and is capable of being defined.... It cannot really be said that we have seen a subject until we have seen its outer limits and thus are able to draw a line between one subject and another.

We might begin to break the problem into its component parts by exploring the distinction between public and private interests.[3] If we can validate this distinction, we shall have established one of the boundaries of the subject.

As a matter of fact, the distinction between *public* and *private* interests is a thoroughly respectable one; it is one of the oldest known to political theory. In the literature of the subject, the public interest refers to general or common interests shared by all or by substantially all members of the community.[4] Presumably no community exists unless there is some kind of community of interests, just as there is no nation without some notion of national interests ....

In the literature of democratic theory the body of common agreement found in the community is known as the "consensus," without which it is believed that no democratic system can survive.

The reality of the common interest is suggested by demonstrated capacity of the community to survive. There must be something that holds people together.

In contrast with the common interests are the special interests. The implication of this term is that these are interests shared by only a few people or a fraction of the community; they *exclude* others and may be *adverse* to them. A special interest is exclusive in about the same way as private property is exclusive. In a complex society it is not surprising that there are some interests that are shared by all or substantially all members of the community and some interests that are not shared so widely. The distinction is useful precisely because conflicting claims are made by people about the nature of their interests in controversial matters.

Perfect agreement within the community is not always possible, but an interest may be said to have become public when it is shared so widely as to be substantially universal. Thus, the difference between 99 percent agreement and perfect agreement is not so great that it becomes necessary to argue that all interests are special, that the interests of the 99 percent are as special as the interests of the 1 percent. For example, the law is probably doing an adequate job of defining the public interest in domestic tranquility despite the fact that there is nearly always one dissenter at every hanging. That is, the law defines the public interest in spite of the fact that there may be some outlaws ....

We can now examine the second distinction, the distinction between organized and unorganized groups.... Organization has been described as "merely a stage or degree of interaction" in the development of a group.[5] ...

Since the beginning of intellectual history, scholars have sought to make progress in their work by distinguishing between things that are unlike and by dividing their subject matter into categories to examine them more intelligently ....

If we are able, therefore, to distinguish between public and private interests and between organized and unorganized groups we have marked out the major boundaries of the subject; *we have given the subject shape and scope.* We are now in a position to attempt to define the area we want to explore. Having cut the pie into four pieces, we can now appropriate the piece we want and leave the rest to someone else. For a multitude of reasons *the most likely field of study is that of the organized, special-interest groups*. The advantage of concentrating on organized groups is that they are known, identifiable, and recognizable. The advantage of concentrating on special-interest groups is that they have one important characteristic in common; they are all exclusive. This piece of the pie (the organized special-interest groups) we shall call the *pressure system* ....

By the time a group has developed the kind of interest that leads it to organize, it may be assumed that it has also developed some kind of political bias because *organization is itself a mobilization of bias in preparation for action*. Since these groups can be identified and since they have memberships (i.e., they include and exclude people), it is possible to think of the *scope* of the system.

When lists of these organizations are examined, the fact that strikes the student most forcibly is that *the system is very small*. The range of organized, identifiable, known groups is amazingly narrow; there is nothing remotely universal about it. There is a tendency on the part of the publishers of directories of associations to place an undue emphasis on business organizations, an emphasis that is almost inevitable because the business community is by a wide margin the most highly organized segment of society ....

The business or upper-class bias of the pressure system shows up everywhere. Businessmen are four or five times as likely to write to their congressmen as manual laborers are. College graduates are far more apt to write to their congressmen than people in the lowest educational category are.[6] ...

Broadly, the pressure system has an upper-class bias. There is overwhelming evidence that participation in voluntary organizations is related to upper social and economic status; the rate of participation is much higher in the upper strata than it is elsewhere. The general proposition is well stated by Lazarsfeld:

> People on the lower SES levels are less likely to belong to any organizations than the people on high SES (Social and Economic Status) levels. (On an A and B level, we find 72 percent of these respondents who belong to one or more organizations. The proportion of respondents who are members of formal organizations decreases steadily as SES level descends until, on the D level only 35 percent of the respondents belong to any associations).[7]

The class bias of associational activity gives meaning to the limited scope of the pressure system, because *scope and bias are aspects of the same tendency*. The data raise a serious question about the validity of the proposition that special-interest groups are a universal form of political organization reflecting *all* interests. As a matter of fact, to suppose that everyone participates in pressure-group activity and that all interests get themselves organized in the pressure system is to destroy the meaning of this form of politics. The pressure system makes sense only as the political instrument of a segment of the community. It gets results by being selective and biased; *if everybody got into the act, the unique advantages of this form of organization would be destroyed, for it is possible that if all interests could be mobilized the result would be a stalemate*.

Special-interest organizations are most easily formed when they deal with small numbers of individuals who are acutely aware of their exclusive interests. To describe the conditions of pressure-group organization in this way is, however, to say that it is primarily a business phenomenon. Aside from a few very large organizations (the churches, organized labor, farm organizations, and veterans' organizations) the residue is a small segment of the population. *Pressure politics is essentially the politics of small groups.*

The vice of the groupist theory is that it conceals the most significant aspects of the system. The flaw in the pluralist heaven is that the heavenly chorus sings with a strong upper-class accent. Probably about 90 percent of the people cannot get into the pressure system.

The notion that the pressure system is automatically representative of the whole community is a myth . . . *Pressure politics is a selective process* ill designed to serve diffuse interests. The system is skewed, loaded, and unbalanced in favor of a fraction of a minority . . . .

One possible synthesis of pressure politics and party politics might be produced by *describing politics as the socialization of conflict.* That is to say, the political process is a sequence: conflicts are initiated by highly motivated, high-tension groups so directly and immediately involved that it is difficult for them to see the justice of competing claims. As long as the conflicts of these groups remain *private* (carried on in terms of economic competition, reciprocal denial of goods and services, private negotiations and bargaining, struggles for corporate control or competition for membership), no political process is initiated. Conflicts become political only when an attempt is made to involve the wider public. Pressure politics might be described as a stage in the socialization of conflict. This analysis makes pressure politics an integral part of all politics, including party politics . . . .

NOTES

1. Pressure groups have been defined by V. O. Key as "private associations . . . (which) promote their interests by attempting to influence government rather than by nominating candidates and seeking responsibility for the management of government," *Politics, Parties, and Pressure Groups,* 4th ed., New York, 1958, p. 23.

   On the other hand, political parties try to get general control of the government by electing their candidates to the most important public offices.

2. Earl Latham, *The Group Basis of Politics,* Ithaca, 1952, pp. 35 and 36, says, "The legislature referees the group struggle, ratifies the victories of the successful coalitions, and records the terms of the surrenders, compromises, and conquests in the form of statutes . . . ." "the legislative vote on which any issue tends to represent the composition of strength, i.e., the balance of power, among the contending groups at the moment of voting."

3. The discussion here refers generally to the analysis made by David Truman in his distinguished volume *The Government Process,* New York, 1951. See especially pp. 50–51, 65.

4. References to the public interest appear under a variety of headings in the literature of political theory.

   See G. D. H. Cole's comment on "the will of all" and the "general will," pp. xxx and xxxi of his introduction to Everyman's edition of Rousseau's *Social Contract,* London, 1913.

   See Ernst Cassirer, *The Myth of the State,* Garden City, 1955, pp. 88–93, for a discussion of Plato's concept of "justice" as the end of the state in his criticism of the sophists.

   See S. D. Lindsay, *The Essentials of Democracy,* Philadelphia 1929, p. 49, for a statement regarding consensus.

5. Truman, *op. cit.,* p. 51.

6. *American Institute of Public Opinion,* May 29, 1946.

7. Lazarsfeld and Associates, *The People's Choice,* p. 145.

6.4 Charles E. Lindblom, "The Privileged Position of Business" (1977)

Charles E. Lindblom's 1977 classic, *Politics and Markets*, argues that all societies must work out a viable relationship between political and economic authority. In some economies, Russia and China come to mind, politics directs the economy with a firm hand, while in societies organized around democracy and capitalism politicians and businessmen share power. Lindblom and others call democratic-free market societies poliarchies, by which they mean societies in which power, both political and economic, is diffuse, divided, checked, and balanced.

Lindblom's key point is that in all economies, centrally directed or capitalist, government is responsible for the performance of the economy, for economic growth, job creation, wages, interest rates, and inflation. In centrally directed economies, these rates, at least for a time, can simply be set by the government. But in capitalist-free market economies, government can influence but cannot command the economy.

Think about the U.S. economy—government is judged by whether its policies promote growth, job creation, rising wages, and prosperity. Government must induce, since it cannot command, businessmen to innovate, hire, and grow. Lindblom's famous phrase, "the privileged position of business," points to the fact that the nation's business interests are in a position to bargain with government for policies designed to produce a positive business climate. No other interests—labor, social welfare, civil rights—are in a similarly privileged position.

We begin the analysis by exploring ... the political role of businessmen in all private enterprise market-oriented societies. This role is different from what it is usually perceived to be. It is not, we shall see, merely an interest-group role.

The Business Executive as Public Official in the Market System

If we can imagine a politico-economic system without money and markets, decisions on the distribution of income would obviously be political or governmental decisions. Lacking markets and wages, income shares would have to be administered by some kind of public authority, perhaps through rationing. Decisions on what is to be produced in the system would also have to be made by political or governmental authority. So also decisions on the allocation of resources to different lines of production, on the allocation of the labor force to different occupations and workplaces, on plant location, the technologies to be used in production, the quality of goods and services, innovation of new products—in short, on every major aspect of production and distribution. All these decisions would be recognized as public policy decisions.

In all societies, these matters have to be decided. They are of momentous consequences for the welfare of any society. But in a private enterprise market system, they are in larger part decided not by government officials but by businessmen. The delegation of these decisions to the businessman does not diminish their importance or, considering their consequences, their public aspect. In communist and socialist systems, heads of enterprises are government officials; it is taken for granted that their functions are governmental. In private enterprise systems, whether polyarchal or not, their functions are no less of public consequence. On all these matters, moreover, not only do business executives make consequential decisions; but, as we have seen in Chapter 11, corporate executives exercise broad discretion in making them.

For example, for a twelve-year period, while European steel companies held outputs and employment relatively stable by permitting prices of steel to fluctuate, American steel companies held prices steady with the result that output and employment fluctuated. It was a discretionary choice full of consequences for jobs, economic growth, prices, and the balance of payments.[1] But it was steel industry executives, not governmental officials, who made the decision.

We hardly need, however, further illustration of the public consequences of discretionary corporate decisions in the market. The major decisions that rest in corporate hands have been outlined in Chapter 11. Corporate executives in all private enterprise systems, polyarchic or not, decide a nation's industrial technology, the pattern of work organization, location of industry, market structure, resource allocation, and, of course, executive compensation and status. They also are the immediate or proximate and discretionary decision makers, though subject to significant consumer control, on what is to be produced and in what quantities.

In short, in any private enterprise system, a large category of major decisions is turned over to businessmen, both small and larger. They are taken off the agenda of government. Businessmen thus become a kind of public official and exercise what, on a broad view of their role, are public functions. The significant logical consequence of this for polyarchy is that a broad area of public decision making is removed from polyarchal control. Polyarchal decision making may of course ratify such an arrangement or amend it through governmental regulation of business decision making. In all real-world polyarchies, a substantial category of decisions is removed from polyarchal control.

The Businessman as Public Official in Government and Politics

What we have just said, however, only begins to describe the public role of businessmen in all private enterprise market-oriented societies. As a result of the "public" responsibilities of businessmen in the market, a great deal more is implied. Businessmen generally and corporate executives in particular take on a privileged role in government that is, it seems reasonable to say, unmatched by any leadership group other than government officials themselves.[2] Let us see, step by step, how this comes about. Every step in the analysis will refer to a familiar aspect of these systems, the implications of which, taken together, have been overlooked by most of us.

Because public functions in the market system rest in the hands of businessmen, it follows that jobs, prices, production, growth, the standard of living, and the economic security of everyone all rest in their hands. Consequently, government officials cannot be indifferent to how well business performs its functions. Depression, inflation, or other economic distress can bring down a government. A major function of government, therefore, is to see to it that businessmen perform their tasks.

Every day about us we see abundant evidence of governmental concern with business performance. In the polyarchies, government responsibility for avoiding inflation and unemployment is a common issue in elections. In all market-oriented systems, a major concern of tax and monetary policy is their effects on business activity. In subsidies and other help to water, rail, highway, and air transport; in patent protection; in fair trade regulation; in tariff policy; in overseas trade promotion through foreign ministries; in subsidized research and development (recently conspicuous, the Concorde in the United Kingdom and France, the aerospace industry in the United States)—in countless ways governments in these systems recognize that businessmen need to be encouraged to perform.

But take particular note of another familiar feature of these systems. Constitutional rules—especially the law of private property—specify that, although governments can forbid certain kinds of activity, they cannot command business to perform. They must induce rather than command.[3] They must therefore offer benefits to businessmen in order to stimulate the required performance. The examples above are all examples of benefits offered, not of commands issued.

One of the great misconceptions of conventional economic theory is that businessmen are induced to perform their functions by purchases of their goods and services, as though the vast productive tasks performed in market-oriented systems could be motivated solely by exchange relations between buyers and sellers. On so slender a foundation no great productive system can be established. What is required in addition is a set of governmentally provided inducements in the form of market and political benefits. And because market demands themselves do not spontaneously spring up, they too have to be nurtured by government. Governments in market-oriented systems have always been busy with these necessary activities. In the eighteenth century, for example, England established almost a thousand local road improvement authorities. When railroads became feasible, special legislation—more than 600 parliamentary acts between 1844 and 1847—granted attractive benefits to railway companies. In late eighteenth and early nineteenth century England, Parliament passed almost 4,000 enclosure acts, both creating a commercial agriculture to replace subsistence farming and driving a labor force off the land into industrial employment.

In the United States, Alexander Hamilton's *Report on Manufactures* put government in an active supportive role for business. So also did early federal policy on banks, canals, and roads; governmental profligacy in indulgences to western railroads; the judicial interpretation of antimonopoly legislation to restrict unions rather than business enterprises; the deployment of Marines to protect American enterprise in Latin America; the use of public utility regulation to protect business earnings; and the diversion of fair trade laws from their ostensible public purposes to the protection of monopolistic privilege.[4]

In the United States, as in all other market systems, the modern corporation could develop only with the assistance of new corporate law in the mid-nineteenth century that limited stockholders liability and in other ways conferred new authority on organizers of large enterprises. In the United States the courts transformed the Fourteenth Amendment, ostensibly written to safeguard the rights of former slaves, into an instrument for the protection of the corporation in its new role as a legal person.

Even more so than in England and America, continental European governments explicitly accepted a responsibility for the development of private enterprise, Germany most conspicuously. Perhaps learning from Europe, Japan went even further with loans, subsidies, and legal privileges for business enterprise.

What, then, is the list of necessary inducements? They are whatever businessmen need as a condition for performing the tasks that fall to them in a market system: income and wealth, deference, prestige, influence, power, and authority, among others. Every government in these systems accepts a responsibility to do what is necessary to assure profits high enough to maintain as a minimum employment and growth. If businessmen say, as they do, that they need tax offsets to induce investment, governments in all these systems seriously weigh the request, acknowledging that the tax concessions may indeed be necessary. In these systems such concessions are in fact granted. If corporation executives say that the chemical industries need help for research and development, governments will again acknowledge the probability that indeed they do and will commonly provide it. If corporate executives want to consult with government officials, including president or prime minister, they will be accommodated. Given the responsibilities of businessmen in these societies, it would be a foolish chief executive who would deny them consultation. If corporate executives ask, as they frequently do, for veto power over government appointments to regulatory positions, it will again be acknowledged that such a concession may be necessary to induce business performance. All this is familiar. And we shall see below that governments sometimes offer to share their formal authority with corporate officials as a benefit offered to induce business performance.

In the eyes of government officials, therefore, businessmen do not appear simply as the representatives of a special interest, as representatives of interest groups do. They appear as functionaries performing functions that government officials regard as indispensable. When a government official asks himself whether business needs a tax reduction, he knows he is asking a question about the welfare of the whole society and not simply about a favor to a segment of the population, which is what is typically at stake when he asks himself whether he should respond to an interest group.

Any government official who understands the requirements of his position and the responsibilities that market-oriented systems throw on businessmen will therefore grant them a privileged position. He does not have to be bribed, duped, or pressured to do so. Nor does he have to be an uncritical admirer of businessmen to do so. He simply understands, as is plain to see, that public affairs in market-oriented systems are in the hands of two groups of leaders, government and business, who must collaborate and that to make the system work government leadership must often defer to business leadership. Collaboration and deference between the two are at the heart of politics in such systems. Businessmen cannot be left knocking at the doors of the political systems, they must be invited in.

A leader of a West German business association comments on the world of politics, "This is not an alien world to the entrepreneur; it is his own. At stake for him is the leadership of the state."[5] Drawing on his experience in Du Pont, an American writes, "the strength of the position of business and the weakness of the position of government is that government needs a strong economy just as much as business does, and the people need it and demand it even more."[6] The duality of leadership is reminiscent of the medieval dualism between church and state, and the relations between business and government are no less intricate than in the medieval duality.

Thus politics in market-oriented systems takes a peculiar turn, one largely ignored in conventional political science. To understand the peculiar character of politics in market-oriented systems requires, however, no conspiracy theory of politics, no theory of common social origins uniting government and business officials, no crude allegation of a power elite established by clandestine forces. Business simply needs inducements, hence a privileged position in government and politics, if it is to do its job.

Mutual Adjustment between the Two Groups

So far we have stressed controls by businessmen over government. But of course controls go in both directions. In briefest outline the reciprocal controls look like the following:

> Government exercises broad authority over business activities.
>
> But the exercise of that authority is curbed and shaped by the concern of government officials for its possible adverse effects of business, since adverse effects can cause unemployment and other consequences that government officials are unwilling to accept.
>
> In other areas of public policy, the authority of government is again curbed and shaped by concern for possible adverse effects on business.
>
> Hence even the unspoken possibility of adversity for business operates as an all-pervasive constraint on government authority.
>
> Mindful of government concern for business performance, businessmen, especially corporate executives, actively voice and negotiate demands on government, with both implicit threat of poor performance if their demands are not met.
>
> For all these reasons, business officials are privileged not only with respect to the care with which government satisfies business needs in general but also in privileged roles as participants in policy deliberations in government.
>
> At least hypothetically, government always has the option, if dissatisfied with business performance, of refusing further privilege and simply terminating private enterprise in a firm, industry or the entire system. Short of taking that course, however, government has to meet business needs as a condition of inducing business performance.

Market and private enterprise thus introduce an extreme degree of mutual adjustment and political pluralism, even in the absence of polyarchy. The mutual adjustment is not always explicit through meetings and actual negotiation. Nor does government usually enter into an explicit exchange with businessmen. Mutual adjustment is often impersonal and distant. It operates through an unspoken deference of administrations, legislatures, and courts to the needs of business. And it relies on a multitude of common tacit understandings shared by the two groups of leaders, business and governmental, with respect to the conditions under which enterprises can or cannot profitably operate.

In addition, business executives come to be admitted to circles of explicit negotiation, bargaining, and reciprocal persuasion, from which ordinary citizens are excluded. Other leaders are admitted—union and farm leaders and other interest-group representatives. In these consultations, however, corporate executives occupy a privileged position, since they and not the interest-group leaders are there mainly in their capacity as "public" officials.

It follows that evidence, which is abundant, of conflict between business and government—and of business defeats—is not evidence of lack of privilege. Knowing that they must have some privileges and knowing that government officials fully understand that simple fact, businessmen ask for a great deal. They also routinely protest any proposal to reduce any of their privileges. They are not highly motivated to try to understand their own needs. It might weaken them in governmental negotiations to do so. Hence they often predict dire consequences when a new regulation is imposed on them, yet thereafter quickly find ways to perform under it.

NOTES

1. U.S. Congress, Senate, Subcommittee on Antitrust and Monopoly of the Committee on the Judiciary: Hearings, Egon Sohmen testimony in *Economic Concentration*, 90th Congress, 2d session, 1968, p. 3446.
2. In contemporary thought, especially democratic thought, "privilege" often connotes something improper. That is not my intention in using the term. Webster says privilege is "right or immunity granted as a peculiar benefit, advantage, or favor; *esp.*: one attached specif. to a position or an office," and something that is privileged is "not subject to the usual rules and penalties because of some special circumstance" (*Webster's Seventh New Collegiate Dictionary* [Springfield, Mass.: G. & C. Merriam]).
3. But private property is not the key to the process being described. For any market system, whether private or public enterprise is the rule, enterprises must have autonomy or "rights" to respond to market cues rather than be obliged to obey governmental commands. See chapter 22.
4. For a long list of U.S. business subsidies, see Clair Wilcox, *Public Policy toward Business*, 4th ed. (Homewood, Ill.: Irwin, 1971), chapter 33. On the variety of promotions, see Murray Weidenbaum, *The Modern Public Sector* (New York: Basic Books, 1969), esp. the table on p. 137.
5. Quoted in Heinz Hartmann, *Authority and Organization in German Management* (Princeton, N.J.: Princeton University Press, 1959), p. 229.
6. Harold Brayman, *Corporate Management in a World of Politics* (New York: McGraw-Hill, 1967), p. 57.

6.5 Richard Harris and Daniel Tichenor, "Organized Interests and American Political Development" (2002–2003)

This modern classic of APD research and the highlight piece of Chapter 6 pushed the inquiry into the origins and impact of the interest group system back into the nineteenth century. The research goal is to ask whether the structure of the interest group system in the nineteenth and early twentieth century was similar to or different from the more studied late twentieth century. Richard Harris and Daniel Tichenor asked whether the expansion of the interest group system occurred simultaneously with or followed the growth of government in the Progressive (1900s and 1910s) and New Deal (1930s) eras.

Harris and Tichenor found that there was a surge of interest group formation and activity in the Progressive era, well before the rapid expansion of government during the New Deal and the social movement activity of the 1960s. Moreover, they found that during some periods certain kinds of interest groups, business groups at some times, citizen groups at others, were more active and influential than their numbers might suggest. Harris and Tichenor demonstrated that "Expanding the time frame of interest group research can elucidate historical patterns and long-term shifts not discernible by relying exclusively on data since the 1950s."

Within very recent years these [interest] groups have increased and multiplied. More important still, they have become highly organized and are today conducted by shrewd and capable leaders . . . .

E. Pendleton Herring, 1928[1]

Ours is an era of vigorous activity by organized interests in national politics. In the past two decades we have witnessed what seems to be a virtual explosion in demands by private interest organizations in Washington . . . .

Kay Schlozman and John Tierney, 1986[2]

The striking resonance of these quotations from leading interest group scholars generations apart suggests that something remarkably similar may have been happening at both ends of the twentieth century. Contemporary political science offers no shortage of careful research on the behavior of organized interest groups and their place in democratic theory. Yet this impressive body of scholarship routinely concentrates on the past half century of interest group politics. This article highlights the need to expand the time horizons of interest group studies by exploring organized interests during the late nineteenth and early twentieth centuries, a watershed period in American political development that receives scant attention in the political science literature on interest groups. Moreover, a perfunctory treatment of the formation, maintenance, and attrition of organized interests before the New Deal (if not the 1960s) imposes a major limitation on theory building in this field. By presenting new research findings on the level and character of interest group activity in the Progressive Era, we hope to illustrate the value of bringing *both* history and theory to bear on the study of interest group politics in America.

It is often assumed that the formation and mobilization of organized interests in U.S. national politics were natural outgrowths of the modern welfare and regulatory state that emerged with the New Deal and expanded in the post-civil rights era. In truth, precious little is known about the relationship between interest groups and federal government activism over time, particularly in the Progressive Era when modern liberalism first began to take shape. More generally, systematic analysis of long-term trends in interest group growth and mortality rates remains a blind spot for most political scientists working in this area . . . .

Building on the historical–institutional work of political scientists studying the Progressive Era, we present fresh research that illuminates significant changes in the nature and impact of group involvement in national politics during the late nineteenth and early twentieth centuries.[3] In this vein, we corroborate the findings of historians who have asserted that the Progressive Era constituted both an "organizational synthesis" and a pivotal time when new interest groups flourished in U.S. politics.[4] Our empirical research underscores the need to reevaluate prevailing accounts and theories of the development of American interest group politics . . . .

Cornerstones of American Politics

While the interest group literature effectively portrays the post-war evolution of interest group politics and offers useful explanations of group formation in that period, we argue that it is historically incomplete. Careful examination of the Progressive Era reveals a highly developed system of interest group politics with its own characteristics and dynamics. This argument is theoretically significant because it points to evidence that organized interests burst onto the national stage before the Progressive agenda had been translated into legislation and programs. Did the rise of big government drive interest group formation in America, as much of the existing literature presumes? If the Progressive Era was the first period of widespread national interest organization, this mobilization predates the realization of the modern welfare and regulatory state during the New Deal and succeeding decades, thereby challenging prevailing causal accounts. Our research findings raise fresh questions about whether increased group formation and political mobilization actually precede, accompany, or follow extensive national policy making and state-building. These questions challenge us to think in broader theoretical terms about the connections and causal dynamics between interest groups and state-building.

More generally, as our data show, the existence of a robust set of organized interests engaged in Progressive Era political life highlights the need for careful, historically-based explanations of the relationship between interest groups and American political development. Expanding the time frame of interest group research can elucidate historical patterns and long-term shifts not discernible by relying exclusively on data since the 1950s. . . . Taking stock of interest group systems that have emerged in American politics over time offers a more promising basis for theory-building that is not constrained by contemporary empirical foundations and thus limited to a particular historical context. . . . In this vein, we devote considerable attention to the rise of a new interest group system in the Progressive Era.

A National Interest Group System Emerges

Clearly, an assessment of interest group activity over time requires the integration of multiple data sources and must be informed by both quantitative and qualitative analysis.[5] Our strategy, therefore, is to use a variety of sources and methods to triangulate our analysis on the research objective of identifying and explicating interest group systems.[6] In the absence of a single reliable data source, we have sought to pull together a wide variety of quantitative and qualitative materials to provide a broader historical view of organized interests in American politics since the late nineteenth century . . . .

Toward that end, we employ a fivefold typology of interest groups: citizens groups, unions, trade associations, professional associations, and "other" groups. We also draw a coarser distinction between private corporations and interest groups . . . .

[Figure 1 presents] the rates at which particular kinds of interest groups first appeared before Congress during the nineteenth and early twentieth centuries. Nearly every interest group category—professional groups, trade associations/economic interests, unions, citizens groups, and other varieties of groups—increased from one decade to the next. Yet the rates of expansion by category were clearly not equal. The number of trade associations and related economic interests that first appeared in each decade were larger in total number than any other interest group category before 1920 . . . .

When we cast our nets more widely to examine the total number of appearances of both interest groups and private corporations at congressional hearings between 1833 and 1917, one of our most significant findings is the sharp increase in the amount of testimony by organized interests in Washington after the turn of the century. As Figure 2 indicates, appearances of interest groups and private corporations more than tripled between 1900 and 1909 from roughly 800 to 3,000. They also increased at a sharp rate in the eight years between 1910 and 1917 from 3,000 to nearly 6,000. This explosion in the representation of organized interests before congressional committees, and by implication within the Washington policy-making community more generally, is unmistakable. One also may note that private corporations appeared at hearings more often than interest groups in these years. However, private corporations tended to testify before Congress only once or twice during the entire period examined. Moreover, most private corporations were local and their appearances were inspired by the narrowest of concerns. That is, most of the private corporations in our data set were focused on how a specific national policy might affect a decidedly local and material interest, such as a

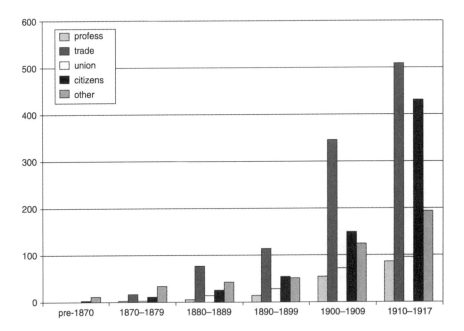

Figure 1 Total Number of Interest Groups Appearing Before Congress by Type, 1833–1917.

Sources: Created by authors from data in *CIS Index for Congressional Hearings*, 23rd–64th Congress (U.S. Government Printing Office, 1985).

local metal screw company testifying on tariffs for metal imports or a small Colorado mining company focused on the acquisition of nearby public lands. By contrast, a large proportion of the interest groups we analyzed appeared at several hearings and were concerned with a broader set of policy issues. This may reflect the fact that roughly half of the interest groups that testified before Congress between 1833 and 1917 were national organizations, whereas only 10 percent of the private corporations could be described as national.

Our findings with regard to an additional measure, the total number of interest groups appearing before Congress in each period, strengthen our conclusion that the early twentieth century polity was a vibrant time for interest group activism at the national level, especially when compared with the nineteenth century (see Figure 2). Whereas 256 interest groups appeared before Congress from 1890 to 1899, that figure rose to 734 between 1900 and 1909, and then nearly doubled to 1,301 over the next eight years. Moreover, when one compares the numbers of first group appearances with the total number of interest groups that testified at legislative hearings, it is striking just how many new interest groups comprised the total of those that testified each decade (1,008 of 1,301 interest groups between 1910 and 1917).

Finally, we found that a comparison of the total number of groups that testified by category with the total number of appearances by group category underscores Berry's recent finding that the kinds of groups with influence in the Washington policy-making setting may not always be proportional to their number (see Table 1). For instance, during the 1900s, trade associations and related economic interests comprised 47 percent

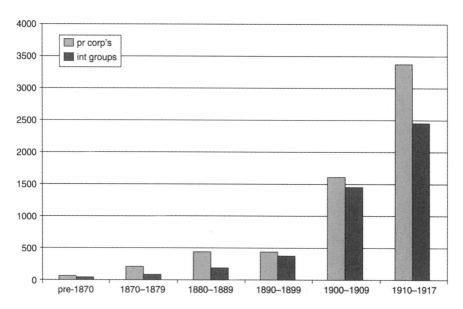

Figure 2 Appearances of Private Corporation and Interest Groups at Congressional Hearings, 1833–1917 (23rd to 24th Congresses.

Source: CIS Index for Congressional Hearings, 23rd–64th Congresses (U.S. Government Printing Office, 1985).

Table 1 Interest Group Appearances at Congressional Hearings, by Category (1889–1917)

Category	1889–1899 (51ˢᵗ–55ᵗʰ Congresses)		1899–1909 (56ᵗʰ–60ᵗʰ Congresses)		1909–1917 (61ˢᵗ–64ᵗʰ Congresses)	
	Group #	*Appearances*	*Group #*	*Appearances*	*Group #*	*Appearances*
Trade Associations	110 (43%)	165 (45%)	342 (47%)	667 (46%)	508 (39%)	715 (29%)
Citizens Groups	53 (21%)	66 (18%)	147 (20%)	262 (18%)	426 (32%)	819 (33%)
Unions	27 (11%)	56 (15%)	72 (9%)	240 (17%)	93 (7%)	479 (17%)
Total	256	367	734	1,442	1,301	2,459

Source: Based on data developed from the *CIS Index for Congressional Hearings*, 23ʳᵈ to 64ᵗʰ Congresses (Washington, DC: Government Printing Office, 1985).

of the groups appearing at hearings and 46 percent of group appearances; citizens groups were 20 percent of all groups and 18 percent of appearances; and unions accounted for 9 percent of all groups and 17 percent of total group appearances. Unions enjoyed similar influence during the next eight years, constituting 7 percent of all groups testifying and 17 percent of all appearances. And while citizens groups made up 32 percent of all groups appearing and 33 percent of all appearances between 1910 and 1917, trade associations had fewer opportunities to testify (29 percent) than their number (39 percent of all groups appearing) may have implied. Finally, the fact that citizens groups appeared more often than any other kind of interest group between 1910 and 1917 is striking, since trade associations represented 7 percent more of the total number of groups testifying. Perhaps most remarkable is that the total number of citizens groups and unions testifying in this period was roughly the same as that of trade associations, but they combined to give 50 percent of all testimony in these years compared to trade associations' 29 percent . . . .

Conclusion

The Progressive Era was a watershed period for organized interests in national political life. One cannot truly understand the origins and development of modern interest group politics in America without taking stock of the crucial transformations ushered in during the late nineteenth and early twentieth centuries. At a time when the nineteenth century "state of courts and parties" was in full retreat and institutions of the national state were undergoing significant change, organized interests—unprecedented in number, variety, and professionalism—became active in federal politics.[7]

As we have shown, more organized interests than ever before emerged on the political stage in these decades. Indeed, the Progressive Era system was animated by aggregate numbers far greater than the standard literature estimates. This finding alone underscores the prospects for more ambitious theory-building when political scientists are attentive to the task of gathering comprehensive historical information about politically active interest groups. It encourages an analytical framework that apprehends not only the long-term trends in group formation and maintenance, but also group attrition. It underscores the possibility that the constellation of organized interests engaged in political life has undergone an intriguing ebb and flow over the years that merits careful theoretical explanation.

Significantly, the surge we found in politicized interest groups during this period was evident across categories, from trade and professional associations to organized labor and citizens groups. One of the defining features of the Progressive Era system is the rich variety of organized interests that mobilized in pursuit of distinct policy goals. It is crucial that the study of interest groups takes into account and seeks explanations for the varying levels of participation and influence by different types of interest groups in given historical periods. Private corporations, trade associations, unions, professional associations, citizens groups, and other organizations emerged at different rates over time and participated at varying levels within historical periods. At particular times, the frequency of participation for given categories of groups can be out of proportion with their numbers. These sorts of categorical comparisons over time hold the promise of drawing out important historical patterns for theoretical analysis, including classic questions of systemic bias in favor of business and upperclass interests.

The Progressive Era system is also characterized by an unprecedented centralization of interest group politics. Long before the New Deal or the social movement insurgency of the 1960s, interest groups of the early twentieth century increasingly focused their activities on federal governmental actors, institutions, and policies. More groups than at any previous time sought to influence policy making within the Washington Beltway in those years, and many established national offices for the first time in the nation's capital. The evidence provided here illustrates that the nationalization of U.S. interest group politics began before the rise of the modern welfare and regulatory state that emerged in later decades. Accordingly, it demonstrates the need for more careful investigation of whether interest group formation and national political mobilization precedes, coincides with, or follows big government programs . . . .

When data on group formation and legislative behavior are brought to bear, we can see a picture of interest group politics that strongly suggests a set of historical patterns worthy of close examination. Organized interests did indeed burgeon in the past half-century as our current interest group literature demonstrates. However, it is equally clear that the beginning of the twentieth century also witnessed a dramatic expansion of organized interest participation in national policy making. In addition, we have shown that the Progressive Era expansion included a disproportionately high rate of citizen groups organizing, foreshadowing the well-documented surge of public interest group formation since the 1960s. Both periods reflects the initial role that citizens groups can play in advancing a national reform agenda. Moreover, our analysis of the attrition rates of Progressive Era organizations suggests that it will be possible to construct a data set that will allow a deeper historical study of interest group politics in America and to draw evolutionary connections both across interest group systems and among interest groups, party politics, and state-building. The most important potential benefit of this historical research, however, is the opportunity to explore broader dynamics of interest group politics over time. Assuming "what's past is prologue," formulating an under-standing of organized interests by analyzing the past forty years is analogous to coming into a play after the second act. We can surely appreciate the dialogue among the actors, but we cannot have a very deep appreciation for the underlying currents that moved the drama to that point.

NOTES

* The authors thank Jeffrey Berry, Elizabeth Clemens, David Hart, Sidney Milkis, Andrew Polsky, and Elizabeth Sanders for their helpful comments on an earlier version of this article.

1. E. Pendleton Herring, *Group Representations Before Congress* (Baltimore: Johns Hopkins University Press, 1929), 2–3.

2. Kay Lehman Schlozman and John Tierney, *Organized Interests and American Democracy* (New York: Harper and Row, 1986), 1–2.

3. See Elisabeth Clemens, *The People's Lobby: Organizational Innovation and the Rise of Interest Group Politics in America, 1890–1925* (Chicago: Chicago University Press, 1997); Elizabeth Sanders, *Roots of Reform: Farmers, Workers, and the American State, 1877–1917* (Chicago: Chicago University Press, 1999); Theda Skocpol, *Protecting Soldiers and Mothers* (Cambridge, MA: Harvard University Press, 1992); and Stephen Skowronek, *Building A New American State: The Expansion of National Administrative Capacities, 1879–1920* (New York: Cambridge University Press, 1982).

4. Arthur Link and Richard L. McCormick, *Progressivism* (Arlington Heights, IL: Harlan Davison, 1983); Robert Wiebe, *The Search for Order* (Westport, CT: Greenwood Press, 1980); and Louis Galambos, "The Emerging Organizational Synthesis in Modern American History," *Business History Review* 44 (1970): 279–290.

5. Berry makes this argument persuasively in *The New Liberalism*.

6. The concept of triangulation is discussed by William Dunn, *Public Policy Analysis*, 4th ed. (Princeton: Prentice-Hall, 1999).

7. Skowronek, *Building a New American State*, 27.

6.6 Elisabeth Clemens, "Politics Without Party: The Organizational Accomplishments of Disenfranchised Women" (1997)

Elisabeth Clemens asked "How were women able to secure a place within the formerly masculine political sphere?" She answered that the organizational evolution of the "woman movement" was from "organizational forms linked to traditional understandings of feminine virtue . . . [to] less feminine but also nonpolitical methods associated with business and education, women activists of the early twentieth century made an oblique entrance into American politics."

Women's organizations were distinctive in that they lacked the aversion that many men's organizations had to dependency on government. Because women's groups lacked access to the partisan structures of the day, they sought the cooperation of government agencies in initiating and administering "programs such as free kindergartens, juvenile courts, . . . support for single mothers . . . [and] laws regulating maximum hours and minimum wages for women . . . ." Unexpectedly, winning suffrage and entering explicitly into partisan politics blunted some of these earlier institutional advantages. New strategies had to be developed.

If the party system suppressed the grievances of many organized workingmen and farmers, for women it did so doubly. Reforming the parties or developing nonpartisan techniques meant little so long as women lacked the primary currency of political life: the vote. But to gain the vote, women had to displace the profoundly fraternal models upon which the parties themselves had been constructed. As women sought new models for organized action, they disrupted the mapping of masculine and feminine onto public and private, onto citizen and dependent, thereby undermining established logics of appropriateness.... How were American women able to secure a place within the formerly masculine political sphere? How did their actions help to define the emerging rules and techniques of a new style of politics in the United States? What do these efforts tell us more generally about the possibilities and processes of institutional change?

These questions are complicated by the fact that much of the "woman movement" adopted seemingly conservative strategies and organizational models. Describing the successful Washington suffrage campaign of 1910, suffragist Emma Smith DeVoe explained, "We worked for our vote in womanly ways, for we weren't men and we didn't want to be men, therefore, we didn't propose to try to get our vote in the way that men would."[1] The use of organizational forms linked to traditional understandings of feminine virtue allowed women to secure an initial public presence. But by relying on forms that invoked norms of difference between men and women, these strategies also created obstacles for women who sought to establish themselves as regular political actors alongside the representatives of business, labor, and agriculture. To move from public service to political action, the middle- and upper-class women who constituted the woman movement increasingly adopted organizational forms less linked to feminine identities than were the philanthropies and reform associations of the late nineteenth century. By gradually adopting the less feminine but also nonpolitical methods associated with business and education, women activists of the early twentieth century made an oblique entrance into American politics ....

Careful to avoid expressions of partisanship so long as women lacked the vote, women's organizations were far less ambivalent in their commitment to nonpartisan and extrapartisan methods than were contemporary associations of workers, farmers, or male reformers. Lacking the aversion to dependency that informed the political visions of many of their male counterparts, women activists were also more open to state regulation and sustained cooperation with government agencies. Programs such as free kindergartens, juvenile courts, probation officers, and the support of single mothers were often established as experimental programs funded by clubwomen and then taken over by public agencies (whose staff frequently included former volunteers).[2] Laws regulating maximum hours and minimum wages for women paved the way for more active state intervention through economic regulation. Because women had long been excluded from the realm of contract, programs advocated by and for women could set important precedents for government action.

In attacking the explicitly masculine world of partisanship, familiar feminine forms of organizations were regularly criticized: "Philanthropic work is not new to women. The woman's club as a means of recreation, intellectual exercise, and growth is a new feature. It seems best to keep the ideas distinct."[3] Records of women's associations document sustained debates over organizational methods, a collective search for models that could define women's common concerns and effectively articulate them with public and political institutions.... Lacking access to party organizations, women constructed cooperative ties between their own organizations and newly created state agencies in the provision of social services.

Viewed from this perspective, the enfranchisement of women and the creation of new capacities for state intervention are not separate problems.... Out of these processes of organization and counterorganization, a new kind of polity emerged: lobbying was legitimated, the politics of education was perfected and gradually shaped into a recognizably modern politics of public opinion and advertising. In the process, however, the explicitly gendered symbols and practices of nineteenth-century politics faded, and gender became a semicovert category of public order, something to be rediscovered by later generations of feminist scholars.[4] ...

Toward a Politics without Parties

Women's influence on the state-building enterprises of the Progressive Era reflected the distinctive cultural and institutional location of their organizing efforts. As an element in the rhetoric of American political reform, women were placed in symbolic opposition to the corrupt mechanisms of late-nineteenth-century politics. As early as 1888, Brother O. F. Alley of the San Jose Grange declared: "We believe that the coming person who shall purify politics, elevate the moral condition of the human race and cultivate and enlarge the spiritual growth, will be a woman, and that this woman will be found in the Grange, a living embodiment of the divine principles of the Patrons of Husbandry."[5] Women's groups reinforced this opposition between women and the existing *partisan* organization of political participation. Claims that these new strategies and models of organization were inappropriate were met with accusations of the vices of political organization among men: "Women are criticized for the methods they pursue to obtain political recognition, also for allowing their impulses rather than their judgment to lead them. Men should remember the beams in their own eyes before pointing out the motes in the eyes of women."[6]

In order to craft new vehicles for political participation, women's groups drew upon forms of organization with which they were already familiar. Thus the central place of education in the women's clubs and moral-reform movements colored the political actions of many women. Prior to gaining the vote, women's groups emphasized civics instruction and discussion of political issues as a means of cultivating informed and independent voters; the same link between education and true citizenship was institutionalized by American farmers, another relatively disenfranchised group. Many women's groups sponsored "civics institutes" prior to the opening of state legislatures or important local elections. This emphasis on the connection of citizenship to education—rather than to party—also informed one of women's most important and enduring contributions to the organizational repertoire of American politics, the nonpartisan forum: "No more amusing or instructive gathering can be imagined than these assemblies of women sitting in judgement while relays of prospective office-holders pass across the stage, explaining each in turn and regardless of his party affiliation, why they should vote for him."[7]

In addition to adopting the practices and imagery of education, women's groups replaced distinctively feminine forms of social organization with organizational models adapted from modern corporations. But while these alternatives muted the opposition of male and female, they heightened that of partisan and nonpartisan. Through a logic of oppositions, where the enemy of my enemy is my friend, these alternatives could be adopted by elite reformers with less experience of popular organizing than their female allies. Thus, at the same time that women drew on forms of economic organization, degendering their associations by imitating the corporations and bureaucracies, they helped to redefine the general terms for political action within the United States.

The organizational and strategic innovations of women's associations were, however, fundamentally limited by their lack of political standing. Without institutionalized opportunities for linking associational resources to public or political goals, women's organizations either stayed with traditional understandings of women's work or explored possible transformations of the domestic sphere or private life. Yet in many states, there were opportunities for organized women to establish a public presence, if only on the margins of the formal polity. Even without the vote, women might establish a public role through their benevolent associations provided that the public sector relied on private associations . . . .

These variations in resources were overlaid by the strikingly different polities that developed in each state. Most obviously, women secured the vote in Washington in 1910 and California in 1911; in Wisconsin, women had to await the 1920 amendment to the U.S. Constitution. This difference in timing was accentuated by the varied opportunities for political action. In California, the party system was largely dismantled; in California and Washington, early passage of the initiative and referendum left state governments open to nonpartisan and extrapartisan pressure politics. Both developments mapped on to the organizational innovations of the national women's associations . . . .

National Ramifications

Success also reflected back on the techniques of nonpartisan and extrapartisan pressure politics that were widely associated with women's groups. The long-standing political exclusion of women ensured that their renewed activism would be particularly disruptive to the culture and structure of political life.[8] Rooted in a subculture that had opposed itself to the fraternal world of partisan politics, women's organizations played a special role in the attack on that system:

> Women are surprisingly quick, perhaps because of their experience with naughty boys, to distrust candidates who try to hypnotize the voters with loud oratory and who dodge straight questions from the floor. Their intuitions seem to make them keenly alive to the dangers of machine politics and they are more and more the despair of politicians who wish to enforce party regularity and to herd voters ignorantly to the polls. . . . [I]n their simplicity they demand *clear* issues and when they understand them vote conscientiously; but rather than be befogged into voting wrong they will stay away from the polls.[9]

This profound antipathy for partisan politics aligned women's groups with both populist antiparty movements and more genteel good government groups. But an alliance of the disenfranchised and an idealistic minority did not offer much hope of success, so women's groups directed much of their energy toward discovering new ways of working within a partisan system.

This reinterpretation is clearest in the case of the lobby. In the Gilded Age, the lobby had belonged to the "Interests," said with a sneer and an implication of bribery. Women took the lobby and transformed it into an everyday interest group—just a collection of concerned citizens trying to make their voices heard. This transformation depended on two qualities that the progressive leadership did not share with organized women. As women, they could claim independence from partisan politics; as leaders of a mass movement,[10] they could claim to represent a large and legitimate (potential) constituency. Once they had gained the right to vote, a purification from within could begin. Some women, notably those most active in the suffrage movement, went so far as to imitate the practices of the despised political machines. In their successful campaign for the vote in 1911, California women adopted a system of precinct canvasing and mobilization that their counterparts in New York had borrowed from the infamous Tammany Hall machine.[11] . . .

Once admitted to electoral competition, women found that the distinctive identities and methods they had cultivated were undermined. Having mobilized around identities and organizational forms defined in opposition to party politics, women activists found it difficult to mobilize as a bloc within the electoral system. The very effort to work within parties appeared at odds with the moral and political rhetorics used to articulate women's distinctive claims upon politics. Arguing that "[w]omen must learn to Play the Game as Men Do," for example, Eleanor Roosevelt urged women to support "women bosses" within the parties rather than pursuing separatist strategies. While "the word 'boss' might 'shock sensitive ears,'" she asserted that "if women believe they have a right and duty in political life today, they must learn to talk the language of men. They must not only master the phraseology, but also understand the machinery which men have built up through years of practical experience. Against the men bosses there must be women bosses who can talk as equals, with the backing of a coherent organization of women voters behind them."[12] But insofar as women accommodated themselves to existing institutions, their insurgent edge was blunted . . . .

NOTES

1. *Milwaukee Free Press*, 7 July 1911.
2. Mary S. Gibson, *A Record of Twenty-five Years of the California Federation of Women's Clubs* (California Federation of Women's Clubs, 1927), 214–16; Mrs. M. Burton, "Ladies' Clubs and Societies in Los Angeles in 1892," reported for the Historical Society of Southern California (Los Angeles: Misses Lillian A. and Estella M. Williamson, 1925), 40.
3. Mrs. J. C. Croly, *The History of the Women's Club Movement in America* (New York: Henry G. Allen and Co., 1898), 125.
4. Nelson, "Two-Channel Welfare State"; Virginia Sapiro, "The Gender Basis of American Social Policy," *Political Science Quarterly* 101, no. 2 (1986): 221–38; Skocpol, *Protecting Soldiers and Mothers*, chaps. 6–9.
5. California State Grange, *Proceedings of the Annual Convention*, 1888, 112.
6. *Wisconsin Citizen*, January 1888, 1.
7. Mary Roberts Coolidge, *What the Women of California Have Done with the Ballot* (San Francisco: n.p., 1916), 4.
8. Symbolically, women had a place in party politics by way of the increasing use of feminine imagery in the "spectacular" campaigns of the late nineteenth century. McGerr, *Decline of Popular Politics*, 208. This changing symbolism corresponded to a reorganization of political solidarities: "Femininity was inducted into politics hand in hand with the ethnic partition of

the public sphere, which was manifested both in partisan rivalries and in violent civil strife.... Gender rose to the surface of political groups within the population, identified as much by their ethnicity and religion as by their opinions on specific questions of public policy." Ryan, *Women in Public*, 140. Thus women were not alone in exporting models of family and kinship into the field of politics.

9. Coolidge, *What Women Have Done*, 4.

10. In California, for example, one paper claimed that "one hundred thousand women in California have, through organizations to which they belong, endorsed the suffrage amendment." The State Federation of Women's Clubs alone claimed a membership of thirty-five thousand. *Western Woman Voter*, September 1911, 8.

11. Schaffer, "Problem of Consciousness"; College Equal Suffrage League of Northern California, *Winning Equal Suffrage*, 107.

12. *Redbook*, April 1928, quoted in Blanche Wiesen Cook, *Eleanor Roosevelt*, vol. 1, *1884–1933* (New York: Viking, 1992), 366–68.

Discussion Questions

1. Are the "factions" that James Madison was worried about in *Federalist* 10 and his convention comments the same thing as what we call interest groups today? How are they similar, how are they different, and should we share his concerns?

2. Do you share Tocqueville's view that freedom of the press is more fundamental to democracy than freedom of association? Why is one more important than the other, or are they equally important? Are limits on either ever justified?

3. Why do you think that groups form around business and corporate interests more readily than they do around interests shared by the poor, the elderly, and the disabled?

4. What was it about the Progressive Era, the New Deal, and the 1960s that seemed to spur organization and increased activity among interest groups?

5. Thinking about the experience of women's groups as described by Elisabeth Clemens, what lessons and skills does group participation teach those who take part?

Suggested Additional Reading

Frank R. Baumgartner and Beth L. Leech, *Basic Interests: The Importance of Groups in Politics and in Political Science* (Princeton, NJ: Princeton University Press, 1998).

Jeffrey Berry and Clyde Wilcox, *Interest Group Society*, 5th ed. (New York: Longman, 2008).

Elizabeth Sanders, *Roots of Reform: Farmers, Workers, and the American State, 1877–1917* (Chicago: University of Chicago Press, 1998).

Mark A. Smith, *American Business and Political Power: Public Opinion, Elections, and Democracy* (Chicago: University of Chicago Press, 2000).

John R. Wright, *Interest Groups and Congress: Lobbying, Contributions, and Influence* (New York: Longman, 2009).

7

Political Parties

Introduction

The history of republican government, ranging from ancient Greece and Rome forward to the American colonial and state governments, convinced the Founders that the self-interest inherent in human nature created factionalism and factionalism created social, economic, and political instability. Factionalism and the instability that it produced had been the bane, often the end, of republican government throughout history. The Founders concluded that political parties, just another name for factions, were a threat rather than a productive element of popular government.

As a result, the U.S. Constitution made no provision for political parties. Almost universally, the Founders saw interest groups and political parties as threats to the common good. In our first selection, James Reichley explained that the Founders crafted "a polity without parties." Their goal in the Constitutional Convention of 1787 was to construct a constitution of distinctly limited powers, with careful separation of powers and checks and balances. The well-balanced institutional structures, they hoped, would allow the new government to withstand the assaults of factions, parties, and other social pressures and tumults.

Nonetheless, the play of politics in the first Washington administration forced a change in thinking. Washington's support for Alexander Hamilton's extensive economic program forced Jefferson and Madison into opposition and led them to organize their supporters, first in Congress and then in the broader public. James Madison, the author of *Federalist* 10, the famous warning against the dangers of faction, explained the necessity for political parties in our second selection, entitled "A Candid State of Parties." Madison claimed that his opponents were aristocrats and monarchists out to do the country ill, while he, Jefferson, and their supporters sought only to protect the public interest and serve the common good. In just a few short years, Jefferson and Madison had concluded that, at least in their hands, a political party might be a vehicle to protect the common good rather than to threaten it.

Our third selection, by Lord James Bryce, from his famous two-volume *The American Commonwealth* (1888), tracks Madison's explanation for the origins of political parties in America, but goes a bit deeper. Bryce was a prominent lawyer and historian who eventually became the British ambassador to the United States.

Much like Madison, Bryce argued that parties have their origin in human psychology—some men distrust human nature and favor strong central government (Hamilton in the U.S.), while others trust human nature and favor weaker decentralized government (Jefferson)—but unlike Madison, for whom parties were an unfortunate necessity, Bryce thought that parties actually held the American separation of powers system together and made it go. Bryce famously said, "In America the great moving forces are the parties. The government counts for less than in Europe, the parties count for more."

For decades, APD scholars have worked to explain both the origins of political parties in the United States and the shape of party competition over the course of the nation's history. In our fourth selection, John Aldrich employs the tools of social choice theory to explain the general circumstances under which parties arise in democratic politics. Aldrich posits that politics without parties are unstable and unpredictable. Self-interested politicians will join like-minded colleagues to create a structure that will limit instability in their favor. Parties bring structure and coherence to politics and allow politicians to better serve their own career interests and their constituent's interests.

Whether United States parties started as vehicles to allow Madison and Jefferson to oppose Washington and Hamilton, or would inevitably have arisen to organize and structure democratic politics in the new nation, scholars have long sought to understand the shape and pattern of party competition. Sidney Milkis argues in our highlight piece that both the historical and institutional origins of U.S. parties create a tension between presidents and parties. Historically, parties arose in the British Parliament to facilitate opposition to the king. Hence, parties have opposition to executive power in their DNA. Moreover, the Founders employed the separation of powers and checks and balances to assure that each branch could defend its own rights and prerogatives. Hence, presidents have rarely been able to lead and control a legislative majority for long. More often, legislative parties, even facing popular presidents of the same party, have sought to maintain their independence. Ask Barack Obama about this.

Our final selection for Chapter 7 draws attention to the fact that throughout American history established political parties have been subject to pressures both from within their ranks and from the society outside. After the Tea Party burst onto the scene in 2009, scholars, journalists, and pundits asked exactly who the Tea Party adherents were, where they came from politically, and what they wanted. Theda Skocpol, a leading APD scholar, and Vanessa Williamson interviewed Tea Party members and scoured public commentary and polling to conclude that the Tea Party was generally the reenergized right wing of the Republican Party. They demonstrated that the Tea Party both supplemented Republican strength and threatened to push the party too far to the right to appeal to moderate voters.

These selections show that political parties are always changing and evolving, sometimes slowly and smoothly, sometimes quickly and roughly. Parties have leaders that try to shape their image and set their direction, but sometimes the energy that swirls around issues like slavery or health care reform, push parties in new and dangerous, or at least uncertain, directions.

7.1 James Reichley "Intention of the Founders: A Polity Without Parties" (2000)

The delegates to the Federal Convention of 1787, led by James Madison, sought to build "a polity without parties" in James Reichley's phrase. Rather than depending simply upon "interests to check interests" as Madison wrote in *Federalist* 10, or parties to check parties, the Founders sought to tame politics and protect liberty by carefully limiting power and building intricate checks and balances into the constitutional structure of the federal government. The Founders looked to constitutional structure—the separation of powers and checks and balances—rather than to the interplay of parties and factions to protect liberty.

Intention of the Founders

A Polity Without Parties

In "government of a monarchical cast," George Washington observed, "Patriotism may look with indulgence, if not with favor, upon the spirit of the party. But in those of popular character, in Governments purely elective, it is a spirit not to be encouraged … A fire not to be quenched; it demands a uniform vigilance to prevent its bursting into a flame, lest instead of warming it should consume."[1] …

The Founders' low regard for parties was in part derived from prejudices formed by their studies of classical writers and British and European political theorists. But they also had before them what they considered the baneful effects of parties in the colonial and state governments: the tendency of parties to sharpen class antagonisms; the emergence of parties, with their attendant functionaries, as interests in themselves; the openness of parties to corruption, and the ease with which they could be mastered by demagogues.

Beyond these acquired biases and empirical observations, the Founders' rejection of parties grew out of their conviction that such political divisions are inherently subversive of republican ideals. The Founders, … realized that any political system will be shaped in part by clashing interests and personal ambitions. But they believed that republican government must finally be rooted in the ideal of a disinterested citizenry coming together, either directly or through elected representatives, to legislate for the common good. They were Lockeans, but Lockeans of the original school, holding, like Locke himself that the social contract once concluded exerts moral authority of its own, rather than merely providing a playing field for unremitting struggle among private interests.

Parties, by framing every issue in terms of winners and losers, the Founders believed, undermine this indispensable willingness to seek at some level the common good rather than the satisfaction of special interests. Parties, therefore, are socially destructive and must be considered, as Madison wrote, a potentially "mortal disease"; as Hamilton claimed, an "avenue to tyranny"; and as Washington insisted, a source of "frightful despotism."[2]

. . .

The delegates who gathered in Philadelphia in the spring of 1787 to consider amendments to the Articles of Confederation, on which such national government as existed was based, were concerned over the growing acrimony among the states. Even more, they were determined to erect constitutional safeguards for social order and established rights, including property rights.

With Washington in the chair, and Hamilton, Madison, James Wilson, and the octogenarian Benjamin Franklin among the delegates, the Philadelphia convention went far beyond its legal mandate and produced a Constitution that embodied the spirit of the Revolution in a moderately conservative structure of national government . . . .

Hamilton, Madison, and John Jay, in their classic defense of the Constitution, *The Federalist,* made no bones about the conservative nature of their objectives. The proposed new structure of government, Hamilton maintained in *Federalist* Number Nine, would be "a barrier against domestic faction and insurrection." A strong national government, insulated against parochial pressures, Jay argued in *Federalist* Number Three, would override the tendency of "the governing party in one or two States to swerve from good faith and justice . . ."[3]

Madison, more than his two colleagues, spelled out the underlying moral, political, and psychological assumptions on which the Constitution is based. The "great object" of the Constitution, Madison wrote in the familiar *Federalist* Number Ten, was to "secure the public good and private rights against the danger of . . . faction, and at the same time to preserve the spirit and the form of popular government. . . ." The causes of faction, "actuated by some common impulse or passion, or of interest, adverse to the rights of other citizens, or to the permanent and aggregate interests of the community," are "sown in the nature of man." Differences over religion and forms of government contribute to the development of faction. "But the most common and most durable source of faction has been the various and unequal distribution of property."[4]

Economic inequality results from "diversity in the faculties of men . . . ." Proponents of pure democracy "have erroneously supposed that by reducing mankind to a perfect equality in their political rights, they would, at the same time, be perfectly equalized and assimilated in their possessions, their opinions, and their passions." Democracies taking this approach "have ever been spectacles of turbulence and confusion; have ever been found incompatible with personal security or the rights of property; and have in general been as short in their lives as they have been violent in their deaths."[5]

Faction growing out of differences in economic interest, though a constant threat to republican government, cannot be avoided without suppressing freedom. "Liberty is to faction what air is to fire . . . ." Since faction in a republic cannot be avoided, its effects must be mitigated through constitutional design. A faction consisting of "less than a majority . . . may clog the administration, . . . may convulse the society," but in the end it must give way to the will of the majority, so long as republican forms are maintained. But "when a majority is included in a faction, the form of popular government . . . enables it to sacrifice to its ruling passion or interest both the public good and the rights of other citizens." It is then that popular government becomes vulnerable to such pernicious schemes as "a rage for paper money, for an abolition of debts, for equal division of property . . . ."[6]

The surest way to avoid this danger, Madison contends, is to make it unlikely that such a majority will form. In relatively small constituencies, like the individual states, the majority of have-lesses will tend to combine politically against the minority of have-mores. But in a nation as large as the federal union to be formed by the new Constitution, economic interests will divide into "a landed interest, a manufacturing interest, a mercantile interest, a moneyed interest, [and] many lesser interests . . . ." Politics, then, will focus on functional and regional differences rather than on class rivalries—a politics, that is, of many minorities, rather than of majority against minority.[7]

Sheer size, moreover, will make it difficult for radical agitators, like the populist leaders coming to power in some of the states, to mobilize the discontented into an effective national majority. "The influence of factious leaders may kindle a flame within their particular states, but will be unable to spread a general conflagration through the other states."[8]

In *Federalist* Number Fifty-one, Madison returned to the need under republican government "to guard one part of the society against the injustice of the other part." . . .

In a republic, the avaricious will of a transitory majority may be countered in part by a system of governmental checks and balances: first dividing "the power surrendered by the people" between the states and the national government; then within the national government balancing the executive against the legislature; and finally by dividing the legislative branch into different houses, rendering "them by different modes of election and different principles of action, as little connected with each other as the nature of their common functions and their common dependence on the society will admit." The surest protection for minorities, however, is extension of governmental authority over a territory so vast and a population so varied that government will have to achieve consensus rather than a simple majority in order to act. Society "will be broken into so many parts, interests, and classes of citizens, that the rights of individuals, or of the minority, will be in little danger from interested combinations of the majority."[9]

Resort to such devices, Madison concedes, may be a reflection on human nature. "But what is government itself, but the greatest of all reflections on human nature? If men were angels, no government would be necessary."[10]

The populist leaders in the states, who had been little represented at the Philadelphia convention, did not have to read *The Federalist* to recognize what the framers of the Constitution were up to. Populist strategists and spokesmen like Samuel Adams in Massachusetts, George Clinton in New York, and Patrick Henry in Virginia fought ratification in their respective states. Among state legislators whose position on the Constitution is known, more than four-fifths of the populists opposed ratification while an even larger share of conservatives were pro-Constitution.[11]

The Antifederalists, as opponents of the Constitution were called, could not match the Federalists' national organization, directed by much of the former high command of the Revolution. The inability of the Antifederalists to mount an effective national campaign provided a demonstration that seemed to bear out Madison's thesis. Populist appeals might work state by state, but when the issue was framed in national terms—in this case, the survival of a united republic—the moderates and conservatives appeared to have the advantage.

The Antifederalists issued propaganda blasts but deployed no intellectual artillery approaching the force of *The Federalist*. Tom Paine, the Revolution's most articulate publicist of equalitarian ideology, had earlier attacked the principles of social balance and mixed government on which the Constitution was based. But in 1787 Paine was otherwise engaged, working on various political and business projects in England, soon to depart for France to participate in the Revolution of 1789. Thomas Jefferson, absent in France as American ambassador but in touch with political associates at home, wrote to friends that he hoped the Constitution would not be ratified—an interesting first effort, he told Madison, but needing another try. Jefferson did not, however, publicly align himself with the Antifederalists. Looking back after the fight for ratification had been won, he maintained that he had been "neither federalist nor antifederalist; . . . of neither party, nor yet a trimmer between parties."[12]

In some states, notably Massachusetts, New Hampshire, New York, and Virginia, the vote on ratification was close. But by March 4, 1789, 11 states had ratified and the Constitution was declared adopted. Eight months later, North Carolina added its vote for ratification. In May 1790, Rhode Island, by a majority at the state convention of only 34 to 32, became the last of the original 13 states to join the federal union. By that time, George Washington had been President for more than a year.

Were the Founders Wrong?

When James Madison argued in *The Federalist* that factions will inevitably develop in a free society, he did not imply approval of political parties nor did he suggest that parties as institutions would necessarily play a major role in the political life of the United States. Like all the other principal Founders, Madison regarded parties as a political evil and believed that a wisely framed constitution would minimize their influence.

The Founders recognized that competition among different economic and social interests was bound to find outlet through politics. But they believed that the varying kinds of representation provided by the states and the federal government, and by the executive and bicameral legislative branches at the federal level, would themselves offer sufficient advocacy for contending interest groups and would make extensive recourse to formally organized parties unnecessary.

Were the Founders, who were right about so many things, simply wrong then when they turned their attention to parties? Did prejudice or lack of experience with how republican government actually works lead them to overlook the valuable role that most political scientists now claim parties play in free societies? Or is it possible that they were in fact right: that the nation would have been better off if the development of institutionalized parties had somehow been avoided; and that parties not only are not necessary to democracy, but also, as many ordinary Americans have always believed, dangerously undermine the efficiency and integrity of republican government?

NOTES

1. Noble E. Cunningham, Jr., *The Jeffersonian Republicans: The Formation of Party Organization, 1789-1801* (U. of North Carolina Press, Chapel Hill, 1957), p. 94.
2. Sisson, *American Revolution*, p. 207; Gerald Stourzh, *Alexander Hamilton and the Idea of Republican Government* (Stanford U. Press, Stanford, CA, 1970), p. 118.
3. *The Federalist* (New York: Modern Library, 1937), pp. 47, 15.
4. *Ibid.*, pp. 55–56.
5. *Ibid.*, p. 58.
6. *Ibid.*, pp. 55–57, 62.
7. *Ibid.*, p. 56.
8. *Ibid.*, p. 61.
9. *Ibid.*, pp. 338–39.
10. *Ibid.*, p. 337.
11. Main, *Political Parties*, pp. 357–58.

12. Wood, *American Republic*, pp. 483–99; Jefferson quoted by Richard Hofstadter, *The Idea of a Party System* (U. of California Press, Berkeley, 1969), p. 123.

7.2 James Madison, "A Candid State of Parties" (1792)

Just five years after James Madison warned of the dangers of factionalism in his convention speech of June 6, 1787 and in the *Federalist* 10 of November 23, 1787, Madison and Jefferson are at the head of a new party taking shape to oppose the tendency of Hamilton's policies in the Washington administration. By September 1792, Madison was the leading figure in the U.S. House of Representatives and Jefferson was Secretary of State. Jefferson was in increasingly direct opposition to Alexander Hamilton, Secretary of the Treasury, in Washington's cabinet. Washington favored Hamilton's counsel. Jefferson resigned his cabinet seat at the end of 1793 to go into more public opposition to Hamilton and Washington.

Madison's "A Candid State of Parties" is a fascinating document, even if more partisan and ideological than candid. Like party politicians from that day to this, Madison seeks to paint his opponents in an unacceptable light and himself and his supporters as the only force for good. Madison described the Federalists as a small, but dangerously clever, band of not-so-secret monarchists, while he described the party taking shape around Jefferson as the true friends of republican government. John Adams and the Federalists beat Jefferson in his first run at the presidency in 1796, but Jefferson came back to defeat Adams in 1800.

A Candid State of Parties[1]

As it is the business of the contemplative statesman to trace the history of parties in a free country, so it is the duty of the citizen at all times to understand the actual state of them. Whenever this duty is omitted, an opportunity is given to designing men, by the use of artificial or nominal distinctions, to oppose and balance against each other those who never differed as to the end to be pursued, and may no longer differ as to the means of attaining it. The most interesting state of parties in the United States may be referred to three periods: Those who espoused the cause of independence and those who adhered to the British claims, formed the parties of the first period; if, indeed, the disaffected class were considerable enough to deserve the name of a party. This state of things was superseded by the treaty of peace in 1783. From 1783 to 1787 there were parties in abundance, but being rather local than general, they are not within the present review.

The Federal Constitution, proposed in the latter year, gave birth to a second and most interesting division of the people. Every one remembers it, because every one was involved in it.

Among those who embraced the constitution, the great body were unquestionably friends to republican liberty; tho' there were, no doubt, some who were openly or secretly attached to monarchy and aristocracy; and hoped to make the constitution a cradle for these hereditary establishments.

Among those who opposed the constitution, the great body were certainly well affected to the union and to good government, tho' there might be a few who had a leaning unfavourable to both. This state of parties was terminated by the regular and effectual establishment of the federal government in 1788; out of the administration of which, however, has arisen a third division, which being natural to most political societies, is likely to be of some duration in ours.

One of the divisions consists of those, who from particular interest, from natural temper, or from the habits of life, are more partial to the opulent than to the other classes of society; and having debauched themselves into a persuasion that mankind are incapable of governing themselves, it follows with them, of course, that government can be carried on only by the pageantry of rank, the influence of money and emoluments, and the terror of military force. Men of those sentiments must naturally wish to point the measures of government less to the interest of the many than of a few, and less to the reason of the many than to their weaknesses; hoping perhaps in proportion to the ardor of their zeal, that by giving such a turn to the administration, the government itself may by degrees be narrowed into fewer hands, and approximated to an hereditary form.

The other division consists of those who believing in the doctrine that mankind are capable of governing themselves, and hating hereditary power as an insult to the reason and an outrage to the rights of man, are naturally offended at every public measure that does not appeal to the understanding and to the general interest of the community, or that is not strictly conformable to the principles, and conducive to the preservation of republican government.

This being the real state of parties among us, an experienced and dispassionate observer will be at no loss to decide on the probable conduct of each.

The anti republican party, as it may be called, being the weaker in point of numbers, will be induced by the most obvious motives to strengthen themselves with the men of influence, particularly of moneyed, which is the most active and insinuating influence. It will be equally their true policy to weaken their opponents by reviving exploded parties, and taking advantage of all prejudices, local, political, and occupational, that may prevent or disturb a general coalition of sentiments.

The republican party, as it may be termed, conscious that the mass of people in every part of the union, in every state, and of every occupation must at bottom be with them, both in interest and sentiment, will naturally find their account in burying all antecedent questions, in banishing every other distinction than that between enemies and friends to republican government, and in promoting a general harmony among the latter, wherever residing, or however employed.

Whether the republican or the rival party will ultimately establish its ascendance, is a problem which may be contemplated now; but which time alone can solve. On one hand experience shews that in politics as in war, stratagem is often an overmatch for numbers; and among more happy characteristics of our political situation, it is now well understood that there are peculiarities, some temporary, others more durable, which may favour that side in the contest. On the republican side, again, the superiority of numbers is so great, their sentiments are so decided, and the practice of making a common cause, where there is a common sentiment and common interest, in spight of circumstantial and artificial distinctions, is so well understood, that no temperate observer of human affairs will be surprised if the issue in the present instance should be reversed, and the government be administered in the spirit and form approved by the great body of the people.

NOTE

1. From *The National Gazette*, September 26, 1792.

7.3 James Bryce, "The American Commonwealth: Political Parties and Their History" (1888)

Lord James Bryce, 1st Viscount Bryce (1838–1922), a British lawyer, historian, and diplomat stands second only to Alexis de Tocqueville as a foreign observer of the American political culture. In preparing to write *The American Commonwealth*, Bryce retraced Tocqueville's U.S. tour. Bryce was disappointed to find that the broad equality that Tocqueville had described in the early 1830s had given way to inequality and the great industrial fortunes of the 1880s.

In this selection, Bryce describes the development of American political parties in the nineteenth century. In a free society, parties develop in response to natural human tendencies. Some men favor centralization, some do not; some men distrust human nature, while others place more confidence in it. Bryce offers compelling character sketches of Alexander Hamilton, skeptical of human nature and favoring centralization, and Thomas Jefferson, confident in human goodness and in distributed local control, as the founders of the Federalist and Jeffersonian Republican parties respectively. Though Bryce thought that parties grew out of natural human inclinations, he also knew that issues played a decisive role. His description of how slavery disrupted both major parties from 1820 to 1860, ultimately shattering the Whig Party and opening the way for the rise of the Republican Party, is instructive. Bryce's *The American Commonwealth*, like Tocqueville's *Democracy in America*, is both good history and good literature.

[T]he spirit and force of party has in America been as essential to the action of the machinery of government as steam is to a locomotive engine; or, to vary the simile, party association and organization are to the organs of government almost what the motor nerves are to the muscles, sinews, and bones of the human body. They transmit the motive power, they determine the directions in which the organs act. A description of them is therefore a necessary complement to an account of the Constitution and government; for it is into the hands of the parties that the working of the government has fallen.

Their ingenuity, stimulated by incessant rivalry, has turned many provisions of the Constitution to unforeseen uses, and given to the legal institutions of the country no small part of their present colour.

In America the great moving forces are the parties. The government counts for less than in Europe, the parties count for more;

In the United States, the history of party begins with the Constitutional Convention of 1787 at Philadelphia. In its debates and discussions on the drafting of the Constitution there were revealed two opposite tendencies, which soon afterwards appeared on a larger scale in the State Conventions, to the new instrument was submitted for acceptance. These were the centrifugal and centripetal tendencies—a tendency to maintain both the freedom of he individual citizen and the independence in legislation, in administration, in jurisdiction, indeed in everything except foreign policy and national defence, of the several States; an opposite tendency to subordinate the States to the nation and vest large powers in the central Federal authority.

The charge against the Constitution that it endangered State rights evoked so much alarm that some States were induced to ratify only by the promise that certain amendments should be added, which were accordingly accepted in the course of the next three years. When the machinery had been set in motion by the choice of George Washington as president, and with him of a Senate and a House of Representatives, the tendencies which had opposed or supported the adoption of the Constitution reappeared not only in Congress but in the President's cabinet, where Alexander Hamilton, secretary of the treasury, counselled a line of action which assumed and required the exercise of large powers by the Federal government, while Jefferson, the secretary of state, desired to practically restrict its action to foreign affairs. The advocates of a central national authority had begun to receive the name of Federalists, and to act pretty constantly together, when an event happened which, while it tightened their union, finally consolidated their opponents also into a party. This was the creation of the French Republic and its declaration of war against England. The Federalists, who were shocked by the excesses of the Terror of 1793, counselled neutrality, and were more than ever inclined to value the principle of authority, and to allow the Federal power a wide sphere of action. The party of Jefferson, who had now retired from the administration, were pervaded by sympathy with French ideas, were hostile to England whose attitude continued to be discourteous, and sought to restrict the interference of the central government with the States, and to allow the fullest play to the sentiment of State independence, of local independence, of personal independence. This party took the name of Republicans or Democratic Republicans, and they are the predecessors of the present Democrats. Both parties were, of course, attached to republican government—that is to say, were alike hostile to a monarchy. But the Jeffersonians had more faith in the masses and in leaving things alone, together with less respect for authority, so that in a sort of general way one may say that while one party claimed to be the apostles of Liberty, the other represented the principle of Order.

These tendencies found occasions for combating one another, not only in foreign policy and in current legislation, but also in the construction and application of the Constitution. Like all documents, and especially documents which have been formed by a series of compromises between opposite views, it was and is susceptible of various interpretations, which the acuteness of both sets of partisans was busy in discovering and expounding. While the piercing intellect of Hamilton developed all those of its provisions which invested the Federal Congress and President with far-reaching powers, and sought to build up a system of institutions which should give to these provisions their full effect, Jefferson and his coadjutors appealed to the sentiment of individualism, strong in the masses of the people, and, without venturing to propose alterations in the text of the Constitution, protested against all extensions of its letter, and against all the assumptions of Federal authority which such extensions could be made to justify....

At first the Federalists had the best of it, for the reaction against the weakness of the old Confederation which the Union had superseded disposed sensible men to tolerate a strong central power. The President, though not a member of either party, was, by force of circumstances, as well as owing to the influence of Hamilton, practically with the Federalists. But during the presidency of John Adams, who succeeded Washington, they committed grave errors. When the presidential election of 1800 arrived, it was seen that the logical and oratorical force of Hamilton's appeals to the reason of the nation told far less than the skill and energy with which Jefferson played on their feelings and prejudices. The Republicans triumphed in the choice of their chief, who retained power for eight years (he was re-elected in 1804), to be peaceably succeeded by his friend Madison for another eight years (elected in 1808, re-elected in 1812), and his disciple Monroe for eight years more (elected in 1816, reelected in 1820). Their long-continued tenure of office was due not so much to their own merits, for neither Jefferson nor Madison conducted foreign affairs with success, as to the collapse of their antagonists. The Federalists never recovered from the blow given in the election of 1800. They lost Hamilton by death in 1803. No other leader of equal gifts appeared, and the party, which had shown little judgment in the critical years 1810–14, finally disappears from sight after the second peace with England in 1815.... This period (1788–1824) may be said to constitute the first act in the drama of American party history?

One cannot note the disappearance of this brilliant figure, to Europeans the most interesting in the earlier history of the Republic, without the remark that his countrymen seem to have never, either in his lifetime or afterwards, duly recognized his splendid gifts. Washington is, indeed, a far more perfect character. Washington stands alone and unapproachable, like a snow-peak rising above its fellows into the clear air of morning, with a dignity, constancy, and purity which have made him the ideal type of civic virtue to succeeding generations. No greater benefit could have befallen the republic than to have such a type set from the first before the eye and mind of the people. But Hamilton, of a virtue not so flawless, touches us more nearly, not only by the romance of his early life and his tragic death, but by a certain ardour and impulsiveness, and even tenderness of soul, joined to a courage equal to that of Washington himself. Equally apt for war and for civil government, with a profundity and amplitude of view rare in practical soldiers or statesmen, he stands in the front rank of a generation never surpassed in history.... Talleyrand, who seems to have fell for him something as near affection as that cold heart could feel, said, after knowing all the famous men of the time, that only Fox and Napoleon were Hamilton's equals, and that he had divined Europe, having never seen it....

Jefferson's importance lies in the fact that he became the representative not merely of democracy, but of local democracy, of the notion that government is hardly wanted at all, that the people are sure to go right if they are left alone, that he who resists authority is *prima facie* justified in doing so, because authority is *prima facie* tyrannical, that a country where each local body in its own local area looks after the objects of common concern, raising and administering any such funds as are needed, and is interfered with as little as possible by any external power, comes nearest to the ideal of a truly free people.

Some intervention on the part of the State there must be, for the State makes the law and appoints the judges of appeal; but the less one has to do with the State, and *a fortiori* the less one has to do with the less popular and more encroaching Federal authority, so much the better. Jefferson impressed this view on his countrymen with so much force and such personal faith that he became a sort of patron saint of freedom in the eyes of the next generation . . . .

The disappearance of the Federal party between 1815 and 1820 left the Republicans masters of the field. But in the United States if old parties vanish nature produces new ones. Sectional divisions soon arose among the men who joined in electing Monroe in 1820, and under the influence of the personal hostility of Henry Clay and Andrew Jackson (chosen President in 1828), two great parties were again formed (about 1830) which some few years later absorbed the minor groups. One of these two parties carried on, under the name of Democrats, the dogmas and traditions of the Jeffersonian Republicans. It was the defender of States' Rights and of a restrictive construction of the Constitution; it leant mainly on the South and the farming classes generally, and it was therefore inclined to free trade. The other section, which called itself at first the National Republican, ultimately the Whig party, represented many of the views of the former Federalists, such as their advocacy of a tariff for the protection of manufactures, and of the expenditure of public money on internal improvements. It was willing to increase the army and navy, and like the Federalists found its chief, though by no means its sole, support in the commercial and manufacturing parts of the country, that is to say, in New England and the middle States. Meantime a new question far more exciting, far more menacing, had arisen. In 1819, when Missouri applied to be admitted into the Union as a State, a sharp contest broke out in Congress as to whether slavery should be permitted within her limits, nearly all the Northern members voting against slavery, nearly all the Southern members for. The struggle might have threatened the stability of the Union but for the compromise adopted next year, which, while admitting slavery in Missouri, forbade it for the future north of lat. 36°30′. The danger seemed to have passed, but in its very suddenness there had been something terrible. Jefferson, then over seventy, said that it startled him "like a fire-bell in the night." . . . The question of the extension of slavery west of the Missouri river had become by 1850 the vital and absorbing question for the people of the United States, and as in that year California, having organized herself without slavery, was knocking at the doors of Congress for admission as a State, it had become an urgent question which evoked the hottest passions, and the victors in which would be victors all along the line. But neither of the two great parties ventured to commit itself either way. The Southern Democrats hesitated to break with those Democrats of the Northern States who sought to restrict slavery. The Whigs of the North, fearing to alienate the South by any decided action against the growing pretensions of the slave-holders, temporized and suggested compromises which practically served the cause of slavery. They did not perceive that in trying to preserve their party they were losing hold of the people, alienating from themselves the men who cared for principle in politics, sinking into a mere organization without a faith worth fighting for. That this was so presently appeared. The Democratic party had by 1852 passed almost completely under the control of the slave-holders, and was adopting the dogma that Congress enjoyed under the Constitution no power to prohibit slavery in the territories. This dogma obviously overthrew as unconstitutional the Missouri compromise of 1820. The Whig leaders discredited themselves by Henry Clay's compromise scheme of 1850, which, while admitting California as a free

State, appeased the South by the Fugitive Slave Law. They received a crushing defeat at the presidential election of 1852; and what remained of their party finally broke in pieces in 1854 over the bill for organizing Kansas as a territory in which the question of slaves or no slaves should be left to the people, a bill which of course repealed the Missouri compromise. Singularly enough, the two great orators of the party, Henry Clay and Daniel Webster, both died in 1852, wearied with strife and disappointed in their ambition of reaching the presidential chair. Together with Calhoun, who passed away two years earlier, they are the ornaments of this generation, not indeed rising to the stature of Washington or Hamilton, but more remarkable than any, save one, among the statesmen who have followed them.[1] With them ends the second period in the annals of American parties, which, extending from about 1820 to 1856, includes the rise and fall of the Whig party.

The Whig party having vanished, the Democrats seemed to be for the moment, as they had been once before, left in possession of the field. But this time a new antagonist was quick to appear. The growing boldness of the slave-owners had begun to alarm the Northern people when they were startled by the decision of the Supreme court, pronounced in the case of the slave Dred Scott, which laid down the doctrine that Congress had no power to forbid slavery anywhere, and that a slave-holder might carry his slaves with him where he pleased, seeing that they were mere objects of property, whose possession the Constitution guaranteed.[2] This hastened the formation out of the wrecks of the Whigs of a new party, which took in 1856 the name of Republican, while at the same time it threw an apple of discord among the Democrats. In 1860 the latter could not agree upon a candidate for President .... Thus the Republicans through the divisions of their opponents triumphed in the election of Abraham Lincoln, presently followed by the secession of eleven slave States.

The Republican party, which had started by denouncing the Dred Scott decision and proclaiming the right of Congress to restrict slavery, was of course throughout the Civil War the defender of the Union and the assertor of Federal authority, stretched, as was unavoidable, to lengths previously unheard of. When the war was over, there came the difficult task of reconstructing the now reconquered slave States, and of securing the position in them of the lately liberated negroes ... the old Democratic party, almost silenced during the war, had now reappeared in full force as the advocate of State rights, and the watchful critic of any undue stretches of Federal authority. It was found necessary to negative the Dred Scott decision and set at rest all questions relating to slavery and to the political equality of the races by the adoption of three important amendments to the Constitution. The troubles of the South by degrees settled down as the whites regained possession of the State governments and the Northern troops were withdrawn. In the presidential election of 1876 the war question and negro question had become dead issues, for it was plain that a large and increasing number of the voters were no longer, despite the appeals of the Republican leaders, seriously concerned about them.

This election marks the close of the third period, which embraces the rise and overwhelming predominance of the Republican party. Formed to resist the extension of slavery, led on to destroy it, compelled by circumstances to expand the central authority in a way unthought of before, that party had now worked out its programme and fulfilled its original mission. The old aims were accomplished, but new ones had not yet been substituted, for though new problems had appeared, the party was not prepared with solutions. Similarly the Democratic party had discharged its mission in defending the rights of the reconstructed States, and criticizing excesses of executive power; similarly it too had refused to grapple either with the fresh questions which had begun to arise since the war, or with those older questions which had now reappeared above the subsiding flood of war days. The old parties still stood as organizations, and still claimed to be the exponents of principles. Their respective principles had, however, little direct application to the questions which confronted and divided the nation. A new era was opening which called either for the evolution of new parties, or for the transformation of the old ones by the adoption of tenets and the advocacy of views suited to the needs of the time. But this fourth period, which began with 1876, has not yet seen such a transformation, and we shall therefore find, when we come to examine the existing state of parties, that there is an unreality and lack of vital force in both Republicans and Democrats, powerful as their organizations are....

Two permanent oppositions may, I think, be discerned running through the history of the parties, sometimes openly recognized, sometimes concealed by the urgency of a transitory question. One of these is the opposition between a centralized or unified and a federalized government. In every country there are centrifugal and centripetal forces at work, the one or the other of which is for the moment the stronger. There has seldom been a country in which something might not have been gained, in the way of good administration and defensive strength, by a greater concentration of power in the hands of the central government, enabling it to do things which local bodies, or a more restricted central government, could not do equally cheaply or well. Against this gain there is always to be set the danger that such concentration may weaken the vitality of local communities and authorities, and may enable the central power to stunt their development. Sometimes needs of the former kind are more urgent, or the sentiment of the people tends to magnify them; sometimes again the centrifugal forces obtain the upper hand.

The other opposition, though it goes deeper and is more pervasive, has been less clearly marked in America, and less consciously admitted by the Americans themselves. It is the opposition between the tendency which makes some men prize the freedom of the individual as the first of social goods, and that which disposes others to insist on checking and regulating his impulses. The opposition of these two tendencies, the love of liberty and the love of order, is permanent and necessary, because it springs from differences in the intellect and feelings of men which one finds in all countries and at all epochs. There are always persons who are struck by the weakness of mankind, by their folly, their passion, their selfishness: and these persons, distrusting the action of average mankind, will always wish to see them guided by wise heads and restrained by strong hands. Such guidance seems the best means of progress, such restraint the only means of security. Those on the other hand who think better of human nature, and have more hope in their own tempers, hold the impulses of the average man to be generally towards justice and peace. They have faith in the power of reason to conquer ignorance, and of generosity to overbear selfishness. They are therefore disposed to leave the individual alone, and to entrust the masses with power. Every sensible man feels in himself the struggle between these two tendencies, and is on his guard not to yield wholly to either, because the one degenerates into tyranny, the other into an anarchy out of which tyranny will eventually spring. The wisest statesman is he who best holds the balance between them.

NOTES

1. Powerful pictures of the political straggles of this time may be found in Mr. Schurz's *Life of Henry Clay*, and Dr. von Hoist's *Life of John C. Calhoun*.

2. This broad doctrine was not necessary for the decision of the case, but delivered as an *obiter dictum* by the majority of the court.

7.4 John H. Aldrich, "Why Parties Form" (2011)

In this modern classic, John Aldrich asks why parties form? In the historical sense, this question has been answered in previous selections—parties formed because Madison and Jefferson opposed Hamilton's fiscal policies and needed help in Congress to block them. Hence, they organized opposition in Congress, which eventually became the Jeffersonian Republican Party (and eventually the Jeffersonian Democrats), and Hamilton organized his Federalist supporters to defeat them. Hamilton wanted to pass his programs and the Jeffersonians were determined to resist—both organized supporters—hence, parties.

Aldrich asks the same historical question, but provides a theoretical answer. The first American parties did not arise simply because Hamilton and his opponents each sought to collect around them those who shared their views. Rather, parties arose because ambitious politicians realized that a stable, coherent party apparatus would help them win more consistently than they could otherwise. Aldrich drew on "the theory of collective goods and collective action, the theory of social choice and voting, and the theory of political ambition" to explain the origins of political parties in the U.S. Political parties form because they enhance the electoral prospects of ambitious politicians and allow them to win more regularly and to govern longer.

Political parties lie at the heart of American politics.[1] E. E. Schattschneider (1942, 1) claimed that "political parties created democracy, and ... democracy is unthinkable save in terms of parties." A fair, if minimal, paraphrase would be to say that democracy is *unworkable* save in terms of parties. All democracies that are Madisonian, extended republics, which is to say all democratic nations, have political parties. To be truly democratic it is necessary for any nation's leadership to be harnessed to public desires and aspirations, at least in some very general sense. The elected leaders, being granted political power by the public, must ultimately be held accountable to that public. It may be that each official can be held accountable for his or her own personal actions by the constituency that elects and reelects that official. But government policy is determined by the collective actions of many individual officeholders. No one person either can or should be held accountable for actions taken by the House, Senate, and president together. The political party as a collective enterprise, organizing competition for the full range of offices, provides the only means for holding elected officials responsible for what they do collectively. Morris P. Fiorina has written (1980, 26) that "the only way collective responsibility has ever existed, and can exist, given our institutions, is through the agency of the political party; in American politics, responsibility requires cohesive parties."

But perhaps there is more. The scholars mentioned above used the plural, "parties." It may be, as V. O. Key Jr. argued (1949), that at least two parties are necessary, that it is the plural parties that lie at the heart of, that make workable, and that provide responsibility for democracy. Indeed, we might have to go even further. It may not be the mere presence of two parties at any one time that matters, for sometimes and in some places parties arise and then disappear from electoral competitiveness rapidly, as the American Independent Party and the Reform Party did in the United States in the 1960s and 1990s, respectively. What matters is the sustained competition that comes from the interaction between or among durable parties, such that it is the fact that any winning party must seriously consider the prospect of losing an election before democracy becomes tenable. A necessary condition for effective democracy, in this view, is that there must be *a party system*, an ongoing set of parties in sustained competition for access to power.

Of course, to think about a system of parties requires understanding the basis of individual political parties. Most of this book examines why the political party exists. It is important to know what the answer to this question is, because it is then a much shorter step than before toward understanding why a party system exists, and hence why some democracies are tenable and potentially durable. In this chapter, we begin by examining the political party and the elements that go into a theory of the political party, from which we can then consider what a party system might be.

The Political Party

With the ability to shape competition for elected office comes responsibility. Many people, whether academics, commentators, politicians, or members of the public, place the political ills of the contemporary scene—a government seemingly unable to solve critical problems and a public distrustful of, apathetic toward, or alienated from politics—on the failures of the two great American parties. Members of Congress are too concerned with their own reelection, in this view, to be able or willing to think of the public good. The president worries about his personal popularity, spends too little time leading the nation, and when he does turn to Congress, finds it impossible to forge majorities—primarily partisan majorities—to pass his own initiatives or to form workable compromises with Congress. Elections are candidate centered, turning on personality, image, and the latest, cleverest ad. Party platforms are little more than the first order of business at national conventions, only to be passed quickly and, party leaders hope, without controversy or media attention, so that the convention can turn to more important business. Ultimate blame for each of these rests, from this perspective, on the major American party.

With few, if important, exceptions, in the 1970s and 1980s the scholarly study of American parties turned from foundational theory to an examination of what appeared to be the central set of issues of the day concerning political parties: party decline, decay, and decomposition.[2] Since then, parties have revitalized. But now there are new ills—extremely polarized "red and blue" politics, bitter public debates that are essentially demagoguery, intractability, and failure to find compromise regardless of the consequences for the public. Where is the bipartisanship of that era of decline, decay, and decomposition? Parties are, in this view, the problem, whether they are too weak or too strong. And yet, whether stronger or weaker, they are there, and thoughtful observers see them as essential.

To address these two questions—how do we understand and evaluate political parties, and how do we understand their role in democracy—I return to consider the foundations of the major American political party and the two-party system (or, more generally, the multiparty system). My basic argument is that the major political party is the creature of the politicians, the partisan activist, and the ambitious office seeker and officeholder. They have created and maintained, used or abused, reformed or ignored the political party when doing so has furthered their goals and ambitions. The political party is thus an "endogenous" institution—an institution shaped by these political actors. Whatever its strength or weakness, whatever its form and role, it is the ambitious politicians' creation.

These politicians, we must understand from the outset, do not have partisan goals per se. Rather, they have more personal and fundamental goals, and the party is only the instrument for achieving them. Their goals are several and come in various combinations. Following Richard Fenno (1973), they include most basically the desire to have a long and successful career in political office, but they also encompass the desire to achieve policy ends and to attain power and prestige within the government. These goals are to be sought in government, not in parties, but they are goals that at times have best been realized *through* the parties. The parties are, as we will see, shaped by these goals in their various combinations, and particularly in the problems politicians most typically encounter when seeking to achieve their goals. Thus, there are three goals, three problems, and three reasons why politicians often turn to the organized party in search for a sustainable way to solve these problems and thus be more likely to achieve these goals.

Ambitious politicians turn to the political party to achieve such goals only when parties are useful vehicles for solving problems that cannot be solved as effectively, if at all, through other means. Thus I believe that the political party must be understood not only in relation to the goals of the actors most consequential for parties, but also in relation to the electoral, legislative, and executive institutions of the government. Fiorina was correct: only given our institutions can we understand political parties.

The third major force shaping the political party is the historical setting. Technological changes, for instance, have made campaigning for office today vastly different than it was only a few decades ago, let alone in the nineteenth century. Such changes have had great consequences for political parties. In the nineteenth century, political parties were the only feasible means for organizing mass elections. Today's technologies allow an individual member of Congress to create a personal, continuing campaign organization, something that was simply unimaginable a century ago. But there is, of course, more to the historical context than technology.

Normative understandings have changed greatly. Even Ronald Reagan, who claimed that "government is not the solution to our problems, government *is* the problem," also held to the value of a "social safety net" provided by the government that is far larger than even the most progressive politician of the nineteenth century could have imagined. Ideas, in short, matter a great deal. Founders had to overcome antipathy verging on disgust over the very idea of political parties in order to create them in the first place, and Martin Van Buren's ideas about the nature and value of the "modern mass party" greatly shaped the nature of Jacksonian Democracy and political parties generally for more than a century. Neither Van Buren nor anyone else set out to create a system of competing mass parties (although he and others of that era recognized the importance of sustained partisan competition, they merely—but always—wanted to win that competiton). But the creation of the modern mass party led quickly to the creation of the first modern mass two-party system.

History matters in yet another way, beyond the ideas, values, and technological possibilities available at any given historical moment. The path of development matters as well. Once a set of institutional arrangements is in place, the set of equilibrium possibilities is greatly reduced, and change from the existing equilibrium path to a new and possibly superior one may be difficult or impossible. In other words, once there are two major parties, their presence induces incentives for ambitious politicians to affiliate with one party or the other, and some of these incentives emerge only because of the prior existence of these two parties.

The combination of these three forces means that the fundamental syllogism for the theory of political parties to be offered here is just what Rohde and Shepsle (1978) originally offered as the basis for the rational-choice-based new institutionalism: political outcomes—here political parties—result from actors' seeking to realize their goals, choosing within and possibly shaping a given set of institutional arrangements, and so choosing within a given historical context. . . .

So why have politicians so often turned to political parties for solutions to these problems? Their existence creates incentives for their use. It is, for example, incredibly difficult to win election to major office without the backing of a major party. It is only a little less certain that legislators who seek to lead a policy proposal through the congressional labyrinth will first turn to their party for assistance. But such incentives tell us only that an ongoing political institution is used when it is useful. Why form political parties in the first place? . . . A brief statement of three points will give a first look at the argument.

First, parties are institutions. This means, among other things, that they have some durability. They may be endogenous institutions, yet party reforms are meant not as short-term fixes but as alterations to last for years, even decades. Thus, for example, legislators might create a party rather than a temporary majority coalition to increase their chances of winning not just today but tomorrow and into the future. Similarly, a long and successful political career means winning office today, but it also requires winning elections throughout that career. A standing, enduring organization makes that goal more likely.

Second, American democracy chooses by plurality or majority rule. Election to office therefore requires broad-based support wherever and from whomever it can be found. So strong are the resulting incentives for a two-party system to emerge that the effect is called Duverger's Law (Duverger 1954). It is in part the need to win vast and diverse support that has led politicians to create political parties.

Third, parties may help officeholders win more, and more often, than alternatives. Consider the usual stylized model of pork barrel politics. All winners get a piece of the pork for their districts. All funded projects are paid for by tax revenues, so each district pays an equal share of the costs of each project adopted, whether or not that district receives a project. Several writers have argued that this kind of legislation leads to "universalism," that is, adoption of a "norm" that every such bill yields a project to every district and thus passes with a "universal" or unanimous coalition. Thus everyone "wins." Weingast proved the basic theorem (1979). His theorem yields the choice of the rule of universalism over the formation of a simple majority coalition, because in advance each legislator calculates the chances of any simple majority coalition's forming as equal to that of any other. As a result, expecting to win only a bit more than half the time and lose the rest of the time, all legislators prefer consistent use of the norm of universalism.[3] But consider an alternative. Suppose some majority agree to form a more permanent coalition, to control outcomes now and into the future, and develop institutional means to encourage fealty to this agreement. If they successfully accomplish this, they will win regularly. Members of this institutionalized coalition would prefer it to universalism, since they always win a project in either case, but they get their projects at lower cost under the institutionalized majority coalition, which passes fewer projects.[4] Thus, even in this case with no shared substantive interests at all, there are nonetheless incentives to form an enduring voting coalition—to form a political party. And those in the excluded minority have incentives to counterorganize. United, they may be more able to woo defectors to their side. If not, they can campaign to throw those rascals in the majority party out of office.

In sum, these theoretical problems affect elective office seekers and officeholders by reducing their chances of winning. Politicians therefore may turn to political parties as institutions designed to ameliorate them. In solving these theoretical problems, however, from the politicians' perspective parties are affecting who wins and loses and what is won or lost. And it is to parties that politicians often turn, because of their durability as institutionalized solutions, because of the need to orchestrate large and diverse groups of people to form winning majorities, and because often more can be won through parties. Note that this argument rests on the implicit assumption that winning and losing hang in the balance. Politicians may be expected to give up some of their personal autonomy only when they face an imminent threat of defeat without doing so or only when doing so can block opponents' ability to build the strength necessary to win.

This is, of course, the positive case for parties, for it specifies conditions under which politicians find them useful. Not all problems are best solved, perhaps even solved at all, by political parties. Other arrangements, perhaps interest groups, issue networks, or personal electoral coalitions, may be superior at different times and under different conditions (see Hansen 1991, for example). The party may even be part of the problem. In such cases politicians turn elsewhere to seek the means to win.[5] Thus this theory is at base a theory of ambitious politicians seeking to achieve their goals. Often they have done so through the agency of the party, but sometimes, this theory implies, they will seek to realize their goals in other ways.

The political party has regularly proved useful. The permanence of parties suggests that the appropriate question is not "When parties?" but "How much parties and how much other means?" That parties are endogenous implies that there is no single, consistent account of the political party—nor should we expect one. Instead, parties are but a (major) part of the institutional context in which current historical conditions—the problems—are set, and solutions are sought with permanence only by changing that web of institutional arrangements. Of these the political party is by design the most malleable, and thus it is intended to change in important ways and with relatively great frequency. But it changes in ways that have, for most of American history, retained major political parties and, indeed, retained two major parties.

NOTES

1. This is an intentional paraphrase of Joseph A. Schlesinger (1966, 1), for reasons that will become evident.
2. Granted, this literature includes important debates about the veracity of such claims.
3. This result does not seem to depend heavily on the assumption that the alternative to universalism is the formation of minimal winning majority coalitions. What does seem to be crucial is the assumption that all coalitions are equally likely a priori.
4. At least they prefer this majority coalition to universalism if the costs of forming and maintaining it are less than the savings from not giving the minority any projects.

5. Once parties have organized, the current institutional arrangements will include those current partisan arrangements. Thus it may be that partisan institutions are part, even much, of the problem. By definition, these current partisan arrangements are at least insufficient to solve that problem. These three recurring problems share at their base something like an impossibility result. That is, no institutional arrangements, partisan or otherwise, that are consistent with republican democracy can solve any of these problems in all circumstances. This logical consequence is the reason partisan institutions are always threatened by, or in a state of, crisis. The party is designed to solve what cannot be permanently solved. The solution is thus contingent. That is, it is the solution that works for the particular set of circumstances currently faced; the same arrangements may not work adequately under other conditions. And in a purely logical sense, any given set of partisan institutions will necessarily fail at some time, if these are indeed true impossibility results. It is in part for this reason that the historical context is so important for understanding political parties.

7.5 Sidney Milkis, "The President and the Parties" (1993)

The Constitution did not anticipate political parties. In our fourth selection, Sidney Milkis argues that political parties in the United States arose as means to coordinate legislative and popular opposition to concentrated executive authority. Parties developed as an adjunct and supplement to the constitutional principles of separation of powers and, even more directly, checks and balances.

What, then, is the relationship between presidents and parties? Is it always confrontational? And how have presidents sought to gain control of their party to enlist it in support of the administration's program? Milkis explains that presidential authority is naturally focused, while legislative authority, especially absent parties, is diffuse. Parties create structure and coherence in legislatures and allow them to play the role that the constitutional principles of separation of powers and checks and balances envision for them. Presidents may gain control of their parties for a time, but strong dynamics central to the American political system make parties in the states and Congress resistant to presidential authority and direction.

On June 24, 1938, Franklin Delano Roosevelt indicated that he intended to participate in the forthcoming Democratic primary elections for Congress. In a national radio address—one of his fabled "fireside chats"—the president told the nation that as "head of the Democratic party, . . . charged with the responsibility of carrying out the definitely liberal declaration of principles set forth in the 1936 Democratic platform," he had "every right" to become involved in the forthcoming primary contests where these principles were at stake between candidates.[1] Roosevelt's message amounted to a public appeal for voters to defeat conservative Democrats, most of them from the southern and border states, who had joined Republicans to defeat or seriously compromise key elements of the administration's program during the 75th Congress, the volatile legislative session that followed the landslide Democratic victory of 1936.

The most dramatic moment of FDR's campaign that summer against recalcitrant Democrats occurred in August when he made a visit to his "other home state" of Georgia. On August 8, Roosevelt endorsed United States Attorney Lawrence Camp for the Senate in a speech at Barnesville, as the conservative incumbent Walter George listened from the same podium. FDR insisted that he felt no personal animosity toward George—he hoped they would "always be good personal friends"—but he was "impelled to make it clear that on most public questions" he and the Georgia Senator did not "speak the same language." The president's "responsibility," Roosevelt told his audience, required that "there be cooperation between members of my own party and myself—cooperation, in other words, within the majority party, between one branch of government, the legislative branch, and the head of the other branch, the Executive." Such cooperation, the President insisted, "was one of the essentials of the party form of government."[2]

Roosevelt's participation in the 1938 primary campaigns, which involved him in one gubernatorial and several congressional contests, represented, as one columnist wrote that October, an unprecedented attempt by a president "to stamp his policies upon his party."[3] Such intervention was not really unprecedented; in particular, William Howard Taft and Woodrow Wilson had made limited efforts to cleanse their parties of recalcitrant members. Yet Roosevelt's campaign took place on an unprecedented scale and, unlike previous efforts, made no attempt to work through the regular party organization. His action was viewed as a shocking departure from the norm: The press labeled it "the purge." . . .

When Roosevelt's "purge" campaign ended unsuccessfully, having failed to weaken the position of conservatives in the Democratic party, the New York *Times* columnist Arthur Krock claimed that the president "has demonstrated in the most public way that the American system and tradition are stronger than he is."[4] In fact, however, the controversy that surrounded Roosevelt's attempt to stamp his policies upon his party is best understood as a dramatic example of the difficulty presidents face in reconciling the roles of party leader and chief executive . . . .

The Modern Presidency and Party Constraints

The essential incompatibility between the modern presidency and party politics is attributable partly to the origins and organizing principles of party government. In English history, the legitimation of party grew out of an effort to curb and regulate the power of the executive.[5] Similarly, Martin Van Buren's efforts to legitimate party competition in the United States during the 1830s rested on an effort to control presidential ambition.[6]

The defense of parties in the Anglo-American tradition conceived of the legislature, which epitomizes public deliberation and choice (the "force of persuasion"), as the preeminent representative institution. But, as Alexander Hamilton argued in his defense of a unified and energetic executive power, legislatures are apt to move slowly, defy consensus, and fail to recognize, let alone protect the society from, peril. At first glance, then, the executive is not only a more efficient institution than the legislature, but more accountable as well.[7] Still, executive power is most needed at times that render accountability most difficult—when differences of opinion must give way to promptitude of decision and action. The people would need a representative legislature to control a representative executive; moreover, this control of presidential prerogative required party politics. As Wilson Carey McWilliams has noted, presidents can be strong, indeed, best display their personal qualities, "above party." By contrast, "Congress cannot be effective, let alone powerful, without the institution of party. . . . A legislature can rival the executive's claims to public confidence only to the extent that it is accountable, which presumes a principle of *collective* responsibility."[8]

The inherent tension between executive power and party politics is exacerbated in the United States by the structure of government, as well as history and tradition. Parliamentary government elsewhere—most notably in Great Britain but in other Western democracies as well—has provided a link between the executive and legislative party government. The American Constitution, with its division and separation of powers, makes difficult the development of party unity in support of strong executive action; the possibility of linking an energetic executive and party politics is further discouraged in the United States, however, by the *interpretation* of the Constitution that gave rise to the American party system.

. . . American political parties matured as the cornerstone of a political order that celebrated democratic individualism and presumed the absence of centralized administrative authority. Both the Democratic and Republican parties were wedded to Jeffersonian principles, dedicated to limiting the role of the national government. Thomas Jefferson, with the invaluable support of James Madison, founded the Democratic—Republican party to rescue the Constitution from a program that would, in their understanding, vitiate popular rule. As Secretary of the Treasury in the Washington administration, Hamilton had proposed an ambitious program, based upon a liberal—"elastic"—interpretation of the national government's powers, that anticipated a significant expansion of executive power. The power of the more democratic and decentralizing institutions— Congress and state governments—were necessarily subordinated in this enterprise. In order to keep power close enough to the people for republican government to prevail, Jefferson and Madison formulated a public philosophy in support of a strict interpretation of the national government's powers. This also became a *party* doctrine, and the principal task of the triumphant Democratic—Republicans after the critical election of 1800 was to dismantle Hamilton's program for a strong executive. The purpose of presidential party leadership in the Jeffersonian mold was to capture the executive office in order to contain and minimize its constitutional potential. As James Piereson has observed in his study of party government in the United States:

> Out of this original clash there developed in America the tension between party politics, on the one hand, and governmental centralization and bureaucracy, on the other. . . . The leaders of the original [Democratic—] Republican party attacked Hamilton's program, and the politics on which it rested, by organizing voters, and by appealing to them on the basis of republican principles, which were inherently decentralizing and hostile to administration, as was the very process of party politics.[9]

The emergence of political parties in the United States, then, grew out of a struggle to curb the power of the executive, especially with respect to expanding national administrative power; accordingly, they have not served as a *link* but as a "wall of separation" between government and society. Jefferson apparently did not expect ongoing party competition to become a permanent part of the American political system. But during the Jacksonian era, Van Buren, supported by a forceful and popular president, defended the party as a legitimate constitutional institution, one that would take its shape from the constitutional principles of Jefferson. It is not surprising, therefore, that the partisan organizations that arose during the Jacksonian era—the Democratic and Whig parties—assumed a form that centered partisan responsibility and practices in the Congress and state governments.[10] American political parties were organized as popular institutions, but they were first organized at a time when popular rule meant the limitation of government power.

The form of party organization that was legitimized during the Jacksonian era endured well into the twentieth century. Even the rise of the Republican party during the 1850s as a result of the slavery controversy, and the subsequent demise of the Whigs, did not alter the essential characteristics of the party system in the United States; and these characteristics—decentralized organization and hostility to administrative centralization—restrained rather than facilitated executive power.[11] . . .

To be sure, there are conflicting and compensating aspects to the American tradition of party politics. Although based on Jeffersonian principles dedicated to decentralized government, the party system has provided presidents with a stable basis of popular support, and, episodically, during critical partisan realignments, with the opportunity to achieve national reform. The executive, through the partisan electoral process, has become the focal point for the usually separated branches of the Constitution to combine during such times, resulting in sharp departures from the prevailing principles, institutions, and policies of government.[12]

The New Deal realignment was the first to challenge fundamentally the partisan emphasis of previous watershed changes in American politics. Although similar in many ways to previous critical partisan chapters in American history, the momentous political developments of the 1930s marked a fundamental change in the relationship between president and party. Prior to the New Deal, none of the programs to which the electorate had subscribed during a realignment had called for a substantial exercise of executive power. Indeed, the thrust of the first realigning movement, which culminated with the Democratic—Republican victory over the Federalists in the election of 1800, had been explicitly in the opposite direction. Whereas the "Revolution of 1800," as Jefferson called it, gave rise to a party system that dismantled Hamilton's program for a strong executive, the New Deal realignment centered on an endeavor to deemphasize party politics and to resurrect the Hamilton executive as the steward of the public welfare. Such an enterprise stemmed from an understanding that the development of industrial capitalism had led to a national economy and concentration of private economic power, requiring strong countervailing action by government to ameliorate unacceptable political and economic inequality. As Herbert Croly wrote in *The Promise of American Life*, the task was to give "democratic meaning and purpose to the Hamiltonian tradition and method," and, thereby, "emancipate American democracy from its Jeffersonian bondage."[13]

The assault on the traditional party system and the emergence of the modern executive did not begin during the 1930s. The Progressive era—especially as shaped by the statesmanship of Theodore Roosevelt and Woodrow Wilson—was an important precursor to the New Deal. The New Deal was sufficiently indebted to Progressive theory to share its view of traditional American party politics as decrepit, as all too compatible with decentralizing constitutional mechanisms such as the separation of powers and federalism, thus preventing the development of an executive-centered national state with the capacity to govern the complex social and economic affairs of the twentieth century.[14] FDR was more effective than TR and Wilson, however, in directing this animus against Jeffersonian parties, making a resurrected Hamiltonianism the focal point of a popular and enduring transformation of the political system. Unlike Theodore Roosevelt and Woodrow Wilson, FDR's leadership was the principal ingredient in a full-scale realignment of the political parties, the first in history that placed executive leadership at the heart of its approach to politics and government. After FDR's long tenure, the logic of presidential responsibilities in the new office would lead even conservative Republican Presidents, such as Nixon and Reagan, to wield executive power according to the vision of the presidency celebrated by their progressive predecessors . . . .

The New Deal Legacy—Party Decline or Transformation

The institutional reforms carried out during the 1930s recast the relationship between political parties and the executive, thus fundamentally redefining the concept of representation in American politics. But this institutional program, designed to transform what New Dealers viewed as a provincial version of popular rule into a progressive democracy, led to two, seemingly contradictory, developments that continue to shape party politics in the United States. . . . Accordingly, the goal of the New Deal institutional program was to reform and extend the reach of *executive administration*, whereby the president and administrative agencies would be delegated the responsibility to shape public policy, thus making ongoing cooperation within the party councils unnecessary.

To a point, these developments—the rise of national parties and the enhancement of executive administration—are complementary and have given rise to a new executive-centered party system. The New Deal accelerated a development that began during the Progressive era, in which each of the parties, instead of being organized in order to enable its members to consult one another and reach an agreement upon differences of opinion, would be subject to the "benevolent dictatorship" of the president. Yet the emergence of an economic constitutional order and the expansion of administrative power during the New Deal did not remove the prohibitive obstacles in the American political system that stand in the way of establishing party government under dominant presidential leadership. As the failed "purge" campaign revealed, the decentralized character of politics in the United States can be modified only by strong presidential leadership, but a president determined to alter fundamentally the connection between the executive and his party will eventually shatter party unity. Given the fundamental resistance to strong partisanship in the United States, and support for the separation and division of powers, "modern" presidents, subject to the enormous programmatic demands of the post-New Deal era, have been encouraged to rely on plebiscitary politics and unilateral executive action to circumvent the regular procedures of constitutional government, as well as formal partisan channels.[15]

NOTES

1. Franklin D. Roosevelt, *Public Papers and Addresses*, ed. Samuel J. Rosenman, 13 volumes (New York: Random House, 1938–50), 7:397–400.
2. Ibid., 7:469.

3. Raymond Clapper, "Roosevelt Tries the Primaries," *Current History*, October, 1938, 16.

4. New York *Times*, September 18, 1938, **4**:3.

5. Harvey C. Mansfield, Jr., *Statesmanship and Party Government* (Chicago: University of Chicago Press, 1965). Mansfield observes that Edmund Burke "conceived the respectability of party because he was willing to accept the less exact principle in exchange for a lessened reliance on statesmen; for great statesmen are unreliable, at least in the sense that they may not always be available" (17–18).

6. James Ceaser, *Presidential Selection: Theory and Development* (Princeton, New Jersey: Princeton University Press, 1979).

7. Alexander Hamilton, James Madison, and John Jay, *The Federalist Papers* (New York: New American Library, 1961), Number 70, 423–31.

8. Wilson Carey McWilliams, "The Anti-Federalists, Representation and Party," *Northwestern University Law Review*, Volume 84, Number 1 (Fall, 1989), 35. For the original constitutional design of the executive, the Founders looked to the concept of "Patriot King" [emphasis in original] provided a half-century earlier by the British author and statesman Lord Bolingbroke. Such an ideal executive stood above the "merely" political conflicts of parties and ruled benevolently in the public interest. See Ralph Ketcham, *Presidents Above Party* (Chapel Hill, North Carolina: University of North Carolina Press, 1984).

9. James Piereson, "Party Government," *The Political Science Reviewer*, **12** (Fall, 1982), 51–52.

10. According to the Whig opposition, the legacy of Jackson's presidency was the dangerous expansion of executive prerogatives. Jackson's aggressive use of the veto and appointment power during the bank controversy, they argued, demonstrated that the Chief Executive now possessed power that dwarfed the influence of Congress as well as the Judiciary, thus undermining the separation of powers. Yet the extension of executive powers during Jackson's presidency did not simply expand unilateral executive action. This extension depended upon the emergence of the president as popular leader that was mediated in critical ways by party organization. And party organization, which took its form from the convention system and patronage, had a decided state and local orientation.

    The powers of the presidency were not only limited by the decentralized character of the party system but by the doctrine of the Democratic party that was organized to advance Jacksonian principles. This doctrine, as evidenced by Jackson's veto of the bank bill, was dedicated to limiting the role of the national government. Jackson defended the principle of union against the extreme states' rights claim of South Carolina in the nullification controversy; generally, however, he was a strong advocate of the rights of the state governments and opposed expanding the responsibilities of the national government and executive. Thus, as Alexis de Tocqueville wrote about the executive of the 1830s, "General Jackson's power is constantly increasing, but that of the president grows less. The federal government is strong in his hands; it will pass to his successor enfeebled." Alexis de Tocqueville, *Democracy in America*, J. P. Mayer, ed. (New York: New American Library, 1969) 395; see also Sidney M. Milkis and Michael Nelson, *The American Presidency: Origins and Development, 1787–1990* (Washington, D.C.: Congressional Quarterly, 1990), Chapter 5.

11. Milkis and Nelson, *The American Presidency*, Chapter 7. The Republicans, like the Democrats, traced their origins to the Jeffersonian era, claiming that as the party opposed to the expansion of slavery in the territories they, and not the Democrats, represented the "republican" principles that defined that era. The restoration of a strong executive as the vital center of a new national program was unanticipated. Most of what Lincoln accomplished in consolidating the executive power during the Civil War, in fact, surprised most of his Republican colleagues in the Congress, who acted forcefully to weaken the presidency after his assassination.

12. The two seminal presentations of critical realignment theory are V. O. Key, Jr., "A Theory of Critical Elections," *Journal of Politics* **17** (February, 1955): 3–18; and Walter Dean

Burnham, *Critical Elections and the Mainsprings of American Politics* (New York: W. W. Norton, 1970). Occurring at critical junctures of American history—1800, 1828, 1860, 1896, and 1932—realignments have resulted in dramatic shifts in voter affiliation, major changes in public policy, and the forging of a new public philosophy. See also Harry Jaffa, "A Phoenix From the Ashes: The Death of James Madison's Constitution (killed by James Madison) and the Birth of Party Government." Paper delivered at the 1977 Annual Meeting of the American Political Science Association, September, Washington, D.C.

13. Herbert Croly, *The Promise of American Life* (New York: G. P. Dutton, 1963, original work published in 1909, by the MacMillan Co.), 169.

14. See, for example, Woodrow Wilson, *Constitutional Government in the United States* (New York: Columbia University Press, 1908), especially Chapters 3 and 8; and Herbert Croly, *Progressive Democracy* (New York: The MacMillan Co., 1914).

15. Jeffrey K. Tulis, *The Rhetorical Presidency*, (Princeton, New Jersey: Princeton University Press, 1987). Tulis argues that the emergence of the president as a leader of public opinion during the twentieth century constitutes the emergence of the "second Constitution." The tendency of the second constitution to make extraordinary executive power routine, Tulis notes, undermines the logic of the original constitutional framework. While Tulis sees the Progressive era as critical to this development, Theodore Lowi links the emergence of a "personal president" and "second republic" to the New deal era. See Lowi, *The Personal President: Power Invested, Promise Unfulfilled* (Ithaca and London: Cornell University Press, 1985). This book suggests that the key to understanding modern presidential leadership is found in the displacement of *party* politics by *administrative* politics, a development that has not always put a premium on active and continuous presidential leadership of public opinion. See Chapter 2.

7.6 Theda Skocpol and Vanessa Williamson, "How the Tea Party Boosts the GOP and Prods It Rightward" (2012)

American political parties generally are broad coalitions of interest groups, activists, and voters. Parties are always changing, usually slowly, but occasionally a wave of social energy will hit one or both parties in ways that drive more rapid change. For example, in 2006 Democrats took control of Congress and in 2008 Obama won the presidency and Democrats extended their congressional majorities. Slow change seemed to be favoring the Democrats until they passed an unpopular stimulus bill and broad health care reforms, which opponents called "Obamacare," setting off a reaction that came to be known as the Tea Party Movement. Who were these tea partiers, how were they organized, and what did they want?

Theda Skocpol and Vanessa Williamson set out to answer these questions through analysis of press accounts, interviews conducted in Massachusetts, Virginia, and Arizona, and survey research results. They found that Tea Party adherents were older, white, fiscal and social conservatives, many of whom had long supported the Republican Party with their contributions and votes. In this selection, Skocpol and Williamson describe the impact of the newly elected Tea Party Members of Congress on the Republican Party in the U.S. House of Representatives. They find that the infusion of Tea Party Members of Congress moved the ideological center of the Republican Party in the House to the right. Finally, they analyze the likely impacts, positive and negative, of the Tea Party Movement on the Republican Party going forward. They argue that Tea Party energy benefits the Republican Party, ideological rigidity—not so much.

The Tea Party includes grassroots activists, conservative media ideologues, and billionaire-backed free-market advocacy groups, all jostling for attention and power. With the Republican victories in the 2010 midterms, Tea Partiers from each of these arenas have felt free to call the shots: to demand immediate measures to slash public spending and taxes, abolish the rights of public sector unions, and eliminate business regulations. Wherever they can weigh in, Tea Partiers loudly tell Republican officeholders to do what they want or else face challenges from the right in the next election.

For the Republican Party, the Tea Party cuts both ways. Certainly, its enthusiasm and resources fuel the GOP. But the story is more complex because the Tea Party is not just a booster organization for Any-Old-Republicans. Tea Party activists at the grass roots and the right-wing advocates roving the national landscape with billionaire backing have designs on the Republican Party. They want to remake it into a much more uncompromising and ideologically principled force. As Tea Party forces make headway in achieving this ideological purification, they spur movement of the Republican Party ever further toward the right, and align the party with a label that principally appeals to older, very conservative white voters.

Tea Party activists, supporters, and funders are not middle-of-the-roaders. With very few exceptions, they are people with long histories of voting for and giving money to Republicans. Even those who have stood apart to the right of the GOP—organizing as Libertarians, for example—certainly have not helped Democrats. At the grass roots as well as in national advocacy circles, Tea Party people aim to defeat Obama and Democrats, and want to curb taxes and government activities at all levels from localities to states to the federal government. To these ends, Tea Partiers reject any notion of organizing a separate third party that would divide forces on the right and clear the way for Democrats.[1] Maneuvering at the rightward end of the GOP, Tea Party participants aim to elect staunchly conservative Republicans. They enjoyed considerable success in 2010, and they aim to do more of the same in 2012.

Yet Tea Partiers also vex "establishment" Republicans. Funders and television hosts and radio jocks brandishing the Tea Party label have undercut longtime Republican officeholders in primaries, including some conservatives who initially enjoyed virtually unanimous backing from Republican Party officials and strategists. Between elections, Tea Party activists are moving in and taking over Republican Party committees in many places. And because Tea Party grassroots participants and elites distrust moderate GOP officeholders, they appoint themselves watchdogs to keep officials "honest," pushing Republican candidates and officials to be more staunchly ultra-conservative.

Above all, Tea Partiers want Republicans in office to refuse compromises with Democrats over the scope and funding of government. They "go nuclear" when GOP officeholders take any steps toward moderation and negotiation. If Tea Party-oriented Republicans have even tiny margins of control, they are expected to ram through maximalist programs. If GOP officials have to coexist with Democrats and moderates, well, as the Tea Party sees it, they should just suck it up and hold firm, until they get their way, or most of it.

Such pressures from the Tea Party can put Republican officeholders and candidates in a bind. What happens if compromises must be made to keep government in operation? Or if candidates looking toward the next election are worried about attracting support from moderate Republicans and middle-of-the-road independents as well as from hard-core GOP conservatives? This question is especially acute for politicians facing election or reelection in the presidential election year of 2012, when voter turnout will be higher, younger, and more diverse than in 2010....

The 112th Congress Lunges Rightward

Determining the degree to which every Republican officeholder across the country is aligned with the Tea Party would be an intricate and protracted challenge. But the Tea Party impact in the 2010 elections comes into sharp focus when we measure shifts in the ideological composition of the House of Representatives from the 111th Congress (of Obama's first two years) to the 112th Congress that arrived in January 2011 and will be in office through the end of 2012. Political scientists use quantitative indices to locate legislators on the left-right spectrum and measure the size of gaps between the two major parties. Adam Bonica has developed a new twist on long-standing measures to provide a clear picture of the Republican-led House installed in DC in January 2011. This GOP House contingent turns out to have ushered in a new phase in the extreme ideological polarization of U.S. politics.[2]

Figure 1 locates the ideological proclivities of legislators who carried over from the 111th to the 112th House of Representatives on both sides of the aisle, and also indicates

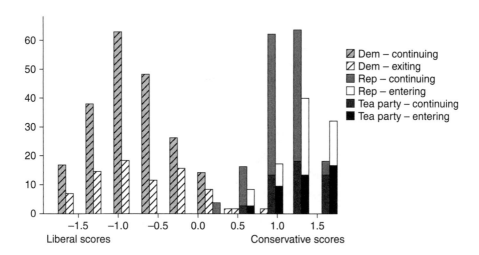

Figure 1 Partisan Shifts in the House of Representatives from 2010 to 2011. *Member Ideology in the 112th Congress Prepared by Adam Bonica, Stanford University.*

the proclivities of those who departed or were newly elected in 2010. Bonica's scale runs from less than –1.5 for extreme liberalism to more than 1.5 for extreme conservatism. On the Democratic side, to the left of the figure, we see what happened with Democrats who stayed in office from the 111th House to the 112th House, versus those who were booted from office by the voters. So many Democrats lost in 2010 that moderates and liberals alike departed. The Democratic contingent in the House became only a smidgen more liberal after 2010.

But the story is very different among Republicans tallied on the right side of the figure. Republicans who stayed in office from the 111th to 112th Congress are all more conservative, mostly much more conservative, than the Democrats. Yet the Republicans newly elected in 2010 are even further to the right than their GOP predecessors. An amazing 77% of the newly arriving Republicans, including dozens of Tea Party-backed Republicans, are to the right of the typical Republican in the previous Congress—and many are to the right of *almost all* continuing Republicans. For both continuing and newly arrived Republicans, Figure 1 indicates how many in each ideological location are aligned with the Tea Party.[3] Clearly, the Tea Party-aligned Republicans are bunched toward the right, and many of the Tea Party solons are new arrivals in the freshman class of the 112th Congress.

The ideological shift from the 111th to the 112th Congress was extraordinary—indeed, larger than any previous shift from one House to the next, including the change that occurred in 1994, when Republicans displaced Democrats from control of the majority for the first time in decades.[4] It is also important to realize that the rightward lunge of the House GOP in 2010 greatly extended a previous rightward trend for House Republicans. Ideological sorting out between the two parties in Congress has been going on for decades, but in recent years virtually all of the incremental polarization comes from Republicans moving ever further rightward while the Democrats mostly stay put. This trend was exacerbated, big time, after the 2010 elections.

Some long-term perspective can be helpful.[5] Back during the New Deal, World War II, and the immediate postwar period, there were moderates and liberals in the Republican Party—just as there were many conservatives, particularly southern conservatives, in the Democratic Party. But after the Civil Rights revolution of the 1960s, activists and voters started sorting themselves out—with the Democratic Party becoming more liberal and Republicans becoming more consistently conservative. For a while, some middle-of-the-roaders remained in each party—moderate Republicans and conservative Democrats. A handful of them are still there in the Senate (for instance, Susan Collins of Maine on the Republican side and Ben Nelson of Nebraska on the Democratic side). But for decades, moderates have been disappearing, especially from the ranks of House Republicans. Recent ideological polarization in the House has been driven primarily by the steady movement of the Republican Party toward the anti-government right.[6] That movement has happened in part through the arrival of more radical right-wing GOP officeholders, and in part because Republican incumbents have shifted their votes toward the right—especially on the key issue of taxes.

Back in the 1980s, President Ronald Reagan dealt with federal budget deficits much as fiscally cautious Republicans before him had done, by arriving at compromises with Democrats that included tax increases as well as spending cuts. President Reagan's approach is currently favored by Democratic President Barack Obama, but today's Republicans insist that all conceivable tax increases must be "off the table" in Congressional discussions about how to tackle federal deficits. Remarkably, GOPers take this extreme stand in lockstep, even though ballooning budget deficits are largely driven by the after-effects of GOP policies and tax cuts pursued during the presidency of George W. Bush from 2000 to 2008.[7] Republicans caused most of the currently projected federal budget problems, but they take a no-compromise stand on how to fix them, demanding that Democrats essentially eviscerate Medicare, Medicaid, and Social Security, so that Republicans can maintain, indeed increase, big tax cuts for businesses and for million-aires and billionaires. Contemporary Republicans are, for the most part, not truly conser-vative, and not really interested in fiscal probity. Their goal is to dismantle much of what the federal government does. . . .

What Next for Republicans and Their Tea Party?

Republican leaders in the 112th Congress have to propitiate the absolutist demands of elite and grassroots Tea Partiers while edging toward compromises with the Obama White House and the Democratic-controlled Senate, if only to keep government func-tioning while policy battles rage. In the months marching toward the critical elections in November 2012, we will repeatedly see Republican Congressional leaders trying to persuade GOP legislators to say no, at least in part, to the most extreme Tea Party demands. But each time a reluctant compromise is struck, it will happen only at the very last minute, after a lot of public posturing and high-wire brinksmanship, some of which surely is dangerous to the economic well-being of the country. As the conservative *Washington Post* commentator Michael Gerson puts it, there "are always compromises in governing. But they are harder to make when one element of a political coalition views compromise itself as the problem."

Theatrical posturing, maximalist demands, and refusals to budge until the last minute (or even beyond)—this formula works to a degree for the Republican Party and its Tea Party allies. Already, national debates have moved far to the right, as most DC office-holders and pundits debate how much to slash from the federal budget, rather than focusing on job creation in a sluggish economy. Nevertheless, even as they gain ground in battles to shape public discussions and cut government, Tea Partiers also risk putting the Republican Party at risk, in two important ways.

In the first place, business interests are increasingly nervous about maximalist, uncom-promising stances in budget battles. Very early in the 112th Congress, demands to slash spending on infrastructure and transportation projects aroused pushback, not just from labor unions, but also from the Chamber of Commerce, speaking for businesses looking forward to profitable contracts on publicly financed projects.[8] Businesses may love the GOP when it guts regulations and cuts taxes, but eliminating funds for public projects that reward contractors is another matter.

An even more spectacular tussle broke out several months later, when GOP Congressional leaders deferring to Tea Party demands threatened to let the United States go into default if they did not get their way in budget negotiations with Democrats. Alarmed by the consequences for credit and the threat to a nascent economic recovery, leading business and industrial associations, including the U.S. Chamber of Commerce and the National Association of Manufacturers, banded together to write a letter to Speaker Boehner urging against such brinksmanship with the U.S. financial system.[9] In the final stages of the debt ceiling battle, business leaders sent another petition to

Congress, and even the *Wall Street Journal* editorial board called for a procedural compromise.[10] In short, GOP business allies do not always see eye to eye with the ideological elites and grassroots populists arrayed in the Tea Party. Whenever two different wings of the usual GOP coalition are at odds, legislators and candidates are sure to be caught awkwardly in the middle.

A second risk for the GOP lies in public opinion and the struggle to attract moderate voters going into 2012. Tea Party extremism exacerbates already considerable public disillusionment with the Republican Party. Not only will many younger, more diverse, less economically well-off voters go to the polls in 2012, "independent" voters who truly are in the middle are also more likely to vote in a presidential election year. Will the Tea Party turn more voters off about the Republican brand? There is significant social science research to suggest this is a serious possibility.[11]

National surveys reveal increasingly negative public evaluations of the Tea Party—with the percent of Americans who tell survey researchers that they are opposed to the Tea Party now surpassing those who say they support it, in some polls by a wide margin.[12] Over the past two and a half years, Americans have gradually firmed up their views of the Tea Party, following an initial period in which many were uncertain about what it was, or undecided in their assessments.[13] As the picture clears, the proportion of Americans saying they like or sympathize with the Tea Party has remained relatively steady at about 25%–30%. (In one surprising poll, from none other than Fox News, the Tea Party's popularity failed to beat out that of the much-maligned Internal Revenue Service![14]) By contrast, the percentage of Americans saying they do not like, or oppose, the Tea Party has increased. Familiarity, in short, seems to have bred dislike. This is a troubling trend for the Republican Party going into 2012 because the party has become so closely identified with Tea Party activism.

During the 2010 election cycle, the GOP strategy was openly to encourage Tea Party activism, on the theory that the party would benefit from highly motivated potential voters and from new infusions of money. No doubt, many GOP leaders still hold this perspective. On the other hand, other GOP leaders and strategists understand that hardcore conservative Republicans who identify with the Tea Party cannot provide enough votes to win all elections, certainly not in swing states and districts, or in the 2012 presidential contest. Many GOP candidates—including eventually the 2012 presidential nominee—will need to appeal not just to Tea Party supporters, but also to non-Tea Party Republicans, independents, and wobbly Democrats.

Consequently, it has to be worrisome for GOP strategists that the views of Tea Party constituents are parting company on many issues with the views of moderate Republicans and independents. American voters can be slow to figure out complicated policy issues, especially when they are fed misleading information by major media outlets. Sooner or later, however, most voters get a bead on things, particularly when real-life matters such as college aid and health care are at issue. As Americans figure out the real choices about the future of social spending and taxes for the United States, the Republican Party may not be in a good place if it continues to defer to the most ideological elements of the Tea Party. Surveys also show that even many Republicans support tax increases along with spending cuts to tackle U.S. budget deficits, a plan anathema to many of the national advocacy organizations stoking Tea Party fervor.[15] When survey-researchers issue reports declaring that the "Tea Party's Hard Line on Spending Divides the GOP," trouble may be brewing.[16] Add to that the likelihood that the style of Tea Party politics—angry, demanding, and absolutist—may be increasingly at odds with the preferences of other citizens. To the degree that Americans want government focus on what works for the economy, the tenor of Tea Party rhetoric wears thin.

For all the hype about the impact of the Tea Party on the fortunes of Republicans versus Democrats, the bigger story, as we have seen, is the impact of the Tea Party on the GOP. The Republican Party has been moving toward the right for some time, and that movement only quickened after the advent of the Tea Party. Although the symbolism of "the Tea Party" is already fading in popularity, the power of hard-right ideologues consolidated during the first years of the Obama Administration is likely to continue to drive Republican politics, crowding Republicans into an ultra-right corner. As American politics marches on, the Tea Party, even if it doggedly persists, will not be able to call all the shots—and Republican leaders will have to decide how far they want to go in the directions Tea Partiers are urging. Before long, the Tea Party ideology and its adherents may shift from an asset to an albatross for many in the Republican Party.

NOTES

1. There have been instances, most notably in upstate New York, where self-declared Tea Party candidates have run along with GOP candidates in general elections, splitting the vote in ways that help Democrats. But occasional instances of this sort are not equivalent to organizing a third party.

2. Adam Bonica, "Introducing the 112th Congress," *Ideological Cartography*, November 5, 2010. Available at http://www.ideologicalcartography.com/2010/11/05/introducing-the-112th-congress/ as of May 22, 2011. Bonica's measures use campaign finance data to pinpoint newly elected legislators on the left-right scale. His measurements correlate closely with well-established political science measures of the left-right voting patterns for sitting legislators. See Bonica, "How to Construct an Ideological Map of Candidates and Contributors Using Campaign Finance Records," *Ideological Cartography*, February 15, 2010; and for a full presentation, Bonica, "Ideology and Interests in the Political Marketplace," unpublished paper, September 2010.

3. Republican Representatives are considered aligned with the Tea Party if they joined the Tea Party caucus by April 2011, or if the *New York Times* listed them prior to the November 2010 elections as receiving clear support from Tea Party groups. See Kate Zernike, "Tea Party Set to Win Enough Races for Wide Influence," *New York Times*, October 14, 2011, including linked list of Tea Party endorsed candidates.

4. Adam Bonica, "Introducing the 112th Congress," *Ideological Cartography* website, November 5, 2010.

5. Nolan McCarty, Keith T. Poole, and Howard Rosenthal, *Polarized Politics: The Dance of Ideology and Unequal Riches* (Cambridge, MA: MIT Press, 2008).

6. The following account draws especially upon Jacob S. Hacker and Paul Pierson, *Off Center: The Republican Revolution and the Erosion of American Democracy* (New Haven, CT: Yale University Press, 2005); and Barbara Sinclair, *Party Wars: Polarization and the Politics of National Policymaking* (Norman, OK: University of Oklahoma Press, 2006).

7. For an analysis of the sources of the current deficit and the debt, see Kathy Ruffing and James R. Horney, "Critics Still Wrong on What's Driving Deficits in Coming Years," *Center on Budget and Policy Priorities*, June 28, 2010.

8. The AFL-CIO and Chamber of Commerce issued a rare joint statement in support of infrastructure spending. Mike Hall, "AFL-CIO and Chamber Agree on Obama's Call for Infrastructure Rebuild," AFL-CIO Now blog, January 26, 2011. Available at http://blog.aflcio.

org/2011/01/26/union-movement-business-back-obamas-call-for-infrastructure-rebuild-and-other-sotu-reactions/ as of May 16, 2011.

9. Jennifer Liberto, "Big Business: Quit Screwing Around on Debt Ceiling," CNN Money, May 12, 2011. Available at http://money.cnn.com/2011/05/12/news/economy/debt_ceiling_big_business/index.htm?section=money_mostpopular as of May 15, 2011.

10. "Debt Limit Harakiri," *Wall Street Journal* editorial, July 13, 2011.

11. Once people have chosen a political party, they tend to be pretty loyal to it. But to the extent that the types of people in the Tea Party come to define what it is to be a Republican, it could have a serious impact on how other people, especially young people, attach themselves to one party or another. "As people reflect on whether they are Democrats or Republicans (or neither), they call to mind some mental image, or stereotype, of what these sorts of people are like and square these images with their own self-conceptions. In effect, people ask themselves two questions: What kinds of social groups come to mind as I think about Democrats, Republicans, and Independents? Which assemblage of groups (if any) best describes me?" Donald P. Green, Bradley Palmquist, and Eric Schickler, *Partisan Hearts and Minds: Political Parties and the Social Identities of Voters* (New Haven, CT: Yale University Press, 2004). Elections can help shape people's view of what "kinds of people" are in each party. In California in the 1990s, the strong anti-immigrant ballot measures championed by Republican elected officials turned Hispanics and younger white people away from the Republican Party. Shaun Bowler, Stephen Nicholson, and Gary Segura, "Earthquakes and aftershocks: Race, direct democracy, and partisan change." *American Journal of Political Science* 50(1): 146–159 (2006).

12. Rachel Weiner, "Tea Party Unpopularity on the Rise," *Washington Post*, March 30, 2011.

13. Nate Silver, "Poll Shows More Americans I-Iave Unfavorable Views of the Tea Party." *FiveTirtyEight* blog, *New York Times*, March 30, 2011.

14. These Fox News results were, unsurprisingly, seized upon by the progressive blogosphere. See Matt Corley, "More Americans have a 'favorable' opinion of the IRS than of the Tea Party," *Think Progress*, April 8, 2010. Available at http://thinkprogress. org/2010/04/08/tea-party-irs-poll/ as of May 11, 2011.

15. Steven Thomma, "Poll: Best Way to Fight Deficits: Raise Taxes on the Rich," *McClatchy Washington Bureau*, April 18, 2011.

16. Pew Research Center, "Tea Party's Hard Line on Spending Divides GOP," February 11, 2011.

Discussion Questions

1. How well does James Reichley's explanation of the surprising rise of parties in the Washington administration comport with James Madison's explanation in "A Candid State of Parties"?

2. Sidney Milkis argues that presidents are structurally limited as party leaders. Should we undertake reforms, and, if so, what reforms, to facilitate presidential leadership of American political parties?

3. Compare and contrast Bryce's description of the origins of U.S. parties with John Aldrich's description. What are the relative strengths and weaknesses of historical versus theoretical analytical approaches?

4. Has the Tea Party been beneficial or detrimental to the Republican Party so far and how is it likely to benefit the party going forward?

5. Do you agree with James Bryce that human nature makes some people prefer centralized government and others prefer more distributed political power?

Suggested Additional Reading

Lewis L. Gould, *Grand Old Party: A History of the Republicans* (New York: Random House, 2003).

John S. Green and Paul S. Herrnson, eds., *Responsible Partisanship?: The Evolution of American Political Parties Since 1950* (Lawrence, KS: University Press of Kansas, 2003).

Jeffrey Layman, *The Great Divide: Religious and Cultural Conflict in American Party Politics* (New York: Columbia University Press, 2002).

Margaret Weir, *The Social Divide: Political Parties and the Future of Activist Government* (Washington, D.C.: Brookings Institution, 1998).

Jules Witcover, *Party of the People: A History of the Democrats* (New York: Random House, 2003).

8

Voting, Campaigns, and Elections

Introduction

Throughout American history politicians and scholars have wondered how voters should relate to candidates and elected officials for democracy to provide stable, intelligent, and efficient government. At some level, the question has always been—do voters know enough to elect the right candidates to office and do those officeholders have the proper incentives to govern well? The United States was the world's first democracy, so it is not surprising that there was early concern about whether "all men" really were capable of participating in their own governance. Even today, surveys of what the average voter knows about the major issues of the day, about who their representatives are, and what the two major parties stand for can be sobering. Where do voters get their information, how do they organize or process it, and do they know enough to fill the roles that democracy expects of them? These are not just interesting questions. They have been the foci of much APD research because a great deal hinges on the answers.

The Founding generation, though they fought and won a revolution for individual rights and liberties, was deeply ambivalent about democracy. Our first selection is drawn from the debates of the Constitutional Convention about who should have the right to vote. Some thought that the common people—emotional, ill-informed, and self-interested—had no role to play in government. Connecticut's Roger Sherman led off the debate on suffrage by saying that "The people . . . should have as little to do as may be about the Government. They want information and are constantly liable to be misled." Others supported a broader role for the people, but universal suffrage, even just for white men, was advocated by very few and was not fully achieved for half a century.

In our second selection and the highlight piece for Chapter 8, Alexander Keyssar traces the progress toward universal suffrage for white men in *The Right to Vote* (2000). Initially, the right to vote was limited, most often by religion and property-holding, to assure that only the stable and right-thinking had access to the ballot. Voting was often public so that it could be monitored by established local leaders. Steadily, from the Revolution through the era we call Jacksonian democracy, the suffrage was expanded to all white male citizens and even a bit beyond. In the mid-nineteenth century some Midwestern states and territories allowed white male immigrants intending to become citizens to vote, but extending the vote to minorities and women was still decades away.

By the mid-twentieth century, with universal suffrage in place or in prospect, scholarly attention turned to how people prepared to vote and then how they vote. Selections by V.O. Key and Samuel L. Popkin explore how citizens collect and process political information and how that information informs and affects their vote. Both Key and Popkin argue that voters act responsibly and reasonably, though not because they are well-informed in any normal sense. Key's book, entitled *The Responsible Electorate* (1960), argued that voters respond to campaigns as responsibly as can be expected given the quality of information that candidates and campaigns present. Voters are constrained to choose between the parties, candidates, and campaigns that are made available to them. If voters are offered silly themes and bumper sticker slogans, it makes no sense to think that they can rise above the process to make an informed and rational choice. In *The Reasoning Voter* (1991), Popkin asks how voters take the partial and inadequate information that campaigns offer them and build around it and add to it to make a reasoned vote choice. Voters are assisted by past knowledge and experience with the parties and candidates, as well as what they hear from family, friends, and trusted media sources, to supplement, check, and help in interpreting what they learn in a particular campaign. Both Key and Popkin conclude that voters do pretty well—considering.

Anthony King and Dennis Johnson raise concerns about how politicians, rather than voters, respond to contemporary campaigns. If voters have trouble getting the information they need from campaigns to make good choices, perhaps it is because the candidates and their handlers have incentives not to give it to them. King argues that American politicians are "running scared" because they face more elections, and, therefore, more career threats, than politicians in any other democracy. Many politicians conclude that obfuscation and avoidance are their best defenses. Finally, Dennis Johnson argues, in *No Place for Amateurs* (2007), that political professionals—campaign managers, media specialists, pollsters, and fund raisers—have taken over modern campaigns above the local level. These professionals are paid to win, not to give voters all the information they might like to have to make an informed decision.

Apparently, the Founders concerns were well-placed and remain with us today.

8.1 Debates at the Constitutional Convention, "Should Common Citizens be Allowed to Vote?" (1787)

The newly independent United States was the world's first democracy, but somewhat uncomfortably so. The colonies and then states were familiar with elections, but the right to vote was usually limited to white, male, property owners. Non-property holders were thought to be unstable because they lacked the permanent and practical "stake in the community" represented by land ownership. Because instability in the states had been one of the problems that had caused the Founders to call for a Constitutional Convention, deciding who should be permitted to vote in the new government proved a contentious issue.

Our first selection presents key exchanges from the suffrage debates in the Convention. Some delegates argued that common voters did not know enough to participate in selecting high government officials and were likely to be duped and misled by demagogues. Others argued that broad participation was the foundation of freedom and democracy and should not be denied. Ultimately, the delegates compromised by agreeing that the right to vote for members of the U.S. House of Representatives would not be set in the Constitution. Rather, eligibility to vote in U.S. House elections would be the same as the right to vote for the lower house of the state legislature. In other words, suffrage would be defined by the states. Some states, such as those in the North and West, might have a broad suffrage while others, mostly in the South, might have a narrower suffrage.

Monday May 31, 1787

In Committee of the whole on Mr. Randolph's propositions.

The 3d. Resolution "that the national Legislature ought to consist of two branches" was agreed to without debate or dissent, except that of Pennsylvania, given probably from complaisance to Docr. Franklin who was understood to be partial to a single House of Legislation.

Resol: 4. first clause "that the members of the first branch of the National Legislature ought to be elected by the people of the several States" being taken up,

Mr. SHERMAN opposed the election by the people, insisting that it ought to be by the State Legislatures. The people he said, immediately should have as little to do as may be about the Government. They want information and are constantly liable to be misled.

Mr. GERRY. The evils we experience flow from the excess of democracy. The people do not want virtue, but are the dupes of pretended patriots. In Massts. it had been fully confirmed by experience that they are daily misled into the most baneful measures and opinions by the false reports circulated by designing men, and which no one on the spot can refute. One principal evil arises from the want of due provision for those employed in the administration of Governmt. It would seem to be a maxim of democracy to starve the public servants. He mentioned the popular clamour in Massts. for the reduction of salaries and the attack made on that of the Govr. though secured by the spirit of the Constitution itself. He had he said been too republican heretofore: he was still however republican, but had been taught by experience the danger of the levelling spirit.

Mr. MASON, argued strongly for an election of the larger branch by the people. It was to be the grand depository of the democratic principle of the Govtt. It was, so to speak, to be our House of Commons—It ought to know & sympathise with every part of the community; and ought therefore to be taken not only from different parts of the whole republic, but also from different districts of the larger members of it, which had in several instances particularly in Virga., different interests and views arising from difference of produce, of habits &c &c. He admitted that we had been too democratic but was afraid we sd. incautiously run into the opposite extreme. We ought to attend to the rights of every class of the people. He had often wondered at the indifference of the superior classes of society to this dictate of humanity & policy; considering that however affluent their circumstances, or elevated their situations, might be, the course of a few years, not only might but certainly would, distribute their posterity throughout the lowest classes of Society. Every selfish motive therefore, every family attachment, ought to recommend such a system of policy as would provide no less carefully for the rights and happiness of the lowest than of the highest orders of Citizens.

Mr. WILSON contended strenuously for drawing the most numerous branch of the Legislature immediately from the people. He was for raising the federal pyramid to a considerable altitude, and for that reason wished to give it as broad a basis as possible. No government could long subsist without the confidence of the people. In a republican Government this confidence was peculiarly essential. He also thought it wrong to increase the weight of the State Legislatures by making them the electors of the national Legislature. All interference between the general and local Governmts. should be obviated as much as possible. On examination it would be found that the opposition of States to federal measures had proceded much more from the officers of the States, than from the people at large.

Mr. MADISON considered the popular election of one branch of the National Legislature as essential to every plan of free Government. He observed that in some of the States one branch of the Legislature was composed of men already removed from the people by an intervening body of electors. That if the first branch of the general legislature should be elected by the State Legislatures, the second branch elected by the first—the Executive by the second together with the first; and other appointments again made for subordinate purposes by the Executive, the people would be lost sight of altogether; and the necessary sympathy between them and their rulers and officers, too little felt. He was an advocate for the policy of refining the popular appointments by successive filtrations, but though it might be pushed too far. He wished the expedient to be resorted to only in the appointment of the second branch of the Legislature, and in the Executive & judiciary branches of the Government. He thought too that the great fabric to be raised would be more stable and durable, if it should rest on the solid foundation of the people themselves, than if it should stand merely on the pillars of the Legislatures.

Mr. GERRY did not like the election by the people. The maxims taken from the British constitution were often fallacious when applied to our situation which was extremely different. Experience he said had shewn that the State legislatures drawn immediately from the people did not always possess their confidence. He had no objection however to an election by the people if it were so qualified that men of honor & character might not be unwilling to be joined in the appointments. He seemed to think the people might nominate a certain number out of which the State legislatures should be bound to choose.

Mr. BUTLER thought an election by the people an impracticable mode.

On the question for an election of the first branch of the national Legislature by the people.

Massts. ay. Connect. divd. N. York ay. N. Jersey no. Pena. ay. Delawe. divd. Va. ay. N. C. ay. S. C. no. Georga. ay.

Wednesday June 6, 1787

IN COMMITTEE OF THE WHOLE

Mr. GERRY. Much depends on the mode of election. In England, the people will probably lose their liberty from the smallness of the proportion having a right of suffrage. Our danger arises from the opposite extreme: hence in Massts. the worst men get into the Legislature. Several members of that Body had lately been convicted of infamous crimes. Men of indigence, ignorance & baseness, spare no pains, however dirty to carry their point agst. men who are superior to the artifices practised. He was not disposed to run into extremes. He was as much principled as ever agst. aristocracy and monarchy. It was necessary on the one hand that the people should appoint one branch of the Govt. in order to inspire them with the necessary confidence. But he wished the election on the other to be so modified as to secure more effectually a just preference of merit. His idea was that the people should nominate certain persons in certain districts, out of whom the State Legislatures shd. make the appointment.

Mr. WILSON. He wished for vigor in the Govt., but he wished that vigorous authority to flow immediately from the legitimate source of all authority. The Govt. ought to possess not only 1st. the force, but 2dly. the mind or sense of the people at large. The Legislature ought to be the most exact transcript of the whole Society. Representation is made necessary only because it is impossible for the people to act collectively.... There is no danger of improper elections if made by large districts. Bad elections proceed from the smallness of the districts which give an opportunity to bad men to intrigue themselves into office.

Monday June 25, 1787

IN CONVENTION

Resolution 4. being taken up.

Mr. PINKNEY spoke as follows—The efficacy of the System will depend on this article. In order to form a right judgmt. in the case, it will be proper to examine the situation of this Country more accurately than it has yet been done. The people of the U. States are perhaps the most singular of any we are acquainted with. Among them there are fewer distinctions of fortune & less of rank, than among the inhabitants of any other nation. Every freeman has a right to the same protection & security; and a very moderate share of property entitles them to the possession of all the honors and privileges the public can bestow: hence arises a greater equality, than is to be found among the people of any other country, and an equality which is more likely to continue— I say this equality is likely to continue, because in a new Country, possessing immense tracts of uncultivated lands, where every temptation is offered to emigration & where industry must be rewarded with competency, there will be few poor, and few dependent—Every member of the Society almost, will enjoy an equal power of arriving at the supreme offices & consequently of directing the strength & sentiments of the whole Community. None will be excluded by birth, & few by fortune, from voting for proper persons to fill the offices of Government—the whole community will enjoy in the fullest sense that kind of political liberty which consists in the power the members of the State reserve to themselves, of arriving at the public offices, or at least, of having votes in the nomination of those who fill them . . . .

Our true situation appears to me to be this.—a new extensive Country containing within itself the materials for forming a Government capable of extending to its citizens all the blessings of civil & religious liberty—capable of making them happy at home. This is the great end of Republican Establishments. We mistake the object of our Government, if we hope or wish that it is to make us respectable abroad. Conquest or superiority among other powers is not or ought not ever to be the object of republican systems. If they are sufficiently active & energetic to rescue us from contempt & preserve our domestic happiness & security, it is all we can expect from them,—it is more than almost any other Government ensures to its citizens . . . .

8.2 Alexander Keyssar, "Democracy Ascendant: The Right to Vote" (2000)

As the new nation grew during the first half of the nineteenth century, democracy was more fully embraced. Four million Americans in 1790 became 20 million by 1850 and 13 states became 31 by 1855. Cheap land in the West encouraged the demand for equal suffrage and for political equality more generally. As the Civil War approached, universal white manhood suffrage was firmly in place.

Other changes in the electoral process also took place. Voice voting—publicly announcing one's choice, common, especially in the South, as late as the 1790s— was generally replaced in the early decades of the nineteenth century by written ballots dropped in a ballot box. Residency requirements were shortened to allow the waves of new immigrants access to the polls. In fact, states in the Midwest, beginning with Wisconsin in 1848 competed for immigrants by passing "alien intent" laws which allowed aliens to vote if they had begun the citizenship process. Turnout approached 80 percent in this newly democratized electorate from the

1830s forward to the Civil War when the electorate would again be expanded by the at least temporary inclusion of black men.

The course of things in this country is for the extension, and not the restriction of popular rights.

Nathan Sanford, New York State Constitutional Convention, 1821

Things changed rapidly in the new nation. The population of the United States was less than four million in 1790; by 1820 it was nearly ten million, and by 1850, more than twenty million. Cities grew, seaboard counties became more densely inhabited, and millions of settlers spilled into the western reaches of Massachusetts, New York, Pennsylvania, Virginia, and the Carolinas. Vast new territories were added by purchase or conquest, and wars were fought against Britain and Mexico. Commerce expanded, thousands of workers carved canals through the earth, steam-powered ships made their way up and down the Mississippi, and the South grew dependent on the cash crop of cotton. In the Northeast, particularly after the War of 1812, manufacturing industries, led by textiles, became increasingly prominent features of the economic and physical landscape.

This fast-moving assembly of changes created pressures for the states to significantly revise the blueprints for governance that they had drawn during the era of the revolution. To many citizens of early-nineteenth-century America, the first state constitutions, written during the tumult of the revolution, appeared either flawed or obsolete—or both. Between 1790 and the 1850s, every state (there were thirty-one by 1855) held at least one constitutional convention, and more than a few held several. The issues addressed by these conventions were many, but almost invariably a key concern was the distribution of political power among the increasingly diverse residents of each state. Indeed, disputes over political power, rights, and influence—including the breadth of the franchise and the apportionment of state legislative seats—were often what prompted states to call constitutional conventions in the first place . . . .

The Course of Things

To attempt to govern men without seeking their consent is usurpation and tyranny, whether in Ohio or in Austria . . . . I was looking the other day . . . into Noah Webster's Dictionary for the meaning of democracy, and I found as I expected that he defines a democrat to be "one who favors universal suffrage."

Norton Townshend, Ohio Constitutional Convention, 1850

Nearly everywhere, the laws governing the right to vote in the United States were greatly elaborated and significantly transformed between 1790 and the 1850s. In addition to the fundamental changes wrought by constitutional conventions, state legislatures frequently supplemented (and sometimes altered) constitutional provisions with statute law; and courts intervened to interpret both the constitutions and the statutes.[1]

One cluster of legal changes involved the physical act of voting. At the nation's founding, the concrete procedures for voting varied widely from state to state and even from town to town. In some locales, particularly in the South, voting was still an oral and public act: men assembled before election judges, waited for their names to be called, and then announced which candidates they supported; in one variant of this process, common in Virginia, men inscribed their names in a poll book underneath the name of the candidate they preferred. Elsewhere, state constitutions or statutes required that voting be conducted by written ballot, to protect voters against intimidation. By the mid-nineteenth century, nearly all states insisted that votes be cast through written ballots, placed in a box or handed to an official. As the number of offices to be filled through elections grew, printed ballots gradually replaced handwritten ones, and political parties themselves began to prepare printed ballots, both to assist and monitor their voters. Abuses of this system were (sometimes) checked by the passage of laws requiring all ballots to be of uniform size and color or by insisting that ballots be placed in envelopes before being deposited. Not surprisingly, the laws governing such procedures were often the subject of partisan wrangling.[2]

Other legal developments were essentially administrative, reflecting a need to translate broad precepts into detailed rules governing the conduct of elections. Most states, for example, had to define what it meant to be a resident or inhabitant. They had to decide how and when lists of eligible voters would be assembled, what documents had to be presented as proof of citizenship, and how challenges to a voter's eligibility should be handled. Some state legislatures also had to specify the ways in which a personal property requirement could be met: Did a promissory note count as personal property? Similarly, race had to be given an operative definition. Just how white did you have to be in order to vote? One half, three quarters? An increasingly voluminous body of law offered answers to such questions.[3]

Far more significant were the substantive changes in voting requirements that marked the era, particularly those that lowered economic barriers to voting. Between the end of the American Revolution and the beginning of the Civil War, the economic and class lines that had so clearly circumscribed the electorate in the eighteenth century became blurred, even indistinct. The sources of this important shift were complex; but first, a brief chronicle of the events.

The property qualifications for suffrage that had begun to erode during the revolution were gradually dismantled after 1790. Delaware eliminated its property requirement in 1792, and Maryland followed a decade later. Massachusetts, despite the eloquent opposition of Adams and Daniel Webster, abolished its freehold or estate qualification in 1821; New York acted in the same year. Virginia was the last state to insist on a real property requirement in all elections, clinging to a modified (and extraordinarily complex) freehold law until 1850. And North Carolina finally eliminated its property qualification for senatorial elections in the mid-1850s.[4] Alongside these developments was another, of equal importance: none of the new states admitted to the union after 1790 adopted mandatory property requirements in their original constitutions.[5] By the end of the 1850s, only two property requirements remained in force anywhere in the United States, one applying to foreign-born residents of Rhode Island and the other to African Americans in New York.

Yet the demise of property requirements was not identical to the eradication of economic qualifications. Several states had taxpaying requirements even in 1790; a number of others instituted such requirements when they abolished property qualifications, and several of the new western states, including Ohio and Louisiana, also insisted that voters be taxpayers. Although taxpaying requirements were conceptually distinct from property qualifications (paying a tax demonstrated one's membership in a community but not one's Blackstonian independence), they nonetheless preserved the link between a person's financial status and his right to vote. Moreover, depending on the size and nature of the tax, these requirements could keep substantial numbers of voters from the polls; ironically, the barrier was lowest in those states that had a regressive (but usually insubstantial) poll tax on all household heads.

The democratic momentum that overwhelmed property requirements, however, also undermined taxpaying qualifications. Between 1830 and 1855, six states relinquished their insistence that voters pay taxes, leaving only six others with taxpaying clauses, several of which were quite minimal. By 1855, thus, there were few formal or explicit economic barriers to voting.

This broadening of state voting requirements was paralleled by changes both in federal policy and in municipal voting laws. In 1808, Congress modified the property qualifications in the Northwest Ordinance; three years later it acted more decisively, enfranchising all free white males who had paid taxes and resided in the territory.[6] Subsequent acts of territorial organization for other regions generally permitted either taxpayer or white male suffrage.[7] Similarly, congressional enabling acts (authorizing territories to become states and to hold constitutional conventions) became increasingly liberal in their suffrage provisions. Representatives to the constitutional conventions of Ohio (1802) and Indiana (1816) were chosen by adult male citizen taxpayers who met a one-year residence requirement; Illinois in 1818 did not even insist on a taxpaying qualification; and several decades later, all free white male inhabitants of Michigan (1835) and Wisconsin (1846) were able to participate in the founding elections.[8] The franchise in the District of Columbia followed a similar path: a taxpaying requirement, adopted in 1802 when the city was first incorporated, was dropped in 1855.[9] ...

In some states, the right to vote also was broadened along axes that were not economic or financial. Almost everywhere states tinkered with their residency rules, which had become increasingly salient once property qualifications had been eliminated. In several states, including Delaware, Pennsylvania, South Carolina, Indiana, and Michigan, residency requirements were shortened, opening the polls to large numbers of migrants who previously had been barred.[10] In Ohio, widespread migration led to a shift in the entire conceptual underpinning of residency rules, increasing the weight given to an individual's right to vote while limiting the power of communities to decide who their official residents were.[11]

Far more dramatic, and perhaps surprising, was the extension of the franchise to aliens—although the history of alien (i.e., noncitizen) voting was anything but unidirectional. At the end of the eighteenth century, the line separating citizens from aliens was not clearly or consistently drawn, either in law or in practice.[12] Some state constitutions specified that voters had to be citizens, while others conferred the franchise on "inhabitants"; the federal government, hoping to encourage settlement, expressly permitted aliens to vote in the Northwest Territories.[13] Thus in many locales, foreign-born men who had not been naturalized by the federal government but who did meet property, taxpaying, and residence requirements were able to participate in elections.[14]

The status of aliens was in flux, however. The federal government changed the procedures and qualifications for naturalization every few years, settling on a durable formula only in 1802, when Congress declared that any foreign-born white male who met a five-year residency requirement could become a citizen three years after formally announcing his intention to do so.[15] In addition, the distinction between citizens and inhabitants became the subject of litigation in Ohio, Illinois, and other jurisdictions.[16]

Between 1800 and 1830, moreover, numerous states opted to clarify ambiguous wording in their constitutions to protect themselves against a perceived or potential influx of (undesirable) foreign-born voters. While revising their constitutions, New York, Massachusetts, Connecticut, Vermont, Maryland, and Virginia all replaced "inhabitant" with "citizen"; New Jersey performed the same alchemy by statute.[17] (New Jersey seemed uniquely cavalier about altering suffrage qualifications by stature rather than constitutional amendment.) Not surprisingly, the western states followed suit: almost all of the new states joining the union between 1800 and 1840 conferred the right to vote exclusively on citizens.[18] (The one exception was Illinois, which permitted aliens to vote for several decades after the state was organized in 1818.) By the Jacksonian era, aliens were barred from the polls nearly everywhere.

Then the pendulum swung back, particularly in the Midwest. Although Illinois by a narrow vote decided to limit the franchise to citizens in 1848, other states in the upper Midwest moved in the opposite direction. Wisconsin was the pioneer, adopting in 1848 what became known as "alien intent" or "declarant non-citizen" suffrage: building on the two-step structure of the naturalization laws, the franchise was extended to aliens who had lived in the United States for two years and who had filed "first papers" declaring their intention to become citizens.[19] Not coincidentally, the population of Wisconsin in 1850 was 35 percent foreign born, the highest of any state.[20] Michigan and Indiana soon passed similar laws, as did the federal government for the territories of Oregon and Minnesota.[21] In the late 1850s, Kansas, Minnesota, and Oregon all adopted alien suffrage, and after the Civil War a dozen more states in the South and the West did likewise (again joined by various territories administered by the federal government). Outside of the Northeast, declarant, noncitizen suffrage therefore became commonplace, permitting hundreds of thousands of previously excluded voters to go to the polls.[22] Although the constitutionality of alien suffrage was heatedly debated in the mid-nineteenth century (opponents often claimed that states were usurping federal power by conferring the franchise on those who were not naturalized), state courts consistently upheld such provisions.[23] In 1840, for example, the Illinois Supreme Court affirmed that the state's constitution granted "the right of suffrage to those who, having by habitation and residence, identified their interests and feelings with the citizenry ... although they may be neither native nor adopted citizens."[24] ...

Ideas and Arguments

Alongside the shifts in the social structure and in political institutions—and surely linked to them—was another factor that played a critical role in the expansion of suffrage: a change in prevailing political ideas and values. Stated simply, more and more Americans came to believe that the people (or at least the male people—"every full-grown featherless biped who wears a hat instead of a bonnet") were and ought to be sovereign and that the sovereign "people" included many individuals who did not own property. Restrictions on the franchise that appeared normal or conventional in 1780 came to look archaic in subsequent decades. Franklin's oft-cited view that the right to vote should belong to the man and not the ass began to look commonsensical rather than radical. The shift in political temper was evident in the decisions of states admitted to the union after 1800 not to impose any pecuniary qualifications on suffrage. It also surfaced throughout the nation in newspapers, in the occasional treatise, in public debate: at William and Mary College, in both 1808 and 1812, the graduating students who gave commencement addresses seized the occasion to proclaim their support for universal suffrage. "The mass of the people," declared one newspaper in 1840, "are honest and capable of self-government." Not everyone embraced such ideas, but the tide of political thought was flowing in the direction of democracy.[25]

This ideological tilt, grounded in social changes that had swept the nation, was readily apparent at numerous constitutional conventions that debated and acted on proposals to enlarge the franchise. These debates generally were heated, and many of the views expressed echoed those heard at the end of the eighteenth century. But the ideological spectrum had shifted, its centerpoint sliding to the left—which was reflected not only in the substance but in the emphases, tones, and language of the debates . . . .

Reform delegates frontally attacked the notion that those who owned property were somehow better qualified to vote than those who did not. "Regard for country," argued J. T. Austin of Boston in 1820, "did not depend upon property, but upon institutions, laws, habits, and associations." William Griffith of New Jersey, writing under the name of Eumenes, declared that it was simply an irrational prejudice, unsupported by any evidence, to claim that the ownership of "fifty pounds clear estate" made someone "more a man or citizen," or "wiser than his neighbor who has but ten pounds," or "more honest." The eloquent nonfreeholders of Richmond went a step further in 1829: "to ascribe to a landed possession, moral or intellectual endowments, would truly be regarded as ludicrous, were it not for the gravity with which the proposition is maintained, and still more for the grave consequences that flow from it." Linked to such views was a complete and sometimes contemptuous dismissal of the Blackstonian notion that only real property ownership gave a man sufficient independence to be a trustworthy voter. One Virginia delegate, after a detailed, logical dissection of the claim that broadening the franchise would permit the rich to manipulate the poor, concluded that the "freehold test" had no merit "unless there be something in the ownership of land, that by enchantment or magic converts frail erring man, into an infallible and impeccable being."[26] . . .

By the middle of the nineteenth century, thus, the nation had taken significant steps in the direction of universal white male suffrage. Spurred by the development of the economy, shifts in the social structure, the dynamics of party politics, the diffusion of democratic ideals, the experiences of war, and the need to maintain militias, the states, the federal government, and municipalities all had dismantled the most fundamental obstacles to the participation of men in elections. The impact of these reforms on the size of the electorate varied from state to state and is difficult to gauge with precision, but it surely was substantial. A careful study of New York before 1820 indicates that two thirds of adult males were unable to meet the freehold requirement to vote for the Senate, and one third were unable to meet the much lower property requirement for voting for the legislature; the reforms therefore tripled the electorate for senatorial elections and increased it by 50 percent for the assembly. Similarly, in North Carolina, abolition of the freehold requirement doubled the electorate for senatorial elections, while the Virginia reforms of 1851, applying to all elections, increased the size of the polity by as much as 60 percent.[27]

The consequences were not everywhere so dramatic (in New Jersey and Massachusetts, for example, the growth of the electorate was more modest), but in every state where property and taxpaying qualifications were abolished, thousands and sometimes tens of thousands of men were enfranchised. The expansion of the suffrage in fact played a key role in the enormous upsurge of political participation in the 1830s and 1840s, when turnout in some locales reached 80 percent of all adult male citizens. De Tocqueville's declaration that "the people reign over the American political world as God rules over the universe" was more than a little hyperbolic; but his celebratory enthusiasm was far more closely matched by the reality of the United States in 1850 than it would have been in 1800.[28]

NOTES

1. Townshend quote from *Report of the Debates and Proceedings of the Convention for the Revision of the Constitution of the State of Ohio, 1850–51*, vol. 2 (Columbus, OH, 1851), 550. The tendency of the courts in general was to protect suffrage, as a constitutional right, from interference by the legislature. In principle, legislatures were permitted to implement and regulate the suffrage but not to change its breadth. See, e.g., Charles Theodore Russell, *The Disfranchisement of Paupers: Examination of the Law of Massachusetts* (Boston, 1878).

2. Eldon C. Evans, *A History of the Australian Ballot System in the United States* (Chicago, 1917), 1–10; L. E. Fredman, *The Australian Ballot: The Story of an American Reform* (Lansing, 1968), 21–23.

3. See, e.g., Massachusetts, *General Laws* (1791), chap. 26; (1793), chap. 40; (1809), chap. 25; (1855), chap. 416; John Duer et al., *The Revised Statutes of the State of New York, As Altered by Subsequent Enactments*, vol. 1 (Albany, 1846), pt. 1, chap. 6, Titles I and IV, 129–37; *Statutes of the State of New York, of a Public and General Character, Passed From 1829 to 1851*, vol. 1, Samuel Blatchford, comp. (Auburn, NY, 1852), Elections, General Elections, Title 1, 435–43; *Supplement to the Fifth Edition of the Revised Statues of the State of New York*, arr. Isaac Edwards (Albany, 1863), 42; *Spragins v. Houghton*, 3 Ill. (2 Scam.) 377 (1840). The emergence of such laws also is reflected in reports on disputed elections; see, e.g., Luther S. Cushing, *Reports of Controverted Elections to the House of Representatives of the Commonwealth of Massachusetts, From 1780 to 1852* (Boston, 1853). For a discussion of the legal history of residence definitions see Kenneth J. Winkle, *The Politics of Community: Migration and Politics in Antebellum Ohio* (Cambridge, UK, 1988), 48–87.

4. Fletcher M. Green, *Constitutional Development in the South Atlantic States, 1776–1860: A Study in the Evolution of Democracy* (Chapel Hill, NC, 1930), 270.

5. Louisiana and Tennessee did make property ownership a means—though not the exclusive means—of qualifying for the franchise. Florida, in its 1838 constitution, notably declared that "no property qualification for eligibility to office, or for the right of suffrage, shall ever be required in this state." *Comparative View of the State Constitutions, Manual for the New York State Constitutional Convention, 1846* (Albany, 1849), 172.

6. Robert M. Taylor, *The Northwest Ordinance 1787: A Bicentennial Handbook* (Indianapolis, 1987), 47–49, 118; Franklin B. Hough, ed., *American Constitutions: Comprising the Constitution of Each State in the Union, and of the United States*, vol. 1 (Albany, 1872), 333; Charles Kettleborough, *Constitution Making in Indiana: A Source Book of Constitutional Documents with Historical Introduction and Critical Notes*, vol. 1 (Indianapolis, 1916), xcii–xciii, 3, 48.

7. Kirk H. Porter, *A History of Suffrage in the United States* (Chicago, 1918), 132–33; Arthur C. Cole, ed., *The Constitutional Debates of 1847* (Springfield, IL, 1919), 536–37; Kettleborough, *Constitution Making in Indiana*, vol. 1, 56, 58; R. H. Thompson, "Suffrage in Mississippi," *Publications of the Mississippi Historical Society*, vol. 1, ed. Franklin L. Riley (Oxford, 1898), 30; Dudley O. McGovney, *The American Suffrage Medley: The Need for a National Uniform Suffrage* (Chicago, 1949), 137; Malcolm C. McMillan, *Constitutional Development in Alabama, 1798–1801: A Study in Politics, the Negro and Sectionalism* (Chapel Hill, NC, 1955), 11–14.

8. Notably, however, Illinois insisted that electors be white, which was not the case in Ohio or Indiana. Richard Peters, ed., *The Public Statutes at Large of the United States of America from the Organization of Government in 1780 to March 3, 1845* (Boston, 1848), vol. 2, 173–75, vol. 3, 289–91, 428–31, vol. 5, 49–50; "An Act in Relation to the Formation of a State Government in Wisconsin," in W. T. Madison, ed., *Laws of the Territory of Wisconsin* (Simeon Mills, WI, 1846), 5–12; George Minot, ed., *The Public Statutes at Large of the United States of America from December 1, 1845 to March 3, 1851* (Boston, 1857), 56–58; "An Act to Enable the People of Michigan to form a Constitution and State Government," *Acts Passed at the Extra and Second Session of the Sixth Legislative Council of the Territory of Michigan* (Detroit, 1835), 72–77.

9. Porter, *History of Suffrage*, 133–34.

10. Green, *Constitutional Development*, 249; Adams, *Suffrage in Michigan*, 37–38; Kettleborough, *Constitution Making in Indiana*, vol. 1, ccxxvi, 106, 304–5; Roy H. Akagi, "The Pennsylvania Constitution of 1838," *Pennsylvania Magazine of History and Biography* 48 (1924): 328.

11. Winkle, *Politics of Community*, 49–65, 83–87, 172–75.

12. Gerald M. Rosberg, "Aliens and Equal Protection: Why Not the Right to Vote?" *Michigan Law Review* 75 (April–May 1977): 1096–97; James H. Kettner, *The Development of American Citizenship, 1608–1870* (Chapel Hill, NC, 1978), 28; H. Sidney Everett, "Immigration and Naturalization," *Atlantic Monthly* 75 (March 1895): 349–50; *Reports of the U.S. Immigration Commission*. Vol. 39, *Immigration Legislation*, Senate Document no. 758 (Washington, DC, 1911), 6.

13. Jamin B. Raskin, "Legal Aliens, Local Citizens: The Historical, Constitutional and Theoretical Meanings of Alien Suffrage," *University of Pennsylvania Law Review* 141 (April 1993): 1402.

14. Gerald L. Neuman, "We Are the People': Alien Suffrage in German and American Perspective," *Michigan Journal of International Law*, 13 (Winter 1992): 291–96; Raskin, "Legal Aliens," 1400–1403.

15. *The Naturalization Laws of the United States*, comp. by "member of the bar," *containing also the Alien Laws of the State of New York* (Rochester, 1855) 9–11; *Immigration Commission*, vol. 39, 6; Everett, "Immigration and Naturalization," 349–50; John P. Gavit, *Americans by Choice* (1922; reprint, Montclair, NJ, 1971), 66–77; Taliesin Evans, *American Citizenship and the Right of Suffrage in the United States* (Oakland, CA, 1892), 14–15.

16. Among the key court cases see *Johnston v. England* (1817), *Ohio Unreported Judicial Decisions Prior to 1823*, ed. Ervin H. Pollack (Indianapolis, 1952), 149–59; or the more widely cited *Spragins v. Houghton*, 3 Ill. (2 Scam.) 377 (1840); and Rosberg, "Aliens and Equal Protection," 1095–96.

17. Raskin, "Legal Aliens," 1403–4; Richard P. McCormick, *The History of Voting in New Jersey: A Study of the Development of Election Machinery, 1664–1911* (New Brunswick, NJ, 1953), 110; Rosberg, "Aliens and Equal Protection," 1097–99.

18. Raskin, "Legal Aliens," 1403–5.

19. For the debate in Wisconsin regarding alien suffrage see Milo M. Quaife, ed., *The Convention of 1846*, Publications of the State Historical Society of Wisconsin, Collections, vol. 27, Constitutional Series, vol. 2 (Madison, 1919), 207–78; *Journal of the Convention to form a constitution for the State of Wisconsin, with a sketch of the debates, begun and held at Madison, on the fifteenth day of December, eighteen hundred and forty-seven* (Madison, 1848), 146–91.

20. Calculated from data in *Naturalization Laws*, 87.

21. For an examination of the politics leading to Michigan's law see Ronald P. Formisano, *The Birth of Mass Political Parties, Michigan, 1827–1861* (Princeton, 1971), 81–101; see also *The Michigan Constitutional Conventions of 1835–36 Debates and Proceedings*, ed. Harold M. Dorr (Ann Arbor, 1940), 177–257, 511; regarding Indiana, see Kettleborough, *Constitution Making in Indiana*, vol. 1, xcvi–xcix, civ–cix; and *Report of the Debates and Proceedings of the Convention for the Revision of the Constitution of the State of Indiana* (Indianapolis, 1850), 1292–1305; for listings of chronology see articles by Raskin, Rosberg, and Neuman.

22. For a partial chronicle of the states that adopted alien suffrage see Neuman, "Alien Suffrage," 297–300; see also Raskin, "Legal Aliens," 1391–1470; and Rosberg, "Aliens and Equal Protection," 1095–99. As Rosberg points out, there is some uncertainty about the number of states that did ever have alien suffrage provisions in part because such provisions may have appeared in statutes rather than constitutional clauses; tables A.4 and A.12 list all of the states in which I found such provisions. See also Albert J. McCulloch, *Suffrage and Its Problems* (Baltimore, 1929), 140–41. For debates regarding alien suffrage see *Debates Indiana 1850*, vol. 2 (Indianapolis, 1850), 1292–1305; *Report of the Debates and Proceedings of the Convention for the Revision of the Constitution of the State of Kentucky, 1849* (Frankfort, 1849), 445–617.

23. Quaife, *Convention of 1846*, 235–38.

24. *Spragins v. Houghton*, 3 Ill. (2 Scam.) 377, 408 (1840); see also Neuman, "Alien Suffrage," 300–310.

25. Chandler, "Suffrage in Virginia," 26; George Ticknor Curtis, *Letters of Phocion* (n.p., n.d., *Daily Advertiser and Courier*, Boston, 1853), 117; Ashworth, "*Agrarians*" and "*Aristocrats*," 10.

26. *Massachusetts Debates 1821*, 252; William Griffith, *Eumenes, being a collection of papers, written for the purpose of exhibiting some of the more prominent errors and omissions of the constitution of New Jersey* (Trenton, 1799), 46; Peterson, *Democracy*, 381–82, 402–3; see also one of the first American treatises on the subject, Isaac Hillard, *The Rights of Suffrage* (Danbury, CT, 1804).

27. Richard P. McCormick, "Suffrage Classes and Party Alignments: A Study in Voter Behavior," *Mississippi Valley Historical Review* 46 (December 1959): 397–410; Williamson, *American Suffrage*, 241.

28. Alexis de Tocqueville, *Democracy in America* (London, 1835), 53; Brooke, *Heart of the Commonwealth*, 325–26; William E. Gienapp, "'Politics Seem to Enter into Everything': Political Culture in the North, 1840–1860," *Essays on American Antebellum Politics, 1840–1860*, ed. Stephen Maizlish and John Kushma (College Station, TX, 1982), 15–22, 62–65; Walter Dean Burnham, "Those High Nineteenth-Century American Voting Turnouts: Fact or Fiction?" *Journal of Interdisciplinary History* 16 (Spring 1986): 613–44; Williamson, *American Suffrage*, 195; Harry Watson, *Liberty and Power: The Politics of Jacksonian America* (New York, 1990), 232; McCormick, "Suffrage Classes," 405–10; idem, "New Perspectives on Jacksonian Politics," *American Historical Review* 65 (January 1960): 291–98; Ronald P. Formisano, "Boston, 1800–1840: From Deferential-Participant to Party Politics," *Boston 1700–1980: The Evolution of Urban Politics*, ed. Ronald P. Formisano and Constance K. Burns (Westport, 1984), 34–35; Walter Dean Burnham, "The Turnout Problem," *Elections American Style*, ed. A. James Reichley (Washington, 1987), 113–15.

8.3 V.O. Key, "The Voice of the People: An Echo" (1966)

By the mid-twentieth century the right to vote was essentially universal, women were added to the electorate in 1920 and minorities were slowly allowed meaningful participation in the 1960s and beyond. Young people, 18 to 21, were added to the voting rolls in the early 1970s. Since then, only those who are institutionalized or fail to register to vote are excluded from the electorate. But how do those who chose to vote make up their minds and what does winning an election actually mean?

V.O. Key throws a certain amount of cold water on the sanctity of elections. Key does not question the capability or motivation of voters. Rather, he describes the electoral process as an echo chamber in which voters can only choose between the candidates, parties, and platforms that are offered to them. If campaigns offer bumper sticker slogans, half truths, and outright lies (Obama pals around with terrorists), the fact that voters chose one candidate over the other says less than is often claimed.

Key's famous summary of the dilemma facing voters is that "voters are not fools . . . the electorate behaves about as rationally and responsibly as we should expect, given the clarity of the alternatives presented to it and the character of the information available to it."

In his reflective moments even the most experienced politician senses a nagging curiosity about why people vote as they do. His power and his position depend upon the outcome of the mysterious rites we perform as opposing candidates harangue the multitudes who finally march to the polls to prolong the rule of their champion, to thrust him, ungratefully, back into the void of private life, or to raise to eminence a new tribune of the people. What kinds of appeals enable a candidate to win the favor of the great god, The People? What circumstances move voters to shift their preferences in this direction or that? What clever propaganda tactic or slogan led to this result? What mannerism of oratory or style of rhetoric produced another outcome? What band of electors rallied to this candidate to save the day for him? What policy of state attracted the devotion of another bloc of voters? What action repelled a third sector of the electorate?

The victorious candidate may claim with assurance that he has the answers to all such questions. He may regard his success as vindication of his beliefs about why voters vote as they do. And he may regard the swing of the vote to him as indubitably a response to the campaign positions he took, as an indication of the acuteness of his intuitive estimates of the mood of the people, and as a ringing manifestation of the esteem in which he is held by a discriminating public. This narcissism assumes its most repulsive form among election winners who have championed intolerance, who have stirred the passions and hatreds of people, or who have advocated causes known by decent men to be outrageous or dangerous in their long-run consequences. No functionary is more repugnant or more arrogant than the unjust man who asserts, with a color of truth, that he speaks from a pedestal of popular approbation.

It thus can be a mischievous error to assume, because a candidate wins, that a majority of the electorate shares his views on public questions, approves his past actions, or has specific expectations about his future conduct. Nor does victory establish that the candidate's campaign strategy, his image, his television style, or his fearless stand against cancer and polio turned the trick. The election returns establish only that the winner attracted a majority of the votes—assuming the existence of a modicum of rectitude in election administration. They tell us precious little about why the plurality was his.

For a glaringly obvious reason, electoral victory cannot be regarded as necessarily a popular ratification of a candidate's outlook. The voice of the people is but an echo. The output of an echo chamber bears an inevitable and invariable relation to the input. As candidates and parties clamor for attention and vie for popular support, the people's verdict can be no more than a selective reflection from among the alternatives and outlooks presented to them. Even the most discriminating popular judgment can reflect only ambiguity, uncertainty, or even foolishness if those are the qualities of the input into the echo chamber. A candidate may win despite his tactics and appeals rather than because of them. If the people can choose only from among rascals, they are certain to choose a rascal.

Scholars, though they have less at stake than do politicians, also have an abiding curiosity about why voters act as they do. In the past quarter of a century they have vastly enlarged their capacity to check the hunches born of their curiosities. The invention of the sample survey—the most widely known example of which is the Gallup poll— enabled them to make fairly trustworthy estimates of the characteristics and behaviors of large human populations. This method of mass observation revolutionized the study of politics—as well as the management of political campaigns. The new technique permitted largescale tests to check the validity of old psychological and sociological theories of human behavior. These tests led to new hunches and new theories about voting behavior, which could, in turn, be checked and which thereby contributed to the extraordinary ferment in the social sciences during recent decades . . . .

Yet, by and large, the picture of the voter that emerges from a combination of the folk-lore of practical politics and the findings of the new electoral studies is not a pretty one. It is not a portrait of citizens moving to considered decision as they play their solemn role of making and unmaking governments. The older tradition from practical politics may regard thevoter as an erratic and irrational fellow susceptible to manipulation by skilled humbugs. One need not live through many campaigns to observe politicians, even successful politicians, who act as though they regarded the people as manageable fools. Nor does a heroic conception of the voter emerge from the new analyses of electoral behavior. They can be added up to a conception of voting not as a civic decision but as an almost purely deterministic act. Given knowledge of certain characteristics of a voter—his occupation, his residence, his religion, his national origin, and perhaps certain of his attitudes—one can predict with a high probability the direction of his vote. The actions of persons are made to appear to be only predictable and automatic responses to campaign stimuli . . . .

Conceptions and theories of the way voters behave . . . touch upon profound issues at the heart of the problem of the nature and work-ability of systems of popular government. Obviously the perceptions of the behavior of the electorate held by political leaders, agitators, and activists condition, if they do not fix, the types of appeals politicians employ as they seek popular support. These perceptions—or theories—affect the nature of the input to the echo chamber, if we may revert to our earlier figure, and thereby control its output. They may govern, too, the kinds of actions that governments take as they look forward to the next election. If politicians perceive the electorate as responsive to father images, they will give it father images. If they see voters as most certainly responsive to nonsense, they will give them nonsense. If they see voters as susceptible to delusion, they will delude them. If they see an electorate receptive to the cold, hard realities, they will give it the cold, hard realities.

In short, theories of how voters behave acquire importance not because of their effects on voters, who may proceed blithely unaware of them. They gain significance because of their effects, both potentially and in reality, on candidates and other political leaders. If leaders believe the route to victory is by projection of images and cultivation of styles rather than by advocacy of policies to cope with the problems of the country, they will project images and cultivate styles to the neglect of the substance of politics. They will abdicate their prime function in a democratic system, which amounts, in essence, to the assumption of the risk of trying to persuade us to lift ourselves by our bootstraps.

Among the literary experts on politics there are those who contend that, because of the development of tricks for the manipulation of the masses, practices of political leadership in the management of voters have moved far toward the conversion of election compaigns into obscene parodies of the models set up by democratic idealists. They point to the good old days when politicians were deep thinkers, eloquent orators, and farsighted statesmen. Such estimates of the course of change in social institutions must be regarded with reserve. They may be only manifestations of the inverted optimism of aged and melancholy men who, estopped from hope for the future, see in the past a satisfaction of their yearning for greatness in our political life.

Whatever the trends may have been, the perceptions that leadership elements of democracies hold of the modes of response of the electorate must always be a matter of fundamental significance. Those perceptions determine the nature of the voice of the people, for they determine the character of the input into the echo chamber. While the output may be governed by the nature of the input, over the longer run the properties of the echo chamber may themselves be altered. Fed a steady diet of buncombe, the people may come to expect and to respond with highest predictability to buncombe. And those leaders most skilled in the propagation of buncombe may gain lasting advantage in the recurring struggles for popular favor.

The perverse and unorthodox argument of this little book is that voters are not fools. To be sure, many individual voters act in odd ways indeed; yet in the large the electorate behaves about as rationally and responsibly as we should expect, given the clarity of the alternatives presented to it and the character of the information available to it. In American presidential campaigns of recent decades the portrait of the American electorate that develops from the data is not one of an electorate strait-jacketed by social determinants or moved by subconscious urges triggered by devilishly skillful propagandists. It is rather one of an electorate moved by concern about central and relevant questions of public policy, of governmental performance, and of executive personality. Propositions so uncompromisingly stated inevitably represent overstatements. Yet to the extent that they can be shown to resemble the reality, they are propositions of basic importance for both the theory and the practice of democracy . . . .

8.4 Samuel L. Popkin, "The Reasoning Voter" (1991)

Like V.O. Key, Samuel Popkin asks how citizens gather, integrate, and evaluate the information they need to formulate their vote. Popkin describes a process of "low information rationality" or "gut reasoning" in which voters use past knowledge and experience, information they came across in the normal course of their day, as well as the opinions of others they trust, in formulating their views about the candidates and parties in a given election. In other words, voting is not a "full information" exercise in which voters intensively gather and analyze relevant information. Instead, it is a "low information" exercise in which information already or easily at hand is the basis for decision. Most of the information voters have comes from the campaigns and from the media.

More formally, Popkin's theory of voting sees the voter as "an investor and the vote as a reasoned investment in collective goods [like good government], made with costly and imperfect information under conditions of uncertainty." Information is costly because it takes time to gather and it is imperfect and uncertain because politicians slant and twist it. Voters are moved by old habits and information embedded in their partisan identification and by new information that comes to hand as part of a given campaign. Party identification is an informational shortcut, a standing decision to vote for one party over the other, that voters use to provide structure and context for what they learn during campaigns.

...I use the term *reasoning voter* because my theory recognizes that voters actually do reason about parties, candidates, and issues. They have premises, and they use those premises to make inferences from their observations of the world around them. They think about who and what political parties stand for; they think about the meaning of political endorsements; they think about what government can and should do. And the performance of government, parties, and candidates affects their assessments and preferences.

The term *low-information rationality*—popularly known as "gut" reasoning—best describes the kind of practical thinking about government and politics in which people actually engage. It is a method of combining, in an economical way, learning and information from past experiences, daily life, the media, and political campaigns.

This reasoning draws on various information shortcuts and rules of thumb that voters use to obtain and evaluate information and to simplify the process of choosing between candidates. People use shortcuts which incorporate much political information; they triangulate and validate their opinions in conversations with people they trust and according to the opinions of national figures whose judgments and positions they have come to know. With these shortcuts, they learn to "read" politicians and their positions ....

Voters have a limited amount of information about politics, a limited knowledge of how government works, and a limited understanding of how governmental actions are connected to consequences of immediate concern to them. Campaigns give them much of the information they reason from as they deal with their uncertainty about these matters ....

Campaigns reach most people through the media. Besides attracting attention to the campaign "horse race," the media play a critical role in shaping voters' limited information about the world, their limited knowledge about the links between issues and offices, their limited understanding of the connections between public policy and its immediate consequences for themselves, and their views about what kind of person a president should be. The campaigns and media, in other words, influence the voter's frame of reference, and can thereby change his or her vote.

Low-Information Rationality

My theory of how voters reason is a theory of low-information rationality which empha-sizes the sources of information voters have about politics, as well as their beliefs about how government works. The theory, as I develop it, is drawn from three main sources: the voting studies done at Columbia University in the 1940s; the theoretical contributions to the economics of information made by Anthony Downs; and certain ideas from modern cognitive psychology, as exemplified in the works of Jerome Bruner, Amos Tversky, and Daniel Kahneman . . . .

Behind every voting theory there is a metaphor or an analogy, either implicit or explicit, about the process of choice. If the analogy is successful, it helps to generate hypotheses and explain voting. I propose to view the voter as an investor and the vote as a reasoned investment in collective goods, made with costly and imperfect information under conditions of uncertainty. This analogy is appropriate because the voter expends time and effort in the expectation of some later return, a return that will depend in large part on what others do. The investor analogy . . . draws attention to the difference between public and private goods and allows us to begin to predict several things: when informa-tion gathering will be searching and when it will be superficial; when voter beliefs will be accurate and when they will be misleading; and, to a lesser extent, when those beliefs will be transient and when they will be stable . . . .

Public choices differ from private choices because the incentives to gather informa-tion are different in each instance. The resources expended to gather and process infor-mation before making personal consumption decisions have a direct effect on the quality of the outcome for the consumer, whereas time and money spent gathering information about candidates leads to a better vote, not necessarily a better outcome. The wrong economic policy or the wrong approach to arms control may in fact have a bigger effect on a voter's life than the wrong choice of home or college, but the expected gains from being an informed consumer remain higher than the gains from being an informed voter. Voters are thus not particularly well informed about the details of public policy and government activities. Everybody's business is nobody's business. If everyone spends an additional hour evaluating the candidates, we all benefit from a better-informed electorate. If everyone but me spends the hour evaluating the candidates and I spend it choosing where to invest my savings, I will get a better return on my investment as well as a better government.

Public choices also differ from private choices because voting is a form of collective action; elections are won only when enough people vote together. Voters focus not only on their own concerns and preferences but on those of others as well. Therefore, in deciding which issues to focus on and which candidates to vote for, voters will be affected by information about what other voters are doing. Information about the preferences and votes of others will help them decide whether there are enough people with the same concerns or preferences to make a critical mass. Learning what government is doing and what government is capable of doing can also affect the issues a citizen will focus on in an election. Information will affect my perception of whether a problem is mine alone or common to many; whether a problem common to many is an individual or a collective problem; and whether a collective problem is "our" problem or our government's problem.

Public choices also differ from some private choices because they involve the provi-sion of services. A politician is promising to deliver a future product about which the voter may have limited understanding, so the vote involves uncertainty about whether the product can be delivered, and, if so, whether it will perform as promised. Thus the voter has to assess the politician's ability to accomplish what he or she promises. Private consumers also face uncertainty in making certain decisions—such as choosing a surgeon to perform a life-threatening operation—but choosing a political leader can be even more complex. To deliver promised benefits, a politician must do more than attract enough votes; he or she must attract the support of other politicians as well. For this reason, voters consider not only the personal characteristics of their candidate, but also the other politicians with whom he or she is affiliated.

Every voting theory begins, implicitly or explicitly, from a question which voters ask as they cast their votes. I suggest that the voter behaves as if asking, "What have you done for me lately?" *What have you done?* stresses feedback from government performance and the need to specify how that performance affects attitudes and expectations. *Lately* raises the issue of time horizons—how voters can discount older information when presented with new claims. In *for me*, however, there is an inherent ambiguity, a tension that cannot be resolved. Doing some things for the voter includes doing the same things for everybody, like reducing pollution. It includes doing things for specific groups, like feeding or housing the homeless. And it involves doing things that protect the voter against future possibilities, like improving Medicare or supporting research into a cure for AIDS. This is an unresolvable ambiguity. In 1952, campaign buttons said "I like Ike," but at rallies people said "*We* like Ike." The very ambiguity in the meaning of *for me*, however, stresses that political leaders seek to create political identities and to forge links between individual and group concerns.

The transformation of "What have you done for me lately?" into "What have you done for *us* lately?" is the essence of campaigning. Transforming unstructured and diverse interests into a single coalition, making a single cleavage dominant, requires the creation of new constituencies and political identities. It requires the aggregation of countless *I*'s into a few *we*'s. Behind the *we*'s, however, are people who are still reasoning about the ways in which their lives and government policies are related. The single most important lesson I have learned from campaigning is never to tell people they are selfish, and never to assume that they aren't.

Communications and Persuasion: The Columbia School

I begin with the original studies of presidential campaigns done at Columbia University's Bureau of Applied Social Research in the 1940s.[1] The Columbia studies took the social reasoning of voters seriously and focused on the relation of the campaign to the final vote. These studies also had a relevant normative concern: the manipulative potential of the media. Today there is widespread concern about the impact of the newest medium, television, on the electoral process. People worry that television is leading to a politics of "spinmasters" and admen who manipulate voters and create "Teflon" presidents. When the first Columbia study was done, there was even more reason to be concerned about the power of radio: Hitler had used it with seeming brilliance to manipulate his countrymen . . . .

The central insight of the Columbia voting studies is captured in one sentence: "The people vote in the same election, but not all of them vote *on it*."[2] This statement recognizes the importance of party identification, of public communication and persuasion, and of the role of issues in elections. It suggests that voters in any one election are being moved not only by new issues of which they are aware but also by old issues that have influenced their party identification. It also stresses that voters are not tabulae rasae when they are exposed to the media barrages of the campaigns; to the contrary, they already have some firm beliefs, so are often not moved at all by campaign propaganda. Finally, the Columbia studies also showed that the effect of the mass media on voters is not direct, but mediated by discussion with others . . . .

Information Shortcuts: The Contributions of Anthony Downs

The central insight of Anthony Downs's pioneering book, *An Economic Theory of Democracy*, is that voters will rely on information shortcuts because they do not have much incentive to gather information about politics solely in order to improve their voting choices.[3] Downs builds on the Columbia studies' findings that voters lack knowledge about the government: "Voters are not always aware of what the government is or could be doing, and often they do not know the relationship between government actions and their own utility incomes."...

Downs's application of the economics of information to politics complements the Columbia studies. Indeed, Downs's central insight about information shortcuts is a generalization of the Columbia findings about the roles of party identification and informal opinion leaders. Party identification, viewed from the perspective of low-information rationality, is an informational shortcut or default value, a substitute for more complete information about parties and candidates. This is a key insight for building a model of the voter that can be used to study the role of campaigns and issues in presidential elections. Party identification is a standing decision; even so, it is affected by voters' beliefs about how government works, by the information they obtain in their daily lives and connect with government policies, and by the information they absorb simply because it is interesting or entertaining.[4]...

Framing and Reasoning: Cognitive Psychology

Contemporary research into the psychology of cognition fills the theoretical gaps left by the original Columbia voting studies and Downs's theoretical reformulation of them. Without cognitive psychology there is no satisfactory way to answer important questions about how people assess meaning and use information. My analysis of campaigns requires an understanding of the role of symbols and stories; to understand people not as naive statisticians, but as symbol processors and naive theorists, requires cognitive psychology. Cognitive psychology's findings about meaning and information usage go beyond cues and information shortcuts to describe modes of reasoning, processing aids, and calculation aids, all of which can be applied to the analysis of reasoning voters' decisions.[5]

Each of the three sources from which I draw provides crucial insights about information and political reasoning. From the Columbia studies, we know that people do not absorb all the information to which they are exposed. From Downs, we know that this happens because people do not have incentives to acquire and absorb much of that information. From cognitive psychology, we know that people do not use all the information they have received, and—paradoxically—that people have not received from outside all the information they use. That is, people take the information they have received and use previous experience to complete the picture.

To study the cues, or informational shortcuts, that people use in voting is to study how people supply themselves with information that fills in their pictures of candidates and governments. Cues enable voters to call on beliefs about people and government from which they can generate or recall scenarios, or "scripts," as they are called in psychology. A little information can go a long way because people have so many scenarios and ideas that they can generate from their cues. They can absorb a few cues and then complete their picture with the help of their "default values."[6]

The claim of political savants and insiders that the right commercials and the right consultants can win any election, particularly any primary, is fed by the self-serving myth that certain "magic moments" on television have turned elections around. I will show that there is no evidence at all for the supposed effects of many of these "magic moments."...

I also object to studies of primaries which suggest that when large numbers of voters suddenly shift their support to new candidates, they are simply jumping on a bandwagon. These jumps to new candidates are in fact attempts to change the direction of the party, or to protest against the established order, and they reflect information that voters use about the issue differences between the new and the old candidates.

I challenge the related fantasies of Democrats who believe that campaign faux pas explain the Republicans' near-monopoly on the White House. Democrats do not lose the presidency because Republicans have better admen. They lose because they have less popular policies on the issues that voters connect to the presidency, notably inflation, national defense, and the role of government in society . . . .

I also challenge the terms of the traditional assessment of voter information. It is certainly true that most citizens do not know many of the basic facts about their government, but assessing voters by civics exams misses the many things that voters *do* know, and the many ways in which they can do without the facts that the civics tradition assumes they should know. Further, the focus on voters' lack of textbook information about many political issues underestimates just how much information they pick up during campaigns and from conventions . . . .

Voters do care about their economic well-being, of course, but they also care about the welfare of others, and when they reason about economic benefits and economic performance, they do not make simplistic connections between their bank balances and the performance of the government . . . .

I believe my theory redeems the voter from some of the blame heaped upon him or her by contemporary criticism of the electoral process. My theory also addresses "loopholes" in voter reasoning that candidates can exploit. However, I hope to show that, in the mixture of trivial and profound issues that will always be found in campaigns, there is more meaning to voting, and less manipulation of voters, than either media-centered analyses or the traditional civics-information focus would have us believe.

NOTES

1. Lazarsfeld, Berelson, and Gaudet, *The People's Choice*; Berelson, Lazarsfeld, and McPhee, *Voting*.
2. Berelson et al., *Voting*, p. 316; emphasis in original.
3. Downs, *An Economic Theory of Democracy*.
4. Fiorina, *Retrospective Voting in American National Elections*, is the most important development of Downs's insights about parties.

5. Discussing advances in psychology, Robyn Dawes notes that much of the early research in psychology did not regard individuals as "decision-making units that weighed the consequences of various courses of action and then chose from among them." Many results in cognitive psychology, however, cannot be explained "without hypothesizing an active, hypothesis-testing mind." Because of these results, Dawes notes, "it is now legitimate for psychologists to talk about thinking, choice, mental representations, plans, goals, mental hypothesis testing, and 'cognitive' biases." Dawes, *Rational Choice in an Uncertain World*, p. 19.
6. Lau and Sears use the notion of "default values" in "Social Cognition and Political Cognition," pp. 347–66, esp. p. 352.

8.5 Anthony King, "Running Scared" (1997)

Anthony King argues that the fact that the United States has more elections than other countries puts our politicians in an off-balance, tentative, and vulnerable position. Always running for election, always making promises to their bored and often hard-pressed constituents, they are too frequently tempted to legislate and govern with an eye on the next election rather than on longer-term effective policymaking and problem solving. King argues that American politics and elections are too democratic and would be more stable and reasonable if they were less so.

Other democratic countries work differently. Some employ a "division of labor" between governors and governed where, following elections, public opinion may be consulted but does not govern. Democracy in the United States takes an "agency" view where elected politicians are to reflect what public opinion shows to be the wishes of their constituents. King suggests that U.S. politicians could be insulated somewhat from public opinion and electoral threat by extending terms. For example, U.S. House terms could be extended from two years to four and U.S. Senate terms from six years to eight. He also proposes "collusion of elites," "putting it into commission," and "thinking big" as ways of reducing electoral vulnerability and the bad policymaking that flows from it.

> Painfully often the legislation our politicians pass is designed less to solve problems than to protect the politicians from defeat in our neverending election campaigns. They are, in short, too frightened of us to govern.

To an extent that astonishes a foreigner, modern America is *about* the holding of elections. Americans do not merely have elections on the first Tuesday after the first Monday of November in every year divisible by four. They have elections on the first Tuesday after the first Monday of November in every year divisible by two. In addition, five states have elections in odd-numbered years. Indeed, there is no year in the United States—ever—when a major statewide election is not being held somewhere. To this catalogue of general elections has of course to be added an equally long catalogue of primary elections (for example, forty-three presidential primaries last year). Moreover, not only do elections occur very frequently in the United States but the number of jobs legally required to be filled by them is enormous—from the presidency of the United States to the post of local consumer advocate in New York. It has been estimated that no fewer than half a million elective offices are filled or waiting to be filled in the United States today.

Americans take the existence of their never-ending election campaign for granted. Some like it, some dislike it, and most are simply bored by it. But they are all conscious of it, in the same way that they are conscious of Mobil, McDonald's, *Larry King Live*, Oprah Winfrey, the Dallas Cowboys, the Ford Motor Company, and all the other symbols and institutions that make up the rich tapestry of American life.

To a visitor to America's shores, however, the never-ending campaign presents a largely unfamiliar spectacle. In other countries election campaigns have both beginnings and ends, and there are even periods, often prolonged periods, when no campaigns take place at all. Other features of American elections are also unfamiliar. In few countries do elections and campaigns cost as much as they do in the United States. In no other country is the role of organized political parties so limited.

America's permanent election campaign, together with other aspects of American electoral politics, has one crucial consequence, little noticed but vitally important for the functioning of American democracy. Quite simply, the American electoral system places politicians in a highly vulnerable position. Individually and collectively they are more vulnerable, more of the time, to the vicissitudes of electoral politics than are the politicians of any other democratic country. Because they are more vulnerable, they devote more of their time to electioneering, and their conduct in office is more continuously governed by electoral considerations. I will argue that American politicians' constant and unremitting electoral preoccupations have deleterious consequences for the functioning of the American system. They consume time and scarce resources. Worse, they make it harder than it would otherwise be for the system as a whole to deal with some of America's most pressing problems. Americans often complain that their system is not sufficiently democratic. I will argue that, on the contrary, there is a sense in which the system is too democratic and ought to be made less so . . . .

How They Came To Be Vulnerable

AMERICAN politicians run scared—and are right to do so. And they run more scared than the politicians of any other democratic country—again rightly. How did this come to be so?

The short answer is that the American people like it that way. They are, and have been for a very long time, the Western world's hyperdemocrats. They are keener on determined that democratic norms and practices should pervade every aspect of national life. To explore the implications of this central fact about the United States, and to see how it came to be, we need to examine two different interpretations of the term "democracy." Both have been discussed from time to time by political philosophers, but they have never been codified and they certainly cannot be found written down in a constitution or any other formal statement of political principles. Nevertheless, one or the other underpins the political practice of every democratic country even if, inevitably, the abstract conception and the day-to-day practice are never perfectly matched.

One of these interpretations might be labeled "division of labor." In this view, there are in any democracy two classes of people—the governors and the governed. The function of the governors is to take decisions on the basis of what they believe to be in the country's best interests and to act on those decisions. If public opinion broadly supports the decisions, that is a welcome bonus. If not, too bad. The views of the people at large are merely one datum among a large number of data that need to be considered. They are not accorded any special status. Politicians in countries that operate within this view can frequently be heard using phrases like "the need for strong leadership" and "the need to take tough decisions." They often take a certain pride in doing what they believe to be right even if the opinion of the majority is opposed to it . . . .

The other interpretation of democracy, the one dominant in America, might be called the "agency" view, and it is wholly different. According to this view, those who govern a country should function as no more than the agents of the people. The job of the governors is not to act independently and to take whatever decisions they believe to be in the national interest but, rather, to reflect in all their actions the views of the majority of the people, whatever those views may be. Governors are not really governors at all; they are representatives, in the very narrow sense of being in office solely to represent the views of those who sent them there . . . .

What, If Anything, Might Be Done?

PRECISELY because American politicians are so exposed electorally, they probably have to display—and do display—more political courage more often than the politicians of any other democratic country. The number of political saints and martyrs in the United States is unusually large . . . .

How, then, might the risks be reduced? What can be done? A number of reforms to the existing system suggest themselves. It may be that none of them is politically feasible—Americans hold tight to the idea of agency democracy—but in principle there should be no bar to any of them. One of the simplest would also be the most radical: to lengthen the terms of members of the House of Representatives from two years to four. The proposal is by no means a new one: at least 123 resolutions bearing on the subject were introduced in Congress in the eighty years from 1885 to 1965, and President Lyndon B. Johnson advocated the change in his State of the Union address in January of 1966.

A congressman participating in a Brookings Institution round table held at about the time of Johnson's message supported the change, saying, "I think that the four years would help you to be a braver congressman, and I think what you need is bravery. I think you need courage." Another congressman on the same occasion cited the example of another bill that he believed had the support of a majority in the House. "That bill is not going to come up this year. You know why it is not coming up? . . . Because four hundred and thirty-five of us have to face election . . . . If we had a four-year term, I am as confident as I can be the bill would have come to the floor and passed."

A similar case could be made for extending the term of senators to eight years, with half the Senate retiring or running for re-election every four years. If the terms of members of both houses were thus extended and made to coincide, the effect in reducing America's never-ending election campaign would be dramatic . . . .

Voter-proofing

...America's politicians ... can try to find alternative ways of insulating at least some aspects of policymaking from the intense campaigning and electioneering pressures they are now under.

Short of taking difficult issues out of electoral politics altogether, there are tactics that could be employed. Most of them are out of keeping with the contemporary American preferences for direct democracy, high levels of political participation, and the maximum exposure of all political processes to the public gaze; but that is precisely their strength ....

One available tactic might be called "the collusion of the elites." There may be occasions on which the great majority of America's politicians, in both the executive and legislative branches, are able to agree that an issue is of such overriding importance to the nation that it must be dealt with at almost any cost; that the politicians involved must therefore be prepared to set aside their ideological and other differences in the interests of finding a workable solution; and that having found a solution, they must stick together in presenting it to what may well be a disgruntled or even hostile electorate. In order to be successful, the collusion-of-elites tactic requires not only a substantial degree of bipartisanship (or, better still, nonpartisanship) but also unusually small teams of negotiators, complete secrecy (not a single ray of "sunshine" must penetrate the proceedings), and the presentation to Congress and the public of a comprehensive, all-or-nothing, take-it-or-leave-it proposal.

The number of occasions on which politicians will be prepared to set aside their ideological differences and pool their political risks in this fashion will inevitably be small ....

One of them occurred in 1983, when representatives of President Reagan and the two party leaderships on Capitol Hill colluded to save the Social Security system, which at that time was in imminent danger of bankruptcy. Paul Light's classic account of the 1983 Social Security reform, *Artful Work* (1985), is in effect a case study of how to conduct collusion-of-elites politics and of the circumstances in which it may succeed ....

Light writes,

> The meetings seemed to inaugurate a new form of presidential-congressional government. The meetings were secret. There were no minutes or transcripts. All conversations were strictly off the record. The gang was free to discuss all of the options without fear of political retaliation. It ... [existed] completely outside of the constitutional system.

Ultimately, as Light relates, the "secret gang built a compromise, wrapped it in a bipartisan flag, and rammed it through Congress. There was no other way to move. It was government by fait accompli." It was also successful government—and none of the participants suffered electoral damage.

Another possible tactic, with many similarities to the collusion of elites, might be called "putting it into commission." ...

[A]n ... example was the procedure adopted by Congress in 1990 for closing redundant military bases. Earlier practice had been almost a caricature of Congress's traditional decision-making process. The Secretary of Defense would propose a program of base closures. Senators and congressmen would immediately leap to the defense of targeted bases in their home states or districts. They of course had the support of their colleagues, who were threatened with or feared base closures in *their* home states or districts. Almost never did anyone manage to close any bases.

Realizing that the process was absurd and that huge sums of taxpayers' money were being wasted in keeping redundant bases open, Congress decided to protect itself from itself. It established the Defense Base Closure and Realignment Commission, which employed an extraordinarily simple formula. The Defense Secretary every two years published a list of the bases he proposed to close, together with a statement of criteria he had used in compiling his list. The commission then examined the list in light of the criteria, held public hearings, and recommended a modified list (with additions as well as deletions) to the President. The President was obliged to accept the commission's list as a whole or reject it as a whole. If, as invariably happened, he accepted it, Congress could intervene only if within forty-five legislative days it passed a bill overriding the President's decision and rejecting the whole list. This it never did.

The formula was a near miracle of voter-proofing. Members of Congress were left free to protest the closure of bases in their home districts or states, but the decision was ultimately taken by the President, who could nonetheless ascribe all blame to the commission, and all Congress had to do for the President's decision to take effect was to do nothing. In the event, hundreds of bases were closed and millions of dollars saved, but no member of Congress ever had to vote—and be seen by his constituents to be voting—in favor of closing a base near home. Beyond any question the results were in America's national interest . . . .

A final tactic, which could also be adopted without major institutional change, might be described as "thinking big." Proposals that are put forward on a piecemeal basis can also be opposed, and in all probability defeated, on a piecemeal basis. In contrast, large-scale, broad-based proposals may have a better chance of success simply by virtue of their comprehensiveness. They can provide something for everyone—conservatives as well as liberals, deficit cutters as well as program defenders, residents of the Sun Belt as well as of the Rust Belt. Gains as well as losses can be broadcast widely. The 1983 Social Security reform and the 1986 tax reform were certainly "big thoughts" of this general type. So, in its way, was the recent base-closure program.

Tactics like these—the collusion of elites, putting issues into commission, and thinking big—all have their virtues, but they also suffer from being tactics in the pejorative as well as the descriptive sense. At bottom they are somewhat cynical devices for getting around the real difficulty, which is the hyper-responsiveness of American politicians that is induced by their having to run scared so much of the time. Although it would be harder, it would be better over the long term to confront this problem directly and try to bring about at least some of the fundamental institutional changes proposed here. [. . .] What America needs today, though it does not seem to know it, is a more realistic and down-to-earth form of division-of-labor democracy.

8.6 Dennis Johnson, "Political Consultants at Work" (2007)

Dennis Johnson explores and analyzes the change in the operation and management of political campaigns over the past half century. Media and polling firms became common in presidential campaigns by 1960. Professional campaign managers and consultants became common over the next couple of decades in presidential, as well as large state gubernatorial and senatorial races, and have since spread to House and medium-sized mayoral elections. Professional campaign operatives have displaced volunteers at the top of all but local campaigns.

The professionalization of political campaigns, as with any arms race, means that candidates facing a professionally managed opponent are under heavy pressure to raise the money required to hire their own professional team. Alternatively, campaign consultants must figure out how to stay busy and profitable between major campaigns. Some companies have sought clients down the political ladder, where races occur on a different cycle, while others have moved from heavy reliance on political campaigns to more reliance on work for trade associations and interest groups. Johnson argues that candidates, not consultants, win or lose elections, but that major elections are too complex and chaotic to win without professional help.

In earlier decades, campaigns were financed and run by local or state political parties. Campaigns were fueled by local party activists and volunteers, by family, friends, and close political supporters. By the early 1960s, presidential campaigns and statewide campaigns for governor and senator began seeking out media and polling firms to help deliver their messages to voters. During the next two decades, there emerged both a new industry (political management) and a new professional (the campaign consultant). By the 1980s, every serious presidential candidate, nearly every statewide candidate, and a large number of congressional candidates were using the services of professional political consultants.[1]

The 1990s witnessed yet another transformation. Candidates for office below the statewide level were beginning to seek the advice of professional political consultants. For many candidates, the dividing line was the $50,000 campaign: Those who could not raise that kind of money had to rely solely on volunteer services, and those above this threshold usually sought professional assistance.[2] In some local political jurisdictions, record amounts of campaign funds were being raised to pay for campaign services, and races for medium-city mayor, county sheriff, or local judge took on the techniques and tactics once seen only in statewide, professionally managed contests. Professional consulting services, such as phone banks, telemarketing, and direct mail, were supplanting the efforts once provided by volunteers and party loyalists. This multibillion-dollar industry is now directed by professional consultants who make the key decisions, determine strategy, develop campaign communications, and carry out campaign tactics for their clients.

Now another transformation is occurring. Individual citizens and groups, empowered by e-mail, the Internet, blogging, text messaging, and other forms of online communication, are adding their voices to campaigns and elections. As the title of a recent book argues, politically active citizens are "crashing the gate" of the traditional political dynamics of candidates and consultants.[3] ...

Many campaign consultants have politics in their blood: They volunteer for candidates and causes while they are in college, work for their political parties in their state capital or in Washington, work for a member of Congress, or toil away at a variety of statewide and local campaigns before striking out on their own. Over 95 percent of political consultants are white and 81 percent of the principals in campaign firms are men. Particularly since the mid-1990s, aspiring political consultants have sought out graduate-level, skills-based training from the University of Florida's Political Campaigning Program, American University's Campaign Management Institute, the George Washington University Graduate School of Political Management, and several other smaller programs.[4]

The influence of political consultants goes well beyond getting candidates elected to office. They play an increased role in ballot measures by helping clients determine ballot strategy, framing issues, and even providing the campaign foot soldiers who gather signatures for ballot petitions. Consultants use marketing and mobilization skills to orchestrate pressure on legislators. Political telemarketers link angered constituents directly with the telephones of members of Congress. Overnight, they can guarantee five thousand constituent telephone calls patched directly to a legislator's office. Political consultants are also finding lucrative markets internationally, serving presidential and other candidates throughout the world.

In the commercial world, a business that generates less than $50 million is considered a small enterprise. By that measure, virtually every political consulting firm is a small business. Most of the estimated three thousand firms that specialize in campaigns and elections have ten or fewer staffers and generate just several hundred thousand dollars in revenue annually. Only a few media firms generate millions of dollars in revenue; most of this money, however, passes through the consultants' hands to pay television advertising costs.

Leading polling firms, such as the Tarrance Group or Public Opinion Strategies, may have forty to eighty employees; most are support staff working the telephones and part of the back office operations. Quite a few firms are cottage enterprises—one- or two-person boutiques, often in specialty markets, such as event planning, opposition research, fundraising, or media buying. Some political consulting firms operate out of the basement of the principal's home with no more than telephone lines, computers, fax machines, and online access. For example, even after he became famous as Clinton's principal political adviser, James Carville and his assistants worked out of the "bat cave," a basement studio apartment on Capitol Hill that served as Carville's home and nerve center for his wide-ranging political operations.

Firms that rely solely on campaign cycles are exposed to the roller coaster of cash flow: Many lean months, with very little money coming in from clients, countered by a few fat months when the bulk of the revenue pours in. In addition to the on-off flow of cash, the firms must deal with the logistical difficulties of juggling many candidates during the crucial last weeks of the campaign cycle and the enormous time pressures of a busy campaign season. Some consulting firms have around-the-clock operations during critical weeks of the campaign. These political emergency rooms are geared to handle any last-minute crisis. During long stretches when there are few campaign opportunities, professionals and support staff may have to be let go until the cycle picks up again.

One of the most difficult but necessary tasks is to even out the steep curves in the election cycle so that money and resources flow more regularly. Consultants have developed several strategies for this: convince candidates to hire consultants earlier in the cycle, stretch out the amount of time they stay with campaigns, and seek out off-year races, especially down the electoral ladder, such as mayoral races, general assembly, and other local contests, many of which in past years would not have sought professional assistance. Consultants are becoming more involved in the growing business of initiatives, referenda, and issues management. Many of these campaigns are tied to the same election cycle as candidate campaigns, but others are tied to local, state, or congressional issue cycles. Political consulting firms also pursue clients from the corporate and trade association world, issue advocacy, and international clients. By spreading out business, consulting firms are able to stay competitive, smooth out the peaks and valleys of the election cycle, and keep their heads above water.

In the 1980s, firms began to shift away from heavy reliance on candidate campaigns. For example, Matt Reese, one of the founders of the political consulting business, who had worked for more than four hundred Democratic candidates, changed direction after the 1982 elections to concentrate on corporate and trade association clients. Republican consultant Eddie Mahe shifted his business from 100 percent candidate-based in 1980 to about 15 percent candidate-based in the early 1990s, picking up corporate and other clients. In the mid-1970s, Walter Clinton's pioneering political telemarketing firm, the Clinton Group, gained 90 percent of its work from candidates, but has since moved away from reliance on candidates to issue advocacy and corporate work. Many successful consulting firms have followed this pattern and now have much of their business coming from noncandidate campaigns.[5]

As corporations have discovered the value of grassroots lobbying and issues management, consultants who specialize in direct mail and political telemarketing have shifted focus to legislative and issues work. Corporate and trade association organizations took special notice of the successful political consultant–orchestrated grassroots campaign run against President Clinton's 1993–1994 healthcare proposal. For political consultants, such work is often far more lucrative, more reliable, and less stress inducing than working for candidates in competitive election cycles. Some of the most successful political consulting firms have less than half of their revenue coming from candidate campaigns.[6] . . .

What Consultants Bring to Campaigns

Candidates, not consultants, win or lose elections. In 2004, voters chose George W. Bush, not campaign manager Ken Mehlman; they rejected John Kerry, not pollster Mark Mellman. Candidates alone face the voters and ultimately bear the responsibility for the tone and expression of their campaign. Sometimes reputations are diminished and images tarnished by the campaign itself. For example, George H. W. Bush will be remembered for permitting a down-and-dirty campaign that included the infamous "revolving door" and Willie Horton commercials in his 1988 presidential campaign. In that same year, Michael Dukakis will be remembered for his ride in a military vehicle, hunkered down in an oversized battle helmet, looking goofy.

While candidates are ultimately responsible for their campaigns, there is no way they can compete, let alone win, without professional help. Professional consultants bring experience, direction, and discipline to the campaign. Few enterprises are as unpredictable, vulnerable, and chaotic as a modern campaign. So much can go wrong. The candidate might go "off message," in which case the campaign loses focus; internal party feuds might threaten the success of the entire campaign; fundraising might fall short of expectations, choking the life out of the entire enterprise. All the while, the opponent's campaign is raising more money, attacking with a sharp and clear message, redefining the race in its own terms, grabbing media attention, and efficiently mobilizing its resources. Campaign professionals are needed to bring order out of chaos, maintain message and strategy discipline, and keep the campaign focused. Republican consultant Lee Atwater was fond of saying that he knew that the message of his campaign was hitting home when he would go to a local Wal-Mart and ask shoppers what they thought of the contest and they'd simply parrot the message he had developed.

In the months before the 2004 Democratic primary, the Howard Dean campaign engaged in a unique experiment: Let the message and direction of the campaign flow from the bottom up, rather from the top down. It was indeed a unique idea, but in the end, a flawed one. To manage the chaos, the competing interests, and messages, the Dean campaign needed, above all, structure and discipline. When it lost these elements, it lost its momentum and ability to win.

Professionals also take campaign burdens off the candidate. Campaigns are exhausting, placing extraordinary physical and emotional demands upon the candidate. The campaign staff, and especially the campaign manager, absorb as much of the stress of the campaign as possible. A campaign manager may serve as official campaign optimist, psychologist, and hand-holder for the candidate or, often, the candidate's spouse. The manager will make the tough personnel and tactical choices when the campaign starts going badly, and be the unofficial heavy (or whipping boy) when needed.

Consultants, particularly those in niche or vendor markets, provide legal, tax, and accounting services for the increasingly complex financial disclosure reporting requirements. They provide expertise in buying television time and placing radio and television commercials. Consulting firms capture and analyze television commercials aired by opponents and other races, and offer both quantitative and qualitative analysis from survey research, focus group, and dial group findings. Increasingly campaigns depend on specialists who also can provide a technological edge. Consultants provide online retrieval systems and websites, computer-assisted telephone technology, voter and demographic databases, and geo-mapping and sophisticated targeting techniques so that a campaign can know, block-by-block and house-by-house, who is likely to vote and for whom they would cast a ballot. Strategists are able to use predictive technologies, traditional statistical techniques, such as regression analysis, and new artificial intelligence technologies, such as neural nets and genetic algorithms to target potential voters.[7]

Above all, consultants bring experience from other campaigns. Every campaign has its unique circumstances, events, and dynamics. But campaigns are also great recycling bins. After a consultant has worked in fifteen or twenty-five races, campaigns begin to fall into predictable patterns: messages and themes, issues, and tactics reappear, taking on slight variations—new twists to old challenges. Veteran consultants can save a candidate from making mistakes, spot opportunities quickly, and take advantage of changing circumstances. As veteran consultant Joseph R. Cerrell put it (tongue in cheek), we need consultants "to have someone handy who has forgotten more about media, mail, fundraising, and strategy than most candidates will ever know."[8]

Growing reliance on professional consultants is costly; the price of admission to elections has risen substantially. The campaign, for many candidates, becomes an exhausting full-time game of chasing dollars. Consultants have seen business grow because of the superheated fundraising activities of the national Democratic and Republican Parties, the explosion of new money raised over the Internet, and issues advocacy.

The best consultants aren't afraid of a fight. They know that, in many cases, an election can be won only if they drop the pretense of reasoned, civilized campaigning and take the gloves off. Campaigns engage in rough tactics because they work. Opposition researchers dig deep into personal lives, seeking out misdeeds and character flaws. Pollsters test-market negative material before focus and electronic dial meter groups. Then the media team cuts slash-and-burn, thirty-second clips, using all the tricks of the trade: unflattering black-and-white photos of the opponent, ominous music and sound effects, and distorted features, salted with authentic-sounding textual material, often taken out of context. The direct mail pieces may get even uglier. The goal is to drive up the opponent's negatives, to paint the opponent in such unflattering ways that enough voters develop only a negative view of that candidate.

Certainly not all campaigns use negative tactics. Candidates are often very reluctant to engage in mudslinging or demagoguery. Voters are turned off by negative campaigns and feel alienated from the democratic process. But campaign consultants see negative campaigning as a tool, not so much a question of political ethics or morality. If the only way to win is to go negative, then negative it is.

Professional consultants bring many weapons to the fight. The campaign's theme and message are communicated through television and radio commercials, through direct mail pieces, and increasingly through campaign websites, blogging, cell phones, and e-mail. These communications are developed and honed through the use of sophisticated research analyses, especially survey research, focus groups, and dial meter sessions. Even more fundamental is the campaign's deadliest weapon—candidate and opposition research.

NOTES

1. Larry Sabato, *The Rise of Political Consultants: New Ways of Winning Elections* (New York: Basic Books, 1981). See also Frank I. Luntz, *Candidates, Consultants, and Elections* (New York: Basil Blackwell, 1988); Karen S. Johnson-Cartee and Gary A. Copeland, *Inside Political Campaigns* (New York: Greenwood Publishing Group, 1997); Robert V. Friedenberg, *Communication Consultants in Political Campaigns: BallotBox Warriors* (Westport, CT.: Praeger, 1997); David A. Dulio, *For Better or Worse? How Political Consultants Are Changing Elections in the United States* (Albany: State University of New York Press, 2004); and Stephen C. Craig, ed., *The Electoral Challenge: Theory Meets Practice* (Washington, D.C.: CQ Press, 2006).
2. Ron Faucheux and Paul S. Herrnson, "See How They Run: State Legislative Candidates," *Campaigns and Elections*, August 1999, 25.
3. Jerome Armstrong and Markos Moulitsas Zuniga, *Crashing the Gate: Netroots, Grassroots, and the Rise of People-Powered Politics* (White River Junction, VT: Chelsea Green, 2006).
4. Dulio, *For Better or Worse?* 45–53; Robin Kolodny, "Electoral Partnerships: Political Consultants and Political Parties," in *Campaign Warriors: Political Consultants in Elections*, James A. Thurber and Candice J. Nelson, eds. (Washington, D.C.: Brookings Institution Press, 2000).
5. Michael Clark, "Selling Issues: Political Consultants Are Shifting Their Business to Include Campaigns without Candidates," *Campaigns and Elections*, April/May 1993. See also David L. Rosenbloom, *The Election Men: Professional Campaign Managers and American Democracy* (New York: Quadrangle Books, 1973), 50.

6. For example, Clinton reelection campaign and second-term pollsters Mark Penn and Doug Schoen also have worked for AT&T, Texaco, Chemical Bank, Citibank, Control Data, Eastman Kodak, Honeywell, Major League Baseball, Nynex, Procter and Gamble, Sony, and the Trump Organization. They also have worked for candidates in Latin America, Israel, Greece, Turkey, and the Philippines. Peter Baker, "White House Isn't Asking Image Advisers to Reveal Assets or Disclose Other Clients," *The Washington Post*, May 19, 1997, A8.

7. Hal Malchow, "The Targeting Revolution in Political Direct Contact," *Campaigns and Elections*, June 1997, 36–9. See chapter 6 for discussion of these new technologies.

8. Joseph R. Cerrell, "Do Political Consultants Harm the Electoral Process?" *CQ Researcher* 6, no. 37 (October 4, 1996): 881.

Discussion Questions

1. Discuss how the Founders were and were not justified in their skepticism about the average citizen's willingness and ability to participate meaningfully in politics and elections.

2. During the middle of the nineteenth century, as Alexander Keyssar explains, many states allowed non-citizens to vote. Why did they do that and do you think the reasons they had for doing it translate well or badly to similar discussions in our own time?

3. Evaluate the arguments that V.O. Key and Samuel Popkin give for thinking that voters are responsible and reasoning. Is Key's declaration that "voters are not fools" convincing or should we be worried that uninformed people are voting and what might we do about it?

4. Anthony King argues that American politics and elections are too democratic. Is King agreeing with the Founders who doubted democracy or do they come to similar conclusions for different reasons?

5. Are candidates or their professional managers and consultants responsible for the negative tone and increasing expense of modern campaigns? Whoever is responsible, are there reforms that might be undertaken?

Suggested Additional Reading

Larry M. Bartels, *Unequal Democracy: The Political Economy of the New Gilded Age* (Princeton, N.J.: Princeton University Press, 2008).

Richard F. Bensel, *The American Ballot Box in the Mid-Nineteenth Century* (New York: Cambridge University Press, 2004).

Michael Lewis-Beck, William G. Jacoby, Helmut Norpoth, and Herbert F. Weisberg, *The American Voter Revisited* (Ann Arbor: University of Michigan Press, 2008).

Nelson W. Polsby and Aaron Wildavsky, *Presidential Elections: Strategies and Structures of American Politics*, 11th ed. (New York: Rowman and Littlefield, 2004).

Richard M. Valelly, *The Two Reconstructions: The Struggle for Black Enfranchisement* (Chicago: University of Chicago Press, 2004).

9

Congress: Lawmaking and Domestic Representation

Introduction

The story of Congress is the story of American political development: difficult questions, continuity and change. The framers' Congress has endured for over two centuries, adapting to changing circumstances with evolving institutions, rules and norms. Nowhere is the interplay of politics and institutions clearer than in the evolution of Congress and its arrival at the point of breakdown in the early twentieth century.

The architects of the U.S. Congress had to address many difficult questions in designing a republican legislature to the nation. What is the chief responsibility of a legislature and its members? Should it be a deliberative assembly that takes its time discussing all points of view about the nation's problems, or should it attack problems by producing laws as swiftly as possible? Should the legislature be a strong, centralized organization tightly controlled by leaders, or should it be decentralized so that each and every member influences the law-making process? Majorities rule in Congress, but how is it possible to slow or stop majorities who are determined to pass laws that will harm the nation? Should individual legislators act as delegates of their constituents and press their preferences faithfully despite their personal opinions, or should they act as trustees of their constituents and exercise their best judgment about the right policy for the nation, even if their constituents disagree? These timeless questions were as important two centuries ago as they are today. In the first reading, Edmund Burke, a member of the British Parliament in the 1770s, grappled with the last of these questions. Burke's widely read speech to his constituents shows how difficult it is to reconcile the cross-pressures put on legislators everywhere, not just in the United States.

The framers of the U.S. Constitution had to grapple with all of these questions. They anticipated that Congress would be the heart of the new American state. Voters would directly choose the U.S. Representatives, and state legislatures would select the U.S. Senators. Based on their personal experience with the state legislatures, the framers were understandably worried about the prospect of a Congress that could create policies that served selfish short-term, parochial interests (a model Burke rejected) rather than the long-term interest of the nation. They feared that Congress might continually change laws to suit shifting public opinion and bully other branches into surrendering even more power. To make these problems less likely, the framers divided Congress into coequal parts, a House of Representatives elected by the people, and a Senate chosen by the state legislatures. Opponents of the Constitution challenged this division of power and the equal role of the Senate. In the second reading, James Madison explained why the Constitutional Convention created a strong Senate and why this additional check on the legislature was so necessary.

While institutions within Congress, such as committees and rules, have evolved considerably since 1789, they have developed along a path adapted to the fundamental framework laid out at the Constitutional Convention. In the early years of the republic, Congress was in session for less than half the year, but today the Congress is in session most of the time.[1] There were no permanent committees in Congress at the start, but now there are dozens, and they are critical decision-makers in the legislative process. Political parties and party leaders did not exist in the first Congress, but now that parties organize Congress the party leaders are crucial for constructing the majorities that allow Congress to make law.

In the highlight piece for this chapter, Ira Katznelson showed the difficulties of building and sustaining these essential majorities in Congress. He explained what happened when the irresistible tide of New Deal reform smashed into the institutional Congress that had been evolving for almost a century and a half. The New Deal was a watershed in American politics. Buoyed by huge majorities in Congress, Franklin Roosevelt and congressional liberals fought for an unprecedented array of reforms that boosted the federal government's power to manage and regulate the American economy, and to provide economic security for individual Americans. But these Democratic majorities concealed deep divisions among Democrats themselves. Northern Democrats from industrial cities sought policies that would benefit their constituents, especially those in the rapidly growing trade unions. But Southern Democrats, representing poorer agricultural areas, strongly resisted policies that would challenge racial segregation and low wages. These differences required compromises *within* the Democratic majority in Congress. These compromises took racial issues off the New Deal agenda and perpetuated segregation in the South. Katznelson's case study shows both the critical role and the difficulties of constructing working majorities in the U.S. Congress.

One thing is clear: by the 1970s, Congress had evolved into an institution that enabled members to build decades-long legislative careers. By the beginning of the twenty-first century, many members of Congress were winning reelection many times over and serving many terms. Most incumbent members of the House of Representatives (and, to a slightly lesser extent, the Senate) do not run much risk of electoral defeat. Over 90 percent of the incumbent members of the House who run for reelection win reelection.[2] In the fourth reading, David Mayhew explained how U.S. Representatives and Senators have been able to use Congress to enhance their own reelection. Members of Congress build strong support among the voters by ensuring that they are well known and liked, that they have helped many voters with problems, and that they have taken positions on issues that are popular locally. The institutional structure of Congress helps individual members by enabling them to run a "candidate-centered" campaign in their quest for reelection. By serving on the committees that deal with policies that help their local constituents (such as serving on an Agriculture Committee for a member from a farm state), members can promote policies that encourage familiarity and gratitude back home.

These developments may have benefited individual members, but they also have made Congress even harder to use and have contributed to a tidal wave of criticism of Congress as an institution. Countless authors have complained that Congress is the "sapless" branch or the "broken" branch. Public opinion polls show that citizens hold their own members of Congress in much higher regard than Congress as an institution.[3] Eric Schickler (reading five) helped understand this frustration by showing how path dependence, political circumstances, and pressures from other institutions have pulled Congress in different directions over time. By the end of the New Deal, for example, committees dominated Congress. Opposition to these committees, in turn, led to institutional reforms that weakened committees and strengthened individual members, while also strengthening leaders. These changes further differentiated the House from the Senate. These houses began as very similar law-making bodies, but they grew into increasingly different—and difficult—legislative institutions.

In the final reading, Sarah Binder showed how one of these rules—the Senate filibuster—contributes to Americans' frustration with Congress as a whole. The filibuster allows a Senator to command the floor of the Senate and prevent action on a proposal she or he opposes. Increasingly, the filibuster has been used as a shield to stop the majority party in the Senate from passing bills. The result is a legislative body often too tied up in knots to act on major issues, and individual Senators whose bitter partisanship contributes to the political polarization that repels many citizens.

Notes

1. Scott C. James, "The Evolution of the Presidency: Between the Promise and the Fear," in Joel D. Aberbach and Mark A. Peterson, eds., *The Executive Branch* (Oxford and New York: Oxford University Press, 2005), 10.
2. Center for Responsive Politics, "Reelection Rates over the Years," www.opensecrets.org/bigpicture/reelect.php (accessed June 9, 2013).
3. Norman Ornstein and Thomas E. Mann, *The Broken Branch: How Congress Is Failing America and How to Get It Back on Track* (Washington, DC: Brookings Institution, 2008); Elizabeth Mendes, "Americans Down on Congress, OK With Own Representative; Congressional approval at 16% in May," *Gallup Politics*, May 9, 2013, http://www.gallup.com/poll/162362/americans-down-congress-own-representative.aspx (accessed June 9, 2013).

9.1 Edmund Burke, "Letter to the Electors of Bristol" (1774)

Edmund Burke was an Irish-born British political philosopher and political leader. In 1774, Burke was elected to Parliament representing the trading city of Bristol,

England. In this speech to his constituents, Burke described the enduring problem that faces legislators anywhere: should they act as their constituents instruct them, or vote as their judgment and conscience require, regardless of the political consequences? Burke told his constituents that he had to act as a trustee for the nation, not just the voters of Bristol. The national legislature, he argued, was "a *deliberative* assembly of *one* nation, with *one* interest, that of the whole . . ." Burke himself took positions controversial in England at the time, such as defending free trade with Ireland, the emancipation of Catholics in Ireland, and the rights of the American colonies. By 1780, Burke's ideas proved to be too controversial for Bristol. He left his seat in that city, and won election to Parliament representing a different location, where his views posed less of a threat to his political career.

I am sorry I cannot conclude without saying a word on a topic touched upon by my worthy colleague. I wish that topic had been passed by at a time when I have so little leisure to discuss it. But since he has thought proper to throw it out, I owe you a clear explanation of my poor sentiments on that subject.

He tells you that "the topic of instructions has occasioned much altercation and uneasiness in this city"; and he expresses himself (if I understand him rightly) in favor of the coercive authority of such instructions.

Certainly, Gentlemen, it ought to be the happiness and glory of a representative to live in the strictest union, the closest correspondence, and the most unreserved communication with his constituents. Their wishes ought to have great weight with him; their opinions high respect; their business unremitted attention. It is his duty to sacrifice his repose, his pleasure, his satisfactions, to theirs,—and above all, ever, and in all cases, to prefer their interest to his own.

But his unbiased opinion, his mature judgment, his enlightened conscience, he ought not to sacrifice to you, to any man, or to any set of men living. These he does not derive from your pleasure,—no, nor from the law and the Constitution. They are a trust from Providence, for the abuse of which he is deeply answerable. Your representative owes you, not his industry only, but his judgment; and he betrays, instead of serving you, if he sacrifices it to your opinion.

My worthy colleague says, his will ought to be subservient to yours. If that be all, the thing is innocent. If government were a matter of will upon any side, yours, without question, ought to be superior. But government and legislation are matters of reason and judgment, and not of inclination; and what sort of reason is that in which the determination precedes the discussion, in which one set of men deliberate and another decide, and where those who form the conclusion are perhaps three hundred miles distant from those who hear the arguments?

To deliver an opinion is the right of all men; that of constituents is a weighty and respectable opinion, which a representative ought always to rejoice to hear, and which he ought always most seriously to consider. But *authoritative* instructions, *mandates* issued, which the member is bound blindly and implicitly to obey, to vote, and to argue for, though contrary to the clearest conviction of his judgment and conscience,—these are things utterly unknown to the laws of this land, and which arise from a fundamental mistake of the whole order and tenor of our Constitution.

Parliament is not a *congress* of ambassadors from different and hostile interests, which interests each must maintain, as an agent and advocate, against other agents and advocates; but Parliament is a *deliberative* assembly of *one* nation, with *one* interest, that of the whole—where not local purposes, not local prejudices, ought to guide, but the general good, resulting from the general reason of the whole. You choose a member, indeed; but when you have chosen him, he is not member of Bristol, but he is a member of *Parliament*. If the local constituent should have an interest or should form an hasty opinion evidently opposite to the real good of the rest of the community, the member for that place ought to be as far as any other from any endeavor to give it effect. I beg pardon for saying so much on this subject; I have been unwillingly drawn into it; but I shall ever use a respectful frankness of communication with you. Your faithful friend, your devoted servant, I shall be to the end of my life: a flatterer you do not wish for. On this point of instructions, however, I think it scarcely possible we ever can have any sort of difference. Perhaps I may give you too much, rather than too little trouble.

From the first hour I was encouraged to court your favor, to this happy day of obtaining it, I have never promised you anything but humble and persevering endeavors to do my duty. The weight of that duty, I confess, makes me tremble; and whoever well considers what it is, of all things in the world, will fly from what has the least likeness to a positive and precipitate engagement. To be a good member of Parliament is, let me tell you, no easy task,—especially at this time, when there is so strong a disposition to run into the perilous extremes of servile compliance or wild popularity. To unite circumspection with vigor is absolutely necessary, but it is extremely difficult. We are now members for a rich commercial *city*; this city, however, is but a part of a rich commercial *nation*, the interests of which are various, multiform, and intricate. We are members for that great nation, which, however, is itself but part of a great *empire*, extended by our virtue and our fortune to the farthest limits of the East and of the West. All these wide-spread interests must be considered,—must be compared,— must be reconciled, if possible. We are members for a *free* country; and surely we all know that the machine of a free constitution is no simple thing, but as intricate and as delicate as it is valuable. We are members in a great and ancient *monarchy*; and we must preserve religiously the true, legal rights of the sovereign, which form the keystone that binds together the noble and well-constructed arch of our empire and our Constitution. A constitution made up of balanced powers must ever be a critical thing. As such I mean to touch that part of it which comes within my reach. I know my inability, and I wish for support from every quarter. In particular I shall aim at the friendship, and shall cultivate the best correspondence, of the worthy colleague you have given me.

I trouble you no farther than once more to thank you all: you, Gentlemen, for your favors; the candidates, for their temperate and polite behavior; and the sheriffs, for a conduct which may give a model for all who are in public stations.

9.2 *Federalist Paper* 62 (1788)

By the end of February, 1788, James Madison's *Federalist* essays turned to the problem of explaining the Senate's role in the proposed Constitution. In *Federalist*

62, Madison cut to the heart of the problem of designing a legislature for a republican government. A republican legislature must respond to the people, but, where there is only a single house in that legislature, the people's representatives are prone "to yield to the impulse of sudden and violent passions." Wily political leaders take advantage of these passions, turning them "into intemperate and pernicious resolutions" that in the long run threaten republican government itself. Rules and policies that are too "mutable," or too easily changed, undermine the authority of government institutions by raising doubts about the durability of the law. To ensure that political leaders are controlled and the laws are stable, Madison insisted that it is essential to include a smaller chamber in Congress, consisting of legislators who serve relatively long terms in office. This Senate can check the temporary passions more likely to emerge from the House of Representatives, bring more expertise to the task of shaping public policy, prevent intemperate government actions, and make national policy much more stable. Here, Madison has made the case that the national laws should influence behavior for long periods of time—in other words, he has argued that Congress's laws *should* create path dependence by making it difficult to change the laws once they are made.

The Federalist No. 62

James Madison

February 27, 1788

To the People of the State of New York.

... The number of senators and the duration of their appointment come next to be considered. In order to form an accurate judgment on both these points, it will be proper to enquire into the purposes which are to be answered by a senate; and in order to ascertain these it will be necessary to review the inconveniencies which a republic must suffer from the want of such an institution.

First. It is a misfortune incident to republican government, though in a less degree than to other governments, that those who administer it, may forget their obligations to their constituents, and prove unfaithful to their important trust. In this point of view, a senate, as a second branch of the legislative assembly, distinct from, and dividing the power with, a first, must be in all cases a salutary check on the government. It doubles the security to the people, by requiring the concurrence of two distinct bodies in schemes of usurpation or perfidy, where the ambition or corruption of one, would otherwise be sufficient. This is a precaution founded on such clear principles, and now so well understood in the United States, that it would be more than superfluous to enlarge on it. I will barely remark that as the improbability of sinister combinations will be in proportion to the dissimilarity in the genius of the two bodies; it must be politic to distinguish them from each other by every circumstance which will consist with a due harmony in all proper measures, and with the genuine principles of republican government.

Secondly. The necessity of a senate is not less indicated by the propensity of all single and numerous assemblies, to yield to the impulse of sudden and violent passions, and to be seduced by factious leaders, into intemperate and pernicious resolutions. Examples on this subject might be cited without number; and from proceedings within the United States, as well as from the history of other nations. But a position that will not be contradicted need not be proved. All that need be remarked is that a body which is to correct this infirmity ought itself be free from it, and consequently ought to be less numerous. It ought moreover to possess great firmness, and consequently ought to hold its authority by a tenure of considerable duration.

Thirdly. Another defect to be supplied by a senate lies in a want of due acquaintance with the objects and principles of legislation. It is not possible that an assembly of men called for the most part from pursuits of a private nature, continued in appointment for a short time, and led by no permanent motive to devote the intervals of public occupation to a study of the laws, the affairs and the comprehensive interests of their country, should, if left wholly to themselves, escape a variety of important errors in the exercise of their legislative trust. It may be affirmed, on the best grounds, that no small share of the present embarrassments of America is to be charged on the blunders of our governments; and that these have proceeded from the heads rather than the hearts of most of the authors of them. What indeed are all the repealing, explaining and amending laws, which fill and disgrace our voluminous codes, but so many monuments of deficient wisdom; so many impeachments exhibited by each succeeding, against each preceding session; so many admonitions to the people of the value of those aids which may be expected from a well constituted senate?

A good government implies two things; first, fidelity to the object of government, which is the happiness of the people; secondly, a knowledge of the means by which that object can be best attained. Some governments are deficient in both these qualities: Most governments are deficient in the first. I scruple not to assert that in the American governments, too little attention has been paid to the last. The federal constitution avoids this error; and what merits particular notice, it provides for the last in a mode which increases the security for the first.

Fourthly. The mutability in the public councils, arising from a rapid succession of new members, however qualified they may be, points out in the strongest manner, the necessity of some stable institution in the government. Every new election in the states, is found to change one half of the representatives. From this change of men must proceed a change of opinions; and from a change of opinions, a change of measures. But a continual change even of good measures is inconsistent with every rule of prudence, and every prospect of success. The remark is verified in private life, and becomes more just as well as more important, in national transactions.

To trace the mischievous effects of a mutable government would fill a volume. I will hint a few only, each of which will be perceived to be a source of innumerable others.

In the first place it forfeits the respect and confidence of other nations, and all the advantages connected with national character. An individual who is observed to be inconstant to his plans, or perhaps to carry on his affairs without any plan at all, is marked at once by all prudent people as a speedy victim to his own unsteadiness and folly. His more friendly neighbours may pity him; but all will decline to connect their fortunes with his; and not a few will seize the opportunity of making their fortunes out of his. One nation is to another what one individual is to another; with this melancholy distinction perhaps, that the former with fewer of the benevolent emotions than the latter, are under fewer restraints also from taking undue advantage of the indiscretions of each other. Every nation consequently whose affairs betray a want of wisdom and stability, may calculate on every loss which can be sustained from the more systematic policy of its wiser neighbours. But the best instruction on this subject is unhappily conveyed to America by the example of her own situation. She finds that she is held in no respect by her friends; that she is the derision of her enemies; and that she is a prey to every nation which has an interest in speculating on her fluctuating councils and embarrassed affairs.

The internal effects of a mutable policy are still more calamitous. It poisons the blessings of liberty itself. It will be of little avail to the people that the laws are made by men of their own choice, if the laws be so voluminous that they cannot be read, or so incoherent that they cannot be understood; if they be repealed or revised before they are promulged, or undergo such incessant changes that no man who knows what the law is to-day can guess what it will be to-morrow. Law is defined to be a rule of action; but how can that be a rule, which is little known and less fixed?

Another effect of public instability is the unreasonable advantage it gives to the sagacious, the enterprising and the moneyed few, over the industrious and uninformed mass of the people. Every new regulation concerning commerce or revenue, or in any manner affecting the value of the different species of property, presents a new harvest to those who watch the change, and can trace its consequences; a harvest reared not by themselves but by the toils and cares of the great body of their fellow citizens. This is a state of things in which it may be said with some truth that laws are made for the *few* not for the *many*.

In another point of view great injury results from an unstable government. The want of confidence in the public councils damps every useful undertaking; the success and profit of which may depend on a continuance of existing arrangements. What prudent merchant will hazard his fortunes in any new branch of commerce, when he knows not but that his plans may be rendered unlawful before they can be executed? What farmer or manufacturer will lay himself out for the encouragement given to any particular cultivation or establishment, when he can have no assurance that his preparatory labors and advances will not render him a victim to an inconstant government? In a word no great improvement or laudable enterprise, can go forward, which requires the auspices of a steady system of national policy.

But the most deplorable effect of all is that diminution of attachment and reverence which steals into the hearts of the people, towards a political system which betrays so many marks of infirmity, and disappoints so many of their flattering hopes. No government any more than an individual will long be respected, without being truly respectable, nor be truly respectable without possessing a certain portion of order and stability.

PUBLIUS.

9.3 Ira Katznelson, "Fear Itself: The New Deal and the Origins of Our Time" (2013)

While Madison and others emphasized the benefits of institutional division in the American Congress, political leaders have had to deal with the problems created by these divisions ever since. In this highlight piece, Ira Katznelson, a leading political scientist and historian, showed how the problem of forming congressional majorities complicated policy-making Congress *even when* one party had an overwhelming majority. During Franklin Roosevelt's presidency, the Democratic Party controlled the House and the Senate. But internally, the party was deeply divided. Democrats had dominated Southern politics for decades when the Depression swept Northern Democrats into office. Southerners who had served for many years became committee chairs because their members had the most seniority. Southerners had enough votes to stymie the president's agenda. When Southern Democrats objected to a New Deal proposal, they could abandon their party and vote down the initiative. Leading Democrats had to confront the reality of their divided majority by proposing laws acceptable to the vital block of Southern Democrats. This necessity resulted in laws that perpetuated legal segregation in the South, and limited African Americans' participation in New Deal programs. Katznelson helped explain not only the problems inherent in getting Congress to act, but also the reasons that some New Deal programs divided citizens by allocating important policy decisions to state policy-makers (reading 3.5).

Much of this volume is devoted to examining how this national state got fashioned. This task leads to Congress, the fulcrum of the book. One cannot understand the New Deal without appreciating the activist lawmaking that resulted from many bouts of arguing, bargaining, and voting in the U.S. Senate and House of Representatives. These policy achievements demonstrably challenged the period's common claim that national legislatures had become incapable and obsolete.

In the United States, the legislature remained an effective center of political life. As evidenced by the welter of lawmaking this book examines, Congress maintained a pride of place in a system of coequal branches. Its constitutional role was not supplanted. The Senate and House of Representatives continued, when they wished, to say no even to presidents at the peak of their popularity. Working through Congress, the New Deal falsified the idea that legislative politics must ensure democratic failure. To the contrary, Congress crafted policies that changed how capitalism worked, in part by promoting unions that gave the working class a voice both at the workplace and in national politics. It also organized responses to the challenges of global violence and national security. It was, in short, the central operative role of Congress that most distinguished the United States from the forces of brutality and the absence of political competition that characterized the dictatorships.[1]

Yet inside Congress, we hear an obbligato—the deep and mournful sound of southern political power determined to hold on to a distinctive way of life that also was indispensable to the era's legislative majorities. The region's representatives were located at the very center of the era's winning coalitions when the country faced a cascade of grave crises, and when its character as a liberal polity was being fundamentally reshaped.

Students of Congress know that, in addition to personal preferences, members of Congress are most influenced by party and constituency pressures. At a time of widespread racial bias and segregated arrangements hardly confined to the South, the men who represented the Jim Crow South constituted the pivotal bloc in the national legislature. With their local constituencies artificially limited through restrictive voting arrangements, and with such institutional rules as the Senate filibuster at their command, the southern bloc gained a key role within Congress, often playing captain to a diverse crew of other officers. Significantly, their votes tended to count for more than one. Buttressed by virtually all-white electorates in one-party constituencies, and possessing the powers of seniority, they dominated the committee system and the leadership of the House and Senate, thus serving as the legislature's main gatekeepers.

In all, the enhanced representation of the South in the powerful national legislature with an internal decision-making structure that experienced southern legislators skillfully negotiated and deployed made questions of region and race matter more than we often have appreciated in shaping what the New Deal could, and did, accomplish. Commanding the institution's lawmaking switchboard, southern members were in a position to determine the shape and content of key legislation. Although they—and the institution in Washington they knew most intimately—did not make the key difference at every turn, the South's capacity to veto what the region did not want and its ability to promote, as a pivotal actor, the policies it did favor mattered regularly and insistently over the course of the Roosevelt and Truman years. As a result, we live in a different country, different from what might have been without the exercise of power by southern members within America's uniquely capable national legislature.

To be sure, the southern region did not exist in isolation.[2] The ability of the House and Senate to refashion American liberal democracy depended on harnessing the Jim Crow South to the majority coalition of the Democratic Party. Without the South, there could have been no New Deal. When southern support was withheld, the outcome was different. With southern support, the New Deal could proceed, but there always was a cost, either tacit or explicit.

Much as the Constitution could never have been adopted without cross-sectional backing, and much as Lincoln understood that he could not win the Civil War without the support of Delaware, Kentucky, Maryland, and Missouri, the slave states that stayed loyal to the Union, so Presidents Roosevelt and Truman recognized their own limitations and how much they needed votes cast by their party's representatives from across the swath of the South to govern effectively. They understood that without the South, the country could not discover policies commanding majorities to steer precariously between the failed or inadequate status quo and nostrums pursued by the world's dictatorships.

Despite its centrality, southern power has always hovered at the fringe of most New Deal portraits.[3] When present at all, the South is usually slotted into a list of elements in the New Deal coalition—"a unique alliance of big city bosses, the white South, farmers and workers, Jews and Irish Catholics, ethnic minorities, and African Americans"[4]—as if these were equivalent units of political power. The failure to place the special, often determining role of the Jim Crow South front and center, I believe, has had much the same effect as the "willful critical blindness" about race that Toni Morrison has identified so tellingly. "It is possible," she mournfully noted, "to read Henry James scholarship exhaustively and never arrive at a nodding mention, much less a satisfactory treatment of the black woman who lubricates the turn of the plot and becomes the agency of moral choice and meaning in *What Maisie Knew*."[5] During the New Deal, it was the white South that acted as the key agent in Congress of just such moral choice and meaning. To record the history of the 1930s, 1940s, and early 1950s as if this were not the case would be as much a distortion as writing American history without its African American sorrow songs.[6]

The South, then, was America's "wild card." Scholarship about the social roots of Fascism in interwar Europe has shown how the fate of democracy frequently hinged on choices made by the leaders and voters from that continent's least prosperous and most "backward" areas, those who were most afflicted by economic volatility, ethnic conflict, demagogic politics, and a sense of isolation from modern life's main currents.[7] This was also the case in Latin America, where agrarian districts, characterized by repressive labor practices, often rejected democratic governance, preferring various forms of authoritarian government.[8]

Both liberal and illiberal, progressive and racist, the large bloc of southern states played more than one role in national life, including that of advancing a radically antiliberal white populism, with a family resemblance to European Fascism that combined "demagogic appeals to lower-income white farmers, bitter denunciations of large corporations and Wall Street, and vitriolic personal abuse of their opponents."[9] This most active form of political racism was perhaps best typified on the national scene by South Carolina governor Strom Thurmond, who ran for president in 1948 and carried four Deep South states, and by Alabama governor George Wallace, who carried five such states in 1968. But such third-party efforts were not the norm. Opting in the main to stay within the Democratic Party, the region empowered most New Deal initiatives in Congress, all the while holding fast to the ideology and institutions of official racism. The result was a Democratic Party—then the party of governance—that internalized the deepest contradictions in American life.

The region's representatives, who manifested strong preferences and effective strategic means to pursue them, imposed their wishes on each facet of New Deal policymaking. They determined which policies were feasible and which were not. The period's remarkable burst of invention reconstituted modern liberalism by reorganizing the country's political rules and public policies, but only within the limits imposed by the most illiberal part of the political order. In yet another ironic turn, these southern politicians helped save liberal democracy so successfully that they ultimately undermined the presuppositions of white supremacy.[10]

Often placing their supremacist values first, these representatives fought fiercely, if ultimately unsuccessfully, to preserve their region's racial tyranny. Their main national instrument, the Democratic Party, confederated two radically disparate political systems. One, northern and western, was primarily rooted in cities that featured urban machines, Catholic and Jewish immigrant populations, labor unions, and the working class. The other, southern, was essentially rural, native, Protestant, antilabor, and exclusively white. Writing about "American liberalism today" shortly after the conclusion of the extended New Deal, Denis Brogan sharply observed in 1957 the dynamics of this cross-sectional coalition:

> The Liberal conscience is most deeply touched and his political behaviour seems (to the unfriendly outsider) most schizophrenic. The representative Liberal is a Democrat, or an ally of the Democrats, but in the ranks of "the Democracy" are most of the most violent enemies of the integration of the Negro into the American community. This is no doubt accidental; it arises from the localization of the most acute form of the colour problem in the region where

the Democratic Party is traditionally strongest. The necessity of holding the national party together makes for strange bedfellows and strange deals.[11]

To properly understand the New Deal, it is just these bedfellows—their deals, successes, and failures—whom we need to place front and center.

But if there is a lesson, it is not one of retrospective judgment, as if the possibility then existed to rescue liberal democracy and pursue racial justice simultaneously. It later turned out that the first would prove to be a condition of the second. But there is no reason not to brood about the confining cage of explicit and willful racism in the Roosevelt and Truman years, or not to weigh its implications.

. . . [I]n *Fear Itself* I examine primarily how the South exercised its critical position to affect decisions concerning global power, national security, civil liberty, unions, and the character of capitalism. The southern wing of the Democratic Party, I show, composed the most persistently effective political force that determined the content and boundaries of this momentous "constitutional moment."[12]

If history plays tricks, southern congressional power in the last era of Jim Crow was a big one. The ability of the New Deal to confront the era's most heinous dictatorships by reshaping liberal democracy required accommodating the most violent and illiberal part of the political system, keeping the South inside the game of democracy. While it would be folly to argue that members of the southern wing of the Democratic Party alone determined the choices the New Deal made, their relative cohesion and their assessment of policy choices through the filter of an anxious protection of white supremacy often proved decisive.

The triumph, in short, cannot be severed from the sorrow. Liberal democracy prospered as a result of an accommodation with racial humiliation and its system of lawful exclusion and principled terror. Each constituted the other like "the united double nature of both soul and body" in Goethe's *Faust*. This combination confers a larger message—a lesson that concerns the persistence of emergency, the inescapability of moral ambiguity, and perhaps the inevitability of a politics of discomfiting allies, abroad as well as at home. It also reminds us that not just whether but also how we find our way truly matters.

. . . Americans with a Difference

Over the arc of an entire half century before the New Deal, every effort in Congress to protect black rights failed . . .

By March 1933, the issue, at least on the political surface, no longer seemed to exist. As the southern region returned to more traditional voting patterns, southern racial confidence seemed safe. FDR—also a New York governor, but a Protestant opposed to Prohibition—won large majorities in every segregated state but Delaware. With Congress also swinging dramatically in a Democratic direction, the 1932 election was an all-too-often-overlooked watershed that thrust the South into a pivotal lawmaking position.

In Congress, southern members held three trump cards: uncommon longevity, disproportionate numbers, and a commitment to racial hierarchy more passionate than that of their opponents. Many key figures—including Senators Ellison "Cotton Ed" Smith of South Carolina, Walter George of Georgia, and Kenneth McKellar of Tennessee, and House members Martin Dies of Texas, Robert Ramspeck of Georgia, and Howard Smith of Virginia—had already become congressional fixtures who were destined to serve over many decades. Often unopposed, southern Senators and members of the House amassed uncommon seniority, the key factor that produced access to the most influential committees and positions. When President Roosevelt was elected, congressional committees had grown more significant and entrenched than they had been during the [Woodrow] Wilson years. Southerners chaired twenty-nine of the forty-seven committees in the House, including Appropriations, Banking and Currency, Judiciary, Foreign Affairs, Agriculture, Military Affairs, and Ways and Means, which handled all tax matters. In the Senate as well, southerners held sway; they headed thirteen of thirty three committees, counting the most significant, including Agriculture, Appropriations, Banking and Currency, Commerce, Finance, and Military Affairs.[13]

With seniority also came experience; with experience, legislative skill based on the command of issues and rules. "With such knowledge and experience in national affairs," moreover, "they become the logical leaders of the Party in Congress," as Marian Irish noted in 1942, when Sam Rayburn of Texas was Speaker of the House and Alben Barkley of Kentucky was majority leader. In all, she concluded, "there is no doubt but that the one-party system enables the South to exert more influence in Congress than it could by any other political means."[14]

Notwithstanding the relatively modest proportion of actual voters in the South, the representation of these districts and states in Washington remained unaffected. Each state automatically secured two U.S. Senate seats, a feature of the Constitution. In turn, seats in the House of Representatives were apportioned by population—the total population, irrespective of who was kept from voting and how many eligible persons actually appeared at the polls on Election Day. As a result, the South achieved numbers and influence in each chamber far in excess of its actual voters. Further, the southern presence in the House and Senate was sanitized. Once a member was sworn in, each chamber repressed any knowledge of racial exclusion, franchise reducing rules, limited voting, or unopposed elections, let alone the pervasive atmosphere of violence that accompanied many, especially rural, southern elections. In Congress, each elected member was treated like every other. Each possessed the same prerogatives. Each was free to play by the same institutional rules.

After the economic and political upheavals of the late nineteenth century, the Democratic Party in Congress came to consist mainly of representatives from the South. From the Democratic Party debacle of 1896 to the election of Franklin Roosevelt in 1932, Democratic congressional candidates outside the South were able to secure only some 40 percent of the popular vote, but the party's vote totals within the South never fell below 86 percent.[15] As a result, during the first three decades of the twentieth century, two out of every three Democrats in Congress were elected from southern constituencies.

With Warren Harding, Calvin Coolidge, and Herbert Hoover in the White House in the 1920s and early 1930s, Republican majorities in the Senate and the House were constant, and often large. As a result, southern members dominated the Democratic Party in both houses of Congress . . . .

The partisan transformation of 1932 altered the region's place in the legislature. Across the country, Democratic Party candidates secured a remarkable 72.4 percent of the vote for the House of Representatives and won fully 63 percent of the ballots cast for the Senate. A House that had been divided between 218 Republicans and 216 Democrats (and one independent) after the midterm election of 1930 was replaced by a chamber with 311 Democrats and just 117 Republicans, so severe was the impact of the Depression and the Roosevelt landslide.[16] In the Senate, the Democrats gained twelve seats, giving them a decisive majority of 59-36.[17] When the Seventy-third Congress assembled in March 1933, the South no longer commanded a majority of Democratic seats; 46 percent of Democrats in the House and 49 percent in the Senate represented southern districts and states. These shares fell further when the party's majorities grew in 1934 and 1936.

Still, southern power persisted. Nonsouthern Democrats could not pass legislation without southern support. At no time during the New Deal did the southern cohort drop below 44 percent of Democrats in the Senate and 41 percent in the House. These numbers were sufficient to block any initiatives they did not approve. During the heyday of the Roosevelt administration's great legislative productivity, every law had to pass southern scrutiny. Even when the presence of Republicans in the House was reduced to a paltry 88 seats after the election of 1936, the 192 nonsouthern Democrats could not muster majorities on their own. Although only 16 Republicans served in the Senate that convened after that Democratic rout, the 43 non southern Democrats likewise constituted only a minority of that chamber. Without southern acquiescence, the party's national program could not pass.

Republicans began a steep comeback in 1938. That midterm election followed President Roosevelt's failed effort to enlarge the Supreme Court, and took place in the context of labor unrest, a severe economic dip (unemployment nearly doubled in the nine months following August 1937, and farm prices fell by some 30 percent), and a foreign policy that many judged to lack a strategy to confront the dictatorships.[18] Despite the Republican Party's gain of eighty seats in the House, the Democrats maintained a comfortable majority, but its composition changed. Southern members once again commanded a majority of their party, 54 percent. Never again during the Roosevelt and Truman administrations did their share fall below half of all House Democrats. Party turnover in the Senate was slower, as the Republicans gained eight seats. A southern majority of Democrats did not emerge until the next election, in 1940. By the end of the Truman administration, fully 63 percent of Democrats in the Senate hailed from the South . . . .

During the course of the New Deal, the character and content of policy majorities depended on these southern decisions. On its own, the region did not command a majority of the House or the Senate. Statistically, representatives from the South were no more central to getting legislation passed than other Democrats or Republicans. In a technical sense, each of these three sets of representatives was pivotal, as each group was in a position to provide the votes that were needed by at least one other to gain a winning margin. Overall, though, the South was the bloc most vital to lawmaking. Unlike other members of the House and Senate, whose substantive preferences and propensity to vote were located predictably on a left-to-right spectrum, southern members were more pliable and less predictable with respect to their views and votes. Unlike the others, they made policy decisions on the basis of two dimensions, not just one, those of partisanship and regional concerns. And when the latter was in play, it almost always took priority over commitments to the national Democratic Party and its policy preferences. The level of intensity felt for each was not symmetrical.[19]

NOTES

1. See Elias Canetti, *Crowds and Power* (New York: Farrar, Straus and Giroux, 1960).
2. [Katznelson compares the South's place in the U.S. to Sicily's place in the Italian polity; Sicily is a poor, underdeveloped region]: "The key problem, however, is that Sicily does not exist in

isolation but rather forms part of the *modern* Italian nation." See Nelson Moe, *The View from Vesuvius: Italian Culture and the Southern Question* (Berkeley: University of California Press, 2002), p. 245.

3. There are partial exceptions, to be sure, including Frank Freidel, *F.D.R. and the South* (Baton Rouge: Louisiana State University Press, 1965). Yet in the larger compass of his work, this remains a peripheral theme.

4. Jean Edward Smith, *FDR* (New York: Random House, 2007), p. 374.

5. Toni Morrison, *Playing in the Dark: Whiteness and the Literary Imagination* (New York: Random House, 1992), pp. 18, 11.

6. W.E.B. Du Bois famously opened each chapter of *The Souls of Black Folk!* with a sorrow song... See Du Bois, *The Souls of Black Folk* (1903; reprint, New York: Penguin, 1996), pp. 204–05 ....

7. Hajo Holborn, *The Political Collapse of Europe* (New York: Alfred A. Knopf, 1965); Gregory M. Luebbert, *Liberalism, Fascism, or Social Democracy: Social Classes and the Political Origins of Regimes in Interwar Europe* (New York: Oxford University Press, 1991); Joseph Rothschild, *East Central Europe between the Two World Wars* (Seattle: University of Washington Press, 1994); MacGregor Knox, *To the Threshold of Power, 1922-1933: Origins and Dynamics of the Fascist and National Socialist Dictatorships*, vol. 1 (Cambridge: Cambridge University Press, 2007).

8. Dietrich Rueschemeyer, Evelyne Huber Stephens, and John D. Stephens, *Capitalist Development and Democracy* (Cambridge: Cambridge University Press, 1992); Linz and Stepan, *The Breakdown of Democratic Regimes*; Lois E. Athey, "Democracy and Populism: Some Recent Studies," *Latin American Research Review* 19, no. 3 (1984): 172–83; Leslie Bethell, ed., *The Cambridge History of Latin America*, vol. 7, *1930 to the Present* (Cambridge: Cambridge University Press, 1990); Ruth Berins Collier and David Collier, *Shaping the Political Arena: Critical Junctures, The Labor Movement, and Regime Dynamics in Latin America: The Labor Movement, and Regime Dynamics in Latin America* (Princeton, NJ: Princeton University Press, 1991); Evelyne Huber and Frank Safford, eds., *Agrarian Structure and Political Power: Landlord & Peasant in the Making of Latin America* (Pittsburgh: University of Pittsburgh Press, 1995); Thomas E. Skidmore and Peter H. Smith, *Modern Latin America*, 6th ed. (New York: Oxford University Press, 2005), pp. 51–54.

9. Anthony J. Badger, "Huey Long and the New Deal," in Badger, *New Deal / New South* (Fayetteville: University of Arkansas Press, 2007), p. 1. Like Thurmond and Wallace, Long was a plausible presidential candidate before his assassination in September 1935.

10. When the Socialist Party leader Norman Thomas implored President Roosevelt to back an anti-lynching bill that had been introduced in the Senate in January 1934, FDR explained why he could not risk offending southern leaders, and added, "Now come, Norman. I'm a damned sight better politician than you are. I know the South, and there is arising a new generation of leaders and we've got to be patient." Cited in David M. Kennedy, *Freedom from Fear: The American People in Depression and War, 1929-1945* (New York: Oxford University Press, 1999), p. 210.

11. D.W. Brogan, "American Liberalism Today," in *British Essays in American History*, ed. H.C. Allen and C.P. Hill (New York: St Martin's Press, 1957), p. 326.

12. Ackerman, *We the People,* 2 vols. (Cambridge: Harvard University Press, 1991–1998).

13. In the early New Deal, the Finance Committee was particularly important. That committee, guided by Harrison, nurtured and reported the National Industrial Recovery Act in 1933, the Reciprocal Trade Act in 1934, and the Social Security Act of 1935—together, the very heart of the New Deal.

14. Marion D. Irish, "The Southern One-Party System and National Politics," *Journal of Politics* 4 (Feb. 1942), 84–85. For a discussion and relevant data on the role of southern Democrats in Congress, see David W. Brady, *Critical Elections and Congressional Policy Making* (Stanford, CA: Stanford University Press, 1988); Sinclair, *Congressional Realignment,* especially the useful table on regional composition on p. 19. See also the discussion on the advantages that accrued

to the South over the long term in Richard L. Watson Jr, "From Populism through the New Deal: Southern Political History," in *Interpreting Southern History: Historiographical Essays in Honor of Sanford W Higginbotham*, ed. John B. Boles and Evelyn Thomas (Baton Rouge: Louisiana State University Press, 1987).

15. Republicans tended to be more competitive in Senate races than in House ones, yet even in that chamber victorious Democratic Party candidates secured 86.4 percent of the vote from 1912 to 1930, dipping below 85 percent only in 1920. The mean percentage of the two-party vote for all candidates in this period outside the South was 58 percent. See Donald Gross and David Breaux, "Historical Trends in U.S. Senate Elections, 1912–1988," *American Politics Quarterly* 19 (1991): 295, 300.

16. There were five Farmer-Labor Party members, as well. This was the composition of the House on March 4, 1933.

17. There was also one Farmer-Labor Party member. This was the composition of the Senate on March 4, 1933.

18. Milton Plesur, "The Republican Congressional Comeback of 1938," *Review of Politics* 24 (1962): 525–62; Clyde P. Weed, *The Nemesis of Reform: The Republican Party during the New Deal* (New York: Columbia University Press, 1994).

19. Southern congressional power peaked during the New Deal era's second decade, from 1943 to 1952. Republicans averaged 43 members (45 percent) in the Senate, compared with 30 (31 percent) for southern Democrats and just 23 (24 percent) for nonsouthern Democrats. In the House, on average, the Republicans held 203 seats (47 percent), while southern Democrats had 133 (31 percent), and nonsouthern Democrats only 97 (23 percent). As a result, the region's representatives became a good deal more than a veto group. Commanding the Democratic Party, the South effectively controlled what Congress would, and would not, accomplish. More than once in his landmark treatment of the growth of congressional conservatism during the New Deal, James Patterson stressed that "too much can be made of the fact" that much of the emergent opposition to the New Deal within the Democratic Party was southern, and he cautioned that "it is easy to simplify the southern role in the conservative bloc" and said that "this factor should not be overemphasized." He rightly noted that, outside explicit race issues or those that elicited racial fears, the South hardly was solid, and, most often, continued to back the New Deal. But that is just the point I wish to stress. The South moved from a core initiator and supporter of the New Deal in the early years to a voting bloc that had to manage to find its way within a two-dimensional map with both party and regional coordinates. I fully agree with Patterson that the South was not the center of a sure and predictable conservative coalition. See James T. Patterson, *Congressional Conservatism and the New Deal* (Lexington: University of Kentucky Press, 1967), pp. 132, 278, 322–23. Patterson first put forth his arguments in the following two articles: "The Failure of Party Realignment in the South, 1937-1939," *Journal of Politics* 27 (1965): 602–17; "A Conservative Coalition Forms in Congress, *1933-1939*," *Journal of American History* 52 (1966): 757–72.

9.4 David Mayhew, "The Electoral Incentive" (1974)

By the middle of the twentieth century, more and more members of Congress viewed office holding as a career that required periodic reelection. Today, most incumbent members of Congress seek reelection, and most who run for reelection win. Political scientist David Mayhew based his path-breaking study of Congress on the assumption that members of Congress focus primarily on reelection before anything else. Even the most idealistic members cannot make a long-term impact on public policy without keeping their seats in Congress. Mayhew explained that members' reelection success depends heavily on their efforts to advertise themselves to their constituents, to claim credit for beneficial public policy, and to take shrewd positions on policy issues. For example, any U.S. Representative's website today will have a link to "services," such as help with government claims and documents, applications to the service academies, and the purchase of a flag flown over the Capitol building. In turn, Congress has evolved in a way that assists these legislators in this behavior. All of these opportunities permit candidates to run "candidate-centered" campaigns. Incumbents highlight the benefits they bring to local constituents, and often downplay their political party affiliation. These electoral incentives create a powerful force of fragmentation in Congress, and this has made the tasks of majority-building, lawmaking, and leadership much more difficult.

The discussion to come will hinge on the assumption that United States congressmen are interested in getting reelected—indeed, in their role here as abstractions, interested in nothing else.

...in the modern Congress the "congressional career" is unmistakably upon us.[1] Turnover figures show that over the past century increasing proportions of members in any given Congress have been holdovers from previous Congresses—members who have both sought reelection and won it. Membership turnover noticeably declined among southern senators as early as the 1850s, among senators generally just after the Civil War.[2] The House followed close behind, with turnover dipping in the late nineteenth century and continuing to decline throughout the twentieth.[3] Average number of terms served has gone up and up, with the House in 1971 registering an all-time high of 20 percent of its members who had served at least ten terms.[4] It seems fair to characterize the modern Congress as an assembly of professional politicians spinning out political careers. The jobs offer good pay and high prestige. There is no want of applicants for them. Successful pursuit of a career requires continual reelection.[5]

...Are, then, congressmen in a position to do anything about getting reelected? If an answer is sought in their ability to affect national partisan percentages, the answer is no. But if an answer is sought in their ability to affect the percentages in their own primary and general elections, the answer is yes. Or at least so the case will be presented here. More specifically, it will be argued that they think that they can affect their own percentages, that in fact they can affect their own percentages, and furthermore that there is reason for them to try to do so . . . .

...when looked at from the standpoint of a career, congressional seats are not as safe as they may seem. Of House members serving in the Ninety-third Congress 58 percent had at least one time in their careers won general elections with less than 55 percent of the total vote, 77 percent with less than 60 percent of the vote. For senators the figures were 70 percent and 86 percent (the last figure including fifteen of the twenty-two southerners). And aside from these November results there is competition in the primaries. The fact is that the typical congressman at least occasionally has won a narrow victory.[6]

...Whether they are safe or marginal, cautious or audacious, congressmen must constantly engage in activities related to reelection. There will be differences in emphasis, but all members share the root need to do things—indeed, to do things day in and day out during their terms. The next step here is to present a typology, a short list of the *kinds* of activities congressmen find it electorally useful to engage in. The case will be that there are three basic kinds of activities. It will be important to lay them out with some care, for arguments in part 2 will be built on them.

One activity is *advertising*, defined here as any effort to disseminate one's name among constituents in such a fashion as to create a favorable image but in messages having little or no issue content. A successful congressman builds what amounts to a brand name, which may have a generalized electoral value for other politicians in the same family. The personal qualities to emphasize are experience, knowledge, responsiveness, concern, sincerity, independence, and the like. Just getting one's name across is difficult enough; only about half the electorate, if asked, can supply their House members' names. It helps a congressman to be known. "In the main, recognition carries a positive valence; to be perceived at all is to be perceived favorably."[7] A vital advantage enjoyed by House incumbents is that they are much better known among voters than their November challengers.[8] They are better known because they spend a great deal of time, energy, and money trying to make themselves better known.[9] There are standard routines—frequent visits to the constituency, nonpolitical speeches to home audiences,[10] the sending out of infant care booklets and letters of condolence and congratulation. Of 158 House members questioned in the mid-1960s, 121 said that they regularly sent newsletters to their constituents;[11] 48 wrote separate news or opinion columns for newspapers; 82 regularly reported to their constituencies by radio or television;[12] 89 regularly sent out mail questionnaires.[13] Some routines are less standard.

...A second activity may be called *credit claiming*, defined here as acting so as to generate a belief in a relevant political actor (or actors) that one is personally responsible for causing the government, or some unit thereof, to do something that the actor (or actors) considers desirable. The political logic of this, from the congressman's point of view, is that an actor who believes that a member can make pleasing things happen will no doubt wish to keep him in office so that he can make pleasing things happen in the future. The emphasis here is on individual accomplishment (rather than, say, party or governmental accomplishment) and on the congressman as doer (rather than as, say, expounder of constituency views). Credit claiming is highly important to congressmen, with the consequence that much of congressional life is a relentless search for opportunities to engage in it.

Where can credit be found? If there were only one congressman rather than 535, the answer would in principle be simple enough.[14] Credit (or blame) would attach to the doings of the government as a whole. But there are 535. Hence it becomes necessary for each congressman to try to peel off pieces of governmental accomplishment for which he can believably generate a sense of responsibility. For the average congressman the staple way of doing this is to traffic in what may be called "particularized benefits."[15] Particularized governmental benefits, as the term will be used here, have two properties: (1) Each benefit is given out to a specific individual, group, or geographical constituency, the recipient unit being of a scale that allows a single congressman to be recognized (by relevant political actors and other congressmen) as the claimant for the benefit (other congressmen being perceived as indifferent or hostile). (2) Each benefit is given out in apparently ad hoc fashion (unlike, say, social security checks) with a congressman apparently having a hand in the allocation. A particularized benefit can normally be regarded as a member of a class. That is, a benefit given out to an individual, group, or constituency can normally be looked upon by congressmen as one of a class of similar benefits given out to sizable numbers of individuals, groups, or constituencies. Hence the impression can arise that a congressman is getting "his share" of whatever it is the government is offering. (The classes may be vaguely defined. Some state legislatures deal in what their members call "local legislation.")

In sheer volume the bulk of particularized benefits come under the heading of "casework"—the thousands of favors congressional offices perform for supplicants in ways that normally do not require legislative action. High school students ask for essay materials, soldiers for emergency leaves, pensioners for location of missing checks, local governments for grant information, and on and on. Each office has skilled professionals who can play the bureaucracy like an organ—pushing the right pedals to produce the desired effects.[16] But many benefits require new legislation, or at least they require important allocative decisions on matters covered by existent legislation. Here the congressman fills the traditional role of supplier of goods to the home district . . . . Shiny construction projects seem especially useful . . . .

The third activity congressmen engage in may be called *position taking*, defined here as the public enunciation of a judgmental statement on anything likely to be of interest to political actors. The statement may take the form of a roll call vote. The most important classes of judgmental statements are those prescribing American governmental ends (a vote cast against the war; a statement that "the war should be ended immediately") or governmental means (a statement that "the way to end the war is to take it to the United Nations"). The judgments may be implicit rather than explicit, as in: "I will support the president on this matter." But judgments may range far beyond these classes to take in implicit or explicit statements on what almost anybody should do or how he should do it: "The great Polish scientist Copernicus has been unjustly neglected"; "The way for Israel to achieve peace is to give up the Sinai."[17] The congressman as position taker is a speaker rather than a doer. The electoral requirement is not that he make pleasing things happen but that he make pleasing judgmental statements. The position itself is the political commodity. Especially on matters where governmental responsibility is widely diffused it is not surprising that political actors should fall back on positions as tests of incumbent virtue. For voters ignorant of congressional processes the recourse is an easy one. The following comment by one of Clapp's House interviewees is highly revealing: "Recently, I went home and began to talk about the—act. I was pleased to have sponsored that bill, but it soon dawned on me that the point wasn't getting through at all. What was getting through was that the act might be a help to people. I changed the emphasis: I didn't mention my role particularly, but stressed my support of the legislation."[18]

The ways in which positions can be registered are numerous and often imaginative. There are floor addresses ranging from weighty orations to mass-produced "nationality day statements."[19] There are speeches before home groups, television appearances, letters, newsletters, press releases, ghostwritten books, *Playboy* articles, even interviews with political scientists. On occasion congressmen generate what amount to petitions;

whether or not to sign the 1956 Southern Manifesto defying school desegregation rulings was an important decision for southern members.[20] Outside the roll call process the congressman is usually able to tailor his positions to suit his audiences. A solid consensus in the constituency calls for ringing declarations; for years the late Senator James K. Vardaman (D., Miss.) campaigned on a proposal to repeal the Fifteenth Amendment.[21] Division or uncertainty in the constituency calls for waffling; in the late 1960s a congressman had to be a poor politician indeed not to be able to come up with an inoffensive statement on Vietnam ("We must have peace with honor at the earliest possible moment consistent with the national interest"). On a controversial issue a Capitol Hill office normally prepares two form letters to send out to constituent letter writers—one for the pros and one (not directly contradictory) for the antis.[22] Handling discrete audiences in person requires simple agility, a talent well demonstrated in this selection from a Nader profile:

> "You may find this difficult to understand," said Democrat Edward R. Roybal, the Mexican-American representative from California's thirtieth district, "but sometimes I wind up making a patriotic speech one afternoon and later on that same day an anti-war speech. In the patriotic speech I speak of past wars but I also speak of the need to prevent more wars. My positions are not inconsistent; I just approach different people differently." Roybal went on to depict the diversity of crowds he speaks to: one afternoon he is surrounded by balding men wearing Veterans' caps and holding American flags; a few hours later he speaks to a crowd of Chicano youths, angry over American involvement in Vietnam. Such a diverse constituency, Roybal believes, calls for different methods of expressing one's convictions.[23]

Indeed it does. Versatility of this sort is occasionally possible in roll call voting. For example a congressman may vote one way on recommittal and the other on final passage, leaving it unclear just how he stands on a bill.[24] Members who cast identical votes on a measure may give different reasons for having done so . . . .

NOTES

1. H. Douglas Price, "The Congressional Career Then and Now," ch. 2 in Nelson W. Polsby (ed.), *Congressional Behavior* (New York: Random House, 1971).
2. H. Douglas Price, "Computer Simulation and Legislative 'Professionalism;' Some Quantitative to Legislative Evolution," paper presented at the annual meeting of the American Political Science Association, 1970, pp. 14–16.
3. Nelson W. Polsby, "The Institutionalization of the U.S. House of Representatives," 62 *American Political Science Review* 146 (1968).
4. Charles S. Bullock III, "House Careerists: Changing Patterns of Longevity and Attrition," 66 *American Political Science Review* 1296 (1972).
5. Indeed, it has been proposed that professional politicians could be gotten rid of by making reelection impossible. For a plan to select one-term legislators by random sampling of the population, see Dennis C. Mueller et al., "Representative Government via Random Selection," 12 *Public Choice* 57–68 (1972).
6. Over the long haul the proportion of seats switching from party to party is quite surprising . . . .
7. Donald E. Stokes and Warren E. Miller, "Party Government and the Saliency of Congress," ch. 11 in Angus Campbell et al. (ed.), *Elections and the Political Order* (New York: Wiley, 1966) p. 205. The same may not be true among, say, mayors.

8. Ibid., p. 204. The likelihood is that senators are also better known than their challengers, but that the gap is not so wide as it is on the House side. There is no hard evidence on the point.

9. In Clapp's interview study, "Conversations with more than fifty House members uncovered only one who seemed to place little emphasis on strategies designed to increase communications with the voter." Charles L. Clapp, *The Congressman: His Work and How He Sees It* (Washington, DC: 1963), p. 88. The exception was an innocent freshman.

10. A statement by one of Clapp's congressmen: "The best speech is a non-political speech. I think a commencement speech is the best of all. X says he has never lost a precinct in a town where he has made a commencement speech." Charles L. Clapp, *The Congressman: His Work as He Sees It* (Washington: Brookings Institution, 1963), p. 96.

11. These and the following figures on member activity are from Donald G. Tacheron and Morris K. Udall, *The Job of the Congressman* (Indianapolis: Bobbs-Merrill, 1966), pp. 281–88.

12. Another Clapp congressman: "I was looking at my TV film today—I have done one every week since I have been here—and who was behind me but Congressman X. I'll swear he had never done a TV show before in his life but he only won by a few hundred votes last time. Now he has a weekly television show. If he had done that before he wouldn't have had any trouble." *The Congressman*, p. 92.

13. On questionnaires generally see Walter Wilcox, "The Congressional Poll—and Non-Poll," in Edward C. Dreyer and Walter A. Rosenbaum (eds.), *Political Opinion and Electoral Behavior* (Belmont, Calif.: Wadsworth, 1966), pp. 390–400.

14. In practice the one might call out the army and suspend the Constitution.

15. These have some of the properties of what Lowi calls "distributive" benefits. Theodore J. Lowi, "American Business, Public Policy, Case-Studies, and Political Theory," 16 *World Politics* 690 (1964).

16. On casework generally see Kenneth G. Olson, "The Service Function of the United States Congress," pp. 337–74 in American Enterprise Institute, *Congress: The First Branch of Government* (Washington, DC: American Enterprise Institute for Public Policy Research, 1966).

17. In the terminology of Stokes, statements may be on either "position issues" or "valence issues." Donald E. Stokes, "Spatial Models of Party Competition," ch. 9 in Campbell et al., *Elections and the Political Order*, pp. 170–74.

18. Clapp, *The Congressman*, p. 108. A difficult borderline question here is whether introduction of bills in Congress should be counted under position taking or credit claiming. On balance, probably under the former. Yet another Clapp congressman addresses the point: "I introduce about sixty bills a year, about 120 a Congress. I try to introduce bills that illustrate, by and large, my ideas—legislative, economic, and social. I do like being able to say when I get cornered, 'yes, boys, I introduced a bill to try to do that in 1954.' To me it is the perfect answer." Ibid., p. 141. But voters probably give claims like this about the value they deserve.

19. On floor speeches generally see Donald R. Matthews, *U.S. Senators and Their World* (Chapel Hill: University of North Carolina Press, 1960), p. 247. On statements celebrating holidays cherished by ethnic groups, Hearings on the Organization of Congress before the Joint Committee on the Organization of the Congress, 89th Cong., 1st sess., 1965, p. 1127; and Arlen J. Large, "And Now Let's Toast Nicolaus Copernicus, the Famous German," *Wall Street Journal*, March 12, 1973, p. 1.

20. Sometimes members of the Senate ostentatiously line up as "cosponsors" of measures—an activity that may attract more attention than roll call voting itself. Thus, in early 1973, seventy-six senators backed a provision to block trade concessions to the USSR until the Soviet government allowed Jews to emigrate without paying high exit fees. "'Why did so many people sign the amendment?' a Northern Senator asked rhetorically. 'Because there is no political advantage in not signing. If you do sign, you don't offend anyone. If you don't sign, you

might offend some Jews in your state.'" David E. Rosenbaum, "Firm Congress Stand on Jews in Soviet Is Traced to Efforts by Those in U.S.," *New York Times*, April 6, 1973, p. 14.

21. "... an utterly hopeless proposal and for that reason an ideal campaign issue." V.O. Key, Jr., *Southern Politics* (New York: Knopf, 1949), p. 232.

22. Instructions on how to do this are given in Donald G. Tacheron and Morris K. Udall, *The Job of the Congressman: An Introduction to Service in the U. S. House of Representatives* (New York: MacMillan, 1970) pp. 73–74.

23. William Lazarus, Nader profile on Edward R. Roybal (D., Cal.), p. 1.

24. On obfuscation in congressional position taking see Raymond A. Bauer, Ithiel de Sola Pool and Lewis A. Dexter, *American Business and Public Policy* (New York: Atherton, 1964), pp. 431–32.

9.5 Eric Schickler, "Institutional Development of Congress" (2004)

The New Deal was a moment in a constantly evolving Congress. Political scientist Eric Schickler stepped back to study the way evolving political pressures and the inherited rules have influenced the development of Congress through time. Over a century ago, political party leaders like House Speakers Thomas Reed and Joseph Cannon centralized power in their own hands. In the early 1910s, members of both the House and Senate revolted against this kind of centralized power, and this revolt decentralized power to committees and spurred the creation of formal rules to protect against arbitrary leadership decisions. When Franklin Roosevelt took office, the dominance of committees and their chairs—often conservative Southern Democrats—was reaching a highpoint. The Reorganization Act of 1946 strengthened committee power further. Reformers in the 1970s—often liberal Northern Democrats—reacted against arbitrary *committee* power. They decentralized power further by protecting congressional subcommittees, while they also empowered their party leaders to exercise more control over legislative outcomes. All these changes played out differently in the House of Representatives and the Senate. Party polarization encouraged stronger majority-party rule in the House, but simply made the Senate a more difficult body for leaders to control.

While the basic constitutional framework governing Congress has changed little over the past two hundred years, a member serving in the 1790s would have considerable difficulty recognizing today's Congress ... Over the past two centuries, both the House and the Senate have fundamentally changed their mode of organization. Each chamber has developed a specialized committee system, which processes most legislation before it reaches the floor. Both chambers now feature elaborate and formalized party structures in which majority-party leaders play a significant role in determining the floor agenda. Individual members in both chambers are now empowered to introduce legislation at will, and each member employs a large personal staff to assist in both legislative activity and constituent service.

Yet the two chambers have also diverged organizationally in important respects. Most notably, majority-party leaders in the House enjoy more prerogatives than their Senate counterparts: their control of the agenda is firmer and their ability to shape committee composition and committee deliberations is greater. The committee system has also traditionally been more powerful in the House than in the Senate. House committees have more extensive property rights over legislation and their proposals are better protected from floor amendments.[1] By contrast, individual members enjoy greater prerogatives in the Senate. In particular, the Senate's tradition of unlimited debate differentiates it from the House. While a determined floor majority can work its will in the House, the filibuster empowers senators to block action indefinitely. A sixty-vote supermajority is required to ensure action in the Senate, and the threat of filibusters leads to the reliance on elaborate unanimous-consent agreements to manage floor deliberations, which give substantial leverage to individual senators.

What were the sources of these major changes in the House and Senate? How did the United States end up with two chambers that differ so much from the original congressional blueprint and from one another? ...

... [S]everal factors have repeatedly proven critical and have, in conjunction, given rise to the contemporary Congress. Members have repeatedly sought to bolster congressional capacity and power in order to maintain their chamber's institutional position. These moves have generally come in response to a burgeoning workload and to threats of executive encroachment. But general concerns with institutional maintenance have rarely proven sufficient on their own to motivate major changes. Instead, partisan interests and members' more personal interest in reelection and exercising power as individuals have also proven critical. Personal power interests have played a more important role in the Senate, due to the chamber's smaller size, which allows greater latitude for individual members. By contrast, partisan calculations have more often proven significant in the House, giving rise to a chamber with tighter agenda control and more limited individual member prerogatives.

These House-Senate differences began to take shape early in the nineteenth century, and have been reinforced by the incentives created by inherited institutions.[2] The options available to decision makers today depend on prior choices. The House early on developed mechanisms for a floor majority, often acting through party leaders, to force a final vote on both policy changes and rules changes. From early in its history, by contrast, the Senate allowed greater latitude for individual members to block action. These inherited institutions have made it more difficult for a floor majority to force institutional changes, thus limiting the majority party's ability to consolidate its power in the upper chamber. As a result, understanding the role of parties, committees, and individual members in today's House and Senate requires attention to historical development ....

Revolt against Centralization, 1910–1930

The late nineteenth and early twentieth centuries represent the historical high water mark for centralized party leadership in both the House and the Senate, even as the upper chamber was well behind the House in terms of the extent of party government. The first decade of the twentieth century, however, featured a move away

from centralization as individual members sought to enhance their own prerogatives . . . .
Members' individual power interests aligned with the policy goals of an ideological
faction to motivate reform . . . .

. . . The critical changes in the House occurred in the final years of Illinois Republican
[Joseph] Cannon's speakership. A series of changes in 1909–1911 took away the Speaker's
control over committee assignments, removed the Speaker from the Rules Committee,
and created mechanisms for a floor majority to force matters to the floor over the
Speaker's opposition. With the Speaker's authority diminished, seniority soon became
the dominant consideration in determining committee leadership positions. This helped
to launch the so-called textbook Congress, in which specialized standing committees
played an especially prominent role and party leaders receded in importance.[3]

Three forces fused to produce the revolt against Cannon. First, starting in 1905,
progressives became more numerous within the Republican Party as President Theodore
Roosevelt began to push for major policy change. These ideological divisions within the
majority party fostered greater resistance to centralized party control, particularly since
Cannon had used that control to push only for conservative policies. When a party is
internally divided on policy, centralized leadership becomes more costly for its members.[4]
Insurgent leader John Nelson, a Republican congressman from Wisconsin, illustrated
progressives' mounting frustration in 1908 when he argued that "President Roosevelt has
been trying to cultivate oranges for many years in the frigid climate of the Committee on
Rules, but what has he gotten but the proverbial lemons?"[5] A second source of dissatisfaction with Cannon was the belief that his tight personal control deprived individual
representatives of opportunities to exert influence. As members began to view Congress
as a career in this era, they sought greater leeway to make a name for themselves without
the Speaker's interference. The insurgents against Cannon included a handful of relatively senior and fairly conservative Republicans who had each seen Cannon comman-
deer legislation from their committees. Weakening the Speaker promised to safeguard
committees from such incursions and thus to allow individual members more opportunities to pursue their own agendas. A third source of Cannon's downfall was the minority
party's reaction to his aggressive leadership. After years of frustration in the minority,
Democrats responded to being shut out of the policy process by attacking the House as
an institution and turning Cannon into the symbol of an undemocratic and unrespon-
sive legislative branch. The Democrats focused heavily on Cannon's leadership style in
the 1908 campaign and planned to continue their attacks in the upcoming 1910 elections. They hoped to identify all Republicans with the increasingly unpopular Speaker
and thereby improve the electoral chances of Democratic candidates. Cannon's mounting
unpopularity eventually forced several vulnerable Midwestern Republicans with no
history of progressivism to back the revolt.

. . . Even though the Senate had never delegated as much power to party leaders, it
moved largely in tandem with the House toward greater decentralization. While
Republicans had enjoyed a reasonable degree of unity on key policy issues in the 1890s
and early 1900s, both parties featured major internal divisions by 1910, which persisted
for the next several decades. This undermined member support for vigorous party leadership . . . The interlocking party and committee leadership of the late 1890s gave way to a
clearer separation of party and committee leadership. By the 1920s, several key committees featured majorities of progressive Republicans and Democrats, notwithstanding the
nominal Republican majority in the chamber as a whole. These committees pursued

policies on issues such as agriculture prices that were out of step with conservative Republican party leaders.[6]

The Senate also emulated the House in providing more formalized floor and agenda management in this period.... A further move toward formalization in the Senate occurred in 1917 with passage of the chamber's first cloture rule. Prior to 1917, the Senate lacked a mechanism for ending debate in the face of minority obstruction. But a series of high-profile filibusters in the early twentieth century brought increased pressure for reform. With World War I rising on the agenda, the Senate's inability to pass much-needed legislation at the end of the Sixty-fourth Congress (1915–1917) led to President Woodrow Wilson's famous attack on the "little group of willful men" who had stood in the way of the majority. The Senate responded in March 1917 with a rule that allowed two-thirds of senators present and voting to adopt a cloture resolution, which provided a timetable for ending debate. It is worth emphasizing that the cloture rule did not curtail the practice of filibustering. Instead, it provided a formal mechanism for ending obstruction, but only in the presence of supermajority support. The 1917 change thus reinforced the contrast with the majoritarian House. Indeed, as the Senate's workload continued to rise after 1917 and as individual senators became more assertive in attempting to make a name for themselves in the political system, filibusters would only become a more prominent feature of Senate lawmaking over time.

Still, although the Senate moved toward greater formalization in the early twentieth century, this shift did not stop the more potent trend toward decentralization. Party floor leaders and the cloture rule allowed for slightly greater predictability and more efficient management of the Senate's agenda, but the basic mode of operations in the upper chamber became ever more individualistic. The constitutional amendment providing for direct election of senators in 1913 likely reinforced the upper chamber's tendency toward individualism and its resistance to collective controls.

Rise of the Modern Presidency and the Legislative Reorganization Act of 1946

The fragmented congressional system that existed in the first decades of the twentieth century came under tremendous challenge with the rise of a far more aggressive and powerful presidency in the 1930s and 1940s. The expansion of federal responsibility during the New Deal, President Franklin Roosevelt's domestic program for economic recovery and social reforms following the onset of the Great Depression, and the unprecedented mobilization effort for World War II combined to lavish immense influence upon Roosevelt and his successors. In the absence of equally strong leaders in the legislature, members of Congress began to worry about the future of their institution. Academic studies, congressional hearings, and journalistic accounts in the 1940s echoed the theme that Congress must reorganize in order to retain its coequal place in the constitutional system. Mike Monroney (a Democrat congressman from Oklahoma), one of the leading advocates of reform, stated the widely held view that "we simply cannot struggle along under this type of workload unless we equip ourselves to answer the challenge that the Constitution's framers intended the Congress to carry."[7] Many reformers called for a return to party government, but in the absence of an internally unified majority party, such calls found little resonance in Congress. The deep Democratic divisions between northern liberals and southern conservatives meant that members had to look elsewhere to create an institutional counterbalance to presidential power.

In response, members chose to streamline and strengthen the congressional committee system by adopting the Legislative Reorganization Act of 1946. The act bolstered the capacity and influence of standing committees in both chambers. It emerged in reaction to the rise of the modern presidency, and reflects how members of Congress sought to defend their institution in ways that were compatible with protecting their existing committee power bases. Members' interest in individual power and improved perquisites fused with their stake in congressional capacity to promote a major institutional renovation.

. . . The Reorganization Act profoundly affected the congressional authority structure by reinforcing the already strong system of standing committees and committee chairmen. By reducing the number of committees and expanding their jurisdictions, the Reorganization Act made each committee a more potent institutional power base for its members and chairman. Since many of these chairmen were conservative southerners, this posed significant problems both for Democratic administrations and for mainstream northern Democrats. Although some reformers attempted to include provisions empowering party leaders to counterbalance the fortified committees, these features were either eliminated before passage or not implemented in practice . . . .

Reform Era of the 1970s

. . . By the early 1970s, the old textbook Congress confronted increasingly sharp challenges from several sources. Liberal Democrats, who augmented their numbers following Democratic sweeps in the 1958 and 1964 elections, were deeply dissatisfied with a committee system that empowered southern conservatives from safe districts, who rarely faced a serious electoral challenge. This dissatisfaction was exacerbated by the shift in the broader political context toward candidate-centered elections, which encouraged members to place a greater premium on gaining rapid access to their own power bases within Congress in order to make a name for themselves. Junior representatives and senators thus sought to undermine the seniority system, which placed disproportionate power in the hands of senior committee chairmen.

Both chambers responded to these pressures in the 1970s with a series of innovations that undercut the seniority system, spread greater resources to subcommittees and individual members, and, particularly in the House, granted new tools to party leaders . . . .

A "subcommittee bill of rights," adopted in January 1973 by the Democratic Caucus, transferred the power to appoint subcommittee chairmen from the full committee chair to the committee's majority-party members. This committee caucus would also set subcommittee jurisdictions. In addition, the bill of rights guaranteed subcommittees an adequate budget and staff, along with automatic referral of legislation. An earlier 1971 caucus reform had limited each member to a single subcommittee chairmanship, thereby spreading access to these influential positions more broadly. A 1975 change adopted by the House further bolstered subcommittee resources by authorizing each subcommittee chairman and ranking member to hire one full-time staff person to handle subcommittee work. Since there were over one hundred subcommittee chairmen and just twenty full committee chairmen, these reforms spread power to more members. Even the most junior Democrat could reasonably aspire to a subcommittee chairmanship within a few terms of entering the House. But the subcommittee reforms did not benefit all junior members equally. Liberals lobbied hardest for the reforms, in part because they believed that strengthening the subcommittees would not only empower them as individual entrepreneurs, but would also weaken conservative committee chairmen, who often blocked liberal legislation. Therefore, the subcommittee changes passed because liberal Democrats had policy reasons to undercut conservative committee chairmen and found that they could forge a broad coalition for doing so by simultaneously appealing to representatives' power-base interests.

A similar confluence of forces generated the revolt against the seniority system for selecting committee chairmen that occurred in 1971–1975 . . . .

The subcommittee and seniority changes contributed to a seismic power shift in the House. Committee chairmen were forced to share power with rank-and-file committee members and to look to the caucus for guidance on important policy issues. Each subcommittee chairman now had a power base that could be used to launch initiatives, claim credit, and gain press attention. Policy entrepreneurship became increasingly widespread, and subcommittees proved a valuable source of programmatic innovation. While subcommittee influence varied across issue areas, subcommittee chairmen now generally had disproportionate access to important resources, such as staff expertise and communication networks. Meanwhile, the roughly twenty committee chairmen who had in the past served as focal points for coalition building suffered greatly reduced stature.

The fragmentation brought about by the rise of subcommittees and the weakening of the chairmen was partially offset by changes that provided new powers to party leaders.[8] . . .

The Senate experienced a movement toward fragmentation in the 1970s that paralleled that of the House, but formal changes empowering party leaders were far more limited. As a result, the reform era deepened the distinctiveness of the chambers, as expanding Senate individualism contrasted with the partial revival of party leadership in the House. Although no Senate chairmen or ranking committee members were deposed, both Democrats and Republicans adopted new rules easing the way for votes on individual chairmen. The Senate also adopted a generous new staffing policy in 1975 that provided each senator on a committee with additional staff assistance independent of the chairmen. This made it easier for junior members to engage in policy entrepreneurship.

The most striking change in Senate operations was an informal one: the filibuster, which had been used relatively sparingly for much of American history, became a routine tool used by individual senators to extract concessions or to block bills entirely. While it is impossible to quantify the amount of obstruction precisely, Sarah Binder and Steven Smith document increasing filibusters in the 1970s and 1980s.[9] They count just 23 "manifest filibusters" in the entire nineteenth century and they report that the typical Congress in the 1940s through the 1960s had about 5 filibusters. By contrast, there were 191 filibusters from 1970 to 1994. In just the 102nd Congress of 1991–1992, there were a record 35 filibusters, and the prevalence of filibusters remained high throughout the remainder of the decade. The boom in obstruction, like the move toward improved staffing for junior senators, was partly rooted in the new, candidate centered political context, which rewarded individual activism.[10] Heightened time pressures, however, added to the temptation to filibuster: as the Senate's schedule became more crowded, the mere threat of a filibuster was often sufficient to extract concessions.[11] As partisan polarization has increased in the chamber, filibusters have also been fueled by the minority party's interest in blocking policies that it opposes. Although partisan filibusters have been a recurrent feature of Senate politics, they have increased in frequency since the 1970s. Since the cloture rule now requires sixty votes to end debate, the routinization of the filibuster means that legislating typically requires supermajority support. Indeed, a 2002 study suggests that roughly half of all major bills encounter filibuster difficulties, often resulting in either defeat or substantial concessions.[12] . . .

Republican "Revolution" of 1995

The institutional development of Congress is ongoing . . . . [after the 1994 elections, and] [u]nder the assertive leadership of Republican Speaker Newt Gingrich of Georgia, Republicans adopted an array of reforms intended to centralize party control. Although the most important changes occurred in the House, Senate Republicans also adopted a handful of innovations meant to strengthen party discipline in the notoriously unruly chamber. Nonetheless, the persistence of the right of unlimited debate has precluded the consolidation of effective party government in the upper chamber. The combination of the filibuster and intense partisan polarization has magnified the challenges facing Senate leaders.

    . . . If the 1910 revolt against centralization presaged the development of a more independent, specialized committee system, the institutional innovations that have occurred since the 1970s suggest a movement in the House back toward the model of leadership offered by Reed and Cannon. Nonetheless, it is an overstatement to claim that Congress has returned to "czar rule." Instead, [Republican House Speaker Dennis] Hastert and his leadership team showed a deep dependence on the ongoing support of rank-and-file Republicans, and they worked assiduously to involve these members in the party machinery. Indeed, the critical shift has been that members' participation now occurs more through party machinery and less through the committee system than in the past.[13]

    The impact of the Republican takeover in the Senate [in the 1994 elections] has been more subtle. Republicans have challenged the seniority system, though more gingerly than in the House. The GOP adopted rules specifying that the party conference would vote on an official legislative agenda prior to selecting committee chairmen, providing a potential benchmark for evaluating their loyalty. Furthermore, the party adopted a term-limit rule of their own for committee chairmen in September 1995, which has forced a handful of longtime chairmen to surrender their posts. The declining independence of committee chairmen was underscored following the 2004 election when Republican senator Arlen Specter headed off a conservative-backed challenge to his ascension to the Judiciary Committee chairmanship by proclaiming that he would work to promote the confirmation of President George W. Bush's judicial nominees. This episode suggests that the majority party in the Senate has become more willing to demand loyalty from committee chairmen . . . .

Lessons for Congressional Reform

Over the past 225 years, the House and Senate have developed an elaborate committee system and party leadership structure to enable members to better pursue their goals. The power of committees and of party leaders has waxed and waned over time, in response to external pressures, such as challenges from the executive branch, and internal dynamics, such as the level of party polarization and individual member careerism. Today's House has returned to a level of party strength not seen in nearly a century, while the Senate remains highly individualistic, notwithstanding its high level of partisan acrimony. Although developments in the two chambers have typically moved in tandem, the general pattern is for formal party leaders to enjoy greater prerogatives in the House, while the smaller Senate has featured greater individual prerogatives, looser rules, and weaker party leaders.

One reason to study the institutional development of Congress is the belief that institutions affect member behavior, and thus that the House-Senate differences described above help explain political outcomes. Yet a cursory examination of roll call voting data suggests that the seemingly sharp institutional differences between the House and Senate do not impact how members vote on the floor, and therefore would appear to have limited importance for policy outcomes. That is, levels of party voting are generally as high in the Senate as in the House, notwithstanding the much greater individualism and weaker party leaders in the upper chamber. For example, the percentage of votes that divided a majority of Democrats against a majority of Republicans reached two-thirds in the Senate in 2003, as compared with 52 percent in the House. In both chambers, approximately 90 percent of the members stuck with their party on these votes.[14] Nonetheless, inherited institutions—such as the filibuster—have had a profound impact on the meaning of this polarization. In the House, as Democrats and Republicans came to represent distinctive constituencies, their policy preferences polarized along party lines, giving members greater incentive to delegate power to party leaders. The majority party has come to dominate the legislative process in the chamber; in the 108th Congress (2003–2004), minority-party Democrats were generally shut out when it came to decision making on most important issues. In the Senate, by contrast, the need for supermajority support for most legislation means that the preference polarization that produces high levels of party voting has not translated into majority-party government. Instead, the minority increasingly uses party-based filibusters to block action. The cloture votes to defeat these filibusters produce numerous sharply partisan roll calls, but in the absence of support from several Democrats, they are doomed to failure. As a result, even perfect party-line votes in the Senate do not necessarily generate majority-party victories, in contrast to the majoritarian House.

In sum, the polarization of party members' preferences has fostered majority-party governance in the House, but has only made the challenges confronting Senate party leaders more daunting. The combination of immense individual prerogatives and polarized party-based teams fighting it out has at times seemed to make the Senate ungovernable, in sharp contrast to the disciplined House. Thus, the filibuster and related institutional differences between the chambers have an enormous impact on policy making, even as voting patterns are broadly similar in the House and Senate.

NOTES

1. *Property rights* refers to each committee's right to have legislation in its jurisdiction referred to it before the bill reaches the floor.
2. See Binder, *Minority Rights, Majority Rule*; and Schickler, *Disjointed Pluralism*.
3. See Kenneth Shepsle, "The Changing Textbook Congress," in *Can the Government Govern?* edited by John E. Chubb and Paul E. Peterson (Washington, DC: Brookings Institution, 1989).
4. See David W. Rohde, *Parties and Leaders in the Postreform House* (Chicago and London: University of Chicago Press, 1991).
5. *Congressional Record*, February 5, 1908, 1652.
6. See Schickler, *Disjointed Pluralism*, chapter 3, and John Mark Hansen, *Gaining Access: Congress and the Farm Lobby, 1919–1981* (Chicago: University of Chicago Press, 1991).

7. *Congressional Record*, July 25, 1946, 10039.
8. The attack on seniority had mixed effects for party leaders. On the one hand, the leaders bene-fited to the extent that the chairmen now had to be responsive to the party caucus. However, key party leaders such as Democratic Speaker Thomas (Tip) O'Neill generally opposed purging the chairmen. This suggests that party leaders believed that weakening the chairmen would make their job of building coalitions more difficult (see Schickler, *Disjointed Pluralism*).
9. Sarah A. Binder and Steven S. Smith, *Politics or Principle?: Filibustering in the United States Senate* (Washington, DC: Brookings Institution, 1997).
10. Bruce I. Oppenheimer, "Changing Time Constraints on Congress: Historical Perspectives on the Use of Cloture," in *Congress Reconsidered*, edited by Lawrence C. Dodd and Bruce I. Oppenheimer, 3rd ed. (Washington, DC: Congressional Quarterly, 1985).
11. Barbara Sinclair, *The Transformation of the U.S. Senate* (Baltimore: Johns Hopkins University Press, 1989).
12. Barbara Sinclair, "The '60-vote Senate,'" in *U.S. Senate Exceptionalism*, edited by Bruce I. Oppenheimer (Columbus: Ohio State University Press, 2002).
13. Barbara Sinclair, *Legislators, Leaders, and Lawmaking: The U.S. House of Representatives in the Postreform Era* (Baltimore: Johns Hopkins University, 1998).
14. See *CQ Weekly*, January 3, 2004.

REFERENCES

Binder, Sarah A. *Minority Rights, Majority Rule: Partisanship and the Development of Congress* (Cambridge, U.K., and New York: Cambridge University Press, 1997).
Cooper, Joseph. *The Origins of the Standing Committees and the Development of the Modern House* (Houston: Rice University Studies, 1971).
Deering, Christopher J. and Steven S. Smith. *Committees in Congress*. 3rd ed. (Washington, DC: Congressional Quarterly, 1997).
Schickler, Eric. *Disjointed Pluralism: Institutional Innovation and the Development of the U.S. Congress* (Princeton, NJ: Princeton University Press, 2001).
Sinclair, Barbara. *The Transformation of the U.S. Senate* (Baltimore and London: Johns Hopkins University Press, 1989).

9.6 Sarah Binder, "Through the Looking Glass, Darkly: What Has Become of the Senate?" (2011)

Schickler emphasizes the way inherited legislative institutions affect political strategy, and political scientist Sarah Binder focused on the Senate to bring this story up to the present-day period of rancorous political polarization. Senators, bolstered by decentralizing reforms and the candidate-centered campaign, became much more individualistic. These Senators, in turn, were willing to use the filibuster more aggressively to achieve the policy results they personally wanted. Senate leaders more often invoked cloture, a rule that allows a majority of 60 Senators to vote to stop a filibuster. But now, ideological partisans are using the filibuster to stop the majority from acting on a much wider array of issues, and partisans are much more likely to vote together against their opponents. The filibuster contributes greatly to the larger stalemate that plagues the Senate and Congress as a whole. Congress, which the framers viewed as the heart of the new government, today has great difficulty addressing any national problems at all.

Some twenty years ago, Richard F. Fenno, Jr., in "The Senate Through the Looking Glass", offered one of the most illuminating and trenchant perspectives on the state of the contemporary Senate. Fenno adroitly used the Senate's debate over the introduction of television into the chamber to take the pulse of the upper body. As he concluded about the Senate of the late 1980s, "External pressures push it toward individualism, but internal concerns produce a countervailing communitarianism. The Senate is still looking for its place in the current U.S. political system" (Fenno 1989, 346) . . . .

In 1989, Fenno saw a Senate well along in its transition from a communitarian past to an individualist present. The communitarian Senate of the 1950s and 1960s had been an inward-looking, committee-dominated body, in which norms of restraint and reciprocity governed senators' behavior. As Huitt (1961) and Matthews (1973) observed, senators rarely exploited their advantages under the rules, lest they disrupt the small-town norms that were essential for making the chamber of informal practices and lax rules function. As Fenno (1989) noted, filibusters were in order only when senators wanted to signal that "the most intensely held interests were at stake" (316). Typically, that meant filibusters by southern conservatives, as the so-called Conservative Coalition sought to block majorities from adopting measures to advance civil rights.

By the late 1980s, an individualistic Senate had emerged, "markedly less self-contained and more outward-looking than the communitarian one" (Fenno 1989, 317). According to Sinclair (1989), the Senate had been transformed. By the 1970s, an emerging liberal Democratic majority inside the Senate and a newly combustible political environment outside had combined to remake the upper chamber. That transformation was evident in both the distribution of power within the chamber and in the changing procedural nature of the body.

Internal influence came to be distributed far more broadly, as senators became champions for groups and causes outside the institution. As Smith (1989) observed, the focus of legislating moved to the floor, undermining long-dominant, conservative committee chairs and weakening committee grasps on the institution. Indeed, we see the Senate's first modern spike in obstructionism in the mid-1970s (Figure 1). Although the Senate's reliance on cloture in that period looks tame compared to recent years, the onset of individualism in the Senate was fully evident in senators' new-found willingness to exploit the rules of the game to block measures they opposed . . . .

The Contemporary Senate

The Senate Fenno saw through the looking glass is hardly recognizable today. A quick glance at Figure 1 shows the path taken by the Senate over the two decades since Fenno wrote. In the 1980s, Senate leaders attempted cloture roughly 15 times a year; today, that number has doubled. Many other metrics show a similar explosion in leaders' reliance on

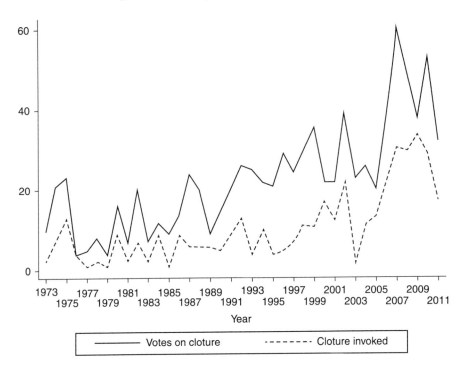

Figure 1 Senate Cloture Trends 1973–2011.

Source: Data compiled by author.

cloture. Steven Smith (2010), for example, records an increase in the percentage of major measures subject to cloture votes over the past forty years—rising from roughly thirty percent when Fenno wrote in the late 1980s to over eighty percent in recent years.

We see the rise as well over this period in leaders' use of cloture, particularly on the motion to proceed, which allows the majority leader to call up bills for consideration on the Senate floor. To be sure, minority leaders have objected to the expanding use of cloture, arguing that majority leaders often file for cloture simply to limit debate and amendments by the minority. In contrast, majority leaders since George Mitchell (D-Maine) in the early 1990s have argued that the move to obstruct measures from coming to the floor—as opposed to launching filibusters only after bills had reached the floor—necessitated more aggressive use of cloture by the majority.

Smith (2010) has aptly captured the contemporary Senate dynamic, dubbing it the "Senate Syndrome":

> In today's Senate, each party assumes that the other party will fully exploit its procedural options—the majority party assumes that the minority party will obstruct legislation and the minority assumes that the majority will restrict its opportunities. Leaders are expected to fully exploit the rules in the interests of their parties. The minority is quick to obstruct and the majority is quick to restrict.

The result has been a parliamentary arms race between the two political parties and their leaders. Whether measured by formal metrics or the informal interactions that take

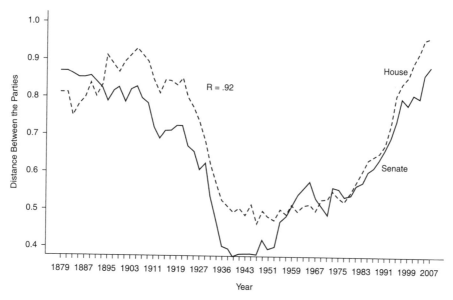

Figure 2 Party Polarization 1879–2008. Distance between Parties First Dimension.

Source: http://www.voteview.com

place between the party leaders on a daily basis, that arms race defines and structures the modern Senate. Both parties expect that the other party will fully exploit its procedural rights, leaving each side to take increasingly aggressive steps that anticipate and attempt to undercut the other party's tactics. Most recently, this anticipatory strategy is seen in majority leaders' willingness to "fill the tree"—to take up available amendment slots with placeholder amendments to prevent the minority from offering amendments to the underlying measure. Coupled with cloture, this maneuver grants majority leaders a modicum of advantage over the minority party—albeit at the expense of the ability of both parties' rank and file to fully debate and amend major bills.

Fenno observed the transformation of a communitarian Senate into a chamber of one hundred senators, each eager to pursue their own policy and political agendas. This second transformation moved the Senate from individualism to a highly partisan legislative body. The key political development over the past two decades that has encouraged this transformation is the increasing polarization of the two major parties in Congress, as mapped by Keith Poole and Howard Rosenthal in Figure 2. Polarization has been underway at least since the early 1980s, when the Democrats' conservative base in the South began voting for Republicans and the GOP's moderate wing in the Northeast all but disappeared from the ranks of Congress. The emergence of polarization reflects increases both in the ideological gap between the two parties and in the exercise of partisan "team play" (Lee 2009).

The parties' disagreements, in short, are both ideological and strategic (Gilmour 1995). To burnish their party's brand name, the parties take opposite positions. As Rep. Jim Jordan (R-Ohio) noted about a House package to extend a payroll tax cut in December of 2011, "The fact that the president doesn't like it makes me like it even more" (Steinhauer and Pear 2011). So long as the two parties each have an opportunity to gain control of government, and so long as party control of government delivers different policy outcomes, each party in Congress has a strategic incentive to disagree with the other party (Fiorina 2006). Unified Republican control under George W. Bush delivered tax cuts opposed by most Democrats; unified Democratic control under Barack Obama delivered healthcare reform opposed by most Republicans. The proceeds of party control create and sustain additional incentives for strategic disagreement even as the parties oppose each other on ideological grounds.

As Smith (2010) has observed, polarization brought significant change to the Senate. Party leaders took on a central role in negotiating major bills, building coalitions for or against those bills, and usurping the role of committee leaders in negotiating agreements with the other chamber. Most importantly, as the parties polarized, rank and file members increasingly coalesced around party positions—meaning that the minority party quite often formed a solid bloc against the majority position on both measures and nominations alike. The impact of rising partisanship is seen clearly in Figure 3, which tracks mean support in the majority party for cloture over the past forty years. In the 1970s, roughly thirty percent of the majority party defected on cloture votes; four decades later, majority party defections dropped to a mere five percent.

Given the Senate's Rule 22 [cloture] that requires sixty votes to overcome debate and given that recent majorities have rarely had sixty within their own party ranks, the polarization of the parties helps to produce stalemate on any controversial issue or

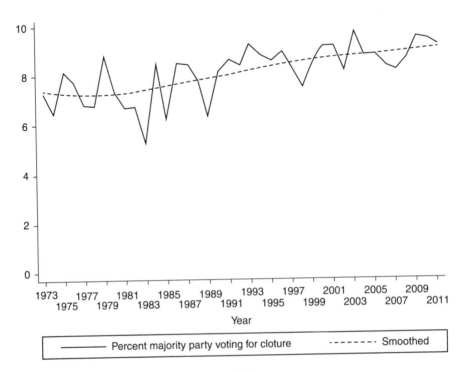

Figure 3 Party Divisions on Cloture Voting, 1973–2011.

Source: Data compiled by author.

nomination the minority chooses to oppose. Sixty votes has become the *de facto* threshold for legislative agreement. The ability of individual senators to place anonymous holds on measures and nominations has only fueled the perception that the Senate is broken—unable to fulfill even its most basic constitutional duty of dispensing advice and consent for the president's appointees.

Efforts amongst Democrats to tighten the rules of debate to make it harder for Republicans to block the majority went largely for naught in January of 2011 (Friel and Lesniewski 2011). Republican capture of the House took the wind out of the sails of many Democratic reform-minded senators and outside liberal groups that had trumpeted reform during Obama's first two years in office, who now saw little need to facilitate Senate action on the House's Tea Party-inspired priorities. No doubt the increased prospects of Republicans gaining control of the Senate in the 2012 elections also diminished enthusiasm amongst Democrats for revising the rules of the Senate.

Instead of formal changes to the Senate's Rule 22, Majority leader Harry Reid (D-Nevada) and Minority leader Mitch McConnell (R-Kentucky) shook hands on an informal agreement for both parties to refrain from fully exploiting the rules in the two congresses to come. Democrats would refrain from filling the amendment tree, and Republicans would refrain from blocking the motion to proceed when the Democrats moved to call up measures to the floor. Moreover, both parties promised not to change Senate rules over the coming four years by "going nuclear"—a tactic through which a majority might attempt to change chamber rules by majority vote (thus circumventing Rule 22's high barrier to cutting off debate on measures to change Senate rules). Few were convinced that this informal agreement could stem the tide of partisanship in the Senate (Friel 2011). And they were right . . . .

Taking Stock of the Senate

With the Senate floor today rarely a venue for true debate or deliberation, legislative deal-making remains in the hands of party leaders. For most major measures, party leaders and their staffs negotiate legislative bargains—which typically come to the Senate floor without opportunity for amendment. Consider, for example, the series of bargains negotiated over the course of 2011: Spending agreements for fiscal years 2011 and 2012, a summer agreement for raising the debt ceiling, and an end of the year deal on extending the payroll tax cut. Had the Joint Committee on Deficit Reduction (otherwise known as the Super Committee) been able to produce a bill under the Budget Control Act in the Fall of 2011, there would have been no surprise that the bill would have been fast-tracked for Senate consideration, without opportunity for amendment or filibuster. Allowing party leaders to negotiate such bargains has made the legislative process on the Hill barely functional. For those matters on which the House plays no role—namely judicial and executive branch nominations—the legislative process has barely worked in recent years. Roughly half of judicial nominees are left in limbo each Congress, with the minority often unwilling to allow votes on even noncontroversial or minor nominees. Other times, the minority has voted lock-step against nominees—whose credentials seemingly made them strong candidates for the bench. The rise of polarized parties has moved legislative deal-making off of the Senate floor and has left the chamber often incapable of completing legislative priorities—even sometimes those with bipartisan support.

When Fenno observed the Senate in the 1980s, he concluded that the body was oscillating somewhere between its communitarian and individualistic modes. External forces pulled the Senate towards individualism, while internal forces could sometimes re-create the communitarian nature of its past. As Fenno concluded, the Senate was "still looking for its place in the current U.S. political system" (Fenno 1989, 346). That uneasy state between individual and institutional obsessions has been derailed over the ensuring two decades by an intense and rising partisanship. Both sides are distrustful of the other's intentions, with each side likely to play tit-for-tat to counter the other's strategic tactics.

In such a Senate, institutional reforms intended to make the Senate work better seem only possible when informally agreed to by a handshake. Still, such informal under-standings in a period of intense ideological and partisan disagreements are fragile, as evidenced by GOP claims that the Democrats had gone nuclear in an effort to shut down the minority and to gain advantage. My sense is that the Senate cannot return to either its communitarian or individualistic past in face of such electorally driven polarization. Although we hear senators on both sides of the aisle share concerns about the degrada-tion of the Senate and its capacity for deliberation, it is hard to fathom how the Senate (at least in the short term) reverses course.

The growth of polarization in the Senate has meant the disappearance of moderates who might have demanded a center-seeking legislative process. Absent a centripetal pull, leaders and their rank and file are free to pursue party-based agendas. And so long as the parties disagree fundamentally about the role of government and plausible solutions to national problems, the legislative process in the Senate is likely to remain dysfunc-tional—particularly in periods of divided party control. The Senate, besieged by its members' and leaders' partisanship, seems barely up to the task of solving vexing national problems, let alone the easy ones.

REFERENCES

Fenno, Richard F., Jr. 1989. "The Senate through the Looking Glass: The Debate over Television," *Legislative Studies Quarterly* 14(3): 313–48.

Fiorina, Morris. 2006. "Parties as Problem Solvers," in Alan S. Gerber and Eric M. Patashnik, eds., *Promoting the General Welfare*. Brookings Institution Press 2006.

Friel, Brian. 2011. "Difficult Tests Ahead for Senate Truce," *CQ Today*, January 28, 2011.

Friel, Brian and Niels Lesniewski, "Senate Adopts Procedural Changes," *CQ Today*, January 27, 2011.

Gilmour, John. 1995. *Strategic Disagreement: Stalemate in American Politics*. University of Pittsburgh Press.

Huitt, Ralph K. 1961. "The Outsider in the Senate: An Alternative Role." *American Political Science Review* 55:566–75.

Lee, Frances. 2009. *Beyond Ideology*. University of Chicago Press 2009.

Matthews, Donald. 1973. *U.S. Senators and Their World*. New York: Norton.

Poole, Keith and Howard Rosenthal. 2010. "Political Polarization in the 110th Congress is the Highest in a 120 Years." http://voteview.com/polarizedamerica.asp#POLITICALPOLARIZATION [Accessed December 18, 2011].

Smith, Steven S. 1989. *Call to Order: Floor Politics in the House and Senate*. Washington, DC: Brookings Institution Press.

Smith, Steven S. 2010. "The Senate Syndrome." http://www.brookings.edu/papers/2010/06_cloture_smith.aspx [Accessed December 18, 2011].

Steinhauer, Jennifer and Robert Pear. 2011. "Republicans Unveil Plans for Payroll Tax." *New York Times*, December 9, 2011. http://www.nytimes.com/2011/12/09/us/politics/house-republicans-unveil-plan-to-extend-payroll-tax-cut.html [Accessed December 18, 2011].

Discussion Questions

1. Does Edmund Burke make a convincing argument that a legislator should decide his vote based on his own reason and judgment, even if that vote is unpopular with his constituents? What rules would you suggest to help a member of Congress decide between his own judgment and his constituents' desires?
2. According to James Madison, what legislative problems does the Senate help prevent? Does the existence of a second house of Congress slow or prevent too much good and necessary legislation? If so, does the Senate do more harm than good, or more good than harm?
3. Ira Katznelson shows that compromise often is essential in Congress even when one party holds a majority. Were the compromises required to get New Deal measures through Congress good or bad for the nation, on the whole? Give both sides.
4. David Mayhew argues that members of the U.S. Congress "are interested in getting reelected" and, in the abstract, "interested in nothing else." What are the costs and benefits for good government if Mayhew is correct? Is this electoral incentive the best way to keep our representatives accountable to the people?
5. How do institutional structure and rules affect the differences in the way the House and Senate work? Would James Madison have been pleased or disappointed with the evolution of the House and Senate?
6. Why are the political parties in Congress so polarized today? Give examples. What can be done to reduce polarization in Congress? What—if anything—should be done?
7. What difference does the path of the development of Congress make for Americans today?

Suggested Additional Reading

Lawrence C. Dodd and Bruce I. Oppenheimer, eds., *Congress Reconsidered*, 10th ed. (Washington, DC: CQ Press, 2012).

Thomas E. Mann and Norman J. Ornstein, *It's Even Worse than It Looks: How the American Constitutional System Collided with the New Politics of Extremism* (New York: Basic Books, 2012).

Eric Schickler, *Disjointed Pluralism: Institutional Innovation and the Development of the U.S. Congress* (Princeton, NJ: Princeton University Press, 2001).

Eric Schickler and Frances E. Lee, eds. *The Oxford Handbook of the American Congress* (Oxford and New York: Oxford University Press, 2011).

Sean M. Theriault, *Party Polarization in Congress* (Cambridge and New York: Cambridge University Press, 2008).

Julian Zelizer, *On Capitol Hill: The Struggle to Reform Congress and its Consequences, 1948–2000* (Cambridge and New York: Cambridge University Press, 2004).

10

The President: Governing in Uncertain Times

Introduction

How much power should a president have? An executive must have the power to protect the citizens of the nation in a crisis. He may have to exceed his authority or violate the letter of the law to do so. A president may have to repel a sudden attack even if Congress cannot act fast enough to authorize his actions. Almost a century before the Constitutional Convention, the British philosopher John Locke acknowledged that a nation's executive needed discretionary power to serve the public good and preserve the nation. Yet there are many examples of kings, presidents and other government leaders around the world who have abused their military and police powers to enrich themselves or amass power over other people. In its indictment of the British monarchy, the Declaration of Independence lists a "long train" of "abuses" (words borrowed directly from Locke) that justified separation from the British state. The Constitutional Convention worried about creating a standing army (see reading 16.1). James Madison later warned that "the fetters imposed on liberty at home have ever been forged out of the weapons provided for defense against real, pretended, or imaginary dangers from abroad . . . there was never a people whose liberties long survived a standing army."[1]

When they designed the U.S. Constitution, Madison and the other framers struggled to find the right balance between congressional control of the president and presidential independence (Gouverneur Morris wrestled with the presidency in reading two). Every question about the design of the presidency raised the fundamental question of the balance of power. Should Congress select the president? Initially, the Convention delegates generally agreed that Congress should choose the president. But, once the Convention actually agreed on the rules for selecting members of Congress, Madison and his allies sought an alternative process of choosing the president that would ensure more presidential independence of the legislature. In the end, the delegates made political compromises to resolve their disagreements about presidential power. The president could veto laws, but Congress could override his veto. Congress could declare war, but the president would conduct it. The president would propose major appointments, but the Senate would confirm them. While Presidential powers, then, were potentially broad, Congress had broad power to rein in the president if it chose to do so.

In the end, the delegates constructed a complex, unfinished set of checks and balances, one that troubled many of the Constitution's opponents. In the *Federalist*, Alexander Hamilton defends the final Constitution against critics who thought it was too dangerous to place presidential power in the hands of a single individual, and who believed that presidents should not be allowed to be reelected to a second term in office.

The development of the American presidency has been shaped from the start by this Constitutional ambivalence about presidential power, by the way presidents have used their office, and by the political opportunities and constraints presidents face over time. Stephen Skowronek argued that presidents "make politics," that is, they use their powers to try either to put their own personal stamp on the political order built by a predecessor, or to construct a new system of enduring political support.[2] By doing so, presidents often stretch the powers of the office itself. No president better illustrates the way presidents make politics than Abraham Lincoln, who became president just as the established political order was collapsing and the nation faced an unprecedented crisis of secession and civil war. In the third reading, Lincoln defended his use of the inherent prerogative powers that Locke described a century and a half earlier.

By the early twentieth century, the nation had changed fundamentally from 1787. The pressure for more activist presidential leadership was irresistible and presidents have learned to expand the powers of the office. Few presidents have reflected about presidential power more thoughtfully than the restless and bold President Theodore Roosevelt. For Roosevelt, presidential power was not limited to specific Constitutional provisions (reading four). Roosevelt believed that the president must be the nation's steward, and must use executive powers to promote the nation's welfare not only in a national security crisis, but in peacetime as well. Beginning with the presidency of Theodore Roosevelt's cousin, Franklin Delano Roosevelt, each president has taken active leadership of the national government's domestic and foreign policy agenda, as well as the leadership of a now vast executive branch.

American politics has adjusted to more activist presidential leadership, but the Constitution's constraints on the president still complicate his ability to make politics and shape policy. Former presidential advisor Richard Neustadt argued that these institutional constraints make the president weaker than he appears. The American system of separated institutions forces the president to exercise power primarily through persuasion and bargaining with other actors, rather than command and control.[3] As the framers expected, Congress and even members of his own cabinet can check the president's ambitions, and force him to compromise to serve their ambitions.

Many American political development scholars point out that the intersection of politics and the office of the presidency has resulted in expanded notions of presidential power over time. A century ago, progressives like Theodore Roosevelt advocated a strong presidential role in political reform and economic management. In our highlight piece, Skowronek showed how the theory of the unitary presidency emerged from the resurgent conservative movement of the last four decades, a movement that drew on progressive era arguments about the president's broad electoral base. Under George W. Bush, these theories flowered. The

hat presidents are the only national officials elected by the nation gives
ilitical authority no other American leader can claim, and allows them
ide to "make politics," particularly through the use of national security
___1's White House forcefully asserted his independence of Congress and
the courts as he executed a worldwide war on terrorism.

Presidents also have steadily increased their efforts to influence domestic policy. In the final reading, Jeffrey Cohen showed that, over time, presidents steadily became more active in sending proposals for Congress to turn into law. While the aspiration to push Congress into action has grown, however, the struggle for activism in a system designed to make cooperation difficult has frustrated presidents of all political stripes.

Notes

1. James Madison, "Political Reflections," *Aurora General Advertiser*, February 23, 1799 [web: http://www.constitution.org/jm/17990223_political.txt; accessed January 25, 2009].
2. Stephen Skowronek, *The Politics Presidents Make: Leadership from John Adams to George W. Bush* (Cambridge, MA: Belknap, 1997).
3. Richard E. Neustadt, *Presidential Power and the Modern Presidents* (New York: Free Press, 1990).

10.1 John Locke, "Of Prerogative" (1690)

As his nation grappled with the problem of limiting the king's prerogatives, the influential British philosopher John Locke addressed a central question of executive power: can an executive act on his own initiative, without the authority of an explicit law or permission from the legislature? Locke argued that the executive unquestionably has this prerogative power when it is used for the common good. If the executive needs to act to preserve society, even laws should "give way" to the nation's leader when he takes the actions necessary to preserve society. The people, after all, would want their leader to use his judgment to protect them. But how do we distinguish between the executive's appropriate use of the prerogative and his abuse of this power for selfish purposes? The laws of nature do not allow humans to submit themselves to such a leader, so they may "Appeal to Heaven," that is, they have the right to rebel against a leader who abuses his prerogative. For Locke, this situation was a real experience, not a theoretical possibility. Locke supported the "Glorious Revolution" of 1688 that removed England's King James II and replaced him with new monarchs. The authors of the U.S. Declaration of Independence used this reasoning, "appealing to the Supreme Judge of the world for the rectitude of our intentions" and asserting that their colonies were "Absolved from all Allegiance to the British Crown . . ."

Where the Legislative and Executive Power are in distinct hands, (as they are in all moderated Monarchies, and well-framed Governments) there the good of the Society requires, that several things should be left to the discretion of him, that has the Executive Power. For the Legislators not being able to foresee, and provide, by Laws, for all, that may be useful to the Community, the Executor of the Laws, having the power in his hands, has by the common Law of Nature, a right to make use of it, for the good of the Society, in many Cases, where the municipal Law has given no direction, till the Legislative can conveniently be Assembled to provide for it. Many things there are, which the Law can by no means provide for, and those must necessarily be left to the discretion of him, that has the Executive Power in his hands, to be ordered by him, as the publick good and advantage shall require: nay, 'tis fit that the Laws themselves should in some Cases give way to the Executive Power, or rather to this Fundamental Law of Nature and Government, *viz.* That as much as may be, *all* the Members of the Society are to be *preserved*. For since many accidents may happen, wherein a strict and rigid observation of the Laws may do harm; (as not to pull down an innocent Man's House to stop the Fire, when the next to it is burning) and a Man may come sometimes within the reach of the Law, which makes no distinction of Persons, by an action, that may deserve reward and pardon; 'tis fit, the Ruler should have a Power, in many Cases, to mitigate the severity of the Law, and pardon some Offenders: For the *end of Government* being the *preservation of all*, as much as may be, even the guilty are to be spared, where it can prove no prejudice to the innocent.

This Power to act according to discretion, for the publick good, without the prescription of the Law, and sometimes even against it, *is* that which is called *Prerogative*. For since in some Governments the Law-making Power is not always in being, and is usually too numerous, and so too slow, for the dispatch requisite to Execution: and because also it is impossible to foresee, and so by laws to provide for, all Accidents and Necessities, that may concern the publick; or to make such Laws, as will do no harm, if they are Executed with an inflexible rigour, on all occasions, and upon all Persons, that may come in their way, therefore there is a latitude left to the Executive power, to do many things of choice, which the Laws do not prescribe.

This power whilst imployed for the benefit of the Community, and suitably to the trust and ends of the Government, *is undoubted Prerogative*, and never is questioned. For the People are very seldom, or never scrupulous, or nice in the point: they are far from examining *Prerogative*, whilst it is in any tolerable degree imploy'd for the use it was meant; that is, for the good of the People, and not manifestly against it. But if there comes to be a *question* between the Executive Power and the People, *about* a thing claimed as a *Prerogative*; the tendency of the exercise of such *Prerogative* to the good or hurt of the People, will easily decide that Question.

It is easie to conceive, that in the Infancy of Governments, when Commonwealths differed little from Families in number of People, they differ'd from them too but little in number of Laws: And the Governours, being as the Fathers of them, watching over them for their good, the Government was almost all *Prerogative*. A few establish'd Laws served the turn, and the discretion and care of the Ruler supply'd the rest. But when mistake, or flattery prevailed with weak Princes to make use of this Power, for private ends of their own, and not for the publick good, the People were fain by express Laws to get Prerogative determin'd, in those points, wherein they found disadvantage from it: And thus declared *limitations of Prerogative* were by the People found necessary in Cases, which they and their Ancestors had left, in the utmost latitude, to the Wisdom of those Princes, who made no other but a right use of it, that is, for the good of their People.

And therefore they have a very wrong Notion of Government, who say, that the People have *incroach'd upon the Prerogative*, when they have got any part of it to be defined by positive Laws. For in so doing, they have not pulled from the Prince any thing, that of right belong'd to him, but only declared, that that Power which they indefinitely left in his, or his Ancestors, hands, to be exercised for their good, was not a thing, which they intended him, when he used it otherwise. For the end of government being the good of the Community, whatsoever alterations are made in it, tending to that end, cannot be an *incroachment* upon any body: since no body in Government can have a right tending to any other end. And those only are *incroachments* which prejudice or hinder the publick good. Those who say otherwise, speak as if the Prince had a distinct and separate Interest from the good of the Community, and was not made for it, the Root and Source, from which spring almost all those Evils, and Disorders, which happen in Kingly Governments. And indeed if that be so, the People under his Government are not a Society of Rational Creatures [entered] into a Community for their mutual good; they are not such as have set Rulers over themselves, to guard, and promote that good; but are to be looked on as an Herd of inferiour Creatures, under the Dominion of a Master, who keeps them, and works them for his own Pleasure or Profit. If Men were so void of Reason, and brutish, as to enter into Society upon such Terms, *Prerogative* might indeed be, what some Men would have it, an Arbitrary Power to do things hurtful to the People.

But since a Rational Creature cannot be supposed when free, to put himself into Subjection to another, for his own harm: (Though where he finds a good and wise Ruler, he may not perhaps think it either necessary, or useful to set precise Bounds to his Power in all things) *Prerogative* can be nothing, but the Peoples permitting their Rulers, to do several things of their own free choice, where the Law was silent, and sometimes too against the direct Letter of the Law, for the publick good; and their acquiescing in it when so done. For as a good Prince, who is mindful of the trust put into his hands, and careful of the good of his People, cannot have too much *Prerogative*, that is, Power to do good: So a weak and ill Prince, who would claim that Power, which his Predecessors exercised without the direction of the Law, as a Prerogative belonging to him by Right of his Office, which he may exercise at his pleasure, to make or promote an Interest distinct from that of the publick, gives the People an occasion, to claim their Right, and limit that Power, which, whilst it was exercised for their good, they were content should be tacitly allowed.

 . . . The old Question will be asked in this matter of *Prerogative*, But *who shall be Judge* when this Power is made a right use of? I Answer: Between an Executive Power in being, with such a Prerogative, and a Legislative that depends upon his will for their convening, there can be no *Judge on Earth*: As there can be none, between the Legislative, and the People, should either the Executive, or the Legislative, when they have got the Power in their hands, design, or go about to enslave, or destroy them. The People have no other remedy in this, as in all other cases where they have no Judge on Earth, but to *appeal to Heaven*. For the Rulers, in such attempts, exercising a Power the People never put into their hands (who can never be supposed to consent, that any body should rule over them for their harm) do that, which they have not a right to do. And where the Body of the People, or any single Man, is deprived of their Right, or is under the Exercise of a power without right, and have no Appeal on Earth, there they have a liberty to appeal to Heaven, whenever they judge the Cause of sufficient moment. And therefore, tho' the *People* cannot be *Judge*, so as to have by the Constitution of that Society any Superiour power, to determine and give effective Sentence in the case; yet they have, by a Law antecedent and paramount to all positive Laws of men, reserv'd that ultimate Determination to themselves, which belongs to all Mankind, where there lies no Appeal on Earth, *viz.* to judge whether they have just Cause to make their Appeal to Heaven. And this Judgment they cannot part with, it being out of a Man's power so to submit himself to another, as to give him a liberty to destroy him; God and Nature never allowing a Man so to abandon himself, as to neglect his own preservation: And since he cannot take away his own Life, neither can he give another power to take it. Nor let any one think, this lays a perpetual foundation for Disorder: for this operates not, till the Inconvenience is so great, that the Majority feel it, and are weary of it, and find a necessity to have it amended. But this the Executive Power, or wise Princes, never need come in the danger of: And 'tis the thing of all others, they have most need to avoid, as of all others the most perilous.

10.2 The Framers and the Presidency (1787–1788)

Gouverneur Morris on "Executive Power" in Constitutional Convention Debates (1787)

By 1787, many of the designers of the new American Constitution were more worried about congressional abuse of power than presidential power. In the middle of the Constitutional Convention, the delegates had tentatively agreed that Congress would appoint the president and could remove him through the impeachment process. Gouverneur Morris, a delegate from Pennsylvania, supported a strong national executive with the power to protect the people from the legislature. He ardently opposed allowing Congress to choose the president, and, at first, he even resisted Congress's power to impeach the president. In this series of speeches, Morris came around to the idea of impeachment, but continued to resist congressional appointment. In the process of explaining his view, he also described how difficult it is for the Convention to determine exactly how much power the president should have.

July 19

Mr. Gouverneur Morris. It is necessary to take into one view all that relates to the establishment of the Executive; on the due formation of which must depend the efficacy & utility of the Union among the present and future States. It has been a maxim in political Science that Republican Government is not adapted to a large extent of Country, because the energy of the Executive Magistracy can not reach the extreme parts of it. Our Country is an extensive one. We must either then renounce the blessings of the Union, or provide an Executive with sufficient vigor to pervade every part of it. This subject was of so much importance that he hoped to be indulged in an extensive view of it. One great object of the Executive is to controul the Legislature. The Legislature will continually seek to aggrandize & perpetuate themselves; and will seize those critical moments produced by war, invasion or convulsion for that purpose. It is necessary then that the Executive Magistrate should be the guardian of the people, even of the lower classes, ag[ain]st Legislative tyranny, against the Great & the wealthy who in the course of things will necessarily compose—the Legislative body.

. . . The Executive therefore ought to be so constituted as to be the great protector of the Mass of the people.—It is the duty of the Executive to appoint the officers & to command the forces of the Republic: to appoint 1. ministerial officers for the administration of public affairs. 2. Officers for the dispensation of Justice—Who will be the best Judges whether these appointments be well made? The people at large, who will know, will see, will feel the effects of them—Again who can judge so well of the discharge of military duties for the protection & security of the people, as the people themselves who are to be protected & secured? He finds too that the Executive is not to be re-eligible [that, will be limited to only one term in office]. What effect will this have? 1. it will destroy the great incitement to merit public esteem by taking away the hope of being rewarded with a reappointment. It may give a dangerous turn to one of the strongest passions in the human breast. The love of fame is the great spring to noble & illustrious actions. Shut the Civil road to Glory & he may be compelled to seek it by the sword. 2. It will tempt him to make the most of the Short space of time allotted him, to accumulate wealth and provide for his friends. 3. It will produce violations of the very constitution it is meant to secure. In moments of pressing danger the tried abilities and established character of a favorite Magistrate will prevail over respect for the forms of the Constitution. The Executive is also to be impeachable. This is a dangerous part of the plan. It will hold him in such dependence that he will be no check on the Legislature, will not be a firm guardian of the people and of the public interest. He will be the tool of a faction, of some leading demagogue in the Legislature. These then are the faults of the Executive establishment as now proposed. Can no better establishm[en]t be devised? If he is to be the Guardian of the people let him be appointed by the people? If he is to be a check on the Legislature let him not be impeachable . . .

July 20

Mr. Govr. Morris's opinion had been changed by the arguments used in the discussion [of executive impeachment]. He was now sensible of the necessity of impeachments, if the Executive was to continue for any time in office. Our Executive was not like a Magistrate having a life interest, much less like one having an hereditary interest in his office. He may be bribed by a greater interest to betray his trust; and no one would say that we ought to expose ourselves to the danger of seeing the first Magistrate in foreign pay without being able to guard ag[ain]st it by displacing him . . . The Executive ought therefore to be impeachable for treachery; Corrupting his electors, and incapacity were other causes of impeachment. For the latter he should be punished not as a man, but as an officer, and punished only by degradation from his office. This Magistrate is not the King but the prime-Minister. The people are the King. When we make him amenable to Justice however we should take care to provide some mode that will not make him dependent on the Legislature.

July 24

Mr. Govr. Morris. Of all possible modes of appointment [of the executive] that by the Legislature is the worst. If the Legislature is to appoint, and to impeach or to influence the impeachment, the Executive will be the mere creature of it. He had been opposed to the impeachment, but was now convinced that impeachments must be provided for, if the app[ointment]t was to be of any duration. No man w[oul]d say, that an Executive known to be in the pay of an Enemy, should not be removable in some way or other. He had been charged heretofore (by Col[onel George] Mason) with inconsistency in pleading for confidence in the Legislature on some occasions, & urging a distrust on others. The charge was not well founded. The Legislature is worthy of unbounded confidence in some respects, and liable to equal distrust in others. When their interest coincides precisely with that of their Constituents, as happens in many of their Acts, no abuse of trust is to be apprehended. When a strong personal interest happens to be opposed to the general interest, the Legislature can not be too much distrusted.

In all public bodies there are two parties. The Executive will necessarily be more connected with one than with the other. There will be a personal interest therefore in one of the parties to oppose as well as in the other to support him. Much had been said of the intrigues that will be practiced by the Executive to get into office. Nothing had been said on the other side of the intrigues to get him out of office. Some leader of party will always covet his seat, will perplex his administration, will cabal with the Legislature, till he succeeds in supplanting him . . .

Our President will be the British [Prime] Minister, yet we are about to make him appointable by the Legislature. Something had been said of the danger of Monarchy—If a good government should not now be formed, if a good organization of the Execu[ti]ve should not be provided, he doubted whether we should not have something worse than a limited Monarchy. In order to get rid of the dependence of the Executive on the Legislature, the expedient of making him ineligible a 2d. time had been devised. This was as much as to say we sh[oul]d give him the benefit of experience, and then deprive ourselves of the use of it. But make him ineligible a 2nd time—and prolong his duration even to 15-years, will he by any wonderful interposition of providence at that period cease to be a man? No he will be unwilling to quit his exaltation, the road to his object thro' the Constitution will be shut; he will be in possession of the sword, a civil war will ensue, and the Commander of the victorious army on which ever side, will be the despot of America. This consideration renders him particularly anxious that the Executive should be properly constituted. The vice here would not, as in some other parts of the system be curable—It is the most difficult of all rightly to balance the Executive. Make him too weak: The Legislature will usurp his powers: Make him too strong. He will usurp on the Legislature. He preferred a short period, a re-eligibility, but a different mode of election. A long period would prevent an adoption of the [Constitution]: it ought to do so. He sh[oul]d himself be afraid to trust it. . . .

Federalist Papers 70 and 72 (1788)

During the ratification debate, some of the Constitution's critics were deeply concerned about the power of the president. Some disparaged the idea of a single person as president (as opposed to a collective presidency of three people, one from each region of the county). Some thought the president's term was too long, or that the president's powers were too extensive. In the *Federalist*, Alexander Hamilton defended the presidential provisions in the Constitution. Republican government, explained Hamilton, requires "energy in the executive" for exactly the reasons Locke gave: the need to protect the people and preserve society. An executive made up of more than one person would invite divisions, weaken presidential authority, make it very difficult for the office to fulfill its role, and, worst, make it hard to hold the president accountable for his actions. In *Federalist 72*, Hamilton argued that the president's four-year term would help ensure stability (a virtue that Madison also saw in the Senate, in reading 9.2). If the president is changed too frequently, national government and policy will be too unstable for the nation's long-term good. Hamilton also made a central point about the process of political development, a point emphasized by political scientist Stephen Skowronek. Every new leader seeks change. Each new president will have an incentive to distance himself from the policies he inherits, to change the direction of policy and administration. Though Hamilton did not put it this way, we can expect each president to try to change politics and to alter the path of American political development.

The Federalist No. 70

Alexander Hamilton

March 15, 1788

To the People of the State of New York.

There is an idea, which is not without its advocates, that a vigorous executive is inconsistent with the genius of republican government. The enlightened well wishers to this species of government must at least hope that the supposition is destitute of foundation; since they can never admit its truth, without at the same time admitting the condemnation of their own principles. Energy in the executive is a leading character in the definition of good government. It is essential to the protection of the community against foreign attacks: It is not less essential to the steady administration of the laws, to the protection of property against those irregular and high handed combinations, which sometimes interrupt the ordinary course of justice, to the security of liberty against the enterprises and assaults of ambition, of faction and of anarchy.

... A feeble executive implies a feeble execution of the government. A feeble execution is but another phrase for a bad execution: And a government ill executed, whatever it may be in theory, must be in practice a bad government.

Taking it for granted, therefore, that all men of sense will agree in the necessity of an energetic executive; it will only remain to inquire, what are the ingredients which constitute this energy—how far can they be combined with those other ingredients which constitute safety in the republican sense? And how far does this combination characterise the plan, which has been reported by the convention?

The ingredients, which constitute energy in the executive, are first unity, secondly duration, thirdly an adequate provision for its support, fourthly competent powers.

The circumstances which constitute safety in the republican sense are, 1st. a due dependence on the people, secondly a due responsibility.

... That unity is conducive to energy will not be disputed. Decision, activity, secrecy, and dispatch will generally characterise the proceedings of one man, in a much more eminent degree, than the proceedings of any greater number; and in proportion as the number is increased, these qualities will be diminished.

This unity may be destroyed in two ways; either by vesting the power in two or more magistrates of equal dignity and authority; or by vesting it ostensibly in one man, subject in whole or in part to the controul and co-operation of others, in the capacity of counsellors to him....

... Wherever two or more persons are engaged in any common enterprize or pursuit, there is always danger of difference of opinion. If it be a public trust or office in which they are cloathed with equal dignity and authority, there is peculiar danger of personal emulation and even animosity. From either and especially from all these causes, the most bitter dissentions are apt to spring. Whenever these happen, they lessen the respectability, weaken the authority, and distract the plans and operations of those whom they divide. If they should unfortunately assail the supreme executive magistracy of a country, consisting of a plurality of persons, they might impede or frustrate the most important measures of the government, in the most critical emergencies of the state.

And what is still worse, they might split the community into the most violent and irreconcilable factions, adhering differently to the different individuals who composed the magistracy.

... But one of the weightiest objections to a plurality in the executive ... is that it tends to conceal faults, and destroy responsibility. Responsibility is of two kinds, to censure and to punishment. The first is the most important of the two; especially in an elective office. Man, in public trust, will much oftener act in such a manner as to render him unworthy of being any longer trusted, than in such a manner as to make him obnoxious to legal punishment. But the multiplication of the executive adds to the difficulty of detection in either case. It often becomes impossible, amidst mutual accusations, to determine on whom the blame or the punishment of a pernicious measure, or series of pernicious measures ought really to fall. It is shifted from one to another with so much dexterity, and under such plausible appearances, that the public opinion is left in suspense about the real author. The circumstances which may have led to any national miscarriage or misfortune are sometimes so complicated, that where there are a number of actors who may have had different degrees and kinds of agency, though we may clearly see upon the whole that there has been mismanagement, yet it may be impracticable to pronounce to whose account the evil which may have been incurred is truly chargeable.

"I was overruled by my council. The council were so divided in their opinions, that it was impossible to obtain any better resolution on the point." These and similar pretexts are constantly at hand, whether true or false. And who is there that will either take the trouble or incur the odium of a strict scrutiny into the secret springs of the transaction? Should there be found a citizen zealous enough to undertake the unpromising task, if there happen to be a collusion between the parties concerned, how easy is it to cloath the circumstances with so much ambiguity, as to render it uncertain what was the precise conduct of any of those parties?

...It is evident from these considerations, that the plurality of the executive tends to deprive the people of the two greatest securities they can have for the faithful exercise of any delegated power; first, the restraints of public opinion, which lose their efficacy as well on account of the division of the censure attendant on bad measures among a number, as on account of the uncertainty on whom it ought to fall; and secondly, the opportunity of discovering with facility and clearness the misconduct of the persons they trust, in order either to their removal from office, or to their actual punishment, in cases which admit of it.

PUBLIUS.

The Federalist No. 72

Alexander Hamilton

March 19, 1788

To the People of the State of New York.
... This view of the subject will at once suggest to us the intimate connection between the duration of the executive magistrate in office, and the stability of the system of administration. To reverse and undo what has been done by a predecessor is very often considered by a successor, as the best proof he can give of his own capacity and desert; and, in addition to this propensity, where the alteration has been the result of public choice, the person substituted is warranted in supposing, that the dismission of his predecessor has proceeded from a dislike to his measures, and that the less he resembles him the more he will recommend himself to the favor of his constituents. These considerations, and the influence of personal confidences and attachments, would be likely to induce every new president to promote a change of men to fill the subordinate stations; and these causes together could not fail to occasion a disgraceful and ruinous mutability in the administration of the government. ...

PUBLIUS

10.3 Abraham Lincoln, "On Suspension of Habeas Corpus" (1861)

For President Abraham Lincoln, the prerogative power was a real, immediate and practical problem. When he was inaugurated in March of 1861, several states had seceded from the union. Congress was not scheduled to convene until December, and could not authorize him to act. Lincoln took forceful action on his own. Without congressional approval, Lincoln reinforced Fort Sumter in South Carolina, called for army recruits to quash the rebellion, blockaded southern ports, and suspended *habeas corpus* in some parts of the country. The Constitution explicitly protected the right of *habeas corpus* (an individual's right not to be held in custody unlawfully) "unless when in cases of rebellion or invasion the public safety may require it." In 1863, federal troops seized Congressman Clement Vallandigham, a very vocal supporter of states' rights and opponent of the Lincoln administration. Vallandigham was tried in a military court and denied *habeas corpus*. Erastus Corning, a wealthy entrepreneur, joined in a letter to Lincoln complaining that the military tribunal's actions violated American freedoms and "strikes a fatal blow at the supremacy of law, and the authority of the State and Federal constitutions."[1] Lincoln answered this accusation in this landmark letter. Lincoln defended the president's prerogative power in a time of crisis, and denied that he used these powers in a way that threatened basic American freedoms.

Note

1. Frank J. Williams, "When Albany Challenged the President," *New York Archives* 8:3 (Winter 2009), 31–36, http://www.archives.nysed.gov/apt/magazine/archivesmag_winter09_Williams.pdf (accessed May 18, 2013).

June 12, 1863
Executive Mansion, Washington
Gentlemen:

Your letter of May 19th. inclosing the resolutions of a public meeting held at Albany, N.Y. on the 16th. of the same month, was received several days ago.

The resolutions, as I understand them, are resolvable into two propositions—first, the expression of a purpose to sustain the cause of the Union, to secure peace through victory, and to support the administration in every constitutional, and lawful measure to suppress the rebellion; and secondly, a declaration of censure upon the administration for supposed unconstitutional action such as the making of military arrests.

. . . The resolutions promise to support me in every constitutional and lawful measure to suppress the rebellion; and I have not knowingly employed, nor shall knowingly employ, any other. But the meeting, by their resolutions, assert and argue, that certain military arrests and proceedings following them for which I am ultimately responsible, are unconstitutional. I think they are not. The resolutions quote from the constitution, the definition of treason; and also the limiting safeguards and guarantees therein provided for the citizen, on trials for treason, and on his being held to answer for capital or otherwise infamous crimes, and, in criminal prosecutions, his right to a speedy and public trial by an impartial jury. They proceed to resolve "That these safe-guards of the rights of the citizen against the pretensions of arbitrary power, were intended more especially for his protection in times of civil commotion." And, apparently, to demonstrate the proposition, the resolutions proceed "They were secured substantially to the English people, after years of protracted civil war, and were adopted into our constitution at the close of the revolution." Would not the demonstration have been better, if it could have been truly said that these safe-guards had been adopted, and applied during the civil wars and during our revolution, instead of after the one, and at the close of the other. I too am devotedly for them after civil war, and before civil war, and at all times "except when, in cases of Rebellion or Invasion, the public Safety may require" their suspension. The resolutions proceed to tell us that these safe-guards "have stood the test of seventy-six years of trial, under our republican system, under circumstances which show that while they constitute the foundation of all free government, they are the elements of the enduring stability of the Republic." No one denies that they have so stood the test up to the beginning of the present rebellion if we except a certain matter [occurrence] at New Orleans hereafter to be mentioned; nor does any one question that they will stand the same test much longer after the rebellion closes. But these provisions of the constitution have no application to the case we have in hand, because the arrests complained of were not made for treason—that is, not for the treason defined in the constitution, and upon the conviction of which, the punishment is death—nor yet were they made to hold persons to answer for any capital, or otherwise infamous crimes; nor were the proceedings following, in any constitutional or legal sense, "criminal prosecutions." The arrests were made on totally different grounds, and the proceedings following, accorded with the grounds of the arrests. Let us consider the real case with which we are dealing, and apply to it the parts of the constitution plainly made for such cases.

Prior to my installation here it had been inculcated that any State had a lawful right to secede from the national Union; and that it would be expedient to exercise the right, whenever the devotees of the doctrine should fail to elect a President to their own liking. I was elected contrary to their liking; and accordingly, so far as it was legally possible, they had taken seven states out of the Union, had seized many of the United States Forts, and had fired upon the United States' Flag, all before I was inaugurated; and, of course, before I had done any official act whatever. The rebellion, thus began soon ran into the present civil war; and, in certain respects, it began on very unequal terms between the parties. The insurgents had been preparing for it more than thirty years, while the government had taken no steps to resist them. The former had carefully considered all the means which could be turned to their account. It undoubtedly was a well pondered reliance with them that in their own unrestricted effort to destroy Union, constitution, and law, all together, the government would, in great degree, be restrained by the same constitution and law, from arresting their progress. Their sympathizers pervaded all departments of the government, and nearly all communities of the people. From this material, under cover of "Liberty of speech" "Liberty of the press" and "Habeas corpus" they hoped to keep on foot amongst us a most efficient corps of spies, informers, suppliers, and aiders and abettors of their cause in a thousand ways. They knew that in times such as they were inaugurating, by the constitution itself, the "Habeas corpus" might be suspended; but they also knew they had friends who would make a question as to who was to suspend it; meanwhile their spies and others might remain at large to help on their cause. Or if, as has happened, the executive should suspend the writ, without ruinous waste of time, instances of arresting innocent persons might occur, as are always likely to occur in such cases; and then a clamor could be raised in regard to this, which might be, at least, of some service to the insurgent cause. It needed no very keen perception to discover this part of the enemies' programme, so soon as by open hostilities their machinery was fairly put in motion. Yet, thoroughly imbued with a reverence for the guaranteed rights of individuals, I was slow to adopt the strong measures, which by degrees I have been forced to regard as being within the exceptions of the constitution, and as indispensable to the public Safety.

Nothing is better known to history than that courts of justice are utterly incompetent to such cases. Civil courts are organized chiefly for trials of individuals, or, at most, a few individuals acting in concert; and this in quiet times, and on charges of crimes well defined in the law. Even in times of peace, bands of horsethieves and robbers frequently grow too numerous and powerful for the ordinary courts of justice. But what comparison, in numbers, have such bands ever borne to the insurgent sympathizers even in many of the loyal states? Again, a jury too frequently have at least one member, more ready to hang the panel than to hang the traitor. And yet again, he who dissuades one man from volunteering, or induces one soldier to desert, weakens the Union cause as much as he who kills a union soldier in battle. Yet this dissuasion, or inducement, may be so conducted as to be no defined crime of which any civil court would take cognizance.

Ours is a case of Rebellion—so called by the resolutions before me—in fact, a clear, flagrant, and gigantic case of Rebellion; and the provision of the constitution that "The privilege of the writ of Habeas Corpus shall not be suspended, unless when in cases of Rebellion or Invasion, the public Safety may require it" is the provision which specially applies to our present case. This provision plainly attests the understanding of those who made the constitution that ordinary courts of justice are inadequate to "cases of Rebellion"—attests their purpose that in such cases, men may be held in custody whom the courts acting on ordinary rules, would discharge. Habeas Corpus, does not discharge men who are proved to be guilty of defined crime; and its suspension is allowed by the constitution on purpose that, men may be arrested and held, who can not be proved to be guilty of defined crime, "when, in cases of Rebellion or Invasion the public Safety may require it." This is precisely our present case—a case of Rebellion, wherein the public Safety does require the suspension. Indeed, arrests by process of courts, and arrests in cases of rebellion, do not proceed altogether upon the same basis. The former is directed at the small percentage of ordinary and continuous perpetration of crime; while the latter is directed at sudden and extensive uprisings against the government, which, at most, will succeed or fail, in no great length of time. In the latter case, arrests are made, not so much for what has been done, as for what probably would be done. The latter is more for the preventive, and less for the vindictive, than the former. In such cases the purposes of men are much more easily understood, than in cases of ordinary crime. The man who stands by and says nothing, when the peril of his government is discussed, can not be misunderstood. If not hindered, he is sure to help the enemy. Much more, if he talks ambiguously—talks for his country with "buts" and "ifs" and "ands." . . . I think the time not unlikely to come when I shall be blamed for having made too few arrests rather than too many.

. . . Long experience has shown that armies can not be maintained unless desertion shall be punished by the severe penalty of death. The case requires, and the law and the constitution, sanction this punishment. Must I shoot a simple-minded soldier boy who deserts, while I must not touch a hair of a wiley agitator who induces him to desert? This is none the less injurious when effected by getting a father, or brother, or friend, into a public meeting, and there working upon his feeling, till he is persuaded to write the soldier boy, that he is fighting in a bad cause, for a wicked administration of a contemptible government, too weak to arrest and punish him if he shall desert. I think that in such a case, to silence the agitator, and save the boy, is not only constitutional, but, withal, a great mercy.

If I be wrong on this question of constitutional power, my error lies in believing that certain proceedings are constitutional when, in cases of rebellion or Invasion, the public Safety requires them, which would not be constitutional when, in absence of rebellion or invasion, the public Safety does not require them—in other words, that the constitution is not in it's application in all respects the same, in cases of Rebellion or invasion, involving the public Safety, as it is in times of profound peace and public security. The constitution itself makes the distinction; and I can no more be persuaded that the government can constitutionally take no strong measure in time of rebellion, because it can be shown that the same could not be lawfully taken in time of peace, than I can be persuaded that a particular drug is not good medicine for a sick man, because it can be shown to not be good food for a well one. Nor am I able to appreciate the danger, apprehended by the meeting, that the American people will, by means of military arrests during the rebellion, lose the right of public discussion, the liberty of speech and the press, the law of evidence, trial by jury, and Habeas corpus, throughout the indefinite peaceful future which I trust lies before them, any more than I am able to believe that a man could contract so strong an appetite for emetics during temporary illness, as to persist in feeding upon them through the remainder of his healthful life....

A. LINCOLN

10.4 Theodore Roosevelt, "Immediate and Vigorous Executive Action" (1909)

Soon after he left the White House in 1909, President Theodore Roosevelt wrote an autobiography that included his view of a vigorous presidency. An energetic, young president, Roosevelt emphasized the need for a view of the presidency elastic enough to lead the nation when its power and its government were growing. The president is a steward of the people, Roosevelt insisted, and is duty bound "to do anything that the needs of the nation demanded" unless forbidden by the Constitution. Presidents such as Andrew Jackson and Abraham Lincoln stretched presidential powers in this way, viewing the Constitution not just as limitation but also a warrant to use presidential power to the extent possible. Roosevelt contrasted this view to the idea that presidential power is strictly limited, a view held by most of Roosevelt's predecessors and by his successor, William Howard Taft. Most presidents since the 1930s have agreed with Roosevelt's expansive view of presidential power.

... My view was that every executive officer, and above all every executive officer in high position, was a steward of the people bound actively and affirmatively to do all he could for the people, and not to content himself with the negative merit of keeping his talents undamaged in a napkin. I declined to adopt the view that what was imperatively necessary for the nation could not be done by the President unless he could find some specific authorization to do it. My belief was that it was not only his right but his duty to do anything that the needs of the nation demanded unless such action was forbidden by the Constitution or by the laws. Under this interpretation of executive power I did and caused to be done many things not previously done by the President and the heads of the departments. I did not usurp power, but I did greatly broaden the use of executive power. In other words, I acted for the public welfare, I acted for the common well-being of all our people, whenever and in whatever manner was necessary, unless prevented by direct constitutional or legislative prohibition. . . .

The course I followed, of regarding the Executive as subject only to the people, and, under the Constitution, bound to serve the people affirmatively in cases where the Constitution does not explicitly forbid him to render the service, was substantially the course followed by both Andrew Jackson and Abraham Lincoln. Other honorable and well-meaning Presidents, such as James Buchanan, took the opposite and, as it seems to me, narrowly legalistic view that the President is the servant of Congress rather than of the people, and can do nothing, no matter how necessary it be to act, unless the Constitution explicitly commands the action. Most able lawyers who are past middle age take this view, and so do large numbers of well-meaning, respectable citizens. My successor in office took this, the Buchanan, view of the President's powers and duties.

For example, under my administration we found that one of the favorite methods adopted by the men desirous of stealing the public domain was to carry the decision of the secretary of the interior into court. By vigorously opposing such action, and only by so doing, we were able to carry out the policy of properly protecting the public domain. My successor not only took the opposite view, but recommended to Congress the passage of a bill which would have given the courts direct appellate power over the secretary of the interior in these land matters. . . . Fortunately, Congress declined to pass the bill. Its passage would have been a veritable calamity.

I acted on the theory that the President could at any time in his discretion withdraw from entry any of the public lands of the United States and reserve the same for forestry, for water-power sites, for irrigation, and other public purposes. Without such action it would have been impossible to stop the activity of the land-thieves. No one ventured to test its legality by lawsuit. My successor, however, himself questioned it, and referred the matter to Congress. Again Congress showed its wisdom by passing a law which gave the President the power which he had long exercised, and of which my successor had shorn himself.

Perhaps the sharp difference between what may be called the Lincoln-Jackson and the Buchanan-Taft schools, in their views of the power and duties of the President, may be best illustrated by comparing the attitude of my successor toward his Secretary of the Interior, Mr. Ballinger, when the latter was accused of gross misconduct in office, with my attitude toward my chiefs of department and other subordinate officers. More than once while I was President my officials were attacked by Congress, generally because these officials did their duty well and fearlessly. In every such case I stood by the official and refused to recognize the right of Congress to interfere with me excepting by impeachment or in other constitutional manner. On the other hand, wherever I found the officer unfit for his position, I promptly removed him, even although the most influential men in Congress fought for his retention. The Jackson-Lincoln view is that a President who is fit to do good work should be able to form his own judgment as to his own subordinates, and, above all, of the subordinates standing highest and in closest and most intimate touch with him. My secretaries and their subordinates were responsible to me, and I accepted the responsibility for all their deeds. As long as they were satisfactory to me I stood by them against every critic or assailant, within or without Congress; and as for getting Congress to make up my mind for me about them, the thought would have been inconceivable to me. My successor took the opposite, or Buchanan, view when he permitted and requested Congress to pass judgment on the charges made against Mr. Ballinger as an executive officer. These charges were made to the President; the President had the facts before him and could get at them at any time, and he alone had power to act if the charges were true. However, he permitted and requested Congress to investigate Mr. Ballinger. The party minority of the committee that investigated him, and one member of the majority, declared that the charges were well-founded and that Mr. Ballinger should be removed. The other members of the majority declared the charges ill-founded. The President abode by the view of the majority. Of course believers in the Jackson-Lincoln theory of the presidency would not be content with this town-meeting majority and minority method of determining by another branch of the government what it seems the especial duty of the President himself to determine for himself in dealing with his own subordinate in his own department . . .

10.5 Stephen Skowronek, "The Conservative Insurgency and Presidential Power: A Developmental Perspective on the Unitary Executive" (2009)

In our highlight piece, political scientist Stephen Skowronek examined the roots of the unitary executive theory aggressively advocated by the administration of George W. Bush. In the broad version of the theory as espoused by Bush and his Vice-President, Dick Cheney, the president is solely responsible for executing the law and is the sole judge of his executive power, particularly his national security power. The advocates of the unitary executive draw heavily on founders such as Alexander Hamilton, who argued for unity in the executive (Andrew Rudalevige traced the unitary executive theory back to John Locke's notion of executive prerogative).[1] Skowronek pointed out that progressives like Theodore Roosevelt ironically prepared the ground for some of these broad unitary executive arguments, because they championed the view that the president was the only official elected by the entire American electorate and had to energize the national government. But it was the resurgent conservative movement that provided the intellectual ammunition for the Bush administration to take claims for the unitary executive and presidential authority further than its predecessors. For these conservatives, a strong president—one like Ronald Reagan—could implement a conservative agenda if he could assert more independent presidential power. Skowronek warned that ideas for expanding presidential prerogatives are developing more rapidly than ideas about controlling presidential power and making the president accountable.

Note

1. Andrew Rudalevige, "Charting a New Imperial Presidency," from "The Contemporary Presidency: The Decline and Resurgence and Decline (And Resurgence?) of Congress: Charting a New Imperial Presidency," *Presidential Studies Quarterly* 36:3 (September 2006), 511–20.

... Time and again, the [American presidency] has proven indispensable to the political ambitions of newly empowered reform movements, and each has brought to it a new set of legitimating ideas and institutional resources designed to attain them. Looking back, it may seem obvious that the presidency is uniquely suited to the promotion of transformative ambitions. But the attraction of insurgent movements to the presidency is, in fact, one of the great paradoxes of American constitutional design. The Framers feared leaders of the sort who would appeal directly to the people on behalf of one political program or another, and they created the presidency in large part to check popular enthusiasms.[1] Far from endorsing presidential leadership, their assumptions in separating executive and legislative power were that Congress, with its vast repository of expressed powers and its close proximity to the people, was the branch most likely to exploit public sentiments, and that a properly constituted executive would help to stabilize the affairs of state.[2] The separation of powers, the provision for indirect presidential elections, the charge to "preserve, protect and defend the Constitution,"[3] the presidential veto of legislation—all marked the presidency as a counterweight to impulsive majorities and a prod to a more deliberative stance in national affairs.[4] It might be said that the Framers anticipated moments like the mid-1860s and the mid-1990s when congressional insurgents flush with power and emboldened by a radical vision of new possibilities squandered precious time and energy trying to weaken and circumvent an uncooperative occupant of the White House.[5] What they did not anticipate was that handicapping the legislative branch in the enactment of popular mandates and reconstructive programs would spur the development of alternative instrumentalities designed to work through the executive. The unintended effect of their division of powers has been to direct proponents of programmatic action to elaborate upon the endowments of the presidency and to refashion that counterweight to insurgency into its cutting edge.

This Essay traces these successive elaborations through to the most recent construction of presidential power, the conservative insurgency's "unitary executive." Work on this construction began in the 1970s and 1980s during the transition from progressive to conservative dominance of the national agenda. A budding conservative legal movement took up the doctrinal challenge as an adjunct to the larger cause, and in the 1990s, it emerged with a fully elaborated constitutional theory. After 2001, aggressive, self-conscious advocacy of the unitary theory in the Administration of George W. Bush put a fine point on its practical implications.[6] The guiding assumption of this analysis is that a new construction of the presidency gains currency when it legitimizes the release of governmental power for new political purposes. . . .

The theory of the unitary executive promotes exactly what the earlier generation of conservatives feared. It is a brief for the President to act as the exclusive manager of all matters that fall within the purview of the instrumentalities of the executive branch. By that premise, contemporary conservatives have sought to limit prerogatives long claimed by the other branches over administrative instruments, procedures, and personnel, to tap the vast repositories of power accumulated in the modern executive establishment, and to expand the capacities of the President to set policy and adjudicate disputes unilaterally. The argument is conservative only in that it draws a hard line against pragmatism and experimentation in institution-building.[7] It rests the case for presidential management squarely on the Constitution as it was originally conceived and ratified.

There are different strands of the unitary theory, and advocates of one do not necessarily endorse all the propositions of another.[8] They do, however, move out from a common core. All proceed upon an elaboration of the principle of the separation of powers, most especially upon the Constitution's grant of independent powers to the President.[9] Of particular importance is the Constitution's vesting of "the executive power" in a single officer, the President, as that is read to imply expansive authority and exclusive responsibility. When the distinctly unqualified wording of Article II's Vesting Clause is figured into other presidential powers derived from the oath of office, the Commander in Chief Clause, and the Take Care Clause, the domain of unfettered action can be broadened along any number of fronts—for example, in interpreting and executing the law, or in conducting foreign relations, or in warmaking and the control of military affairs. The theory has been invoked to justify unilateral warmaking powers for the President.[10] It has been used to expand presidential discretion with signing statements that defend executive prerogatives against possible infringement by specific parts of the legislation being enacted into law.[11] Even in its more modest forms, the theory undercuts administrative arrangements designed to secure the independence of prosecutors, regulators, accountants, forecasters, personnel officers, scientists, and the like. It discounts the notion of objective, disinterested administration in service to the government as a whole and advances in its place the ideal of an administration run in strict accordance with the President's priorities. The principal claim is that the Constitution mandates an integrated and hierarchical administration—a unified executive branch—in which all officers performing executive business are subordinate to the President, accountable to his interpretations of their charge, and removable at his discretion. The overall effect is to authorize the President to capitalize on all that the historical development of national power has created while leaving to others the Constitution's most rudimentary and combative instruments: term limits and quadrennial elections, congressional control of the purse and Senate review of appointments, judicial intervention and the threat of impeachment.

. . . The new conservatives . . . have reinvigorated traditional conservative arguments for resting power on original understandings of the Constitution, but they have jettisoned traditional conservative reservations about the modern presidency, and they have extended the progressive paradigm of presidency-centered government while jettisoning the distinctly progressive premises on which it was built. . . .

. . . today's conservative construction of presidential power is hardly unfamiliar. Advocates of the unitary theory have a long, if contentious, history on which to draw.

During the Washington Administration, Alexander Hamilton ventured that when the Framers of the Constitution vested "the Executive Power" in the President, they had in mind a well-established model of what those powers encompassed. It followed that the clauses of Article II should be read expansively in light of what the "general theory and practice" of other nations at the time considered the executive's "natural" domain, and that presidential powers were limited only narrowly by the qualifications stipulated in the rest of document.[12] This argument was reworked at the height of the progressive movement by Theodore Roosevelt in his "stewardship theory" of the presidency.[13] Drawing upon Hamilton's broad reading of the Vesting Clause and celebrating what he called the "Jackson-Lincoln" school of presidential practice, Roosevelt asserted that the American President was free to do anything on behalf of the nation except what the Constitution and the laws explicitly proscribed.[14] The companion notion of "departmentalism" also has a long and distinguished pedigree. It holds that the presidency, as an equal and coordinate branch of government, cannot be subordinated to interpretations of the Constitution and the laws proffered by the other branches but must remain free to interpret both by its own lights in the fulfillment of its executive responsibilities.[15] . . .

Previously, presidential empowerment in America has been accompanied by insurgent campaigns to democratize the government more thoroughly; that is to say, new power claims by the President were accommodated by the political movements that supported them in alternative governing arrangements designed to surround and regulate the release of that power from outside the Constitution proper. The Jeffersonians, Jacksonians, and Progressives, though markedly different from one another in their immediate programmatic objectives, each coupled enthusiasm for a more expansive reading of executive prerogatives with innovations designed to render the control of power more collective and cooperative. . . .

. . . Successive waves of progressive reform extending over the first two-thirds of the twentieth century expanded the domain of national action, constructed an extensive administrative apparatus for intervention at home and abroad, and concentrated power in the presidency on a scale that dwarfs nineteenth-century precedents. This concerted shift toward national, executive, and presidential power marked a pivotal turn in American political development. . . . .[16]

. . . [T]he progressives seized upon the possibility of constructing a presidential democracy: they singled out the chief executive as the instrument around which to build their new national polity. Parties were too decentralized; courts were too tied to precedent; Congress was too cumbersome and beholden to special interests. Only the presidency had the national vision to articulate the public's evolving interests, the political incentive to represent those interests in action, and the wherewithal to act upon them with dispatch. The progressives put the President to work accordingly. They constructed an office in which incumbents would be duty-bound to assume political leadership of the nation on an ongoing basis. Each was individually charged to test his skills in keeping national opinion mobilized behind great public purposes and to overcome thereby the constitutional obstacles in its path.[17] As Woodrow Wilson saw it, Presidents would make their proposals irresistible to Congress insofar as they reached out to the people directly, articulated their common concerns, and garnered their support.[18] As Henry Jones Ford put it, the work of the presidency was "the work of the people, breaking through the constitutional form."[19]

... But as the progressives [in the 1970s] were recoiling and the intellectual foundations of their "modern" presidency were foundering, another insurgency began to rework the case for presidential power. Given past episodes, it is no surprise that these new advocates have been impatient with checks and balances. Like all empowered movements, this one has sought to unleash the presidency against reigning political priorities, to break through the thicket of institutions that has grown up around them, and to reconfigure American government around their own. The only curious thing is the indifference of these new insurgents to the challenge of inventing alternative machinery to surround presidential power and call it to account, machinery that might justify easing checks and balances with superior forms of external supervision, institutional coordination, and collective control. Their premise cuts the other way. It is that everything needed to justify an expansive indulgence of presidential prerogatives today is to be found in "the text, structure, and ratification history of the Constitution."[20]

With both critics and advocates of presidential power now appealing to the formalities of the Constitution, the progressives' insight that modern governance demands both an unprecedented concentration of power in the executive and new mechanisms for calling that power to account has fallen by the wayside. ...

The critical intellectual move in the unitary theory is a relocation of the dispositive action to the years prior to the inauguration of George Washington. By elevating the significance of the prehistory of the office, the new conservatives undercut the notion that the powers of the "modern" presidency have "developed" over time. The principal claim is that those powers have been there all along and only need to be recovered in their full significance.[21] To this end, the new construction scouts European developments in the theory and practice of executive power leading up to the American Revolution.[22] Advocates observe the clear rejection of that line of development in the Declaration of Independence and the constitutions of the post-Revolutionary period, but they then dwell on the deliberate reintroduction of independent executive authority in the figure of a president in the new Constitution of 1787. The unitary theory rests at bottom on an interpretation of this early developmental sequence. The contention is that the Constitution of 1787 broke decisively with the unorthodox principles of executive organization ushered in by the American Revolution, and that in ratifying the Constitution, the people repaired to the more familiar historical model of a unitary executive authority. Put another way, in repudiating their post-Revolutionary experiments in collective control of the executive power, the people allegedly repudiated all but the rudimentary forms of collective control specified in the rest of the document and foreclosed any future experimentation along those lines.[23] By implication, the efforts of every subsequent generation to qualify the President's unilateral control of executive power stand discredited as a betrayal of the intent of the American people at their most authoritative moment. All told, it is not the powers of the presidency that have developed over time, only illegitimate constraints on those powers.[24]

... Public opinion, pluralism, publicity, openness, empiricism, science, technical expertise, professionalism, administrative independence, freedom of information—all the operating norms and intermediary authorities on which the progressives pegged their faith in a "modern" presidency—are short-circuited by this appeal back to the formalities of the Constitution. While disillusioned progressives have been lamenting the inadequacy of these old nostrums in recent decades and calling for new forms of institutional restraint, insurgent conservatives have been busy crafting an alternative that renders those nostrums irrelevant and experimentation with new constraints unduly intrusive. When an interviewer pressed Vice President Cheney on the decisive turn of public opinion against Bush Administration war policies, the quick retort—"So?"— offered a pointed lesson on the distance that has been traveled between these two constructions.[25] Democracy's claims on presidential power now end with the administration of the oath of office.

...As a rarefied legal brief for the President's unilateral claims to rule, it is not clear why anyone besides the president would support it. If new constructions of presidential power rise to prominence on the heels of major reform insurgencies, how are we to credit a construction so indifferent to matters of collective control? How does an ideologically charged political movement maximize its leverage in a democratic polity by advancing a closed system of personal rule?

Answers to these questions are to be found in the peculiar circumstances in which the conservative insurgency gestated. In the 1970s, suspicion of the sprawling bureaucratic state spawned by the progressives, anger at the progressives' repudiation of the Vietnam War, resistance to the progressives' penchant for market regulations, and rejection of their social and cultural permissiveness all came together in a formidable political tide. The election landslide of 1972 amply demonstrated the potential of this new coalition to dominate presidential contests. And yet, in the short run at least, any hope of its gaining control of Congress appeared a pipe dream. American politics entered into a long period in which conservatives were on the offensive ideologically but unable to consolidate their hold on national power. Shorn of an interbranch consensus on foreign and economic policy and faced with the stubborn persistence of divided government, they could anticipate little but frustration for their new national majority. The alterations conservative intellectuals made in the ideational foundations of presidential power follow directly. The return to formalism in defense of expansive presidential prerogatives facilitated programmatic action in the absence of an overarching political consensus; a unitary executive promised to ease the way to the political reconstruction of a divided polity.[26] The quest for unity, which since the time of Jefferson had prompted political solutions to the problem of constitutional divisions, now prompted a constitutional solution to the problem of political divisions. Given all that had developed in the interim, the difference was easy to miss.

Like all previous constructions, this one played to the political strengths of the insurgent movement behind it. Conservatives could not but notice that the progressives' main stipulation for the release of presidential power—a clear public voice—had become more difficult to meet. In effect, they seized upon the instrument in hand—a presidency-centered government—for an alternative. The new construction sought unity in the executive because there was little prospect of institutional collaboration or political cooperation. It demanded strict administrative subordination to the will of the President because the ideal of administration in service to government as a whole had become vacuous. It was cast as a lawyer's brief because the new insurgents, unlike previous ones, saw no final victory on the horizon; they anticipated a future of ongoing political division, institutional confrontation, and, ultimately, judicial intervention.[27]

The political context also offered something of a democratic defense for the conservatives' assault on collective control, and it was on this count perhaps that the legacy of progressivism was most deeply implicated. It is not just that the presidency centered government built by the progressives made it easier to imagine incumbents resourceful enough to reconstruct priorities on their own. At least as important was the fact that progressives had raised the political profile of Presidents, foisting them on the public and charging them to act as spearheads of a "continual process of internal reformation." ...

All the conservatives needed to do to tap this sense of democracy was to constitutionalize the public voice, to tie the fact that the President is the only officer in American government who represents the nation as a whole more closely to the notion that the selection of the President had become, in effect, the only credible expression of the public's will. ...

The Nixon Administration anticipated at a practical level what the new theory would soon seek to elevate as a standard of rule. While he was quick to remind his critics of precedents from his progressive predecessors for everything he sought to do, Nixon was also acutely aware of the very different circumstances in which he was invoking them: he was acting in a government otherwise controlled by his political enemies; there was no cohesive national sentiment on which to base expansive claims to power; his was a "silent" majority. Faced with these circumstances and emboldened by his lopsided victory in 1972, Nixon tapped the historical development of presidency-centered government to sharpen the argument for presidential independence and to press forward on his own with a transformation of American government and politics. Using many of the tools already available, he worked to undercut institutions put in place to foster interbranch collaboration and collective control. The statutory offices of the EOP [Executive Office of the Presidency] were downgraded by compromising their neutrality and negating their promise of cooperative action.[28] At the same time, Nixon worked to bolster institutions put in place to enhance his own governing capacities. He concentrated resources in the White House Office itself and extended the political supervision of the White House deeper into the permanent bureaucracy.[29] When asked what was to prevent a President so empowered from overreaching, Nixon invoked the retroactive sanction of voters: "[A] President has to come up before the electorate."[30] Here then was a clear road map showing how to move away from the idea of governing more collectively through the presidency toward the idea of governing more exclusively within the presidency.

The key assertions in what would become the unitary theory of the executive circulated through the conservative movement in the tumultuous years between the precipitous collapse of the Nixon presidency at the hands of the political enemies he so feared and the capitulation of George H.W. Bush to a Democratic Congress on the signal conservative issue of taxes in the budget agreement of 1990. In this period of persistent political division and stiff institutional resistance to the conservative turn, arguments circulated in and around the White House for the subordination of executive power to presidential will. ...

Had the ambitions of the conservative insurgency not met such stubborn resistance for so long, it would be harder to credit its heavy investment in the exclusivity of presidential control. As it stands, the unitary theory is a high-stakes gamble that leaves movement priorities no more secure than the next election cycle. More striking still is the theory's pretension to upholding constitutional intent, for its personalization of executive power renders the whole of modern American government more volatile.[31] When the notion of a presidential stewardship is stripped of progressive provisions for collective oversight by the nation's prudentes, when the notion of a politicized bureaucracy is stripped of Jacksonian provisions for collective oversight by the party, when the notion of a concert of power is stripped of Jeffersonian provisions for collective oversight by

Congress—when the extra-constitutional ballast for presidential government is all stripped away and the idea is formalized as fundamental law, the original value of stability in government is all but lost from view. It is this confounding of constitutional ideals that points us, in the final analysis, to the limits of construction as a rejuvenating political process . . . .

. . . The theory of the unitary executive is effective because in doubling back to the predemocratic foundations of executive power, it both extends powers gained through the democratization of the presidency and changes the meaning of democracy itself. The democracy that ratified the creation of the presidency is not the same as the democracy that politicized central administration in the Jacksonian era, nor is it the same as the democracy that nationalized governmental power in the Progressive era. By some unstated transitive property of construction, however, the original act of ratification now provides democratic sanction to unbridled presidential control over the vast powers that have accumulated in the executive branch.

Constitutional construction is an American political tradition, perhaps the American political tradition. It is at the core of the successful adaptation of American government to the changing circumstances of its operation. But in the case of the presidency, as in other aspects of constitutional government where construction has been piled upon construction, the interpretive standards appear increasingly problematic. Future insurgents will surely find plausibility an easy discipline to master in asserting presidential power. By combining in their own way the full array of premises now in play, they will, in effect, be freer than ever before just to make things up as they go along. This is the final triumph of construction and the limit of its capacity to legitimate new forms of national government. Once a presidency-centered system of government built on the rejection of formalism and originalism is recast as the very expression of formalism and originalism—once the fruit of democracy's claims against limits are redeployed to limit democracy's claims—there is little left that appears reliable or settled.

One thing that does seem clear is that new ideas about how to assert presidential power are now fast outpacing new ideas about how to hold that power to account. . . . On the one side, developmental analysis suggests that the efforts of contemporary critics of the modern presidency to get Congress to reclaim its original role and to reinvigorate checks and balances are unlikely to get very far. Ever since the rise of parties in the nineteenth century, democratic reformers have been seeking ways to ease checks and balances, and the mechanisms they have developed have so altered the operations of American government that going back hardly seems a practical option. On the other side, developmental analysis suggests that contemporary advocates who claim the Constitution as a safe, familiar, and wholly adequate ground on which to venture a further expansion of executive prerogatives are, in fact, pushing down a road that is neither restorative nor well-anchored. There may be good reasons to alter the terms and conditions under which presidential power extended its reach in the twentieth century and American government as a whole reoriented its operations. But the time has long passed when doing so in the name of reclaiming the wisdom of the Framers was a straightforward proposition.[32] The more sober option for twenty first-century governance may be the one that reckons with political development more directly and follows the example of the institution builders who transformed American government in the nineteenth and twentieth centuries. They did not resist new claims of presidential power, but neither did they accept them before staking out fresh claims of their own.

NOTES

1. See, e.g., James W. Ceaser, *Presidential Selection* 51–75 (1979); Jeffrey K. Tulis, *The Rhetorical Presidency* 27–45 (1987); cf. James W. Ceaser et al., "The Rise of the Rhetorical Presidency," in *Rethinking the Presidency* 233 (Thomas E. Cronin ed., 1982) (discussing a doctrinal shift in the twentieth century away from the original constitutional ideal and the "increasing pressure" on modern Presidents "to demonstrate their leadership capacity through an ever growing number of rhetorical performances," id. at 236).

2. See, e.g., *The Federalist* No. 48, at 306 (James Madison) (Clinton Rossiter ed., 1999) ("It is against the enterprising ambition of [the legislative] department that the people ought to indulge all their jealousy and exhaust all their precautions."). Hamilton defended the separation of powers as essential to control an overweening legislature. *The Federalist* No. 71 (Alexander Hamilton), supra, at 432 ("The tendency of the legislative authority to absorb every other has been fully displayed and illustrated by examples in some preceding numbers. In governments purely republican, this tendency is almost irresistible. The representatives of the people ... seem sometimes to fancy that they are the people themselves...."); see also Abner S. Greene, "Checks and Balances in an Era of Presidential Lawmaking," 61 *U. Chi. L. Rev.* 123, 140–53 (1994) (discussing the Framers' assumptions).

3. U.S. Const. art. II, § 1, cl. 8.

4. On enduring tensions in relations between Presidents and movements, see Sidney M. Milkis, "The President in the Vanguard: Lyndon Johnson and the Civil Rights Insurgency," in *Formative Acts: American Politics in the Making* 269 (Stephen Skowronek and Matthew Glassman eds., 2007) [hereinafter *Formative Acts*]; Elizabeth Sanders, "Presidents and Social Movements: A Logic and Preliminary Results," in *Formative Acts*, supra, at 223; and Daniel J. Tichenor, "Leaders, Citizenship Movements, and the Politics Rivalries Make," in *Formative Acts*, supra, at 241.

5. On Andrew Johnson's efforts to contain and stigmatize the ambitions of congressional Republicans for a more radical reconstruction of the South in the mid-1860s, see, for example, Nicole Mellow and Jeffrey K. Tulis, "Andrew Johnson and the Politics of Failure," in *Formative Acts*, supra note 4, at 153. On Bill Clinton's efforts to contain and stigmatize the ambitions of congressional Republicans working on behalf of the conservative agenda of the mid-1990s, see, for example, Elizabeth Drew, *Showdown: The Struggle Between the Gingrich Congress and the Clinton White House* (1996).

6. See John P. MacKenzie, *Absolute Power: How the Unitary Executive Theory is Undermining the Constitution* 1–4, 31–62 (2008); James P. Pfiffner, *Power Play: The Bush Presidency and the Constitution* (2008); Steven E. Schier, "George W. Bush and Washington Governance: Effective Use of a Self-Limiting Style," 6 *Forum*, Issue 2, art. 2, 2008, available at http://www.degruyter. com.ezproxy.umsl.edu/view/j/for.2008.6.2_20120105083453/for.2008.6.2/for.2008.6.2.1243/ for.2008.6.2.1243.xml?format=INT.

7. See, e.g., Steven G. Calabresi, "Political Parties as Mediating Institutions," 61 *U. Chi. L. Rev.* 1479 (1994) (indicating how a unitary theorist might accommodate the improvisational developments that have come to surround presidential power over time).

8. For a description of the range of views, see Steven G. Calabresi and Christopher S. Yoo, *The Unitary Executive* 18–21 (2008).

9. See, e.g., Steven G. Calabresi, "Some Normative Arguments for the Unitary Executive," 48 *Ark. L. Rev.* 23, 45–70 (1995); Steven G. Calabresi, "The Vesting Clauses As Power Grants," 88 *Nw. U. L. Rev.* 1377, 1395–1400 (1994); Steven G. Calabresi and Saikrishna B. Prakash, "The President's Power To Execute the Laws," 104 *Yale L.J.* 541, 570–99 (1994); Steven G. Calabresi and Kevin H. Rhodes, "The Structural Constitution: Unitary Executive, Plural Judiciary," 105 *Harv. L. Rev.* 1153 (1992); see also John Yoo, *The Powers of War and Peace: The Constitution and Foreign Affairs After 9/11* (2005) [hereinafter Yoo, *The Powers of War and Peace*]; John Yoo, *War by Other Means: An Insider's Account of the War on Terror* (2006).

10. See Yoo, *The Powers of War and Peace*.

11. See Curtis A. Bradley and Eric A. Posner, "Presidential Signing Statements and Executive Power," 23 *Const. Comment*. 307, 308, 318, 328–29 (2006); Steven G. Calabresi and Daniel Lev, "The Legal Significance of Presidential Signing Statements," 4 *Forum*, Issue 2, art. 8, 2006, available at http://www.degruyter.com.ezproxy.umsl.edu/view/j/for.2006.4.2_20120105083451/for.2006.4.2/for.2006.4.2.1131/for.2006.4.2.1131.xml?format=INT.

12. See Alexander Hamilton, *Pacificus* No. 1 (June 29, 1793), reprinted in 1 *Classics of American Political and Constitutional Thought* 634, 636 (Scott J. Hammond, Kevin R. Hardwick and Howard L. Lubert eds., 2007).

13. William H. Harbaugh, "The Constitution of the Theodore Roosevelt Presidency and the Progressive Era," in *The Constitution and the American Presidency* 63, 67 (Martin L. Fausold and Alan Shank eds., 1991); see also id. at 66–68.

14. Theodore Roosevelt, *An Autobiography* 380 (Da Capo Press 1985) (1913); accord id. at 371–72, 379–80.

15. See Keith E. Whittington, "Political Foundations of Judicial Supremacy: The Presidency, the Supreme Court, and Constitutional Leadership," in *U.S. History* xi, 14–18 (2007); Walter F. Murphy, "Who Shall Interpret? The Quest for the Ultimate Constitutional Interpreter," 48 *Rev. Pol.* 401, 411–12 (1986).

16. See, e.g., Stephen Skowronek, *Building a New American State: The Expansion of National Administrative Capacities, 1877-1920* (1982); Fred I. Greenstein, "Change and Continuity in the Modern Presidency," in *The New American Political System* 45, 45–86 (Anthony King ed., 1978).

17. See, generally, James MacGregor Burns, *The Deadlock of Democracy: Four-Party Politics in America* (1963); Richard E. Neustadt, *Presidential Power: The Politics of Leadership* (1960).

18. Woodrow Wilson, *Constitutional Government in the United States* 68 (1908) ("If [the President] rightly interprets the national thought and boldly insists upon it, he is irresistible . . . ."); id. at 70–71 ("If Congress be overborne by him, it will be no fault of the makers of the Constitution,—it will be from no lack of constitutional powers on its part, but only because the President has the nation behind him, and Congress has not. He has no means of compelling Congress except through public opinion.").

19. Henry Jones Ford, *The Rise and Growth of American Politics* 292–93 (1898).

20. Yoo, *The Powers of War and Peace*, supra note 10, at 5.

21. In a similar spirit, see David K. Nichols, *The Myth of the Modern Presidency* (1994).

22. See Harvey C. Mansfield, Jr., *Taming the Prince: The Ambivalence of Modern Executive Power* (1989); Forrest McDonald, *The American Presidency: an Intellectual History* 9–97 (1994); Nichols, supra note 21, at 139–61; see also Benjamin A. Kleinerman, "Can the Prince Really Be Tamed? Executive Prerogative, Popular Apathy, and the Constitutional Frame in Locke's Second Treatise," 101 *Am. Pol. Sci. Rev.* 209 (2007); Sheldon S. Wolin, "Executive Liberation," 6 *Stud. Am. Pol. Dev.* 211, 211–16 (1992) (reviewing Mansfield, supra).

23. See, e.g., Calabresi and Yoo, supra note 17, at 30–36; see also Yoo, *The Powers of War and Peace*, supra note 18, at 30–142 (discussing these early developments with respect to the President's foreign affairs power).

24. See Hadley Arkes, "On the Moral Standing of the President As an Interpreter of the Constitution: Some Reflections on Our Current 'Crises,'" 20 *PS: Pol. Sci. & Pol.* 637 (1987).

25. Interview by Martha Raddatz with Richard Cheney, Vice President of the United States, in Muscat, Oman (March 19, 2008) (transcript available at http://abcnews.go.com/politics/story?id=4481568).

26. Instructive on this point is Daryl J. Levinson and Richard H. Pildes, "Separation of Parties, Not Powers," 119 *Harv. L. Rev.* 2311 (2006).

27. See, e.g., Phillip J. Cooper, *By Order of the President: The Use and Abuse of Executive Direct Action 201-03* (2002) (describing the Reagan Administration's strategic thinking about signing statements).

28. See, e.g., Hugh Heclo, *A Government of Strangers* 78–80 (1977).

29. See, generally, Richard P. Nathan, *The Administrative Presidency* (1983); Richard P. Nathan, *The Plot that Failed* (1975). Note the Nixon-era breakpoints in the organization history as reviewed by John Hart, *The Presidential Branch* 52–53, at 1–147; see also Heclo, supra note 28, at 13, 75; and Karen M. Hult and Charles E. Walcott, *Empowering the White House* 166–72 (2004).

30. Christopher H. Pyle and Richard M. Pious, *The President, Congress, and the Constitution* 74 (1984) (quoting Interview by David Frost with Richard Nixon (May 19, 1977)).

31. See Jeremy D. Bailey, "The New Unitary Executive and Democratic Theory: The Problem of Alexander Hamilton," 102 *Am. Pol. Sci. Rev.* 453 (2008).

32. For an interesting response to this conundrum, see Greene, supra note 2, at 153–96.

10.6 Jeffrey E. Cohen, "The Size of the President's Agenda, 1789–2002" (2012)

In *Federalist* 70, Alexander Hamilton wrote that "all men of sense will agree in the necessity of an energetic executive." Political scientist Jeffrey Cohen analyzed the growth of presidential energy in proposing an agenda for Congress. Cohen found that the president's role as "chief legislator" dates to the administration of George Washington, and developed steadily thereafter. It is hardly surprising that Theodore Roosevelt, the advocate of "immediate and vigorous executive action", would significantly boost the number of presidential proposals to Congress. Cohen's evidence revealed just how important the growth of the presidential establishment has been for expanding the president's agenda, and how that agenda expanded after the nation assumed a more activist global role in World War II.

This chapter looks at perhaps the most basic characteristic of the president's legislative agenda, the number of legislative proposals that the president submits to Congress, what Cameron and Park (2008) term *legislative activism*. The conventional wisdom holds that modern presidents, those from FDR onward, have been more active in the legislative policy-making process than their predecessors. Theories of the modern presidency often cite increased presidential involvement in the legislative process as a characteristic that distinguishes modern presidents from traditional ones (Greenstein, 1988; Pfiffner, 2008; Shaw, 1987; Wayne, 1978) . . .

From George Washington until the 1940s, there was . . . a slow, steady increase in the number of presidential proposals submitted to Congress. Traditional presidents were not as legislatively inactive, in terms of submitting proposals for legislation to Congress, as conventional wisdom portrays. These proposal data, spanning nearly the entire history of the office and the nation, lead us to revise our understanding of the presidency with regard to legislative activism. The first part of this chapter details the trends in presidential legislative activism.

Although precisely describing trends in legislative activism is important, more important is identifying the factors that affect presidential activism over both the long and the short haul. This chapter raises the following questions: Why the long-term secular increase in proposals across the first 150 years of presidential history? Why the abrupt surge in legislative proposing in the late 1940s? Why has that higher rate of legislative proposing persisted to the present? Why does presidential legislative activism rise and fall in the short run, from congress to congress? . . .

Trends in Presidential Proposal Activity: The Long View

Figure 1 plots the number of presidential requests for legislation by Congress from the first Congress (1789–1790) through the 107th (2001–2002). I use "congress" as the temporal unit for several reasons. First, the two calendar years that make up each congress is the legislature's natural time unit. Proposals submitted by any member[1] during the congress remain alive until the end of that congress, when all bills that Congress did not enact and the president did not sign into law die. Someone must reintroduce those bills in the next congress to keep them on the legislative agenda. Presidents are obviously aware of this temporal structure.

Rethinking the Modern Presidency
Figure 1 illustrates the conventional wisdom of the higher legislative activism of modern compared with traditional presidents. There is a remarkable surge in presidential proposing beginning in the mid-twentieth century. Given the importance of Franklin Roosevelt in establishing the modern presidency (Greenstein, 1988), we might expect to see the upsurge in proposal activity during his term of office; however, it might take time for the executive branch to acquire the institutional support and foundation necessary to sustain a high level of legislative proposing. Although FDR might have set the seeds for presidential modernity during his tenure, to submit a large volume of legislative proposals to Congress would require staff resources that would take time to accumulate and to organize behind such a task. Thus we might expect the surge in legislative proposing to begin sometime after the establishment of the Executive Office of the Presidency (EOP) in 1939. With the EOP came the recognition that the presidency had fundamentally transformed, and that the office would need to be reorganized and staffed in accord with that transformation. The EOP would provide the institutional platform for the modern presidency.

The proposal data support neither of these hypotheses, the first that we should see a great rise in legislative activism early in FDR's term, the second that the upsurge should commence soon after the establishment of the EOP in 1939. Rather, the steep rise in presidential proposal activity does not begin until the end of the Second World War, during the Truman administration. The big jump in proposal activity begins with the 79th Congress (1947–1948) and continued with the 80th. During the 78th Congress (1943–1944), in the midst of war, FDR submitted forty-six legislative proposals to Congress. The next Congress, the 79th (1945–1946), the last year of war and first post-year, FDR and Truman together submitted 137 proposals. Proposal activity continued to climb steeply during the 80th Congress (1947–1948), with 225 submissions. Thereafter

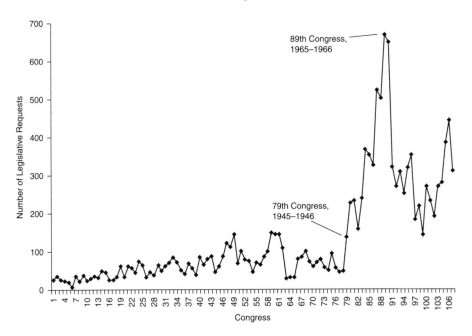

Figure 1 The Number of Presidential Legislative Requests, 1st to 107th Congresses (1789–2002).

proposal activity leveled off until the mid-to-late 1950s and 1960s, another period when presidential submissions to Congress rose dramatically.

The 79th and 80th Congresses (1945–1948) mark a transition period in legislative activism. During these four years, presidential submission rates to Congress rose steeply, and subsequent presidents maintained that high level of proposal activity to the present. The high rate of proposing for the 79th and 80th Congresses is not a short-term spike in legislative activism but began a new period of presidential legislative activity. From the 68th to the 77th Congresses (1923–1944), presidents submitted on average 69.7 proposals, somewhat higher than the 46 of the 78th Congress. Truman's proposal rate during the 79th Congress is twice as high as the average for the 68th to the 77th Congresses. His proposal rate for the 80th Congress is nearly three times the rate for presidents from the 68th to 77th Congresses. What accounts for this abrupt and sustained change in presidential proposal activity beginning with the 79th and 80th Congresses?

Two conventional answers for Truman's unprecedented degree of legislative proposing consider the impact of the Second World War and political conditions in Congress during the 80th Congress (1947–1948). First, the Second World War might have constrained the amount of presidential proposal activity as the president and the nation focused more on the war effort.[2] Once the war ended, pent-up demand from several years of a restricted agenda and limited governmental resources to handle anything other than war-related matters might have led to the increase in presidential proposal activity. Proposal rates during the war years do appear slightly lower than for the late New Deal, but not by much. The war constraint-pent-up demand hypothesis predicts an uptick in proposal activity soon after the cessation of the Second World War, and this is basically what we see.

Secondly, political conditions during the next Congress (80th, 1947–1948) might have also spurred the increase in Truman's proposal activity. Republicans controlled the 80th Congress, blocking numerous policy initiatives from the Truman administration. Looking weak to voters because of these defeats in Congress, Truman decided to try to back the Republican Congress into a corner, submitting proposals for legislation that he knew would be defeated but that were popular with voters. This legislative strategy allowed him to build a campaign theme to run against the Republicans in the 1948 presidential elections (Hartmann, 1971; Rudalevige, 2002, p. 118), a strategy that proved effective. Not only was he reelected, but voters turned out the Republicans in Congress, giving Truman Democratic majorities for the 81st Congress (1949–1950).

Both of these impulses toward greater presidential proposal activity must also be understood in the context of a more institutionally resourceful presidency. Although postwar pent-up demand and a resistant Congress might have led Truman in the short term to submit large legislative agendas to Congress, to sustain that level of proposing required both the means (e.g., staff resources) and the motivations to do so.

The motivation for presidential legislative leadership comes primarily from a change in the nation's public philosophy (Beer, 1978), allowing for a larger federal government and public expectations for presidential leadership of this enlarged governmental establishment. These legislative proposal data lead us to reinterpret the transformation of the presidency into its modern form, at least as it pertains to the legislative presidency. Several elements needed to come together. As is often mentioned in the modern presidency literature, the political culture needed to change. In this new political culture, presidents would be expected to be policy leaders, and the public would also expect greater effort on the part of the federal government to handle national problems.

Second, for the president to be a legislative activist would also require staff and other institutional resources. It would take the FDR administration some time to learn the importance of additional staffing for modern presidential leadership. These cultural-institutional factors alone would have probably led to an increase in presidential activism but do not adequately account for the timing of the upsurge in legislative activism. The Second World War also might have dampened presidential legislative activism. Soon after the war ended, we see an upturn in the number of presidential proposals. Finally, the political circumstances associated with the 80th Congress interacted with the cultural expectations for presidential leadership and the stronger institutional presidency to spike presidential activism in 1947/1948. Truman's successful reelection strategy, along with expectations for presidential leadership and a strong presidential institution, provided the incentive for continued high levels of legislative activism by presidents.

To maintain that high level of activism would require presidential resources devoted to that task, however. As the theory of congressional anticipations argues, presidents look to the likelihood that Congress will enact their proposals in deciding what to submit for legislative consideration. The greater their expectation of success with Congress, the larger the legislative agenda is. Central clearance and the presidential program gave the president control over an important resource that could affect his bargaining situation with Congress, bureaucratic expertise. Prior to the creation of these processes, Congress could solicit input from the bureaucracy directly, whenever its members thought that they needed the bureaucracy's expertise to inform the crafting of legislation.

With central clearance procedures in place, the president could regulate all bureaucratic contact with Congress. Presidents could deny the provision of bureaucratic expertise to Congress and perhaps more crucially could bias the type of information that the bureaucracy would pass along to Congress—providing Congress with only the expertise supportive of the president's policy goals. Inasmuch as bureaucratic expertise is important to Congress for policy making, the presidential bargaining situation with Congress is strengthened by the establishment of central clearance. The rise of presidential activism in the postwar years therefore must be seen as both the presidential response to demands for legislative and policy leadership and the acquisition of resources that enhance the president's ability to bargain successfully with Congress.[3]

Rethinking the Legislative Activism of Traditional Presidents

Figure 1 obscures as much as it reveals because the level of proposal activity in the post-War World Two era dwarfs that of the previous years, visually compressing the variability in proposal activity from 1789 to 1944. There are a few notable short-term spikes in legislative activity prior to 1946 (e.g., 49th Congress, 1885–1886; 59th–61st, 1905–1910). There also appears to be an upward slope in proposal activity across these first 150 years of the presidency. The data on Figure 1 are so compressed, however, that one cannot see clearly what is going on. To give a clearer picture of the trend in proposal activity before the great postwar upsurge, Figure 2 plots just the years from 1789 to 1944, the 1st to the 78th Congresses.

First, Figure 2 reveals that early presidents might have been more legislatively active, in the sense of submitting requests to Congress, than conventional understandings of the early presidency suggest. George Washington, for instance, submitted on average twenty-six requests per Congress, ranging from twenty-two to thirty-four. His volume of request activity might be a function of his being the first president and the problems that

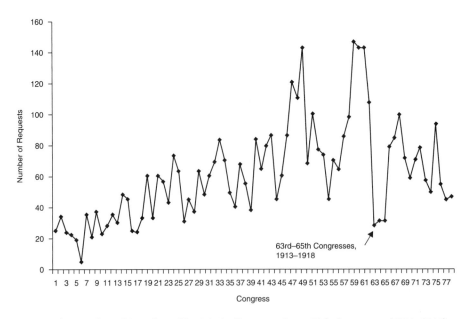

Figure 2 The Number of Presidential Legislative Requests, 1st to 78th Congresses (1789–1944).

had mounted during the Articles of Confederation period. The inability of the government under the Articles of Confederation to produce necessary legislation (e.g., policy) to handle issues such as defense, western uprisings, and economic distress provided the major rationale for the Philadelphia Constitutional convention. With this as a backdrop, a major task of the first president and the earliest congresses was to address problems that had been festering and worsening during the Confederation period. The first president and early congresses confronted a large problem stream (Kingdon, 1995).

The early presidents after Washington, except for John Adams, showed no signs of reducing the number of proposals, however. Although John Adams averaged only 12 proposals per Congress, about half of Washington's rate, Jefferson averaged 29 per Congress, Madison 35, Monroe 32, and John Quincy Adams 46.5. Even the supposedly "do-nothing" Monroe submitted legislative proposals at the rate equal to these other early presidents. Admittedly these totals pale when compared with those of twentieth-century presidents, who average more than 200 requests per Congress, but these numbers are far from trivial.[4]

These figures should lead us to rethink the legislative activity of early presidents. Accounts of presidential-congressional interactions in the early period generally stress two points: presidential fidelity to separation of powers and that presidents tended to refrain from becoming heavily involved in the legislative policy-making process. Most early presidents were not as involved in legislative processes as are modern presidents (Greenstein, 2009; McCarty, 2009). George Washington usually sat on the sidelines after making legislative requests to Congress (Chernow, 2010). His Treasury Secretary, Alexander Hamilton, spearheaded the administration's legislative efforts, sometimes directing legislative strategies and coordinating them with friendly members of Congress (McDonald, 1974). Jefferson too was sometimes deeply involved in legislative matters, although he too tended to work with and through the party leadership in Congress, rather than publicly (McDonald, 1976).

Figure 2 also shows that presidential request levels steadily climbed from the First until the 78th Congress (1943–1944). Where Washington through John Quincy Adams proposed on average thirty requests per Congress, presidents of the 1890s submitted on average sixty-six proposals, twice the rate of the earliest presidents. The supposedly inactive, restrained Republican presidents of the 1920s and early 1930s (i.e., Harding, Coolidge, and Hoover) proposed on average seventy-seven items, again a marked increased from late nineteenth-century presidents, and surprisingly more than Franklin Roosevelt from 1933 to 1944, who averaged only fifty-seven. Even if we exclude the war years from FDR's totals and look only at the congresses from 1933 to 1940 (73rd–77th), FDR merely issued sixty-three proposals per congress, lower than the Republican presidents who preceded him. If FDR altered the relationship between the president and Congress, it is not because he made more legislative proposals to Congress than his predecessors.

Furthermore, Figure 2 reveals several spikes in proposal activity across the first seventy-eight congresses. One spike occurs with the 49th Congress (1885–1886), the first two years of Grover Cleveland's first term of office. Cleveland's election was the first time that a Democrat sat in the Oval Office since James Buchanan (1857–1860). Perhaps the spike in Cleveland's proposal activity is a function of Democrats being out of the presidency for such a long time (Welch, 1988). Not only is Cleveland at times a "high-rate proposer," but he is also a "low-rate proposer," as is the case for his very low proposal rate during the 54th Congress (1895–1896), the last two years of his second term. The economic panic of those years and strong Republican control of both houses of Congress might have dampened Cleveland's proposal activity rate compared with his other years in office.

Another spike in activity occurs during the 56th to the 61st Congresses (1905–1910), the last four years of Theodore Roosevelt's administration and the first two for his successor, Taft. Although Roosevelt's activity here could be predicted from his steward-ship conception of the presidency, Taft, famously associated with the clerkship perspec-tive on the presidency, appears more active than expected (Korzi, 2003). Soon after, however, from 1913 to 1918 (63rd–65th Congresses), the first six Wilson years, we see a sharp decline in proposal activity, despite Wilson's reputation as a legislative leader with an expansive agenda. These figures somewhat belie conventional views of Wilson as an activist and progressive, but other accounts suggest that Wilson's legislative agenda was not large in terms of the number of proposals, although it was bold and innovative in terms of policy ambition (Macmahon, 1956).

Post-World War Two Proposal Activity: A Closer Look

As noted, legislative activism surges with Harry Truman in the postwar years and continues to the present. From Truman's initial full Congress, the 79th (1945–1946) through the 89th (1965–1966), LBJ's remarkably productive Congress, there is a massive and steady increase in presidential proposal activity. Truman averaged 187 proposals per Congress, three times the rate of FDR. Republican Eisenhower not only maintained Truman's rate but also increased it to 320 per Congress, 70% higher than for Truman. Kennedy and Johnson from 1961 to 1964 submitted even more, 511 on average. The peak in proposal activity came with LBJ's two full congresses (1965–1968) with 665 proposals in 1965/1966 and 646 in 1967/1968, a tenfold increase compared with FDR. The approx-imately twenty years from 1947 through 1968 represents, at least with regard to presiden-tial legislative activism, a remarkable transformation of the presidency.

High levels of legislative activism persist to the present, although not at LBJ's remark-ably high levels. Proposal activity drops off steeply with LBJ's Republican successors, Nixon and Ford, whose activity levels of 286 proposals on average between them compare somewhat with Eisenhower. The post-LBJ decline in proposal activity is not just a Republican phenomenon, however. Democrat Jimmy Carter averaged 333, closer to Nixon and Ford than LBJ. Republicans Reagan and the first Bush scaled back their proposing levels to about Truman's level, 202 and 210. Clinton increased the average number of proposals to Carter's level, 342, still a far cry from LBJ, and during his first congress, George W. Bush made 309 proposals, more in line with the post-LBJ Democrats than Republicans. Compared with LBJ, these presidents look modest in their legislative activism, but they still appear highly active when compared to the pre-Truman presi-dents, with a proposal rate about five times as high as the most legislatively active premodern presidents.

The post-World War Two trend shows high proposal activity for both Democrats and Republicans, although Republicans appear to propose legislation at lower rates than Democrats. Democrats averaged 366 proposals per congress to 264 for Republicans. A simple regression analysis for the postwar years, with a dummy for presidential party and controls for a linear time trend and a square of the linear trend (to account for the decline in activity after LBJ), indicates a significant difference in partisan proposal activity. The regression results suggest that Democrats issue about 140 more proposals per congress than Republicans.[5]

A "big bang" did occur in presidential legislative activism, but it commenced more than a decade after the beginning of FDR's presidency, with Truman in the late 1940s. Legislative activism is only one aspect of presidential legislative leadership, however. Other aspects, such as active lobbying of Congress and focusing congressional and public attention on the president's legislative priorities, might have begun earlier, during FDR's tenure, as historical accounts suggest. The "big bang" in legislative activism is not simply a story of presidential activity rates jumping to a higher level under Truman and settling at that level. For the twenty years after Truman, the level of presidential activism grew at a rapid pace, peaking with LBJ, whose activity rate was more than three times greater than Truman's. After LBJ, presidential activism receded to about one-half of Johnson's rate, still quite high by historical standards.

NOTES

1. The president cannot formally submit legislation directly to Congress; this must be done by a member of Congress.
2. One hypothesis that we entertain later is that war constrains the agenda to policies directly relevant to the war effort. This war effect would have implications for several attributes of the president's legislative agenda, including its size.
3. Congress would come to realize the bias in bureaucratic information coming to it once central clearance was in place; still, there would be times when Congress would rely on such biased information. Congress can to some degree offset this presidential advantage by building its own expertise, as it has done for instance with the Congressional Budget Office (CBO). Congress cannot match the expertise of the executive branch—the bureaucracy is just too large. Moreover, presidents can also respond to congressional attempts to narrow the expertise gap between the branches (Epstein and O'Halioran, 1999; Krause, 2002).
4. For a reinterpretation of the leadership of the early presidents see Greenstein, 2009.
5. The regression results (SE) are: Proposal Level = 90.0 (83.6) Constant + 139.6 (46.2) Democrat + 28.6 (11.4) Time - 0.9 (0.4) Time Squared; $R2$ = 0.32, n = 29. All independent variables are statistically significant at the 0.01 level or better.

REFERENCES

Beer, Samuel. 1978. "In Search of a New Public Philosophy." In Anthony King, ed. *The New American Political System*. Washington, DC: American Enterprise Institute, pp. 5–44.

Cameron, Charles M. and Jee-Kwang Park. 2008. "A Primer on the President's Legislative Program." In Bert A. Rockman and Richard W. Waterman, eds. *Presidential Leadership: The Vortex of Power*. New York: Oxford University Press, pp. 45–80.

Chernow, Ron. 2010. *Washington: A Life*. New York: Penguin Books.

Epstein, David and Sharyn O'Halloran. 1999. *Delegating Powers: A Transaction Cost Politics Approach to Policy Making Under Separate Powers*. New York: Cambridge University Press.

Greenstein, Fred I., ed. 1988. *Leadership and the Modern Presidency*. Cambridge, MA: Harvard University Press.

——. 2009. *Inventing the Presidency: Leadership Style from George Washington to Andrew Jackson*. Princeton, NJ: Princeton University Press.

Hartmann, Susan M. 1971. *Truman and the 80th Congress*. Columbia: University of Missouri Press.

Kingdon, John W. 1995. *Agendas, Alternatives, and Public Policies*. 2nd ed. New York: HarperCollins.

Korzi, Michael J. 2003. "Our Chief Magistrate and his Powers: A Reconsideration of William Howard Taft's 'Whig' Theory of Presidential Leadership," *Presidential Studies Quarterly*, 33 (June): 305–324.

Krause, George A. 2002. "Separated Powers and Institutional Growth in the Presidential and Congressional Branches: Distinguishing between Short-Run versus Long-Run Dynamics." *Political Research Quarterly* 55 (March): 27–57.

Macmahon, Arthur W. 1956. "Woodrow Wilson as Legislative Leader and Administrator." *American Political Science Review* 50 (September): 641–675.

McCarty, Nolan M. 2009. "Presidential Vetoes in the Early Republic: Changing Constitutional Norms or Electoral Reform." *Journal of Politics* 71 (April): 369–384.

McDonald, Forrest. 1974. *The Presidency of George Washington.* Lawrence: University Press of Kansas.

——. 1976. *The Presidency of Thomas Jefferson.* Lawrence: University Press of Kansas.

Pfiffner, James P. 2008. *The Modern Presidency*, 5th ed. New York: Wadsworth.

Rudalevige, Andrew. 2002. *Managing the President's Program: Presidential Leadership and Legislative Policy Formulation.* Princeton, NJ: Princeton University Press.

Shaw, Malcolm. 1987. "The Traditional and Modern Presidencies." In Shaw, Malcolm, ed. *The Modern Presidency: From Roosevelt to Reagan.* New York: Harper and Row, pp. 244–310.

Wayne, Stephen. 1978. *The Legislative Presidency.* New York: HarperCollins.

Welch, Richard E., Jr. 1988. *The Presidencies of Grover Cleveland.* Lawrence: University Press of Kansas.

Discussion Questions

1. John Locke argues that the executive sometimes has to break the law, but that executives can only use this power legitimately to preserve society. Does Abraham Lincoln provide a good example of this use of prerogative power? Does Lincoln sufficiently justify his actions? Why or why not?

2. At the Constitutional Convention, Gouverneur Morris struggled with the problem of ensuring that the president would be accountable. But in the *Federalist*, Alexander Hamilton seems confident that the Constitution's framers had struck the right balance by creating a single executive. How would the United States have developed differently if the framers had created a presidency consisting of three leaders instead of one?

3. Do all new presidents try to prove themselves by trying "To reverse and undo what has been done by a predecessor," as Hamilton puts it in *Federalist 72*? Is this claim true of recent presidents? If so, what are the consequences?

4. Does the president have the right measure of power to protect the nation in a time of terrorism? Does he have too much power? Too little? What specific additional limitations or new powers does the president need, if any?

5. Is it a problem that "new ideas about how to assert presidential power are now fast outpacing new ideas about how to hold that power to account," as Skowronek puts it? What kinds of ideas about increasing presidential accountability could improve the situation?

7. What difference does the path of the development of the presidency make for Americans today?

Suggested Additional Reading

James Bryce, *The American Commonwealth*, vol. 1, chap. 8, "Why Great Men Are Not Chosen President," 3rd ed. (New York: Macmillan, 1901), 78–85.

Richard Ellis, *The Development of the American Presidency* (Abingdon, UK, and New York: Routledge, 2012).

Doris Kearns Goodwin, *Team of Rivals: The Political Genius of Abraham Lincoln* (New York: Simon & Schuster, 2005).

Lori Cox Han, ed., *New Directions in the American Presidency* (Abingdon, UK, and New York: Routledge, 2010).

Sidney M. Milkis, *The President and the Parties: The Transformation of the American Party System since the New Deal* (Oxford and New York: Oxford University Press, 1993).

Stephen Skowronek, *The Politics Presidents Make: Leadership from John Adams to Bill Clinton* (Cambridge, MA: Belknap Press, 1997).

Jeffrey K. Tulis, *The Rhetorical Presidency* (Princeton University Press, 1987).

11

Bureaucracy: Shaping Government for the Twenty-first Century

Introduction

The American republic was founded on rule by the people and the rule of law. Yet, like every other national government, the United States quickly came to rely on unelected public administrators to put those laws into effect. A year before it declared independence from Great Britain, the Continental Congress chose George Washington—a leader with military experience—to lead the Continental Army and implement the defense of the nation during the American Revolution. By 1781, Congress was deeply in debt, and created the office of Superintendent of Finance to do the vital work of ensuring that the fledgling government would have the funds to carry on. They chose Robert Morris, a wealthy merchant with international commercial ties, to implement this sensitive task.

Since the Founding, Americans have grappled with the fit between democracy and bureaucracy. The expansion of the nation, its economy, its problems and its laws also has expanded American bureaucracy. Today, the federal government employs 2.8 million civilians; together, the federal, state and local governments employ almost 22 million people (a number that includes many teachers). No elected official could directly control all these employees. Besides the sheer number of government employees, no single elected official could master the diverse expertise of these workers, from meteorologists at the National Weather Service to physicians at the Centers for Disease control, cybersecurity experts at the Department of Homeland Security, lawyers in the Department of Justice, Forest Service officers at the Department of Agriculture and skilled diplomats at the State department. These experts must have discretion to do their jobs. Their work is scattered across the nation and the world.

Bureaucracy is here to stay. In the first reading, Anthony Downs emphasized that bureaucracy is indispensable in modern society. Government must do tasks that business cannot or will not do, at least on the necessary scale: defend the nation, protect property and commerce, regulate dangers in the environment, teach the young, and provide help for those who cannot provide for themselves. James Q. Wilson (reading two) stressed that bureaucracy exists both in government and in large private businesses like McDonald's. Both public and private bureaucracies are big, complex and run according to many detailed rules and procedures. But public bureaucracy cannot operate in the way bureaucracies operate in private businesses, because public bureaucracy is judged by many (often conflicting) standards, and not just profits. Public bureaus operate under much more complicated constraints and uncertainties than private bureaus. And public bureaus must be sensitive to politics.

The problem of maintaining bureaucracy in a republic also is here to stay. The United States became a democracy early in its history, before the expansion of bureaucracy. This sequence meant that control of the bureaucracy became intertwined with intense party competition to win elections. Party leaders used appointment to federal administrative offices, such as local postmasters, as rewards for faithful supporters of the party. This patronage (or "spoils") system distinguished the United States from many European nations, where bureaucracy was established well before democracy took root, and preceded the robust political party jostling characteristic of America.

For reformers like Woodrow Wilson (reading three) and many who have followed, patronage was unacceptable. For them, bureaucracy could only be reconciled with democracy if politics and administration were kept as separate as possible. First, elected officials would negotiate public policy through the political process. Only after politics had determined policy would expert administrators, selected for their competence rather than their political loyalty, implement this policy with efficiency and strict political neutrality.

While appealing in theory, the actual process of reconciling bureaucracy and democracy has been much more complicated. In our highlight piece, political scientist Michael Nelson (reading four) traced the actual sequence of key bureaucratic developments in the United States. Over and over again, efforts to reconcile bureaucracy with democracy have had unanticipated—and ironic—consequences that strengthened bureaucracy. For example, efforts by reformers helped create a civil service system that only increased the independence of administrators, making it more difficult for elected officials to hold the bureaucracy accountable.

In reading five, Daniel Carpenter showed that the subsequent growth of American bureaucracy has responded to the growing need for non-market administration (as Downs points out) as well as the forces set in motion by politics and political reform (as Nelson argues). Entrepreneurial administrators themselves often have led the expansion of bureaucracy. While bureaucratic growth is more limited at present, the problem of reconciling democracy and bureaucracy persists. Barack Obama was the most recent president to try to tackle this problem. In our sixth reading, Laurence Lynn, one of the most prominent scholars of public administration, assessed Obama's approach to the bureaucracy in the first few months of his presidency. For Lynn, Obama marked a return to ideas of progressive-era administrative reform. This approach, cautions Lynn, has its own problems and limitations.

11.1 Anthony Downs, "Why Bureaus Are Necessary" (1967)

Economist Anthony Downs applied his expertise to the fundamental problems of democracy and bureaucracy. In this selection from his landmark book, *Inside*

Bureaucracy, Downs explained why a modern economy requires public bureaucracy. For Downs, a bureaucracy is a large organization with a full-time, paid workforce that is assessed on performance and that produces goods or services that are not evaluated by simple market values. Government has many such organizations because government must see to it that essential tasks of protecting citizens and nurturing prosperity get done. Private business alone will not meet these needs. Nothing illustrates the demand for public bureaucracy better than the American experience after 9/11, when the federal government expanded the military and established a new Department of Homeland Security. Such bureaus have to be large; federal government activities inevitably involve implementation across the nation, and, in the case of the military, diplomacy and many other tasks, across the globe.

Bureaucracy Is Here to Stay

Many people regard bureaucracy and bureaucrats as necessary evils at best. In fact, there is a widespread feeling that their extent and influence should be minimized. This chapter will show why it is not possible to eliminate bureaus from modern societies. Certain vital social functions must be performed by nonmarket-oriented organizations that possess all the traits defined as characterizing bureaus.

Social Functions in Modern Societies That Must Be Performed by Nonmarket-oriented Organizations

Major Causes of Governmental Functions in Democracies Containing Private Markets

Large External Benefits or Costs

Some important social functions cannot be performed adequately by market-oriented organizations because they involve external costs or benefits. An external cost or benefit does not reflect itself in market prices, but is felt directly or indirectly outside of markets. For example, the exhaust fumes from automobiles which create smog cause certain nonmarket costs of living in Los Angeles.

When there are divergencies between internal and total costs or benefits because of external elements, private agents operating solely through markets tend to make decisions that do not take account of all the relevant effects of their behavior. In some cases, this results in socially undesirable outcomes. Either private agents carry out policies that are profitable to them but inflict unduly heavy costs on others, or they fail to carry out policies unprofitable to them that would result in great benefits to others.

To avoid both of these outcomes, society must develop nonmarket-oriented organizations that can intervene in markets to help insure that all the relevant costs and benefits enter into the decisionmaking process. This is often done when there are large divergencies between internal and total costs or benefits. Examples are zoning controls, traffic regulations, and smoke suppression laws.

Indivisible Benefits

An extreme type of external benefits important enough to consider separately results from what some economists have called "collective goods." A collective good provides indivisible benefits. As soon as it exists, everyone is able to benefit from it regardless of whether he himself has paid for it and regardless of how many others are also benefiting from it.

Provision of the proper amount of indivisible benefits cannot be handled by the allocation mechanisms of private-markets. The beneficiaries are motivated to conceal their true preferences in order to avoid their share of the costs. For example, national defense benefits every citizen. But each person finds it advantageous to evade paying for such benefits. Instead, he assumes that others will bear the costs and he will still benefit. In a free-market everyone makes the same assumption so no one bears any of the costs and none of the benefits are forthcoming.

Thus nonmarket-oriented organizations capable of using coercion are required to allocate appropriate resources to collective goods. Such vital services as national defense, maintenance of law and order, enforcement of contracts, and education all involve some indivisible benefits.

Redistribution of Incomes

The members of a society may decide to redistribute their incomes so that certain individuals (usually those with low incomes) are benefited at the expense of others (those with high incomes). Some such redistribution can be accomplished voluntarily through small-scale private charity. However, the citizenry may decide that such action is insufficient. Therefore, private citizens may institute large-scale charities, which by nature are nonmarket-oriented. Or the citizenry may wish to take additional money away from some citizens and transfer it to others, as in the case of unemployment compensation, medical care for the poor, and aid to dependent children. The persons from whom money is so taken will usually not yield it without being required to do so by law (backed ultimately by the threat of coercion). Since markets are based upon voluntary transactions, nonmarket-oriented organizations are necessary for such policies.

Regulation of Monopolies

For technical reasons, some operations must be monopolies (such as the telephone company or the electric power supplier in a given area); in other industries, economies of scale or patent controls create strong monopolistic tendencies. Nonmarket regulatory agencies are often established in such monopolistic markets to protect the consuming public.

Protection of Consumers from Their Own Ignorance or Incompetence

Some products might be very harmful to their consumers if they were not properly prepared, but the consumers cannot measure the quality of their preparation because of technical incompetence or practical difficulties. In this category are foods, drugs, water supplies, and cigarettes. To protect themselves from harmful exploitation by producers in such instances, consumers in a democracy often have the government establish regulatory or inspection agencies which must be insulated from market pressures.

Compensation for Aggregate Instabilities or Deficiencies in a Market Economy

The overall performance of a market economy may differ widely from what is considered socially desirable, as in the Great Depression of the Thirties. To prevent this outcome, or to correct it if it occurs, governments establish nonmarket agencies to measure the performance of the economy (as does the National Income Section of the Department of Commerce), to make recommendations regarding compensatory steps to be taken (as does the President's Council of Economic Advisors), or to take such steps (as does the Federal Reserve Board).

Areas of Producer Disorganization
In some industries, particularly agriculture, producers are so fragmented that the competitive market may create no incentive for research and development. As a result, governments may devise nonmarket agencies to carry out research in such fields and to reduce the shock caused therein by the resulting technical changes in production.

Creation of a Framework of Law and Order
Most democratic and many nondemocratic societies are based upon the ethical premise that men are of inherently equal value in some ultimate sense. Therefore, such societies seek to create systems of law and order that apply a single set of rules impartially to everyone. However, markets respond to money signals given to them by potential buyers and sellers, and money is very unequally distributed in almost every society. Therefore, systems of law and order cannot be based upon markets if they are to treat all citizens as equal before the law.

Maintenance of the Government Itself
Creation, organization, operation, and financing of the many nonmarket organizations described above requires other nonmarket organizations. Such bureaus as the Treasury Department, the General Services Administration, the Bureau of the Budget, and the General Accounting Office all perform necessary "housekeeping" operations for the entire "family" of government agencies. Since none of the primary government agencies sell most of their outputs through voluntary *quid pro quo* transactions, those agencies devoted to "housekeeping" functions are also unable to operate through markets.

The above list of government activities that only nonmarket organizations can carry out could be longer or shorter, depending on the type of government. However, all governments must perform a great many of these activities, because they include the major reasons why governments exist. . . .

Other Traits of Bureaus in Nonmarket-oriented Organizations

Bureaus as we have defined them have three basic traits other than nonmarket orientation. Many of the nonmarket-oriented organizations that societies need to perform the functions described above must have all three of these traits; therefore they are bureaus.

Why Most Are Large
Most of the social functions described in the preceding section must be carried out on a very large scale—at least in the many societies in the world that have several million members or more. The mere size of the tasks involved requires large organizations to perform them. Although many of these giant tasks . . . can be broken down into thousands of smaller ones, the smaller tasks cannot be assigned to completely separate, small organizations because they must be closely coordinated by a single overall policy.

Why They Employ Full-time, Paid Personnel

Another characteristic of these functions is that most of them require almost continuous attention from trained specialists. This is necessary either because their services cannot be interrupted without harmful consequences (such as the provision of law and order) or because only sustained efforts can maintain the expert knowledge required ... The personnel who carry out such functions must have received adequate training and must be extremely reliable in the performance of their jobs. These traits are not likely to be possessed by dilettantes or persons working for purely honorific reasons.

This is not to say that noneconomic incentives are unimportant in such organizations; in some cases they are vital. Moreover, a few individuals can be relied upon to do their best merely because they enjoy their work, have a strong sense of duty, or get a feeling of power from their activities. But most large organizations responsible for a wide variety of jobs, from low-level labor to high-level policy planning, cannot depend upon personal inclinations as the main motives for getting these jobs done continuously, and under all conditions. Such reliability is most likely to be exhibited by people who must work because they need the money. This need also increases their general willingness to obey orders. As Max Weber observed, "Other circumstances being equal, only economically independent officials, that is, officials who belong to the propertied strata, can permit themselves to risk the loss of their offices. Today as always recruitment of officials from among the propertyless strata increases the power of the rulers."[1]

Why Their Personnel Policies Are Based on Role Performance

Officials are motivated to perform their roles with energy and competence insofar as promotion is based on these two traits. Both are extremely important to large nonmarket-oriented organizations. These organizations are entrusted with complex tasks in a changing and uncertain environment; hence they need members who will exhibit initiative and imagination. Moreover, they require considerable delegation of authority; hence they also need mechanisms for insuring that the discretion of lower-level officials is at least partly used to carry out the orders and intentions of their superiors.

Why Governmental Nonmarket Functions Cannot Be Performed by Nonbureaucratic Organizations

Some critics of government activity have argued that many governmental nonmarket functions need not actually be carried out by bureaucratic organizations. For example, Milton Friedman has espoused leaving the operation of educational facilities entirely to private firms.[2] Similarly, other economists have proposed private operation of the post office and fire and police departments.

Private firms could undoubtedly carry out through voluntary *quid pro quo* transactions many of the service functions now entrusted to government agencies. Provision of electric power or first-class mail service are examples of such potentially marketable services. Nevertheless, shifting certain marketable services from government agencies to private firms would not eliminate the need for a significant number of large nonmarket-oriented organizations, that is, bureaus. This is true for three reasons. First, certain nonmarketable benefits now produced by government agencies as joint products with marketable benefits would still have to be furnished by bureaus. For example, the Post Office Department provides subsidies to several activities (such as Rural Free Delivery) that are not self-supporting on a voluntary *quid pro quo* basis, but produce external benefits regarded by Congress as significant.

Second, bureaus would be needed to regulate the production of some marketable benefits that cannot be separated from the production of joint nonmarketable benefits. For example, assume that the government paid lump-sum cash grants to all parents for the education of their children, but left selection of educational facilities entirely up to the parents. If no regulations were imposed upon the production of education by private entrepreneurs, then some might succeed in selling shoddy education to irresponsible or ignorant parents. In this case, society would be ignoring certain important indivisible benefits of providing a minimum quality of education to every child. To take account of such benefits, a nonmarketoriented agency would have to be created to set and enforce minimum educational standards.

Third, many governmental functions described earlier have no marketable components at all; hence they would have to be carried out entirely by bureaus. Examples are regulating "natural" monopolies and compensating for the aggregate deficiencies of a market economy.

This reasoning does not imply that all bureaus required by society must be owned or operated by governments. Privately run bureaus (such as Federal Reserve Banks) can perform important regulatory and other nonmarket-oriented functions, so long as they are ultimately backed by government's power of coercion. Thus the question of who should own and operate bureaus is different from the question of whether they need to exist. Similarly, the fact that society needs bureaus to perform some governmental functions does not imply that all functions now performed by the government must be carried out by bureaus. Undoubtedly some could be shifted to market-oriented organizations. But these qualifications do not alter the basic conclusion that bureaus are a necessity in modem societies.

NOTES

1. Max Weber, "Bureaucracy," in *Essays in Sociology*, translated by H. H. Gerth and C. Wright Mills (New York: Oxford University Press, 2962), p. 235.
2. Milton Friedman, "The Role of Government in Education," *Capitalism and Freedom* (Chicago: University of Chicago Press, 1962).

11.2 James Q. Wilson, "Bureaucracy" (1989)

Political scientist James Wilson explains why these inevitable public bureaucracies fundamentally cannot be run like private businesses. The very notion of democratic control of public bureaucracy makes it impossible for public bureaucracy to have the power to control its fate, as a private bureaucracy often can do. Unlike large businesses, bureaucracy does not fully control the keys to autonomy: money, personnel and investments. Legislatures and elected executives control budgets, and appropriations usually reflect the political priorities of elected officials rather than the performance of the agency. Managers in public bureaucracies also are more subject to outside intervention, whether from other agencies, legislators, courts or constituents, than are managers of private organizations. Their performance is difficult to measure, because bureaus are judged in many different ways by different legislators, executives, interest groups and clients. These constraints, Wilson contends, make managers within public bureaucracies much more rule and process oriented and much more risk averse than managers in private or corporate bureaucracies. Public managers are more attuned to issues of process and equity than to the issues of innovation and efficiency that drive the best of their private counterparts.

BY THE TIME the office opens at 8:45 A.M., the line of people waiting to do business at the Registry of Motor Vehicles in Watertown, Massachusetts, often will be twenty-five deep. By midday, especially if it is near the end of the month, the line may extend clear around the building. Inside, motorists wait in slow-moving rows before poorly marked windows to get a driver's license or to register an automobile. When someone gets to the head of the line, he or she is often told by the clerk that it is the wrong line: "Get an application over there and then come back," or "This is only for people getting a new license; if you want to replace one you lost, you have to go to the next window." The customers grumble impatiently. The clerks act harried and sometimes speak brusquely, even rudely. What seems to be a simple transaction may take 45 minutes or even longer. By the time people are photographed for their driver's licenses, they are often scowling. The photographer valiantly tries to get people to smile, but only occasionally succeeds.[1]

Not far away, people also wait in line at a McDonald's fast-food restaurant. There are several lines; each is short, each moves quickly. The menu is clearly displayed on attractive signs. The workers behind the counter are invariably polite. If someone's order cannot be filled immediately, he or she is asked to step aside for a moment while the food is prepared and then is brought back to the head of the line to receive the order. The atmosphere is friendly and good-natured. The room is immaculately clean.

Many people have noticed the difference between getting a driver's license and ordering a Big Mac. Most will explain it by saying that bureaucracies are different from businesses. "Bureaucracies" behave as they do because they are run by unqualified "bureaucrats" and are enmeshed in "rules" and "red tape."

But business firms are also bureaucracies, and McDonald's is a bureaucracy that regulates virtually every detail of its employees' behavior by a complex and all-encompassing set of rules. Its operations manual is six hundred pages long and weighs four pounds.[2] In it one learns that french fries are to be nine-thirty-seconds of an inch thick and that grill workers are to place hamburger patties on the grill from left to right, six to a row for six rows. They are then to flip the third row first, followed by the fourth, fifth, and sixth rows, and finally the first and second. The amount of sauce placed on each bun is precisely specified. . . . There are plenty of rules governing the Registry, but they are only a small fraction of the rules that govern every detail of every operation at McDonald's. Indeed, if the DMV manager tried to impose on his employees as demanding a set of rules as those that govern the McDonald's staff, they would probably rebel and he would lose his job. . . .

In short, many of the popular stereotypes about government agencies and their members are either questionable or incomplete. To explain why government agencies behave as they do, it is not enough to know that they are "bureaucracies"—that is, it is not enough to know that they are big, or complex, or have rules. What is crucial is that they are *government* bureaucracies.... [and] all government agencies have in common certain characteristics that tend to make their management far more difficult than managing a McDonald's. These common characteristics are the constraints of public agencies.

The key constraints are three in number. To a much greater extent than is true of private bureaucracies, government agencies (1) cannot lawfully retain and devote to the private benefit of their members the earnings of the organization, (2) cannot allocate the factors of production in accordance with the preferences of the organization's administrators, and (3) must serve goals not of the organization's own choosing. Control over revenues, productive factors, and agency goals is all vested to an important degree in entities external to the organization—legislatures, courts, politicians, and interest groups. Given this, agency managers must attend to the demands of these external entities. As a result, government management tends to be driven by the *constraints* on the organization, not the *tasks* of the organization....

Acquiring and Using the Factors of Production

A business firm acquires capital by retaining earnings, borrowing money, or selling shares of ownership; a government agency (with some exceptions) acquires capital by persuading a legislature to appropriate it. A business firm hires, promotes, demotes, and fires personnel with considerable though not perfect freedom; a federal government agency is told by Congress how many persons it can hire and at what rate of pay, by the Office of Personnel Management (OPM) what rules it must follow in selecting and assigning personnel, by the Office of Management and Budget (OMB) how many persons of each rank it may employ, by the Merit Systems Protection Board (MSPB) what procedures it must follow in demoting or discharging personnel, and by the courts whether it has faithfully followed the rules of Congress, OPM, OMB, and MSPB.... When a business firm finds that certain offices or factories are no longer economical it will close or combine them; when a government agency wishes to shut down a local office or military base often it must get the permission of the legislature....

... These complexities in hiring, purchasing, contracting, and budgeting often are said to be the result of the "bureaucracy's love of red tape." But few, if any, of the rules producing this complexity would have been generated by the bureaucracy if left to its own devices, and many are as cordially disliked by the bureaucrats as by their clients. These rules have been imposed on the agencies by external actors, chiefly the legislature. They are not bureaucratic rules but *political* ones.... The reason is politics, or more precisely, democratic politics....

Contextual Goals

An agency's primary goal may be clear or vague, but its primacy usually is not in dispute. "Educate children," "prevent crime," "maintain relations with other nations"—ambiguous as these objectives may be, they nonetheless justify the existence of school systems, police forces, and the State Department.

But these primary goals are not the only ones an agency is expected to serve. In addition it must serve a large number of contextual goals—that is, descriptions of desired states of affairs other than the one the agency was brought into being to create. For example, a police department not only must try to prevent crime and catch criminals, it must protect the rights of the accused, safeguard the confidentiality of its records, and provide necessary health services to arrestees. These other goals define the context within which the primary goals can be sought.

The number and importance of contextual goals has risen dramatically in recent years. The Administrative Procedure Act (APA), passed in 1946, requires most federal agencies to observe certain standards of procedural fairness. They cannot adopt a new rule or policy without first giving written notice of their intention to do so (usually by publishing a "notice of proposed rulemaking" in the *Federal Register*) and soliciting comments from interested parties. If the agencies hold hearings, they must allow interested parties to appear and introduce evidence. In 1981, President Reagan required that the regulations an agency proposed to adopt also would have to be submitted to the Office of Information and Regulatory Affairs in the Office of Management and Budget. OMB had the power to block regulations if in its judgment the costs exceeded the benefits.

The Freedom of Information Act (FOIA), passed in 1966–67 and amended in 1986, gives citizens the right to inspect almost all government records with the exception of military, intelligence, trade secrets, and those files the disclosure of which reasonably could be expected to constitute an invasion of privacy or compromise a law-enforcement investigation.[3] . . .

These contextual goals have two principal, and somewhat different, motivations. The first is a desire to insure procedural fairness. (For example: "Give notice." "Hold hearings." "Encourage participation." "Consider evidence." "Reveal records." "Allow arrested persons a chance to talk to a lawyer.") The second is a desire to favor certain interests over others. (For example: "Buy American." "Buy from small businesses owned by women.") The first motive might be described as an effort to produce a level playing field, the second as an effort to tilt the playing field.

The Effects of Constraints and Context

The existence of so many contextual goals and political constraints has several consequences for the management of public agencies. First, managers have a strong incentive to worry more about constraints than tasks, which means to worry more about processes than outcomes. Outcomes often are uncertain, delayed, and controversial; procedures are known, immediate, and defined by law or rule. It is hard to hold managers accountable for attaining a goal, easy to hold them accountable for conforming to the rules. Even when a bureau's primary goals are clear and progress toward them measurable, the managers of the bureau cannot be content with achieving them with the least use of resources; they also must worry about serving the contextual goals of the agency. These contextual goals are defended by powerful interests or by individuals and groups with access to important centers of power—the courts and congressional committees. The Army Corps of Engineers can describe exactly how a dam should be built and verify that it was built that way, but woe betide it if it goes ahead with the dam without extensive public consultation and close attention to environmental issues.[4]

Second, the multiplicity of constraints on an agency enhances the power of potential intervenors in the agency. Every constraint or contextual goal is the written affirmation of the claim of some external constituency. Thus the agency has weak boundaries and a large, variegated "membership" consisting of all who have a stake in the maintenance of one or more constraints. In the United States, where courts have great authority and access to them is relatively easy, the multiplication of constraints enhances the power of the courts over bureaucratic processes. If an agency is bound by a procedural rule, such as the obligation to hold hearings, people affected by that agency's decisions can enforce the procedural rule by going to court. The rules have conferred rights; courts exist to enforce rights. If an interest (say, the clean-air interest) has acquired special legal status, then that claim to a special status can be enforced by appeal to the courts. Between 1963 and 1983, the number of appeals from the decisions of federal administrative agencies heard by U.S. courts of appeal nearly tripled.[5]

Third, equity is more important than efficiency in the management of many government agencies. This follows from the first two consequences: if managers must follow the correct procedures and if courts exist to enforce those procedures, then a procedural rule often will be defended by claiming that it is essential to the fair or equitable treatment of agency members or clients. Equity issues always seem easier to judge than efficiency issues: We cannot easily say whether the pupils were educated, the streets made safer, or some diseases prevented; but we can say whether every pupil got the same textbook, every citizen got the same police response, and every patient got the same vaccine....

Fourth, the existence of many contextual goals, like the existence of constraints on the use of resources, tends to make managers more risk averse. Police administrators rarely lose their jobs because the crime rate has gone up or win promotions because it has gone down. They can easily lose their jobs if somebody persuasively argues that the police department has abused a citizen, beaten a prisoner, or failed to answer a call for service.[6] School administrators rarely lose their jobs when their pupils' reading scores go down or win promotions when scores go up. But they can lose their jobs or suffer other career-impeding consequences if students are punished, controversial textbooks assigned, or parents treated impolitely. Under these circumstances it is hardly surprising that police captains spend a lot of their time trying to make certain that their officers follow the rules and that school principals spend a lot of their time cultivating the goodwill of parents....

Finally, the more contextual goals and constraints that must be served, the more discretionary authority in an agency is pushed upward to the top. In most organizations, front-line operators are in a better position to exercise judgment about operating problems than upper-level managers, who can know of a problem, if at all, only through delayed and much-condensed reports. It is easier to allow front-line operators to exercise discretion when only one clear goal is to be attained. The greater the number and complexity of those goals, the riskier it is to give authority to operators....

NOTES

1. "The Registry of Motor Vehicles: Watertown Branch," Case number C16–84–580, prepared at the John F. Kennedy School of Government, Harvard University, 1984.
2. John F. Love, *McDonald's: Behind the Arches* (New York: Bantam Books, 1986), 140ff.
3. *5 U.S. Code* 552.

4. Cf. Daniel A. Mazmanian and Jeanne Nienaber, *Can Organizations Change?* (Washington, DC: The Brookings Institution, 1979).

5. Robert A. Carp and Ronald Stidham, *The Federal Courts* (Washington, DC: CQ Press, 1985), 42.

6. James Q. Wilson, *Varieties of Police Behavior* (Cambridge, Mass.: Harvard University Press, 1968), 70–71.

11.3 Woodrow Wilson, "The Study of Administration" (1887)

Before Woodrow Wilson (1856–1924) became reform-minded governor of New Jersey and President of the U.S., he was a pioneering political scientist. In this 1887 article, Wilson noted that far more scholarly time and attention had been spent on the origins and constitutional structure of government than on its efficient daily operation. But the administration of government, he argued, "is government in action" and "the most visible side of government." Wilson's article illustrates how reformers were developing a powerful alternative to the patronage-based system for filling public offices with party loyalists in late nineteenth-century America. He makes the point that "politics sets the tasks for administration" but politics "should not be suffered to manipulate its offices. . ." He insisted that administration should instead be placed in the hands of those with professional skills, who would be impartial, trustworthy, and professionally skilled. They would faithfully and effectively execute the will of the people, translated into government policies by the people's chosen leaders. Wilson's article gave more momentum to civil service reform, which already had begun in the federal Pendleton Civil Service Act (1883) and would come to full fruition during the Progressive Era of the early 1900s. Wilson's assertion that politics and administration *can* be separated has remained controversial for over a century.

I SUPPOSE that no practical science is ever studied where there is no need to know it. . . . It is the object of administrative study to discover, first, what government can properly and successfully do, and, secondly, how it can do these proper things with the utmost possible efficiency and at the least possible cost either of money or of energy. On both these points there is obviously much need of light among us; and only careful study can supply that light. . . .

I.

Administration is the most obvious part of government; it is government in action; it is the executive, the operative, the most visible side of government, and is of course as old as government itself. . . .

This is why there should be a science of administration which shall seek to straighten the paths of government, to make its business less unbusinesslike, to strengthen and purify its organization, and to crown its duties with dutifulness. This is one reason why there is such a science....

The field of administration is a field of business. It is removed from the hurry and strife of politics; it at most points stands apart even from the debatable ground of constitutional study. It is a part of political life only as the methods of the counting-house are a part of the life of society; only as machinery is part of the manufactured product. But it is, at the same time, raised very far above the dull level of mere technical detail by the fact that through its greater principles it is directly connected with the lasting maxims of political wisdom, the permanent truths of political progress.

The object of administrative study is to rescue executive methods from the confusion and costliness of empirical experiment and set them upon foundations laid deep in stable principle....

Let me expand a little what I have said of the province of administration....; namely, that administration lies outside the proper sphere of *politics*. Administrative questions are not political questions. Although politics sets the tasks for administration, it should not be suffered to manipulate its offices.

This is distinction of high authority; eminent German writers insist upon it as of course. Bluntschli,[1] for instance, bids us separate administration alike from politics and from law. Politics, he says, is state activity "in things great and universal," while "administration, on the other hand," is "the activity of the state in individual and small things. Politics is thus the special province of the statesman, administration of the technical official." "Policy does nothing without the aid of administration"; but administration is not therefore politics. But we do not require German authority for this position; this discrimination between administration and politics is now, happily, too obvious to need further discussion.

There is another distinction which must be worked into all our conclusions, which, though but another side of that between administration and politics, is not quite so easy to keep sight of: I mean the distinction between *constitutional* and administrative questions, between those governmental adjustments which are essential to constitutional principle and those which are merely instrumental to the possibly changing purposes of a wisely adapting convenience....

A clear view of the difference between the province of constitutional law and the province of administrative function ought to leave no room for misconception; and it is possible to name some roughly definite criteria upon which such a view can be built. Public administration is detailed and systematic execution of public law. Every particular application of general law is an act of administration. The assessment and raising of taxes, for instance, the hanging of a criminal, the transportation and delivery of the mails, the equipment and recruiting of the army and navy, *etc.*, are all obviously acts of administration; but the general laws which direct these things to be done are as obviously outside of and above administration. The broad plans of governmental action are not administrative; the detailed execution of such plans is administrative. Constitutions, therefore, properly concern themselves only with those instrumentalities of government which are to control general law. Our federal constitution observes this principle in saying nothing of even the greatest of the purely executive offices, and speaking only of that President of the Union who was to share the legislative and policy-making functions of government, only of those judges of highest jurisdiction who were to interpret and guard its principles, and not of those who were merely to give utterance to them. . . .

There is, indeed, one point at which administrative studies trench on constitutional ground—or at least upon what seems constitutional ground. The study of administration, philosophically viewed, is closely connected with the study of the proper distribution of constitutional authority. To be efficient it must discover the simplest arrangements by which responsibility can be unmistakably fixed upon officials; the best way of dividing authority without hampering it, and responsibility without obscuring it. And this question of the distribution of authority, when taken into the sphere of the higher, the originating functions of government, is obviously a central constitutional question. If administrative study can discover the best principles upon which to base such distribution, it will have done constitutional study an invaluable service. Montesquieu did not, I am convinced, say the last word on this head.

To discover the best principle for the distribution of authority is of greater importance, possibly, under a democratic system, where officials serve many masters, than under others where they serve but a few. All sovereigns are suspicious of their servants, and the sovereign people is no exception to the rule; but how is its suspicion to be allayed by *knowledge?* If that suspicion could but be clarified into wise vigilance, it would be altogether salutary; if that vigilance could be aided by the unmistakable placing of responsibility, it would be altogether beneficent. Suspicion in itself is never healthful either in the private or in the public mind. *Trust is strength* in all relations of life; and, as it is the office of the constitutional reformer to create conditions of trustfulness, so it is the office of the administrative organizer to fit administration with conditions of clear-cut responsibility which shall insure trustworthiness. . . .

But is the whole duty of administrative study done when it has taught the people what sort of administration to desire and demand, and how to get what they demand? Ought it not to go on to drill candidates for the public service?

There is an admirable movement towards universal political education now afoot in this country. The time will soon come when no college of respectability can afford to do without a well-filled chair of political science. But the education thus imparted will go but a certain length. It will multiply the number of intelligent critics of government, but it will create no competent body of administrators. It will prepare the way for the development of a sure-footed understanding of the general principles of government, but it will not necessarily foster skill in conducting government. It is an education which will equip legislators, perhaps, but not executive officials. If we are to improve public opinion, which is the motive power of government, we must prepare better officials as the *apparatus* of government. If we are to put in new boilers and to mend the fires which drive our governmental machinery, we must not leave the old wheels and joints and valves and bands to creak and buzz and clatter on as best they may at bidding of the new force. We must put in new running parts wherever there is the least lack of strength or adjustment. It will be necessary to organize democracy by sending up to the competitive examinations for the civil service men definitely prepared for standing liberal tests as to technical knowledge. A technically schooled civil service will presently have become indispensable.

I know that a corps of civil servants prepared by a special schooling and drilled, after appointment, into a perfected organization, with appropriate hierarchy and characteristic discipline, seems to a great many very thoughtful persons to contain elements which might combine to make an offensive official class,—a distinct, semi-corporate body with sympathies divorced from those of a progressive, free-spirited people, and with hearts narrowed to the meanness of a bigoted officialism. Certainly such a class would be altogether hateful and harmful in the United States. Any measures calculated to produce it would for us be measures of reaction and of folly.

But to fear the creation of a domineering, illiberal officialism as a result of the studies I am here proposing is to miss altogether the principle upon which I wish most to insist. That principle is, that administration in the United States must be at all points sensitive to public opinion. A body of thoroughly trained officials serving during good behavior we must have in any case: that is a plain business necessity. But the apprehension that such a body will be anything un-American clears away the moment it is asked, What is to constitute good behavior? For that question obviously carries its own answer on its face. Steady, hearty allegiance to the policy of the government they serve will constitute good behavior. That *policy* will have no taint of officialism about it. It will not be the creation of permanent officials, but of statesmen whose responsibility to public opinion will be direct and inevitable. Bureaucracy can exist only where the whole service of the state is removed from the common political life of the people, its chiefs as well as its rank and file. Its motives, its objects, its policy, its standards, must be bureaucratic. It would be difficult to point out any examples of impudent exclusiveness and arbitrariness on the part of officials doing service under a chief of department who really served the people, as all our chiefs of departments must be made to do. It would be easy, on the other hand, to adduce other instances like that of the influence of Stein in Prussia, where the leadership of one statesman imbued with true public spirit transformed arrogant and perfunctory bureaux into public-spirited instruments of just government.

The ideal for us is a civil service cultured and self-sufficient enough to act with sense and vigor, and yet so intimately connected with the popular thought, by means of elections and constant public counsel, as to find arbitrariness or class spirit quite out of the question. . . .

NOTE

1. Politik, 5. 467.

11.4 Michael Nelson, "A Short, Ironic History of American National Bureaucracy" (1982)

In the highlight piece for this chapter, political scientist Michael Nelson placed bureaucracy into the larger story of American political development. He saw many ironies in the sequence of bureaucratic development and reform. The biggest irony of all is that, throughout American history, efforts to increase popular control of the bureaucracy unintentionally prepared the way for more bureaucratic power. For example, the creation of a spoils system in the presidential administration of Andrew Jackson was accompanied by more record-keeping and monitoring, two of the building blocks for bureaucracy in the future. Nelson also emphasized the sequence of political events. The fact that popular elections and democracy came so early in American history prompted the development of politically driven administrative appointments. This spoils system, in turn, retarded the growth of a more professionalized bureaucracy and stimulated the progressive era desire to separate politics and administration—an aspiration that, ironically, contributed further to bureaucratic power. Nelson's piece illustrates the value of understanding the path and the unanticipated consequences of political change over time.

... [T]he argument has been made that, for American bureaucracy, the present really is the sum of the past. Stephen Skowronek contends that one must return to the 1877–1920 period to find the "systemic changes in long-established political and institutional arrangements which first had to be negotiated in order to begin to accommodate an expansion of national administrative capacities in American government."[1] Matthew Crenson goes further, suggesting that the roots of modern bureaucracy are to be found in the Jackson administration, "when ... bureaucratic forms of organization were superimposed upon the business of the national government."[2] Leonard White's tetralogy on pre-twentieth-century national administration takes us all the way to 1789: "Washington, Hamilton, Jefferson, ... and many others dealt with most of the administrative problems that presidents and department heads face today" and developed an approach "to public management that is untouched by time and valid even on the scale of modern administration."[3]

In a chronological sense, at least, White is closest to the mark.[4] Although American national bureaucracy did not spring full-grown from the head of the First Continental Congress in 1775, its fundamental nature, and structure began to develop then and substantially were formed well before the New Deal. Further, at almost every critical turn in American bureaucratic history, the efforts of public officials and organized political groups to enhance popular control of government inadvertently planted the seeds of modern bureaucratic power. This is grand irony in the sense that Reinhold Niebuhr uses the word: an "apparently fortuitous incongruit[y]" between what one intends and what one actually achieves that is not fortuitous at all, but rather is caused by a "hidden relationship" that experience reveals.[5]

Seven particular ironies of pre-1933 American bureaucratic history—ironies of "Revolution," of "Jacksonian Democracy," of "Reform," and of "Representation"—form the heart of this essay....

Ironies of Revolution: 1775–1828

The colonies' distasteful experience with British executive power caused many Americans to reject all executive forms as potentially tyrannical. Thus, though the sole task of the provisional government established by the First Continental Congress in 1775 was an executive one—to raise, support, and direct an army of revolution—it was made purely legislative in structure....

This form of decisionmaking ... exasperated almost everyone [other than the British military]. " 'Inefficiency and waste, if not downright peculation and corruption' were the rule, writes Charles Thach ... After much debate, Congress ... finally, in 1781 ...

established separate departments of Foreign Affairs, War, Marine, and Finance (later Treasury).[6] They were headed by single executives, elected by and accountable to Congress, but otherwise in full control of their jurisdictions, at least until war's end." ...

In creating the departments, following a pattern which would become typical, Congress inaugurated the First Irony of American bureaucratic history, by which *the revolt against the old administrative order planted the seeds of a new administrative order.* The political goal of securing American independence from British administrative power led Congress to give to the new country administrative institutions of its own ...

[During the first decades of American government under the Constitution, early U.S. presidents found that they could not fully control their cabinet secretaries, and] those secretaries could not exercise unfettered control of their departments. Beginning in earnest during the War of 1812, Congress had organized itself into specialized committees that corresponded functionally to the departments and whose purpose was to direct and oversee them .... Through the committee system, Congress used its clear constitutional powers, such as investigation, to dominate administration, and claimed near-monopolistic control over the statute-writing and appropriations powers shared with the president....

... In all this, there was a Second Irony: *the system of dual control of administration became one of limited control.* The Constitutional Convention, in loosing the agencies from their old legislative moorings ... without tying them securely to the presidency ... forced agencies to find and exercise relatively independent power. Agencies began to learn to play one branch off against the other; if neither president nor Congress was supreme, then law was, and the agencies interpreted and implemented the law.

Ironies of Jacksonian Democracy: 1829–1860

[President Andrew Jackson announced in his 1829 inaugural address that] "The duties of all public officers are, or at least admit of being made, so plain and simple that men of intelligence may readily qualify themselves for their performance; and I cannot but believe that much more is lost by the long continuance of men in office than is generally to be gained by their experience."[7]

Rotation in office was the elevated description of this philosophy ... "To the victor belong the spoils of the enemy" was Democratic Senator William Marcy's blunt corollary.[8] In eight years, Jackson removed 252 "presidential officers," more than his six predecessors combined had in forty years ...

... it is the Third Irony of American bureaucratic history that *spoils bred bureaucracy*: Jackson's patronage system helped to hasten the reorganization of federal administrative agencies along bureaucratic lines.

... [T]he Democrats [faced a] dilemma: satisfaction of the party faithful seemed to require the appointment of incompetent officials whose poor performance eventually might bring on a popular backlash fatal to the party. After all, more voters send mail than deliver it.

Jackson's remedy lay in the key phrase of his message to Congress: federal jobs "admit of being made" so simple that any intelligent person could do them.... Labor was to be divided, tasks defined, jobs simplified. "In this system, individuals could be placed or replaced [after an election] without upsetting the integrity of the whole.... It was the administrative counterpart of the interchangeability of machine parts.[9] Consequently, it also was an impetus, however inadvertent, to bureaucratic organization in American government."[10] ...

The second source of the bureaucratization of administration that took place under Andrew Jackson also was the second of his supporters' expressly governmental concerns: rampant corruption in the executive agencies.... Amos Kendall, Jackson's political adviser and Postmaster-General ... was the first to see what had to be done to restrain official thievery. He reorganized the Post Office into an elaborate system of administrative checks and balances among newly organized offices of Accounts, Appointment, Contract, and Inspection, each watchful of the others.... Carefully kept records of every official action were required of employees, and auditors were hired to pore over them. In the new system, the locals spoke only to the auditors, and the auditors spoke only to Kendall.... His innovations spread to the other departments.[11]

... Form follows function in bureaucracy; agencies designed to prevent internal fraud look and act differently from those designed to promote efficiency, coordination, responsiveness, or some other value. All those internal checks and balances took time. For example, when the House Ways and Means Committee convened in 1836 to investigate complaints about the Treasury Department's excruciating slowness in releasing funds, it found that in order to prevent embezzlement five internal clearances had to be made prior to any departmental financial transaction.[12]—hence, the Fourth Irony: *agencies organized to avoid evil became that much less able to do good.* The popular political demand for honest bureaucracy restricted the possibility for efficient and responsive bureaucracy that could satisfactorily meet other, later popular political demands....

An Irony of Reform: 1861–1932

... [M]id-nineteenth-century advocates of a merit-selected civil service sold their proposal with the argument that honest administration and efficient, politically responsive administration were one and the same. Their case, according to Herbert Kaufman, rested on a view of "policy and administration as distinct and separate, though related, activities, and they wanted to restrict partisanship to the policy-makers in order to provide a superlative mechanism by which the voters' mandates could be carried out.[13] ... In short, reformers seemed to feel, a bureaucracy devoid of political appointees would be like a royal guard of eunuchs—an agency with no distracting wants of its own to impede the execution of its assigned tasks." Or, in Kaufman's more subdued analogy, "... the civil service was like a hammer or a saw; it would do nothing at all by itself, but it would serve any purpose, wise or unwise, good or bad, to which any user put it."

Admittedly, spoils had become an easy target in the years after Jackson .... despite the success of the new bureaucratic checks and balances at reducing internal peculation, there was wide corruption at the hiring stage.... And some political leaders were known to feather-bed agencies in order to free employees' time for party labors.... Meritless employees, reformers argued, had so prolonged the Civil War by their incompetence that thousands of soldiers had died needlessly.

... The Pendleton Act passed soon after [the assassination of President James Garfield by Charles Guiteau, a "disappointed office seeker"], in 1883, giving birth to the modern civil service. In the half-century that followed, a Fifth Irony emerged: *reformers' efforts to make the civil service more responsive to the political branches made it less responsive.* This was true in part because, as Richard Schott states, the new civil service's "emphasis on merit in hiring promoted the development of a professional, specialized bureaucracy whose expertise [could] not be matched either by president or Congress. Its emphasis on tenure and permanence in office built into this bureaucracy an insensitivity toward and protection from direct overhead political control."[14]

Also, tenured public employees, unlike eunuchs or hammers, developed interests of their own that impeded the efforts of elected officials to have their decisions implemented faithfully. This was possible because the Act was unclear as to which political branch the new Civil Service Commission was to be primarily responsive. When Presidents Theodore Roosevelt and William Howard Taft tried to increase presidential control over federal employees by, among other things, making dismissals for cause easier to obtain, employee unions played on Congress's jealousy of its institutional power to beat their efforts back.... These and future efforts by one or the other political branches left the civil service more autonomous, prosperous, and unionized than it had been before.

Ironies of Representation: 1861–1932

... The rise of a national market economy produced new demands on government for "clientele" agencies that would represent and support society's increasingly distinct economic groups. It also generated a second set of demands for regulation, in part to protect weak, albeit large, groups from more powerful ones.

... American government at rest tends to stay at rest; except in unusual times, its inertial resistance is overcome only when a powerful group is able to press the kind of claim on government that other powerful groups do not strenuously oppose. Such was the birth of the federal government's first important clientele agency, the Agriculture Department, in 1862.[15] Farmers had organized a lobby, the United States Agricultural Society, to press for the creation of a department that would represent their interests in the administrative realm.

The story of what happened will sound familiar to observers of modern bureaucracy, but it doubtless astonished the political Newtonians of the day. For, once in motion, the new Department of Agriculture not only stayed in motion but accelerated, snowballing in size and eventually in function. By 1901 it had added divisions of Forestry, Animal Husbandry, Entomology, Pomology, Ornithology and Mammalogy, and Plant Industry, as well as the Weather Bureau and an Office of Experiment Stations. The politics of this process were as follows: the new department was staffed, for obvious and entirely innocent reasons, by friends of agriculture. The legislative committees with jurisdiction over the department attracted sympathetic congressmen from farm districts, eager to advance their constituents' and thus the department's interests. The agriculture lobby grew in influence; its new power in Washington made it more powerful with the folks back home; the latter's support made it even more influential in Washington, and so on. Keller notes that during this period, "an agricultural establishment consisting of the department, land grant colleges, and agricultural experiment stations took form."[16] Other groups [such as veterans, educators, organized labor and business] followed agriculture's lead and demanded agencies of their own.[17]

A century ago, the creation of client agencies must have seemed like democracy at its best—worthy groups in society demanding, government responding—but once again things turned out less than happily. The Sixth Irony of American bureaucratic history, in fact, is that *client agencies, created to enhance political representation in government, often became almost independent from general political branch control.* "Subgovernments" consisting of constituencies, agencies, and committees grew secure from the direction of either distracted presidents or apathetic majorities of congressmen, whose districts directed their attention to the advancement of other interests, perhaps through sub-governments of their own.[18]

The other set of demands born of the rise of a national industrial economy was for the restriction of economic power; it resulted in the creation of the first independent regulatory agencies. Railroads, which not only were the fastest growing enterprise in the new inter-regional commerce but its very foundation, also were the first objects of federal regulation. ... [The monopolistic pricing and cooperative "pooling" of the large railroads] enraged the Grange-represented dirt farmers, western merchants, Pennsylvania independent oil producers and refiners, New York businessmen, and others who shipped their products by rail.[19] ...

To mute these mass protests, Congress created the ICC [Interstate Commerce Commission] and charged it to block pooling and to regulate rates. Then, in the familiar manner of "majoritarian politics," the triumphant small shippers, rendered "quiescent" by their legislative victory in Murray Edelman's phrase, happily abandoned political affairs and went on about their business.[20] Who was left to provide the new commission with the political support it needed to survive? Who was to influence its staffing and monitor its activities? Who, aided by a sympathetic Supreme Court, was to dominate its legalistic rate-setting proceedings? The railroad lobby that had "lost" the war found the peace that followed to be its for the asking. By the time of its second annual report, the Commission already was saying ... that pooling was permissible in its eyes ... In 1920, Congress succumbed; the Transportation Act passed that year authorized the ICC to approve such proposals for railroad pooling as it deemed desirable. As for rates, the Commission now was authorized to set minimum as well as maximum limits. Thus, the Seventh, and familiar, Irony is *regulatory agencies created in response to popular political movements often became, in effect, client agencies of the regulated* ...

Grand Irony, Unintended Consequences, and The "Hidden Relationship"

... [In] at least one area of surpassing modern concern, the past seems to speak convincingly. "Unintended consequences" are the bane of the modern policy process: programs are established by law with certain purposes in mind; their actual effects, however, are not (or are not only) those that were intended....

Most efforts to account for these breakdowns in the policy process come in two parts: first, the self-interest of implementing agencies, which adds goals of organizational preservation and growth to those provided by the program statute; and second, the lack of care and specificity characteristic of many such statutes themselves. But the questions again are why? Why is the organizational self-interest of bureaucratic agencies such a powerful force in the American policy process? Why are American legislators and political executives so inattentive to program design?

It is possible that history offers the answers to these questions. If nothing else, history shows that unintended consequences are nothing new; the evolution of American bureaucracy has been marked by one ironic failure after another, the "grand irony" of which is that repeated efforts to bring government under political branch control have enhanced the power of bureaucracy. In particular, I would argue that clues to the nature of the "hidden relationship" discussed in the introduction to this essay that causes this irony are to be found in historical *sequence*, the order in which things happened in the country's political development. The importance of historical sequence becomes apparent through comparison. In Western Europe, a monarchical past meant that the democratization of national political systems occurred long after their bureaucratization. Because the legitimate presence and power of bureaucratic organizations were given by the time democracy came along, the primary democratic task was to control and direct their activities to popular ends. One of the reasons that European political parties developed as programmatic, disciplined organizations was to provide the kind of clear, sustained external direction that bureaucratic agencies need if their organizational goals are to be overcome. The strict internal hierarchy of these agencies, a carry-over from pre-democratic days, facilitated this effort: to appoint or control the agency heads was a giant step toward controlling the agency. In the United States, however, the establishment of democratic political institutions *preceded* the establishment of administrative ones. The latter, which were resisted strenuously in the Continental Congress and scarcely mentioned in the Constitution, have remained somewhat illegitimate in American political culture ever since.[21] From the start, this has forced bureaucratic agencies to build independent political bases to provide sustenance to their pursuit of organizational goals, an endeavor encouraged by the constitutional system of divided political control. "The development of political skills," writes Rourke, "was part of the process by which executive agencies adapted to their environment in order to survive in the egalitarian democratic society in which they found themselves."[22]

The order of American political development (democracy before bureaucracy) also affected the country's political parties (which, in turn, affected the later development of national bureaucracy which, in turn, affected the parties, and so on). Early American parties, quite understandably, had little of the European concern for curbing and directing bureaucratic power. To them, administrative agencies were sources of bounty (pork and patronage), not loci of power in need of control; indeed, Jackson's Democrats fostered the process of bureaucratization in order to reap the harvest of spoils such organizational changes allowed. In part, because bureaucracy was looked at this way, parties also had no incentive to develop as programmatic organizations. This meant, for example, that unlike Great Britain where civil service reform followed the establishment of central party leadership and really did turn British bureaucracy into a "hammer and saw" for the elected government, the American civil service took shape with no vision at all from the parties as to what policy purposes it should serve. This made it a good deal easier for it to foster purposes of its own.

In recent years, as the size and complexity of governmental tasks have increased, the technical expertise to handle them has become an added source of power for bureaucratic agencies.... Without clear policy direction from the parties or their elected officials, organizational self-interest has been able to thrive. And so have unintended consequences.

NOTES

1. Stephen Skowronek, *Building a New American State: The Expansion of National Administrative Capacities, 1877-1920* (New York: Cambridge University Press, 1982), x.
2. Matthew A. Crenson, *The Federal Machine: Beginnings of Bureaucracy in Jacksonian America* (Baltimore: Johns Hopkins University Press, 1975), ix.
3. Leonard D. White, *The Federalists* (New York: Macmillan, 1948), vii, viii. The other three volumes of his "Study in Administrative History" series, all published by Macmillan, are *The Jeffersonians* (1951); *The Jacksonians* (1954); and *The Republican Era* (1958).
4. White's notion of "modern administration" seems concerned more with executive leadership of administration by the president and department heads than with

bureaucracy as a form of organization or a force in society. [Max] Weber, for example, is nowhere cited.

5. Reinhold Niebuhr, *The Irony of History* (New York: Charles Scribner's Sons, 1952), viii.

6. Charles C. Thach, Jr, *The Creation of the Presidency, 1775-1789* (Baltimore: Johns Hopkins University Press, 1923), 67.

7. Quoted in David H. Rosenbloom, *Federal Service and the Constitution: The Development of the Public Employee Relationship* (Ithaca, N.Y.: Cornell University Press, 1971), 49.

8. William Safire, *Safire's Political Dictionary* (New York: Random House, 1978), 679.

9. Lynn Marshall, "The Strange Stillbirth of the Whig Party," *American Historical Review*, LXXII (January 1967), 455–56.

10. This is the view of Marshall, ibid., 468.

11. Crenson, *The Federal Machine*, 136–39.

12. Ibid.

13. Herbert Kaufman, "The Growth of the Federal Personnel System," in *The Federal Government Service: Its Character, Prestige, and Problems*, ed. Wallace S. Sayre (New York: American Assembly, 1954), 36.

14. Lawrence C. Dodd and Richard L. Schott, *Congress and the Administrative State* (New York: John Wiley & Sons, 1979), 25.

15. This discussion of the Agriculture Department is based largely on James Q. Wilson, "The Rise of the Bureaucratic State," in *The American Commonwealth*, eds. Nathan Glazer and Irving Kristol (New York: Basic Books, 1976); and Morton A. Keller, *Affairs of State: Public Life in Late Nineteenth Century America* (Cambridge: Harvard University Press, 1977), ch. 8.

16. Keller, *Affairs*, 314.

17. Theodore Lowi, *The End of Liberalism* (New York: W.W. Norton, 1969).

18. The term is Douglass Cater's. *Power in Washington* (New York: Random House, 1964). But the concept is J. Leiper Freeman's. See *The Political Process: Executive Bureau-Legislative Committee Relations* (New York: Doubleday, 1955).

19. Solon Buck, *The Granger Movement: A Study of Agricultural Organization and Its Political, Economic and Social Manifestations, 1870-1880* (Lincoln: University of Nebraska Press, 1913); George Miller, *Railroads and the Granger Laws* (Madison: University of Wisconsin Press, 1971); Gerald D. Nash, "Origins of the Interstate Commerce Act of 1887," *Pennsylvania History*, XXIV (1957); Lee Benson, *Merchants, Farmers and Railroads: Railroad Regulation and New York Politics* (Cambridge: Harvard University Press, 1955).

20. Wilson, "Rise," 96–97; Murray Edelman, "Symbols and Political Quiescence," *American Political Science Review*, LIV (September 1960), 695–704.

21. Michael Nelson, "Holding Bureaucracy Accountable: The Search for a Model," in *Accountability in the American Policy Process*, ed. George J. Graham (forthcoming); "Power to the People: The Crusade for Direct Democracy," *Saturday Review* (November 24, 1979), 12–17.

22. Francis E. Rourke, *Bureaucracy, Politics, and Public Policy*, 2nd ed. (Boston: Little, Brown, 1976), 73.

11.5 Daniel Carpenter, "The Evolution of the National Bureaucracy" (2005)

Political scientist Daniel Carpenter studied the growing influence of bureaucracy on public policy. For a century, public administrators have played a major role in cultivating policy innovation. The federal bureaucracy became more capable of leading innovation as it became more professional and managerial. The ranks of social scientists and physical scientists have increased in federal agencies. These government-employed professionals are motivated more by reputation, prestige and autonomy than by the more classic bureaucratic motivations for salary and budgetary growth. In recent decades, the aspiration for bureaucratic reform took a new direction. The idea that government could be "reinvented" and run like a business was ascendant. But, in Carpenter's view, these business models have run their course. They have left a legacy of government by contract with private providers, such as contracts with private security firms during the war in Iraq. These contracts, however, have added to the difficulty of making bureaucracy accountable. These developments have set the stage for a return to progressive era principles for reconciling bureaucracy and democracy.

The Rise and Persistence of the Executive Policy-making State

What sort of impact do bureaucratic agencies exercise upon policy, and upon social and economic outcomes? No one doubts that the influence of federal agencies is immense today, yet an important historical point is that bureaucratic influence upon policy has changed immensely in the past 150 years. Executive branch agencies today engage in two activities—planning and policy making—in which independent commissions and other sorts of agencies now play a lesser role, and which executive agencies themselves used to do a lot less of. In some respects, this represents a departure from traditional models of policy making that students learn in civics classes. For much of the past century, executive agencies have been the fount of numerous bills, influential policy ideas, and executive plans. Not all of these have been politically successful, and in some cases, poor public policies have resulted. Yet the fact of extensive bureaucratic involvement in policy innovation is today undeniable. Think tanks and interest groups have certainly diminished the dominant role of the agencies in some areas, but it remains true that in policy domains such as food and pharmaceutical safety, transportation, energy, security, and intelligence, the federal bureaucracy continues to play a crucial planning role.

The Historical Form of Bureaucratic Policy Innovation

Executive agencies are sometimes as powerful in creating new programs as in administering them, as powerful in innovation as in execution. In the late 1800s and early 1900s, the Agriculture Department and the Post Office Department were home to considerable policy innovation of this sort. Long-tenured career federal officials (protected by the Pendleton Act, and reinforced through the bureau-based system of hiring and retention) launched new programs and offices, ranging from the anti-pornography and anti-lottery laws of postal inspector Anthony Comstock to the pure food and drug regulation championed by the Department of Agriculture's Harvey Wiley. Postal bureaucrats took the lead in launching the rural free delivery service, postal savings banks, and parcel post. Agriculture Department officials inaugurated the farm extension system, programs in agricultural economics and planning, and numerous applied scientific programs (soil surveys, insect and pest studies, forestry regulation, and others).

In one of the best-known examples of bureaucratic policy innovation, Social Security administrators such as Arthur Altmeyer, Robert Ball, and others helped to transform the Old-Age and Survivors Disability Insurance (OASDI) program into the dominant income protection program of the federal government of the United States. Some of these moves were made during the formative years of the Social Security program in the 1930s, when Altmeyer and his lieutenants at the Social Security Board (SSB) carefully chose the personnel who would guide the program's development in the ensuing decades and orchestrated an agency-wide plan for program stability followed by growth. Other administrative moves occurred after the World War II—in 1946, the SSB was transformed into the Social Security Administration (SSA) that exists today— including the SSA's active role in promoting union- and corporate-based income protection programs that were jointly negotiated by labor and management (beginning with the United Mine Workers in 1947) and the deployment of the Social Security Administration's expertise in statistics and actuarial science in managing field offices and state income-protection programs.[1]

Such bureaucratic innovation is not confined to the domestic agencies. In the middle of World War II, Navy Department administrators fundamentally changed the way that American militaries procured their supplies. Under the leadership of Undersecretary of the Navy James V. Forrestal (later appointed the first secretary of Defense in 1947), Navy bureaus such as the Bureau of Ships and the Bureau of Aeronautics sidestepped the earlier regime of competitive bidding and began to take active and discretionary control over naval procurement. Naval attorneys developed the first incentive-based contracts for construction and supply. Naval offices used direct and indirect price controls to capture "excess profits" from naval contractors. The bureaus induced their contractors to further subcontract their work as a way of reducing costs. And, as World War II ended, the Navy Department launched its own "deprocurement program" that terminated tens of thousands of contracts with suppliers. After the 1947 National Security Act, which unified the armed forces in a new Department of Defense, the Navy retained many of its procurement capacities even as the Army surrendered its capacities to the new department. The result, as Bartholomew Sparrow describes it, is that naval procurement was a strong exception to the general characterization of a "military-industrial complex" during and after World War II.[2] . . .

To observers of recent presidencies, and especially of the George W. Bush and Reagan administrations, this characterization of agencies as policy innovators may seem problematic. It is apparent, for instance, that there has been considerable centralization of policy making in the White House under the administration of President George W. Bush. Observers of the federal government routinely note that Bush has distanced the making of administration policy and new rules from career civil servants, instead concentrating authority in the top (political) echelons of the federal bureaucracy. The Bush Administration has also encouraged and strengthened the hand of the Office of Management and Budget in reviewing new proposed rules proffered by lower-level bureaus and agencies.

Yet in two respects, the administration of George W. Bush is a continuation of earlier trends.[3] For one, it was a considered reaction to the prominence of executive departments in policy making that led the Bush Administration to move policy-making authority ever higher in the federal administrative hierarchy. Bush's centralization, then, followed upon the Reagan Administration's reaction to a received status quo in which executive agencies played a prominent role. Second, even as the Bush Administration has centralized policy making in the higher echelons of the federal bureaucracy, it has also begun to rely more heavily upon executive agencies for planning and executing federal government activity. Examples here include: the role of the new Center for Medicare and Medicaid Services (CMS) in administering the complex prescription-drug benefit from the Medicare reforms of 2002; the enhanced role of the Department of Transportation; the role of its Federal Aviation Administration (FAA) in coordinating airline schedules (particularly at the nation's most crowded and delayed airports, such as Chicago's O'Hare Field); and the role of the Environmental Protection Agency in proposing and administering new emissions-trading and other deregulatory programs, such as the Administration's Clear Skies Initiative. . . .

The Role and Distribution of Expertise

An increasingly prominent feature of national bureaucracies in the United States, as Patricia Ingraham points out . . . is the professional and scientific composition of their workforce. Government positions are ever more characterized by personnel with highly specialized educations and extensive training and specific experience. This transformation is not unlike many sectors of the U.S. and global economies, but unlike the U.S. economy, the federal bureaucracy has seen little expansion of the "service sector" in the government labor system. This profession- and science-based transformation of American national bureaucracy has had several identifiable implications. First, it has led to increasing average pay scales. The average salary of federal government workers (though not the salaries of high-level federal executives) exceeds that of private sector workers by a fair margin. Observers of American bureaucracy often note facts such as these and decry the pay disparity between the public and private sectors, but unless education and training are accounted for, the wrong conclusion will be reached: the typical federal employee is more educated and more specifically trained than is the typical private sector employee. Indeed, when "human capital" is accounted for, federal government pay is less (and has been increasing more slowly) than pay for comparable positions in the private sector.[4] Second, this specificity and expert nature of federal employment creates a massive personnel problem in the federal government. The training that federal employees receive is very highly valued in private sector positions, whether the skills be those of nuclear engineering (personnel in the Navy and the Department of Energy), pharmacology and chemistry (chemists and physicians employed at the U.S. Food and Drug Administration), law (antitrust specialists in the Department of Justice, or pension lawyers in the Department of Labor's Pension Benefit Guaranty Corporation) or finance (employees of the Federal Reserve Bank or the Treasury Department). Specialized positions in the U.S. federal government are often characterized by high levels of turnover that disrupt the continuity of administrative operations and exacerbate the liabilities of organizational memory. The problem is not easy to solve: the positions created in public agencies target skills that are well remunerated in private and nonprofit positions.

There is a political element to these linkages as well, noticeable especially in hiring within the social sciences. Within the federal government bureaucracy a slow but steady shift in hiring practices has replaced sociologists and demographers with economists. Indeed, the demand for skills in economics is much greater in the public sector of government (and in the nonprofit world of academia and think tanks) than it is in the for-profit private sector. Along with the rise in economic analysis (particularly the cost-benefit analysis of new federal rules and existing policies) has come a sharp rise in the demand for statistical training. With the 1960s and 1970s, American government was newly infused with professional statisticians, who now command a presence in health sciences (biostatisticians) as well as in welfare and budget agencies. Where sociologists played important policy-making roles in the federal bureaucracy in the 1950s through the 1970s, their power has waned considerably since the early 1980s. The influence and number of lawyers and political scientists (international relations and security specialists, for example) in the federal government has plateaued. Beyond these "social-scientific" professionals, there have also been broad expansions of the scientific work-force in U.S. government, marked by an increasing flow of natural and physical scientists to government positions ranging from agricultural chemists (USDA) to geologists and engineers (Interior, Mines, Reclamation) to nuclear and high-energy physicists (Atomic Energy Commission and NASA) to chemists and toxicologists (EPA, USDA) to pharma-cologists and molecular chemists (FDA).

Today the bureaucratic policy-making state is more constrained than it used to be, for three reasons. First, the fiscal constraints operating at all levels of government have combined to reduce discretionary spending and programs. The primary constraint upon discretionary bureaucracies comes not from deficits but from entitlement programs that take up an increasing share of federal spending. Put differently, the growth of entitlement government has limited the growth of administrative government. Second, bureaucra-cies are under increasing "competition" from think tanks and interest groups for the roles of specialization and information provision that they have enjoyed in the past century. Even expert bureaucracies rarely enjoy information monopolies in the contemporary political system. Finally, the waning of the traditional merit system in civil service has made federal bureaucracies much more top-heavy and answerable to the White House.

WHAT DO BUREAUCRATS VALUE? The emergence of greater administrative discretion, and of policy-making roles, among federal officials suggests something striking about what bureaucrats really value. Since a greater and greater fraction of federal employees work in professional positions, intangibles such as autonomy, reputation, esteem, and policy influence loom much larger in the bureaucratic calculus than do budgets and power. Most federal bureaucrats do not maximize budgets, and they do not uniformly attempt to expand their turf. Federal officials are instead "maximizers" of their reputa-tion, their esteem, and their autonomy.[5] This reputation-maintenance dynamic prevails among military and intelligence officials, among Department of Justice attorneys, among National Institutes of Health (NIH) and FDA scientists, and among social workers.

War, Bureaucracy Building, and the Security-Domestic Spillover

Numerous agencies—military, diplomatic, and domestic—have been created and remade in the face of civil and international wars. War often makes new demands upon national governments, commonly met through the creation of new administrative organizations or the refinement of existing agencies. . . . World War I roiled domestic markets for agri-cultural labor and threw farm commodity prices into a period of extreme variation, events that eventually enabled the U.S. Department of Agriculture to expand its regulatory powers over farm labor and enhance its forecasting and planning powers in preparation for the New Deal. World War II pressed new social and economic demands upon the federal government that transformed the Social Security Administration, the National Labor Relations Board, and the Navy. Most recently, the exigencies of the global fight against terrorism have resulted in the wholesale merger of previous intelligence agencies into the Department of Homeland Security and the creation of new discretionary agencies devoted to transportation security.[6]

If the past of American bureaucracy is any guide to its future, one relevant point may be that national security politics "spill over" into domestic politics. Repeatedly in the political history of the United States, seemingly "domestic" agencies have responded opportunistically to war and security threats to expand or refine their activities and their influence. Examples of such abound, particularly in the twentieth century.

- the USDA and agricultural production coordination in World War I and II;
- the development and regulation of nuclear weapons by the Department of Energy in the Cold War;
- the coordination of civilian defense and transportation security by the Federal Security Administration and later the Department of Transportation during the Cold War and in response to the terrorist attacks of September 11, 2001;
- the role of the Food and Drug Administration, USDA, and Environmental Protection Agency in planning and preparing for acts of bioterrorism.

In summary, wars and national security crises often provide an opening for bureaucratic agencies to expand and redefine their missions in creative ways. They also provide opportunities for politicians and interest groups to refashion agencies and give them new mandates. Exactly who controls these processes depends upon the agency in question, and upon history. The key point is that agencies have interests in intentionally blurring the line between domestic and foreign policy, and astute bureaucratic entrepreneurs are sometimes responsible for this blurring. . . .

The Emergence of the Contracting State, and the Plateau of "Government as Business" Models

In the last decades of the twentieth century, a turn against government, and against "big, bureaucratic government" in particular, suffused the American political landscape. Among the products of this political turn were the elimination and privatization of numerous government services and capacities (regulation of commercial airline entry and pricing, government provision of legal services for the poor, government provision of public housing for low-income families). Along with this reduction in government capacity has come a general reduction in government offices and personnel. Many agencies have been downsized, including the Agriculture Department, the Department of Housing and Urban Development, and much of the nation's military. The nation's civilian federal workforce is now about 2 million persons, or less than 2 percent of the total working age population in the United States. But Professor Paul Light has shown that nine times as many people work for the federal government through the "shadow government" of contractors implementing federal programs.[7]

Perhaps the biggest structural change in American national government is the increasing reliance upon contractors for the provision of government service. Accompanying and reinforcing this "contracting out" revolution is the growing reliance of the national government upon state and local government to perform functions that were once centralized at the federal level. Contractor firms now conduct most government construction, much billing and auditing, and even provide security in domestic and overseas government activities. The administration of President George W. Bush has accelerated this trend, although recent figures suggest that it may be reaching a plateau of sorts.

Along with changes in government procedure have come changes in the metaphors we use to understand government bureaucracy. The past two decades have witnessed a resurgence of "government as business" metaphors that were in parlance in the Progressive Era and again in the 1950s. Beginning in 1993, Vice President Albert Gore Jr. launched a "Reinventing Government" campaign that emphasized government offices as entrepreneurial businesses and cast American citizens as "customers" of government bureaucracies. The Price Waterhouse Coopers firm (now owned by IBM) launched a "Foundation for the Business of Government," awarding grants to researchers and agencies for the furtherance of business-like reforms in government agencies, and bestowing awards and publicity upon particularly entrepreneurial government administrators.[8]

It seems likely that these "business" and "reinvention" models of administration have run their course and will be ever less helpful to the U.S. government. (I am not persuaded that they were of much help over the last twenty years, for that matter.) It seems incredibly problematic to apply these metaphors to crucial policy arenas such as homeland security, counterterrorism, environmental protection, or food and drug regulation. While there has been significant privatization and outsourcing of government work, these activities still do not appropriately define the U.S. citizen as a "customer" of government services. The "Contracting State" is real and will endure. "Government as business" will endure in rhetoric only.

Conclusion: Recombination and Reputation

... There are at least three general historical lessons to be derived from a survey of American national bureaucracy. First, agencies are rarely created anew but are usually "recombined" from parts or wholes of existing administrative institutions.... We see it even in the creation of the Department of Homeland Security in 2002.

The meaning of this continuity is that much of our current executive bureaucracy has been around for quite some time. Agencies draw upon laws, norms, and traditions that reach back into the nineteenth and twentieth centuries and, in some cases, to the very beginnings of the Republic. We also see that the "creation" of new agencies does not always add to the overall size of government.

Second, the historical study of government bureaucracy consistently reveals the importance of such intangibles as reputation, prestige, professional esteem, and historical legacy as motivating factors driving bureaucratic behavior. Attention to the history of administrative agencies—ranging from military agencies to large departments to small government bureaus—alerts us to dynamics of administrative behavior that differ materially from the standard views. Scholars studying bureaucracy have posited variously that bureaucrats try to enhance their budgets, their power, and their turf. Yet the history of American bureaucracy provides case after case in which these generalizations fail utterly. Agencies often resist new powers that seductively come with bigger budgets (the Federal Emergency Management Agency and the Social Security Administration are examples). Agencies often seek a *reduction* of responsibilities to their core missions in which they have demonstrated and observed competence. Agencies and their leaders are just as likely to take steps to build, protect, and enhance their reputations as they are to seek new authority, try to expand their pay and their budgets, and move up the ladder of hierarchy and power.

If nothing else, a historical perspective on American bureaucracy is useful for combating the hubris that observers of American government often have in thinking that a simple set of generalizations can explain behavior and operations across diverse agencies or over centuries of time. Too often, pundits and scholars will try to generalize about bureaucratic organizations, as if the USDA of today were equivalent to the Agriculture Department of the Progressive Era, as if the same principles and norms governing the behavior of the Federal Trade Commission also explain behavior at the Department of Housing and Urban Development, the Department of Defense, or the Environmental Protection Agency.

If we pay attention to the specific reputations and cultures of different bureaucratic organizations, we can engage in more accurate analysis of bureaucratic behavior while combining the general and specific. The pursuit and crafting of reputation—the reputation of individual officers, of their bureaus, or of their entire agency—is something that federal administrators engage in all the time. Yet because the reputation and culture of each agency are different, the way that one agency (a military intelligence bureau, say) shapes its identity is invariably different from the way that others do so (a social welfare agency, for example). . . .

NOTES

1. See Martha Derthick, *Policymaking for Social Security* (Washington, D.C.: The Brookings Institution, 1979); Jerry R. Cates, *Insuring Inequality: Administrative Leadership in Social Security, 1935–1954* (Ann Arbor: University of Michigan Press, 1984); and Sparrow, "Social Security's Missing Years," ch. 2 of his *From the Outside In.*

2. See Bartholomew Sparrow's excellent chapter "The Transformation of Navy Procurement," pages 161–257 in his book *From the Outside In.*

3. See Richard Nathan, *The Plot That Failed: Nixon and the Administrative Presidency* (New York: John Wiley & Sons, 1975); and Joel Aberbach and Bert Rockman, *In the Web of Politics: Three Decades of the U.S. Federal Executive* (Washington, D.C.: The Brookings Institution, 2000).

4. See the memorandum of the Congressional Budget Office, "Comparing Federal Salaries with Those in the Private Sector," CBO Memorandum, June 1999 (Washington, D.C.: Congressional Budget Office). Available at http://www.cbo.gov/ftpdocs/5xx/doc599/fedsal.pdf (accessed March 13, 2005).

5. See Daniel P. Carpenter, *The Forging of Bureaucratic Autonomy: Reputations, Networks, and Policy Innovation in Executive Agencies, 1862–1928* (Princeton, N.J.: Princeton University Press, 2001); and James Q. Wilson, *Bureaucracy: What Government Agencies Do and Why They Do It* (New York: Basic Books, 1989)

6. See Robert V. Remini, *Andrew Jackson and His Indian Wars* (New York: Viking Penguin, 2001); Richard Franklin Bensel, *Yankee Leviathan: The Origins of Central State Authority, 1857–1877* (New York: Cambridge University Press, 1990).

7. Paul C. Light, *The True Size of Government* (Washington, D.C.: Brookings Institution Press,1999).

8. See the chapter by Donald Kettl in this volume. On the prevalence of government as business metaphors in Progressive Era administrative discourse, see Carpenter, *The Forging of Bureaucratic Autonomy*.

11.6 Laurence E. Lynn, Jr, "Theodore Roosevelt Redux: Barack Obama Confronts American Bureaucracy" (2009)

Laurence Lynn is a renowned public administration scholar who has held high level positions in the federal government. In this piece, published during the first year of the Obama presidency, Lynn examined President Obama's campaign rhetoric and his first actions in office to assess Obama's administrative approach. Lynn found echoes of Theodore Roosevelt and Woodrow Wilson in Obama's approach to bureaucracy. Obama seeks a government that is more efficient and less wasteful, and that conducts its business with as much transparency as possible. Lynn saw trouble ahead for Obama's managerial philosophy, in part because the administration was understandably focused on the substantive problems of recession and war, and in part because it added new criteria of performance (such as job creation) to existing agencies. These additional criteria echo the differences between public and private bureaucracy that James Q. Wilson emphasized in the second reading for this chapter.

> It yet remains true that there is a good deal of duplication of work, a good deal of clumsiness of work, and, above all, the inevitable tendency toward mere bureaucratic methods against which every Government official should be perpetually on his guard.
>
> President Theodore Roosevelt
> *New York Times*, March 23, 1906

"The question we ask today is not whether our government is too big or too small, but whether it works." With these words, just-inaugurated President Barack Obama signaled the no-nonsense, nuts-and-bolts approach to public management revealed during his campaign for the presidency. Two weeks earlier, the President-elect had announced his intention to nominate a senior executive from a prominent management consulting firm to the newly created position of "chief performance officer" (CPO). Thus on "day one" of the new administration, momentum had begun to build toward the fulfillment of campaign themes: creating a high-performance government, eliminating ineffective and wasteful programs, and ensuring transparency of government operations.

At the 100-day mark of the Obama administration, preoccupation with the tsunami of crises largely inherited from his predecessor—the collapse of the financial services industry, a rapidly deepening recession, dangerous instability in the Middle East, looming bankruptcies among automobile manufacturers—had undercut the likelihood of the kind of deliberate approach to public management reform taken by his two immediate predecessors. . . .

Obama's broad political strategy seems clear enough. Following the precept, "never waste a good crisis," the administration is viewing the urgent necessity for financial system stabilization and economic recovery as an opportunity to begin a determined pursuit of long-term goals in health, energy, education, regulatory reform, defense, and other high priority areas. The administration's approach to public management, embedded in lengthy and detailed statutes and directives, is shaped by political necessity as well: to assuage fears of mind-boggling levels of government spending and escalating national indebtedness, Obama promises unprecedented transparency of government operations and sleepless vigilance—by additional thousands of investigators, auditors, and contract officers, whistleblowers, and citizens at large—toward all forms of waste, fraud, and abuse.

While the administration is necessarily making it up as it goes along, there is nevertheless an evident consistency in Obama's managerial philosophy, if not yet in its implementation. To get a sense of this philosophy, it is necessary to search not only campaign promises but hundreds of decisions made pursuant to confronting the unfolding crises: implementing the Emergency Economic Stabilization Act (EESA), which authorized the Troubled Assets Relief Program (TARP) and the Public-Private Investment Program (PPIP); the nearly $800 billion "stimulus" package titled the American Recovery and Reinvestment Act (ARRA); the President's budget message for fiscal year 2010, "A New Era of Responsibility: Renewing America's Promise" and the "Concurrent Budget Resolution Explanatory Statement" enacted by Congress; and numerous letters, guidelines, statements, blogs, and comments of the president, the director of the Office of Management and Budget (OMB), and other senior government officials.

What is clear is that, of Paul Light's four "tides of reform" (Light, 2008), Obama has initiated a fully-mobilized "war on waste" under the "watchful eye" of legislators, auditors, whistleblowers, and citizens who will be provided with unprecedented amounts of information on government operations.

What Candidate Obama Promised

In accepting the Democratic nomination in August 2008, Obama pledged to "go through the federal budget line by line, eliminating programs that no longer work and making the ones we do need work better and cost less because we cannot meet 21st century challenges with a 20th century bureaucracy.". . . As his statements and actions have consistently shown, Obama is a disciple of Theodore Roosevelt and those among his successors, including Ronald Reagan, who distrusted wasteful and ingrown bureaucrats and were determined to thwart their tendencies toward inefficiency and keep their workplaces brightly lit by public scrutiny.

A comprehensive September 2008 Obama/Biden campaign statement, "Stop Wasteful Spending and Curb Influence of Special Interests so Government Can Tackle Great Challenges," provided a clear indication of Obama's main idea:

> The lack of accountability and efficiency not only robs money from critical programs, it also erodes taxpayers' confidence that Washington can be responsible stewards of their money.

When people lose faith in their government, it is hard to build the consensus needed to tackle our great problems: ensuring affordable, accessible health care for all, eliminating our addiction to foreign oil, securing our homeland, educating our children and rebuilding our crumbling infrastructure.

The statement is replete with promises to ensure transparency: to open closed doors to the public, to shine a light on spending and tax breaks, to ensure "sunlight before signing" enacted legislation. Performance would be emphasized through the creation of White House-based Chief Performance Officer assisted by expert teams that would work with OMB and the agencies to "improve results and outcomes . . . while eliminating waste and inefficiency" and "set tough performance targets and hold managers accountable for progress."

Rather than scrapping the Bush administration's OMB-administered Program Assessment Rating Tool (PART), Obama promised to "fundamentally reconfigure it," to

open up the insular performance measurement process to the public, Congress and outside experts, [and] eliminate ideological performance goals and replace them with goals Americans care about and that are based on congressional intent and feedback from the people served by government programs. [I] will also ensure that programs are not only measured in isolation, but are assessed in the context of other programs that are serving the same population or meeting the same goals. (OMB, 2009)

Obama also promised to "work with Congress to enable the president to take steps like sending in performance teams to reform programs; replacing existing management; demanding improvement action plans; and cutting program budgets or eliminating programs entirely:" all such actions would be transparent and visible to the public.

Obama also promised (cf. T. Roosevelt) to

conduct an immediate and periodic public inventory of administrative offices and functions and require agency leaders to work together to root out redundancy. Where consolidation is not the right strategy to improve efficiency, [I] will improve information sharing and use of common assets to minimize wasteful duplication.

Other promises dealt with expanded whistleblower protection, streamlining government procurement, "line-by-line review" of spending, restoring the government's capacity to manage and provide oversight of contractors, reducing no-bid and cost-plus contracts, and reducing reliance on contractors in general.

What President Obama is Doing

An important source of insights into how these promises are being translated into action is Obama's initial budget message (OMB, 2009). The promised line-by-line review of the budget for waste is announced, along with a variety of reforms in budget administration. But it is the subsection on "Making Government More Effective" that specifically echoes campaign promises. These include, in addition to reforming federal contracting and acquisition, enforcing standards, measuring performance by opening up the "insular" PART process to "the public, the Congress and outside experts" and replacing ideological goals with "goals Americans care about."

A second significant source of insights into the new administration's public management is the text of the ARRA. This 407-page statute is dense with directives, delegations of authority, new offices, definitions, constraints, criteria, report requirements, and standards—some highly detailed, others vague and ambiguous—which, though intended to produce short-term impact, are also expected to have important long-term consequences for public management practice and policy achievement.

The act creates, for example, a Recovery Accountability and Transparency Board within OMB "to coordinate and conduct oversight of covered funds to prevent fraud, waste, and abuse." Comprising federal inspectors general (IGs), the Board, which is authorized to operate until September 30, 2013, is chaired by a highly regarded veteran IG in the "junkyard dog" tradition. In addition to the usual organization matters, including subpoena authority, the act directs that the Board

> submit to the President and Congress . . . reports, to be known as "flash reports," on potential management and funding problems that require immediate attention. The Board also shall submit to Congress such other reports as the Board considers appropriate on the use and benefits of funds made available in this Act.

The Board is instructed to "coordinate its oversight activities with the Comptroller General of the United States [who heads the Government Accountability Office (GAO)] and State auditors."

Another important indicator of Obama's view of management is his nomination of an individual with no government experience whatever, not even as an advisor or consultant, to be the first CPO. A specialist in performance benchmarking and best practices in the corporate sector, the new CPO is charged with reforming contracting and procurement, rooting out error and waste, building a performance agenda, and enhancing the transparency of the government's finances. For Obama, public management is good, old-fashioned public administration, not the gauzy, new-age homilies of the consultancies.

Obama has clearly indicated that his highest long-term priories are substantive: health, energy, and education. In February 2009, he convened a bipartisan "Fiscal Responsibility Summit" of political leaders from across the country. In releasing the report of this summit a month later, OMB Director Orszag emphasized policy: "The single most important thing we can do to put this nation back on a sustainable long-term fiscal course is to slow the growth rate of health care costs."

The Obama budget message suggested that health care costs could be reduced by 30 percent. Thus, in addition to expanding medical insurance, the President promised a focus on computerizing medical records and on developing and disseminating information on effective medical interventions. The ARRA has already appropriated $19 billion to promote electronic medical records and $1.1 billion for conducting "comparative medical effectiveness research".

Obama as a Public Manager

The optimism of Obama and his advisors concerning what they intend to achieve has yet to be tested by reality. More questions have been raised than answered by the statements and actions of the first 100 days. For example, counting on unprecedented increases in government efficiency to pay for high priority policy initiatives such as expanding health coverage has elicited deserved skepticism. The extraordinary new information demands imposed on all levels of government as conditions for receiving stimulus funds are likely to produce more noise than good data. The bold quasi-nationalization of the finance and automobile sectors has yet to be disciplined by an exit strategy.

At a distance from the overwhelming number and detail of the new initiatives, one can discern some tendencies in Obama's managerialism. A consequence of Obama's decisions is a considerable centralization of deliberation and decision making in the Executive Office of the President. "The buck stops with me," he has said. A panoply of "special envoys," "czars," and "chiefs" with various titles, along with a plethora of lawyers, have engorged the White House organization chart. These positions are said to be necessary to coordinate the traditional executive departments and agencies on behalf of holistic problem solving. Whether and how coordination will overcome the inevitable competition and confusion among strong-minded, experienced, and ambitious officials remains to be seen.

Obama also favors sweeping declarations of principles, standards, goals, and priorities that are short on detail. Such statements invite critics on both the left and the right to find the inconsistencies between the bold proclamations and actual practice: appointees who have proscribed lobbying backgrounds; policies not fully reflective of promised "scientific integrity," continued use of the reviled state secrets privilege, continued much-criticized reliance on private contractors in war zones, economic policy making that is anything but transparent, tolerating earmarks that he has promised to ban. The possibly criminal activities of those engaged in authorizing and conducting detainee interrogations will be revealed but not prosecuted. Subtle erosions in presidential credibility can result as what may be relatively small and nuanced deviations from principle begin to accumulate.

In general, Obama emphasizes the prevention of waste, fraud, and abuse to the point that one wonders if he is advocating a Wilsonian separation of politics and administration. Apparently not, because at the same time, he emphasizes the transparency of operations and broad participation in policy making by street-level bureaucrats and by citizens at large, a direct democracy that is antithetical to the technical rationality required by the efficiency he so urgently advocates. It is already apparent that striking a balance will be governed by pragmatism more than principle, but tensions and political controversy are inevitable.

Muddling Through?

The administration of George W. Bush was widely derided for managerial incompetence so pervasive that it seriously undermined his presidency. Yet on the home page of the whitehouse.gov website, his successor's agenda contains no specific reference to management reform, competent administration, effective government, or any other overt indication of the priority he places on the competence of public administration and management on his watch. The priority is on policies and actions that are linked to achieving "Fiscal Responsibility," a campaign promise made politically essential by the speed and depth of the economic and financial crisis and the deficit spending needed to confront it.

The course on which Obama has embarked, which features bold promises, ambitious goals, and institutional reforms, launches him into a minefield of risks large and small. The unqualified commitments to efficiency and transparency have about them the herbal aroma of inexperience and naïvety: who could have promised opening up the technical PART process to Congress and the public with a straight face? Public managers across the executive branches of every level of government confront the challenge of spending unprecedented increases in their budgets rapidly but wisely, crafting long-term investments that have high short-term economic impact—the National Endowment for the Arts must now report on job creation—often with organizational capacity that was already inadequate and cannot be augmented rapidly. In America's Madisonian politics, Republicans, watchdog groups, and non-partisan specialists are poised to ferret out and publicize every voucher for a "wasteful" purchase, every failure to deliver, every retreat from principle, every delay, every cost overrun.

Enveloping the Obama administration's bright promise, then, is a penumbra of uncertainty. Can a new strategy for the war in Afghanistan succeed? Will the emergency fiscal and economic measures lead to significant recovery? Can the growth in health care costs be attenuated and then reversed by digitizing medical records? Likewise, whether a more effective infrastructure of administrative structures, technologies, and practices, and a government that works, materialize from a crisis-dominated, private-sector inspired, and still uncoordinated blitz of reforms, remains to be seen.

REFERENCES

Brodsky, R., Rosenberg, A, and Shoop, T. (2008). "Obama calls for end of 20th century bureaucracy," GovernmentExecutive.com, August 29, 2008. Retrieved June 19, 2009, from http://www.govexec.com

Light, P. C. 2008. *A Government Ill-Executed: The Decline of the Federal Service and How to Reverse It.* Cambridge, MA: Harvard University Press.

U.S. Office of Management and Budget (OMB). 2009. Budget of the United States Government, Fiscal Year 2010. Retrieved June 19, 2009, from http:// whitehouse.gov/omb/

Discussion Questions

1. How do public and private organizations differ and why? What could we do to make public bureaus act more like businesses? Would Americans like these changes if they were made?

2. What are the strengths and weaknesses of Woodrow Wilson's view that politics and administration are separate activities? Is this separation possible in the American political system? If it were, would it satisfactorily solve the problem of reconciling bureaucracy and democracy?

3. James Q. Wilson says the lack of a profit motive explains why public bureaucracies seem slow, slovenly and risk averse. Carpenter says federal bureaucrats care more about autonomy and prestige than money and power. Explain whether they actually disagree, and, if so, why and to what effect?

4. Michael Nelson writes that many efforts to reform bureaucracy have had unanticipated consequences that strengthened bureaucracy. Looking back at these reforms, did they do more good than harm, or more harm than good? How can reformers today do a better job of anticipating all the consequences of change when they recommend reforms in any aspect of American government?

5. Is a more educated, professional and expert bureaucracy overseeing legions of private contractors and state and local government program managers a good or bad development for our democracy?

6. What difference does the path of American bureaucratic development make for Americans today?

Suggested Additional Reading

Daniel P. Carpenter, *Reputation and Power: Organizational Image and Pharmaceutical Regulation at the FDA* (Princeton, NJ: Princeton University Press, 2010).

Martha Derthick, *Policy-Making for Social Security* (Washington, DC: Brookings Institution Press, 1979).

Robert Durant, ed., *The Oxford Handbook of American Bureaucracy* (Oxford University Press, 2010).

Joanna Grisinger, *The Unwieldy American State: Administrative Politics since the New Deal* (New York: Cambridge University Press, 2012).

Paul C. Light, *A Government Ill Executed: The Decline of the Federal Service and How to Reverse It* (Cambridge, MA: Harvard University Press, 2008).

Stephen Skowronek, *Building A New American State: The Expansion of National Administrative Capacities, 1877–1920* (New York: Cambridge University Press, 1982).

12

The Federal Courts: Activism v. Restraint

Introduction

The judicial branch of government, the courts, is often juxtaposed to the political branches of the government, the legislative and executive branches. The juxtaposition is apt in many respects, but not, obviously, in all. The president and members of Congress are elected, rather than appointed, and must stand for reelection. Their terms of office are fixed, rather than indeterminate. And the president and Congress must mind their political constituencies and coalitions if they intend to stay in office and succeed in their policy goals.

Federal judges, on the other hand, are appointed by the president with the advice and consent of the Senate. Once appointed, they serve during good behavior, which means, in practice, until they chose to retire or die in office. Judges are expected to apply the law impartially and to compare particular acts of government to the Constitution to insure that they are legitimate and enforceable. Nonetheless, judges are actors in the American political system, and while means and ends are not, or not often, explicitly political, they must still keep the goals of other actors and the shape of public opinion in mind—and they do.

Thinking about the role of judges in politics and government was evolving during the Founding period. In Europe, judges were appointed by monarchs and were understood to serve at pleasure as members of the executive branch. During the Founding period, the idea of an independent judiciary, a third branch of government, independent of the executive and legislative branches, had emerged but had not yet taken solid shape either intellectually or institutionally. In Article III of the Constitution, the Founders created an independent judiciary with seemingly broad powers. Article III, section 2, reads: "The judicial power shall extend to all cases, in law and equity, arising under this Constitution, the laws of the United States, and treaties made, or which shall be made, under their authority."

But judicial independence was a fairly new idea and the Founders were uncertain how it would work and how the judiciary would stand up to opposition from the political branches. Alexander Hamilton famously called the judiciary "the least dangerous branch," because it lacked anything equivalent to the executive's power of the sword or the legislature's power of the purse. Our first selection,

Hamilton's *Federalist* 81, reflects uncertainty as to the role the federal courts would play in the new national government. Hamilton knew that many readers of the *Federalist* still believed that the nation's highest court, as in Britain, should be the upper house of the legislature, rather than the independent Supreme Court described in the proposed Constitution. Critics worried that the Supreme Court would dominate the legislature and would shape the Constitution to its preference. Hamilton sought to soothe the critics by reminding them that courts are inherently weak and that the legislature had many ways to fight back against a court that strayed beyond its constitutional mandate.

In our second selection, the famous case of *Marbury v. Madison* (1803), Chief Justice John Marshall provided the foundation for independent judicial authority. *Marbury v. Madison* established the federal court's power of judicial review—the legal and political right to declare acts of government unconstitutional (and, therefore, null, void, and of no effect) if outside the legislative and executive powers granted in the Constitution. Some feared that judicial review threatened judicial supremacy as it presumed the judicial right to overturn acts of Congress signed by the president. Scholars since have argued both about how the courts should wield their authority—aggressively or passively—and what the courts can and do achieve in exercising their authority.

Our third selection and the highlight piece for Chapter 12 is by Akhil Amar, a Yale law professor and one of the leading experts on the U.S. Constitution. Amar identifies and explains the constitutional sources and foundation of judicial power in the U.S. political system. He points to Articles III and VI of the Constitution, the judiciary article and the "supremacy clause" as the foundations of "Judicial Power Under the Constitution." Article III gives the federal courts jurisdiction over cases arising under "this Constitution" and Article VI declares the Constitution the "supreme Law of the land" and requires government official, federal and state, to pledge allegiance to it. Federal courts don't just interpret the Constitution; they apply it in precedents that other courts, other branches and levels of government, and all public officials must follow.

Jeffrey Rosen, in selection 12.3, lays out the political and legal issues that confronted Chief Justice Marshall and the Supreme Court in *Marbury v. Madison*. The facts in *Marbury* threatened a conflict between Chief Justice Marshall and President Thomas Jefferson, both newly ensconced in their offices. President Jefferson did not want to seat newly appointed Federalist judges that seemed to have a right to their appointments. If Marshall ordered Jefferson to deliver the appointments, the president could simply refuse and the weakness of the Court would be displayed publicly. In a sense, Marshall outfoxed Jefferson by declaring that the Court could not order the appointments delivered (the outcome Jefferson wanted) because the law under which the appointments had been made was unconstitutional and therefore void (Jefferson denied that the court was the final arbiter of what was constitutional and what was not). Jefferson took the political win, but Marshall won the far larger point on judicial review. Rosen argues that the courts have protected their constitutional role, political authority, and public support by being careful not to get too far ahead of the political consensus. Rather than forcing social change, the courts generally have waited for a political consensus to emerge and then validated it and embedded it in the law.

Howard Gillman and Thomas Keck argue that the modern court has strayed from the careful moderation of earlier courts by allowing partisanship and ideology too large a role in their thinking. In our fourth selection, Howard Gillman recounts the court battles that resolved the disputed 2000 presidential election. While judges were involved in earlier presidential election disputes, especially the Hayes/Tilden race in 1876, they never decided those disputes themselves. Gillman is concerned that *Bush v. Gore* (2001) was decided on what looked like a 5–4 partisan vote. Thomas Keck, in our fifth selection, agrees, arguing that the modern federal courts are both more activist and more political than previous courts. Liberals and conservatives, using the courts to press for political advantage and each side willing to charge the other with political motivation, have undercut the legitimacy of the courts.

12.1 *Federalist Paper* 81 (1788)

Federalist 78 through 83 deal with the structure and power of the judiciary in the new Constitution. *Federalist* 81 deals with the distribution of judicial authority between different levels and types of federal courts. The concern treated in *Federalist* 81 is that the Supreme Court will overpower and control the Congress if it has the ultimate authority to declare laws unconstitutional. Hamilton concludes that such a power is safer in the hands of an independent Supreme Court, rather than with some part of the legislature, as with the House of Lords in Great Britain, and is necessary to the idea and practice of limited government. Hamilton argued that the danger of judicial usurpation of legislative authority is a phantom as the Congress has many ways of repelling such assaults.

Federalist Paper 81 (1788)

Alexander Hamilton

May 28, 1788

Let us now return to the partition of the judiciary authority between different courts, and their relations to each other.

"The judicial power of the United States is (by the plan of the convention) to be vested in one supreme court, and in such inferior courts as the congress may from time to time ordain and establish."*

That there ought to be one court of supreme and final jurisdiction is a proposition which has not been, and is not likely to be contested. . . . The only question that seems to have been raised concerning it, is whether it ought to be a distinct body, or a branch of the legislature. . . .

The arguments or rather suggestions, upon which this charge is founded, are to this effect: "The authority of the proposed supreme court of the United States, which is to be a separate and independent body, will be superior to that of the legislature. The power of construing the laws, according to the *spirit* of the constitution, will enable that court to mould them into whatever shape it may think proper; especially as its decisions will not be in any manner subject to the revision or correction of the legislative body. This is as unprecedented as it is dangerous. In Britain, the judicial power in the last resort, resides in the house of lords, which is a branch of the legislature; and this part of the British government has been imitated in the state constitutions in general. The parliament of Great-Britain, and the legislatures of the several states, can at any time rectify by law, the exceptionable decisions of their respective courts. But the errors and usurpations of the supreme court of the United States will be uncontrolable and remediless." This, upon examination, will be found to be altogether made up of false reasoning upon misconceived fact.

In the first place, there is not a syllable in the plan under consideration, which *directly* empowers the national courts to construe the laws according to the spirit of the constitution, or which gives them any greater latitude in this respect, than may be claimed by the courts of every state. I admit however, that the constitution ought to be the standard of construction for the laws, and that wherever there is an evident opposition, the laws ought to give place to the constitution. But this doctrine is not deducible from any circumstance peculiar to the plan of the convention; but from the general theory of a limited constitution; and as far as it is true, is equally applicable to most, if not to all the state governments. There can be no objection therefore, on this account, to the federal judicature, which will not lie against the local judicatures in general, and which will not serve to condemn every constitution that attempts to set bounds to the legislative discretion.

But perhaps the force of the objection may be thought to consist in the particular organization of the proposed supreme court; in its being composed of a distinct body of magistrates, instead of being one of the branches of the legislature, as in the government of Great-Britain and in that of this state. To insist upon this point, the authors of the objection must renounce the meaning they have laboured to annex to the celebrated maxim requiring a separation of the departments of power. It shall nevertheless be conceded to them, agreeably to the interpretation given to that maxim in the course of these papers, that it is not violated by vesting the ultimate power of judging in a *part* of the legislative body. But though this be not an absolute violation of that excellent rule; yet it verges so nearly upon it, as on this account alone to be less eligible than the mode preferred by the convention. From a body which had had even a partial agency in passing bad laws, we could rarely expect a disposition to temper and moderate them in the application. The same spirit, which had operated in making them, would be too apt to operate in interpreting them: Still less could it be expected, that men who had infringed the constitution, in the character of legislators, would be disposed to repair the breach, in the character of judges. Nor is this all: Every reason, which recommends the tenure of good behaviour for judicial offices, militates against placing the judiciary power in the last resort in a body composed of men chosen for a limited period. . . .

These considerations teach us to applaud the wisdom of those states, who have committed the judicial power in the last resort, not to a part of the legislature, but to distinct and independent bodies of men. Contrary to the supposition of those, who have represented the plan of the convention in this respect as novel and unprecedented, it is but a copy of the constitutions of New-Hampshire, Massachusetts, Pennsylvania, Delaware, Maryland, Virginia, North-Carolina, South-Carolina and Georgia; and the preference which has been given to these models is highly to be commended.

It is not true, in the second place, that the parliament of Great Britain, or the legislatures of the particular states, can rectify the exceptionable decisions of their respective courts, in any other sense than might be done by a future legislature of the United States. The theory neither of the British, nor the state constitutions, authorises the revisal of a judicial sentence, by a legislative act. Nor is there any thing in the proposed constitution more than in either of them, by which it is forbidden. In the former as well as in the latter, the impropriety of the thing, on the general principles of law and reason, is the sole obstacle. A legislature without exceeding its province cannot reverse a determination once made, in a particular case; though it may prescribe a new rule for future cases. This is the principle, and it applies in all its consequences, exactly in the same manner and extent, to the state governments, as to the national government, now under consideration. Not the least difference can be pointed out in any view of the subject.

It may in the last place be observed that the supposed danger of judiciary encroachments on the legislative authority, which has been upon many occasions reiterated, is in reality a phantom. Particular misconstructions and contraventions of the will of the legislature may now and then happen; but they can never be so extensive as to amount to an inconvenience, or in any sensible degree to affect the order of the political system. This may be inferred with certainty from the general nature of the judicial power; from the objects to which it relates; from the manner in which it is exercised; from its comparative weakness, and from its total incapacity to support its usurpations by force. And the inference is greatly fortified by the consideration of the important constitutional check, which the power of instituting impeachments, in one part of the legislative body, and of determining upon them in the other, would give to that body upon the members of the judicial department. This is alone a complete security. There never can be danger that the judges, by a series of deliberate usurpations on the authority of the legislature, would hazard the united resentment of the body entrusted with it, while this body was possessed of the means of punishing their presumption by degrading them from their stations. While this ought to remove all apprehensions on the subject, it affords at the same time a cogent argument for constituting the senate a court for the trial of impeachments. . . .

NOTE

*   Article 3. Sec. 1. (Publius)

12.2 *Marbury v. Madison* (1803)

Marbury v. Madison (1803) is likely the most famous and most important decision of the U.S. Supreme Court. *Federalist* 81 discussed the role of the federal courts in deciding the constitutionality of the actions of the legislative and executive branches, but alternative views remained into the Jefferson administration and beyond. President Jefferson believed that each branch of government was the best judge of its own constitutional powers and the judiciary had no particular insight or wisdom regarding these issues. Chief Justice John Marshall disagreed.

The facts of the case and the politics surrounding it are fascinatingly complex, but space requires that we leave the telling of them to teachers (and to Jeffrey Rosen in selection 12.3). Here suffice it to say that Chief Justice Marshall, writing for a unanimous court, declared sections of a law passed by the Congress and signed by the president to be unconstitutional. Marshall's decision held that the courts had a peculiar expertise and responsibility to declare when laws violated the Constitution. He declared that "It is emphatically the province and duty of the judicial department to say what the law is."

SUPREME COURT OF THE UNITED STATES

WILLIAM MARBURY

v.

JAMES MADISON, Secretary of State of the United States.

February Term, 1803

(Cite As: 5 U.S. 137)

AT the December term 1801, William Marbury, Dennis Ramsay, Robert Townsend Hooe, and William Harper, by their counsel severally moved the court for a rule to James Madison, secretary of state of the United States, to show cause why a mandamus should not issue commanding him to cause to be delivered to them respectively their several commissions as justices of the peace in the district of Columbia.

This motion was supported by affidavits of the following facts:

that notice of this motion had been given to Mr. Madison;

that Mr. Adams, the late president of the United States, nominated the applicants to the senate for their advice and consent to be appointed justices of the peace of the district of Columbia;

that the senate advised and consented to the appointments;

that commissions in due form were signed by the said president appointing them justices, &c. and that the seal of the United States was in due form affixed to the said commissions by the secretary of state;

that the applicants have requested Mr. Madison to deliver them their said commissions, who has not complied with that request;

and that their said commissions are withheld from them; . . .

To enable the court to issue a mandamus to compel the delivery of the commission of a public office, by the secretary of state, it must be shown, that it is an exercise of appellate jurisdiction, or that it be necessary to enable them to exercise appellate jurisdiction.

It is the essential criterion of appellate jurisdiction that it revises and corrects the proceedings in a cause already instituted, and does not create the cause.

The authority given to the supreme court by the act establishing the judicial system of the United States, to issue writs of mandamus to public officers, appears not to be warranted by the constitution.

It is emphatically the duty of the judicial department to say what the law is. Those who apply the rule to particular cases, must of necessity expound and interpret the rule. If two laws conflict with each other, the court must decide on the operation of each.

If courts are to regard the constitution, and the constitution is superior to any ordinary act of the legislature; the constitution, and not such ordinary act, must govern the case to which they both apply.

Mr. Chief Justice MARSHALL delivered the opinion of the court. . . .

This, then, is a plain case of a mandamus, either to deliver the commission, or a copy of it from the record; and it only remains to be inquired, Whether it can issue from this court.

The act to establish the judicial courts of the United States authorizes the supreme court 'to issue writs of mandamus, in cases warranted by the principles and usages of law, to any courts appointed, or persons holding office, under the authority of the United States.'

The secretary of state, being a person, holding an office under the authority of the United States, is precisely within the letter of the description; and if this court is not authorized to issue a writ of mandamus to such an officer, it must be because the law is unconstitutional, and therefore absolutely incapable of conferring the authority, and assigning the duties which its words purport to confer and assign.

The constitution vests the whole judicial power of the United States in one supreme court, and such inferior courts as congress shall, from time to time, ordain and establish. This power is expressly extended to all cases arising under the laws of the United States; and consequently, in some form, may be exercised over the present case; because the right claimed is given by a law of the United States.

In the distribution of this power it is declared that 'the supreme court shall have original jurisdiction in all cases affecting ambassadors, other public ministers and consuls, and those in which a state shall be a party. In all other cases, the supreme court shall have appellate jurisdiction.' . . .

If congress remains at liberty to give this court appellate jurisdiction, where the constitution has declared their jurisdiction shall be original; and original jurisdiction where the constitution has declared it shall be appellate; the distribution of jurisdiction made in the constitution, is form without substance. . . .

When an instrument organizing fundamentally a judicial system, divides it into one supreme, and so many inferior courts as the legislature may ordain and establish; then enumerates its powers, and proceeds so far to distribute them, as to define the jurisdiction of the supreme court by declaring the cases in which it shall take original jurisdiction, and that in others it shall take appellate jurisdiction, the plain import of the words seems to be, that in one class of cases its jurisdiction is original, and not appellate; in the other it is appellate, and not original. If any other construction would render the clause inoperative, that is an additional reason for rejecting such other construction, and for adhering to the obvious meaning.

To enable this court then to issue a mandamus, it must be shown to be an exercise of appellate jurisdiction, or to be necessary to enable them to exercise appellate jurisdiction. . . .

It is the essential criterion of appellate jurisdiction, that it revises and corrects the proceedings in a cause already instituted, and does not create that case. Although, therefore, a mandamus may be directed to courts, yet to issue such a writ to an officer for the delivery of a paper, is in effect the same as to sustain an original action for that paper, and therefore seems not to belong to appellate, but to original jurisdiction. Neither is it necessary in such a case as this, to enable the court to exercise its appellate jurisdiction.

The authority, therefore, given to the supreme court, by the act establishing the judicial courts of the United States, to issue writs of mandamus to public officers, appears not to be warranted by the constitution; and it becomes necessary to inquire whether a jurisdiction, so conferred, can be exercised.

The question, whether an act, repugnant to the constitution, can become the law of the land, is a question deeply interesting to the United States; but, happily, not of an intricacy proportioned to its interest. It seems only necessary to recognise certain principles, supposed to have been long and well established, to decide it.

That the people have an original right to establish, for their future government, such principles as, in their opinion, shall most conduce to their own happiness, is the basis on which the whole American fabric has been erected. The exercise of this original right is a very great exertion; nor can it nor ought it to be frequently repeated. The principles, therefore, so established are deemed fundamental. And as the authority, from which they proceed, is supreme, and can seldom act, they are designed to be permanent.

This original and supreme will organizes the government, and assigns to different departments their respective powers. It may either stop here; or establish certain limits not to be transcended by those departments.

The government of the United States is of the latter description. The powers of the legislature are defined and limited; and that those limits may not be mistaken or forgotten, the constitution is written. To what purpose are powers limited, and to what purpose is that limitation committed to writing; if these limits may, at any time, be passed by those intended to be restrained? The distinction between a government with limited and unlimited powers is abolished, if those limits do not confine the persons on whom they are imposed, and if acts prohibited and acts allowed are of equal obligation. It is a proposition too plain to be contested, that the constitution controls any legislative act repugnant to it; or, that the legislature may alter the constitution by an ordinary act.

Between these alternatives there is no middle ground. The constitution is either a superior, paramount law, unchangeable by ordinary means, or it is on a level with ordinary legislative acts, and like other acts, is alterable when the legislature shall please to alter it.

If the former part of the alternative be true, then a legislative act contrary to the constitution is not law: if the latter part be true, then written constitutions are absurd attempts, on the part of the people, to limit a power in its own nature illimitable.

Certainly all those who have framed written constitutions contemplate them as forming the fundamental and paramount law of the nation, and consequently the theory of every such government must be, that an act of the legislature repugnant to the constitution is void.

This theory is essentially attached to a written constitution, and is consequently to be considered by this court as one of the fundamental principles of our society. It is not therefore to be lost sight of in the further consideration of this subject.

If an act of the legislature, repugnant to the constitution, is void, does it, notwithstanding its invalidity, bind the courts and oblige them to give it effect? Or, in other words, though it be not law, does it constitute a rule as operative as if it was a law? This would be to overthrow in fact what was established in theory; and would seem, at first view, an absurdity too gross to be insisted on. It shall, however, receive a more attentive consideration.

It is emphatically the province and duty of the judicial department to say what the law is. Those who apply the rule to particular cases, must of necessity expound and interpret that rule. If two laws conflict with each other, the courts must decide on the operation of each. . . .

Thus, the particular phraseology of the constitution of the United States confirms and strengthens the principle, supposed to be essential to all written constitutions, that a law repugnant to the constitution is void, and that courts, as well as other departments, are bound by that instrument.

The rule must be discharged.

12.3 Akhil Reed Amar, "Judicial Power Under the Constitution" (2012)

The point is often made that the U.S. federal courts wield more legal and political power than courts in any other country in the world. How can this be? Hamilton in Federalist # 81 described the courts as "the least dangerous branch" and Jeffrey Rosen, in the next reading, will call them "the most democratic branch." Neither description suggests great sway or power. What kind of power do U.S. courts wield and from whence does this power flow?

Akhil Amar, one of the leading constitutional scholars of the day, points to the interlocking provisions of Articles III and VI as the sources of federal court authority. These two articles declare the Constitution to be "the supreme Law of the land" and Chief Justice Marshall, in *Marbury v. Madison* (immediately above), declared the federal courts to be the final arbiter of the Constitution's meaning. After exploring the role of the Constitution as "supreme law," Amar describes five distinct components of Article III judicial power. Judicial power under the Constitution involves the rightful authority to declare the meaning of the Constitution's text, implement the Constitution's meaning through specific legal practices and decisions, declare precedents, and define remedies for violations of legal rights. Amar gives weight and meaning to the abstract phrases "judicial supremacy" and "judicial power."

"THIS CONSTITUTION ... shall be the supreme Law of the Land." "The Senators and Representatives ..., and the Members of the several State Legislatures, and all executive and judicial Officers, both of the United States and of the several States, shall be bound by Oath or Affirmation, to support this Constitution."

With this pair of self-referential sentences in the closing paragraphs of Article VI, the Constitution crowns itself king. Judges and other officials must pledge allegiance to the document. These crowning words recapitulate the Constitution's basic architecture and enactment history. In his 1803 opinion in *Marbury v. Madison*, John Marshall declared that the Constitution's supremacy would have arisen even without specific language because of the very nature of the document as approved by the American people: "Certainly all those who have framed written constitutions contemplate them as forming the fundamental and paramount law of the nation."

Of course, any document can claim to be supreme law. Something more is needed to make it so. That something is social convention. Underpinning the Constitution's self-proclaimed supremacy is the basic social fact that Americans generally accept the document's pretensions. Ordinary citizens view the Constitution as authoritative, and power-wielding officials everywhere take solemn oaths to support the Constitution, as commanded by the document itself. . . .

THE CONSTITUTION'S REFERENCE TO ITSELF as "supreme law" in Article VI textually interlocked with an earlier self-reference in the document's Article III, its Judicial Article. Both articles specified the hierarchy of law in America and did so in virtually identical language. Consider first the text of Article III, which extends the federal judicial power to lawsuits arising under "this Constitution, the Laws of the United States, and Treaties made, or which shall be made, under their Authority." Now, compare Article VI, which specifies America's supreme law as comprising "[t]his Constitution, and the Laws of the United States which shall be made in Pursuance thereof; and all Treaties made, or which shall be made, under the Authority of the United States."

This textual interlock between Articles III and Article VI was no mere coincidence. The Philadelphia framers purposely chose matching language to make clear that the supreme law of the Constitution would come before federal judges in garden-variety lawsuits, either at trial or on appeal from state court rulings. Thus, the clauses referring to "this Constitution" in Article III and the closing paragraphs of Article VI did not simply float freely in constitutional space; rather, they formed a tight textual triangle, with two vertices positioned in close Article VI proximity and the third located in Article III.[1]

Here is how the triangle worked: Immediately after specifying the hierarchy of America's supreme law, Article VI added that all state judges would "be bound" by this supreme law, notwithstanding any contrary command in a state law or even a state constitution. In the next sentence, Article VI went on to oblige every judge, along with other state and federal officials, to swear a personal oath to support "this Constitution." Lest state judges fail to enforce the Constitution properly—either by willfully defying the

Constitution, and thus dishonoring their oaths, or by simply misconstruing the document in good faith—Article III's language stood as a backstop to Article VI, ensuring that federal courts could review and, if necessary, reverse any state court decision involving a dispute about the meaning of "this Constitution." This tight triangle of self-referential provisions thus made clear that the Constitution would operate not merely as law, not merely as supreme law, but also as everyday law—as courtroom law that could be invoked by ordinary parties in ordinary lawsuits.

The Founders understood that grand constitutional questions could arise in the humblest of places. Imagine an agreement between two small farmers, in which Jones promises to sell five acres to Smith. Before money changes hands and the deed is transferred, Jones gets a better offer and wants out of the deal. And he has an argument: Smith has recently arrived from England, and state law forbids foreigners from owning real estate. But Smith has a counterargument: Congress has enacted an immigration law giving all lawful aliens the right to hold real property despite any state rule. But is this federal law constitutional? Does it properly fall within the powers of the federal government? In a suit brought by Smith against Jones, these are the constitutional issues a court would need to address to decide whether Smith or Jones should win the case. These momentous questions, pitting state against federal power, could arise in either state or federal court, at trial or on appeal, and would need to be decided by the court even if neither the state nor the federal government formally intervened as a party to the lawsuit, and indeed even if neither government bothered to file an amicus brief.

But exactly what would and what should happen when the Constitution goes to court in this hypothetical constitutional case, or in any other case "arising under this Constitution"? How do and how should judges turn the document into workable court-law—that is, doctrine?

"The judicial Power"

Via it's tight triangle of self-referential clauses dealing with "law" and "judges," the Constitution envisioned that in deciding cases arising under the supreme law of the land, judges would offer interpretations of the document's meaning, give reasons for those interpretations, develop mediating principles, and craft implementing frameworks enabling the document to work as in-court law. These interpretations, reasons, principles, and frameworks are what lawyers call *doctrine*.

The basic need for doctrine arises because the terse text is and must remain terse. Concision is constitutionally constitutive. Had America's written Constitution tried to specify every detail, it would have lost its strength as a document that could be voted on in the 1780s—and that could thereafter be read and reread—by ordinary Americans. (This was John Marshall's profound insight in *McCulloch v. Maryland*, where he declared that the Constitution could not properly "partake of the prolixity of a legal code," because if it did, it would "never be understood by the public.") Because terseness is necessary, the document is importantly and intentionally underspecified. Judicial doctrine helps fill in the gaps, translating the Constitution's broad dictates into law that works in court, in keeping with the vision of Article III.

Article III "judicial power" comprises at least five distinct components.

First, "judicial Power" encompasses the power of constitutional interpretation and exposition—the power of judges to decide for themselves and to declare what the Constitution as law means. As Marshall famously put the point in *Marbury*, "It is emphatically the province and duty of the judicial department to say what the law is."

Marshall here built his church on the solid rock of the word "jurisdiction," a word that explicitly appeared in the Judicial Article as a facet of "judicial Power." Specifically, the Judicial Article vested "judicial Power" in federal courts; declared that this very same "judicial Power" had to extend to all legal and equitable cases arising under "this Constitution"; and then specified that the Supreme Court would generally have "appellate Jurisdiction" in these cases. Thus, "judicial Power" encompassed "Jurisdiction." "Jurisdiction" in turn encompassed the power to speak the law. As Alexander Hamilton, writing as Publius, reminded readers in *The Federalist* No. 81, the very word "jurisdiction" is "a compound of JUS and DICTO, juris, dictio, or a speaking or pronouncing of the law." Accordingly, Article III authorized any federal court hearing *Smith v. Jones* to declare its own answer to the relevant constitutional questions raised by the case.

A second and hugely significant component of "judicial Power" is the power not merely to interpret and declare the Constitution's meaning, but to implement the Constitution. This component involves taking the abstract meanings of the Constitution and making them work as actual rules of decision in the courtroom itself and in the real world beyond the courtroom. For example, in *Smith v. Jones*, what specific test should a court use to decide how broadly to construe the scope of congressional power under the Constitution? Who should bear the burden of proving what in the courtroom? What kind of evidence should count in favor of or against various factual assertions made in court? In order to decide the case at hand, a court will typically need to develop a set of tools for its own use and for the use of lawyers, litigants, and lower courts. These tools translate the core meanings of the Constitution into sub-rules, formulas, and tests that can be applied in the courtroom. Among other things, these various sub-rules and tests are necessary so that a court may go beyond abstract opining on the meaning of the Constitution and actually decide the case at hand.[2]

This need to decide also brings into view a third component of "judicial Power"—the power to adjudicate a proper constitutional case and to award a binding judgment to the prevailing party. In our hypothetical, a federal court would have the power to rule in favor of either Smith or Jones and to order that the disputed property be disposed of accordingly. So long as a lawsuit is properly before a federal court—that is, so long as the court has "jurisdiction" in the broadest sense of the word, jurisdiction as provided for in the Judicial Article and appropriate implementing legislation—the court's rulings must be respected by private citizens and enforced by public officials, even if those citizens and officials believe (quite plausibly or even correctly from a God's-eye point of view) that the court has erred and the wrong party has won. In this sense, jurisdiction and "judicial Power" encompass the judiciary's right to be wrong, its right to err and nevertheless have that error be honored as the law of the case. This is what lawyers call *res judicata*, an "adjudicated thing," the law governing the parties to the case. Thus, a federal court hearing *Smith v. Jones* could definitively determine the status of the disputed acreage between these two men.[3]

Beyond a court's legal authority to bind the parties in the case at hand, there exists a fourth component of "judicial Power," encompassing the authority to lay down a decisional precedent that will be entitled to a certain amount of legal weight in later cases.

This is what lawyers call *stare decisis*. But how much weight should precedent carry? What kind of weight? Alongside the power to set precedents for the future, the judiciary also has the power to overturn past precedents. When and how should it exercise this power? We shall return to these momentous questions at the conclusion of this chapter.

Fifth and finally, the "judicial Power" encompasses authority to fashion traditional judicial remedies for the violations of legal rights. In our hypothetical, if a court rules for Smith, it will need to decide whether Smith should receive the land itself or merely money damages. If the latter, the court must also decide whether the damages should aim simply to compensate Smith for his loss or also to penalize Jones for his breach.

Although the written Constitution says little about remedies, a powerful regulatory ideal and background legal principle (rather like the precept that no man should be a judge in his own case) prevailed at the Founding: For every legal right there should be a judicial remedy. Just as Blackstone's *Commentaries* had highlighted the *nemo judex in causa sua* principle, so, too, the *Commentaries* emphasized the remedial imperative: "[I]t is a general and indisputable [!] rule, that where there is a legal right, there is also a legal remedy, by suit or action at law, whenever that right is invaded." Several Revolutionary-era state constitutions featured similar language in their bills of rights, and Madison/Publius invoked the principle—"But a right implies a remedy"—in a passage whose very casualness indicated the uncontroversial nature of the proposition.[4]

In *Marbury v. Madison*, Marshall waxed eloquent on the point. He began as fallows: "The very essence of civil liberty certainly consists in the right of every individual to claim the protection of the laws, whenever he receives an injury. One of the first duties of government is to afford him that protection." After quoting Blackstone's "indisputable" rule and invoking additional language from the *Commentaries*, Marshall concluded with a flourish: "The government of the United States has been emphatically termed a government of laws, and not of men. It will certainly cease to deserve this high appellation, if the laws furnish no remedy for the violation of a vested legal right."

In short, the general authority of federal judges to fashion proper judicial remedies is a core feature of America's Constitution, whether we locate this remedial authority of judges (and the corresponding right of litigants to judicial redress) in the explicit phrase "judicial Power" or treat it as an implicit element of our unwritten Constitution in the spirit of Blackstone and the Ninth Amendment.

NOTES

1. *Farrand's Records*, 2:389, 417, 430–431 (rewording the Judicial Article and the supremacy clause so as to "conform[]" and interlock); Amar, *ACAB*, 576–577 n. 47.
2. Important scholarly analyses of the need for and significance of doctrine of this sort include Keith E. Whittington, *Constitutional Construction: Divided Powers and Constitutional Meaning* (1999); Richard H. Fallon Jr., *Implementing the Constitution* (2001); Richard H. Fallon Jr., *The Dynamic Constitution: An Introduction to American Constitutional Law* (2004); Jed Rubenfeld, *Revolution by Judiciary: The Structure of American Constitutional Law* (2005); Kermit Roosevelt, *The Myth of Judicial Activism: Making Sense of Supreme Court Decisions* (2006); Jack M. Balkin, *Living Originalism* (2011); David A. Strauss, "The Ubiquity of Prophylactic Rules," *U. of Chicago LR 55* (1988): 190; Mitchell N. Berman, "Constitutional Decision Rules," *Virginia LR 90* (2004): 1. Special mention must also be made of the extraordinary contributions of Professors Tribe,

Bobbitt, and Currie. See Laurence H. Tribe, *American Constitutional Law* (1978); ibid., 2d ed. (1988); ibid., 3d ed. (2000); Philip Bobbitt, *Constitutional Fate: Theory of the Constitution* (1982); Philip Bobbitt, *Constitutional Interpretation* (1991); David P. Currie, *The Constitution in the Supreme Court: The First Hundred Years, 1789–1888* (1992); David P. Currie, *The Constitution in the Supreme Court: The Second Century, 1888–1986* (1994).

3. See William Baude, "The Judgment Power," *Georgetown LJ* 96 (2008): 1807.
4. *Blackstone's Comm.* 3:23; Del. Const. (1776), Declaration of Rights, sec. 12; Md. Const. (1776), Declaration of Rights, art. XVII; Mass. Const. (1780), pt. I, art. XI; *Federalist* No. 43. See also *Elliot's Debates*, 3:658 (twelfth item of proposed bill of rights of the Virginia ratifying convention).

12.4 Jeffrey Rosen, "The Most Democratic Branch" (2005)

Many have called the federal judiciary the least democratic branch because its members are appointed, rather than elected, and they hold office during good behavior (for life) rather than for a fixed term. Jeffrey Rosen, a professor of law at George Washington University, uses a detailed discussion of *Marbury v. Madison* (1803) to argue that, following Chief Justice Marshall's early example, the Supreme Court has nurtured its prestige and authority by regularly deferring to congressional and popular majorities on what today we would call hot button issues. "In the end," Rosen claims, "Marshall realized, a determined majority in Congress can and will enforce its constitutional vision, and the Court attempts to thwart it at its peril."

John Marshall, America's greatest chief justice, took office in 1801 at the most vulnerable moment in the Supreme Court's history. Jeffersonian Republicans were determined to attack the independence of the largely Federalist bench by making judges entirely subservient to popular will; high Federalists, by contrast, viewed the judiciary as a monarchical protection against mob rule. Marshall's genius as chief justice was to find a middle ground between the populist and aristocratic positions, establishing judicial independence by avoiding judicial unilateralism. In case after case, he reinforced the paradoxical lesson that courts can best serve democracy by enforcing only those limitations on governmental power that national majorities have already approved.

Marshall succeeded in molding the Court in his own image as a result of his temperament as much as his constitutional philosophy: a genial, outgoing, and convivial man, he insisted that the justices board together so they could discuss cases over glasses of his excellent Madeira. Using the chief justice's most important power—the ability to assign cases when he is in the majority or to select a justice who will best reflect his views—Marshall persuaded colleagues of different ideological inclinations to join him in a series of unanimous opinions. He established judicial independence by repudiating the claim of radical Jeffersonians—that constitutional values should be enforced exclusively by legislatures, who were ultimately accountable to public opinion. But although Marshall established the power of independent judges to ignore public opinion in theory, he declined to press this power very far in practice, always taking care to defer to Congress on questions that the nation cared intensely about, and confining his invalidation of laws to cases affecting basic principles—such as federal power and property rights—that the nation as a whole was willing to support. In this sense, Marshall cannily achieved the Federalist vision of judicial independence by adopting the Jeffersonian counsel of judicial deference to the constitutional views of the people.

Marbury v. Madison

Marbury v. Madison (1803) is a monument to the inherent weakness of courts when challenged by a determined Congress and a popular president. *Marbury* recognized the power of courts to strike down laws inconsistent with the Constitution. This power, known as judicial review, may have been uncertain at the founding, but it became broadly accepted over the next fifteen years and was relatively uncontroversial when the case was decided.[1]

After losing the election of 1800 in an electoral cliff-hanger, President John Adams immediately signed the Judiciary Act of 1801, passed by the lame-duck Federalist Congress on February 13. The act expanded the judiciary by creating sixteen new circuit judges, who the Federalists would appoint. And it reduced the size of the Supreme Court after the next vacancy, to deny Jefferson the right to fill the seat. Two weeks later, Congress created the new position of justices of the peace for the District, who would serve for five-year terms.[2]

On March 1, Adams sent the Senate his nominations for the new justices of the peace, including that of William Marbury. By the next day, the Senate had confirmed Adams's nominees, and Adams stayed up late signing commissions which were then brought to the State Department and notarized by the secretary of state, John Marshall. Some of the commissions were immediately delivered to their recipients by Marshall's brother James, but others, including Marbury's, were not. When Jefferson took office on March 4, 1801, he ordered Lincoln Levi, the acting secretary of state, not to deliver the remaining commissions, and he replaced some of Adams's appointees with loyal Republicans (but not all—in the bipartisan spirit of his inaugural address, Jefferson was trying to be moderate). He also campaigned against the Federalist judiciary, encouraging Congress to repeal the Judiciary Act of 1801, thereby abolishing the nationwide circuit courts the Federalists had established and tossing the newly appointed Federalist judges out of office.[3]

It was the constitutionality of this Repeal Act—not the constitutional questions at issue in *Marbury*—that was intensely contested in Congress as John Marshall, the new chief justice whom Adams had appointed weeks before Jefferson's inauguration, prepared to decide the case. *Marbury* involved the relatively narrow question of whether or not an Adams appointee was entitled to his commission; by contrast, Congress was focused on the broader question of whether courts should be ultimately accountable to elected representatives. The Federalists predicted that a Congress unconstrained by judicially enforced constitutional limits might run roughshod over the liberties of the states and the people, as state legislatures had done in their assaults on property rights during the 1780s under the Articles of Confederation. The most sober Republicans, while conceding the authority of courts to strike down acts of Congress, emphasized that since the founding, Americans had tended to settle their constitutional disputes through the political process rather than in courts. In the long run, they emphasized, engaged citizens and representatives would prove to be more effective guardians of constitutional liberties than would unelected judges.[4] Over the course of American history, both the Federalists and Republicans proved half right: independent courts tended to enforce constitutional limitations, but only those that the people were willing to accept.

By the time the Court met again in February 1803, the *Marbury* case put the Court in an especially awkward position. If Marshall ordered Madison to deliver Marbury's commission, the order would be ignored and the Court's weakness exposed. If, by contrast, Marshall refused to order the delivery of the commission to which Marbury was arguably entitled, the Court would appear to be capitulating in the face of political pressure.[5]

Faced with two dangerous alternatives, Marshall deftly avoided both. And he did so with the combination of personal cunning and judicial modesty that was the touchstone of his legacy. By modern standards, he should never have agreed to hear the case in the first place: he himself had been the official responsible for the strategic error that gave rise to the dispute—the failure to deliver the commissions—and his own conflict of interest was hard to ignore. But Marshall minimized the inherent awkwardness of his position with his extravagant deference to the prerogatives of Congress and the executive. By appearing to rule against Marbury, a Federalist office holder, and in favor of Madison, the Republican secretary of state, he confounded his political enemies. And by pulling out of his hat a constitutional objection that hadn't occurred to the parties to the case, he enhanced judicial power over the long run.

In recognizing the power of judges to refuse to enforce clearly unconstitutional laws, Chief Justice Marshall claimed to be stating the obvious. "The question, whether an act, repugnant to the constitution, can become the law of the land, is a question deeply interesting to the United States; but, happily, not of an intricacy proportioned to its interest," he wrote.[6] All the conventional tools of constitutional interpretation—text as well as original understanding and pragmatic considerations—supported this modest conception of judicial review. As Marshall noted, for a judge to allow a law not made in pursuance of the Constitution to trump the Constitution would be to deny the Constitution's status as fundamental law, undermining the very purpose of a written Constitution, which is to maintain limits on enumerated powers of government.[7]

What made *Marbury* a perilous test for Marshall was not his relatively uncontroversial assertion of the power of judges to refuse to enforce unconstitutional laws that affected their own jurisdiction. It was, instead, the danger that the Court would issue an order to Jefferson to deliver Marbury's commission that the new president and his congressional supporters were determined to resist. In sidestepping a potential conflict between the Court and the political branches, Marshall displayed judicial statesmanship of the shrewdest kind.[8]

In Marshall's opinion, he took care to distinguish between the president's "political" or discretionary powers, for which he was "accountable only to his country in his political character,"[9] and his legal or nondiscretionary powers, for which he was answerable to judges. This formal distinction was another sign of Marshall's humility: he made clear that not all of the president's actions were reviewable in court, but only those "affecting the absolute rights of individuals."[10] And in a judicial arabesque—or perhaps an act of jujitsu—at the end of his opinion, he held that although Jefferson was illegally violating Marbury's rights by refusing to deliver his commission, the Supreme Court had no power to grant him the remedy he sought. Section 13 of the Judiciary Act of 1789, passed by the First Congress, appeared to give the Supreme Court the power to order Jefferson to deliver the commission. Although Marshall read the Judiciary Act to confer jurisdiction in this case, however, he emphasized that this case did not fall within the narrow categories of the Court's original jurisdiction set out in the Constitution. Therefore, he concluded, Section 13 of the Judiciary Act was unconstitutional.

Marshall's constitutional conclusion may have been open to question, but no one had a political incentive to question it. He had given the Jeffersonians the result they hoped for on several levels (Republicans had questioned Section 13 when it was being debated, while Federalists defended it) and declined to issue an order that would have been defied. He avoided judicial unilateralism, since the constitutionality of Section 13 of the Judiciary Act of 1789 was not a question that engaged the passions of the current Congress, which was focused instead on defending its power to abolish the national circuit courts. As a result, neither Republicans nor Federalists in the House or Senate offered any criticism of *Marbury* after it was decided. And a week later, in a far more politically charged case than *Marbury*, the Marshall Court deferred to Congress on the constitutional question that Congress cared about intensely, unanimously upholding the constitutionality of the Repeal Act in *Stuart v. Laird*. The Court had retreated in the face of Republican opposition, but by avoiding a direct confrontation, it had enhanced its power in the long term. *Marbury* is the paradigmatic example of how the Court can strengthen itself by restraining itself. In the end, Marshall realized, a determined majority in Congress can and will enforce its constitutional vision, and the Court attempts to thwart Congress at its peril.

During the rest of Marshall's chief justiceship, he kept these lesson firmly in mind: judicial authority could best be enhanced by deference to the democratizing forces of national sovereignty; and (conversely) the cause of national democracy is best served by a strong but restrained judiciary. For this reason, Marshall's greatest judicial achievements consisted not of attempts to challenge Congress but instead of simply getting out of its way. He upheld congressional authority after a consensus about broad national powers had crystallized in Congress and only struck down state laws in the name of the broader constitutional consensus that Congress had endorsed. . . .

This, then, is the achievement of John Marshall: he expanded judicial authority by declining to exercise it in a heavy-handed manner. He was generally deferential to assertions of broad national power, where judicial activism would have created a national backlash, and he reserved his judicial invalidations for surgical strikes against local laws that could plausibly be attacked as special privileges. By staking the enhancement of judicial power to the enhancement of congressional power, he gained a crucial ally in his efforts to establish the judicial branch as fully coequal to the president and Congress. His combination of legal precision and political sophistication is unmatched in American history, except, as we will see, in the hands of our most constitutionally precise president, Abraham Lincoln. . . .

NOTES

1. Michael Klarman, *How Great Were Those 'Great' Marshall Court Decisions?*, 87 Vᴀ. L. Rᴇᴠ. 1111, 1120 and n. 42 (2001).
2. Michael W. McConnell, "The Story of Marbury v. Madison: Making Defeat Look Like Victory," in *Constitutional Law Stories* (New York: Foundation Press, 2004), pp. 14–16.
3. Ibid., pp. 19–22.
4. James M. O'Fallon, *Marbury*, 44 Sᴛᴀɴ L. Rᴇᴠ. 219, 258 (1992).
5. McCloskey, *The American Supreme Court*, p. 26.
6. Marbury v. Madison, 5 U.S. (1 Cranch) 137, 176 (1803).
7. Ibid., p. 177.
8. McCloskey, *The American Supreme Court*, p. 25.
9. Marbury, 3 U.S. (1 Cranch) at 166.
10. Ibid. p. 171.

12.5 Howard Gillman, "The Courts and the 2000 Election" (2001)

Howard Gillman compares disputed presidential elections of the past, especially the Rutherford B. Hayes (R) v. Samuel Tilden (D) election of 1876, with the George W. Bush (R) v. Al Gore (D) election of 2000. Judges were involved in the outcome of the 1876 election dispute, but their involvement was at the invitation of Congress and the ultimate resolution of the dispute was congressional and political. In the 2000 election dispute, for the first time in U.S. history, courts, both in Florida and in Washington, D.C., struggled to decide the outcome of a presidential election.

Gillman asks whether this is what the Founders intended, whether courts had been so involved in previous election disputes, and whether the Supreme Court's deep and eventually definitive involvement in 2000 damaged the image of the high court or popular confidence in it. Generally, the answer to all of these questions seems to be no.

None are more conscious of the vital limits on judicial authority than are the members of this Court, and none stand more in admiration of the Constitution's design to leave the selection of the President to the people, through their legislatures, and to the political sphere. When contending parties invoke the process of the courts, however, it becomes our unsought responsibility to resolve the federal and constitutional issues the judicial system has been forced to confront.

Bush v. Gore (2000), per curiam opinion

Although we may never know with complete certainty the identity of the winner of this year's Presidential election, the identity of the loser is perfectly clear. It is the Nation's confidence in the judge as an impartial guardian of the rule of law.

Bush v. Gore (2000), Justice John Paul Stevens, dissenting

U.S. courts have been at the center of many high-stakes political disputes. But even seasoned court-watchers were transfixed at the end of 2000 when the outcome of a presidential election was thrown into one courtroom after another.

The postelection struggle between Republican governor George W. Bush of Texas and Democratic vice president Al Gore of Tennessee to become president of the United States unfolded like a ridiculously implausible hypothetical question on a college examination designed to test our faith in courts. The outcome in the key Electoral College battleground state of Florida was unbelievably close—initially a matter of a few thousand votes, and then a few hundred—and there were apparent problems with confusing ballots, error-prone vote-counting machines, and untallied votes. Claims were made that some of these problems violated Florida election law, and lawsuits were filed in state courts. Efforts were also made to have certain ballots manually recounted, and lawsuits were filed in federal courts to stop that from happening. Additional lawsuits were filed in state courts when state election officials attempted to certify the Florida election results without including the results of recounts. And this was only the beginning.

I offer an explanation and an assessment of how courts responded to the legal and political challenges associated with this historic presidential election dispute. The explanation requires attention not only to the law but also to judicial politics—the various ways in which judicial ideologies, partisan preferences, public opinion, and larger political and historical contexts shape how judges view the law and decide cases. . . .

Most of the courts involved in the election 2000 dispute resisted the pressures and met our expectations. The decisions of these judges on important questions about election law and (by extension) the workings of American democracy are historic case studies of the legal and political elements that create something that looks like the rule of law. However, even more compelling and, perhaps, more important to discuss, are those examples in which judges appeared to risk their reputations, and maybe even the authority of their institutions, by giving in to the pressures for partisan justice. Election 2000 provides a few suspects, but the most notorious are, of course, the justices of the Florida and U.S. Supreme Courts.

It would be easy to treat these battling supreme courts as equivalent examples of the influence of political preference on judicial decision-making. After all, the Florida Supreme Court, controlled by Democrats, handed down some decisions that proved helpful to Al Gore, and the Republican-controlled U.S. Supreme Court handed down decisions that protected Bush's lead and then ensured his victory. But before reaching this conclusion, and before embracing the irredeemable view of judicial politics implied by it, we should review more carefully the records of these courts and the legal and political justifications offered for their decisions. . . . In the end, I will argue that the behavior of these high courts is not equivalent, and that there is only one court that acted in ways that were uniquely partisan and outside what should be considered the acceptable boundaries of judicial power. It was the court that decided the outcome of the 2000 presidential election.

It is not that unusual for judges to become involved in election disputes when results are very close and questions are raised about the legality of the process.[1] But presidential elections have been a different matter. The United States has held such elections for 212 years, and not one was ever previously resolved by a court.[2] This made perfect sense under our constitutional design, which gave states the responsibility to appoint electors to the Electoral College—either by direct action of the state legislature or, if they so chose, in an election that would be run in accordance with state election laws—and Congress the authority to count the electors' votes and announce the result. If a problem arose, it was generally assumed that Congress would resolve it, for better or worse, often by facilitating overt political bargains among competing political factions.[3]

Prior to election 2000, the most conspicuous attempt at a "judicious" resolution of a disputed presidential election was the 1876 contest between Rutherford B. Hayes, the Republican governor of Ohio, and Democrat Samuel J. Tilden, the Democratic governor of New York. Eerie parallels exist between that controversy and the 2000 dispute. In the 1876 presidential election, the Electoral College vote was so close that problems with the outcomes in a few key states were enough to hold up the final result.[4] The Democratic candidate had reason to believe that he had won the national popular vote as well as the votes in the states he needed in order to win the Electoral College. However, the Republican candidate used political operatives in key states, including Florida, to have needed electors delivered to him without regard to alleged voting irregularities. Democrats insisted that the election results announced by Republican operatives were simply wrong—an attempt to steal the election by refusing to count all legitimate ballots—and so they arranged for the appointment of their own slate of Tilden electors.[5] The votes of two competing slates of electors were sent to the Congress. As in 2000, different political parties controlled the House of Representative and the Senate.[6]

Rather than hand this dispute over to the judiciary—which would have struck most officeholders back then as absurd and even unconstitutional—congressional leaders established a bipartisan electoral commission to determine which slates of electors Congress should count. Five members of the commission were appointed by the Democratic House of Representatives (three Democrats and two Republicans), five were appointed by the Republican Senate (three Republicans and two Democrats), and then five U.S. Supreme Court justices were asked to participate—two Democrats (Nathan Clifford and Stephen Field), two Republicans (Samuel Miller and William Strong), and a fifth justice to be chosen by the other four justices (Justice Joseph Bradley, a Republican).

There was some hope that the members of this commission might be able to transcend their partisan divisions, but in the end they decided on a strict party-line vote (8 to 7) to give all the disputed electoral votes to Hayes—despite the fact that state judges in Florida had ruled in favor of the Democratic candidate.[7] These nineteen votes gave Hayes a bare majority in the Electoral College. Congressional Democrats eventually agreed to accept a Hayes presidency after Republicans agreed to stop further efforts at so-called Reconstruction, which essentially meant ending the federal government's short-lived post-Civil War commitment to black civil rights.[8]

In the wake of the Hayes-Tilden election, Congress spent several years debating how to create a more regular process for handling these sorts of controversies. Before long they passed the Electoral Count Act of 1887. It made no provision for the participation of an electoral commission or any other national tribunal. Instead, state governments were encouraged to resolve controversies on their own. The promise was that if the states could clean up all disputes within six days of the scheduled Electoral College vote—"by judicial or other methods or procedures" that were based on "laws enacted prior to the day fixed for the appointment of the electors"—then Congress would not challenge their electoral votes.[9] If there was still a controversy, and more than one slate of electors ended up in Congress, then the slate of electors that was "certified by the executive of the State" would be counted, unless both houses of Congress decided differently.[10] If for some reason this did not provide a clear standard for resolving the election (perhaps because controversy remained over which slate of electors was properly certified by the chief executive of the state) then the dispute would presumably stay in the two houses of Congress until a decision could be reached.

Thus, our common experiences, combined with the history of presidential election disputes and the processes laid out in existing federal law, gave us good reasons to assume that judges, particularly federal judges, were unlikely ever to play a significant role in the election of a president—at least not without an explicit, bipartisan invitation from Congress for assistance in the performance of its constitutional responsibilities.[11]

It was against this backdrop that the country reacted to the courtroom battles surrounding the 2000 presidential election. Because of the razor-thin margin of difference in the vote totals any court decision that would result in the recounting of a few more votes or the disqualification of a handful of votes could mean the difference between President Bush and President Gore. Thus, courts became the eye of a political storm as well as the objects of an extensive and divisive debate on the idea of "the judge as an impartial guardian of the rule of law." This theme was articulated by U.S. Supreme Court Justice John Paul Stevens during the culminating event of this dispute, when an ideologically divided Supreme Court handed down its decision in the aptly named case *Bush v. Gore*. In that decision, the five most conservative justices, ending what would have otherwise been an ongoing political dispute, used a number of unprecedented constitutional arguments as a basis for issuing a ruling that effectively handed the presidency to Bush. This was done over the objections of the four less conservative justices, who insisted that the Court had no business interfering in a ballot recount that may have shown that Gore had actually won the popular vote in Florida and had thus earned the presidency.

While the decision brought some relief to an increasingly weary public, the outcome was dispiriting to those who were hopeful that the justices could avoid a result that appeared so overtly political. Many commentators predicted that the decision would have a devastating effect on the Court's reputation and authority. At the same time, there were those who rushed to defend the Court's integrity by claiming, not just that the majority's legal arguments were sound, but that they acted appropriately to stop a politically biased state supreme court from stealing an election for its favorite candidate. In other words, the very act that critics claimed was an example of illegitimate judicial activism was seen by supporters as a statesmanlike effort to put an end to illegitimate judicial activism.

As everyone knew at the time, the question of whether judicial power reflected partisan considerations is an obvious starting point for any discussion of the role of courts in the election 2000 dispute. Still, this question is only the beginning of an analysis of the judicial politics surrounding this event. . . .

The Challenge Facing Courts in the Election 2000 Disputes

Given that courts are fully integrated into larger structures of power, judicial decision-making can never be considered apolitical or truly impartial. Still, the activity of judging does not normally "become politicized" in a way that threatens the judiciary's "natural reservoir of goodwill." . . .

As it turned out, the specific legal questions that arose in the state courts were unprecedented, and so there was no established procedure to which judges could refer as neutral justification for a decision. . . . Even when there seemed to be very clear precedents—for example, the precedents for federal courts that balloting and vote-counting procedures were matters to be handled by the states without federal interference or that disputes over presidential elections would be resolved by the Congress—the lawyers had enormous incentives to proffer innovative lines of argument, and their stature, and the stature of their clients, allowed interested judges to take these arguments more seriously than would normally be the case when lawyers try to get fancy with judges.

Also, at various times during this process, representatives of both campaigns, but in particular those of George W. Bush,[12] were willing publicly to question the good faith of judges who handed down adverse decisions. These accusations had more resonance than they might in other cases because it was almost always plausible to claim that a judge was motivated by an illegitimate political bias and not merely by a disagreeable ideology.[13] Moreover, given assumptions about the importance of fast-approaching deadlines, these judges often faced enormous time constraints in reaching decisions, and this may have undermined opportunities for deliberation and judicial bargaining across partisan lines. For example, *Bush v. Gore* was the fastest modern U.S. Supreme Court decision handed down on the merits of an argued case, coming only three days after the justices agreed to hear it.[14] By contrast, Chief Justice Earl Warren lobbied Justice Stanley Reed for months to talk him out of issuing a dissent in *Brown v. Board of Education*.

Finally, the U.S. Supreme Court was up against one political challenge that was not faced by other courts. Of all the judges involved in the election dispute, these justices were the only ones who had not only an abstract political bias in favor of one candidate but also a direct personal stake in the outcome. After all, the president that the Court might help choose would, in turn, choose future justices. At a personal level this affected the well-being of justices who might have been waiting for the election of a Republican president so that they could retire from the Court without giving their seat to a Democratic appointee. More generally, the justices also understood that the election outcome could have a dramatic impact on the direction of the Court's decision-making and its future role in the political system, especially in light of the range of important legal issues on which this particular Court was closely divided along ideological lines. In other words, election 2000 would most likely determine which wing of the Court would control its policy-making for years or even decades to come.

NOTES

1. For an overview of election law and examples of judicial decisions, see Issacharoff, Karlan, and Pildes (1998). This is not to say that judges have authority to resolve all election disputes. For example, the U.S. Constitution delegates to the House of Representatives the authority to resolve disputes involving the election of House members. The Florida Legislature, like other state legislatures, had similar authority over the election of its members. However, the existence

of these special exceptions makes it clear that the involvement of judges in other election controversies reflects a typical and uncontroversial policy choice rather than an extraordinary occurrence.

2. Because only fifty-four presidential elections have taken place prior to 2000, some might suggest that presidential elections are thrown into court at a rate of once every fifty-five elections. But we should keep in mind that because of the Electoral College every presidential election is actually made up of many separate local decisions. That makes this development even more rare than it might appear when we say that it has happened once every 212 years (although there have been a few times, most notably in 1876 and 1960, when state courts have participated in some aspects of a dispute over presidential electors). In fact, just since 1980 we have had more than three hundred elections for president (held six separate times in each of the fifty states plus the District of Columbia) and only one of them has ended up in the court system. Then again, most elections are not close enough to make judicial battles over a few votes worthwhile.

3. An example of "better" might be the selection of Thomas Jefferson over Aaron Burr when these two candidates tied in 1800 (because of a defect in the original design of the Electoral College that instructed electors to cast two votes for president rather than one vote for president and one for vice president). Some people think an example of "worse" was the decision to pass over Andrew Jackson in favor of John Quincy Adams in 1824, despite Jackson's greater number of popular votes; however, the long-standing view that this represented a "corrupt bargain" between Adams and Henry Clay (rather than an example of representatives voting their constituents' preferences) has recently been challenged (see Jenkins and Sala 1998).

4. There have been other times when questions were raised about the electoral votes of a state but the election was nevertheless concluded since there were enough undisputed electoral votes to determine a winner. For example, in 1873 Congress refused to accept results from Arkansas and Louisiana, mostly because of the disruptive conditions associated with Reconstruction; they also decided not to count Georgia's three votes for Horace Greeley, who had died after the election but before the Electoral College met. Still, this has little effect on Grant's landslide Electoral College victory.

5. The original results were announced by the Republican state canvassing board, which reached its decision after discarding returns it considered fraudulent; this was enough to change a 94-vote lead by Tilden into a 922-vote margin of victory for Hayes. In December, the outgoing Republican governor certified the Hayes electors as duly appointed. A Florida circuit court ruled in January that the Tilden electors were duly elected, and in January the new Democratic governor sent a new certification to the Congress in favor of the Tilden electors.

6. In 2000, Republicans had a narrow majority in the House of Representatives. The Senate was evenly divided, but it was presided over by the vice president of the United States. Until the new administration was elected, this presiding officer was candidate Al Gore, and this gave Democrats control of the Senate for this period.

7. Explaining his decision against Tilden, Justice Miller said that the state court decisions might have been determinative if they had been handed down before the day when the electors cast their votes for president, but since it followed it by a month, it seemed too much like an attempt after the fact to change the results. Justice Clifford responded by noting that the state canvassing board did not announce its pro-Hayes decision until the day that the presidential electors were scheduled to vote, thus making it impossible for a court challenge to have been completed earlier.

8. For more on the election of 1876, see Fairman (1988), Dougherty (1906), Woodward (1951), and Haworth (1906); for a synthesis, see Stoner (2001).

9. 3 U.S.C. § 5. The 1887 act was folded into this statute, which is known as Title III of the U.S. Code (see appendix B).

10. 3 U.S.C. § 15.

11. Before 2000, the only other post-Electoral Count Act controversy over competing slates of electors occurred in 1960, when two slates came in from the new state of Hawaii under the signature of the same governor. The first slate went for the Republican candidate, but the governor sent a second slate right before Congress was scheduled to count the votes, after a court-ordered recount resulted in a razor-thin victory for the Democrats. The presiding officer of the Senate, presidential candidate Richard Nixon, declared that he would count the Democratic slate, and there was no objection from either House of Congress.

12. This will be illustrated in the course of the narrative, but for now it is worth noting that the Gore campaign's greater willingness to show respect for judicial authority was mostly due to the fact that courts were his best hope at winning; by contrast, the vote leader Bush knew that litigation was a threat to his nominal victory, unless the point was to get a federal court to stop recount efforts.

13. As the respected authors of an election law casebook on this dispute summarized it, "once the votes are counted, every potential procedural and substantive decision becomes outcome determinative. There are ample reasons to believe that every claim put forward and every decision made will be the product of an attentive eye to the bottom-line result—or at least will be publicly perceived as such" (Issacharoff, Karlan, and Pildes 2001:3). They added that because of this, "this is an area in which courts have been acting and must continue to act with tremendous circumspection" since "the adjudication of claims that will alter the outcomes of high-profile elections threatens significant damage to the integrity of courts." The paradox, though, is that "the failure to provide for a judicial forum threatens to undermine the legitimacy of the political process itself" (3).

14. The previous record was thirty years earlier in the Pentagon Papers case, *New York Times v. United States* (1971), involving an ongoing injunction preventing a newspaper from publishing a story, in which a ruling was handed down five days after the appeal was granted.

12.6 Thomas M. Keck, "Modern Conservatism and Judicial Power" (2004)

The common wisdom is that liberal jurists are likely to favor dynamic or activist courts, while conservative jurists are likely to favor courts that exercise judicial restraint. Thomas Keck argues that in recent decades conservatives have expanded judicial power and turned it to achieving conservative political goals. While judicial activism benefited conservatives in *Bush v. Gore* (2000) and in areas like federalism, it has made conservative preferences more vulnerable in areas like abortion and gay rights.

Keck argues that Supreme Court justices appointed by Republican presidents have been no more restrained than justices appointed by Democratic presidents—both have used judicial review to promote their political preferences. He argues that conservative jurists would have been better off, both in terms of philosophical consistency and political results if they had continued to argue for judicial restraint and for the resolution of contentious social issues by the political branches of government and elected officials. Keck favorably quotes Louis Seidman saying "the real dispute in modern constitutional law is not between

advocates of activism and restraint, but between advocates of liberal and conservatism activism."

Sandra Day O'Connor has played such a decisive role since 1994 that this Supreme Court
more truly belongs to her than to the chief justice. And the most significant feature of
constitutional development on the "O'Connor Court" has been the success on the part
of conservatives in expanding judicial power and exercising that power on behalf of
conservative ends. This Court's expansive vision of judicial power was clear before
December 12, 2000, but *Bush v. Gore* brought it into sharp relief. Rights-based judicial
activism has become so firmly entrenched in the American polity that the Court was
able to settle a narrowly divided national election without provoking any serious threat
to its own power. In fact, while some scholars (and some dissenting justices) speculated
that the decision might amount to a "self-inflicted wound," it has paradoxically had the
effect of increasing national support for judicial power. The public's overall support for
the Supreme Court has remained relatively steady in the wake of *Bush v. Gore*, but the
aggregate numbers mask a dramatic increase in support among Republicans. For
example, from June 2000 to mid-December 2000 (right after the decision), the percentage
of Gallop Poll respondents who had either "a great deal" or "quite a lot" of confidence in
the Supreme Court rose slightly, from 47 percent to 49 percent. By June 2001, it had risen
to 50 percent. Among Republicans, however, this degree of confidence jumped from 48
to 67 percent, and then settled back down to 62 percent. During the same period,
Democratic support dropped from 44 to 40 percent, but then rebounded to 46 percent.[1]

In sum, liberal and Democratic support for the Court took a temporary hit from *Bush
v. Gore*, but it quickly rebounded and is likely to remain strong over the long term, in
large part because Justices O'Connor and Anthony Kennedy have preserved so much of
the Warren Court legacy. The election decision has been roundly criticized, but most
contemporary American liberals remain firmly committed to a vigorous independent
judiciary as an important bulwark of liberty. All *Bush v. Gore* appears to have done is to
solidify the commitment of contemporary conservatives to this same principle, thus
making even less likely the development of an influential political constituency for
curbing the Court. Just as the Marshall Court expanded federal judicial power in the
early years of the nineteenth century by issuing decisions that "swelled (or at least did not
diminish) the ranks of influential politicians who favored that power" (Graber 1999: 39),
so too with the O'Connor Court in the early years of the twenty-first. The current Court's
continued willingness to exercise its power on behalf of liberal as well as conservative
ends has tended to reinforce support for judicial power among political elites.

The nation's ever-firmer commitment to rights-based activism, in turn, has undermined the continued conservative calls for judicial restraint in contexts such as abortion
and gay rights. Put another way, the conservatives' abandonment of restraint has enabled
them to influence the law in a number of areas, but has unintentionally constrained their
influence in others. By turning away from the path of Felix Frankfurter, conservatives
were able to revive the federalism-based limits on congressional power, but had they
continued along that path, their long-standing demands for judicial deference in the
abortion and gay rights contexts might have proven more successful. Instead, the
dramatic rise of conservative activism has weakened the rhetorical force of judicial

restraint arguments throughout constitutional discourse, thus facilitating the Court's liberal decisions in such cases as *Planned Parenthood v. Casey, Romer v. Evans*, and *Lawrence v. Texas*. The current Court is the most activist in American history, and the justices with the swing votes have been willing to engage in this activism to serve a variety of constitutional ends. O'Connor's and Kennedy's decisions to extend meaningful scrutiny to laws that restrict reproductive rights or discriminate against gays and lesbians would have proven much more difficult had judicial restraint survived as the principal ideal of constitutional conservatism.

It has not so survived, and we cannot understand the current Court if we continue to insist that it has. A number of scholars had noted the rise of conservative activism before *Bush v. Gore*, and this observation has been even more widespread in that decision's wake (Seidman 1996; Rosen 2000; Posner 2001; Balkin and Levinson 2001). Still, other scholars have continued to deny or understate the extent of this activism, particularly by minimizing the scope of the federalism revolution (Silverstein 2003; Whittington 2003; Rossum 2003; Tushnet 2003). While the reach of the O'Connor Court's activism is a matter for continuing debate, there is no realistic sense in which this Court can be described as a tribunal committed to restraint. Supreme Court justices appointed by Republican presidents have been no more restrained than those appointed by Democrats. They exercise judicial review just as frequently, and they are no more reluctant to enter political thickets.

Contemporary judicial conservatism is a rights-based conservatism. When the conservative justices have asserted their own power, they have generally justified such assertions on either originalist or rights-protecting grounds. In *Bush v. Gore*, for example, the per curiam opinion relied on a new and potentially sweeping equal protection claim, while William Rehnquist's concurring opinion emphasized the original text of Article II. These two sorts of justifications have often overlapped, with the conservative justices mobilizing originalist arguments on behalf of conservative rights claims. Even in the federalism cases, which have primarily implicated arguments of constitutional structure, the conservatives have still defended their decisions in part on rights-protecting grounds. And even when their principal goal has been to thwart congressional efforts to expand legal rights guarantees, the conservative justices have relied on rights-protecting doctrines in doing so. So while many of the Court's conservative activist holdings can be described as efforts to limit rights granted by other institutions—the federalism-based limits on congressional civil rights statutes, the freedom-of-association limits on state civil rights statutes, the color-blind limits on affirmative action policies, the free-speech limits on sexual harassment laws, and so forth—these have still been (in the conservative mind) rights-protecting decisions. They have generally been initiated by aggrieved rights-bearers (such as rejected white university applicants), have generally been supported by rights-based organizations (such as the Center for Individual Rights), and have generally been defended by the conservative justices in the language of constitutional rights.

We cannot evaluate the O'Connor Court's jurisprudence if we do not have an accurate picture of it. There are a number of grounds on which contemporary constitutional conservatism might be defended, but judicial restraint is not one of them. The conservative justices continue to speak in the language of Frankfurterian self-restraint, but since none of them actually advocates a posture of across-the-board deference, this language has become more misleading than helpful. As advanced by conservatives, both on and off the Court, the demand for restraint is often couched as a shrill denunciation of their opponents for usurping the popular will, and in this form, the argument is particularly unconducive to constitutional dialogue. As I have noted at some length, Antonin Scalia has become notorious for such shrill denunciations, and they are in fact a defining feature of contemporary conservatism. . . .

These regular denunciations of judicial power are misleading at best and profoundly destructive of constitutional politics at worst. They preempt a more productive conversation about constitutional meaning, distracting our attention from the actual locus of constitutional conflict. While we still tend to associate judicial restraint arguments with conservatives, the O'Connor Court's liberal justices have taken to responding to the rise of conservative activism by quoting Alexander Bickel, Louis Brandeis, and Harlan Stone on the merits of restraint. Their rhetoric is usually more tempered, but such arguments are just as misleading in their hands as in Scalia's or Bork's. In *Bush v. Gore*, for example, Stephen Breyer looked to Bickel in noting that "[t]hose who caution judicial restraint in resolving political disputes have described the quintessential case for that restraint as [one] . . . marked, among other things, by the 'strangeness of the issue,' its 'intractability to principled resolution,' its 'sheer momentousness, . . . which tends to unbalance judicial judgment,' and 'the inner vulnerability, the self-doubt of an institution which is electorally irresponsible and has no earth to draw strength from.' Those characteristics mark this case." Quoting Stone and then Brandeis, Breyer continued: "I fear that in order to bring this agonizingly long election process to a definitive conclusion, we have not adequately attended to that necessary 'check upon our own exercise of power,' 'our own sense of self-restraint.' Justice Brandeis once said of the Court, 'The most important thing we do is not doing.' What it does today, the Court should have left undone."[2]

Breyer is in fact one of the current Court's most deferential justices, but as Richard Epstein (2000) has noted, it is disingenuous for either liberals or conservatives to claim "that judicial restraint is the hallmark of sound judicial construction" because no judges any longer believe it. Louis Seidman observed as early as 1996 that "the real dispute in modern constitutional law is not between advocates of activism and restraint, but between advocates of liberal and conservative activism." He noted even then that there was no "significant difference between 'liberal' and 'conservative' Justices with regard to the frequency with which they support 'activist' results. Both liberals and conservatives can regularly be found arguing for activism and for restraint in various contexts" (1996:87–88). All of the justices see the Constitution as a charter of fundamental principles which it is the Court's painful duty to enforce whenever the elected branches attempt to violate them. The real disagreement between liberals and conservatives is over what those principles are.

Put another way, while constitutional conservatives continue to emphasize the long-standing critique of "government by judiciary," their primary concern is more often with liberalism than with judicial power. The conservatives who have criticized the Court most sharply in the past decade—Scalia, Bork, and their allies—have been concerned with abortion and euthanasia and gay rights, not judicial activism itself (Whittington 1998b). . . .

Moreover, the overall effect of these constant critiques of judicial power—particularly when combined with the ongoing active exercise of that power by liberal and conservative justices alike—has been to normalize the impression that the justices are simply seeking to write their own views into the Constitution. Bork and the advocates of the "attitudinal model," for instance, are united in their critique of every Supreme Court justice since John Marshall as dishonest, deceitful, and motivated only by a pursuit of his own preferred policy outcomes (Bork 1996b, 1990; Segal and Spaeth 1993: 74–124). This link between the critique of judicial activism, on the one hand, and instrumental accounts of judicial decisionmaking, on the other, is not a new one. In his 1964 *Harvard Law Review* foreword, Philip Kurland ended his long denunciation of Warren Court activism by noting that the political scientists may well be right that the quantitative measurement of judicial results is more important than the Court's rationalizing legal fictions (1964:175). A few years earlier, political scientist Sidney Ulmer began his article on "Supreme Court Behavior and Civil Rights" (1960) by quoting one of Frankfurter's many denunciations of his colleagues for result-oriented decision-making, and then provided statistical evidence to suggest that this was in fact what Frankfurter's colleagues had been doing.

It remains true today that opponents of judicial decisions tend to denounce them as result-oriented, that such denunciations tend to operate as self-fulfilling prophecies, and that such prophecies may have the effect of undermining judicial authority.[3] Since constitutional conservatives have made such attacks on judicial power ubiquitous, but have not actually succeeded in curtailing the exercise of judicial activism, we now have a system of federal courts that are as activist as ever, but whose legitimacy is perpetually under attack. Assessing the impact of such attacks is beyond the scope of this study, but they have the potential to undermine judicial authority in our constitutional democracy. After all, if the nine unelected members of the Supreme Court are simply imposing their personal preferences on the nation as a whole, then there is of course no justification whatsoever for the power of judicial review, let alone the active employment of that power.[4] ...

NOTES

1. Similarly, aggregate response to the question "Do you approve or disapprove of the way the Supreme Court is handling its job?" was quite steady from August/September 2000, to January 2001, and then to June 2001, with approval percentages of 62, 59, and 62 percent, respectively. Among Republicans, however, the approval skyrocketed from 60 to 80 percent, and then settled back down to 74 percent. Among Democrats, approval of the Court plummeted from 70 to 42 percent, before partially rebounding to 54 percent (Kritzer 2001; see also Levinson 2002:21–28).
2. 531 U.S. 98, 157–58 (2000).
3. As Bruce Ackerman has noted, the legal realist view that "[t]here is no such thing as legal interpretation distinct from political preference" tends to operate as "a self-fulfilling prophecy ... : the more lawyers and judges believe in realism, the more they vindicate its predictions by playing politics" (1998:418). See also Seidman and Tushnet 1996:35–48.
4. Bickel made a similar point forty years ago, noting that "[i]t was never altogether realistic to conclude that behind all judicial dialectic there was personal preference and personal power and nothing else. In any event, that is a reality, if it be true, on which we cannot allow the edifice of judicial review to be based, for if that is all judges do, then their authority over us is totally intolerable and totally irreconcilable with the theory and practice of political democracy" (1986:80). For a different view, see Peretti 1999.

REFERENCES

Balkin, Jack M., and Sanford Levinson. 2001. "Understanding the Constitutional Revolution." *Virginia Law Review* 87 (October): 1045–1109.

Bork, Robert H. 1996b. "Our Judicial Oligarchy." In *The End of Democracy? The Judicial Usurpation of Politics*, ed. Mitchell S. Muncy, 10–17. Dallas: Spence Publishing.

Epstein, Richard A. 2000. "Undue Restraint: Why Judicial Activism Has Its Place." *National Review* 52(25) (December 31).

Graber, Mark A. 1999. "The Problematic Establishment of Judicial Review." In *The Supreme Court in American Politics: New Institutionalist Interpretations*, ed. Howard Gillman and Cornell W. Clayton, 28–42. Lawrence: University Press of Kansas.

Kurland, Philip B. 1964. "Foreword: 'Equal in Origin and Equal in Title to the Legislative and Executive Branches of the Government.'" *Harvard Law Review* 78: 143–76.

Posner, Richard A. 2001. *Breaking the Deadlock: The 2000 Election, the Constitution, and the Courts*. Princeton: Princeton University Press.

Rosen, Jeffrey. 2000. "Hyperactive: How the Right Learned to Love Judicial Activism." *New Republic* (January 31): 20–21.

Rossum, Ralph A. 2003. "Text and Tradition: The Originalist Jurisprudence of Antonin Scalia." In *Rehnquist Justice: Understanding the Court Dynamic*, ed. Earl Maltz, 34–69. Lawrence: University Press of Kansas.

Segal, Jeffrey A., and Harold J. Spaeth. 1993. *The Supreme Court and the Attitudinal Model*. New York: Cambridge University Press.

Seidman, Louis Michael. 1996. "*Romer's* Radicalism: The Unexpected Revival of Warren Court Activism." *Supreme Court Review* 1996: 67–121.

Seidman, Louis Michael, and Mark V. Tushnet. 1996. *Remnants of Belief: Contemporary Constitutional Issues*. New York: Oxford University Press.

Silverstein, Mark. 2003. "Conclusion: Politics and the Rehnquist Court." In *Rehnquist Justice: Understanding the Court Dynamic*, ed. Earl Maltz, 277–92. Lawrence: University Press of Kansas).

Tushnet, Mark V. 2003. *The New Constitutional Order*. Princeton: Princeton University Press.

Ulmer, Sidney. 1960. "Supreme Court Behavior and Civil Rights." *Western Political Quarterly* 13:288.

Whittington, Keith E. 2003. "William H. Rehnquist: Nixon's Strict Constructionist, Reagan's Chief Justice." In *Rehnquist Justice: Understanding the Court Dynamic*, ed. Earl Maltz, 8–33. Lawrence: University Press of Kansas.

——. 1998b. "Review of *The End of Democracy? The Judicial Usurpation of Politics: The Celebrated* First Things *Debate with Arguments Pro and Con*, by Mitchell S. Muncy." *Review of Politics* 60(3) (Summer): 597–99.

Discussion Questions

1. The U.S. federal courts have been described as the bedrock of democracy and as undemocratic. There is probably a kernel of truth in each view. How do you see the balance?

2. You have read *Marbury v. Madison* and Jeffrey Rosen's discussion of it. As law, *Marbury v. Madison* established the court's power of judicial review. But thinking politically, what were the strategic opportunities and dangers facing Chief Justice Marshall and President Jefferson and how did they play their respective hands?

3. Howard Gillman argues that the U.S. Supreme Court overstepped in *Bush v. Gore* to assure their partisan preference for Bush? Do you agree? And, if they did, why didn't they pay a higher price in terms of reputation and prestige? If you disagree, why did they stop the vote counting when they did?

4. Jeffrey Rosen says the court is most successful when it reflects an existing consensus. Should the court act strategically, waiting for consensus to form on controversial issues before they move, or should it just decide cases according to the Constitution as they arise?

5. Should courts exercise judicial restraint, deciding only the cases that come before them, or should they be activist, reaching out for cases that allow them to address important social problems and advance fairness, equity, and justice?

Suggested Additional Reading

Bruce Ackerman, *We The People: Transformations* (Cambridge, MA: Harvard University Press, 1998).

Kermit L. Hall and Kevin T. McGuire, eds., *The Judicial Branch* (New York: Oxford University Press, 2005).

Ronald Kahn and Ken I. Kersch, eds., *The Supreme Court and American Political Development* (Lawrence, KS: University of Kansas Press, 2006).

Peter F. Nardulli, ed., *The Constitution and American Political Development: An Institutional Perspective* (Urbana, IL: University of Illinois Press, 1991).

Charles D. Shipan, *Designing Judicial Review* (Ann Arbor, MI: University of Michigan Press, 1997).

13

Civil Liberties

Introduction

Today, Americans tend to think of civil liberties and civil rights as at least compatible if not mutually supportive and reinforcing. Civil liberties, also called individual rights or personal liberties, provide the space within which to make individual choices. Obvious examples of civil liberties are the famous First Amendment freedoms of religion, speech, press, assembly, petition, and the like. Others include the right to a speedy trial by a jury of one's peers, the right against self-incrimination, to say nothing of the right to be free from cruel and unusual punishment. These are personal, individual, rights and protections. Civil rights, which we treat in the next chapter, promise all individuals, but more importantly, all groups, including groups defined by race, ethnicity, gender, and sexual preference, the right to be treated like others in the society.

Civil liberties were a major concern of Americans in the colonial and Founding generations, though, as we shall see, early generations took a narrower view of civil liberties than we do today. Civil rights did not become a major concern until the mid-nineteenth century, when different kinds of Americans, black ones as well as white ones, women as well as men, began pushing for "equal" rights. In our first selection, we are again introduced to John Winthrop, the Puritan leader that we met in Chapter 1. There Winthrop was delivering his speech, "A Model of Christian Charity," to awe-struck Puritans not yet landed in the wilderness of Massachusetts Bay. Here, Winthrop's "Little Speech on Liberty" (1645) is delivered to a citizenry in partial rebellion against the high-handed, they think, behavior of the magistrates. Though Winthrop has been cleared by a court of charges brought against him, he is eager to limit citizen's sense of their "liberty" and push them back toward obedience to their elected leaders and, behind them, God.

In our second selection, the Baron de Montesquieu, another writer we met in Chapter 1, wrestles with the idea of civil liberty almost exactly a century after Winthrop. Recall that Montesquieu is a Frenchman, living under a centralized monarchical government, and not an Englishman, let alone a colonial American, so his sense of civil liberties is as close to Winthrop's as it is the

Founders, let along ours. Nonetheless, Montesquieu made two important points, that civil liberties depend upon the rule of law and that the rule of law depends upon separation of powers in government. Finally, Montesquieu's definition of political liberty as "the opinion that each person has of his safety" is still fascinating.

We reach the American Founding period in our third reading and begin to see the initial outlines of our modern sense of civil liberties. That modern sense is that in certain areas central to personal autonomy, such as belief and expression, government must respect a zone of individual discretion and choice. This zone will broaden over time, but we see it first in James Madison's famous "Memorial and Remonstrance Against Religious Assessments" (1785). Madison presents the classic argument against government support of religion. He argues that religious belief and non-belief are private matters in which government should not be involved—even when the involvement is meant to be positive and supportive.

Our fourth selection, John Stuart Mill's iconic "On Liberty," is the classic statement of the nineteenth-century liberal individualist defense of liberty. Mill's broadest claim is that society and government have no right to limit, through law or social pressure, individual liberty except for the protection of others. Mill makes two important arguments, with which you may or may not agree. One is that the state should leave individuals completely free in regard to matters that affect only themselves, but may regulate actions that affect others. Is this an easy or a hard line to draw? Drug use? Abortion? The other is that the truth thrives best in an arena in which free thought and expression are unhindered. Slander? Lies?

Our fifth selection brings the points raised by and about Mill's argument to life. *New York Times v. Sullivan* (1964) is perhaps the most important civil liberties U.S. Supreme Court decision of the twentieth century. L.B. Sullivan was the police commissioner in Montgomery, Alabama, during the civil rights movement. Civil rights demonstrators were harassed and arrested, as they were throughout the South, and a group of local ministers took out a full page ad in the *New York Times* challenging police behavior. Commissioner Sullivan, citing factual errors in the *Times*, sued for libel and sought damages, claiming that his professional reputation had been besmirched. Not surprisingly, the Alabama courts sided with the commissioner. The U.S. Supreme Court, citing the First and Fourteenth Amendments, declared that the right to criticize public officials was general, limited only by malicious intent, and not simple misstatements of fact.

Finally, in our sixth selection and the focus piece for this chapter, Ken Kersch traces the historical development of the idea of a "right to privacy." Americans long assumed they had a right to privacy, grounded, for example, in the Bill of Rights prohibition against "unreasonable searches and seizures," but to the discomfort of some, that right has come to include contraception and abortion services. Kersch shows how even familiar ideas, like the right to privacy, shift and evolve over time in ways that make tracking them difficult unless one is alert and careful.

13.1 John Winthrop, "Little Speech on Liberty" (1645)

John Winthrop arrived with the first wave of Puritan immigrants to the Massachusetts Bay Colony in 1630. Winthrop served as a leading magistrate, sometimes governor, sometimes deputy-governor, until his death in 1649. By 1645, the colony was settled and dispersed and the magistrates' authoritarian rule, accepted in the dangerous early days, began to grate on some residents. When Winthrop and the colonial magistrates interfered in a local election, they were challenged and it took a court of inquiry three months to decide in the magistrates' favor and clear their names.

Following the court's announcement of his acquittal, Winthrop offered the following observations on the interplay of political authority and personal liberty. Winthrop explained that magistrates are elected and their election is evidence of God's will acting through the community. More to the point here, Winthrop distinguished between natural liberty, the right to do as one wishes, enjoyed equally with the beasts of the field, and civil or moral liberty, which he defines as the liberty to do what is right according to the laws of God and man. The examples that Winthrop gives of liberty under good law are the church's subjection to God and the wife's subjection to her husband. The latter example strikes the modern ear strangely, but echoes of it are still heard in some modern marriage vows.

[In 1645, while he was deputy-governor of Massachusetts, John Winthrop and his fellow-magistrates had interfered in a local election of a militia officer. When the dispute flared into a war of words, the magistrates bound over some of the dissidents to the next court and summoned others to appear. In this controversy the magistrates were accused of having exceeded their powers, and Winthrop was impeached. After a controversy of almost three months Winthrop was fully acquitted and some of his opponents fined. It was after this test and vindication that Winthrop made his famous "little speech" here quoted.]

It may be of some good use, to inform and rectify the judgments of some of the people, and may prevent such distempers as have arisen amongst us. The great questions that have troubled the country are about the authority of the magistrates and the liberty of the people. It is yourselves who have called us to this office, and, being called by you, we have our authority from God, in way of an ordinance, such as hath the image of God eminently stamped upon it, the contempt and violation whereof hath been vindicated with examples of divine vengeance. I entreat you to consider that, when you choose magistrates, you take them from among yourselves, men subject to like passions as you are. Therefore, when you see infirmities in us, you should reflect upon your own, and that would make you bear the more with us, and not be severe censurers of the failings of your magistrates, when you have continual experience of the like infirmities in yourselves and others. We account him a good servant who breaks not his covenant. The covenant between you and us is the oath you have taken of us, which is to this purpose: that we shall govern you and judge your causes by the rules of God's laws and our own, according to our best skill. When you agree with a workman to build you a ship or house, etc., he undertakes as well for his skill as for his faithfulness, for it is his profession, and you pay him for both. But when you call one to be a magistrate, he doth not profess nor undertake to have sufficient skill for that office, nor can you furnish him with gifts, etc., therefore you must run the hazard of his skill and ability. But if he fail in faithfulness, which by his oath he is bound unto, that he must answer for. If it fall out that the case be clear to common apprehension, and the rule clear also, if he transgress here, the error is not in the skill, but in the evil of the will: it must be required of him. But if the case be doubtful, or the rule doubtful, to men of such understanding and parts as your magistrates are, if your magistrates should err here, yourselves must bear it.

For the other point concerning liberty, I observe a great mistake in the country about that. There is a twofold liberty, natural (I mean as our nature is now corrupt) and civil or federal. The first is common to man with beasts and other creatures. By this, man, as he stands in relation to man simply, hath liberty to do what he lists; it is a liberty to evil as well as to good. This liberty is incompatible and inconsistent with authority and cannot endure the least restraint of the most just authority. The exercise and maintaining of this liberty makes men grow more evil and in time to be worse than brute beasts: *omnes sumus licentia deteriores*. This is that great enemy of truth and peace, that wild beast, which all of the ordinances of God are bent against, to restrain and subdue it. The other kind of liberty I call civil or federal; it may also be termed moral, in reference to the covenant between God and man, in the moral law, and the politic covenants and constitutions amongst men themselves. This liberty is the proper end and object of authority and cannot subsist without it; and it is a liberty to that only which is good, just, and honest. This liberty you are to stand for, with the hazard (not only of your goods, but) of your lives, if need be. Whatsoever crosseth this is not authority but a distemper thereof. This liberty is maintained and exercised in a way of subjection to authority; it is of the same kind of liberty wherewith Christ hath made us free. The women's own choice makes such a man her husband; yet, being so chosen, he is her lord, and she is to be subject to him, yet in a way of liberty, not of bondage; and a true wife accounts her subjection her honor and freedom and would not think her condition safe and free but in her subjection to her husband's authority. Such is the liberty of the church under the authority of Christ, her king and husband; his yoke is so easy and sweet to her as a bride's ornaments; and if through forwardness or wantonness, etc., she shake it off, at any time, she is at no rest in her spirit, until she take it up again; and whether her lord smiles upon her and embraceth her in his arms, or whether he frowns, or rebukes, or smites her, she apprehends the sweetness of his love in all, and is refreshed, supported, and instructed by every such dispensation of his authority over her. On the other side, ye know who they are that complain of this yoke and say, Let us break their bands, etc.; we will not have this man to rule over us. Even so, brethren, it will be between you and your magistrates. If you want to stand for your natural corrupt liberties, and will do what is good in your own eyes, you will not endure the least weight of authority, but will murmur, and oppose, and be always striving to shake off that yoke; but if you will be satisfied to enjoy such civil and lawful liberties, such as Christ allows you, then will you quietly and cheerfully submit unto that authority which is set over you, in all the administrations of it, for your good. Wherein, if we fail at any time, we hope we shall be willing (by God's assistance) to hearken to good advice from any of you, or in any other way of God; so shall your liberties be preserved in upholding the honor and power of authority amongst you.

13.2 Montesquieu, "Of the Laws Which Establish Political Liberty" (1748)

Charles Secondat, Baron de Montesquieu, argued that the spirit of the laws, the title of his most famous book, had to match constitutions and laws to the social and economic characteristics of the people. Montesquieu's point was that only people with experience of individual choice and responsibility can operate and maintain democratic and republican political institutions. Montesquieu would not have been surprised that Iraqis and Afghans have a hard time running free institutions, but he might have been surprised that we American seem not to know this.

In this selection, from Chapters XI and XII of volume I of *The Spirit of the Laws*, Montesquieu describes the constitutional and legal foundations of political liberty. Montesquieu defined political liberty, as we saw in the chapter introduction, as "the opinion that each person has of his safety." Constitutionally, a citizen's confidence as to his personal safely depends on the separation of legislative, executive, and judicial authority. Legally, the well-administered rule of law, as opposed to men, is the foundation of political liberty. Montesquieu counsels patience and moderation on the part of governments and their officials in regard to freedom of thought, including religious thought, speech, and writing.

Book XI

1. A general Idea

I make a distinction between the laws that establish political liberty, as it relates to the constitution, and those by which it is established, as it relates to the citizen. The former shall be the subject of this book; the latter I shall examine in the next.

2. Different Significations of the word Liberty

There is no word that admits of more various significations, and has made more varied impressions on the human mind, than that *of Liberty*. Some have taken it as a means of deposing a person on whom they had conferred a tyrannical authority; others for the power of choosing a superior whom they are obliged to obey; others for the right of bearing arms, and of being thereby enabled to use violence; others, in fine, for the privilege of being governed by a native of their own country, or by their own laws. A certain nation for a long time thought liberty consisted in the privilege of wearing a long beard. Some have annexed this name to one form of government exclusive of others: those who had a republican taste applied it to this species of polity; those who liked a monarchical state gave it to monarchy. Thus they have all applied the name of *liberty* to the government most suitable to their own customs and inclinations: and as in republics the people have not so constant and so present a view of the causes of their misery, and as the magistrates seem to act only in conformity to the laws, hence liberty is generally said to reside in republics, and to be banished from monarchies. In fine, as in democracies the people seem to act almost as they please, this sort of government has been deemed the most free, and the power of the people has been confounded with their liberty.

3. In what Liberty consists

It is true that in democracies the people seem to act as they please; but political liberty does not consist in an unlimited freedom. In governments, that is, in societies directed by laws, liberty can consist only in the power of doing what we ought to will, and in not being constrained to do what we ought not to will.

We must have continually present to our minds the difference between independence and liberty. Liberty is a right of doing whatever the laws permit, and if a citizen could do what they forbid he would be no longer possessed of liberty, because all his fellow-citizens would have the same power.

4. The same Subject continued

Democratic and aristocratic states are not in their own nature free. Political liberty is to be found only in moderate governments; and even in these it is not always found. It is there only when there is no abuse of power. But constant experience shows us that every man invested with power is apt to abuse it, and to carry his authority as far as it will go. Is it not strange, though true, to say that virtue itself has need of limits?

To prevent this abuse, it is necessary from the very nature of things that power should be a check to power. A government may be so constituted, as no man shall be compelled to do things to which the law does not oblige him, nor forced to abstain from things which the law permits.

5. Of the End or View of different Governments

Though all governments have the same general end, which is that of preservation, yet each has another particular object. Increase of dominion was the object of Rome; war, that of Sparta; religion, that of the Jewish laws; commerce, that of Marseilles; public tranquillity, that of the laws of China: navigation, that of the laws of Rhodes; natural liberty, that of the policy of the Savages; in general, the pleasures of the prince, that of despotic states; that of monarchies, the prince's and the kingdom's glory; the independence of individuals is the end aimed at by the laws of Poland, thence results the oppression of the whole.

One nation there is also in the world that has for the direct end of its constitution political liberty. We shall presently examine the principles on which this liberty is founded; if they are sound, liberty will appear in its highest perfection.

To discover political liberty in a constitution, no great labour is requisite. If we are capable of seeing it where it exists, it is soon found, and we need not go far in search of it.

6. Of the Constitution of England

In every government there are three sorts of power: the legislative; the executive in respect to things dependent on the law of nations; and the executive in regard to matters that depend on the civil law.

By virtue of the first, the prince or magistrate enacts temporary or perpetual laws, and amends or abrogates those that have been already enacted. By the second, he makes peace or war, sends or receives embassies, establishes the public security, and provides against invasions. By the third, he punishes criminals, or determines the disputes that arise between individuals. The latter we shall call the judiciary power, and the other simply the executive power of the state.

The political liberty of the subject is a tranquillity of mind arising from the opinion each person has of his safety. In order to have this liberty, it is requisite the government be so constituted as one man need not be afraid of another.

When the legislative and executive powers are united in the same person, or in the same body of magistrates, there can be no liberty; because apprehensions may arise, lest the same monarch or senate should enact tyrannical laws, to execute them in a tyrannical manner.

Again, there is no liberty, if the judiciary power be not separated from the legislative and executive. Were it joined with the legislative, the life and liberty of the subject would be exposed to arbitrary control; for the judge would be then the legislator. Were it joined to the executive power, the judge might behave with violence and oppression.

There would be an end of everything, were the same man or the same body, whether of the nobles or of the people, to exercise those three powers, that of enacting laws, that of executing the public resolutions, and of trying the causes of individuals. ...

Book XII

1. Idea of this Book

It is not sufficient to have treated of political liberty in relation to the constitution; we must examine it likewise in the relation it bears to the subject.

We have observed that in the former case it arises from a certain distribution of the three powers; but in the latter, we must consider it in another light. It consists in security, or in the opinion people have of their security.

The constitution may happen to be free, and the subject not. The subject may be free, and not the constitution. In those cases, the constitution will be free by right, and not in fact; the subject will be free in fact, and not by right.

It is the disposition only of the laws, and even of the fundamental laws, that constitutes liberty in relation to the constitution. But as it regards the subject: manners, customs, or received examples may give rise to it, and particular civil laws may encourage it, as we shall presently observe.

Further, as in most states liberty is more checked or depressed than their constitution requires, it is proper to treat of the particular laws that in each constitution are apt to assist or check the principle of liberty which each state is capable of receiving.

2. Of the Liberty of the Subject

Philosophic liberty consists in the free exercise of the will; or at least, if we must speak agreeably to all systems, in an opinion that we have the free exercise of our will. Political liberty consists in security, or, at least, in the opinion that we enjoy security.

This security is never more dangerously attacked than in public or private accusations. It is, therefore, on the goodness of criminal laws that the liberty of the subject principally depends.

Criminal laws did not receive their full perfection all at once. Even in places where liberty has been most sought after, it has not been always found. Aristotle informs us that at Cum the parents of the accuser might be witnesses. So imperfect was the law under the kings of Rome that Servius Tullius pronounced sentence against the children of Ancus Martius, who were charged with having assassinated the king, his father-in-law. Under the first kings of France, Clotarius made a law that nobody should be condemned without being heard; which shows that a contrary custom had prevailed in some particular case or among some barbarous people. It was Charondas that first established penalties against false witnesses. When the subject has no fence to secure his innocence, he has none for his liberty.

The knowledge already acquired in some countries, or that may be hereafter attained in others, concerning the surest rules to be observed in criminal judgments, is more interesting to mankind than any other thing in the world. ...

4. That Liberty is favoured by the Nature and Proportion of Punishments

Liberty is in perfection when criminal laws derive each punishment from the particular nature of the crime. There are then no arbitrary decisions; the punishment does not flow from the capriciousness of the legislator, but from the very nature of the thing; and man uses no violence to man.

There are four sorts of crimes. Those of the first species are prejudicial to religion, the second to morals, the third to the public tranquillity, and the fourth to the security of the subject. The punishments inflicted for these crimes ought to proceed from the nature of each of these species.

In the class of crimes that concern religion, I rank only those which attack it directly, such as all simple sacrileges. For as to crimes that disturb the exercise of it, they are of the nature of those which prejudice the tranquillity or security of the subject, and ought to be referred to those classes.

In order to derive the punishment of simple sacrileges from the nature of the thing, it should consist in depriving people of the advantages conferred by religion in expelling them out of the temples, in a temporary or perpetual exclusion from the society of the faithful, in shunning their presence, in execrations, comminations, and conjurations....

11. Of Thoughts

Marsyas dreamed that he had cut Dionysius's throat. Dionysius put him to death, pretending that he would never have dreamed of such a thing by night if he had not thought of it by day. This was a most tyrannical action: for though it had been the subject of his thoughts, yet he had made no attempt towards it. The laws do not take upon them to punish any other than overt acts.

12. Of indiscreet Speeches

Nothing renders the crime of high treason more arbitrary than declaring people guilty of it for indiscreet speeches. Speech is so subject to interpretation; there is so great a difference between indiscretion and malice; and frequently so little is there of the latter in the freedom of expression, that the law can hardly subject people to a capital punishment for words unless it expressly declares what words they are.

Words do not constitute an overt act; they remain only in idea. When considered by themselves, they have generally no determinate signification; for this depends on the tone in which they are uttered. It often happens that in repeating the same words they have not the same meaning; this depends on their connection with other things, and sometimes more is signified by silence than by any expression whatever. Since there can be nothing so equivocal and ambiguous as all this, how is it possible to convert it into a crime of high treason? Wherever this law is established, there is an end not only of liberty, but even of its very shadow....

Overt acts do not happen every day; they are exposed to the eye of the public; and a false charge with regard to matters of fact may be easily detected. Words carried into action assume the nature of that action. Thus a man who goes into a public market-place to incite the subject to revolt incurs the guilt of high treason, because the words are joined to the action, and partake of its nature. It is not the words that are punished, but an action in which words are employed. They do not become criminal, but when they are annexed to a criminal action: everything is confounded if words are construed into a capital crime, instead of considering them only as a mark of that crime.

13. Of Writings
In writings there is something more permanent than in words, but when they are in no way preparative to high treason they cannot amount to that charge. ...

18. How dangerous it is in Republics to be too severe in punishing the Crime of High Treason
As soon as a republic has compassed the destruction of those who wanted to subvert it, there should be an end of terrors, punishments, and even of rewards.

Great punishments, and consequently great changes, cannot take place without investing some citizens with an exorbitant power. It is, therefore, more advisable in this case to exceed in lenity than in severity; to banish but few, rather than many; and to leave them their estates, instead of making a vast number of confiscations. Under pretence of avenging the republic's cause, the avengers would establish tyranny. The business is not to destroy the rebel, but the rebellion. They ought to return as quickly as possible into the usual track of government, in which every one is protected by the laws, and no one injured.

13.3 James Madison, "Memorial and Remonstrance Against Religious Assessments" (1785)

Before the Revolution, most colonies had formal religious establishments; meaning that most colonies, with tax dollars, supported an official religion. In much of New England, the official religion was Congregationalism, while in much of the South it was Anglicanism. The official religion was the only one to receive state financial support, though people were free to practice other religions (mostly other Christian denominations) if they wished. If they did practice other denominations or religions, their tax dollars would go to the official church and they would have to contribute other money to their own church.

In 1779, Thomas Jefferson drafted a "Virginia Act for Establishing Religious Freedom" but the state legislature never passed it. In the mid-1780s, Patrick Henry led a movement to use tax dollars to support "teachers of religion." Henry's idea was to assure public support of religion, without placing one denomination above the rest. When Henry submitted his bill, James Madison (Jefferson was in Paris as Ambassador to France) wrote and published the "Memorial and Remonstrance" declaring religion a private and personal matter not subject to state interference, even when that interference takes the guise of assistance. Madison's "Remonstrance" is one of the great American defenses of religious freedom. Four years later, these ideas were embedded in the First Amendment to the U.S. Constitution.

To the Honorable the General Assembly of the Commonwealth of Virginia A Memorial and Remonstrance Against Religious Assessments

We the subscribers, citizens of the said Commonwealth, having taken into serious consideration, a Bill printed by order of the last Session of General Assembly, entitled "A Bill establishing a provision for Teachers of the Christian Religion," and conceiving that the same if finally armed with the sanctions of a law, will be a dangerous abuse of power, are bound as faithful members of a free State to remonstrate against it, and to declare the reasons by which we are determined. We remonstrate against the said Bill,

1. **Because** we hold it for a fundamental and undeniable truth, "that religion or the duty which we owe to our Creator and the manner of discharging it, can be directed only by reason and conviction, not by force or violence." The Religion then of every man must be left to the conviction and conscience of every man; and it is the right of every man to exercise it as these may dictate. This right is in its nature an unalienable right. It is unalienable, because the opinions of men, depending only on the evidence contemplated by their own minds cannot follow the dictates of other men: It is unalienable also, because what is here a right towards men, is a duty towards the Creator. It is the duty of every man to render to the Creator such homage and such only as he believes to be acceptable to him. This duty is precedent, both in order of time and in degree of obligation, to the claims of Civil Society. ... We maintain therefore that in matters of Religion, no man's right is abridged by the institution of Civil Society and that Religion is wholly exempt from its cognizance. ...

2. **Because** Religion be exempt from the authority of the Society at large, still less can it be subject to that of the Legislative Body. The latter are but the creatures and viceregents of the former. Their jurisdiction is both derivative and limited: it is limited with regard to the co-ordinate departments, more necessarily is it limited with regard to the constituents. The preservation of a free Government requires not merely, that the metes and bounds which separate each department of power be invariably maintained; but more especially that neither of them be suffered to overleap the great Barrier which defends the rights of the people. The Rulers who are guilty of such an encroachment, exceed the commission from which they derive their authority, and are Tyrants. The People who submit to it are governed by laws made neither by themselves nor by an authority derived from them, and are slaves.

3. **Because** it is proper to take alarm at the first experiment on our liberties. We hold this prudent jealousy to be the first duty of Citizens, and one of the noblest characteristics of the late Revolution. The free men of America

did not wait till usurped power had strengthened itself by exercise, and entangled the question in precedents. They saw all the consequences in the principle, and they avoided the consequences by denying the principle. We revere this lesson too much soon to forget it. Who does not see that the same authority which can establish Christianity, in exclusion of all other Religions, may establish with the same ease any particular sect of Christians, in exclusion of all other Sects? ...

4. **Because** ... "all men are to be considered as entering into Society on equal conditions; as relinquishing no more, and therefore retaining no less, one than another, of their natural rights. Above all are they to be considered as retaining an "equal title to the free exercise of Religion according to the dictates of Conscience." Whilst we assert for ourselves a freedom to embrace, to profess and to observe the Religion which we believe to be of divine origin, we cannot deny an equal freedom to those whose minds have not yet yielded to the evidence which has convinced us. If this freedom be abused, it is an offence against God, not against man: To God, therefore, not to man, must an account of it be rendered....

5. **Because** the Bill implies either that the Civil Magistrate is a competent Judge of Religious Truth; or that he may employ Religion as an engine of Civil policy. The first is an arrogant pretension falsified by the contradictory opinions of Rulers in all ages, and throughout the world: the second an unhallowed perversion of the means of salvation.

6. **Because** the establishment proposed by the Bill is not requisite for the support of the Christian Religion. To say that it is, is a contradiction to the Christian Religion itself, for every page of it disavows a dependence on the powers of this world: it is a contradiction to fact; for it is known that this Religion both existed and flourished, not only without the support of human laws, but in spite of every opposition from them, and not only during the period of miraculous aid, but long after it had been left to its own evidence and the ordinary care of Providence....

7. **Because** experience witnesseth that ecclesiastical establishments, instead of maintaining the purity and efficacy of Religion, have had a contrary operation. During almost fifteen centuries has the legal establishment of Christianity been on trial. What have been its fruits? More or less in all places, pride and indolence in the Clergy, ignorance and servility in the laity, in both, superstition, bigotry and persecution. Enquire of the Teachers of Christianity for the ages in which it appeared in its greatest lustre; those of every sect, point to the ages prior to its incorporation with Civil policy....

8. **Because** the establishment in question is not necessary for the support of Civil Government.... What influence in fact have ecclesiastical establishments had on Civil Society? In some instances they have been seen to erect a spiritual tyranny on the ruins of the Civil authority; in many instances they have been seen upholding the thrones of political tyranny: in no instance have they been seen the guardians of the liberties of the people. Rulers who wished to subvert the public liberty, may have found an established Clergy convenient auxiliaries. A just Government instituted to secure & perpetuate it needs them not. Such a Government will be best supported by protecting every Citizen in the

enjoyment of his Religion with the same equal hand which protects his person and his property; by neither invading the equal rights of any Sect, nor suffering any Sect to invade those of another.

9. **Because** the proposed establishment is a departure from the generous policy, which, offering an Asylum to the persecuted and oppressed of every Nation and Religion, promised a lustre to our country, and an accession to the number of its citizens. What a melancholy mark is the Bill of sudden degeneracy? . . . The maganimous sufferer under this cruel scourge in foreign Regions, must view the Bill as a Beacon on our Coast, warning him to seek some other haven, where liberty and philanthrophy in their due extent, may offer a more certain respose from his Troubles.

10. **Because** it will have a like tendency to banish our Citizens. The allurements presented by other situations are every day thinning their number. To superadd a fresh motive to emigration by revoking the liberty which they now enjoy, would be the same species of folly which has dishonoured and depopulated flourishing kingdoms.

11. **Because** it will destroy that moderation and harmony which the forbearance of our laws to intermeddle with Religion has produced among its several sects. Torrents of blood have been split in the old world, by vain attempts of the secular arm, to extinguish Religious discord, by proscribing all difference in Religious opinion. Time has at length revealed the true remedy. Every relaxation of narrow and rigorous policy, wherever it has been tried, has been found to assuage the disease. The American Theatre has exhibited proofs that equal and compleat liberty, if it does not wholly eradicate it, sufficiently destroys its malignant influence on the health and prosperity of the State. If with the salutary effects of this system under our own eyes, we begin to contract the bounds of Religious freedom, we know no name that will too severely reproach our folly. . . .

12. **Because** the policy of the Bill is adverse to the diffusion of the light of Christianity. The first wish of those who enjoy this precious gift ought to be that it may be imparted to the whole race of mankind. . . . Instead of Levelling as far as possible, every obstacle to the victorious progress of Truth, the Bill with an ignoble and unchristian timidity would circumscribe it with a wall of defence against the encroachments of error.

13. **Because** attempts to enforce by legal sanctions, acts obnoxious to so great a proportion of Citizens, tend to enervate the laws in general, and to slacken the bands of Society. If it be difficult to execute any law which is not generally deemed necessary or salutary, what must be the case, where it is deemed invalid and dangerous? And what may be the effect of so striking an example of impotency in the Government, on its general authority?

14. **Because** a measure of such singular magnitude and delicacy ought not to be imposed, without the clearest evidence that it is called for by a majority of citizens, and no satisfactory method is yet proposed by which the voice of the majority in this case may be determined, or its influence secured. The people of the respective counties are indeed requested to signify their opinion respecting the adoption of the Bill to the next Session of Assembly." . . . Our hope is that neither of the former will, after due consideration, espouse the dangerous principle of the Bill. Should

the event disappoint us, it will still leave us in full confidence, that a fair appeal to the latter will reverse the sentence against our liberties.

15. **Because** finally, "the equal right of every citizen to the free exercise of his Religion according to the dictates of conscience" is held by the same tenure with all our other rights. If we recur to its origin, it is equally the gift of nature; if we weigh its importance, it cannot be less dear to us; if we consult the "Declaration of those rights which pertain to the good people of Virginia, as the basis and foundation of Government," it is enumerated with equal solemnity, or rather studied emphasis.... Either we must say, that they may controul the freedom of the press, may abolish the Trial by Jury, may swallow up the Executive and Judiciary Powers of the State; nay that they may despoil us of our very right of suffrage, and erect themselves into an independent and hereditary Assembly or, we must say, that they have no authority to enact into the law the Bill under consideration.

We the Subscribers say, that the General Assembly of this Commonwealth have no such authority: And that no effort may be omitted on our part against so dangerous an usurpation, we oppose to it, this remonstrance; earnestly praying, as we are in duty bound, that the Supreme Lawgiver of the Universe, by illuminating those to whom it is addressed, may on the one hand, turn their Councils from every act which would affront his holy prerogative, or violate the trust committed to them: and on the other, guide them into every measure which may be worthy of his [blessing, may re]dound to their own praise, and may establish more firmly the liberties, the prosperity and the happiness of the Commonwealth.

13.4 John Stuart Mill, "On Liberty" (1860)

John Stuart Mill (1806–1873) was the nineteenth century's most prominent advocate of individualism and personal liberty. In the previous generation, Jeremy Bentham and James Mill, John Stuart Mill's father, developed the Benthamite or utilitarian tradition. Utilitarianism was a version of individualism which held that persons were the best judges of their own interests and the best public policy was that which brought the greatest benefit to the greatest number. "On Liberty" is Mill's most famous political exposition.

In the selection below, Mill makes several arguments. One is that individuals should be free to think and act as they wish in all cases that affect only themselves. If an individual's actions threaten harm to someone else, society may intervene, but not otherwise. Another is that "the appropriate region of human liberty" includes freedom of consciousness, thought, speech, press, and assembly. And yet another is the liberty "of framing the plan of our life to suit our own character." John Stuart Mill's argument is that insight, judgment, and truth are best served by the free and open competition of ideas. This still comports well with our modern commitments to individualism, empiricism, and the scientific method.

Chapter I

The object of this Essay is to assert one very simple principle, as entitled to govern absolutely the dealings of society with the individual in the way of compulsion and control, whether the means used be physical force in the form of legal penalties, or the moral coercion of public opinion. That principle is, that the sole end for which mankind are warranted, individually or collectively in interfering with the liberty of action of any of their number, is self-protection. That the only purpose for which power can be right-fully exercised over any member of a civilized community, against his will, is to prevent harm to others. His own good, either physical or moral, is not a sufficient warrant. He cannot rightfully be compelled to do or forbear because it will be better for him to do so, because it will make him happier, because, in the opinions of others, to do so would be wise, or even right. These are good reasons for remonstrating with him, or reasoning with him, or persuading him, or entreating him, but not for compelling him, or visiting him with any evil, in case he do otherwise. To justify that, the conduct from which it is desired to deter him must be calculated to produce evil to some one else. The only part of the conduct of any one, for which he is amenable to society, is that which concerns others. In the part which merely concerns himself, his independence is, of right, absolute. Over himself, over his own body and mind, the individual is sovereign.

It is, perhaps, hardly necessary to say that this doctrine is meant to apply only to human beings in the maturity of their faculties. We are not speaking of children, or of young persons below the age which the law may fix as that of manhood or womanhood. Those who are still in a state to require being taken care of by others, must be protected against their own actions as well as against external injury....

It is proper to state that I forego any advantage which could be derived to my argu-ment from the idea of abstract right as a thing independent of utility. I regard utility as the ultimate appeal on all ethical questions; but it must be utility in the largest sense, grounded on the permanent interests of man as a progressive being. Those interests, I contend, authorize the subjection of individual spontaneity to external control, only in respect to those actions of each, which concern the interest of other people. If any one does an act hurtful to others, there is a prima facie case for punishing him, by law, or, where legal penalties are not safely applicable, by general disapprobation. There are also many positive acts for the benefit of others, which he may rightfully be compelled to perform; such as, to give evidence in a court of justice; to bear his fair share in the common defence, or in any other joint work necessary to the interest of the society of which he enjoys the protection; and to perform certain acts of individual beneficence, such as saving a fellow-creature's life, or interposing to protect the defenceless against ill-usage, things which whenever it is obviously a man's duty to do, he may rightfully be made responsible to society for not doing. A person may cause evil to others not only by his actions but by his inaction, and in neither case he is justly accountable to them for the injury. The latter case, it is true, requires a much more cautious exercise of compulsion than the former. To make any one answerable for doing evil to others, is the rule; to make him answerable for not preventing evil, is, comparatively speaking, the exception....

But there is a sphere of action in which society, as distinguished from the individual, has, if any, only an indirect interest; comprehending all that portion of a person's life and conduct which affects only himself, or, if it also affects others, only with their free, volun-tary, and undeceived consent and participation. When I say only himself, I mean directly, and in the first instance: for whatever affects himself, may affect others through himself; and the objection which may be grounded on this contingency, will receive consideration in the sequel. This, then, is the appropriate region of human liberty. It comprises, first, the inward domain of consciousness; demanding liberty of conscience, in the most comprehensive sense; liberty of thought and feeling; absolute freedom of opinion and sentiment on all subjects, practical or speculative, scientific, moral, or theological. The liberty of expressing and publishing opinions may seem to fall under a different principle, since it belongs to that part of the conduct of an individual which concerns other people; but, being almost of as much importance as the liberty of thought itself, and resting in great part on the same reasons, is practically inseparable from it.

Secondly, the principle requires liberty of tastes and pursuits; of framing the plan of our life to suit our own character; of doing as we like, subject to such consequences as may follow; without impediment from our fellow-creatures, so long as what we do does not harm them even though they should think our conduct foolish, perverse, or wrong. Thirdly, from this liberty of each individual, follows the liberty, within the same limits, of combination among individuals; freedom to unite, for any purpose not involving harm to others: the persons combining being supposed to be of full age, and not forced or deceived.

No society in which these liberties are not, on the whole, respected, is free, whatever may be its form of government; and none is completely free in which they do not exist absolute and unqualified. The only freedom which deserves the name, is that of pursuing our own good in our own way, so long as we do not attempt to deprive others of theirs, or impede their efforts to obtain it. Each is the proper guardian of his own health, whether bodily, or mental or spiritual. Mankind are greater gainers by suffering each other to live as seems good to themselves, than by compelling each to live as seems good to the rest.

Though this doctrine is anything but new, and, to some persons, may have the air of a truism, there is no doctrine which stands more directly opposed to the general tendency of existing opinion and practice. Society has expended fully as much effort in the attempt (according to its lights) to compel people to conform to its notions of personal, as of social excellence . . .

[T]here is also in the world at large an increasing inclination to stretch unduly the powers of society over the individual, both by the force of opinion and even by that of legislation: and as the tendency of all the changes taking place in the world is to strengthen society, and diminish the power of the individual, this encroachment is not one of the evils which tend spontaneously to disappear, but, on the contrary, to grow more and more formidable. The disposition of mankind, whether as rulers or as fellow-citizens, to impose their own opinions and inclinations as a rule of conduct on others, is so energetically supported by some of the best and by some of the worst feelings incident to human nature, that it is hardly ever kept under restraint by anything but want of power; and as the power is not declining, but growing, unless a strong barrier of moral conviction can be raised against the mischief, we must expect, in the present circumstances of the world, to see it increase.

It will be convenient for the argument, if, instead of at once entering upon the general thesis, we confine ourselves in the first instance to a single branch of it, on which the principle here stated is, if not fully, yet to a certain point, recognized by the current opinions. This one branch is the Liberty of Thought: from which it is impossible to separate the cognate liberty of speaking and of writing. Although these liberties, to some considerable amount, form part of the political morality of all countries which profess religious toleration and free institutions, the grounds, both philosophical and practical, on which they rest, are perhaps not so familiar to the general mind, nor so thoroughly appreciated by many even of the leaders of opinion, as might have been expected. Those grounds, when rightly understood, are of much wider application than to only one division of the subject, and a thorough consideration of this part of the question will be found the best introduction to the remainder. Those to whom nothing which I am about to say will be new, may therefore, I hope, excuse me, if on a subject which for now three centuries has been so often discussed, I venture on one discussion more.

Chapter II

Of the Liberty of Thought and Discussion

The time, it is to be hoped, is gone by when any defence would be necessary of the "liberty of the press" as one of the securities against corrupt or tyrannical government. No argument, we may suppose, can now be needed, against permitting a legislature or an executive, not identified in interest with the people, to prescribe opinions to them, and determine what doctrines or what arguments they shall be allowed to hear. This aspect of the question, besides, has been so often and so triumphantly enforced by preceding writers, that it needs not be specially insisted on in this place. Though the law of England, on the subject of the press, is as servile to this day as it was in the time of the Tudors, there is little danger of its being actually put in force against political discussion, except during some temporary panic, when fear of insurrection drives ministers and judges from their propriety; and, speaking generally, it is not, in constitutional countries, to be apprehended that the government, whether completely responsible to the people or not, will often attempt to control the expression of opinion, except when in doing so it makes itself the organ of the general intolerance of the public. Let us suppose, therefore, that the government is entirely at one with the people, and never thinks of exerting any power of coercion unless in agreement with what it conceives to be their voice. But I deny the right of the people to exercise such coercion, either by themselves or by their government. The power itself is illegitimate. The best government has no more title to it than the worst. It is as noxious, or more noxious, when exerted in accordance with public opinion, than when in opposition to it. If all mankind minus one, were of one opinion, and only one person were of the contrary opinion, mankind would be no more justified in silencing that one person, than he, if he had the power, would be justified in silencing mankind. Were an opinion a personal possession of no value except to the owner; if to be obstructed in the enjoyment of it were simply a private injury, it would make some difference whether the injury was inflicted only on a few persons or on many. But the peculiar evil of silencing the expression of an opinion is, that it is robbing the human race; posterity as well as the existing generation; those who dissent from the opinion, still more than those who hold it. If the opinion is right, they are deprived of the opportunity of exchanging error for truth: if wrong, they lose, what is almost as great a benefit, the clearer perception and livelier impression of truth, produced by its collision with error.

It is necessary to consider separately these two hypotheses, each of which has a distinct branch of the argument corresponding to it. We can never be sure that the opinion we are endeavouring to stifle is a false opinion; and if we were sure, stifling it would be an evil still.

First the opinion which it is attempted to suppress by authority may possibly be true. Those who desire to suppress it, of course deny its truth; but they are not infallible. They have no authority to decide the question for all mankind, and exclude every other person from the means of judging. To refuse a hearing to an opinion, because they are sure that it is false, is to assume that their certainty is the same thing as absolute certainty. All silencing of discussion is an assumption of infallibility. Its condemnation may be allowed to rest on this common argument, not the worse for being common. . . .

The objection likely to be made to this argument, would probably take some such form as the following. There is no greater assumption of infallibility in forbidding the propagation of error, than in any other thing which is done by public authority on its own judgment and responsibility. Judgment is given to men that they may use it. Because it may be used erroneously, are men to be told that they ought not to use it at all? To prohibit what they think pernicious, is not claiming exemption from error, but fulfilling the duty incumbent on them, although fallible, of acting on their conscientious conviction. If we were never to act on our opinions, because those opinions may be wrong, we should leave all our interests uncared for, and all our duties unperformed. An objection which applies to all conduct can be no valid objection to any conduct in particular.

It is the duty of governments, and of individuals, to form the truest opinions they can; to form them carefully, and never impose them upon others unless they are quite sure of being right. But when they are sure (such reasoners may say), it is not conscientiousness but cowardice to shrink from acting on their opinions, and allow doctrines which they honestly think dangerous to the welfare of mankind, either in this life or in another, to be scattered abroad without restraint, because other people, in less enlightened times, have persecuted opinions now believed to be true. . . . We may, and must, assume our opinion to be true for the guidance of our own conduct: and it is assuming no more when we forbid bad men to pervert society by the propagation of opinions which we regard as false and pernicious.

I answer, that it is assuming very much more. There is the greatest difference between presuming an opinion to be true, because, with every opportunity for contesting it, it has not been refuted, and assuming its truth for the purpose of not permitting its refutation. Complete liberty of contradicting and disproving our opinion, is the very condition which justifies us in assuming its truth for purposes of action; and on no other terms can a being with human faculties have any rational assurance of being right. . . .

The whole strength and value, then, of human judgment, depending on the one property, that it can be set right when it is wrong, reliance can be placed on it only when the means of setting it right are kept constantly at hand. In the case of any person whose judgment is really deserving of confidence, how has it become so? Because he has kept his mind open to criticism of his opinions and conduct. Because it has been his practice to listen to all that could be said against him; to profit by as much of it as was just, and expound to himself, and upon occasion to others, the fallacy of what was fallacious. Because he has felt, that the only way in which a human being can make some approach to knowing the whole of a subject, is by hearing what can be said about it by persons of every variety of opinion, and studying all modes in which it can be looked at by every character of mind. No wise man ever acquired his wisdom in any mode but this; nor is it in the nature of human intellect to become wise in any other manner. The steady habit of correcting and completing his own opinion by collating it with those of others, so far from causing doubt and hesitation in carrying it into practice, is the only stable foundation for a just reliance on it: for, being cognizant of all that can, at least obviously, be said against him, and having taken up his position against all gainsayers knowing that he has sought for objections and difficulties, instead of avoiding them, and has shut out no light which can be thrown upon the subject from any quarter—he has a right to think his judgment better than that of any person, or any multitude, who have not gone through a similar process.

13.5 *New York Times v. Sullivan* (1964)

Public officials are reluctant to be criticized either in speech or in the press. Recall John Winthrop's admonition (reading 13.1 above) to his fellow Puritans that having been elected to his position, he held it by God's will, so citizens should be careful in questioning or criticizing authority. John Stuart Mill, in the preceding reading, argued that society in general benefits from a free competition of ideas in which truth will eventually triumph of falsehood and error.

In *New York Times v. Sullivan*, the Supreme Court reads Mill's view into the Constitution. The Sullivan case arises out of the civil rights protests in the early 1960s south. Montgomery, Alabama, police commissioner L.B. Sullivan filed and won in the Alabama courts a civil libel suit against several civil rights activists and the *New York Times*. Sullivan claimed that public criticism, containing several errors of fact, had libeled him and harmed his public reputation. Alabama courts agreed, holding that criticisms of public officials had to be true to be legally protected. The U.S. Supreme Court held that error crept into all animated public debate and to make it punishable would unconstitutionally limit free expression. Nonetheless, the court held that "actual malice," not just error, was punishable. Justices Arthur Goldberg, Hugo Black, and William O. Douglas, concurred in the majority opinion, but advocated a broader rule in which all criticism of public officials, true or not, malicious or not, was protected by the First and Fourteenth Amendments to the U.S. Constitution.

---

376 U.S. 254 (1964)

NEW YORK TIMES CO.
v.
SULLIVAN

No. 39

Supreme Court of United States.

Argued January 6, 1964.
Decided March 9, 1964.

MR. JUSTICE BRENNAN delivered the opinion of the Court.

We are required in this case to determine for the first time the extent to which the constitutional protections for speech and press limit a State's power to award damages in a libel action brought by a public official against critics of his official conduct.

Respondent L. B. Sullivan is one of the three elected Commissioners of the City of Montgomery, Alabama. He testified that he was "Commissioner of Public Affairs and the duties are supervision of the Police Department, Fire Department, Department of Cemetery and Department of Scales." He brought this civil libel action against the four individual petitioners, who are Negroes and Alabama clergymen, and against petitioner the New York Times Company, a New York corporation which publishes the New York Times, a daily newspaper. A jury in the Circuit Court of Montgomery County awarded him damages of $500,000, the full amount claimed, against all the petitioners, and the Supreme Court of Alabama affirmed. 273 Ala. 656, 144 So. 2d 25.

Respondent's complaint alleged that he had been libeled by statements in a full-page advertisement that was carried in the New York Times on March 29, 1960. Entitled "Heed Their Rising Voices," the advertisement began by stating that "As the whole world knows by now, thousands of Southern Negro students are engaged in widespread non-violent demonstrations in positive affirmation of the right to live in human dignity as guaranteed by the U. S. Constitution and the Bill of Rights." It went on to charge that "in their efforts to uphold these guarantees, they are being met by an unprecedented wave of terror by those who would deny and negate that document which the whole world looks upon as setting the pattern for modern freedom. . . ." Succeeding paragraphs purported to illustrate the "wave of terror" by describing certain alleged events. The text concluded with an appeal for funds for three purposes: support of the student movement, "the struggle for the right-to-vote," and the legal defense of Dr. Martin Luther King, Jr., leader of the movement, against a perjury indictment then pending in Montgomery.

The text appeared over the names of 64 persons, many widely known for their activities in public affairs, religion, trade unions, and the performing arts. Below these names, and under a line reading "We in the south who are struggling daily for dignity and freedom warmly endorse this appeal," appeared the names of the four individual petitioners and of 16 other persons, all but two of whom were identified as clergymen in various Southern cities. The advertisement was signed at the bottom of the page by the "Committee to Defend Martin Luther King and the Struggle for Freedom in the South," and the officers of the Committee were listed.

Of the 10 paragraphs of text in the advertisement, the third and a portion of the sixth were the basis of respondent's claim of libel. They read as follows:

Third paragraph:

"In Montgomery, Alabama, after students sang My Country, 'Tis of Thee' on the State Capitol steps, their leaders were expelled from school, and truckloads of police armed with shotguns and tear-gas ringed the Alabama State College Campus. When the entire student body protested to state authorities by refusing to re-register, their dining hall was padlocked in an attempt to starve them into submission."

Sixth paragraph:

"Again and again the Southern violators have answered Dr. King's peaceful protests with intimidation and violence. They have bombed his home almost killing his wife and child.

They have assaulted his person. They have arrested him seven times—for 'speeding,' 'loitering' and similar 'offenses.' And now they have charged him with 'perjury'—a *felony* under which they could imprison him for *ten years* . . . ."

Although neither of these statements mentions respondent by name, he contended that the word "police" in the third paragraph referred to him as the Montgomery Commissioner who supervised the Police Department, so that he was being accused of "ringing" the campus with police. He further claimed that the paragraph would be read as imputing to the police, and hence to him, the padlocking of the dining hall in order to starve the students into submission. As to the sixth paragraph, he contended that since arrests are ordinarily made by the police, the statement "They have arrested [Dr. King] seven times" would be read as referring to him; he further contended that the "They" who did the arresting would be equated with the "They" who committed the other described acts and with the "Southern violators." Thus, he argued, the paragraph would be read as accusing the Montgomery police, and hence him, of answering Dr. King's protests with "intimidation and violence," bombing his home, assaulting his person, and charging him with perjury. Respondent and six other Montgomery residents testified that they read some or all of the statements as referring to him in his capacity as Commissioner.

It is uncontroverted that some of the statements contained in the paragraphs were not accurate descriptions of events which occurred in Montgomery. Although Negro students staged a demonstration on the State Capitol steps, they sang the National Anthem and not "My country, 'Tis of Thee." Although nine students were expelled by the State Board of Education, this was not for leading the demonstration at the Capitol, but for demanding service at a lunch counter in the Montgomery County Courthouse on another day. Not the entire student body, but most of it, had protested the expulsion, not by refusing to register, but by boycotting classes on a single day; virtually all the students did register for the ensuing semester. The campus dining hall was not padlocked on any occasion, and the only students who may have been barred from eating there were the few who had neither signed a preregistration application nor requested temporary meal tickets. Although the police were deployed near the campus in large numbers on three occasions, they did not at any time "ring" the campus, and they were not called to the campus in connection with the demonstration on the State Capitol steps, as the third paragraph implied. Dr. King had not been arrested seven times, but only four; and although he claimed to have been assaulted some years earlier in connection with his arrest for loitering outside a courtroom, one of the officers who made the arrest denied that there was such an assault. . . .

II

Under Alabama law as applied in this case, a publication is "libelous per se" if the words "tend to injure a person . . . in his reputation" or to "bring [him] into public contempt"; the trial court stated that the standard was met if the words are such as to "injure him in his public office, or impute misconduct to him in his office, or want of official integrity, or want of fidelity to a public trust. . . ." The jury must find that the words were published "of and concerning" the plaintiff, but where the plaintiff is a public official his place in the governmental hierarchy is sufficient evidence to support a finding that his reputation has been affected by statements that reflect upon the agency of which he is in charge. Once "libel per se" has been established, the defendant has no defense as to stated facts unless he can persuade the jury that they were true in all their particulars. *Alabama Ride Co. v. Vance*, 235 Ala. 263, 178 So. 438 (1938); *Johnson Publishing Co. v. Davis*, 271 Ala. 474, 494–495, 124 So. 2d 441, 457–458 (1960). His privilege of "fair comment" for expressions of opinion depends on the truth of the facts upon which the comment is based. *Parsons v. Age-Herald Publishing Co.*, 181 Ala. 439, 450, 61 So. 345, 350 (1913). Unless he can discharge the burden of proving truth, general damages are presumed, and may be awarded without proof of pecuniary injury. A showing of actual malice is apparently a prerequisite to recovery of punitive damages, and the defendant may in any event forestall a punitive award by a retraction meeting the statutory requirements. Good motives and belief in truth do not negate an inference of malice, but are relevant only in mitigation of punitive damages if the jury chooses to accord them weight. *Johnson Publishing Co. v. Davis, supra*, 271 Ala., at 495, 124 So. 2d, at 458.

*268 The question before us is whether this rule of liability, as applied to an action brought by a public official against critics of his official conduct, abridges the freedom of speech and of the press that is guaranteed by the first and Fourteenth Amendments....

The general proposition that freedom of expression upon public questions is secured by the First Amendment has long been settled by our decisions. The constitutional safeguard, we have said, "was fashioned to assure unfettered interchange of ideas for the bringing about of political and social changes desired by the people." *Roth v. United States*. 354 U. S. 476. 484. "The maintenance of the opportunity for free political discussion to the end that government may be responsive to the will of the people and that changes may be obtained by lawful means, an opportunity essential to the security of the Republic, is a fundamental principle of our constitutional system." *Stromberg v. California*. 283 U. S. 359, 369. "[I]t is a prized American privilege to speak one's mind, although not always with perfect good taste, on all public institutions," *Bridges v. California*. 314 U. S. 252, 270, and this opportunity is to be afforded for "vigorous advocacy" no less than "abstract discussion." *N. A. A. C. P. v. Button*. 371 U. S. 415, 429. The First Amendment, said Judge Learned Hand, "presupposes that right conclusions are more likely to be gathered out of a multitude of tongues, than through any kind of authoritative selection. To many this is, and always will be, folly; but we have staked upon it our all." *United States v. Associated Press*, 52 F. Supp. 362, 372 (D. C. S. D. N. Y. 1943). Mr. Justice Brandeis, in his concurring opinion in *Whitney v. California*, 274 U. S. 357. 375–376, gave the principle its classic formulation:

> "Those who won our independence believed . . . that public discussion is a political duty; and that this should be a fundamental principle of the American government. They recognized the risks to which all human institutions are subject. But they knew that order cannot be secured merely through fear of punishment for its infraction; that it is hazardous to discourage thought, hope and imagination; that fear breeds repression; that repression breeds hate; that hate menaces stable government; that the path of safety lies in the opportunity to discuss freely supposed grievances and proposed remedies; and that the fitting remedy for evil counsels is good ones. Believing in the power of reason as applied through public discussion, they eschewed silence coerced by law—the argument of force in its worst form. Recognizing the occasional tyrannies of governing majorities, they amended the Constitution so that free speech and assembly should be guaranteed."

Thus we consider this case against the background of a profound national commitment to the principle that debate on public issues should be uninhibited, robust, and wide-open, and that it may well include vehement, caustic, and sometimes unpleasantly sharp attacks on government and public officials. See *Terminiello v. Chicago.* 337 U. S. 1. 4: *De Jonge v. Oregon.* 299 U. S. 353, 365. The present advertisement, as an expression of grievance and protest on one of the major public issues of our time, would seem clearly to qualify for the constitutional protection. The question is whether it forfeits that protection by the falsity of some of its factual statements and by its alleged defamation of respondent.

Authoritative interpretations of the First Amendment guarantees have consistently refused to recognize an exception for any test of truth—whether administered by judges, juries, or administrative officials—and especially one that puts the burden of proving truth on the speaker. Cf. *Speiser v. Randall.* 357 U. S. 513, 525–526. The constitutional protection does not turn upon "the truth, popularity, or social utility of the ideas and beliefs which are offered." *N. A. A. C. P. v. Button.* 371 U. S. 415, 445. As Madison said, "Some degree of abuse is inseparable from the proper use of every thing; and in no instance is this more true than in that of the press." 4 Elliot's Debates on the Federal Constitution (1876), p. 571. In *Cantwell v. Connecticut*, 310 U. S. 296, 310. the Court declared:

> "In the realm of religious faith, and in that of political belief, sharp differences arise. In both fields the tenets of one man may seem the rankest error to his neighbor. To persuade others to his own point of view, the pleader, as we know, at times, resorts to exaggeration, to vilification of men who have been, or are, prominent in church or state, and even to false statement. But the people of this nation have ordained in the light of history, that, in spite of the probability of excesses and abuses, these liberties are, in the long view, essential to enlightened opinion and right conduct on the part of the citizens of a democracy."

That erroneous statement is inevitable in free debate, and that it must be protected if the freedoms of expression are to have the "breathing space" that they "need ... to survive," *N. A. A. C. P. v. Button,* 371 U. S. 415, 433, was also recognized by the Court of Appeals for the District of Columbia Circuit in *Sweeney v. Patterson.* 76 U. S. App. D. C. 23, 24, 128 F. 2d 457, 458 (1942), cert. denied, 317 U. S. 678. Judge Edgerton spoke for a unanimous court which affirmed the dismissal of a Congressman's libel suit based upon a newspaper article charging him with anti-Semitism in opposing a judicial appointment. He said:

> "Cases which impose liability for erroneous reports of the political conduct of officials reflect the obsolete doctrine that the governed must not criticize their governors.... The interest of the public here outweighs the interest of appellant or any other individual. The protection of the public requires not merely discussion, but information. Political conduct and views which some respectable people approve, and others condemn, are constantly imputed to Congressmen. Errors of fact, particularly in regard to a man's mental states and processes, are inevitable.... Whatever is added to the field of libel is taken from the field of free debate."

Injury to official reputation affords no more warrant for repressing speech that would otherwise be free than does factual error. Where judicial officers are involved, this Court has held that concern for the dignity and reputation of the courts does not justify the punishment as criminal contempt of criticism of the judge or his decision. *Bridges v. California,* 314 U. S. 252. This is true even though the utterance contains "half-truths" and "misinformation." *Pennekamp v. Florida*, 328 U. S. 331, 342, 343, n. 5, 345. Such repression can be justified, if at all, only by a clear and present danger of the obstruction of justice.

See also *Craig v. Harney*, 331 U. S. 367; *Wood v. Georgia*, 370 U. S. 375. If judges are to be treated as "men of fortitude, able to thrive in a hardy climate," *Craig v. Harney, supra*, 331 U. S., at 376, surely the same must be true of other government officials, such as elected city commissioners. Criticism of their official conduct does not lose its constitutional protection merely because it is effective criticism and hence diminishes their official reputations....

We conclude that such a privilege is required by the First and Fourteenth Amendments.

III

We hold today that the Constitution delimits a State's power to award damages for libel in actions brought by public officials against critics of their official conduct. Since this is such an action, the rule requiring proof of actual malice is applicable. While Alabama law apparently requires proof of actual malice for an award of punitive damages, where general damages are concerned malice is "presumed." Such a presumption is inconsistent with the federal rule....

Reversed and remanded
MR. JUSTICE BLACK, with whom MR. JUSTICE DOUGLAS joins, concurring.

I concur in reversing this half-million-dollar judgment against the New York Times Company and the four individual defendants. In reversing the Court holds that "the Constitution delimits a State's power to award damages for libel in actions brought by public officials against critics of their official conduct." *Ante*, p. 283. I base my vote to reverse on the belief that the First and Fourteenth Amendments not merely "delimit" a State's power to award damages to "public officials against critics of their official conduct" but completely prohibit a State from exercising such a power. The Court goes on to hold that a State can subject such critics to damages if "actual malice" can be proved against them. "Malice," even as defined by the Court, is an elusive, abstract concept, hard to prove and hard to disprove. The requirement that malice be proved provides at best an evanescent protection for the right critically to discuss public affairs and certainly does not measure up to the sturdy safeguard embodied in the First Amendment. Unlike the Court, therefore, I vote to reverse exclusively on the ground that the Times and the individual defendants had an absolute, unconditional constitutional right to publish in the Times advertisement their criticisms of the Montgomery agencies and officials....

We would, I think, more faithfully interpret the First Amendment by holding that at the very least it leaves the people and the press free to criticize officials and discuss public affairs with impunity. This Nation of ours elects many of its important officials; so do the States, the municipalities, the counties, and even many precincts. These officials are responsible to the people for the way they perform their duties. While our Court has held that some kinds of speech and writings, such as "obscenity," *Roth v. United States*, 354 U. S. 476, and "fighting words," *Chaplinsky v. New Hampshire*, 315 U. S. 568, are not expression within the protection of the First Amendment, freedom to discuss public affairs and public officials is unquestionably, as the Court today holds, the kind of speech the First Amendment was primarily designed to keep within the area of free discussion. To punish the exercise of this right to discuss public affairs or to penalize it through libel judgments is to abridge or shut off discussion of the very kind most needed. This Nation, I suspect, can live in peace without libel suits based on public discussions of public affairs and public officials. But I doubt that a country can live in freedom where its people can be made to suffer physically or financially for criticizing their government, its actions, or its officials. "For a representative democracy ceases to exist the moment that the public functionaries are by any means absolved from their responsibility to their constituents; and this happens whenever the constituent can be restrained in any manner from speaking, writing, or publishing his opinions upon any public measure, or upon the conduct of those who may advise or execute it." An unconditional right to say what one pleases about public affairs is what I consider to be the minimum guarantee of the First Amendment.

I regret that the Court has stopped short of this holding indispensable to preserve our free press from destruction.

MR. JUSTICE GOLDBERG, with whom MR. JUSTICE DOUGLAS joins, concurring in the result.

The Court today announces a constitutional standard which prohibits "a public official from recovering damages for a defamatory falsehood relating to his official conduct unless he proves that the statement was made with 'actual malice'—that is, with knowledge that it was false or with reckless disregard of whether it was false or not." *Ante*, at 279–280. The Court thus rules that the Constitution gives citizens and newspapers a "conditional privilege" immunizing nonmalicious misstatements of fact regarding the official conduct of a government officer. The impressive array of history and precedent marshaled by the Court, however, confirms my belief that the Constitution affords greater protection than that provided by the Court's standard to citizen and press in exercising the right of public criticism.

In my view, the First and Fourteenth Amendments to the Constitution afford to the citizen and to the press an absolute, unconditional privilege to criticize official conduct despite the harm which may flow from excesses and abuses. The prized American right "to speak one's mind," cf. *Bridges v. California*. 314 U. S. 252, 270, about public officials and affairs needs "breathing space to survive," *N. A. A. C. P. v. Button*. 371 U. S. 415, 433. The right should not depend upon a probing by the jury of the motivation of the citizen or press. The theory of our Constitution is that every citizen may speak his mind and every newspaper express its view on matters of public concern and may not be barred from speaking or publishing because those in control of government think that what is said or written is unwise, unfair, false, or malicious. In a democratic society, one who assumes to act for the citizens in an executive, legislative, or judicial capacity must expect that his official acts will be commented upon and criticized. Such criticism cannot, in my opinion, be muzzled or deterred by the courts at the instance of public officials under the label of libel.

13.6 Ken I. Kersch, "The Right to Privacy" (2008)

When one traces an idea over broad stretches of time, as Ken Kersch does here with the idea of a right to privacy, the meaning of words central to understanding that idea may change from one historical era to the next. Note that in this selection

Kersch talks about how Democrats and Republicans have differed over the right to privacy in cases dealing with contraception and abortion and then talks about the liberal principles underlying the right to privacy. To the modern ear, the words liberal and Democrat seem to go together, but Kersch's discussion of liberal principles refers to Lockean individualist principles prominent from the seventeenth century onward. Always be alert to the meaning of words, even seemingly familiar words like liberal, when the discussion crosses several eras.

In this selection, Ken Kersch examines the tension within democratic government between the citizen's desire "to be left alone" and government desire and responsibility to lead, guide, and, sometimes, coerce citizens. Kersch highlights the state's response to broad scale social, economic, and demographic change in the late nineteenth and early twentieth centuries. Urbanization, industrialization, and immigration forced a redrawing of the line between the public and the private. When these lines shift, courts have to devise and revise principles, doctrine, and rules. The right to privacy, the right to be left alone, is still an important constitutional value, but more explicitly defined than in earlier centuries.

From the moment it was pronounced fundamental by the Supreme Court in the mid-1960s, the "right to privacy" has been one of American constitutional law's most prominent paradoxes and flash points. The word "privacy," after all, appears neither in the body of the Constitution nor in the Bill of Rights. For this reason, many have lambasted the Court's invocation of the privacy right in voiding an 1879 Connecticut law banning the use of contraception *(Griswold v. Connecticut* [1965]) as a paradigmatically "activist" judicial concoction.[1] When, only a few years later, the Court went on to hold that the privacy right was so expansive as to protect a woman's right to end her pregnancy by abortion,[2] ...commentators pointed to *Griswold* and *Roe* as prime exhibits for the proposition that Americans were once again being governed by unelected, life-tenured federal judges, ... writing their own time-bound elite values into the Constitution under the guise of interpreting it.[3]

Ever since, debates about the *right* to privacy have extended well beyond considerations of the *value* of privacy and its reach. The right to privacy invoked in *Griswold* and *Roe* has become central to a set of broader institutional questions concerning the proper role for the courts in the American constitutional order. It has also been at the core of contemporary methodological debates about the way for a judge to best interpret a constitutional text.[4] The privacy right, moreover, has assumed a starring role on the marquee of electoral politics—placing it in rarefied company for a judicial pronouncement. The modern Republican Party rose to power in significant part by campaigning against activist judges handing down willful decisions like *Griswold* and *Roe*. Liberal Democrats lost political power in the late twentieth century in no small part through their defense of those decisions, and of the style of judging that underwrote them. Given this trajectory, it is no exaggeration to conclude that, despite its absence from the constitutional text—or, perhaps, because of it—the "right to privacy" (like the Lochnerite "liberty of contract" before it) has stood at the core of contemporary constitutional debates for nearly half a century.

The controversy over the privacy right is, in many respects, surprising. This is because, despite the above-mentioned disputes, Americans have always held privacy itself in high esteem. Americans of divergent political leanings would probably approve of the sentiments expressed by the iconic liberal justice Louis D. Brandeis: "The makers of our Constitution conferred, as against the government, the right to be let alone—the most comprehensive of rights and the right most valued by civilized men."[5] Americans converge on the value of being left alone because that value is a touchstone of liberal political thought, which accords foundational value to individual freedom. And, as many have observed, the United States is the most ideologically liberal nation on earth.[6]

Prior to the ascendancy of liberal political outlooks in the seventeenth century, a person's place in the world—economic, cultural, and political—was set almost universally, and irremediably, by his assigned place in a hierarchical, feudal social order. In this world, political authority, typically monarchical, issued from on high. In such a world, a "right to be let alone" was scarcely imaginable. The rise of liberalism, closely associated with the Protestant Reformation and the rise of market capitalism, placed new value on an individual's private beliefs, claims of individual conscience, and worldly wants and responsibilities. Under liberal theories of government, legitimate political authority derived not from God, but rather from the consent of individuals joining together to form an autonomous political community.

Of course, the decision to erect a government meant that individuals, by their own consent, would no longer be "left alone." Indeed, so long as the government did not become abusive of the collective ends for which it was created—the protection of an individual and his rights—the individual was under an obligation to obey the rightful government, and its laws. But determining when the government was working to advance its rightful ends and when it was being abusive has often been hotly contested in liberal societies. Individuals—and political parties—have disagreed vehemently about when it is appropriate to coerce individuals for the purpose of advancing the collective public safety and peace. They have disagreed vehemently, moreover, about when it is appropriate to coerce individuals for the purpose of advancing public morals—also a strong consideration in a polity, like the United States that, while clearly liberal, is both religious and shaped by supplementary strains of a civic republicanism that emphasizes the importance of virtue to the preservation of liberty. Contemporary arguments in the U.S. about the "right to be let alone" and the "right to privacy" begin with the tension at the heart of liberal political cultures between their animating commitment to the prerogative of the individual concerning his conscience and his choices, and the recognition that healthy, and stable governments, created by independent individuals, do not function by leaving people alone—put otherwise, that the essence of government is to guide and to coerce.

The question of the scope of the protection to be afforded to the value of privacy, or the right to be "let alone," will inevitably turn on broader social, cultural, and political considerations concerning when it is appropriate to seek to advance collective social purposes (peace, safety, health, morality) through coercion, and when it is not. Some—be they statists or libertarians—hold strong, principled views on these matters that vary little with the temper of the times. Most, however, simply accept the status quo conventions of the public-private divide of their age. Most interesting, perhaps, are periods of rapid social, economic, and political change, when questions concerning the appropriate divide between the public and private, either generally or as applied to particular social problems, become hotly debated, and the lines are ripe for redrawing. In those periods, some will insist that the old lines be held. Others will demand radical change. Still others are willing to listen and consider arguments on both sides.

As a practical matter, these arguments will often be subsumed within arguments about law, be it (judge-made) common, statutory, or constitutional. For example, it was no accident that the Supreme Court discovered the constitutional privacy right in a birth control case, and extended it in an abortion case, at the height of the sexual revolution, when the women's movement (and other social changes) brought traditional sex roles under siege, and agitated on behalf of a revolutionary new commitment to sexual autonomy.[7] In fact, in a reflection of this genesis, the constitutional right to privacy in its contemporary guise has become identified almost exclusively with claims to bodily freedom (including not just sex, but also end-of-life decisions). If we take a longer view and consider privacy not simply as a constitutional *right*, but as a constitutional *value*, we are forced to consider a much broader range of questions.

Privacy, the New American State, and the Modern Supreme Court

The sense by individuals that they have a "right to be let alone"—that there is an important distinction to be drawn between the public and private spheres, and the claims of the public sphere are to be strictly limited—is inherent in the liberal worldview. But contemporary questions concerning constitutional privacy are defined by the terms, not simply by the liberal outlook generally, but by what has been called the "New Liberalism." In the United States, prior to the late nineteenth century, state, local, and common law rules provided a relatively stable (if not unchanging) framework for regulating the boundaries between the public and private spheres. This framework was informed, in significant part, by traditional moral and religious understandings of the nature of the broader public good. *Salus populi suprema lex est*—the welfare of the people is the supreme law—was the era's guiding maxim. Under the prevailing constitutional understandings of that same era, the national government was conceived of as having been delegated enumerated and limited powers for specified purposes (such as the regulation of interstate commerce and foreign trade). Unlike the states and localities, it was not charged with sweeping, more general powers to advance the broader public health, safety, and morals.[8]

The massive economic and social changes of the late nineteenth century—industrialization, urbanization, and immigration among them—threw up a set of national social problems that either were new or dwarfed in scale the effects of their predecessors. Advances in science and in the new social sciences suggested to many that a government of expert professionals might very well be capable of eliminating some of the problems created by the unprecedented conditions, and of managing or mitigating others. Robust constituencies began to insist that they do so. Many social and economic problems once conceived of as either local or inevitable were re-conceptualized as national and solvable. In this context, the potential claims of government—its possibility for advancing the public good—seemed to many all but unlimited. The decision to build a modern, centralized administrative state revolutionized traditional understandings of the relative claims of the public and private spheres. This, of course, required that traditional constitutional understandings implicating privacy be radically reworked.

It was at this time that the public/private divide was reimagined in constitutional terms as pitting the newly broadened claims of national power to advance the collective public good against an individual asserting constitutional rights, with the competing claims of the state and the individual ultimately adjudicated by the U.S. Supreme Court. It was at this time that constitutional rights claims became central to the Supreme Court's jurisprudence, and when the Court began to hold the provisions of the Bill of Rights enforceable not just against the conduct of the federal government but also against that of the states (in the process, creating a nationwide definition of rights). This was the time, moreover, that, in a long line of cases, the Court set out to promulgate elaborate doctrine concerning the meaning of the most broadly worded Bill of Rights provisions, giving rise to the complex jurisprudence concerning the meaning of the Constitution's civil liberties provisions. In short, it was in the crucible of "New Liberal" thinking that modern constitutional rights were invented.[9]

In the late nineteenth and early twentieth centuries, there was initially staunch resistance on privacy grounds to many efforts by the government to collect facts that we would now consider routine. There was resistance, for example, to the government's right to know whether or not you had been vaccinated for a disease, or how much money you made. The most sustained and significant constitutional resistance to the rise of the modern state in the name of privacy came where the push for regulation was most vigorous: the regulation of business. To effectively regulate private business at the national level, the state needed to know what businesses were doing behind closed doors; it needed access to their records. Traditionally, the government could gain access to these only through court order, on a case-by-case basis, pursuant to the investigation of a crime. To create a fully functioning regulatory order, however, the modern administrative state needed routine access to this information as a matter of course.

In *Boyd v. United States* (1886), a case involving government efforts to acquire business records in a customs dispute, the Supreme Court, citing privacy concerns, dealt what might have been a crippling blow to the entire state-building process. Traditionally, courts had held that the Fifth Amendment's privilege against self-incrimination protected only criminal defendants called upon to testify at their own trials. Writing for the Court in *Boyd*, however, Justice Joseph Bradley held that the privilege could be invoked by a nondefendant in a civil proceeding, and fused that privilege with the Fourth Amendment's protection against unreasonable searches and seizures. "The principles laid down in this opinion," Bradley wrote, "affect the very essence of constitutional liberty and security. It is not the breaking of his doors, and the rummaging of his drawers, that constitutes the essence of the offence; but it is the invasion of the indefeasible right of personal security, personal liberty, and private property."[10]

In subsequent years, in a series of cases involving novel efforts at regulating railroads and trusts, the Supreme Court gradually worked through the question of whether *Boyd's* staunchly pro-privacy ruling would be interpreted strictly—which would have placed perhaps insuperable legal barriers in the face of the newly developing modern administrative state—or more flexibly. But the Court ultimately arrived at a modus vivendi friendly to the claims of the modern administrative state: while deeming privacy important, and the Fourth and Fifth Amendments relevant, it bowed to perceived necessity, holding repeatedly that if the government followed proper procedures in advancing legitimate ends, it would be given the power necessary to collect all of the formerly private information necessary to regulate in what it took to be the broader public interest.[11] As the regulatory ambitions of the centralized modern American state expanded to include not just economic regulation but "police" matters concerning health, safety, and morals,[12] and as the growth of government required ever more aggressive federal efforts to extract tax revenues to feed the Leviathan, the Supreme Court was led into forging its modern understandings of privacy.

The Court created the exclusionary rule (providing that illegally seized evidence may not be introduced in court as evidence against a criminal defendant) in a 1914 case in which the police had entered the defendant's house without a warrant while he was at work, and rifled through his room and drawers searching for illegal lottery tickets.[13] The national ban on alcohol—Prohibition—inaugurated the Court's modern efforts to craft constitutional criminal procedure doctrine, including that involving the Fourth Amendment. Home searches, automobile searches, wiretapping—all were undertaken in the effort to enforce the new alcohol ban, raising a spectrum of questions about the practicalities of protecting personal privacy. As government efforts to enforce Prohibition spiraled wildly out of hand, the Court became increasingly protective of Fourth Amendment personal privacy.[14] As the abuses under the government's war on alcohol grew, even some progressives, like Louis D. Brandeis, came to understand that the incursions into personal privacy under the banner of advancing the public interest had gone too far. In the late Prohibition wiretapping case, for instance, Justice Brandeis penned his famous dissent praising "the right to be let alone."[15] By the time of Prohibitions repeal in the early 1930s, the Court had laid the doctrinal foundations for the later privacy-protecting innovations in constitutional doctrine undertaken in support of the civil rights movement of the 1950s and 1960s.[16] These efforts were advanced further when the Court assumed greater responsibilities for the supervision of the conduct of law enforcement officials in the South—especially as concerned their treatment of blacks.[17] The Court subsequently undertook a sustained process of gradually forging a code of constitutional Fourth Amendment doctrine. That doctrine set the rules that we live under today concerning when the police can detain a person, search him, his possessions, and his personal property (like his backpack, his car, or his home), as well as when, under the terms of the exclusionary rule, the fruits of an illegal search can be properly admitted into evidence.

NOTES

1. *Griswold v. Connecticut*, 381 U.S. 479 (1965).
2. *Roe v. Wade*, 410 U.S. 113 (1973).
3. *Lochner v. New York*, 198 U.S. 45 (1905).
4. See, e.g., John Hart Ely, "The Wages of Crying Wolf: A Comment on *Roe v. Wade*," *Yale Law Journal* 82 (1973): 920–49; John Hart Ely, *Democracy and Distrust: A Theory of Judicial Review* (Cambridge, Mass.: Harvard University Press, 1980).
5. *Olmstead v. United States*, 277 U.S. 438, 478 (1928).
6. See John Locke, *Second Treatise of Government* (1690; repr., Indianapolis: Hackett, 1980); Louis Hartz, *The Liberal Tradition in America: An Interpretation of American Political Thought since the Revolution* (1955; repr., New York: Harcourt Brace, 1991); David Hackett Fiseher, *Liberty and Freedom: A Visual History of America's Founding Ideas* (New York: Oxford University Press, 2005).
7. See Lucas A. Powe, Jr., *The Warren Court and American Politics* (Cambridge, Mass.: Belknap Press of Harvard University Press, 2000).
8. See William J. Novak, *The People's Welfare: Law and Regulation in Nineteenth Century America* (Chapel Hill: University of North Carolina Press, 1996).

9. See Howard Gillman, "Preferred Freedoms: The Progressive Expansion of State Power and the Rise of Modern Civil Liberties Jurisprudence," *Political Research Quarterly 47* (1994): 623–53.

10. *Boyd v. United States*, 116 U.S. 616, 630 (1886). On the protection of property rights as a crucial component of the protection of the value of privacy, see James W. Ely, Jr., *The Guardian of Every Other Right: A Constitutional History of Property Rights*, 3rd ed. (New York: Oxford University Press, 2007).

11. Ken I. Kersch, *Constructing Civil Liberties: Discontinuities in the Development of American Constitutional Law* (New York: Cambridge University Press, 2004), 49–52. As William Stuntz has observed, after many years of the government insisting, at the behest of progressives and liberals, that more and more private entities and individuals be rendered legible as a prerequisite to supervising and regulating them, business interests and conservatives, in turn, insisted that the regulatory activities of the government itself be opened to public scrutiny and supervision through the requirements of the Administrative Procedure Act (1946). Stuntz, "Secret Service: Against Privacy and Transparency," *The New Republic* (April 17, 2006), 12–15.

12. See *Champion v. Ames*, 188 U.S. 321 (1903).

13. *Weeks v. United States*, 232 U.S. 383 (1914).

14. Kersch, *Constructing Civil Liberties*, 72–84; Wickersham Commission Report, 57. See Kenneth M. Murchison, *Federal Criminal Law Doctrines: The Forgotten Influence of Prohibition* (Durham, N.C.: Duke University Press, 1994).

15. *Olmstead v. United States*, 277 U.S. 438 (1928).

16. See generally, Powe, *Warren Court and American Politics*; Michael J. Klarman, *From Jim Crow to Civil Rights: The Supreme Court and the Struggle for Racial Equality* (New York: Oxford University Press, 2006).

17. See, e.g., *Powell v. Alabama*. 287 U.S. 45 (1932). See generally Kersch, *Constructing Civil Liberties*, 88–112; Klarman, *From Jim Crow to Civil Rights*.

Discussion Questions

1. John Winthrop distinguished between natural liberty and civic or moral liberty. We sometimes talk about the distinction between liberty and license. To what extent do we really agree or disagree with Winthrop about the nature of liberty?

2. James Madison opposed government support for religion on the grounds that belief is a personal matter and that government involvement in religion weakened both government and religion. What then would Madison have thought about the "faith-based initiatives" of Presidents Clinton, Bush, and Obama?

3. John Stuart Mill argues that in a fair contest, truth will overcome falsehood and error. Mark Twain once said a good lie could circle the globe before truth could get its shoes tied. Who's closest to being right?

4. Montgomery, Alabama, police commissioner L.B. Sullivan is not a particularly sympathetic character, but does he have a point in arguing that public officials should be protected against false criticisms and charges? Why or why not?

5. How does the nineteenth-century liberal individualist desire "to be let alone" show up in modern liberal and conservative discussions of size of government? How about access to abortion services?

Suggested Additional Reading

David J. Bodenhamer and James W. Ely, Jr., eds., *Bill of Rights in Modern America* (Bloomington: Indiana University Press, 2008).

Ronald Kahn and Kenneth I. Kersch, eds., *The Supreme Court and American Political Development* (Lawrence: University Press of Kansas, 2006).

Alexander Keyssar, *The Right to Vote: The Contested History of Democracy in America* (New York: Basic Books, 2000).

Frank Lambert, *The Founding Fathers and the Place of Religion in America* (Princeton, NJ: Princeton University Press, 2003).

Geoffrey R. Stone, *Perilous Times: Free Speech in Wartime* (New York: Norton, 2004).

14

Civil Rights

Introduction

As we saw in Chapter 13, civil liberties generally involve the right to be left alone. Civil rights, on the other hand, is the assurance that government will intervene to see that all citizens have equal rights and basic opportunities in the society. Civil rights include the right to enjoy due process of law and equal protection of the laws; the right to vote and stand for office; and the right to buy a home, get a loan, or eat lunch under the same terms and conditions that others enjoy.

Our first selection, "On the Equality of the Sexes" (1790), by Judith Sargent Murray, highlights the fact that throughout our history, especially early, questions of equality and inequality have been fraught with tension. Murray's point is that although women are the intellectual equals of men, they are denied the right to develop their capabilities. The loss to women themselves is great, but so is the loss to their husbands, families, and society. Murray wrote the first draft of "On the Equality of the Sexes" in 1779, not too long after Abigail Adams (see reading 4.1) wrote her famous plea to her husband, John Adams, that after independence the Congress "remember the ladies," but there is more of an edge to Murray's writing.

While tensions over individual liberties have been present throughout American history, race is the scar that cleaves American history. Thomas Jefferson luminously declared that "all men are created equal," but he owned slaves all of his life. Abraham Lincoln's "Speech on the Dred Scott Decision" (1857, after the Supreme Court declared that blacks, slave or free, could not be U.S. citizens), began the argument for civic recognition of blacks. Abraham Lincoln's political genius was to lead without getting so far ahead of the public that he lost touch with them. Lincoln's speeches were meant to shape and direct the public mind, in the North at least, feeling its way toward freedom if not equality for blacks. The "Gettysburg Address" (1863), made to commemorate a cemetery for the dead of a great Civil War battle, is perhaps the most memorable piece of civic poetry in the American lexicon. The "Second Inaugural" (1865), equally stirring, suggests that the Civil War might have been visited by God on the nation as recompense for the sin of slavery.

Though blacks were freed in the immediate wake of the Civil War, within a few short years Jim Crow segregation, the legally enforced separation of the races in public places, had settled over the land. The Supreme Court formally adopted the doctrine of "separate but equal" in *Plessy v. Ferguson* (1896). The Supreme Court declared that racial segregation of blacks and whites in trains and other public places did not violate the 13th and 14th Amendment rights of blacks to "equal protection of the laws." The court reasoned that both blacks and whites had access to train travel and both blacks and whites were barred from riding in cars marked for the other race—hence, no discrimination. It took more than half a century for the court to overturn *Plessy* and put the country on a track to real civil equality in *Brown v. Board* (1954). In *Brown* the Supreme Court finally declared that separation of black and white children in public schools was detrimental to black children and, therefore, inherently discriminatory and illegal in light of the 14th Amendment promise of "equal protection of the laws."

APD scholars Richard Valelly and Desmond King and Rogers Smith ask what broad social and political dynamics have structured, directed, and shaped American history in regard to race. Valelly contends that institutions either facilitate or limit political and policy reform. In the first reconstruction, in the immediate wake of the Civil War, a party system had to be constructed essentially from scratch to support Republican reconstruction of the South. The task was too difficult and reconstruction failed. When the second reconstruction dawned in the mid-twentieth century, the Democratic Party was well-developed and willing to support the demand for civil rights. The second reconstruction, though its progress was slow and halting, was more successful. Valelly's important point is that social change is much more likely to succeed when institutions are in place and receptive to the calls for change.

Desmond King and Rogers Smith, in this chapter's highlight piece, argue that American history in regard to race, but more broadly as well, is best understood as an ongoing clash between two racial orders or visions. One is the white supremacist racial order that thought slavery and black subordination natural. The other was the egalitarian order anticipated by Jefferson's declaration that all men are created equal and Lincoln's second inaugural address. Though the egalitarian racial order has certainly gained ground, many, including King and Smith, argue that vestiges of the white supremacist order are all about and the fight is not won.

14.1 Judith Sargent Murray, "On the Equality of the Sexes" (1790)

Judith Sargent Murray (1751–1820) was the oldest of eight children born to Winthrop and Judith Saunders Sargent in Gloucester, Massachusetts. Winthrop Sargent was a ship owner and captain and an active member of the Massachusetts political elite. Judith and her brother Winthrop, two years younger, were initially educated together at home. Judith learned to read and write and to speak some French, but Winthrop received a more advanced education and eventually went on to study at Harvard. Judith married at 18 but continued her self-education, becoming one of the new nation's most prominent female writers by the 1790s.

Judith Sargent Murray wrote an early version of her famous essay, "On the Equality of the Sexes," in 1779, but a revised version of the essay was first published in the *Massachusetts Magazine* in 1790. Murray challenged the widely accepted view that God had created men and women with separate natures and talents. Men were rational and aggressive, best fitted for commerce, politics, and war, while women were emotional and nurturing, best fitted for domestic and family life. Murray did not reject these views out of hand, but she did argue that men and women were equal intellectually. Moreover, she argued that both men and women would benefit if women's capabilities were more fully developed. Murray, more assertive than Abigail Adams (see reading 4.1), still was constrained by the convention of her day. Nonetheless, she is often credited with being among the earliest American feminists and the first to declare men and women "equal."

Is it upon mature consideration we adopt the idea, that nature is thus partial in her distributions? Is it indeed a fact, that she hath yielded to one half of the human species so unquestionable a mental superiority? I know that to both sexes elevated understandings, and the reverse, are common. But, suffer me to ask, in what the minds of females are so notoriously deficient, or unequal. May not the intellectual powers be ranged under these four heads—imagination, reason, memory and judgment. The province of imagination hath long since been surrendered to us, and we have been crowned and undoubted sovereigns of the regions of fancy. Invention is perhaps the most arduous effort of the mind; this branch of imagination hath been particularly ceded to us, and we have been time out of mind invested with that creative faculty. Observe the variety of fashions (here I bar the contemptuous smile) which distinguish and adorn the female world: how continually are they changing, insomuch that they almost render the wise man's assertion problematical, and we are ready to say, *there is something new under the sun*. Now what a playfulness, what an exuberance of fancy, what strength of inventine imagination, doth this continual variation discover? . . . Perhaps it will be asked if I furnish these facts as instances of excellency in our sex. Certainly not; but as proofs of a creative faculty, of a lively imagination. Assuredly great activity of mind is thereby discovered, and was this activity properly directed, what beneficial effects would follow. Is the needle and kitchen sufficient to employ the operations of a soul thus organized? I should conceive not, Nay, it is a truth that those very departments leave the intelligent principle vacant, and at liberty for speculation. Are we deficient in reason? we can only reason from what we know, and if an opportunity of acquiring knowledge hath been denied us, the inferiority of our sex cannot fairly be deduced from thence. Memory, I believe, will be allowed us in common, since everyone's experience must testify, that a loquacious old woman is as frequently met with, as a communicative man; their subjects are alike drawn from the fund of other times, and the transactions of their youth, or of maturer life, entertain, or perhaps fatigue you, in the evening of their lives.

"But our judgment is not so strong—we do not distinguish so well."—Yet it may be questioned, from what doth this superiority, in this determining faculty of the soul, proceed. May we not trace its source in the difference of education, and continued advantages? Will it be said that the judgment of a male of two years old, is more sage than that of a female's of the same age? I believe the reverse is generally observed to be true. But from that period what partiality! how is the one exalted, and the other depressed, by the contrary modes of education which are adopted! the one is taught to aspire, and the other is early confined and limitted, As their years increase, the sister must be wholly domesticated, while the brother is led by the hand through all the flowery paths of science. Grant that their minds are by nature equal, yet who shall wonder at the *apparent* superiority, if indeed custom becomes *second nature*; nay if it taketh place of nature, and that it doth the experience of each day will evince. At length arrived at womanhood, the uncultivated fair one feels a void, which the employments allotted her are by no means capable of filling. What can she do? to books she may not apply; or if she doth, *to those only of the novel kind*, lest she merit the appellation of a *learned lady*; and what ideas have been affixed to this term, the observation of many can testify. . . . Is she united to a person whose soul nature made equal to her own, education hath set him so far above her, that in those entertainments which are productive of such rational felicity, she is not qualified to accompany him. She experiences a mortifying consciousness of inferiority, which embitters every enjoyment. Doth the person to whom her adverse fate hath consigned her, possess a mind incapable of improvement, she is equally wretched, in being so closely connected with an individual whom she cannot but despise. Now, was she permitted the same instructors as her brother, (with an eye however to their particular departments) for the employment of a rational mind an ample field would be opened. In astronomy she might catch a glimpse of the immensity of the Deity, and thence she would form amazing conceptions of the august and supreme Intelligence. In geography she would admire Jehovah in the midst of his benevolence; thus adapting this globe to the various wants and amusements of its inhabitants. In natural philosophy she would adore the infinite majesty of heaven, clothed in condescension; and as she traversed the reptile world, she would hail the goodness of a creating God. A mind, thus filled, would have little room for the trifles with which our sex are, with too much justice, accused of amusing themselves, and they would thus be rendered fit companions for those, who should one day wear them as their crown. Fashions, in their variety, would then give place to conjectures, which might perhaps conduce to the improvements of the literary world; and there would be no leisure for slander or detraction. Reputation would not then be blasted, but serious speculations would occupy the lively imaginations of the sex. Unnecessary visits would only be indulged by way of relaxation, or to answer the demands of consanguinity and friendship. Females would become discreet, their judgments would be invigorated, and their partners for life being circumspectly chosen, an unhappy Hymen would then be as rare, as is now the reverse.

Will it be urged that those acquirements would supersede our domestick duties. I answer that every requisite in female economy is easily attained; and, with truth I can add, that when once attained, they require no further *mental attention*. Nay, while we are pursuing the needle, or the superintendency of the family, I repeat, that our minds are at full liberty for reflection; that imagination may exert itself in full vigor; and that if a just foundation is early laid, our ideas will then be worthy of rational beings. If we were industrious we might easily find time to arrange them upon paper, or should avocations press too hard for such an indulgence, the hours allotted for conversation would at least become more refined and rational. Should it still be vociferated, "Your domestick employments are sufficient"—I would calmly ask, is it reasonable, that a candidate for immortality, for the joys of heaven, an intelligent being, who is to spend an eternity in contemplating the works of the Deity, should at present be so degraded, as to be allowed no other ideas, than those which are suggested by the mechanism of a pudding, or the sewing the seams of a garment? Pity that all such censurers of female improvement do not go one step further, and deny their future existence; to be consistent they surely ought.

Yes, ye lordly, ye haughty sex, our souls are by nature *equal* to yours; the same breath of God animates, enlivens, and invigorates us; and that we are not fallen lower than yourselves, let those witness who have greatly towered above the various discouragements by which they have been so heavily oppressed; and though I am unacquainted with the list of celebrated characters on either side, yet from the observations I have made in the contracted circle in which I have moved, I dare confidently believe, that from the commencement of time to the present day, there hath been as many females, as males, who, by the *mere force of natural powers*, have merited the crown of applause; who, *thus unassisted*, have seized the wreath of fame. I know there are who assert, that as the animal power of the one sex are superiour, of course their mental faculties also must be stronger; thus attributing strength of mind to the transient organization of this earth born tenement. But if this reasoning is just, man must be content to yield the palm to many of the brute creation, since by not a few of his brethren of the field, he is far surpassed in bodily strength. Moreover, was this argument admitted, it would prove too much, for occular demonstration evinceth, that there are many robust masculine ladies, and effeminate gentlemen. Yet I fancy that Mr. Pope, though clogged with an enervated body, and distinguished by a diminutive stature, could nevertheless lay claim to greatness of soul; and perhaps there are many other instances which might be adduced to combat so unphilosophical an opinion. Do we not often see, that when the clay built tabernacle is well nigh dissolved, when it is just ready to mingle with the parent soil, the immortal inhabitant aspires to, and even attaineth heights the most sublime, and which were before wholly unexplored. Besides, were we to grant that animal strength proved any thing, taking into consideration the accustomed impartiality of nature, we should be induced to imagine, that she had invested the female mind with superior strength as an equivalent for the bodily powers of man. But waving this however palpable advantage, for *equality only*, we wish to contend.

14.2 Abraham Lincoln, "Speech on the Dred Scott Decision" (1857)
"The Gettysburg Address" (1863)
"Second Inaugural Address" (1865)

Abraham Lincoln had less formal education than virtually any other American president. But he was among the most literate and intellectual of American presidents. Thomas Jefferson, with the best formal education available in America at the time, may be Lincoln's only peer as a man of the mind. Below are three brief excerpts from Lincoln's political writings.

In the "Speech on the Dred Scott Decision," the U.S. Supreme Court had recently declared that Dred Scott, a slave taken into free territory, was property and, therefore, remained a slave wherever he resided. Illinois Senator Stephen A. Douglas (Lincoln refers to him as Judge Douglas as he had served briefly on the Illinois Supreme Court fifteen years earlier) had endorsed the Supreme Court's decision. Douglas, first elected to the U.S. Senate in 1847, would seek a third term in 1858 and Lincoln was positioning to be his opponent. As you will see, political positioning does not preclude heroic ideas. "The Gettysburg Address" and Lincoln's "Second Inaugural Address" are iconic examples of American political thought and expression and deserve your full attention.

––––––––––––––––––––

Speech on the Dred Scott Decision

June 26, 1857

Speech at Springfield, Illinois

FELLOW CITIZENS:—I am here to-night, partly by the invitation of some of you, and partly by my own inclination. Two weeks ago Judge Douglas spoke here on ... the Dred Scott decision, and Utah. I listened to the speech at the time, and have read the report of it since. It was intended to controvert opinions which I think just, and to assail (politically, not personally,) those men who, in common with me, entertain those opinions. For this reason I wished then, and still wish, to make some answer to it, which I now take the opportunity of doing.

... The Dred Scott decision ... declares two propositions—first, that a negro cannot sue in the U.S. Courts; and secondly, that Congress cannot prohibit slavery in the Territories. It was made by a divided court—dividing differently on the different points. Judge Douglas does not discuss the merits of the decision; and, in that respect, I shall follow his example, believing I could no more improve on McLean and Curtis, than he could on Taney.

He denounces all who question the correctness of that decision, as offering violent resistance to it. But who resists it? Who has, in spite of the decision, declared Dred Scott free, and resisted the authority of his master over him?

Judicial decisions have two uses—first, to absolutely determine the case decided, and secondly, to indicate to the public how other similar cases will be decided when they arise. For the latter use, they are called "precedents" and "authorities."

We believe, as much as Judge Douglas, (perhaps more) in obedience to, and respect for the judicial department of government. We think its decisions on Constitutional questions, when fully settled, should control, not only the particular cases decided, but the general policy of the country, subject to be disturbed only by amendments of the Constitution as provided in that instrument itself. More than this would be revolution. But we think the Dred Scott decision is erroneous. We know the court that made it, has often over-ruled its own decisions, and we shall do what we can to have it to over-rule this. We offer no resistance to it.

Judicial decisions are of greater or less authority as precedents, according to circumstances. That this should be so, accords both with common sense, and the customary understanding of the legal profession.

If this important decision had been made by the unanimous concurrence of the judges, and without any apparent partisan bias, and in accordance with legal public expectation, and with the steady practice of the departments throughout our history, and had been in no part, based on assumed historical facts which are not really true; or, if wanting in some of these, it had been before the court more than once, and had there been affirmed and re-affirmed through a course of years, it then might be, perhaps would be, factious, nay, even revolutionary, to not acquiesce in it as a precedent.

But when, as it is true we find it wanting in all these claims to the public confidence, it is not resistance, it is not factious, it is not even disrespectful, to treat it as not having yet quite established a settled doctrine for the country . . .

I have said, in substance, that the Dred Scott decision was, in part, based on assumed historical facts which were not really true; and I ought not to leave the subject without giving some reasons for saying this; I therefore give an instance or two, which I think fully sustain me. Chief Justice Taney, in delivering the opinion of the majority of the Court, insists at great length that negroes were no part of the people who made, or for whom was made, the Declaration of Independence, or the Constitution of the United States.

On the contrary, Judge Curtis, in his dissenting opinion, shows that in five of the then thirteen states, to wit, New Hampshire, Massachusetts, New York, New Jersey and North Carolina, free negroes were voters, and, in proportion to their numbers, had the same part in making the Constitution that the white people had. He shows this with so much particularity as to leave no doubt of its truth; and, as a sort of conclusion on that point, holds the following language:

"The Constitution was ordained and established by the people of the United States, through the action, in each State, of those persons who were qualified by its laws to act thereon in behalf of themselves and all other citizens of the State. In some of the States, as we have seen, colored persons were among those qualified by law to act on the subject. These colored persons were not only included in the body of 'the people of the United States,' by whom the Constitution was ordained and established; but in at least five of the States they had the power to act, and, doubtless, did act, by their suffrages, upon the question of its adoption."

Again, Chief Justice Taney says: "It is difficult, at this day to realize the state of public opinion in relation to that unfortunate race, which prevailed in the civilized and enlightened portions of the world at the time of the Declaration of Independence, and when the Constitution of the United States was framed and adopted." And again, after quoting from the Declaration, he says: "The general words above quoted would seem to include the whole human family, and if they were used in a similar instrument at this day, would be so understood."

In these the Chief Justice does not directly assert, but plainly assumes, as a fact, that the public estimate of the black man is more favorable now than it was in the days of the Revolution. This assumption is a mistake. In some trifling particulars, the condition of that race has been ameliorated; but, as a whole, in this country, the change between then and now is decidedly the other way; and their ultimate destiny has never appeared so hopeless as in the last three or four years. In two of the five States—New Jersey and North

Carolina—that then gave the free negro the right of voting, the right has since been taken away; and in a third—New York—it has been greatly abridged; while it has not been extended, so far as I know, to a single additional State, though the number of the States has more than doubled. In those days, as I understand, masters could, at their own pleasure, emancipate their slaves; but since then, such legal restraints have been made upon emancipation, as to amount almost to prohibition. In those days, Legislatures held the unquestioned power to abolish slavery in their respective States; but now it is becoming quite fashionable for State Constitutions to withhold that power from the Legislatures. . . .

It is grossly incorrect to say or assume, that the public estimate of the negro is more favorable now than it was at the origin of the government. . . .

There is a natural disgust in the minds of nearly all white people, to the idea of an indiscriminate amalgamation of the white and black races; and Judge Douglas evidently is basing his chief hope, upon the chances of being able to appropriate the benefit of this disgust to himself. . . . He finds the Republicans insisting that the Declaration of Independence includes ALL men, black as well as white; and forth-with he boldly denies that it includes negroes at all, and proceeds to argue gravely that all who contend it does, do so only because they want to vote, and eat, and sleep, and marry with negroes! He will have it that they cannot be consistent else. Now I protest against that counterfeit logic which concludes that, because I do not want a black woman for a slave I must necessarily want her for a wife. I need not have her for either, I can just leave her alone. In some respects she certainly is not my equal; but in her natural right to eat the bread she earns with her own hands without asking leave of any one else, she is my equal, and the equal of all others.

Chief Justice Taney, in his opinion in the Dred Scott case, admits that the language of the Declaration is broad enough to include the whole human family, but he and Judge Douglas argue that the authors of that instrument did not intend to include negroes, by the fact that they did not at once, actually place them on an equality with the whites. Now this grave argument comes to just nothing at all, by the other fact, that they did not at once, or ever afterwards, actually place all white people on an equality with one or another. And this is the staple argument of both the Chief Justice and the Senator, for doing this obvious violence to the plain unmistakable language of the Declaration. I think the authors of that notable instrument intended to include all men, but they did not intend to declare all men equal in all respects. They did not mean to say all were equal in color, size, intellect, moral developments, or social capacity. They defined with tolerable distinctness, in what respects they did consider all men created equal—equal in "certain inalienable rights, among which are life, liberty, and the pursuit of happiness." This they said, and this meant. They did not mean to assert the obvious untruth, that all were then actually enjoying that equality, nor yet, that they were about to confer it immediately upon them. In fact they had no power to confer such a boon. They meant simply to declare the right, so that the enforcement of it might follow as fast as circumstances should permit. They meant to set up a standard maxim for free society, which should be familiar to all, and revered by all; constantly looked to, constantly labored for, and even though never perfectly attained, constantly approximated, and thereby constantly spreading and deepening its influence, and augmenting the happiness and value of life to all people of all colors everywhere. The assertion that "all men are created equal" was of no practical use in effecting our separation from Great Britain; and it was placed in the Declaration, nor for that, but for future use. Its authors meant it to be, thank God, it is now proving itself, a stumbling block to those who in after times might seek to turn a free people back into the hateful paths of despotism. They knew the proneness of prosperity to breed tyrants, and they meant when such should re-appear in this fair land and commence their vocation they should find left for them at least one hard nut to crack....

Gettysburg Address

November 19, 1863

Four score and seven years ago our fathers brought forth on this continent, a new nation, conceived in Liberty, and dedicated to the proposition that all men are created equal.

Now we are engaged in a great civil war, testing whether that nation, or any nation so conceived and so dedicated, can long endure. We are met on a great battle-field of that war. We have come to dedicate a portion of that field, as a final resting place for those who here gave their lives that that nation might live. It is altogether fitting and proper that we should do this.

But, in a larger sense, we can not dedicate—we can not consecrate—we can not hallow—this ground. The brave men, living and dead, who struggled here, have consecrated it, far above our poor power to add or detract. The world will little note, nor long remember what we say here, but it can never forget what they did here. It is for us the living, rather, to be dedicated here to the unfinished work which they who fought here have thus far so nobly advanced. It is rather for us to be here dedicated to the great task remaining before us—that from these honored dead we take increased devotion to that cause for which they gave the last full measure of devotion—that we here highly resolve that these dead shall not have died in vain—that this nation, under God, shall have a new birth of freedom—and that government of the people, by the people, for the people, shall not perish from the earth.

Second Inaugural Address

March 4, 1865

Fellow Countrymen:
At this second appearing to take the oath of the presidential office, there is less occasion for an extended address than there was at the first. Then a statement, somewhat in detail, of a course to be pursued, seemed fitting and proper. Now, at the expiration of four years, during which public declarations have been constantly called forth on every point and phase of the great contest which still absorbs the attention, and engrosses the energies of the nation, little that is new could be presented. The progress of our arms, upon which all else chiefly depends, is as well known to the public as to myself; and it is, I trust, reasonably satisfactory and encouraging to all. With high hope for the future, no prediction in regard to it is ventured.

On the occasion corresponding to this four years ago, all thoughts were anxiously directed to an impending civil war. All dreaded it, all sought to avert it. While the inaugeral [*sic*] address was being delivered from this place, devoted altogether to *saving* the Union without war, insurgent agents were in the city seeking to *destroy* it without war—seeking to dissole [*sic*] the Union, and divide effects, by negotiation. Both parties deprecated war; but one of them would *make* war rather than let the nation survive; and the other would *accept* war rather than let it perish. And the war came.

One eighth of the whole population were colored slaves, not distributed generally over the Union, but localized in the Southern part of it. These slaves constituted a peculiar and powerful interest. All knew that this interest was, somehow, the cause of the war. To strengthen, perpetuate, and extend this interest was the object for which the insurgents would rend the Union, even by war; while the government claimed no right to do more than to restrict the territorial enlargement of it. Neither party expected for the war, the magnitude, or the duration, which it has already attained. Neither anticipated that the *cause* of the conflict might cease with, or even before, the conflict itself should cease. Each looked for an easier triumph, and a result less fundamental and astounding. Both read the same Bible, and pray to the same God; and each invokes His aid against the other. It may seem strange that any men should dare to ask a just God's assistance in wringing their bread from the sweat of other men's faces; but let us judge not that we be not judged. The prayers of both could not be answered; that of neither has been answered fully. The Almighty has His own purposes. Woe unto the world because of offences! for it must needs be that offences come; but woe to that man by whom the offence cometh! If we shall suppose that American Slavery is one of those offences which, in the providence of God, must needs come, but which, having continued through His appointed time, He now wills to remove, and that He gives to both North and South, this terrible war, as the woe due to those by whom the offence came, shall we discern therein any departure from those divine attributes which the believers in a Living God always ascribe to Him? Fondly do we hope, fervently do we pray, that this mighty scourge of war may speedily pass away. Yet, if God wills that it continue, until all the wealth piled by the bond-man's two hundred and fifty years of unrequited toil shall be sunk, and until every drop of blood drawn with the lash, shall be paid by another drawn with the sword, as was said three thousand years ago, so still it must be said "the judgments of the Lord, are true and righteous altogether."

With malice toward none; with charity for all; with firmness in the right, as God gives us to see the right, let us strive on to finish the work we are in; to bind up the nation's wounds; to care for him who shall have borne the battle, and for his widow, and his orphan—to do all which may achieve and cherish a just and a lasting peace, among ourselves, and with all nations.

14.3 *Plessy v. Ferguson* (1896)

Plessy v. Ferguson (1896), along with *Dred Scott* (1857), is among the most infamous decisions of the U.S. Supreme Court. Nonetheless, it was the law of the land until overturned by *Brown v. Board* (1954). *Plessy v. Ferguson* established the doctrine of "separate but equal"; declaring that state laws mandating separation of the races in public settings such as transportation, hotels and restaurants, and schools did not violate the Constitution.

In 1890 Louisiana passed a statute requiring that trains have separate passenger cars for whites and blacks and that the railroads and police enforce racial separation. Homer Plessy, one-eighth black and light-skinned, decided to challenge the law by buying a ticket and attempting to enter the white coach. Officials were ready for him as he had announced his intention and he was arrested. Plessy sued on equal protection grounds and the Supreme Court upheld the Louisiana law, declaring that separation of the races in public places was a reasonable exercise of the state's "police power" and was no denial of equal protection as both races had access, in this case, to train travel.

There was one dissenter, Associate Justice John Marshall Harlan. Justice Harlan memorably excoriated his colleagues, arguing that no legislature or court has the right to consider race in regard to the common rights of citizens. Harlan famously declared that "Our Constitution is color-blind." But Harlan was a minority of one in 1896 and his view would not prevail for more than half a century.

No. 210

Argued April 18, 1896
Decided May 18, 1896
163 U.S. 537

Error to the Supreme Court of the State of Louisiana

Syllabus

The statute of Louisiana, acts of 1890, c. 111, requiring railway companies carrying passengers in their coaches in that State, to provide equal, but separate, accommodations for the white and colored races, by providing two or more passenger coaches for each passenger train, or by dividing the passenger coaches by a partition so as to secure separate accommodations; and providing that no person shall be permitted to occupy seats in coaches other than the ones assigned to them, on account [163 U.S. 538] of the race they belong to; and requiring the officer of the passenger train to assign each passenger to the coach or compartment assigned for the race to which he or she belong; and imposing fines or imprisonment upon passengers insisting on going into a coach or compartment other than the one set aide for the race to which he or she belongs; and conferring upon officers of the train power to refuse to carry on the train passengers refusing to occupy the coach or compartment assigned to them, and exempting the railway company from liability for such refusal, are not in conflict with the provisions either of the Thirteenth Amendment or of the Fourteenth Amendment to the Constitution of the United States. . . .

BROWN, J., lead opinion

MR. JUSTICE BROWN, after stating the case, delivered the opinion of the court. . . .

By the Fourteenth Amendment, all persons born or naturalized in the United States and subject to the jurisdiction thereof are made citizens of the United States and of the

State wherein they reside, and the States are forbidden from making or enforcing any law which shall abridge the privileges or immunities of citizens of the United States, or shall deprive any person of life, liberty, or property without due process of law, or deny to any person within their jurisdiction the equal protection of the laws. . . .

The object of the amendment was undoubtedly to enforce the absolute equality of the two races before the law, but, in the nature of things, it could not have been intended to abolish distinctions based upon color, or to enforce social, as distinguished from political, equality, or a commingling of the two races upon terms unsatisfactory to either. Laws permitting, and even requiring, their separation in places where they are liable to be brought into contact do not necessarily imply the inferiority of either race to the other, and have been generally, if not universally, recognized as within the competency of the state legislatures in the exercise of their police power. The most common instance of this is connected with the establishment of separate schools for white and colored children, which has been held to be a valid exercise of the legislative power even by courts of States where the political rights of the colored race have been longest and most earnestly enforced. . . .

Laws forbidding the intermarriage of the two races may be said in a technical sense to interfere with the freedom of contract, and yet have been universally recognized as within the police power of the State. State v. Gibson, 36 Indiana 389. . . .

In the Civil Rights Case, 109 U.S. 3, it was held that an act of Congress entitling all persons within the jurisdiction of the United States to the full and equal enjoyment of the accommodations, advantages, facilities and privileges of inns, public conveyances, on land or water, theatres and other places of public amusement, and made applicable to citizens of every race and color, regardless of any previous condition of servitude, was unconstitutional and void upon the ground that the Fourteenth Amendment was prohibitory upon the States only, . . . In delivering the opinion of the court, Mr. Justice Bradley observed that the Fourteenth Amendment

> does not invest Congress with power to legislate upon subjects that are within the [163 U.S. 547] domain of state legislation, but to provide modes of relief against state legislation or state action of the kind referred to. It does not authorize Congress to create a code of municipal law for the regulation of private rights, but to provide modes of redress against the operation of state laws and the action of state officers, executive or judicial, when these are subversive of the fundamental rights specified in the amendment. Positive rights and privileges are undoubtedly secured by the Fourteenth Amendment, but they are secured by way of prohibition against state laws and state proceedings affecting those rights and privileges, and by power given to Congress to legislate for the purpose of carrying such prohibition into effect, and such legislation must necessarily be predicated upon such supposed state laws or state proceedings, and be directed to the correction of their operation and effect. . . .

. . . So far, then, as a conflict with the Fourteenth Amendment is concerned, the case reduces itself to the question whether the statute of Louisiana is a reasonable regulation, and, with respect to this, there must necessarily be a large discretion on the part of the legislature. In determining the question of reasonableness, it is at liberty to act with reference to the established usages, customs, and traditions of the people, and with a view to the promotion of their comfort and the preservation of the public peace and good order. Gauged by this standard, we cannot say that a law which authorizes or even requires the separation of the two races in public conveyances [163 U.S. 551] is unreasonable, or more obnoxious to the Fourteenth Amendment than the acts of Congress requiring separate schools for colored children in the District of Columbia, the constitutionality of which does not seem to have been questioned, or the corresponding acts of state legislatures.

We consider the underlying fallacy of the plaintiff's argument to consist in the assumption that the enforced separation of the two races stamps the colored race with a badge of inferiority. If this be so, it is not by reason of anything found in the act, but solely because the colored race chooses to put that construction upon it. The argument necessarily assumes that if, as has been more than once the case and is not unlikely to be so again, the colored race should become the dominant power in the state legislature, and should enact a law in precisely similar terms, it would thereby relegate the white race to an inferior position. We imagine that the white race, at least, would not acquiesce in this assumption. The argument also assumes that social prejudices may be overcome by legislation, and that equal rights cannot be secured to the negro except by an enforced commingling of the two races. We cannot accept this proposition. If the two races are to meet upon terms of social equality, it must be the result of natural affinities, a mutual appreciation of each other's merits, and a voluntary consent of individuals. As was said by the Court of Appeals of New York in People v. Gallagher, 93 N. Y. 438, 448,

> this end can neither be accomplished nor promoted by laws which conflict with the general sentiment of the community upon whom they are designed to operate. When the government, therefore, has secured to each of its citizens equal rights before the law and equal opportunities for improvement and progress, it has accomplished the end for which it was organized, and performed all of the functions respecting social advantages with which it is endowed.

Legislation is powerless to eradicate racial instincts or to abolish distinctions based upon physical differences, and the attempt to do so can only result in accentuating the difficulties of the present situation. If the civil and political rights of both races be equal, one cannot be inferior to the other civilly [163 U.S. 552] or politically. If one race be inferior to the other socially, the Constitution of the United States cannot put them upon the same plane....

The judgment of the court below is, therefore,

Affirmed.

Harlan, J., Dissenting

MR. JUSTICE HARLAN, dissenting.

...In respect of civil rights common to all citizens, the Constitution of the United States does not, I think, permit any public authority to know the race of those entitled to be protected in the enjoyment of such rights. Every true man has pride of race, and, under appropriate circumstances, when the rights of others, his equals before the law, are not to be affected, it is his privilege to express such pride and to take such action based upon it as to him seems proper. But I deny that any legislative body or judicial tribunal may have regard to the [163 U.S. 555] race of citizens when the civil rights of those citizens are involved. Indeed, such legislation as that here in question is inconsistent not only with that equality of rights which pertains to citizenship, National and State, but with the personal liberty enjoyed by everyone within the United States.

The Thirteenth Amendment does not permit the withholding or the deprivation of any right necessarily inhering in freedom. It not only struck down the institution of slavery as previously existing in the United States, but it prevents the imposition of any burdens or disabilities that constitute badges of slavery or servitude. It decreed universal civil freedom in this country. This court has so adjudged. But that amendment having been found inadequate to the protection of the rights of those who had been in slavery, it was followed by the Fourteenth Amendment, which added greatly to the dignity and glory of American citizenship and to the security of personal liberty by declaring that

> all persons born or naturalized in the United States, and subject to the jurisdiction thereof, are citizens of the United States and of the State wherein they reside,

and that

> no State shall make or enforce any law which shall abridge the privileges or immunities of citizens of the United States; nor shall any State deprive any person of life, liberty or property without due process of law, nor deny to any person within its jurisdiction the equal protection of the laws.

These two amendments, if enforced according to their true intent and meaning, will protect all the civil rights that pertain to freedom and citizenship. Finally, and to the end that no citizen should be denied, on account of his race, the privilege of participating in the political control of his country, it as declared by the Fifteenth Amendment that

> the right of citizens of the United States to vote shall not be denied or abridged by the United States or by any State on account of race, color or previous condition of servitude.

These notable additions to the fundamental law were welcomed by the friends of liberty throughout the world. They removed the race line from our governmental systems. . . . They declared, in legal effect, this court has further said, ·

> that the law in the States shall be the same for the black as for the white; that all persons, whether colored or white, shall stand equal before the laws of the States, and, in regard to the colored race, for whose protection the amendment was primarily designed, that no discrimination shall be made against them by law because of their color.

. . . It was said in argument that the statute of Louisiana does [163 U.S. 557] not discriminate against either race, but prescribes a rule applicable alike to white and colored citizens. But this argument does not meet the difficulty. Everyone knows that the statute in question had its origin in the purpose not so much to exclude white persons from railroad cars occupied by blacks as to exclude colored people from coaches occupied by or assigned to white persons. Railroad corporations of Louisiana did not make discrimination among whites in the matter of accommodation for travelers. The thing to accomplish was, under the guise of giving equal accommodation for whites and blacks, to compel the latter to keep to themselves while traveling in railroad passenger coaches. No one would be so wanting in candor as to assert the contrary. The fundamental objection, therefore, to the statute is that it interferes with the personal freedom of citizens. "Personal liberty," it has been well said,

> consists in the power of locomotion, of changing situation, or removing one's person to whatsoever places one's own inclination may direct, without imprisonment or restraint unless by due course of law.

1 Bl.Com. *134. If a white man and a black man choose to occupy the same public conveyance on a public highway, it is their right to do so, and no government, proceeding alone on grounds of race, can prevent it without infringing the personal liberty of each.

It is one thing for railroad carriers to furnish, or to be required by law to furnish, equal accommodations for all whom they are under a legal duty to carry. It is quite another thing for government to forbid citizens of the white and black races from traveling in the same public conveyance, and to punish officers of railroad companies for permitting persons of the two races to occupy the same passenger coach. If a State can prescribe, as a rule of civil conduct, that whites and blacks shall not travel as passengers in the same railroad coach, why may it not so regulate the use of the streets of its cities and towns as to compel white citizens to keep on one side of a street and black citizens to keep on the other? Why may it not, upon like grounds, punish whites and blacks who ride together in streetcars or in open vehicles on a public road [163 U.S. 558] or street? Why may it not require sheriffs to assign whites to one side of a courtroom and blacks to the other? And why may it not also prohibit the commingling of the two races in the galleries of legislative halls or in public assemblages convened for the consideration of the political questions of the day? Further, if this statute of Louisiana is consistent with the personal liberty of citizens, why may not the State require the separation in railroad coaches of native and naturalized citizens of the United States, or of Protestants and Roman Catholics? ...

The white race deems itself to be the dominant race in this country. And so it is in prestige, in achievements, in education, in wealth and in power. So, I doubt not, it will continue to be for all time if it remains true to its great heritage and holds fast to the principles of constitutional liberty. But in view of the Constitution, in the eye of the law, there is in this country no superior, dominant, ruling class of citizens. There is no caste here. Our Constitution is color-blind, and neither knows nor tolerates classes among citizens. In respect of civil rights, all citizens are equal before the law. The humblest is the peer of the most powerful. The law regards man as man, and takes no account of his surroundings or of his color when his civil rights as guaranteed by the supreme law of the land are involved. It is therefore to be regretted that this high tribunal, the final expositor of the fundamental law of the land, has reached the conclusion that it is competent for a State to regulate the enjoyment by citizens of their civil rights solely upon the basis of race.

In my opinion, the judgment this day rendered will, in time, prove to be quite as pernicious as the decision made by this tribunal in the Dred Scott Case. It was adjudged in that case that the descendants of Africans who were imported into this country and sold as slaves were not included nor intended to be included under the word "citizens" in the Constitution, and could not claim any of the rights and privileges which that instrument provided for and secured to citizens of the United States; that, at the time of the adoption of the Constitution, they were

> considered as a subordinate and inferior class of beings, who had been subjugated by the dominant [163 U.S. 560] race, and, whether emancipated or not, yet remained subject to their authority, and had no rights or privileges but such as those who held the power and the government might choose to grant them.

19 How. 393, 404. The recent amendments of the Constitution, it was supposed, had eradicated these principles from our institutions. But it seems that we have yet, in some of the States, a dominant race—a superior class of citizens, which assumes to regulate the

enjoyment of civil rights, common to all citizens, upon the basis of race. The present decision, it may well be apprehended, will not only stimulate aggressions, more or less brutal and irritating, upon the admitted rights of colored citizens, but will encourage the belief that it is possible, by means of state enactments, to defeat the beneficent purposes which the people of the United States had in view when they adopted the recent amendments of the Constitution, by one of which the blacks of this country were made citizens of the United States and of the States in which they respectively reside, and whose privileges and immunities, as citizens, the States are forbidden to abridge. Sixty millions of whites are in no danger from the presence here of eight millions of blacks. The destinies of the two races in this country are indissolubly linked together, and the interests of both require that the common government of all shall not permit the seeds of race hate to be planted under the sanction of law. What can more certainly arouse race hate, what more certainly create and perpetuate a feeling of distrust between these races, than state enactments which, in fact, proceed on the ground that colored citizens are so inferior and degraded that they cannot be allowed to sit in public coaches occupied by white citizens. That, as all will admit, is the real meaning of such legislation as was enacted in Louisiana.

The sure guarantee of the peace and security of each race is the clear, distinct, unconditional recognition by our governments, National and State, of every right that inheres in civil freedom, and of the equality before the law of all citizens of the United States, without regard to race. . . .

I am of opinion that the statute of Louisiana is inconsistent with the personal liberty of citizens, white and black, in that State, and hostile to both the spirit and letter of the Constitution of the United States. If laws of like character should be enacted in the several States of the Union, the effect would be in the highest degree mischievous. Slavery, as an institution tolerated by law would, it is true, have disappeared from our country, but there would remain a power in the States, by sinister legislation, to interfere with the full enjoyment of the blessings of freedom to regulate civil rights, common to all citizens, upon the basis of race, and to place in a condition of legal inferiority a large body of American citizens now constituting a part of the political community called the [163 U.S. 564] People of the United States, for whom and by whom, through representatives, our government is administered. Such a system is inconsistent with the guarantee given by the Constitution to each State of a republican form of government, and may be stricken down by Congressional action, or by the courts in the discharge of their solemn duty to maintain the supreme law of the land, anything in the constitution or laws of any State to the contrary notwithstanding.

For the reasons stated, I am constrained to withhold my assent from the opinion and judgment of the majority.

14.4 *Brown v. Board of Education* (1954)

Brown v. Board of Education (1954) overturned *Plessy v. Ferguson* (1896) and outlawed legal segregation of the races in America. Though some states and districts complied with *Brown* immediately, others, mostly in the South, undertook a program of "massive resistance" which did not end until Congress brought additional pressure in the mid-1960s. Even then, with legal or de jure segregation ended, de facto or on the ground racial separation based on comfort, not so subtle pressure, and income continued and still continues.

Brown was one of four cases tailored to challenge Plessy's "separate but equal" doctrine directly. Previous cases had been decided in favor of the plaintiffs when they showed that separate schools for blacks and whites were not, in fact, equal—the black schools were inferior. In Brown and its companion cases, the schools in question were separate, but they were, in fact, equal in every meaningful way. So the issue before the court was—is separate inherently unequal and, therefore, unconstitutional. The U.S. Supreme Court declared that separation of the races was inherently unequal and discriminatory and must end.

---

347 U.S. 483

Argued December 9, 1952
Reargued December 8, 1953
Decided May 17, 1954

Appeal from the United States District Court for the District of Kansas*

Syllabus

Segregation of white and Negro children in the public schools of a State solely on the basis of race, pursuant to state laws permitting or requiring such segregation, denies to Negro children the equal protection of the laws guaranteed by the Fourteenth Amendment—even though the physical facilities and other "tangible" factors of white and Negro schools may be equal.

(a) The history of the Fourteenth Amendment is inconclusive as to its intended effect on public education.

(b) The question presented in these cases must be determined not on the basis of conditions existing when the Fourteenth Amendment was adopted, but in the light of the full development of public education and its present place in American life throughout the Nation.

(c) Where a State has undertaken to provide an opportunity for an education in its public schools, such an opportunity is a right which must be made available to all on equal terms.

(d) Segregation of children in public schools solely on the basis of race deprives children of the minority group of equal educational opportunities, even though the physical facilities and other "tangible" factors may be equal.

(e) The "separate but equal" doctrine adopted in Plessy v. Ferguson, 163 U.S. 537, has no place in the field of public education.

(f) The cases are restored to the docket for further argument on specified questions relating to the forms of the decrees.

Opinion

Warren

MR. CHIEF JUSTICE WARREN delivered the opinion of the Court.

These cases come to us from the States of Kansas, South Carolina, Virginia, and Delaware. They are premised on different facts and different local conditions, but a common legal question justifies their consideration together in this consolidated opinion.

In each of the cases, minors of the Negro race, through their legal representatives, seek the aid of the courts in obtaining admission to the public schools of their community on a nonsegregated basis. In each instance, they had been denied admission to schools attended by white children under laws requiring or permitting segregation according to race. This segregation was alleged to deprive the plaintiffs of the equal protection of the laws under the Fourteenth Amendment. In each of the cases other than the Delaware case, a three-judge federal district court denied relief to the plaintiffs on the so-called "separate but equal" doctrine announced by this Court in Plessy v. Fergson, 163 U.S. 537. Under that doctrine, equality of treatment is accorded when the races are provided substantially equal facilities, even though these facilities be separate. In the Delaware case, the Supreme Court of Delaware adhered to that doctrine, but ordered that the plaintiffs be admitted to the white schools because of their superiority to the Negro schools.

The plaintiffs contend that segregated public schools are not "equal" and cannot be made "equal," and that hence they are deprived of the equal protection of the laws. Because of the obvious importance of the question presented, the Court took jurisdiction. Argument was heard in the 1952 Term, and reargument was heard this Term on certain questions propounded by the Court.

Reargument was largely devoted to the circumstances surrounding the adoption of the Fourteenth Amendment in 1868. It covered exhaustively consideration of the Amendment in Congress, ratification by the states, then-existing practices in racial segregation, and the views of proponents and opponents of the Amendment. This discussion and our own investigation convince us that, although these sources cast some light, it is not enough to resolve the problem with which we are faced. At best, they are inconclusive. The most avid proponents of the post-War Amendments undoubtedly intended them to remove all legal distinctions among "all persons born or naturalized in the United States." Their opponents, just as certainly, were antagonistic to both the letter and the spirit of the Amendments and wished them to have the most limited effect. What others in Congress and the state legislatures had in mind cannot be determined with any degree of certainty.

An additional reason for the inconclusive nature of the Amendment's history with respect to segregated schools is the status of public education at that time. In the South, the movement toward free common schools, supported by general taxation, had not yet taken hold. Education of white children was largely in the hands of private groups. Education of Negroes was almost nonexistent, and practically all of the race were illiterate. In fact, any education of Negroes was forbidden by law in some states. Today, in contrast, many Negroes have achieved outstanding success in the arts and sciences, as well as in the business and professional world. It is true that public school education at the time of the Amendment had advanced further in the North, but the effect of the Amendment on Northern States was generally ignored in the congressional debates.

Even in the North, the conditions of public education did not approximate those existing today. The curriculum was usually rudimentary; ungraded schools were common in rural areas; the school term was but three months a year in many states, and compulsory school attendance was virtually unknown. As a consequence, it is not surprising that there should be so little in the history of the Fourteenth Amendment relating to its intended effect on public education.

In the first cases in this Court construing the Fourteenth Amendment, decided shortly after its adoption, the Court interpreted it as proscribing all state-imposed discriminations against the Negro race. The doctrine of "separate but equal" did not make its appearance in this Court until 1896 in the case of Plessy v. Ferguson, supra, involving not education but transportation. American courts have since labored with the doctrine for over half a century. In this Court, there have been six cases involving the "separate but equal" doctrine in the field of public education. In Cumming v. County Board of Education, 175 U.S. 528, and Gong Lum v. Rice, 275 U.S. 78, the validity of the doctrine itself was not challenged. In more recent cases, all on the graduate school level, inequality was found in that specific benefits enjoyed by white students were denied to Negro students of the same educational qualifications. Missouri ex rel. Gaines v. Canada, 305 U.S. 337; Sipuel v. Oklahoma, 332 U.S. 631; Sweatt v. Painter, 339 U.S. 629; McLaurin v. Oklahoma State Regents, 339 U.S. 637. In none of these cases was it necessary to reexamine the doctrine to grant relief to the Negro plaintiff. And in Sweatt v. Painter, supra, the Court expressly reserved decision on the question whether Plessy v. Ferguson should be held inapplicable to public education.

In the instant cases, that question is directly presented. Here, unlike Sweatt v. Painter, there are findings below that the Negro and white schools involved have been equalized, or are being equalized, with respect to buildings, curricula, qualifications and salaries of teachers, and other "tangible" factors. Our decision, therefore, cannot turn on merely a comparison of these tangible factors in the Negro and white schools involved in each of the cases. We must look instead to the effect of segregation itself on public education.

In approaching this problem, we cannot turn the clock back to 1868, when the Amendment was adopted, or even to 1896, when Plessy v. Ferguson was written. We must consider public education in the light of its full development and its present place in American life throughout the Nation. Only in this way can it be determined if segregation in public schools deprives these plaintiffs of the equal protection of the laws.

Today, education is perhaps the most important function of state and local governments. Compulsory school attendance laws and the great expenditures for education both demonstrate our recognition of the importance of education to our democratic society. It is required in the performance of our most basic public responsibilities, even service in the armed forces. It is the very foundation of good citizenship. Today it is a principal instrument in awakening the child to cultural values, in preparing him for later professional training, and in helping him to adjust normally to his environment. In these days, it is doubtful that any child may reasonably be expected to succeed in life if he is denied the opportunity of an education. Such an opportunity, where the state has undertaken to provide it, is a right which must be made available to all on equal terms.

We come then to the question presented: Does segregation of children in public schools solely on the basis of race, even though the physical facilities and other "tangible" factors may be equal, deprive the children of the minority group of equal educational opportunities? We believe that it does.

In Sweatt v. Painter, supra, in finding that a segregated law school for Negroes could not provide them equal educational opportunities, this Court relied in large part on "those qualities which are incapable of objective measurement but which make for greatness in a law school." In McLaurin v. Oklahoma State Regents, supra, the Court, in requiring that a Negro admitted to a white graduate school be treated like all other students, again resorted to intangible considerations: "... his ability to study, to engage in discussions and exchange views with other students, and, in general, to learn his profession." Such considerations apply with added force to children in grade and high schools. To separate them from others of similar age and qualifications solely because of their race generates a feeling of inferiority as to their status in the community that may affect their hearts and minds in a way unlikely ever to be undone. The effect of this separation on their educational opportunities was well stated by a finding in the Kansas case by a court which nevertheless felt compelled to rule against the Negro plaintiffs:

> Segregation of white and colored children in public schools has a detrimental effect upon the colored children. The impact is greater when it has the sanction of the law, for the policy of separating the races is usually interpreted as denoting the inferiority of the negro group. A sense of inferiority affects the motivation of a child to learn. Segregation with the sanction of law, therefore, has a tendency to [retard] the educational and mental development of negro children and to deprive them of some of the benefits they would receive in a racial[ly] integrated school system.

Whatever may have been the extent of psychological knowledge at the time of Plessy v. Ferguson, this finding is amply supported by modern authority. Any language in Plessy v. Ferguson contrary to this finding is rejected.

We conclude that, in the field of public education, the doctrine of "separate but equal" has no place. Separate educational facilities are inherently unequal. Therefore, we hold that the plaintiffs and others similarly situated for whom the actions have been brought are, by reason of the segregation complained of, deprived of the equal protection of the laws guaranteed by the Fourteenth Amendment. This disposition makes unnecessary any discussion whether such segregation also violates the Due Process Clause of the Fourteenth Amendment.

Because these are class actions, because of the wide applicability of this decision, and because of the great variety of local conditions, the formulation of decrees in these cases presents problems of considerable complexity. On reargument, the consideration of appropriate relief was necessarily subordinated to the primary question—the constitutionality of segregation in public education. We have now announced that such segregation is a denial of the equal protection of the laws. In order that we may have the full assistance of the parties in formulating decrees, the cases will be restored to the docket, and the parties are requested to present further argument on Questions 4 and 5 previously propounded by the Court for the reargument this Term. The Attorney General of the United States is again invited to participate. The Attorneys General of the states requiring or permitting segregation in public education will also be permitted to appear as amici curiae upon request to do so by September 15, 1954, and submission of briefs by October 1, 1954.

It is so ordered.

NOTE

* Together with No. 2, Briggs et al. v. Elliott et al., on appeal from the United States District Court for the Eastern District of South Carolina, argued December 9–10, 1952, reargued December 7–8, 1953; No. 4, Davis et al. v. County School Board of Prince Edward County, Virginia, et al., on appeal from the United States District Court for the Eastern District of Virginia, argued December 10, 1952, reargued December 7–8, 1953, and No. 10, Gebhart et al. v. Belton et al., on certiorari to the Supreme Court of Delaware, argued December 11, 1952, reargued December 9, 1953.

_____

14.5 Richard M. Valelly, "Institutions and Enfranchisement" (2004)

Richard Valelly describes how institutions affect political outcomes by comparing the first reconstruction, in the immediate wake of the Civil War, with the second reconstruction, following *Brown v. Board*. Valelly asks how the initial decisions made by the federal courts in regard to voting rights in the first and second reconstruction affected the flow of events and political outcomes thereafter. An initially unfavorable ruling throws sand in the gears and requires that valuable time and effort be lost in cleaning and repairing legal equipment, while a favorable ruling acts as a lubricant to further change.

Valelly concludes that the collapse of the first reconstruction meant that the United States lost a century on the road to full democracy; making it among the last developed nation to still be working on democratic inclusion. This left the United States with a post-slavery century of minority political, economic, and social exclusion that must be undone before an unfettered democracy will be in place.

_____

. . . I offer a distinctive view of what institutions do in politics. One viewpoint stresses the way institutions force political actors to adopt perspectives on their strategic and political situations that differ from those they would hold in the absence of these institutions. The Madisonian separation of powers does this, in theory at least, by channeling self-interested political behavior into a system of complex interactions, out of which arises an ensemble of broad representational perspectives on policy questions.[1]

Another classic conjecture is that institutions enable coordination. They permit mutually beneficial arrangements between rational actors who otherwise would have difficulty achieving their goals—often, paradoxically, because of the actors' very rationality. The political party has been portrayed as such an institution. It critically introduces a time horizon into actors' calculations about how to realize their goals. A party permits better political bargains for its members across time, as it were. They are superior to the deals that would be negotiated by these same actors if they tried instead for one intricate and uncertain logroll after another.[2]

Yet a third hypothesis is that institutions are really not joint "solutions" for helping all similarly situated rational actors so much as subtle allocators of advantage and disadvantage whose effects escape detection in the short run but not in the long run. For instance, the internal committee structure and parliamentary rules of the U.S. House will periodically change in ways that solve problems for a majority coalition at the time of solution. But the losers will eventually realize that they lost and will seek later to renegotiate the partial equilibrium.[3]

The analysis in this book sees institutions in a way somewhat different from these. It builds on a core idea in each of the other views, namely, that institutions mesh with political action. I see institutions as a kind of technology that allows actors in a difficult and challenging situation to gain leverage—a fulcrum, as it were—on a demanding enterprise that they have set for themselves.[4]

Party System Structure and Institutionalizing the Biracial Coalition

In the first reconstruction, the southern party system's institutional baseline was unpromising for the coalition of 1867–1868. For nearly a decade before the first reconstruction the South lacked strongly competitive two-party politics. The collapse of the Whig Party splintered southern politics. One-partyism then emerged during the Civil War. Only late in the life of the Confederacy was there factional opposition to the Davis administration. The Confederacy's Civil War experience with a "politics above parties" subtly framed any competitive organized opposition to the southern elite as an illegitimate politics.[5]

In this forbidding context the coalition poured enormous energy into building eleven state-level parties as rapidly as possible. Although essential for giving enfranchisement substance and meaning, this was very difficult business. The development of competitive, mass political parties before the Civil War took several decades. Now something similar needed to be set up almost overnight in the former Confederacy.

During the second reconstruction, in contrast, the coalition-making between the Democratic party's New Deal faction and black southerners only required them to take over long-standing, long-accepted party organizations. As early as 1961, such a strategy was in fact explicit. Harris Wofford, John F. Kennedy's civil rights advisor, urged the president during the period between election and inauguration to focus on black voter registration in order to strengthen white southern moderates' electoral chances: "[B]ehind their back, with their open or tacit approval, the Executive will be increasing the Negro vote which can help re-elect them." He noted that the southern conservatives "who oppose any form of Federal action on civil rights are against most of the social legislation of the new administration anyway." The idea was to take their historic party away from them and give it to new people.[6]

Had the structural context for party-building been more favorable during the first reconstruction, the coalition of 1867–1868 would have become better institutionalized. When they are well-developed, political parties allow voters to clearly grant authority for using governmental resources in socially useful ways. Parties do this because they channel the ambition of talented political entrepreneurs into mobilizing the loyalty and participation of ordinary citizens on a regular basis. But such attractive properties of party politics did not fully emerge during the first reconstruction, given the structural context. They have, however, characterized southern party politics to a greater extent during the second reconstruction.[7]

Jurisprudence-Building

...During both reconstructions, the key factor in the evolution of voting rights jurisprudence was the first stance taken by a majority of the Supreme Court, that is, when the constitutional and statutory products of coalition-making first received Court scrutiny. At such moments informed observers were both highly uncertain and highly self-conscious. Coalition-making was, after all, contentious; it altered power relations.

Which side of the post-coalition struggle would the Court's majority join? It had to choose. Protecting black voting and office-holding either appeared valid and commanding or it did not. Minimum political requirements—that constitutional amendments be taken seriously and that new statutes be respected by the courts—were either met or not met. For these reasons, the initial signal from the Court had one of two further effects during the two reconstructions. At the least, the favorable stance (the second reconstruction) generated pressure for compliance with the new policies. But the initially *un*favorable stance (the first reconstruction) produced something different than pressure for compliance. It created new and difficult follow-on tasks. It placed pressure on the incorporating coalition to (1) undertake some new litigation strategy or (2) change the Court's composition.

In other words, an unfavorable ruling did not mean the end of reform. It instead meant much more work. As we will see for the case of the first reconstruction, the Supreme Court's initially hostile rulings did *not* foreclose an ultimately favorable position on the national protection of black voting rights. This is rarely remarked. By the late 1880s, an alternative (though also more limited) constitutional basis for the protection of black voting rights became available within the original Constitution, not in the Reconstruction Amendments. The result was to encourage the Republican Party's final attempt to save some of the political gains of Reconstruction, namely, the Federal Elections Bill of 1890.

But by then a great deal of time had been lost. The coalition of 1867–1868 was much weaker. The jurisprudential opportunity cost, as it were, of the Supreme Court's initially unfavorable position was therefore high. Time and effort that could have gone into strengthening, revising, and advancing the legal basis for electorally including African Americans had to go toward solving the problem of the Court's hostility.

Progress and Policy

Taking notice of the similarities and differences of the two reconstructions has many implications. Perhaps the most important is that as a nation we have only just begun to truly experience the kind of full political democracy that we might have had if the first reconstruction had not collapsed. The United States is among the last of the advanced democracies to still be at the business of fully including all of its citizens in its electoral politics. The United States is the only democracy in which a major social group entered the electorate en masse and then was extruded via legislation, referendum, and constitutional revision, forcing that group to start all over again.

Consequently, as a country we still have very important business to do: we have to overcome the social and economic legacies of disenfranchisement. It is often thought that the persistence of black disadvantage is rooted in the experience of African American enslavement. But disenfranchisement is also an important cause. It may even be more significant than the experience of enslavement.[8]

Once black southerners were disenfranchised by the early 1900s, the stage was set for a systematic entrenchment of white supremacist norms and public policies. These exercised considerable influence over national public policy. This is because southern states escaped the representational penalty for disenfranchisement established in the second section of the Fourteenth Amendment. The former Confederacy's Democratic politicians thus received a political bonus in the census enumeration, bringing more of them to the U.S. House than they might otherwise have had. One-partyism in the South also assured long political careers for southern Democrats in Congress. They gained special advantages in congressional leadership politics into the early 1960s.

Not coincidentally, color lines grew brighter in the District of Columbia, the federal civil service, the dining rooms of Congress, and the armed forces. Such highly symbolic national segregation tacitly legitimated northern de facto segregation in public employment, schooling, and housing. Examples of de facto racial exclusions also occurred in old-age income security, collective bargaining, direct housing subsidies, mortgage credit, insurance regulation, banking regulation, medical care, and government jobs. Statutory design reflected who was represented—and who was not. This remarkable state of affairs lasted into the mid-1960s.[9]

Racial hierarchy, in short, got a very strong second wind. As a result, when the coalition of 1961–1965 emerged, the second reconstruction had its work cut out for it. Because the links between electoral politics and policy impact are not tight and immediate, the beginning of full electoral inclusion circa 1965 could not quickly dissolve disenfranchisement's legacies. The second reconstruction has been instead a gradual solvent of economic and educational inequality.[10]

One day the hateful inequalities that disenfranchisement did so much to create or to entrench—in housing, jobs, medical care, and education—may be gone. When that happens the second reconstruction will finally be over. But not until then will it be over. And this has clear implications, I believe, for voting rights policy. The temporary provisions of the Voting Rights Act will come up for congressional consideration no later than 2007. When they do, they must not be allowed to lapse—at least not without putting protections of equal strength in their place.

There is an attitude that may tempt members of Congress and much of the public when the Voting Rights Acts temporary sections require reconsideration. In an essay in *Collier's Weekly* in 1906, W. E. B. Du Bois put his finger on it. "We have a way in America," he wrote, "of wanting to be 'rid' of problems. It is not so much a desire to reach the best and largest solution as it is to clean the board and start a new game. For instance, most Americans are simply tired and impatient over our . . . social problem, the Negro. They do not want to solve it, they do not want to understand it, they want to simply be done with it and hear the last of it. Of all possible attitudes, this is the most dangerous." Du Bois recommended instead a policy of—to use his Victorian but apt language—"Freedom and Friendship."[11]

Abraham Lincoln also understood the special obligations of our national history. As is well known, Lincoln's Second Inaugural offered the most soaring, historicist sorts of ideas, even speculating that divine providence might prolong the Civil War for another two and a half centuries. But Lincoln ended on just the right note. His voice will serve

Congress and the president well when they reconsider the Voting Rights Act: "With malice toward none, with charity for all, with firmness in the right as God gives us to see the right, let us strive on to finish the work we are in."[12]

NOTES

1. Thus *Federalist* 51 concludes: "In the extended republic of the United States, and among the great variety of interests, parties, and sects which it embraces, a coalition of a majority of the whole society could seldom take place on any other principles than those of justice and the general good." Alexander Hamilton, John Jay, and James Madison, *The Federalist: A Commentary on the Constitution of the United States*, pp. 335–341 (New York: Modern Library College Editions, published by Random House, n.d.), pp. 340–341.

2. John H. Aldrich, *Why Parties? The Origin and Transformation of Party Politics in America* (Chicago: University of Chicago Press, 1995), pp. 33–36.

3. Eric Schickler, *Disjointed Pluralism: Institutional Innovation and the Development of the U.S. Congress* (Princeton University Press, 2001).

4. See Jon Elster, *Nuts and Bolts for the Social Sciences* (Cambridge: Cambridge University Press, 1989), pp. 13–21.

5. Daniel W. Crofts, "Politics in the Antebellum South," in *A Companion to the American South*, ed. John B. Boles, pp. 176–190, Blackwell Companions to American History (Malden, Mass.: Blackwell, 2002), esp. pp. 181–185; James M. McPherson, *Battle Cry of Freedom: The Civil War Era* (New York: Oxford University Press, 1988), pp. 689–692; Peyton McCrary, Clark Miller, and Dale Baum, "Class and Party in the Secession Crisis: Voting Behavior in the Deep South, 1856–1861," *Journal of Interdisciplinary History* 8 (Winter 1978): 429–457.

6. Carl M. Brauer, *John F. Kennedy and the Second Reconstruction* (New York: Columbia University Press, 1977), pp. 112–113.

7. Thomas R. Rochon and Ikuo Kabashima, "Movement and Aftermath: Mobilization of the African-American Electorate, 1952–1992," in *Politicians and Party Politics*, ed. John Geer, pp. 102–124 (Baltimore: Johns Hopkins University Press, 1998); Harold W. Stanley, *Voter Mobilization and the Politics of Race: The South and Universal Suffrage, 1952–1984* (New York: Praeger, 1987).

8. In this connection, see Robert A. Margo, *Race and Schooling in the South, 1880–1950: An Economic History* (Chicago: University of Chicago Press, 1990), which underscores the relation between disenfranchisement and the sharp drop in state and local educational expenditures on African Americans in the South.

9. See, among others, Michael Jones-Correa, "The Origins and Diffusion of Racial Restrictive Covenanting," *Political Science Quarterly* 115 (Winter 2000–2001): 541–568; Gareth Davies and Martha Derthick, "Race and Social Welfare Policy: The Social Security Act of 1935," *Political Science Quarterly* 112 (Summer 1997): 217–235; Michael Klarman, "The Puzzling Resistance to Political Process Theory," *Virginia Law Review* 77 (May 1991): 747–832; Dona Cooper Hamilton and Charles V. Hamilton, *The Dual Agenda: The African-American Struggle for Civil and Economic Equality* (New York: Columbia University Press, 1997).

10. Jennifer L. Hochschild, "You Win Some, You Lose Some: Explaining the Pattern of Success and Failure in the Second Reconstruction," in *Taking Stock: American Government in the Twentieth Century*, ed. R. Shep Melnick and Morton Keller (New York: Cambridge University Press for the Woodrow Wilson Center, 1999), pp. 219–246, esp. p: 238.

11. W.E.B. Du Bois, "The Color Line Belts the World," in *W.E.B. Du Bois—A Reader*, ed. David Levering Lewis (New York: Holt, 1995), pp. 42–43.

12. John Gabriel Hunt, ed., *The Essential Abraham Lincoln* (Avenel, N.J.: Portland House, 1993), pp. 330–331.

14.6 Desmond King and Rogers Smith, "Racial Orders in American Political Development" (2005)

King and Smith contend that race permeates American political life in ways that cannot be, but frequently are, ignored. They contend that American political development is best understood as a continuous interaction between two racial orders— two broad patterns of racial ideas, assumptions, and patterns of advantage. One racial order is the "egalitarian-transformative" order of our best aspirations and the other is the "white supremacist" order of much of our national history and our political, social, and economic present. Both orders are continuously with us, always interacting, and they vary in influence and importance at various stages in our history.

King and Smith highlight the role of racial orders, "racial concepts, commitments, and aims," in holding together political coalitions, adopting political institutions, and shaping political, social, and economic outcomes. They argue that the American story is one of early dominance, never uncontested, of a white supremacist racial order in conflict with an "incipient" egalitarian transformative order. While the egalitarian racial order has gained strength and made progress over time, King and Smith argue that students of American politics ought always to look and look again for the impact of exclusivist racial orders.

———————————

American political science has long struggled to deal adequately with issues of race. Many studies inaccurately treat their topics as unrelated to race. Many studies of racial issues lack clear theoretical accounts of the relationships of race and politics. Drawing on arguments in the American political development literature, this essay argues for analyzing race, and American politics more broadly, in terms of two evolving, competing "racial institutional orders": a "white supremacist" order and an "egalitarian transformative" order. This conceptual framework can synthesize and unify many arguments about race and politics that political scientists have advanced, and it can also serve to highlight the role of race in political developments that leading scholars have analyzed without attention to race. The argument here suggests that no analysis of American politics is likely to be adequate unless the impact of these racial orders is explicitly considered or their disregard explained.

Whether race is *the* "American Dilemma," racial inequities have been and remain confounding features of U.S. experience. Has racial injustice been a great aberration within a fundamentally democratic, rights-respecting regime? Has the United States instead been an intrinsically racist society? Has racial discrimination been the spawn of psychological or cultural pathologies, or a tool of class exploitation, or a political "card" to be played in power games, or something else?

One might expect political science in the United States to be the center of debates, if not answers, on such questions. But American political scientists have historically not been much more successful than America itself in addressing racial issues. We seek to do so by connecting theoretical frameworks emerging in the subfield of American political development, including King (1995), Lieberman (2002), Orren and Skowronek (1994, 1996, 1999, 2002), and Smith (1997), with insights from scholars of race in other areas of political science and other disciplines (e.g., Dawson and Cohen 2002, Omi and Winant 1994, and Wacquant 2002). We argue that American politics has historically been constituted in part by two evolving but linked "racial institutional orders": a set of "white supremacist" orders and a competing set of "transformative egalitarian" orders. Each of these orders has had distinct phases, and someday the United States may transcend them entirely—though that prospect is not in sight.

This "racial orders" thesis rejects claims that racial injustices are aberrations in America, for it elaborates how the nation has been pervasively constituted by systems of racial hierarchy since its inception. Yet more than many approaches, it also captures how those injustices have been contested by those they have injured and by other political institutions and actors. It does not deny that the nation's "white supremacist" racial orders have often served vicious economic exploitation or that their persistence reveals psychological and cultural pathologies. Instead it provides a framework to organize empirical evidence of the extent and manner in which structures of racial inequalities have been interwoven with economic as well as gender and religious hierarchies and social institutions.

But more than many scholars, our approach analyzes the "political economy" of American racial systems by stressing the "political," not the "economy." We see all political institutional orders as *coalitions of state institutions and other political actors and organizations that seek to secure and exercise governing power in demographically, economically, and ideologically structured contexts that define the range of opportunities open to political actors.* "Institutional orders" are thus more diversely constituted and loosely bound than state agencies; but they are also more institutionalized, authoritatively empowered, and enduring than many political movements. *Racial* institutional orders are ones in which political actors have adopted (and often adapted) racial concepts, commitments, and aims in order to help bind together their coalitions and structure governing institutions that express and serve the interests of their architects. As in any coalition, the members of a racial order support it out of varied motives. Economic aims are central for many, but others seek political power for its own sake, or to quiet social anxieties, or to further ideological goals. Leaders hold them together by gaining broad agreement on the desirability of certain publicly authorized arrangements that predictably distribute power, status, and resources along what are seen as racial lines. . . .

To sketch the argument developed here: at the nation's founding, a political coalition of Americans formed that gained sufficient power to direct most governing institutions, and also economic, legal, educational, residential, and social institutions, in ways that established a hierarchical order of white supremacy, though never without variations, inconsistencies, and resistance. That order was so bound up with the institutional order of chattel slavery, which it legitimated, as to seem identical to it—but never wholly so. White supremacist structures often subordinated putatively free Native Americans and many "nonwhite" immigrants as well as African Americans. And again, this order also always included some white racists, whose numbers grew over time, who opposed slavery, seeing it as the source of a dangerous black presence. Their hope was to "get shut of the Negro," not to be his master.

Yet at least from the time the Declaration claimed that all men are created equal, the nation also displayed an incipient "transformative egalitarian" order, one that some soon applied to racial hierarchies. This order had its governmental institutionalization in legal guarantees of equal rights that were sometimes implemented in judicial rulings and legislative statutes, often under the pressure of religious groups, black and white. Initially, to be sure, this political order was far weaker than white supremacist actors and institutions. Conflicts between proslavery and antislavery forces, not white supremacists and racial egalitarians, formed the central axis of, especially, late antebellum politics. But in context, the antislavery alliance was undeniably a force for egalitarian racial transformation; and though some of its partisans were strongly racist, and most were only moderately egalitarian, some opposed white supremacy in Congress, on state courts, and in state legislatures. The triumph of the antislavery forces greatly strengthened the position of these more racially egalitarian actors and the institutions they occupied.

After the Civil War, this revised transformative alliance built new constitutional, administrative, political, economic, educational, and social institutions to promote greater racial equality. Most important were the Fourteenth and Fifteenth Amendments, along with new schools, political organizations, and civic associations for blacks. But the allies and institutions that made up the "white supremacist" racial order were far from eradicated. They eventually regained dominance in the modified form of the Jim Crow system of segregation and disfranchisement that largely prevailed until the civil rights era of the 1960s. Substantial further development came only when, in light of new national and international political contexts, some who had long been complicit in white supremacy, especially northern Democrats, chose from mixed tactical and moral motives to join heightening black resistance to those arrangements. Gaining executive, judicial, and finally legislative support, proponents of the nation's resurgent "transformative egalitarian" racial order succeeded in discrediting explicitly "white supremacist" policies definitively and expanding their own institutional order more than ever. But despite these triumphs, still-valorized "antitransformative" institutions of racial inequality have continued to play major roles in American life, while leaders of "transformative egalitarian" institutions have struggled more than ever to decide what further changes should be pursued.

Useful as this framework is for making sense of racial development, our main claim here is that a "racial institutional orders" approach helps explain many features of American politics that may appear *unrelated* to race, such as congressional organization, bureaucratic autonomy, and modern immigration priorities. We conclude that the internal developments, clashes, and broader impacts of American racial orders have been and remain so central that all scholars of American politics ought always to consider how far "racial order" variables affect the phenomena they examine. Analysts should inquire whether the activities of institutions and actors chiefly concerned either to protect or to erode white supremacist arrangements help to account for the behavior and changes in the nation's political institutions, coalitions, and contests they study. Any choice not to consider racial dimensions requires explicit justification. . . .

The Unseen Impacts of Racial Orders

Many features of the U.S. political system, from national powers over commerce and other economic concerns, to states' rights and voting rights, to structures of congressional representation, to immigration and naturalization, the scope of free expression, criminal justice procedures, and much more, have never developed apart from pressures to alter or to maintain the nation's racial ordering. The pattern continues today. The operations of the federal civil service; the organization of Congress; the content of major pieces of social policy during the New Deal and the War on Poverty; the opposition to "big government," "tax and spend programs," and "welfare" from the Reagan administration on; and the activism of modern courts, among other matters, have all been driven in major ways by battles over how far racial hierarchies would be kept or changed.

When political scientists ignore these impacts, or analyze them without a suitable theoretical framework, they often neglect or misunderstand the conduct of actors who are responding to the tensions and opportunities generated by America's racial orders. As a result, not only are these writings inadequate in their discussions of race, but they fall short in their accounts of the apparently nonracial topics they address. . . .

Immigration

In common with too many other policy topics, immigration policies are often analyzed separately from domestic racial issues. Yet from the 1882 Chinese Exclusion Act, through the Johnson–Reed 1924 Immigration Act establishing race-based national origins criteria, to the Immigration and Naturalization Act of 1952 affirming racial discrimination, domestic racial institutions and their proponents have interacted profoundly with immigration policy (Ngai 1999). For many, Chinese exclusion fit with displacing western American Indians. Constitutional endorsement of segregation sustained the legitimacy of racial naturalization restrictions. It is doubtful that the prorestriction immigration regime, initiated in 1882 and in place until 1965, could have existed without a white supremacist alliance in Congress of southern Democrats and western Republicans, a coalition that provided successive chairs of the two houses' Immigration Committees. They gained further reinforcement from northeastern nativist elites. These "strange bedfellow" alliances show that the racial order promoted linkages across diverse political groupings that, in turn, helped maintain that order. . . .

Yet many scholars persist in analyzing immigration in nonracial economic, cultural, and institutional terms. In *Dividing Lines* (2002), Daniel Tichenor provides the most thorough scholarly narrative of American immigration policy yet available, and his approach is suitably more complex. He explains the major shifts in policy in terms of four factors: the fragmentation of the U.S. polity that permits unequal patterns of access for lobbyists, the tendency for politically unusual coalitions to form around immigration policy issues, the influence of professional experts' views in policy choices, and the effect of international crises. This framework enables a comprehensive account of U.S. immigration policies from the late eighteenth century to the present. However, because it does not include recognition of racial orders, it again fails to highlight how these patterns of unequal access, unusual coalitions, expert opinion, and responses to international pressures have often been products of racial aims, alliances, and institutional structures. Thus at times Tichenor does not bring out fully the roles that actors within those orders have played in shaping and contesting the politics of immigration and the ways in which immigration policies have in turn affected America's domestic racial structures. . . .

Tichenor's account of the national origins system implemented from the late 1920s through the mid-1960s highlights the influence of its founders' "xenophobic and racist intentions" (147). But Tichenor fails to explore African American political responses at the time, articulated at annual NAACP conferences and in the Association's lobbying, or the implications for black-white configurations of the law's racial "architecture" (Ngai 1999). The NAACP deplored the system of "race classification" embodied in the national origins quota system as "naïve and untechnical" (3), for good reason. That system expressed and reinforced the nation's domestic racial order, working with, for example, the Supreme Court's decisions upholding naturalization preferences for whites to maintain the vision of the United States as an essentially white country. Some white supremacists saw in immigration policy a chance to achieve greater national "whitening" and even contemplated the removal of all African Americans from the United States via either forcible or voluntary emigration. A bill passed by the Senate in 1914 but rejected by the House, after intense NAACP lobbying, sought to exclude all black immigrants and to permit the exclusion of African Americans who traveled abroad (King 2000, 153–55)....

And though the old quota system codified theories of racial and ethnic differences more explicitly than modern laws do, current policies have fostered discourses about the "new immigrants," principally Asian Americans and Hispanics, that perpetuate stereotyped notions of racial identities. Contemporary debates repeatedly air implicit or explicit concerns about how these groups will fit into or reconfigure America's still-contesting racial systems.... The politics of immigration and new immigrants, like issues of bureaucracy, congressional structure, and many other topics, thus can be better grasped if we consider the roles of racial orders in shaping past and current political institutions, policies, and conduct.

Conclusion

...Our argument has not been that race explains everything in American politics, or even that race is always important for every dimension of American political development.... But we maintain that the internal dynamics of American racial orders, and their interactions with each other and with other aspects of American political life, have so often been so important that the question of what role race may be playing should always be part of political science inquiries. The failure of political scientists to deal adequately with race in their scholarship has been all too much a part of the failure of Americans to deal adequately with race in their common lives. That is why this failure is one that our discipline has a special need, and a special duty, to rectify.

REFERENCES

Dawson, Michael C., and Cathy Cohen. 2002. "Problems in the Study of the Politics of Race." In *Political Science: The State of the Discipline*, ed. I. Katznelson and H. V. Milner. New York: W. W. Norton, 488–510.

King, Desmond. 1995. *Separate and Unequal: Black Americans and the US Federal Government*. Oxford: Oxford University Press.

———. 2000. *Making Americans: Immigration, Race, and the Origins of the Diverse Democracy*. Cambridge, MA: Harvard University Press.

Lieberman, Robert. 2002. "Ideas, Institutions, and Political Order: Explaining Political Change." *American Political Science Review* 96 (December): 697–712.

Logan, Rayford W. (1954) 1965. *The Betrayal of the Negro from Rutherford B. Hayes to Woodrow Wilson*. New York: Collier Books.

Ngai, Mai M. 1999. "The Architecture of American Immigration Law: A Reexamination of the Immigration Act of 1924." *Journal of American History* 86 (June): 67–92.

Omi, Michael, and Howard Winant. 1994. *Racial Formation in the United States: From the 1960s to the 1990s*. 2nd ed. New York: Routledge.

Orren, Karen, and Stephen Skowronek. 1994. "Beyond the Iconography of Order: Notes for a 'New Institutionalism.'" In *The Dynamics of American Politics: Approaches and Interpretations*, ed. L. C. Dodd and C. Jillson. Boulder, CO: Westview Press, 311–30.

——. 1996. "Institutions and Intercurrence: Theory Building in the Fullness of Time." In *Nomos XXXVIII: Political Order*, ed. I. Shapiro and R. Hardin. New York: New York University Press, 111–46.

——. 1999. "In Search of Political Development." In *The Liberal Tradition in American Politics: Reassessing the Legacy of American Liberalism*, ed. D. F. Ericson and L. E. Bertch Green. New York: Routledge, 29–41.

——. 2002. "The Study of American Political Development." In *Political Science: The State of the Discipline*, ed. I. Katznelson and H. V. Milner. New York: W. W. Norton, 722–54.

Smith, Rogers M. 1997. *Civic Ideals: Conflicting Visions of Citizenship in U.S. History*. New Haven, CT: Yale University Press.

Tichenor, Daniel J. 2002. *Dividing Lines: The Politics of Immigration Control in America*. Princeton, NJ: Princeton University Press.

Wacquant, Loïc. 2002. "From Slavery to Mass Incarceration: Rethinking the 'Race Question' in the U.S." *New Left Review* 13: 41–60.

Discussion Questions

1. One of the great puzzles of American history is what Thomas Jefferson, a life long slave owner, was thinking when he penned the words "all men are created equal" in the Declaration of Independence. Many think they know—what do you think?

2. Judith Sargent Murray argued that women are just as naturally intelligent and talented as men, but are denied the opportunity for education and training. What parts of Murray's critique holds true today?

3. Both *Plessy v. Ferguson* and *Brown v. Board* discuss whether the fact of segregation has a negative impact on black self-esteem and achievement. How do these two historic Supreme Court decisions differ on this question and what are the strengths and weaknesses of each argument?

4. Describe Abraham Lincoln's understanding of the appropriate role for blacks within the American society of the mid-nineteenth century. Where do you think Lincoln would have been on the issues in the early twentieth century? How about the late twentieth century?

5. King and Smith argue that no inquiry in American politics should proceed without stopping to ask whether the white supremacist racial order may be playing an unseen and unexpected role. Some would say there is no harm in looking for racism in any inquiry, while others would say that the concern is overblown. What do you think?

Suggested Additional Reading

Edward G. Carmines and James A. Stimson, *Issue Evolution: Race and Transformation in American Politics* (Princeton, N.J.: Princeton University Press, 1989).

J. Morgan Kousser, *Colorblind Justice: Minority Voting Rights and the Undoing of the Second Reconstruction* (Chapel Hill, N.C.: University of North Carolina Press, 1999).

Michael J. Klarman, From Jim Crow to Civil Rights: The Supreme Court and the Struggle for Racial Equality (New York: Oford University Press, 2004).

Robert C. Lieberman, *Shaping Race Policy: The U.S. in Comparative Perspective* (Princeton, N.J.: Princeton University Press, 2005).

Rogers Smith, *Civic Ideals: Conflicting Visions of Citizenship in U.S. History* (New Haven, CT: Yale University Press, 1997).

15

Government, the Economy, and Domestic Policy

Introduction

What is the state's role in ensuring the prosperity and well-being of its citizens? How much should the government regulate economic behavior? How much should government protect citizens who cannot be expected to work in private employment because they are too young, too old or too disabled? How much should government invest in public education, public parks, public roads or health research?

The framers of the U.S. Constitution insisted that protecting private property and fostering commerce were high priorities for the new government. Many believed that the British colonial system, in which trade was tightly controlled by the British government, had held back American prosperity. While the Constitution laid the basis for protecting private property, it did not specify much about the additional economic tasks the new national government could or should undertake.

As soon as the federal government organized, some of its leaders pressed for more active economic policy. The first Secretary of the Treasury, Alexander Hamilton, asserted that the United States government should take a very active role in building American industry and ensuring that it could compete with nations like Britain. According to Hamilton (reading one), the U.S. government had to use public subsidies, tax breaks, trade restrictions and other tools to aid manufacturing because other nations used these tools to boost their own industries. Hamilton's ideas on manufacturing, and his plans for a national bank, sparked strong opposition from James Madison, Thomas Jefferson and other Americans who thought agriculture offered a better route to national prosperity. Madison and Jefferson advocated a much less active national government that would leave most economic development to the states. Their view generally prevailed until the Civil War. When Abraham Lincoln and a Republican Congress took power in 1861, they pursued more active government policies, including land grants to homesteaders, to railroad companies, and to states for the purpose of building new colleges.

As U.S. industry grew and the capitalist economy expanded in the late nineteenth and early twentieth centuries, the economy fundamentally changed. New, large corporations built unprecedented economic power. Commerce transcended state borders. Fewer Americans worked on farms and more in cities. Urban workers depended on wages from private businesses. Government afforded few protections for those who could not work, even though many workers endured terrible hardships in the slumps of the 1870s, the 1890s, the Panic of 1907, and the sharp recession after World War I. These problems stoked many proposals for reforms that would counter corporate power and improve the lot of the urban masses. In 1910, former president Theodore Roosevelt gave a momentous speech in Osawatomie, Kansas, that laid out the ideas for a "New Nationalism" (reading two). Roosevelt broke with the traditional belief in limited government, asserting the need for a much more active national government role. He forcefully argued that the federal government should impose progressive income taxes, control the large corporations, and provide for the welfare of the general public. Some of these reforms became law during the presidency of Woodrow Wilson (1913–1921). In a 2011 speech also given in Osawatomie, President Obama purposely invoked the "New Nationalism" speech in arguing that fundamental economic change again requires a more active government.[1]

The unprecedented economic disaster of the Great Depression of the 1930s unraveled prosperity for millions of workers and their employers. In the terrible winter of 1932–1933, a quarter of American workers were jobless and millions more were working shorter hours and absorbing pay cuts. In March of 1933, Franklin D. Roosevelt (Theodore Roosevelt's cousin) became president and immediately set to work and began to change the path of American economic and domestic policy. Since then, Americans generally have come to accept that the national government has a responsibility to help support those who have suffered economically through no fault of their own.

In the third reading, Roosevelt explains this federal responsibility and the role of the Social Security plan to fulfill it. The Social Security Act of 1935 was not just a plan for old-age insurance; it also provided for unemployment insurance, aid for the blind and aged, and aid "for services for the protection and care of homeless, neglected, dependent, and crippled children." Thus, the Social Security Act laid the foundation for the American welfare state. Roosevelt's New Deal also established the federal government role as a more active manager of the economy. National institutions of economic management, such as the Federal Reserve Board, gained new economic powers. New regulatory agencies, such as the Securities and Exchange Commission, began to police and stabilize markets. In the financial crisis and Great Recession of 2008–2009, most American leaders and citizens accepted the need for these government institutions to devise ways to prevent or mitigate economic disaster.

The fourth and fifth readings examine the impact of these newer government policies. Political scientists Benjamin Page and James Simmons argued that federal programs such as Social Security have a proven record of mitigating the problems of poverty and inequality by providing income support and preparation for the workforce. John Kingdon, a foremost public policy scholar, examined the differences between public policy in the United States and policy in other wealthy democracies. Public policy has grown in all these nations, he noted, but the United States spends and taxes less than these other nations, and provides a less inclusive social "safety net" of programs for those adversely affected by expansion of the market economy. This difference does not seem to stem from policies that are unusually ineffective in the United States.

In our highlight piece, Suzanne Mettler shows how the design of domestic policy over the last twenty-five years has hidden the role government plays in encouraging economic security and opportunity. She describes the growth of a "submerged" welfare state, consisting of tax breaks, subsidies and other benefits that are delivered indirectly to Americans. Many of those who benefit from such programs, such as college savings programs, have no idea that government is responsible for them. The Obama administration's signature health care policy perpetuates some of these features of the American domestic policy. Mettler concludes that this "submerged" welfare state will strongly influence the future development of American domestic policy.

The broader lesson is that policy always makes politics, by changing the coalitions that support political parties and the array of interest groups with a stake in government efforts. For example, the Obama health care proposals affected every interest in the health care sector (over 17 percent of the U.S. economy), from doctors to insurance companies to hospitals and any private business that has workers that need health insurance. By affecting these coalitions and interests, new policies—like the Obama health care reform—will shape the new developments in future American politics.

Note

1. "Text: Obama's Speech in Kansas," *New York Times*, December 6, 2011, http://www.nytimes.com/2011/12/07/us/politics/text-obamas-speech-in-kansas.html?pagewanted=all&_r=0 (accessed June 11, 2013).

15.1 Alexander Hamilton, "Report on Manufactures" (1791)

President George Washington appointed Alexander Hamilton to serve as his Secretary of the Treasury. As if fulfilling his observations in *Federalist* 72, the ambitious Hamilton soon put his own stamp on American economic policy with a new national bank, national assumption of responsibility for state debts, and a proposal for encouraging the development of American manufactures. In this excerpt from his proposal to promote manufacturing, Hamilton argues that the U.S. government cannot simply allow the unpredictable play of free markets to determine the course of American economic development. Instead, the United States had to employ all of the policy tools that other nations were using to shape "free" markets, including protective tariffs (taxes on imported products that raised the prices of competitive goods from abroad), bans on and inspections of imported products, business subsidies (bounties), the encouragement of inventions, and the development of transportation infrastructure (then, roads and canals, and today, highways, rail lines, seaports and airports). American governments have used these tools throughout American history, and will continue to use them in the future.

December 5, 1791

The expediency of encouraging manufactures in the United States, which was not long since deemed very questionable, appears at this time to be pretty generally admitted. The embarrassments, which have obstructed the progress of our external trade, have led to serious reflections on the necessity of enlarging the sphere of our domestic commerce: the restrictive regulations, which in foreign markets abrige the vent of the increasing surplus of our Agricultural produce, serve to beget an earnest desire, that a more extensive demand for that surplus may be created at home . . .

[One objection to government encouragement of manufacturing is] that Industry, if left to itself, will naturally find its way to the most useful and profitable employment: whence it is inferred, that manufactures without the aid of government will grow up as soon and as fast, as the natural state of things and the interest of the community may require. [But several factors counter that logic. T]he strong influence of habit and the spirit of imitation—the fear of want of success in untried enterprises—the intrinsic diffi-culties incident to first essays towards a competition with those who have previously attained to perfection in the business to be attempted—the bounties premiums and other artificial encouragements, with which foreign nations second the exertions of their own Citizens in the branches, in which they are to be rivalled.

Experience teaches, that men are often so much governed by what they are accus-tomed to see and practice, that the simplest and most obvious improvements, in the [most] ordinary occupations, are adopted with hesitation, reluctance and by slow grada-tions. The spontaneous transition to new pursuits, in a community long habituated to different ones, may be expected to be attended with proportionably greater difficulty. When former occupations ceased to yield a profit adequate to the subsistence of their followers, or when there was an absolute deficiency of employment in them, owing to the superabundance of hands, changes would ensue; but these changes would be likely to be more tardy than might consist with the interest either of individuals or of the Society . . . To produce the desireable changes, as early as may be expedient, may therefore require the incitement and patronage of government.

The apprehension of failing in new attempts is perhaps a more serious impediment. There are dispositions apt to be attracted by the mere novelty of an undertaking—but these are not always those best calculated to give it success. To this, it is of importance that the confidence of cautious sagacious capitalists both citizens and foreigners, should be excited. And to inspire this description of persons with confidence, it is essential, that they should be made to see in any project, which is new, and for that reason alone, if, for no other, precarious, the prospect of such a degree of countenance and support from government, as may be capable of overcoming the obstacles, inseparable from first experiments.

The superiority antecedently enjoyed by nations, who have preoccupied and perfected a branch of industry, constitutes a more formidable obstacle, than either of those, which have been mentioned, to the introduction of the same branch into a country, in which it did not before exist. To maintain between the recent establishments of one country and the long matured establishments of another country, a competition upon equal terms, both as to quality and price, is in most cases impracticable. The disparity in the one, or in the other, or in both, must necessarily be so considerable as to forbid a successful rivalship, without the extraordinary aid and protection of government.

But the greatest obstacle of all to the successful prosecution of a new branch of industry in a country, in which it was before unknown, consists, as far as the instances apply, in the bounties premiums and other aids which are granted, in a variety of cases, by the nations, in which the establishments to be imitated are previously introduced. It is well known (and particular examples in the course of this report will be cited) that certain nations grant bounties on the exportation of particular commodities, to enable their own workmen to undersell and supplant all competitors, in the countries to which those commodities are sent. Hence the undertakers of a new manufacture have to contend not only with the natural disadvantages of a new undertaking, but with the gratuities and remunerations which other governments bestow. To be enabled to contend with success, it is evident, that the interference and aid of their own government are indispensable.

Combinations by those engaged in a particular branch of business in one country, to frustrate the first efforts to introduce it into another, by temporary sacrifices, recompensed perhaps by extraordinary indemnifications of the government of such country, are believed to have existed, and are not to be regarded as destitute of probability. The existence or assurance of aid from the government of the country, in which the business is to be introduced, may be essential to fortify adventurers against the dread of such combinations, to defeat their effects, if formed and to prevent their being formed, by demonstrating that they must in the end prove fruitless. . . .

In order to a better judgment of the means proper to be resorted to by the United States, it will be of use to advert to those which have been employed with success in other countries. The principal of these are:

1. *Protecting duties—or duties on those foreign articles which are the rivals of the domestic ones intended to be encouraged.*

Duties of this nature evidently amount to a virtual bounty on the domestic fabrics; since, by enhancing the charges on foreign articles, they enable the, national manufacturers to undersell; all their foreign competitors. The propriety of this species of encouragement need not be dwelt upon, as it is not only a clear result from . . . numerous topics which have been suggested, but is sanctioned by the laws of the United States, in a variety of instances; it has the additional recommendation of being a resource of revenue. Indeed, all tile duties imposed on imported articles, though with an exclusive view to revenue, have the effect, in contemplation, and, except where they fill on raw materials, wear a beneficent aspect towards the manufacturers of the country.

2. *Prohibitions of rival articles, or duties equivalent to prohibitions.*

This is another and an efficacious means of encouraging national manufactures; but, in general, it is only fit to be employed when a manufacture has made such progress, and is in so many hands, as to insure a due competition, and an adequate supply on reasonable terms . . .

3. *Prohibitions of the exportation of the Materials of Manufactures . . .*

4. *Pecuniary bounties.*
This has been found one of the most efficacious means of encouraging manufactures, and is, in some views, the best. Though it has not yet been practised upon by the Government of the United States (unless the allowance on the expiration of dried and pickled fish and salted meat could be considered as a bounty), and though it is less favored by public opinion than some other modes, its advantages are these:

1. It is a species of encouragement more positive and direct than any other, and, for that very reason, has a more immediate tendency to stimulate and uphold new enterprises, increasing the chances of profit, and diminishing the risks of loss, in the first attempts.

2. It avoids the inconvenience of a temporary augmentation of price, which is incident to some other modes; or it produces it to, a less degree, either by making no addition to the charges on the rival foreign article, as in the case of protecting duties, or by making a smaller addition. The first happens when the fund for the bounty is derived from a different object (which may or may not increase the price of some other article, according to the nature of that object), the second, when the fund is derived from the same, or a similar object, of foreign manufacture. One percent. duty on the foreign article, converted into a bounty on the domestic, will have an equal effect with a duty of two percent., exclusive of such bounty; and the price of the foreign commodity is liable to be raised, in the one case, in the proportion of one percent.; in the other in that of two percent. Indeed the bounty, when drawn from another source, is calculated to promote a reduction of price; because, without laying any new charge on the foreign article, it serves to introduce a competition with it, and to increase the total quantity of the article in the market.

3. Bounties have not, like high protecting duties, a tendency to produce scarcity. An increase of price is not always the immediate, though, where the progress of a domestic manufacture does not counteract a rise, it is, commonly, the ultimate effect of an additional duty. In the interval between the laying of the duty and the proportional increase of price, it may discourage importation, by interfering with the profits to be expected from the sale of the article.

4. Bounties are, sometimes, not only the best, but the only proper expedient for uniting the encouragement of a new object of agriculture with that of a new object of manufacture. It is the interest of the farmer to have the production of the raw material promoted by counteracting the interference of the foreign material of the same kind. It is the interest of the manufacturer to have the material abundant and cheap. . . .

5. *Premiums*
. . . Bounties are applicable to the whole quantity of an article produced, or manufactured, or exported, and involve a correspondent expense. Premiums serve to reward some particular excellence or superiority, some extraordinary exertion or skill, and are dispensed only in a small number of cases . . .

6. *The exemption of the materials of manufactures from duty* . . .

7. *Drawbacks of the duties which are imposed on the materials of manufactures.*

[An example of drawback would be a repayment to a manufacturer who has paid a tariff on materials that he uses to manufacture products that are later exported to other countries].

8. *The encouragement of new intentions and discoveries at home, and of the introduction into the United States of such as may have been made in other countries; particularly, those which relate to machinery.*

This is among the most useful and unexceptionable of the aids which can be given to manufactures. The usual means of that encouragement are pecuniary rewards, and, for a time, exclusive privileges [such as patents] . . .

9. *Judicious regulations for the inspection of manufactured commodities.*

This is not among the least important of the means by which the prosperity of manufactures may be promoted. It is, indeed, in many cases, one of the most essential. Contributing to prevent frauds upon consumers at home, and exporters to foreign countries; to improve the quality, and preserve the character of the national manufactures; it cannot fill to aid the expeditious and advantageous sale of them, and to serve as a guard against successful competition from other quarters. The reputation of the flour and lumber of some States, and of the potash of others, has been established by an attention to this point.

10. *The facilitating of pecuniary remittances from place to place –*

[If bills of exchange and other forms of monetary payments] drawn in one State, payable in another, were made negotiable everywhere, and interest and damages allowed in case of protest, it would greatly promote negotiations between the citizens of different States, by rendering them more secure, and with it the convenience and advantage of the merchants and manufacturers of each.

11. *The facilitating of the transportation of commodities.*

Improvements favoring this object intimately concern all the domestic interests of a community; but they may, without impropriety, be mentioned as having, an important relation to manufactures. There is, perhaps, scarcely any thing which has been better calculated to assist the manufacturers of Great Britain, than the melioration of the public roads of that kingdom, and the great progress which has been of late made in opening canals. Of the former, the United States stand much in need; for the latter, they present uncommon facilities.

15.2 Theodore Roosevelt, "The New Nationalism" (1910)

Consistently with his view that the president was the nation's steward (reading 10.4), President Theodore Roosevelt assumed broad responsibility for steering domestic policy. He arbitrated a major labor dispute, pressed for railroad safety regulations, took legal action against some large monopoly corporations, advocated a compensation program for injured workers, extended conservation and national parks, and put the problems of child welfare on the national agenda. After leaving office, Roosevelt sought to further expand the national agenda, declaring that "I believe in shaping the ends of government to protect property as well as human welfare . . ." in this speech at an event commemorating civil war veterans in Osawatomie, Kansas. Roosevelt argued that equal opportunity requires national government action. By 1912, Roosevelt ran for president on the ticket of the new Progressive Party, whose platform advanced the goal of social and industrial justice. Roosevelt lost to Democratic presidential candidate Woodrow Wilson, but received more votes than incumbent Republican President William Howard Taft.

In every wise struggle for human betterment one of the main objects, and often the only object, has been to achieve in large measure equality of opportunity. In the struggle for this great end, nations rise from barbarism to civilization, and through it people press forward from one stage of enlightenment to the next. One of the chief factors in progress is the destruction of special privilege. The essence of any struggle for healthy liberty has always been, and must always be, to take from some one man or class of men the right to enjoy power, or wealth, or position, or immunity, which has not been earned by service to his or their fellows. . . .

At many stages in the advance of humanity, this conflict between the men who possess more than they have earned and the men who have earned more than they possess is the central condition of progress. In our day it appears as the struggle of freemen to gain and hold the right of self-government as against the special interests, who twist the methods of free government into machinery for defeating the popular will. At every stage, and under all circumstances, the essence of the struggle is to equalize opportunity, destroy privilege, and give to the life and citizenship of every individual the highest possible value both to himself and to the commonwealth. . . .

Practical equality of opportunity for all citizens, when we achieve it, will have two great results. First, every man will have a fair chance to make of himself all that in him lies; to reach the highest point to which his capacities, unassisted by special privilege of his own and unhampered by the special privilege of others, can carry him, and to get for himself and his family substantially what he has earned. Second, equality of opportunity means that the commonwealth will get from every citizen the highest service of which he is capable. No man who carries the burden of the special privileges of another can give to the commonwealth that service to which it is fairly entitled.

. . . [W]hen I say that I am for the square deal, I mean not merely that I stand for fair play under the present rules of the games, but that I stand for having those rules changed so as to work for a more substantial equality of opportunity and of reward for equally good service....

Now, this means that our government, national and State, must be freed from the sinister influence or control of special interests. Exactly as the special interests of cotton and slavery threatened our political integrity before the Civil War, so now the great special business interests too often control and corrupt the men and methods of government for their own profit. We must drive the special interests out of politics.... [E]very special interest is entitled to justice, but not one is entitled to a vote in Congress, to a voice on the bench, or to representation in any public office. The Constitution guarantees protections to property, and we must make that promise good. But it does not give the right of suffrage to any corporation. The true friend of property, the true conservative, is he who insists that property shall be the servant and not the master of the commonwealth; who insists that the creature of man's making shall be the servant and not the master of the man who made it.

Combinations in industry are the result of an imperative economic law which cannot be repealed by political legislation. The effort at prohibiting all combination has substantially failed. The way out lies, not in attempting to prevent such combinations, but in completely controlling them in the interest of the public welfare....

The absence of effective State, and, especially, national, restraint upon unfair money-getting has tended to create a small class of enormously wealthy and economically powerful men, whose chief object is to hold and increase their power. The prime need is to change the conditions which enable these men to accumulate power which is not for the general welfare that they should hold or exercise.... We grudge no man a fortune in civil life if it is honorably obtained and well used. It is not even enough that it should have gained without doing damage to the community. We should permit it to be gained only so long as the gaining represents benefit to the community. This, I know, implies a policy of a far more active governmental interference with social and economic conditions in this country than we have yet had, but I think we have got to face the fact that such an increase in governmental control is now necessary.

No man should receive a dollar unless that dollar has been fairly earned.... Therefore, I believe in a graduated income tax on big fortunes, and in another tax which is far more easily collected and far more effective—a graduated inheritance tax on big fortunes, properly safeguarded against evasion and increasing rapidly in amount with the size of the estate....

But I think we may go still further. The right to regulate the use of wealth in the public interest is universally admitted. Let us admit also the right to regulate the terms and conditions of labor, which is the chief element of wealth, directly in the interest of the common good. The fundamental thing to do for every man is to give him a chance to reach a place in which he will make the greatest possible contribution to the public welfare. Understand what I say there. Give him a chance, not push him up if he will not be pushed. Help any man who stumbles; if he lies down, it is a poor job to try to carry him; but if he is a worthy man, try your best to see that he gets a chance to show the worth that is in him. No man can be a good citizen unless he has a wage more than sufficient to cover the bare cost of living, and hours of labor short enough so that after his day's work is done he will have time and energy to bear his share in the management of the community, to help in carrying the general load. We keep countless men from being good citizens by the conditions of life with which we surround them. We need comprehensive workmen's compensation acts, both State and national laws to regulate child labor and work for women, and, especially, we need in our common schools not merely education in booklearning, but also practical training for daily life and work. We need to enforce better sanitary conditions for our workers and to extend the use of safety appliances for our workers in industry and commerce, both within and between the States. Also, friends, in the interest of the working man himself we need to set our faces .... against violence and injustice and lawlessness by wage-workers just as much as against lawless cunning and greed and selfish arrogance of employers....

I do not ask for overcentralization; but I do ask that we work in a spirit of broad and far-reaching nationalism when we work for what concerns our people as a whole.... The national government belongs to the whole American people, and where the whole American people are interested, that interest can be guarded effectively only by the national government. The betterment which we seek must be accomplished, I believe, mainly through the national government.

... The New Nationalism puts the national need before sectional or personal advantage. It is impatient of the utter confusion that results from local legislatures attempting to treat national issues as local issues. It is still more impatient of the impotence which springs from overdivision of governmental powers, the impotence which makes it possible for local selfishness or for legal cunning, hired by wealthy special interests, to bring national activities to a deadlock. This New Nationalism regards the executive power as the steward of the public welfare.

15.3 Franklin Delano Roosevelt, "Message to Congress on Social Security" (1935)

The 1932 presidential election took place in the depths of the Great Depression, and, as a presidential candidate, Franklin Roosevelt insisted that the federal government must take responsibility for Americans who are starving or who want "to maintain themselves but cannot." As Hamilton believed that the government had to intervene to encourage economic growth, Roosevelt argued that the national government had to help sustain people during economic crises. Less than two years after taking office as president, Roosevelt proposed a Social Security Act that would reduce the dangers of future economic depressions and protect Americans against the economic hazards that were disrupting millions of lives. This Social Security Act would both prevent future need and alleviate current needs. It would be a kind of constitution for the American welfare state, including old age insurance for those who grew too old to work, unemployment compensation for those who involuntarily lost their jobs, and federal aid to needy mothers to protect "homeless, neglected, dependent and crippled children." This law established the enduring, basic framework for income support in the United States;

later programs and reforms, such as Medicare for the aged and Medicaid for the poor, were built on the path laid out by the Social Security Act of 1935.

In addressing you on June 8, 1934, I summarized the main objectives of our American program. Among these was, and is, the security of the men, women, and children of the Nation against certain hazards and vicissitudes of life. This purpose is an essential part of our task. In my annual message to you I promised to submit a definite program of action. This I do in the form of a report to me by a Committee on Economic Security, appointed by me for the purpose of surveying the field and of recommending the basis of legislation.

I am gratified with the work of this Committee and of those who have helped it: The Technical Board on Economic Security drawn from various departments of the Government, the Advisory Council on Economic Security, consisting of informed and public-spirited private citizens and a number of other advisory groups, including a committee on actuarial consultants, a medical advisory board, a dental advisory committee, a hospital advisory committee, a public-health advisory committee, a child welfare committee and an advisory committee on employment relief. All of those who participated in this notable task of planning this major legislative proposal are ready and willing, at any time, to consult with and assist in any way the appropriate Congressional committees and members, with respect to detailed aspects.

It is my best judgment that this legislation should be brought forward with a minimum of delay. Federal action is necessary to, and conditioned upon, the action of States. Forty-four legislatures are meeting or will meet soon. In order that the necessary State action may be taken promptly it is important that the Federal Government proceed speedily.

The detailed report of the Committee sets forth a series of proposals that will appeal to the sound sense of the American people. It has not attempted the impossible, nor has it failed to exercise sound caution and consideration of all of the factors concerned: the national credit, the rights and responsibilities of States, the capacity of industry to assume financial responsibilities and the fundamental necessity of proceeding in a manner that will merit the enthusiastic support of citizens of all sorts.

It is overwhelmingly important to avoid any danger of permanently discrediting the sound and necessary policy of Federal legislation for economic security by attempting to apply it on too ambitious a scale before actual experience has provided guidance for the permanently safe direction of such efforts. The place of such a fundamental in our future civilization is too precious to be jeopardized now by extravagant action. It is a sound idea—a sound ideal. Most of the other advanced countries of the world have already adopted it and their experience affords the knowledge that social insurance can be made a sound and workable project.

Three principles should be observed in legislation on this subject. First, the system adopted, except for the money necessary to initiate it, should be self-sustaining in the sense that funds for the payment of insurance benefits should not come from the proceeds of general taxation. Second, excepting in old-age insurance, actual management should be left to the States subject to standards established by the Federal Government. Third, sound financial management of the funds and the reserves, and protection of the credit structure of the Nation should be assured by retaining Federal control over all funds through trustees in the Treasury of the United States.

At this time, I recommend the following types of legislation looking to economic security:

1. Unemployment compensation.
2. Old-age benefits, including compulsory and voluntary annuities.
3. Federal aid to dependent children through grants to States for the support of existing mothers' pension systems and for services for the protection and care of homeless, neglected, dependent, and crippled children.
4. Additional Federal aid to State and local public-health agencies and the strengthening of the Federal Public Health Service. I am not at this time recommending the adoption of so-called "health insurance," although groups representing the medical profession are cooperating with the Federal Government in the further study of the subject and definite progress is being made ...

... States will largely administer unemployment compensation, assisted and guided by the Federal Government. An unemployment compensation system should be constructed in such a way as to afford every practicable aid and incentive toward the larger purpose of employment stabilization. This can be helped by the intelligent planning of both public and private employment. It also can be helped by correlating the system with public employment so that a person who has exhausted his benefits may be eligible for some form of public work as is recommended in this report. Moreover, in order to encourage the stabilization of private employment, Federal legislation should not foreclose the States from establishing means for inducing industries to afford an even greater stabilization of employment.

In the important field of security for our old people, it seems necessary to adopt three principles: First, noncontributory old age pensions for those who are now too old to build up their own insurance. It is, of course, clear that for perhaps 30 years to come funds will have to be provided by the States and the Federal Government to meet these pensions. Second, compulsory contributory annuities which in time will establish a self-supporting system for those now young and for future generations. Third, voluntary contributory annuities by which individual initiative can increase the annual amounts received in old age. It is proposed that the Federal Government assume one-half of the cost of the old-age pension plan, which ought ultimately to be supplanted by self-supporting annuity plans ...

The establishment of sound means toward a greater future economic security of the American people is dictated by a prudent consideration of the hazards involved in our national life. No one can guarantee this country against the dangers of future depressions but we can reduce these dangers. We can eliminate many of the factors that cause economic depressions, and we can provide the means of mitigating their results. This plan for economic security is at once a measure of prevention and a method of alleviation.

We pay now for the dreadful consequence of economic insecurity—and dearly. This plan presents a more equitable and infinitely less expensive means of meeting these costs. We cannot afford to neglect the plain duty before us. I strongly recommend action to attain the objectives sought in this report.

15.4 Benjamin I. Page and James R. Simmons, "Is American Public Policy Effective?" (2000)

Did government efforts to mitigate poverty and inequality work? Political scientists Benjamin Page and James Simmons argued that they did. In the process of making their argument, they showed the many ways in which government has intervened in markets to mitigate the worst consequences of "creative destruction" for individuals. By ensuring a basic standard of living for many elderly Americans, the Social Security program is a very successful, extensive and popular program for reducing poverty and inequality. The U.S. government sets a floor under wages, and helps those with little means to purchase food. States provide the education that can propel many to advance economically. Despite the complexity and political contentiousness of American government, then, it has sustained enduring and respected efforts to help its citizens prosper.

At the beginning of this book, we asked what, if anything, government can do about poverty and inequality. Our answer is clear: government can do a great deal. It can do so while preserving other things we value, including liberty, economic efficiency, and general prosperity.

Persistent poverty and a high level of income inequality in the United States cast a dark shadow over our otherwise great achievements. When ... about one-fifth of American children live in families with incomes below the poverty line, when the top fifth of families receive about half of all the income in the country but the bottom fifth get less than 4 percent of it, something is seriously wrong. No doubt a substantial degree of inequality would be tolerable, so long as the lot of those on the bottom was satisfactory and steadily improving. But that has not been the case. Inequality has increased sharply over the past three decades, with big gains for the wealthy, while most people's incomes stagnated or declined. We are troubled by the extraordinary extent of disparities in income and wealth, by the persistence of absolute poverty, and by the fact that many millions of working people have to struggle desperately in order to make ends meet.

Such extensive poverty and inequality waste lives and cause unnecessary suffering. They limit freedom. They prevent full individual development, impair a sense of community, upset social stability, make a mockery of the idea of equal opportunity, and unnecessarily reduce human happiness.

Private markets and free-enterprise capitalism, for all their virtues, plainly do not themselves keep the levels of poverty and inequality within acceptable bounds. Even to the extent that markets accurately reward individual skills and efforts—and the most eloquent defenders of markets admit that they do not invariably do so—huge inequalities in "rewards" cannot be considered fair or just. Many factors that lead to high or low incomes are beyond individuals' control. To a great extent, they reflect happy or unhappy chance, the results of nature, nurture, and social arrangements: the fortune or misfortune of genes, upbringing, parents, peers, good breaks, catastrophic accidents, economic fluctuations, global trends.

Nor is poverty or extreme inequality necessary in order to motivate people to learn, to work hard, and to do their best. Duty, pride, love of family, aspirations for achievement, and self-fulfillment are excellent motivators. We do not need to use unlimited greed or fear of starvation. Given encouragement and opportunities—the opportunities are crucial—the vast majority of people will work hard and productively.

There are many reasons therefore to think that governments *should* act to reduce poverty and inequality, if they can do so in ways that do not entail too many costs: without too much inefficiency, for example, and without seriously infringing on individual liberties. Our review of the evidence indicates that government *can* in fact do so. The old canard that governments cannot do anything right is simply not correct. Nor is the newer claim that globalization renders national governments completely impotent. Yes, globalization does exert pressure against certain types of egalitarian programs, but those pressures are much less overpowering than is often supposed. Some important kinds of egalitarian programs (investment in education, for example; childhood health and nutrition; income supplements for low-wage work) actually can confer global competitive advantages, rather than disadvantages. Yes, it requires creativity and care to design programs to maximize their effectiveness, while minimizing red tape and bureaucratic interference. But such creativity and care are well within the reach of our experts, political leaders, and citizenry.

Right now, in fact, the U.S. federal, state, and local governments *do*, in many efficient and effective ways, contribute to the reduction of poverty and inequality. At the same time, there remains much more that can and should be done. To make further progress requires recognizing and surmounting certain political and economic obstacles.

Programs That Work

... U.S. social insurance programs, which offer certain kinds of protection that private insurance markets cannot provide, make very significant contributions to reducing poverty and inequality. Social Security in particular—the very foundation of American social policy—does more than any other government program to keep people's incomes above the poverty line. Without Social Security old age benefits, many more millions of elderly Americans would be poor, as many millions were before the enactment and expansion of the program.

That great reduction in poverty has been accomplished with a high degree of efficiency. Social Security's administrative costs amount to only about 1 percent of total payments. The poverty reduction has been achieved through a near-universal system of forced savings linked to work, in which people contribute while they are working and then quite properly feel entitled to benefits when they retire. The antipoverty effects are real; payroll contributions to Social Security have not merely replaced private savings that would have occurred without the program.

To be sure, Social Security is largely a middle-class program designed to smooth out individuals' earnings over their life cycles and to prevent disastrous losses of income upon retirement. It only modestly reduces inequality between the lifetime earnings of high- and low-income people. True also, the long-term financial health of the program will probably require some new resources, but those can be obtained relatively easily through such methods as extending the payroll tax to higher incomes, drawing on general tax revenues, and/or investing some tax revenues in higher-yield securities. The chief challenge for Social Security right now is simply to keep the program intact against forces working for benefit cuts or destructive privatization schemes.

Similarly, U.S. social insurance programs do a reasonably good job of helping Americans who have severe disabilities that prevent them from working. Together with the Americans with Disabilities Act's legal provisions for nondiscrimination and mainstreaming, the benefits of Social Security's Disability Insurance (DI) and Supplemental Security Income (SSI) have helped most gravely disabled Americans to avoid impoverishment.

Again, the Medicare program for the aged, despite its gaps in coverage, has greatly helped the elderly with medical expenses and (together with Medicaid) has prevented millions of people from sinking into poverty under the weight of bills for hospitals, doctors, and nursing homes. Although Medicare's scope and efficiency could be bettered by a universal health insurance system, the first task for the twenty-first century is simply to augment its financial resources and protect the program from benefit cutting or privatizing.

... It is possible to operate a fair tax system that sets tax rates according to ability to pay and reduces the inequality of after-tax incomes. A progressive personal income tax—at one time reviled as a form of "communism"—can accomplish those aims, as is clear from several periods of our history. It can do so at rather low administrative expense (vigorous enforcement efforts more than pay for themselves, though anti-government legislators have cut back enforcement in recent years) and without serious negative effects on work efforts or savings.

The income tax is also a useful vehicle for what may be the most effective of all work-encouraging antipoverty programs, the Earned Income Tax Credit (EITC). The refundable EITC has brought the total earnings of millions of low-wage workers close to or just above the poverty threshold. The EITC puts some reality behind the all-too-facile American promise that everyone who works hard can get a decent income. It does so in a way that is cheap to administer, reduces income maintenance expenses, and encourages increased work effort, thus increasing economic output and helping rather than hurting the United States in global competition.

In education and training, too, ... various U.S. government policies have enjoyed a great deal of success: considerably more success than they are usually given credit for. It is fashionable to disparage the U.S. system of public elementary and secondary education as ineffective, internationally inferior, and perhaps hopeless. But this trashing—sometimes inflicted by armchair critics who are less than fully committed to a multi-cultural, egalitarian society—ignores the awesome magnitude of the tasks we want our schools to perform. It slights the schools' real achievements in accomplishing those tasks. We ask our public schools to teach everyone the basics, to socialize children of diverse cultural and linguistic backgrounds, to cope with economic and racial segregation, and to make up for absent or neglectful parents, all while working with limited amounts of unequally distributed money. The federal Elementary and Secondary Education Act has provided important resources for poor students and poor school districts. With federal government help, the system of higher education, too, has done a great deal of excellent teaching and research and has provided pathways to upward mobility for many Americans of modest background. Educational opportunities are certainly not equal for all Americans, and much needs to be done to improve this situation, but our educational system has the potential—to some extent already realized—to build up nearly everyone's skills and talents.

Several programs specifically designed to help educate and train the disadvantaged have demonstrated the capacity to do so. Head Start, despite surprisingly pinched funding, has helped prepare millions of poor children for school. Childhood health and nutrition programs provide some of the food and medical care that is essential for the development of sound minds in sound bodies. Special education helps many disabled children to acquire cognitive and social skills and the ability to function in mainstream society. Vocational education, apprenticeships, retraining, and welfare-to-work programs (particularly those that offer help with day care and transportation, as well as job training) have all demonstrated the capacity to prepare even severely disadvantaged Americans for useful work. Some of these programs require a substantial investment of resources in each trainee, but the trainees and society as a whole generally get good returns on the investment in terms of lifelong reductions in income maintenance payments, increased productive work, and more fulfilling lives.

... U.S. public policies have fallen considerably short of the ideal of providing jobs for everyone at good wages. Yet here, too, effective policy tools are available and have been successful when used. The trick is to use them. When the U.S. Congress, the president, and the Federal Reserve Board encourage economic growth through moderately expansive fiscal policies and low interest rates, for instance, the economy does tend to grow, unemployment falls, and the lowest-wage workers do better. (On the other hand, obsession with deficits and inflation has sometimes led to excessively tight money and unnecessarily steep recessions, in which low-income workers have suffered most.) Job creation through public service employment, when tried, has worked fairly well, and it could easily be made to work better. The minimum wage (when set at a reasonable level and not allowed to fall behind increases in the cost of living), together with the EITC, does a great deal to make sure that all work is rewarded by a living wage. Antidiscrimination laws and regulations have helped reduce employment discrimination based on arbitrary factors like race and gender.

United States government policies have even successfully provided at least one important part of a minimal standard of living.... The Food Stamps program, our only near-comprehensive effort to provide an essential good to everyone in need, has sharply reduced the extent of hunger and malnutrition in America from the outrageously high levels that existed in the 1960s. Weathering years of ideological attacks and misleading rhetoric, Food Stamps have accomplished this very important task with limited and declining levels of fraud and with administrative costs that are reasonable, given the difficulty of determining eligibility and enforcing complex rules (some administrative costs could be saved by simplifying the rules and making Food Stamps universal). The much smaller and more grudging program of rental vouchers, and the experience of other countries like Canada with universal health insurance, makes clear that governments also have the capacity—not yet realized in the United States—to provide everyone with the basic necessities of shelter and medical care....

We see no reason at all to despair about the capacity of governments to deal with the problems of poverty and inequality. The challenge is to make better use of that capacity.

15.5 John W. Kingdon, "American Public Policy in Comparative Perspective" (1999)

Political scientist John Kingdon asked why the American state taxes less, spends less, and provides less domestic policy than do comparably wealthy democracies. While similar nations have long ensured universal access to health care for their citizens, the United States has not. It provided health insurance only for elderly Social Security recipients (Medicare) and for the poor (Medicaid) until the enactment of the broader Affordable Care Act ("Obamacare") in 2010. While governments in similar nations have provided extensive public transportation and utilities, the United States has provided fewer such services through the public sector, which is much smaller in the United States than it is abroad. But in other areas—defense, criminal justice and regulation—the United States stands out in its exceptionally extensive policy efforts. In the "big policy picture," American public policy is very unusual—a puzzle that has motivated many American political development scholars.

First, let's look at the big picture. In his 1996 State of the Union address, President Clinton declared that "the era of big government is over." But the fact is that American government has never been as big as in other industrialized countries. That's true not just of the federal government. Combining federal, state, and local activity, government is much less involved in most aspects of social and economic problems than it is in other industrialized countries. Contrary to many Americans' assumptions, the state is less intrusive, our government programs are smaller and less far-reaching, our public sector is smaller relative to the private sector, and yes, our taxes are lower.

Some Examples

Consider medical care (see White 1995a). In every industrialized country in the world except for the United States, the entire population is covered by health insurance. Some countries have government-run national health insurance. Others require employers to provide insurance for their employees and fill in the gaps with government programs. Most finance long-term care, which in the United States is government-financed only through Medicaid for the poor. Not only do these other countries cover the entire population with health insurance, but they also do it at far less total cost (government plus private cost) than we spend for health care in the United States.

Take transportation (Weaver 1985; King 1973). While not universal, government-owned and -operated railroads are common in other industrialized countries. Many of their governments sponsor national airlines. Mass transit is more completely developed in more of their cities than it is in American cities. Freight moves in and out of central terminals, coordinated across rail, truck, and other modes by government. Now this sort of transportation structure, both infrastructure and operation, costs a lot. The Swiss rail system, for instance, is fabulously convenient for passengers but also fabulously expensive. But it represents the collective Swiss decision to spend part of their national treasure on that sort of government program. Americans have not made such a collective decision.

This picture of transportation extends to public utilities in general, including not only transportation industries like railroads but also communications (e.g., telephones, cable television) and power generation and distribution (Temin 1991:88). In many other countries, utilities are either owned and operated by government, or are government sponsored monopolies. Instead of imposing nationalization or direct government control, the United States keeps such activities in the private sector, but regulates them through both federal and state regulatory commissions. Over the last couple of decades, furthermore, the deregulation movement has resulted in even less government involvement in regulation of utilities.

Beyond utilities, the United States ranks at the bottom of Western industrialized countries in the percentage of capital formation invested in, and the percentage of the work force employed in, public enterprises of all kinds (Weaver 1985: 71). The absence of state-owned enterprises (e.g., nationalized industries or railroads) in America compared to many other countries adds to the relatively large private sector in the United States.

Let's turn to welfare (Lipset 1996:71, 289). Americans complain about the top-heavy welfare state. But it pales in comparison with welfare programs in other industrialized nations. Most countries provide family allowances, paid maternal leave and day care, longer annual vacations, and more generous old age pensions than the United States does.... However, they pay dearly for them.

It isn't as though the United States has no welfare state at all. Starting with soldiers and mothers (Skocpol 1992), we have provided some sorts of benefits to some people. We do have AFDC (or its post-welfare reform substitute), food stamps, disability benefits, social security pensions, Medicare for the elderly, and Medicaid for the poor. There have also been fluctuations in our public policies over time. The New Deal period of the 1930s, for instance, introduced some radical public employment programs and social security provisions to deal with the Great Depression that were unknown in many other countries. And Americans provide for some sorts of welfare-state benefits privately, such as health insurance and pensions, as union-negotiated fringe benefits rather than government programs.

Despite that, however, it's still true that compared to other countries, the American welfare system, at the federal, state, and local levels combined, remains less ambitious, provides fewer types of benefits, makes fewer people eligible for those benefits, and costs less per capita or as a proportion of gross domestic product (GDP). And as the enactment of welfare reform legislation in 1996 indicates, the United States is currently reinforcing that pattern. Further, employer-paid fringe benefits, including health insurance and pensions, have been shrinking as the unionized proportion of the labor force has fallen. As Weir, Orloff, and Skocpol (1988:xi) summarize it, "The United States never has had, and is not likely to develop, a comprehensive national welfare state along West European lines."

I'm not necessarily arguing here that the United States should adopt programs to provide for a more lavish welfare state. I'm just highlighting the fact that our welfare programs are much less comprehensive, and cover fewer people and fewer sorts of contingencies, than welfare programs in other countries. Many other countries really do have what one of my respondents in an earlier study called a "lust-to-dust" welfare state, the likes of which Americans would hardly contemplate.

Look at housing (Heidenheimer, Heclo, and Adams 1983: 88). In many countries, government owns and manages a fair chunk of housing units or provides various forms of encouragement (e.g., favorable tax treatment and subsidies) to cooperatives, unions, and other nonprofits to build housing. While there is some public housing in the United States, it's not nearly as extensive, does not house as large a proportion of the population, and does not account for as large a proportion of the housing stock as in other countries. Whereas nearly all housing in the United States is constructed by private builders, it is not uncommon in European countries for a third or half of dwellings to be built by government or by nonprofits with the aid of government (Heidenheimer et al. 1983:102). Indeed, the first Clinton budget provided for even less public housing in the United States, proposing instead to provide vouchers to poor people for use in the private housing marketplace. While there are American government housing subsidies (e.g., the income tax deduction for home mortgage interest), there still is less government involvement in housing than in other countries.

Exceptions

So far, our examples have pointed in the same direction. Public policies, we have seen, are less ambitious, and the reach of government is less broad-ranging in the United States than in most other industrialized countries. But there are some policy areas that seem to be exceptions to this picture of unrelieved limited government.

One of those exceptions is education (Heidenheimer et al. 1983:21; King 1973). America has a long tradition of public elementary and secondary schools. Most of their financing and policy control rests at the local and state levels, with fairly limited and recent federal involvement. Still, this long and revered tradition of public schools in America stands in contrast to many other countries' reliance on private and religious schools. There's also a long American tradition of public higher education: universities, colleges, and normal schools, financed from state, and sometimes local, tax revenues. In England, for a contrasting example, public universities are a comparatively recent development.

Another exception to the pattern of limited government in the United States seems to be government regulation (Nivola 1997). Other countries do regulate some sectors of the economy (e.g., labor relations and retail trade) much more heavily than we do. But in certain areas (e.g., banking, securities, environmental, civil rights regulation) our regulatory regimes seem to be quite thorough. A considerable deregulation movement in the United States, dating to the early 1970s, has actually accomplished a substantial degree of deregulation in such areas as transportation, communications, and banking. Still, in some respects, the reach of government regulation remains quite extensive. In broad outline, the United States has deregulated in economic spheres but has maintained a considerable apparatus of social regulation (e.g., environmental regulation, civil rights) (Nivola 1997).

The question of regulation is accompanied by a much broader phenomenon, the much-discussed litigiousness of America. Americans sue one another a lot more than do people in other countries, and therefore spend a lot more in anticipating, avoiding, defending against, and prosecuting lawsuits. There were about three thousand lawyers for every million Americans in 1990, about twice as many per capita as in 1970. The United States has three times as many lawyers per thousand persons as Germany, ten times as many as Sweden, and twenty times as many as Japan (Nivola 1997:75). Tort costs were 2.3 percent of American GDP in 1991, nearly twice the rate of the next-ranking country. Comparable rates were 1.2 percent for Germany; 0.9 percent for France, Canada, and Australia; 0.7 percent for Japan; and 0.6 percent for the United Kingdom (Nivola 1997:27).

Litigation and government regulation add considerable costs to doing business in the United States. Some of the litigation is strictly private. But much of it springs directly from deliberate government policies, providing for class-action suits and enforcement of civil rights, consumer protection, malpractice, and other statutes by creating the right to bring suit rather than by relying on other sorts of enforcement practices. In America, lawyers do things that bureaucrats do in other countries (Kagan and Axelrad 1997).

Actually, litigation is built into our Constitution. We provide for a Bill of Rights, enforceable in court. Our tradition of civil liberties, including the rights accorded criminal defendants, is much more rigorous than in many other countries. The equal protection and due process clauses of the Fourteenth Amendment have generated tremendous volumes of litigation. More broadly, the United States is built on a regime of individual rights, which requires a considerable legal apparatus to implement. As Tocqueville (1835) observed long ago, "There is hardly a political question in the United States which does not sooner or later turn into a judicial one."

Another exception can be found in the criminal justice system. Our rate of incarceration is by far the highest in the Western world. The various levels of government in the United States spend considerably more on police, courts, and prisons than other countries do, and those expenditures are growing. Some of the difference might be due to higher crime rates and stiffer penalties. But we also criminalize some activities (e.g., prostitution, gambling, marijuana use, environmental damage, some abortions) that other countries do not treat as criminal. We even tried prohibition of alcoholic beverages by constitutional amendment.

A final exception to the general maxim of limited government is, of course, the defense establishment. The United States maintains a much larger military than most other countries, with military expenditure consuming a substantial portion of the federal budget and GDP. Spending on national defense and veterans, for instance, accounted for about one-fifth of total federal government outlays in the fiscal year 1996. That proportion has been declining over the last several years, but it is still substantial.

All of these examples—education, regulation, litigation, criminal justice, and defense— seem to be exceptions to the rule of limited government in the United States compared to other countries. What accounts for these apparent anomalies? Actually, it turns out that most of them flow quite naturally and consistently from American conceptions of the proper role of government. Let's leave that observation dangling tantalizingly for now, and return to it in the next chapter.

The Size of the Public Sector

Stepping back from the examples of public policy differences, what do they all add up to? How big is American government? The short answer is that American government is smaller, relative to the total size of the economy, than government in other countries.

American government has grown during the twentieth century. Although some of this expansion has been gradual, other growth has come along in big spurts. In the 1930s, the federal government added social security, agricultural assistance, several types of economic regulation, and other government programs to the total. In the 1960s it added Medicare, Medicaid, federal aid to education, and civil rights laws to the books. So we should notice first that government is bigger than it used to be.

But the total is still small by world standards. Let's look at some numbers. In 1995, the general government total outlays were 33 percent of GDP in the United States (federal, state, and local combined), 43 percent in Great Britain, 50 percent in Germany, 54 percent in France, 61 percent in Denmark, and 66 percent in Sweden (OECD 1996). To make this comparison less tied to these particular countries, the total of general government outlays throughout all the European Union countries amounted to 50 percent, compared to the 33 percent figure for the United States—a difference of 17 percentage points. Lest readers think that this picture is a peculiarity of 1995, the percentage point difference between the United States and Europe has been roughly similar every year since the late 1970s—ranging from a low of 13 percentage points in one year (1980) to a high of 17 in three years (1993, 1994, 1995), and averaging a 15 percentage point difference. In general, the difference between the United States and Europe has been widening, not narrowing (see also Rose 1991)....

The differences in government outlays are doubly striking because the portion of the American budget allocated for defense is larger than in most other countries (Rose, 1991). In other words, if we were simply to compare nonmilitary outlays as a percentage of GDP, the American government would look even smaller in comparison to other industrialized countries.

These figures on government outlays do not include the effects of tax expenditures. It's possible that in the United States, we might provide government help for certain activities in the form of tax deductions or tax credits rather than direct government subsidies. Instead of government payments to the opera, for instance, we allow a charitable deduction for those who choose to contribute to the opera, but it's a government subsidy either way—whether as a direct payment or as tax revenue forgone. Instead of building a great deal of public housing, to take another example, we provide homeowners with a mortgage interest tax deduction.

Howard (1997) argues that including tax expenditures in the total would boost the size of the American welfare state. While it is probably true that taking account of tax expenditures closes some of the gap between the American and European public sectors, the general picture of a smaller American government is still largely accurate. Other countries also use tax expenditures to some degree, for one thing. And other countries start with such a markedly different approach to government authority and responsibilities that we would have to go a great distance through tax expenditures to close the gap.

Furthermore, the fact that the United States tries to accomplish collective purposes through tax deductions and credits rather than direct government subsidies more than other countries do is an interesting commentary on the American way of doing business. We shy away from "big government" in the form of subsidies, in other words, and try to hide such expenditures by subsidizing various sorts of activities through manipulating the tax code. In the process, ironically, we make the tax code grotesquely complex and government far less efficient.

Tax expenditures are also more regressive than direct government subsidies would be. "Regressive" means that wealthier people benefit more than poorer people do, proportionate to their income. Take the tax deduction for mortgage interest, for example.

Because wealthy people are in higher tax brackets than poorer people, they get a larger percentage tax expenditure subsidy for equal amounts of mortgage interest. They also purchase more expensive houses and have larger mortgages, adding to the subsidy they receive in the form of their mortgage interest deduction.

Much of the time, it would be more straightforward to subsidize than to provide for tax deductions and credits. Instead of enacting the complicated provisions for tax deductions and credits for higher education that President Clinton proposed, for instance, he could much more simply have proposed straight subsidies and scholarships. As the example of mortgage interest deduction shows, furthermore, subsidies are also sometimes fairer. But the American impulse to avoid "big government" leads to some peculiar distortions.

If one compares total government tax receipts, rather than total government outlays, to GDP in these same countries, the picture is roughly similar. To return to our comparison year of 1995, the tax receipts in the United States (federal, state, and local) totaled 31 percent of GDP, compared to 45 percent for the total of European Union countries (OECD 1996). Some European countries were lower than the overall European percentage (e.g., Great Britain at 38 percent), and others were considerably higher (e.g., Sweden at 58 percent). Again, the estimates and projections into 1996 through 1998 were almost exactly the same, the differences between the American and European numbers have been maintained with minor year-to-year variations since the late 1970s, and the gap between the United States and the European countries has widened slightly over that period.

The Big Public Policy Picture

The public policy differences between the United States and other industrialized countries can be summarized quite simply without doing much violence to reality. Other countries provide more government services, pay higher taxes, and have larger public sectors relative to their private sectors. There seem to be a few exceptions to that general picture, but mostly, those are the facts.

Not every scholar interprets the data in the same way as I have here. Rose (1991), for example, argues that America is not alone in being what he calls a "Rich Nation with a Not-So-Big Government." Other such countries are non-European nations along the Pacific Rim, such as Canada, Japan, and Australia; the European ones are Switzerland and Finland. He thus calls into question the notion that America is unique. Wilson (1998) also questions the idea that America is the world's exception. Indeed, it has become common in the literature on "American exceptionalism" to claim that all countries are exceptional in some respects, and therefore to deny the notion that America is different.

I think this is all a matter of comparison. Some countries, like the Scandinavian ones, are extremely far from the United States on all of the indicators, quantitative and nonquantitative, that we have been discussing. Other countries are closer to the United States, and they make up Rose's category of "Rich Nations with a Not-So-Big Government." But in some respects, some of these countries are still very different from America, despite being included in the same category. Canada has universal single-payer health insurance, for instance; Japan has a much more centralized economy and governmental decision-making process than America; and Switzerland has a far more complete system of public transportation. The United States also devotes much much more of its public expenditure (as a percentage of GDP) to defense than other countries do, as Rose points out, which means that on most major nonmilitary programs, the United States is not nearly as ambitious as the overall figures might indicate.

REFERENCES

Heidenheimer, Arnold J., Hugh Heclo, and Carolyn Teich Adams, 1983. *Comparative Public Policy: The Politics of Social Choice in Europe and America* (St. Martin's Press, Second Edition).

Howard, Christopher, 1997. *The Hidden Welfare State* (Princeton University Press).

Kagan, Robert A. and Lee Axelrad, 1997. "Adversarial Legalism: An International Perspective," in Pietro S. Nivola, editor, *Comparative Disadvantages? Social Regulations and the Global Economy* (The Brookings Institution), Chapter 4.

King, Anthony, 1973. "Ideas, Institutions, and the Policies of Governments: A Comparative Analysis:" *British Journal of Political Science*, 3:291–313, and 409–423.

Lipset, Seymour Martin, 1996. *American Exceptionalism: A Double-Edged Sword* (W.W. Norton).

Nivola, Pietro S., editor, 1997. *Comparative Disadvantages: Social Regulations and the Global Economy* (The Brookings Institution).

OECD, 1996. Organisation for Economic Co-Operation and Development, OECD *Economic Outlook*, December 1996, Annex Tables 28 and 29.

Rose, Richard, 1991. "Is American Public Policy Exceptional?", in Byron E. Shafer, editor, *Is America Different? A New Look at American Exceptionalism* (Oxford University Press).

Skocpol, Theda, 1992. *Protecting Soldiers and Mothers: The Political Origins of Social Policy in the United States* (Harvard University Press).

Temin, Peter, ed. 1991. *Inside the Business Enterprise: Historical Perspectives on the Use of Information* (University of Chicago Press).

Tocqueville, Alexis de, 1835. *Democracy in America* (edited by Richard Heffner, Penguin, 1956).

Weaver, R. Kent, 1985. *The Politics of Industrial Change* (The Brookings Institution).

Weir, Margaret, Ann Shola Orloff, and Theda Skocpol, editors, 1988. *The Politics of Social Policy in the United States* (Princeton University Press).

White, Joseph, 1995a. *Competing Solutions: American Health Care Proposals and International Experience* (The Brookings Institution).

Wilson, Graham K., 1998. *Only in America: The Politics of the United States in Comparative Perspective* (Chatham House).

15.6 Suzanne Mettler, "Reconstituting the Submerged State: The Challenges of Social Policy Reform in the Obama Era" (2010)

Many observers would add another exceptional feature of American social policy; one suggested by John Kingdon in the previous reading. In our highlight piece, Suzanne Mettler described this feature as "the submerged state." Many Americans do not know about a number of government programs that benefit them. Public policies provide tax breaks for home mortgages, or for saving for a college education. Other government programs provide subsidies or guarantees to private lenders who arrange financing for some activity. These activities constitute a kind of hidden welfare state—in the sense that many Americans do not know what popular programs benefit them. For example, a majority of people in her survey who had taken student loans say that they have never used a government program. These programs have dramatically expanded over the past 25 years, and that expansion has changed the politics of social policy. The banks, medical providers and others who benefit as middlemen in this system have strong incentives to use political muscle against any proposed reform that challenges their role or their profits. The design of important American domestic programs, then, tends to conceal their benefits and costs from those who use them, but to mobilize special interests to defend and expand them. The Obama administration's policy initiatives will change politics, not just policy. Health care reform, for example, will alter the future path of health care politics in the United States.

———————————

Barack Obama ran for president on the platform of change, and social welfare policies ranked among his top priorities for reform. During his campaign he denounced tax breaks and recent tax cuts that benefit the most affluent, even amidst rising economic inequality; he condemned the deteriorating condition of education, including reduced affordability of and access to higher education among those from low to moderate income households; and he excoriated the skyrocketing costs of health care, the growing numbers of the uninsured, and the poor treatment Americans often receive from insurance companies. These issues resonated with the public, because most Americans are aware of and concerned about economic inequality, and most support expanded government programs to mitigate it, particularly in the areas of education and health care.[1] . . .

Yet, as would soon become evident, established political arrangements present formidable obstacles to would-be reformers once they attempt the work of governance. Change requires not only new ideas and determination but also the arduous reconstitution of pre-established political relationships and modes of operation. . . . In each area he sought to reform, Obama confronted an existing state that is at once formidable and elusive, and thus the quest required engagement in treacherous political battles. Remarkably, his administration has now succeeded in achieving several of its major goals with respect to social welfare policy. Even so, for much of the public, the delivery on those promises fails to meet the high expectations that surrounded the president when he first took office. What can explain the shape that reform has taken and the formidable challenges Obama has faced in accomplishing his agenda? Further, how can we make sense of why even after scoring key victories, he has had to try to convince the public of the value of what he has achieved?

Obama confronted an established and complex policy thicket that presents tremendous challenges to reform. By contrast to presidents such as Franklin D. Roosevelt and Lyndon B. Johnson, Obama did not aim to create major new direct visible government social programs. Neither did he seek to terminate or dramatically alter such programs, as did Ronald Reagan, who told the nation that "government is not the solution to our problem; government is the problem," or Bill Clinton, who vowed to "end welfare as we know it." Rather, Obama's policy objectives involved primarily attempts to reconstitute the *submerged state*—policies that lay beneath the surface of US market institutions and within the federal tax system.

While its origins are not new—they date back to the middle and even early twentieth century—the "submerged state" has become a formidable presence in the United States particularly over the past twenty-five years. I am referring here to a conglomeration of federal social policies that incentivize and subsidize activities engaged in by private actors and individuals. These feature a variety of tools, including social benefits in the form of tax breaks for individuals and families; the regulation and tax free nature of benefits provided by private employers, including health care benefits in the form of insurance; and the government-sponsored enterprises and third party organizations that receive federal subsidies in exchange for carrying out public policy goals, such as the banks and lending associations that have administered student loans.

Over time, the policies of the submerged state have reshaped politics in two ways, both of which presented profound challenges to Obama as he sought to accomplish reform and which, paradoxically, also imperil the success of his greatest achievements thus far. First, especially during the past two decades, the submerged state has nurtured particular sectors of the market economy and they have in turn invested in strengthening their political capacity for the sake of preserving existing arrangements. As a result, the alteration of such arrangements has required either defeating entrenched interests—which has proven impossible in most cases—or, more typically, negotiating with and accommodating them, which hardly appears to be the kind of change Obama's supporters expected when he won office. Second, such policies have shrouded the state's role, making it largely invisible to most ordinary citizens, even beneficiaries of existing policies. As a result, the public possesses little awareness of such policies, nor are most people cognizant of either what is at stake in reform efforts or the significance of their success . . .

While the foundations of the "submerged state" were established in the early and mid-twentieth century, its size and costliness have grown especially in recent decades. Overall, as of 2006, social (non-business) tax expenditures accounted for 5.7 percent of GDP, up from 4.2 percent in 1976.[2] Today, the largest of these—as seen in Table 1—emanates from the non-taxable nature of health insurance benefit provided by employers, followed by the home mortgage interest deduction, and then by tax-free employer-provided retirement benefits. Indicating the scope of these "submerged" dimensions relative to the clearly visible components of social welfare spending, Jacob Hacker calculated that

Table 1 Largest Individual Tax Expenditures: Year of Enactment and Cost in 2011

Tax Expenditure	Year of Enactment	Estimated Cost in 2011 (billions of dollars)
Exclusion of employer contributions for medical insurance	1954	177.0
Deductibility of Mortgage interest on owner-occupied homes	1913	104.5
Net exclusion of contributions and earnings for retirement plans	1974	67.1
Deduction of state and local taxes	1913	46.5
Pensions	1914–1926	44.6
Step-up basis of capital gains at death	1921	44.5
Lower tax rates on long-term capital gains	1921	44.3
Deductibility of charitable contributions (other than ed and health)	1917	43.9

Sources: US Budget, Analytical Perspectives, FY 2011; Howard 1997, 176–77.

whereas traditional social public welfare expenditures amounted to 17.1 percent of GDP in the United States in 1995, making the nation a laggard relative to other OECD nations, the inclusion of tax expenditures and other private social welfare expenditures brought the total to 24.5 percent of GDP, placing U.S. spending slightly above average.[3] Among tax expenditures, health care costs especially have ballooned over time, growing (in nominal dollars) from 77.3 billion in 1995 to 137.3 billion in 2007.[4] Meanwhile, through another policy vehicle that also subsidizes private actors to provide social benefits, the Higher Education Act of 1965 gave incentives to banks to lend to students at low rates of interest by offering that the federal government would pay half the interest on such loans.[5] In 1972, policymakers provided further impetus to student lending by creating the Student Loan Marketing Association (SLM, otherwise known as "Sallie Mae"), to provide a "secondary market" and warehousing facility.[6] By the 1980s and 1990s, student lending became highly lucrative for lenders but costly to the federal government; in 2009, the Congressional Budget Office estimated that $87 billion could be saved over 10 years if the system of subsidizing lenders was terminated entirely and replaced by direct lending.[7]

Although some individual features of the submerged state—most notably, the Earned Income Tax Credit— mitigate inequality, on net, these policies exacerbate it....

Interest Group Politics and the Submerged State

... the Obama Administration confronted highly sophisticated efforts to protect the status quo....

Take, for example, student lending, administered by banks and organizations within the financial sector. During the 1980s and 1990s, tuition outpaced inflation and policymakers at the national and state level failed to maintain a constant level of funding for grants and public universities and colleges.[8] Amid the growing partisan divide in Congress, policymakers found consensus more easily on student loans, for which they expanded borrowing limits and loosened eligibility requirements. As a result, the number and average amount of loans grew dramatically, as did lenders' profits....

Mass Politics and the Submerged State

... [i]n taking on the submerged state, Obama engaged in a set of battles over policies that are obscure if not invisible to much of the public. In fact, even individuals who have themselves utilized such policies may have little awareness of them as public social benefits. Because few existing surveys permit us to examine citizens' perceptions and experiences of such policies compared to more visible ones, I designed the Social and Governmental Issues and Participation Study of 2008 (hereafter, referred to as "Governmental Issues Survey") to do so.[9] Respondents were asked, first, whether they had "ever used a government social program, or not." Later, they were asked whether they had ever benefitted personally from any of 19 federal social policies, including some that belong to the "submerged state" and others that are visible and direct in their design and delivery. Table 2 presents the percentage of beneficiaries of each of several policies who reported that they had never used a federal social program. Notably, the six italicized policies that head the list are precisely those belonging to the submerged state: tax-deferred savings accounts, several tax expenditures, and student loans. Given the design

Table 2 Percentage of Program Beneficiaries Who Report that they "Have Not Used a Government Social Program"

Program	"No, Have Not Used a Government Social Program"
529 or Coverdell	64.3
Home Mortgage Interest Deduction	60.0
Hope or Lifetime Learning Tax Credit	59.6
Student Loans	53.3
Child and Dependent Care Tax Credit	51.7
Earned Income Tax Credit	47.1
Social Security—Retirement & Survivors	44.1
Pell Grants	43.1
Unemployment Insurance	43.0
Veterans Benefits (other than G.I. Bill)	41.7
G.I. Bill	40.3
Medicare	39.8
Head Start	37.2
Social Security Disability	28.7
SSI—Supplemental Security Income	28.2
Medicaid	27.8
Welfare/Public Assistance	27.4
Government Subsidized Housing	27.4
Food Stamps	25.4

Source: Social and Governmental Issues and Participation Study, 2008. Note: Submerged state policies shown in italics.

and manner of delivery of these policies, few individuals seem to perceive them to be social benefits. Such dynamics may imperil the political effectiveness of reforms that are limited to expansions or modifications of the submerged state....

Taking Stock

Obama came into office with ambitious plans for restructuring tax expenditures and undercutting their upwardly redistributive bias. In his first year, he succeeded only in his goal of creating new tax breaks—at least temporary ones—for low to middle-income households. But these policies further add to the size and scope of the submerged state, and they are imperceptible to most Americans....

Higher Education Policy

... Obama's ambition to restore American leadership in college graduation rates required, first, a restructuring of entrenched policy arrangements, namely a subsidized lending system that has consumed funds that could have been spent instead to foster access, and which has, meanwhile, fostered increasingly divisive politics over the past decade and a half.

... As student lenders' profits soared between 1995 and 2006, they invested in strengthening their political capacity. In campaign financing, Sallie Mae [the Student Loan Marketing Association, a corporation that originates, services, and collects repayment of student loans], established a [political action committee, or] PAC in the late 1990s, and by 2006 it emerged as the top donor within the entire finance and credit industry.[10] ... In lobbying, Sallie Mae began to rank among the top five finance and credit companies, outspending even Mastercard and American Express.[11] Lenders also worked together to create several new organizations to represent their interests in Washington, DC. Over this period, Republicans in Congress increasingly worked in tandem with lenders, attempting to seek favorable rates and terms for them....

Taking on the Lenders

Just a few months into his presidency, Obama ... directly and forcefully took on the lenders:

> The banks and the lenders who have reaped a windfall from these subsidies have mobilized an army of lobbyists to try to keep things the way they are. They are gearing up for battle. So am I. They will fight for their special interests. I will fight for ... American students and their families. And for those who care about America's future, this is a battle we can't afford to lose.[12] ...

[Democratic l]eaders [in the U.S. Senate] realized that they might ultimately need to combine elements of the higher education policy with health care reform in such a bill, so they delayed action throughout the autumn (of 2009)....

The Lenders Fight Back

Lenders used the delay to organize the opposition, both at the grassroots and elite levels....

By November, the lenders appeared to be gaining ground: analysts predicted that Obama's proposal lacked the support of enough Senators to pass.[13] ... Similar to the tax policy realm, vested interests of the submerged state seemed far more aware of what was at stake in reform efforts than did ordinary citizens, and they were mobilized whereas the general public remained quiescent.

Remarkably, however, in an eleventh hour stroke of good fortune for the Obama administration, Democratic leaders ultimately found that including the higher education legislation with health care reform in the March 2010 budget reconciliation bill helped it to meet the criteria for cost savings that would help ensure passage. Despite the dim prospects in December for the administration's higher education proposals to acquire support from even 50 Democratic Senators, 56 came on board when the direct lending plan that some disliked was combined with the party's top agenda item, health care reform. In what represented the most significant shift from submerged to visible governance achieved by Obama to date, the existing system of student lending was terminated and replaced entirely by direct lending.

... Visible and Submerged Success

In the realm of social welfare issues, Barack Obama set out to transform existing policies within the submerged state. He sought to harness this vast set of arrangements and to make it more inclusive and responsive to the needs of ordinary citizens, and to curtail the extent to which it channels public funds toward powerful sectors of the economy and affluent citizens. This has been an ambitious reform agenda. Such change requires the reconstitution of long-established relationships between government and economic actors. Organizations and industries that have long benefitted from the established system of public subsidies and incentives have been willing and able to invest tremendous resources in preserving those arrangements. Paradoxically, in defending them, they and their allies in elective office officials have routinely depicted reform proposals as attempts at "government takeovers," as if to imply that government were not already central to the existing arrangements.

Reconstituting the submerged state has been doubly difficult because while the stakes have been highly apparent to the groups that have benefitted from them, they were not very visible to most Americans. Most people perceived only the market at work: they have little awareness that many social benefits they receive emanate from a submerged state that is structured by public policy and subsidized by government. Neither do they realize that many such policies disproportionately benefit wealthy citizens. They are unlikely to know the extent to which government policy promotes the profitability of some industries by offsetting their costs in serving citizens, whether as consumers or borrowers. The functioning and effects of the submerged state remain murky, if not largely hidden, to most citizens.

Yet despite the shrouded nature of the submerged state, citizens have been able to observe—illuminated in the media's spotlight—the activities of reformers who attempt to engage in its reconstitution. The problem is that without perceiving what is at stake, citizens likely viewed reformers as simply playing "politics as usual," making deals with powerful interests. The process of reforming the submerged state is inherently messy and conflictual, far from idealized notions of change. It may have reinforced some citizens' views that government should not be trusted with complicated matters, that the private sector can handle them better and without such controversy.

In his first fourteen months in office, Barack Obama accomplished numerous of his major goals with respect to social welfare policy, as we have seen. Yet . . . the scorecard indicates that new policies do as much or more to expand the submerged state as they do to reduce its scope. The end of the existing bank-based system of student lending and its replacement with direct lending represents the most significant curtailment of the submerged state—even though lenders will continue to have a role in servicing loans. In the area of tax expenditures, the Obama administration achieved the creation of new and expanded policies for low to moderate income people. Several aspects of health care reform, as discussed above, also expand on the submerged state. Thus, the submerged state endures, albeit in altered form. The political dynamics that it engenders will continue to challenge reformers.

Successful reconstitution of the submerged state requires reformers to accomplish several tasks. First, they must either *regroup or defeat* the interest groups that have been empowered by existing arrangements. If circumstances allow and meaningful agreements can be reached, some groups might be brought on board to cooperate in reform, as the Obama Administration succeeded in doing with respect to health care reform. Outright defeat of groups that benefit from current policies is unlikely, given the extent to which they were empowered. It worked in 2010 with respect to student lenders only because those groups had already been weakened substantially over time: the creation of pilot programs for direct lending in the early 1990s created an entering wedge, a base on which reformers could build until their ideas became more widely acceptable. As this indicates, a new policy alternative can be established alongside existing arrangements as an interim approach that can facilitate more extensive reform later on.

Second, reformers must *reveal* to the public how existing policies of the submerged state function and who benefits, what is at stake in reform, who will gain and what the costs will be. In each of the three policy areas considered here, Obama has done more than other political leaders to expose the deeply obscured arrangements, but more focused and sustained attention is warranted. The tasks of reform may have proceeded more easily throughout 2009–2010 if political leaders had attempted to communicate to the public earlier, more often, and more deliberately about these matters. Even now that reform has been achieved, political leaders need to continue to inform the public about what has changed and how new policies will function.

Third, reformers must *revamp policies*, either through redesigning them or at least by guiding their delivery to make them more visible to citizens. The primary way to engage in this meaningfully is for policies to be restructured so that they no longer subsidize the interests and groups they have promoted in the past, or at least so that such support is curtailed. The change to direct lending represents quite a complete reconstitution of one policy area. The health care reform bill offers a more modified approach by retaining the existing system of private health insurance, but making it subject to mechanisms that regulate private actors and slightly curtail the extent of subsidization. But administrators should seek means to make the benefits of the submerged state more evident to citizens, for example by providing a summary sheet to individuals with their tax return that notes the amount accrued through each type of tax expenditure, or by indicating what private health insurance would cost individuals in the absence of public subsidies. . . .

NOTES

1. Page and Jacobs 2009.
2. Hacker 2002, also see Gottschalk 2000.
3. Hacker 2002, 13–16; Garfinkel, Rainwater, and Smeeding 2006, 904.
4. Howard 1997, 21; Burman, Toder, and Geissler 2008.
5. Mettler and Rose 2009.
6. Gladieux and Wolanin 1976, 61–62.
7. U.S. Congressional Budget Office 2009.
8. National Center for Public Policy and Higher Education 2002, 8–9, 12, 22–30.
9. The Social and Governmental Issues and Participation Study of 2008 consisted of a telephone survey of 1,400 Americans, including a national random sample of 1,000 plus oversamples of 200 low-income individuals and 200 25–34 year olds. It was conducted by the Cornell Survey Research Institute, from August–September 2008. The response rate was 34 percent, calculated according to AAPOR [American Association for Public Opinion Research] guidelines.
10. OpenSecrets.org 2010.
11. Ibid.
12. Obama 2009.
13. Dreas 2009.

REFERENCES

Burman, Leonard, Eric Toder, and Christopher Geissler. 2008. "How Big Are Total Individual Income Tax Expenditures, and Who Benefits from Them?" Discussion Paper No. 31. The Urban-Brookings Tax Policy Center. http://www.taxpolicycenter.org/UploadedPDF/1001234_tax_expenditures.pdf, accessed March 1, 2010.

Dreas, Maryann. 2009. "Private Lenders Focus on Jobs in Student Loan Fight." *The Hill.* http://thehill.com/business-a-lobbying/69873-private-lenders-focus-onjobs-in-student-loan-fight, accessed March 1, 2010.

Garfinkel, Irwin, Lee Rainwater, and Timothy M. Smeeding. 2006. "A Re-examination of Welfare States and Inequality in Rich Nations: How In-Kind Transfers and Indirect Taxes Change the Story." *Journal of Policy Analysis and Management* 25(4): 897–919.

Gladieux, Lawrence E., and Thomas R. Wolanin. 1976. *Congress and the Colleges: The National Politics of Higher Education.* Lexington, MA: Lexington Books.

Gottschalk, Marie. 2000. *The Shadow Welfare State: Labor, Business, and the Politics of Health Care in the United States.* Ithaca, NY: Cornell University Press.

Hacker, Jacob S. 2002. *The Divided Welfare State: The Battle Over Public and Private Social Benefits in the United States.* New York: Cambridge University Press.

Howard, Christopher. 1997. *The Hidden Welfare State: Tax Expenditures and Social Policy in the United States.* Princeton, NJ: Princeton University Press.

Mettler, Suzanne, and Deondra Rose. 2009. "Unsustainability of Equal Opportunity: The Development of the Higher Education Act, 1965–2008." Prepared for delivery at the Annual Meeting of the American Political Science Association. Toronto, Ontario, Canada. Sept. 3–6.

National Center for Public Policy and Higher Education. 2002. *Losing Ground: A National Status Report on the Affordability of American Higher Education.* San Jose, CA: National Center for Public Policy and Higher Education.

Obama, Barack. 2009. "Remarks by the President on Higher Education" April 24, 2009. http://www.whitehouse.gov/the_press_office/Remarks-by-the-President-on-Higher-Education, accessed February 26, 2010.

OpenSecrets.org. 2010. *Center for Responsive Politics.* Available at: http://www.opensecrets.org/, accessed January 29, 2010.

Page, Benjamin I., and Lawrence R. Jacobs. 2009. "No Class War: Economic Inequality and the American Public." In *The Unsustainable American State,* ed. Lawrence Jacobs and Desmond King. New York: Oxford University Press.

U.S. Congressional Budget Office. 2009. "An Analysis of the President's Budgetary Proposals for FY2010." http://www.cbo.gov/ftpdocs/102xx/doc10296/TablesforWeb.pdf, accessed June 15, 2010.

Discussion Questions

1. Which of Hamilton's policy recommendations are still appropriate for American economic policy in the twenty-first century? Should government try to help specific industries? Which ones, and how?

2. Does the federal government have the responsibility for the welfare of its citizens, as Theodore Roosevelt suggests? If so, what does that federal responsibility include? Better access to higher education? To health care? To a "living" minimum wage set at or above the poverty line?

3. Do you agree with Benjamin Page and James Simmons that programs such as Social Security prove that the U.S. government has the capacity to deal with the problems of poverty and inequality? As you think about the answer, remember the articles by Margaret Weir and Suzanne Mettler in Chapter 3.

4. How has the "submerged" state affected public opinion and interest groups in the United States? Is that likely to change in the near future?

5. Explain how past events have shaped the current American welfare state. Draw on the lessons of the past to explain how the domestic change is likely to unfold over the next decade.

Suggested Additional Reading

Martha Derthick, *Policymaking for Social Security* (Washington: Brookings Institution, 1979).

Jacob Hacker, *The Great Risk Shift* (Oxford and New York: Oxford University Press, 2006).

Robert C. Lieberman, *Shifting the Color Line: Race and the American Welfare State* (Cambridge, MA: Harvard University Press, 1998).

Suzanne Mettler, *The Submerged State: How Invisible Government Policies Undermine American Democracy* (University of Chicago Press, 2011).

Karl Polanyi, *The Great Transformation* (Boston: Beacon Press, 1944).

Monica Prasad, *The Land of Too Much: American Abundance and the Paradox of Poverty* (Cambridge, MA: Harvard University Press, 2012).

Theda Skocpol, *Protecting Soldiers and Mothers: The Political Origins of Social Policy in the United States* (Cambridge, MA: Belknap / Harvard University Press, 1992).

16

America's Place in a Dangerous World

Introduction

How should the United States deal with foreign nations and military threats? The United States of America was born vulnerable, but the vast Atlantic Ocean insulated it from Europe's great armies. Should the United States isolate itself from international power politics and remain neutral, or should it take sides and actively engage with other nations to achieve its international goals? If the nation engages in international conflicts, should it rely more heavily on diplomatic negotiations, or should it rely primarily on its military power to accomplish its goals? Should the U.S. act alone, unilaterally, or should it act in concert with other nations? Should the nation maintain a powerful military, and, if so, would a strong military itself become a threat to American democracy, as it often has been in Latin America, Africa and Asia?

When the Constitution's framers tried to write specific rules for national military and diplomatic power, they faced a dilemma. On the one hand, they agreed on the urgent need for more national power to defend Americans; on the other, they insisted on restraining that power so that the national government itself would not abuse its new authority. The first reading shows that the Convention, worried about the war powers, refused to limit the size of the military, but made it more difficult for the government to use troops by splitting the formal power to *declare* war and to *conduct* war between the legislative and executive branches, respectively, and by prohibiting the national government from deploying troops within the nation without the consent of the affected states. The Civil War, and many military actions in the twentieth century, not only have stretched these original rules to the breaking point, but also have resulted in a military whose size would shock and trouble the framers. A strong military has continued to raise troubling questions for democracy. Half a century later, French author and social analyst Alexis de Tocqueville (reading three) made the provocative suggestion that democratic nations like the United States are prone to peace—but democratic armies are prone to war.

After the Constitution's ratification, the new nation almost immediately confronted controversies in foreign affairs. President Washington in 1793 declared that the United States would remain neutral in the war between Britain and

France, a position that created a storm over the president's foreign policy role. President Washington himself warned Americans to resist "the insidious wiles of foreign influence" that would lure the United States into European politics, and to "steer clear of permanent alliances with any portion of the foreign world" (reading two).

The United States generally followed this advice in military affairs for the next century. It remained isolated from conflicts with European powers until it committed to war with Spain in 1898. But strong and distinctive ideas about international engagement shaped American political development. As David C. Hendrickson explained (reading four), the successful struggle to unify the American states provided American foreign policy-makers with a template for ideal international peace and cooperation under the rule of law. Freer international commerce could improve prosperity internationally, just as it was improving it among the states. Nations could remain self-governing and unique, but, by partnering with each other as did the states, they might subdue international disorder and war. These ideas help explain why the United States has been so committed to building international organizations and agreements over the last century.

In the twentieth century, American expansion and new war-making technologies and tactics, like planes, nuclear weapons and terrorism, have exposed the nation to new, immediate threats. Americans learned this lesson in 1941, when Japanese planes attacked the distant American naval base at Pearl Harbor, Hawaii, and again on September 11, 2001, when terrorists seized domestic aircraft and used them as weapons against the World Trade Center and the Pentagon. During and since World War II, the United States built the world's more powerful military, and it has maintained military superiority ever since. About half of all the military expenditure in the world is spent by the United States.

Reading five shows how three presidents dealt with the Cold War and its aftermath. For Harry Truman, still the commander-in-chief of thousands of American troops fighting in Korea, the United States had to lead an alliance of free nations to block Communist expansion anywhere in the world. For George Bush, who committed American troops to wars in both Afghanistan and Iraq, the nation had to fight terrorism on a broad scale, much like it fought the Cold War. But, for Barack Obama, the United States was overextended, and the nation had to rebalance its military commitments to fight a more narrowly defined war on terror.

In our highlight piece, Peter Trubowitz put such presidential strategies in historical context. Truman, Bush and Obama, along with other presidents, have had to take *both* domestic politics and national security into account in their foreign policies. History shows that political parties, interest groups, elections, Congress, and national economic health—that is, all the topics discussed in this book—influence presidential choices in dealing with international threats. Across time, differences in foreign policy reflect differences in political circumstances at home as well as differences in foreign threats abroad. Historical perspective, then, can help us make sense of the past, present and future foreign commitments that affect and will affect American life.

16.1 The Constitutional Convention Debates the Military (1787)

The delegates to the Constitutional Convention began to debate specific powers of the national government in August, 1787. Several distrusted the national power to maintain an army. Unlike a navy, a national army could invade and occupy any part of American territory to subdue it (as the British army had done in Boston before the American Revolution). The problem of balancing democracy and national security has remained difficult since the Founding. James Madison warned in 1795 that "no nation could preserve its freedom in the midst of continual warfare."

August 17, 1787

[The delegates took up a proposed Constitutional provision allowing Congress] "To subdue a rebellion in any State, on the application of its legislature" [with military force].

Mr. [Charles] Pinckney moved to strike out "on the application of its legislature" . . .

Mr. L[uther] Martin opposed it as giving a dangerous & unnecessary power. The consent of the State ought to precede the introduction of any extraneous force whatever. . . .

Mr. [Oliver] Ellsworth proposed to add after "legislature" "or Executive".

Mr. [Gouverneur] Morris. The Executive may possibly be at the head of the Rebellion. The Gen[era]l Gov[ernmen]t should enforce obedience in all cases where it may be necessary.

Mr. Ellsworth. In many cases The Gen[era]l Govt. ought not to be able to interpose unless called upon. He was willing to vary his motion so as to read, "or without it when the legislature cannot meet."

Mr. [Elbridge] Gerry was against letting loose the myrmidons [mythical robotic soldiers] of the U. States on a State without its own consent. The States will be the best Judges in such cases. More blood would have been spilt in Mass[achuset]ts in the late insurrection [Shays's Rebellion], if the Gen[era]l authority had intermeddled.

Mr. [John] Langdon was for striking out as moved by Mr. Pinkney. The apprehension of the national force, will have a salutary effect in preventing insurrections.

Mr. [Edmund] Randolph—If the Nat[iona]l. Legislature is to judge whether the State legislature can or cannot meet, that amendment would make the clause as objectionable as the motion of Mr. [Gouverneur] Morris. We are acting a very strange part. We first form a strong man to protect us, and at the same time wish to tie his hands behind him. The legislature may surely be trusted with such a power to preserve the public tranquillity.

[But the delegates deadlocked on accepting the possibility of national military intervention when a state legislature could not meet to approve the intervention].

[Next, the delegates took up a proposed Constitutional provision allowing Congress "To make war"].

Mr. Pinckney opposed the vesting this power in the Legislature. Its proceedings were too slow. It w[oul]d meet but once a year. The H[ouse] of Rep[resentative]s would be too numerous for such deliberations. The Senate would be the best depositary, being more acquainted with foreign affairs, and most capable of proper resolutions. If the States are equally represented in Senate, so as to give no advantage to large States, the power will notwithstanding be safe, as the small have their all at stake in such cases as well as the large States. It would be singular for one authority to make war, and another peace.

Mr. [Pierce] Butler. The Objections ag[ain]st the Legislature lie in a great degree ag[ain]st the Senate. He was for vesting the power in the President, who will have all the requisite qualities, and will not make war but when the Nation will support it.

Mr. [James] Madison and Mr. Gerry moved to insert "declare," striking out "make" war; leaving to the Executive the power to repel sudden attacks.

Mr. [Roger] Sherman thought it stood very well. The Executive sh[oul]d be able to repel and not to commence war. "Make" better than "declare" the latter narrowing the power too much.

Mr. Gerry never expected to hear in a republic a motion to empower the Executive alone to declare war.

Mr. Ellsworth: there is a material difference between the cases of making *war*, and making *peace*. It sh[oul]d be more easy to get out of war, than into it. War also is a simple and overt declaration. peace attended with intricate & secret negociations.

Mr. George Mason was ag[ain]st giving the power of war to the Executive, because not safely to be trusted with it; or to the Senate, because not so constructed as to be entitled to it. He was for clogging rather than facilitating war; but for facilitating peace. He preferred "declare" to "make".

[The Convention approved the Motion to replace "make" with "declare." The delegates next took up the provision that Congress have the authority "To raise armies".]

August 18, 1787

Mr. Gerry took notice that there was no check here ag[ain]st standing armies in time of peace. The existing Cong[res]s is so constructed that it cannot of itself maintain an army. This w[oul]d. not be the case under the new system. The people were jealous on this head, and great opposition to the plan would spring from such an omission. He suspected that preparations of force were now making ag[ain]st it.... He thought an army dangerous in time of peace & could never consent to a power to keep up an indefinite number. He proposed that there shall not be kept up in time of peace more than _____ thousand troops. His idea was that the blank should be filled with two or three thousand.

Mr. Luther Martin and Mr. Gerry now regularly moved "provided that in time of peace the army shall not consist of more than _____ thousand men."

General Pinkney asked whether no troops were ever to be raised untill an attack should be made on us?

Mr. Gerry. if there be no restriction, a few States may establish a military Gov[ernmen]t.

(In response to Gerry's motion of this day that no standing army exceed 3,000 men ..., Washington is alleged to have suggested a counter-motion that "no foreign enemy should invade the United States at any time, with more than three thousand troops.")

Mr. Williamson, reminded him of Mr. Mason's motion for limiting the appropriation of revenue as the best guard in this case.

Mr. Langdon saw no room for Mr. Gerry's distrust of the Representatives of the people.

Mr. Dayton. preparations for war are generally made in peace; and a standing force of some sort may, for ought we know, become unavoidable. He should object to no restrictions consistent with these ideas.

[The Convention rejected the proposal to set a Constitutional limit on the size of the American army.]

August 24

[The Convention discussed a proposal authorizing the president to appoint military officers.] Mr. Sherman objected to the sentence "and shall appoint officers in all cases not otherwise provided for by this Constitution". He admitted it to be proper that many officers in the Executive Department should be so appointed—but contended that many ought not, as general officers in the Army in time of peace [and so on]. Herein lay the corruption in G[reat] Britain. If the Executive can model the army, he may set up an absolute Government; taking advantage of the close of a war and an army commanded by his creatures. [King] James [II of Britain] was not obeyed by his officers because they had been appointed by his predecessors not by himself [a critical factor in the success of Britain's "Glorious Revolution" of 1688 that overthrew the overbearing King James. [The Convention voted to clarify the language to prevent the president from creating new military offices that had not been authorized by Congress].

16.2 George Washington, "Farewell Address" (1796)

At the end of his second term as president, George Washington advised Americans to steer clear of foreign military entanglements so that the United States could develop in peace. For Washington, the United States "should have as little political connection as possible" with foreign nations such as Britain or France. As a nation insulated from European warfare by the Atlantic Ocean, the United States needed only to nurture its economy and trade to build its defenses. If the nation remained united and stayed out of foreign wars and focused on building its economic capacity, its strong economy would deter belligerent nations from attacking it. Note that Washington defended his controversial Neutrality Proclamation on grounds of American political development: it aimed "to gain time to our country to settle and mature its yet recent institutions. . . ."

September 19, 1796

Observe good faith and justice towards all nations; cultivate peace and harmony with all. Religion and morality enjoin this conduct; and can it be, that good policy does not equally enjoin it—It will be worthy of a free, enlightened, and at no distant period, a great nation, to give to mankind the magnanimous and too novel example of a people always guided by an exalted justice and benevolence.

... [N]othing is more essential than that permanent, inveterate antipathies against particular nations, and passionate attachments for others, should be excluded; and that, in place of them, just and amicable feelings towards all should be cultivated. The nation which indulges towards another a habitual hatred or a habitual fondness is in some degree a slave. It is a slave to its animosity or to its affection, either of which is sufficient to lead it astray from its duty and its interest. Antipathy in one nation against another disposes each more readily to offer insult and injury, to lay hold of slight causes of umbrage, and to be haughty and intractable, when accidental or trifling occasions of dispute occur. Hence, frequent collisions, obstinate, envenomed, and bloody contests. The nation, prompted by ill-will and resentment, sometimes impels to war the government, contrary to the best calculations of policy. The government sometimes participates in the national propensity, and adopts through passion what reason would reject; at other times it makes the animosity of the nation subservient to projects of hostility instigated by pride, ambition, and other sinister and pernicious motives. The peace often, sometimes perhaps the liberty, of nations, has been the victim.

... Against the insidious wiles of foreign influence (I conjure you to believe me, fellow-citizens) the jealousy of a free people ought to be constantly awake, since history and experience prove that foreign influence is one of the most baneful foes of republican government. But that jealousy to be useful must be impartial; else it becomes the instrument of the very influence to be avoided, instead of a defense against it. Excessive partiality for one foreign nation and excessive dislike of another cause those whom they actuate to see danger only on one side, and serve to veil and even second the arts of influence on the other. Real patriots who may resist the intrigues of the favorite are liable to become suspected and odious, while its tools and dupes usurp the applause and confidence of the people, to surrender their interests.

The great rule of conduct for us in regard to foreign nations is in extending our commercial relations, to have with them as little political connection as possible. So far as we have already formed engagements, let them be fulfilled with perfect good faith. Here let us stop. Europe has a set of primary interests which to us have none; or a very remote relation. Hence she must be engaged in frequent controversies, the causes of which are essentially foreign to our concerns. Hence, therefore, it must be unwise in us to implicate ourselves by artificial ties in the ordinary vicissitudes of her politics, or the ordinary combinations and collisions of her friendships or enmities.

Our detached and distant situation invites and enables us to pursue a different course. If we remain one people under an efficient government, the period is not far off when we may defy material injury from external annoyance; when we may take such an attitude as will cause the neutrality we may at any time resolve upon to be scrupulously respected; when belligerent nations, under the impossibility of making acquisitions upon us, will not lightly hazard the giving us provocation; when we may choose peace or war, as our interest, guided by justice, shall counsel.

Why forego the advantages of so peculiar a situation? Why quit our own to stand upon foreign ground? Why, by interweaving our destiny with that of any part of Europe, entangle our peace and prosperity in the toils of European ambition, rivalship, interest, humor or caprice?

It is our true policy to steer clear of permanent alliances with any portion of the foreign world; so far, I mean, as we are now at liberty to do it; for let me not be understood as capable of patronizing infidelity to existing engagements. I hold the maxim no less applicable to public than to private affairs, that honesty is always the best policy. I repeat it, therefore, let those engagements be observed in their genuine sense. But, in my opinion, it is unnecessary and would be unwise to extend them.

Taking care always to keep ourselves by suitable establishments on a respectable defensive posture, we may safely trust to temporary alliances for extraordinary emergencies.

Harmony, liberal intercourse with all nations, are recommended by policy, humanity, and interest. But even our commercial policy should hold an equal and impartial hand; neither seeking nor granting exclusive favors or preferences; consulting the natural course of things; diffusing and diversifying by gentle means the streams of commerce, but forcing nothing; establishing (with powers so disposed, in order to give trade a stable course, to define the rights of our merchants, and to enable the government to support them) conventional rules of intercourse, the best that present circumstances and mutual opinion will permit, but temporary, and liable to be from time to time abandoned or varied, as experience and circumstances shall dictate; constantly keeping in view that it is folly in one nation to look for disinterested favors from another; that it must pay with a portion of its independence for whatever it may accept under that character; that, by such acceptance, it may place itself in the condition of having given equivalents for nominal favors, and yet of being reproached with ingratitude for not giving more. There can be no greater error than to expect or calculate upon real favors from nation to nation. It is an illusion, which experience must cure, which a just pride ought to discard.

In offering to you, my countrymen, these counsels of an old and affectionate friend, I dare not hope they will make the strong and lasting impression I could wish; that they will control the usual current of the passions, or prevent our nation from running the course which has hitherto marked the destiny of nations. But, if I may even flatter myself that they may be productive of some partial benefit, some occasional good; that they may now and then recur to moderate the fury of party spirit, to warn against the mischiefs of foreign intrigue, to guard against the impostures of pretended patriotism; this hope will be a full recompense for the solicitude for your welfare, by which they have been dictated.

How far in the discharge of my official duties I have been guided by the principles which have been delineated, the public records and other evidences of my conduct must witness to you and to the world. To myself, the assurance of my own conscience is, that I have at least believed myself to be guided by them.

In relation to the still subsisting war in Europe, my proclamation [of neutrality] of the twenty-second of April, 1793, is the index of my plan. Sanctioned by your approving voice, and by that of your representatives in both houses of Congress, the spirit of that measure has continually governed me, uninfluenced by any attempts to deter or divert me from it.

After deliberate examination, with the aid of the best lights I could obtain, I was well satisfied that our country, under all the circumstances of the case, had a right to take, and was bound in duty and interest to take, a neutral position. Having taken it, I determined, as far as should depend upon me, to maintain it, with moderation, perseverance, and firmness.

The considerations which respect the right to hold this conduct, it is not necessary on this occasion to detail. I will only observe that, according to my understanding of the matter, that right, so far from being denied by any of the belligerent powers, has been virtually admitted by all.

The duty of holding a neutral conduct may be inferred, without anything more, from the obligation which justice and humanity impose on every nation, in cases in which it is free to act, to maintain inviolate the relations of peace and amity towards other nations.

The inducements of interest for observing that conduct will best be referred to your own reflections and experience. With me a predominant motive has been to endeavor to gain time to our country to settle and mature its yet recent institutions, and to progress without interruption to that degree of strength and consistency which is necessary to give it, humanly speaking, the command of its own fortunes . . .

16.3 Alexis de Tocqueville, "Why Democratic Nations Naturally Desire Peace, and Democratic Armies, War" (1840)

In *Democracy in America* (1835), French traveler and author Alexis de Tocqueville examined the "evils" and "advantages" of democracy, the safeguards put in place to protect against its excesses, and the dangers that remained. In this selection, Tocqueville reflected on democracy's influence on a society's preference for peace or war. American democracy, he argued, fosters a love of peace in the American people. The institution of the military, however, has opposite incentives. Military officers in a democratic army can advance in rank more quickly in war than in peace, which makes the military in a republic an organization more prone to war than peace. Within the following thirty years, American officers would get their opportunities—first in a war with Mexico, and then in the American Civil War.

The same interests, the same fears, the same passions that deter democratic nations from revolutions deter them also from war; the spirit of military glory and the spirit of revolution are weakened at the same time and by the same causes. The ever increasing numbers of men of property who are lovers of peace, the growth of personal wealth which war so rapidly consumes, the mildness of manners, the gentleness of heart, those tendencies to pity which are produced by the equality of conditions, that coolness of understanding which renders men comparatively insensible to the violent and poetical excitement of arms, all these causes concur to quench the military spirit. I think it may be admitted as a general and constant rule that among civilized nations the warlike passions will become more rare and less intense in proportion as social conditions are more equal.

War is nevertheless an occurrence to which all nations are subject, democratic nations as well as others. Whatever taste they may have for peace, they must hold themselves in readiness to repel aggression, or, in other words, they must have an army. Fortune, which has conferred so many peculiar benefits upon the inhabitants of the United States, has placed them in the midst of a wilderness, where they have, so to speak, no neighbors; a few thousand soldiers are sufficient for their wants. But this is peculiar to America, not to democracy.

The equality of conditions and the manners as well as the institutions resulting from it do not exempt a democratic people from the necessity of standing armies, and their armies always exercise a powerful influence over their fate. It is therefore of singular importance to inquire what are the natural propensities of the men of whom these armies are composed.

Among aristocratic nations, especially among those in which birth is the only source of rank, the same inequality exists in the army as in the nation; the officer is noble, the soldier is a serf; the one is naturally called upon to command, the other to obey. In aristocratic armies the private soldier's ambition is therefore circumscribed within very narrow limits. Nor has the ambition of the officer an unlimited range. An aristocratic body not only forms a part of the scale of ranks in the nation, but contains a scale of ranks within itself; the members of whom it is composed are placed one above another in a particular and unvarying manner. Thus one man is born to the command of a regiment, another to that of a company. When once they have reached the utmost object of their hopes, they stop of their own accord and remain contented with their lot.

There is, besides, a strong cause that in aristocracies weakens the officer's desire of promotion. Among aristocratic nations an officer, independently of his rank in the army, also occupies an elevated rank in society; the former is almost always, in his eyes, only an appendage to the latter. A nobleman who embraces the profession of arms follows it less from motives of ambition than from a sense of the duties imposed on him by his birth. He enters the army in order to find an honorable employment for the idle years of his youth and to be able to bring back to his home and his peers some honorable recollections of military life; but his principal object is not to obtain by that profession either property, distinction, or power, for he possesses these advantages in his own right and enjoys them without leaving his home.

In democratic armies all the soldiers may become officers, which makes the desire of promotion general and immeasurably extends the bounds of military ambition. The officer, on his part, sees nothing that naturally and necessarily stops him at one grade more than at another; and each grade has immense importance in his eyes because his rank in society almost always depends on his rank in the army. Among democratic nations it often happens that an officer has no property but his pay and no distinction but that of military honors; consequently, as often as his duties change, his fortune changes and he becomes, as it were, a new man. What was only an appendage to his position in aristocratic armies has thus become the main point, the basis of his whole condition.

Under the old French monarchy officers were always called by their titles of nobility; they are now always called by the title of their military rank. This little change in the forms of language suffices to show that a great revolution has taken place in the constitution of society and in that of the army.

In democratic armies the desire of advancement is almost universal: it is ardent, tenacious, perpetual; it is strengthened by all other desires and extinguished only with life itself. But it is easy to see that, of all armies in the world, those in which advancement must be slowest in time of peace are the armies of democratic countries. As the number of commissions is naturally limited while the number of competitors is almost unlimited, and as the strict law of equality is over all alike, none can make rapid progress; many can make no progress at all. Thus the desire of advancement is greater and the opportunities of advancement fewer there than elsewhere. All the ambitious spirits of a democratic army are consequently ardently desirous of war, because war makes vacancies and warrants the violation of that law of seniority which is the sole privilege natural to democracy.

We thus arrive at this singular consequence, that, of all armies, those most ardently desirous of war are democratic armies, and of all nations, those most fond of peace are democratic nations; and what makes these facts still more extraordinary is that these contrary effects are produced at the same time by the principle of equality.

All the members of the community, being alike, constantly harbor the wish and discover the possibility of changing their condition and improving their welfare; this makes them fond of peace, which is favorable to industry and allows every man to pursue his own little undertakings to their completion. On the other hand, this same equality makes soldiers dream of fields of battle, by increasing the value of military honors in the eyes of those who follow the profession of arms and by rendering those honors accessible to all. In either case the restlessness of the heart is the same, the taste for enjoyment is insatiable, the ambition of success as great; the means of gratifying it alone are different.

These opposite tendencies of the nation and the army expose democratic communities to great dangers. When a military spirit forsakes a people, the profession of arms immediately ceases to be held in honor and military men fall to the lowest rank of the public servants; they are little esteemed and no longer understood. The reverse of what takes place in aristocratic ages then occurs; the men who enter the army are no longer those of the highest, but of the lowest class. Military ambition is indulged only when no other is possible. Hence arises a circle of cause and consequence from which it is difficult to escape: the best part of the nation shuns the military profession because that profession is not honored, and the profession is not honored because the best part of the nation has ceased to follow it.

It is then no matter of surprise that democratic armies are often restless, ill-tempered, and dissatisfied with their lot, although their physical condition is commonly far better and their discipline less strict than in other countries. The soldier feels that he occupies an inferior position, and his wounded pride either stimulates his taste for hostilities that would render his services necessary or gives him a desire for revolution, during which he may hope to win by force of arms the political influence and personal importance now denied him.

The composition of democratic armies makes this last-mentioned danger much to be feared. In democratic communities almost every man has some property to preserve; but democratic armies are generally led by men without property, most of whom have little to lose in civil broils. The bulk of the nation is naturally much more afraid of revolutions than in the ages of aristocracy, but the leaders of the army much less so.

Moreover, as among democratic nations (to repeat what I have just remarked) the wealthiest, best-educated, and ablest men seldom adopt the military profession, the army, taken collectively, eventually forms a small nation by itself, where the mind is less enlarged and habits are more rude than in the nation at large. Now, this small uncivilized nation has arms in its possession and alone knows how to use them; for, indeed, the pacific temper of the community increases the danger to which a democratic people is exposed from the military and turbulent spirit of the army. Nothing is so dangerous as an army in the midst of an unwarlike nation; the excessive love of the whole community for quiet continually puts the constitution at the mercy of the soldiery.

It may therefore be asserted, generally speaking, that if democratic nations are naturally prone to peace from their interests and their propensities, they are constantly drawn to war and revolutions by their armies. Military revolutions, which are scarcely ever to be apprehended in aristocracies, are always to be dreaded among democratic nations. These perils must be reckoned among the most formidable that beset their future fate, and the attention of statesmen should be sedulously applied to find a remedy for the evil.

When a nation perceives that it is inwardly affected by the restless ambition of its army, the first thought which occurs is to give this inconvenient ambition an object by going to war. I do not wish to speak ill of war: war almost always enlarges the mind of a people and raises their character. In some cases it is the only check to the excessive growth of certain propensities that naturally spring out of the equality of conditions, and it must be considered as a necessary corrective to certain inveterate diseases to which democratic communities are liable.

War has great advantages, but we must not flatter ourselves that it can diminish the danger I have just pointed out. That peril is only suspended by it, to return more fiercely when the war is over; for armies are much more impatient of peace after having tasted military exploits. War could be a remedy only for a people who were always athirst for military glory.

... The remedy for the vices of the army is not to be found in the army itself, but in the country. Democratic nations are naturally afraid of disturbance and of despotism; the object is to turn these natural instincts into intelligent, deliberate, and lasting tastes. When men have at last learned to make a peaceful and profitable use of freedom and have felt its blessings, when they have conceived a manly love of order and have freely submitted themselves to discipline, these same men, if they follow the profession of arms, bring into it, unconsciously and almost against their will, these same habits and manners. The general spirit of the nation, being infused into the spirit peculiar to the army, tempers the opinions and desires engendered by military life, or represses them by the mighty force of public opinion. Teach the citizens to be educated, orderly, firm, and free and the soldiers will be disciplined and obedient.

16.4 David C. Hendrickson, "American Internationalism" (2009)

Historian David Hendrickson argued that many American leaders always have had strong interest in the international role of the United States and the best way to organize international relations. For Hendrickson, the union of the states in the Constitution provided a template for American engagement in the world. The Constitution created the world's largest free trade zone among the American states. Similarly, the new nation would benefit from free trade with the other nations (a point George Washington made in his Farewell Address). All sought a peaceful world in which commerce and trade could flourish (to the benefit of the U.S.). Such ideas about internationalism under law have endured, and since World War II they have influenced American leaders to champion durable institutions and international agreements for advancing peaceful economic growth globally. These include the United Nations, the World Bank, the International Monetary Fund, the General Agreement on Tariffs and Trade (GATT), the North American Free Trade Agreement (NAFTA) and the World Trade Organization (WTO), among many others.

AMERICAN INTERNATIONALISM, as it came of age in the first four decades of the twentieth century, was associated with a cluster of related ideas. It was committed to the peaceful settlement of disputes and held forth the ultimate ideal of a world at peace under the reign of law. It saw freer commerce as the indispensable means of maximizing wealth and making the nations useful to one another. It identified liberal democracy as the preferred method for organizing political life within nations and saw leadership in a partnership of democratic nations as the primary basis of America's world role. It emphasized both independence and union, recognizing that each of the peoples was entitled to rule itself according to its own forms and fastening on aggression as the key specter against which international society must unite. It envisaged forms of cooperative partnership as against the nightmares of international anarchy and imperial domination. It "rejected the idea of peace by universal empire or by the diplomatic juggle of balance of power," adopting instead "the ideal of the cooperative peace—the ideal which is the great contribution of the Americas to world thought."[1]

The quintessential expressions of the internationalist ethos in the twentieth century were Woodrow Wilson's embrace of the League of Nations and Franklin Roosevelt's championing of the United Nations, but it would be a mistake to identify internationalism solely with Wilson and Roosevelt or the international institutions they promoted. There were Republicans, such as William Howard Taft and Elihu Root, who also considered themselves internationalists. Internationalists divided on the portion of sovereignty or untrammeled discretion that would need to be ceded to any international body, they divided between "particularists" and "universalists" in their conception of the international community, and they divided over the degree to which the United States must pledge itself to the use of U.S. military force (as against economic sanctions and public opinion) in vindication of internationalist ideals. Despite these divergences, which made for a fairly big tent, internationalists held in common the vision of a peaceful world ordered by law and believed that America must play a vital role in bringing it about. Trying to put his finger on the phenomenon, George Kennan called it the "legalistic-moralistic approach to international relations" in his famous 1951 lectures on American diplomacy, and he noted that it had run "like a red skein through our foreign policy of the last fifty years." The tradition, Kennan observed, had in it "something of the old emphasis on arbitration treaties, something of the Hague Conferences and schemes for universal disarmament, something of the more ambitious American concepts of the role of international law, something of the League of Nations and the United Nations, something of the Kellogg Pact, something of the idea of a universal 'Article 51' pact, something of the belief in World Law and World Government." The essence of the idea, which

Kennan shrewdly located in the historic experience of federal union, lay in the belief "that it should be possible to suppress the chaotic and dangerous aspirations of governments in the international field by the acceptance of some system of legal rules and restraints."[2]

As Kennan recognized, internationalism need not take a universal form, and to identify it simply with enthusiasts of the League of Nations or the United Nations is too restrictive an interpretation of the phenomenon. In the first part of the twentieth century, American internationalists imagined or projected various communities—the community of English-speaking peoples, a universal association for collective security, a Western Hemisphere community, an Atlantic Community, a Great Power Concert—and the study of internationalism must fully register that variety. But if our understanding of the internationalist idea must be broadened in some respects, it must be narrowed in another. Unless there is a conception of mutual exchange and reciprocal benefit within these various communities, sustained by pledges of good faith and commitment, internationalism can hardly be said to be present.

The internationalist insists that there is a community beyond the nation, within which good faith, cooperation, and law are deemed essential. Internationalism is distinct from cosmopolitanism on the one hand and nationalism and imperialism on the other. Whereas cosmopolitanism postulates a global society in which national identities and loyalties are abandoned, internationalism accepts that national loyalties are and will continue to be important. The internationalist does not seek a world from which nations are absent, but rather one in which they are enabled to flourish. Commitment to internationalism does not require states to cease pursuing their national interest, but only to pursue this interest in an enlightened way—that is, by taking account of the interests of others and requiring that the national interest be pursued within the limitations of justice and good faith. It is "the ideology of international bonding."[3]

Internationalism also stands in sharp opposition to the characteristic claims of nationalism and imperialism. The internationalist rejects a world in which egotistical nations pursue their interest without regard to a common international interest in the principles of a just and stable world order. That is the way of anarchy, a condition that invariably gives succor to forces at odds with free government. Equally rejected, however, is the proposition that the world of anarchy can or should be mastered through imperial methods. From an internationalist perspective, any condition of unbound power, such as "empire" frequently connotes, is a remedy as fatal as the disease.

The most characteristic idea in the architecture of American diplomatic history is that internationalism did not make its appearance until the twentieth century. It is, so to speak, a Johnny-come-lately whose impact before 1900 was minimal. Whereas nationalism and imperialism are well-traveled historical routes, internationalism has been viewed as almost wholly a phenomenon of the twentieth century. . . . Once we were "isolationist," then we became "internationalist."[4]

These accounts are not wrong in stressing the revolutionary and epochal change represented by the abandonment in the 1940s of America's historic political detachment from overseas alliances, but they are wrong in dismissing the significance of internationalist currents in what may be termed the long nineteenth century (that is, from 1789 to 1914). In fact, all the big themes registered in twentieth-century internationalism—the league of free peoples, the peaceful settlement of disputes, the "commitment to the idea of commitment,"[5] the aspiration to bring the international anarchy under the "empire of law," the self-determination of nations, the preference for liberal democracy, the advantages of mutual exchange—are plainly registered in the eighteenth and nineteenth centuries. The normative order to which American internationalists appealed in the twentieth century had very deep roots in the American past. . . . .

The American statesman who contributed most to the development of American internationalism in the twentieth century, Woodrow Wilson, was himself emphatic on his debt to traditional American beliefs of a just world order. With every fiber of his being, he claimed in his great speaking tour on behalf of the League of Nations, he "shouted out" the traditions of the United States. Wilson once observed that because America was "compounded out of the peoples of the world her problem is largely a problem of union all the time, a problem of compounding out of many elements a single triumphal force."[6] That, in a nutshell, was his idea of the League of Nations. Historical judgments of Wilson emphasize the sheer novelty of his internationalism, but Wilson saw himself as a conservative who sought to apply old principles to new circumstances.[7]

One legacy of the eighteenth and nineteenth centuries was the traditional American commitment to international law. This "old internationalism" professed fidelity to the law of nations—the mother of multilateral norms—and was thoroughly committed to the "society of states" tradition. American diplomats attached vital significance to the law of nations in various spheres, especially the law of neutrality. They also sought to infuse into the law of nations "a spirit," in James Madison's words, "which may diminish the frequency or circumscribe the calamities of war." The "great increase which has taken place in the intercourse among civilized and commercial states," as Daniel Webster noted, had connected the United States "with other nations, and given us a high concern in the pres-ervation of those salutary principles upon which that intercourse is founded. We have as clear an interest in international law, as individuals have in the laws of society." This posture is distinguishable, on the one hand, from an outlook, customarily identified with realpolitik, that sees the interstate world as an anarchy in which moral and legal restraints are irrelevant; and, on the other, from a cosmopolitan or revolutionary outlook that looks forward to the transcendence of the state system and its replacement by a new ordering of human relations. With but few exceptions this commitment to "the constitutional tradition in diplomacy" may be considered the characteristic worldview of American diplomatists in the eighteenth and nineteenth centuries, and the embrace of it by twentieth-century American internationalists requires no special explanation.[8]

A second feature of eighteenth- and nineteenth-century internationalism was the commitment to free trade. Throwing open the doors of commerce and breaking off its shackles was a deep impulse of the American Revolution. Among the bundle of argu-ments for free trade throughout the eighteenth and nineteenth centuries was the contri-bution it would make to repressing otherwise pronounced tendencies toward war and conflict. This vision of a liberal trading regime based on mutual interest and reciprocal benefit, and excluding all ideas of domination, was thought to offer a great contribution to international peace. America, as John Adams expressed that early faith, "will grow with astonishing Rapidity and England France and every other Nation in Europe will be the better for her prosperity. Peace which is her dear Delight will be her Wealth and Glory."[9]

These free trade visions, offering "a sort of Protestantism" in political economy, were sharply dented after the American Revolution by Europe's still deep attachment to the protective system, and there arose a school of American protectionists, whose early leaders were Alexander Hamilton and Henry Clay, that challenged the verities of the free trade gospel. In the confines of what might, from one perspective, appear the driest subject on the face of the earth—the discussion of the tariff—there arose a profound and fascinating argument concerning the relationship among free trade, protection, and peace, over which nationalists and internationalists waged ferocious battles.[10] Though the protectionists emerged as dominant during and after the Civil War, the American union was sufficiently big and diverse as to itself constitute an argument for free trade within the confines of an enlarged political community. "Inside of the union," noted William Graham Sumner in 1899, "we have established the grandest experiment in absolute free trade that has ever existed." The commitment to a vast free trade area behind high protective tariffs was the pattern that emerged after 1865, and it was, as Sumner observed, a very peculiar combination, "an interesting result of the presence in men's minds of two opposite philosophies, the adjustment of which has never yet been fought out."[11]

Though these ideas of the society of states and of free trade attest to the existence of strong internationalist currents in the eighteenth and nineteenth centuries, the phenomenon that most attracted to it the central perturbations of internationalist thought was the American federal union. We saw in the preface how the categories of thought radiating outward from the union had a decidedly internationalist tenor, in which the problem of cooperation among refractory states was of fundamental importance. Ideas commonly thought of as a special preserve of twentieth-century internationalism are given continual registration in this context. While the name—internationalism—did not yet exist, just about everything that came to be associated with the internationalist idea did exist. But instead of a "security community" or "international regime," the thing was called a "federative system."[12]

At the root of "the federal principle," writes one political scientist, was the notion of a covenant or *foedus* (its etymological root). This and "synonymous ideas of promise, commitment, undertaking, or obligating, vowing and plighting one's word" were joined together with two other things: "the idea of cooperation, reciprocity, mutuality," and "the need for some measure of predictability, expectation, constancy, and reliability in human relations."[13] These three concepts—commitment, reciprocity, predictability—are closely associated with contemporary ideas of international cooperation, and they were endlessly elaborated in debates over the nature and character of federal union from 1776 to 1861. A similar definition (serviceable, like the previous one, for "internationalism" as well) sees the federative principle as emphasizing "the political relation of adjustment among equals rather than the political relationships of inferiority and superiority, and methods of law rather than methods of force."[14] Both federalism and internationalism ... propose union partly to aggregate power and partly to maintain distinctness. Each may be conceived as "an exercise in the difficult art of separation," as a "coming together to stay apart," as proposing devices "to cope with the problem of how distinct communities can live a common life together without ceasing to be distinct communities."[15] ...

... That the making of the American Constitution formed a template for the problems of world order was an oft-reiterated thought in the second decade of the twentieth century, as well known then as the "clash of civilizations" or the "end of history" theses are today. The inescapable reality, it seemed to internationalists, was that the threat of international anarchy or imperial domination, in a world now made suddenly compact by economic interdependence and revolutions in military technology and communications, required a union of some kind that would tame these malign forces of international anarchy and world empire. All internationalists saw that parallel and believed their world in need of union as an antidote to international anarchy and imperial despotism.

This sense of déjà vu all over again, that the breakdown of the European and world order had returned the United States to its founding predicament, was basic to the internationalist sensibility. As Horace Kallen, a member of Wilson's "Inquiry," put it in 1918, the independent states of America after 1776 "were in precisely the same position and confronted precisely the same problems, in principle, as the present states and governments of the world." James Brown Scott, the eminent authority on international law, gave voice to the same idea. Scott himself was no enthusiast of a federal state for the world, but he saw that the makers of the American Constitution had in fact mapped out the entire terrain regarding the possibilities and limits of international cooperation. Though acknowledging that the "Society of Nations may not be willing, and indeed even with good will may not be able, to go so far now or at any time as have the States forming the American Union," he insisted that "however many steps they may take or however few toward the closer Union, the experience of the framers of the Constitution who traversed the entire path should be as a lamp to their feet."[16]

As fraught with meaning as that parallel was, it was associated with one very troubling paradox. The more one traded on the analogy between the circumstances of 1787 and 1919, the more problematic the entire enterprise appeared. The problem, as Kallen observed, was in principle the same, but the solution—if there was a solution—would have to be different. However loose the old federal union was intended to be at the beginning, it had become much closer over time, and few wanted a degree of intimacy within "the civilized powers" or "the free world" that approached a common nationality. Certainly the American people did not want that. Off the table, therefore, was any international commitment that made a union as tight in its bonds as the Constitution of 1787—that is, which created state institutions and a community from which secession was, or might prove to be, impossible. Between the exigent need for a union among the peace-loving nations and the no less obvious foreclosure of a world state, American internationalism would have to carve out a new path. In responding to the potentialities and necessities of America's new world role in the twentieth century, the unionist paradigm was neither abandoned nor uncritically accepted, but rather modified and restated to fit the new circumstances of the case.[17]

NOTES

1. A.A. Berle Jr., assistant secretary of state, "No, Says Berle," *New York Times,* January 14, 1940.
2. Kennan, *American Diplomacy,* 95–96. . . . A good short introduction, though at odds with my approach in certain respects, is Warren F. Kuehl and Gary B. Ostrower, "Internationalism," *Encyclopedia of American Foreign Policy,* 2nd ed., ed. Alexander Decode et al. (New York, 2002).
3. Cars ten Holbraad, *Internationalism and Nationalism in European Political Thought* (New York, 2003), I.
4. For various expressions of this pervasive theme, see, for example, Kuehl, *Seeking World Order;* McDougall, *Promised Land;* and Prestowitz, *Rogue Nation.* . . .
5. A felicitous expression of Ninkovich, *Modernity and Power,* 173.
6. Memorial Day Address, May 30, 1916, *Wilson Speeches,* 197–98.
7. Burke's idea of "conservative reform" always had great appeal to Wilson. . . . The towering figures of early twentieth-century diplomacy, Theodore Roosevelt and Woodrow Wilson, are invariably seen as anticipations of things to come later, and justly so. But there is value also in seeing them from the vantage point of the long nineteenth century. Wilson, Roosevelt and

Henry Cabot Lodge were keen students of American history and had spent years absorbing its debates and contestations. . . . .

8. Madison, Eighth Annual Message, December 3, 1816; Webster, "The Revolution in Greece," January 19, 1824, *Webster Works* (1890), 3: 75. . . .

9. John Adams to James Warren, *Adams Papers*, 6: 348. See further Onuf and Onuf, *Federal Union*, 103–08.

10. The definitive review, though stopping at 1861, is Onuf and Onuf, *Nations, Markets, and War.* . . .

11. William Graham Sumner, *War, and Other Essays* (New Haven, CT, 1911), 317. . . .

12. On "security communities" and "international regimes," see G. John Ikenberry, *After Victory: Institutions, Strategic Restraint, and the Rebuilding of Order after Major Wars* (Princeton, NJ, 2001), and Helga Haftendorn, Robert O. Keohane and Celeste A. Wallender, eds., *Imperfect Unions: Security Institutions over Time and Space* (New York, 1999).

13. Davis, *Federal Principle*, 38, 3, 215–16.

14. Robert C. Binkley, *Realism and Nationalism, 1852-1871* (New York, 1935), XIX.

15. Samuel V. LaSelva, *The Moral Foundations of Canadian Federalism* (Montreal, 1996), 40, 46.

16. Horace Kallen, *The Structure of a Lasting Peace: An Inquiry into the Motives of War and Peace* (Boston, 1918), 136–37; Lewis S. Feuer, "Horace M. Kallen on War and Peace," *Modern Judaism* 4 (1984): 201; James Brown Scott, *The United States of America: A Study in International Organization* (New York, 1920); and idem, *James Madison's Notes of Debates in the Federal Convention of 1787 and Their Relation to a More Perfect Society of Nations* (New York, 1918). This essential continuity is emphasized by Daniel Deudney, *Bounding Power*, 186–87, who argues that the liberal internationalist agenda advanced by Wilson was "Madisonianism in the context of global interdependence . . . the continuation of isolationist republicanism in interdependent circumstances." . . .

17. The cluster of values I am identifying with union, the federal principle, and internationalism is also registered in liberalism and republicanism. . . .

16.5 Presidential Policy from the Cold War to the War on Terror

Presidents Harry Truman (1945–1953), George W. Bush (2001–2009) and Barack Obama (2009–) all confronted monumental foreign policy problems. These excerpts from their key speeches demonstrate the critical role that past historical experience plays in current policy choices. As Truman, Bush and Obama interpret the problems they face, each tried to explain their root causes to the American people. Truman's comments were typical of Cold War thinking. The problem was the threat of relentless expansion by communism, a problem that led to American involvement in the Korean War (1950–1953). The remedy, said Truman, is vigilance to prevent another Pearl Harbor, the expansion of the American military to meet the expansion of Soviet military power, and the development of solidarity among democratic nations opposed to communism. Consistent with the Truman Doctrine of containment (1947), the forces of democracy must stave off communist expansion anywhere in the world (including Southeast Asia, already a concern for American policy makers more than a decade before ground troops). For Bush, who had to deal with the terrorist attacks of 9/11 during his first year in office, the problem was terrorism, which, like communism, is driven by a totalitarian ideology. Just like the Cold War, the United States must be prepared to confront the threat across the globe, to preempt terrorist attacks and to be constantly vigilant to a very wide range of dangers. For Obama in 2013, the threat of a strong Al-Qaeda organization had receded, but the United States faced the more diverse terrorist threats that already occurred before 9/11. The remedy is not a perpetual, "boundless, 'global war on terror,' " or massive military intervention, such as occurred in the tragic Vietnam War. Congress should cut back on the Authorization to Use Military Force, enacted three days after 9/11 to give President Bush broad latitude to use military force to combat terrorism. Instead, if other nations are not capable of dealing with Al-Qaeda and its affiliates within their borders, the United States must pursue targeted, surgical strikes against these terrorists.

President Harry S. Truman, "The State of the Union" (1952)

Peace depends upon the free nations sticking together, and making a combined effort to check aggression and prevent war. In this respect, 1951 was a year of great achievement.

In Korea the forces of the United Nations turned back the Chinese Communist invasion—and did it without widening the area of conflict. The action of the United Nations in Korea has been a powerful deterrent to a third world war. However, the situation in Korea remains very hazardous. The outcome of the armistice negotiation still remains uncertain.

In Indochina and Malaya, our aid has helped our allies to hold back the Communist advance, although there are signs of further trouble in that area....

The United Nations, the world's greatest hope for peace, has come through a year of trial stronger and more useful than ever....

During this past year we added more than a million men and women to our Armed Forces. The total is now nearly 3½ million. We have made rapid progress in the field of atomic weapons. We have turned out billion worth of military supplies and equipment, three times as much as the year before....

The outstanding fact to note on the debit side of the ledger is that the Soviet Union, in 1951, continued to expand its military production and increase its already excessive military power.

... It is still producing more war planes than the free nations. It has set off two more atomic explosions. The world still walks in the shadow of another world war....

Taking the good and bad together, we have made real progress this last year along the road to peace. We have increased the power and unity of the free world. And while we were doing this, we have avoided world war on the one hand, and appeasement on the other. This is a hard road to follow, but the events of the last year show that it is the right road to peace.

We cannot expect to complete the job overnight. The free nations may have to maintain for years the larger military forces needed to deter aggression. We must build steadily, over a period of years, toward political solidarity and economic progress among the free nations in all parts of the world....

... [I]f there are any among us who think we ought to ease up in the fight for peace, I want to remind them of three things—just three things.

First: The threat of world war is still very real. We had one Pearl Harbor—let's not get caught off guard again. If you don't think the threat of Communist armies is real, talk to some of our men back from Korea.

Second: If the United States had to try to stand alone against a Soviet-dominated world, it would destroy the life we know and the ideals we hold dear. Our allies are essential to us, just as we are essential to them. The more shoulders there are to bear the burden the lighter that burden will be.

Third: The things we believe in most deeply are under relentless attack. We have the great responsibility of saving the basic moral and spiritual values of our civilization. We have started out well—with a program for peace that is unparalleled in history. If we believe in ourselves and the faith we profess, we will stick to that job until it is victoriously finished. . . .

We went into Korea because we knew that Communist aggression had to be met firmly if freedom was to be preserved in the world. We went into the fight to save the Republic of Korea, a free country, established under the United Nations. These are our aims. We will not give up until we attain them.

Meanwhile, we must continue to strengthen the forces of freedom throughout the world. . . .

In Europe we must go on helping our friends and allies to build up their military forces. This means we must send weapons in large volume to our European allies. I have directed that weapons for Europe be given a very high priority. Economic aid is necessary, too, to supply the margin of difference between success and failure in making Europe a strong partner in our joint defense.

In Asia the new Communist empire is a daily threat to millions of people. The peoples of Asia want to be free to follow their own way of life. They want to preserve their culture and their traditions against communism, just as much as we want to preserve ours. They are laboring under terrific handicaps—poverty, ill health, feudal systems of land ownership, and the threat of internal subversion or external attack. We can and we must increase our help to them.

This means military aid, especially to those places like Indochina which might be hardest hit by some new Communist attack. . . .

Turning from our foreign policies, let us consider the jobs we have here at home as a part of our program for peace. The first of these jobs is to move ahead full steam on the defense program.

Our objective is to have a well-equipped active defense force large enough—in concert with the forces of our allies—to deter aggression and to inflict punishing losses on the enemy immediately if we should be attacked. This active force must be backed by adequate reserves, and by the plants and tools to turn out the tremendous quantities of new weapons that would be needed if war came. We are not building an active force adequate to carry on full scale war, but we are putting ourselves in a position to mobilize very rapidly if we have to.

As a part of our program to keep our country strong, we are determined to preserve the financial strength of the Government. This means high taxes over the next few years. We must see to it that these taxes are shared among the people as fairly as possible. . . .

President George W. Bush, Remarks at the Ribbon-Cutting Ceremony for the Air Force One Pavilion [at the Reagan Library] (2005)

... At the beginning of his presidency, Ronald Reagan declared that the years ahead would be great ones "for the cause of freedom and the spread of civilization." He dismissed communism as "a bizarre chapter in human history whose last pages were being written." For eight years he acted on that conviction, and shortly after he left office, the Berlin Wall came down, the "Evil Empire" collapsed, and the cause of liberty prevailed in the Cold War. ...

Because of Ronald Reagan's leadership, America prevailed in the twentieth century's great struggle of wills. And now in this new century, our freedom is once again being tested by determined enemies. The terrorists who attacked us on September the 11th, 2001, are followers of a radical and violent ideology. They exploit the religion of Islam to serve a violent political vision, the establishment of a totalitarian empire that denies all political and religious freedom. These extremists distort the idea of jihad into a call for terrorist murder against Christians and Jews and Hindus, and against Muslims from other traditions who they regard as heretics.

Like the ideology of communism, our new enemy is elitist, led by a self-appointed vanguard of Islamic militants that presume to speak for the Muslim masses. Like the ideology of communism, our new enemy teaches that the innocent can be murdered to serve a political vision. Like the ideology of communism, our new enemy pursues totalitarian aims. Like the ideology of communism, our new enemy is dismissive of free peoples, claiming that men and women who live in liberty are weak and decadent. And like the ideology of communism, Islamic radicalism is doomed to fail.

It will fail because it undermines the freedom and creativity that makes human progress possible and human societies successful. The only thing modern about our enemy's vision is the weapons they want to use against us. The rest of their grim vision is defined by a warped image of the past, a declaration of war on the idea of progress, itself. And whatever lies ahead in the war against this ideology, the outcome is not in doubt: Those who despise freedom and progress have condemned themselves to isolation, decline, and collapse. Because free peoples believe in the future, free peoples will own the future.

We didn't ask for this global struggle, but we are answering history's call with confidence and a comprehensive strategy. We're working to prevent the attacks of terrorist networks before they occur. We're determined to deny weapons of mass destruction to outlaw regimes and to their terrorist allies who would use them without hesitation. We're depriving radical groups of support and sanctuary from outlaw regimes. We're stopping the militants from gaining control of any nation which they would use as a home base and a launching pad for terror. And we're draining the militants of future recruits by replacing hatred and resentment with democracy and hope and freedom across the broader Middle East.

We will prevail in the war on terror, because this generation is determined to meet the threats of our time. We understand our duty; we understand our responsibility to the American people. There will be tough moments ahead on this path to victory. Yet, we have confidence in our cause because we have seen America face down brutal enemies before. We have confidence in our cause because we have seen the power of freedom to overcome the dark ideologies of tyranny and terror. And we have confidence in our cause because we believe, as President Ronald Reagan did, that freedom is "one of the deepest and noblest aspirations of the human spirit."

President Barack Obama, Remarks at the National Defense University (2013)

... Americans are deeply ambivalent about war, but having fought for our independence, we know a price must be paid for freedom. From the Civil War to our struggle against fascism, on through the long twilight struggle of the Cold War, battlefields have changed and technology has evolved. But our commitment to constitutional principles has weathered every war, and every war has come to an end.

With the collapse of the Berlin Wall, a new dawn of democracy took hold abroad, and a decade of peace and prosperity arrived here at home. And for a moment, it seemed the 21st century would be a tranquil time. And then, on September 11, 2001, we were shaken out of complacency. Thousands were taken from us, as clouds of fire and metal and ash descended upon a sun-filled morning. This was a different kind of war. No armies came to our shores, and our military was not the principal target. Instead, a group of terrorists came to kill as many civilians as they could.

... [M]ake no mistake, our nation is still threatened by terrorists. From Benghazi to Boston, we have been tragically reminded of that truth. But we have to recognize that the threat has shifted and evolved from the one that came to our shores on 9/11. With a decade of experience now to draw from, this is the moment to ask ourselves hard questions—about the nature of today's threats and how we should confront them.

... For over the last decade, our nation has spent well over a trillion dollars on war, helping to explode our deficits and constraining our ability to nation-build here at home. Our service members and their families have sacrificed far more on our behalf. Nearly 7,000 Americans have made the ultimate sacrifice. Many more have left a part of themselves on the battlefield, or brought the shadows of battle back home. From our use of drones to the detention of terrorist suspects, the decisions that we are making now will define the type of nation—and world—that we leave to our children.

So America is at a crossroads. We must define the nature and scope of this struggle, or else it will define us. We have to be mindful of James Madison's warning that "No nation could preserve its freedom in the midst of continual warfare." Neither I, nor any President, can promise the total defeat of terror. We will never erase the evil that lies in the hearts of some human beings, nor stamp out every danger to our open society. But what we can do— what we must do—is dismantle networks that pose a direct danger to us, and make it less likely for new groups to gain a foothold, all the while maintaining the freedoms and ideals that we defend. And to define that strategy, we have to make decisions based not on fear, but on hard-earned wisdom. That begins with understanding the current threat that we face.

... [T]he current threat [is] lethal yet less capable al Qaeda affiliates; threats to diplomatic facilities and businesses abroad; homegrown extremists. This is the future of terrorism. We have to take these threats seriously, and do all that we can to confront them. But as we shape our response, we have to recognize that the scale of this threat closely resembles the types of attacks we faced before 9/11.

Moreover, we have to recognize that ... [m]ost, though not all, of the terrorism we faced is fueled by a common ideology—a belief by some extremists that Islam is in conflict with the United States and the West, and that violence against Western targets, including civilians, is justified in pursuit of a larger cause. Of course, this ideology is based on a lie, for the United States is not at war with Islam. And this ideology is rejected by the vast majority of Muslims, who are the most frequent victims of terrorist attacks.

I want to discuss . . . the components of such a comprehensive counterterrorism strategy.

First, we must finish the work of defeating al Qaeda and its associated forces [in Afghanistan].

Beyond Afghanistan, we must define our effort not as a boundless "global war on terror," but rather as a series of persistent, targeted efforts to dismantle specific networks of violent extremists that threaten America. In many cases, this will involve partnerships with other countries. . . .

. . . But despite our strong preference for the detention and prosecution of terrorists, sometimes this approach is foreclosed. Al Qaeda and its affiliates try to gain foothold in some of the most distant and unforgiving places on Earth. . . . In some of these places—such as parts of Somalia and Yemen—the state only has the most tenuous reach into the territory. In other cases, the state lacks the capacity or will to take action. . . .

So it is in this context that the United States has taken lethal, targeted action against al Qaeda and its associated forces, including with remotely piloted aircraft commonly referred to as drones. . . . [O]ur actions are effective. . . . Moreover, America's actions are legal. . . .

And yet, . . . [t]o say a military tactic is legal, or even effective, is not to say it is wise or moral in every instance. For the same human progress that gives us the technology to strike half a world away also demands the discipline to constrain that power—or risk abusing it. [O]ver the last four years, my administration has worked vigorously to establish a framework that governs our use of force against terrorists—insisting upon clear guidelines, oversight and accountability that is now codified in Presidential Policy Guidance that I signed yesterday. . . .

Beyond the Afghan theater, we only target al Qaeda and its associated forces. And even then, the use of drones is heavily constrained. America does not take strikes when we have the ability to capture individual terrorists; our preference is always to detain, interrogate, and prosecute . . .

[I]t is a hard fact that U.S. strikes have resulted in civilian casualties, a risk that exists in every war. And for the families of those civilians, no words or legal construct can justify their loss. For me, and those in my chain of command, those deaths will haunt us as long as we live, just as we are haunted by the civilian casualties that have occurred throughout conventional fighting in Afghanistan and Iraq.

But as Commander-in-Chief, I must weigh these heartbreaking tragedies against the alternatives. To do nothing in the face of terrorist networks would invite far more civilian casualties—not just in our cities at home and our facilities abroad, but also in the very places like Sana'a and Kabul and Mogadishu where terrorists seek a foothold. Remember that the terrorists we are after target civilians, and the death toll from their acts of terrorism against Muslims dwarfs any estimate of civilian casualties from drone strikes. So doing nothing is not an option.

[I]t is false to assert that putting boots on the ground is less likely to result in civilian deaths or less likely to create enemies in the Muslim world. . . .

Our efforts must be measured against the history of putting American troops in distant lands among hostile populations. In Vietnam, hundreds of thousands of civilians died in a war where the boundaries of battle were blurred. In Iraq and Afghanistan, despite the extraordinary courage and discipline of our troops, thousands of civilians have been killed. So neither conventional military action nor waiting for attacks to occur offers moral safe harbor, and neither does a sole reliance on law enforcement in territories that have no functioning police or security services—and indeed, have no functioning law. . . .

And for this reason, I've insisted on strong oversight of all lethal action. After I took office, my administration began briefing all strikes outside of Iraq and Afghanistan to the appropriate committees of Congress. Let me repeat that: Not only did Congress authorize the use of force, it is briefed on every strike that America takes. . . .

Going forward, I've asked my administration to review proposals to extend oversight of lethal actions outside of warzones that go beyond our reporting to Congress. . . .

[F]or all the focus on the use of force, force alone cannot make us safe. We cannot use force everywhere that a radical ideology takes root; and in the absence of a strategy that reduces the wellspring of extremism, a perpetual war—through drones or Special Forces or troop deployments—will prove self-defeating, and alter our country in troubling ways.

So the next element of our strategy involves addressing the underlying grievances and conflicts that feed extremism—from North Africa to South Asia. As we've learned this past decade, this is a vast and complex undertaking. We must be humble in our expectation that we can quickly resolve deep-rooted problems like poverty and sectarian hatred. . . .

And success on all these fronts requires sustained engagement, but it will also require resources. . . .

Foreign assistance cannot be viewed as charity. It is fundamental to our national security. And it's fundamental to any sensible long-term strategy to battle extremism.

. . . Thwarting homegrown plots presents particular challenges in part because of our proud commitment to civil liberties for all who call America home. That's why, in the years to come, we will have to keep working hard to strike the appropriate balance between our need for security and preserving those freedoms that make us who we are. That means reviewing the authorities of law enforcement, so we can intercept new types of communication, but also build in privacy protections to prevent abuse.

That means . . . means finally having a strong Privacy and Civil Liberties Board to review those issues where our counterterrorism efforts and our values may come into tension.

Now, all these issues remind us that the choices we make about war can impact—in sometimes unintended ways—the openness and freedom on which our way of life depends. And that is why I intend to engage Congress about the existing Authorization to Use Military Force, or AUMF, to determine how we can continue to fight terrorism without keeping America on a perpetual wartime footing.

The AUMF is now nearly 12 years old. The Afghan war is coming to an end. . . .

So I look forward to engaging Congress and the American people in efforts to refine, and ultimately repeal, the AUMF's mandate. And I will not sign laws designed to expand this mandate further. Our systematic effort to dismantle terrorist organizations must continue. But this war, like all wars, must end. That's what history advises. That's what our democracy demands.

16.6 Peter Trubowitz, "Politics and Strategy: Partisan Ambition and American Statecraft" (2011)

In his book *Politics and Strategy*, political scientist Peter Trubowitz explained why some American presidents pursue more aggressive, far-reaching American foreign policies than others. Using history to compare several presidencies, Trubowitz argued that these different strategies can only be understood by taking into account *both* domestic politics and the international vulnerability of the United States. A president may have to deal with a poor economy or a political party that does not support an aggressive foreign policy; conversely, the president's party may support a military buildup. The United States may face immediate, serious foreign threats, or it may not face such threats and may enjoy more freedom (Trubowitz calls it "slack") to pursue a variety of international goals. These two factors—domestic and foreign—account for the way different presidents approach foreign policy in different ways. For example, with his party supporting military growth and the U.S. facing the threat of terrorism, George W. Bush could pursue an expansive foreign policy that defined the national security threats very broadly. But Barack Obama, focused on a deep economic recession and the cost of wars initiated by the Bush administration, pursued a more "balancing" strategy that aims to reduce American exposure to foreign threats. Both of these strategies are understandable, given the domestic concerns and international problems that faced these two presidents (compare the Bush and Obama statements in the preceding section).

The Two Faces of Grand Strategy

Two general approaches dominate the study of grand strategy in international relations.[1] The first draws on the tradition known as Realpolitik or realism. It argues that grand strategies are determined by a country's geopolitical circumstances and especially by its position in the international system. Scholars in the realist tradition stress international factors such as a state's relative material power (e.g., military strength, gross national product, population size), whether prevailing military technology favors the offense or defense in fighting wars, and the distribution of power among states in the international system ... These and other international constraints, realists argue, shape states' ambitions and possibilities, defining what strategies their leaders might reasonably expect to succeed in a world that is fundamentally anarchical. These considerations determine leaders' foreign policy strategies and choices.

Realist explanations of statecraft differ sharply from a second approach that argues that grand strategy has a domestic face. Scholars in this domestic politics or Innenpolitik tradition point to pressures within states, rather than pushes and pulls from the outside, to explain leaders' choices. The domestic politics approach starts from the premise that societal interests (e.g., industrialists, bankers, merchants, interest groups) have a stake in whether a nation's foreign policy is expensive or cheap, offensive or defensive, or coercive or cooperative. Leaders are thought to respond to these interests in setting grand strategy and choosing national priorities in international affairs. In Innenpolitik accounts of grand strategy, states' foreign policy choices are thus constrained, and perhaps even distorted, by societal interests and pressures. Innenpolitikers argue, for example, that the roots of the classic problem of "strategic overextension," in which a state's reach exceeds its grasp, lie on the domestic side: the combination of powerful economic interests and weak, ineffectual governing institutions allow narrow special interests to push political leaders into overly ambitious foreign policies ...

GRAND STRATEGY REFERS TO THE PURPOSEFUL use of military, diplomatic, and economic tools of statecraft to achieve desired ends. Scholars often define these goals in terms of national security, power, or wealth, but the ends can also refer to other valued goods such as national honor, prestige, and profit. In this book, I argue that grand strategy can also be viewed as a means by which national leaders strive to maintain or strengthen their hold on executive power. . . .

Many grand strategies are status quo-oriented in nature. Balancing is perhaps the best-known defensive grand strategy, though scholars disagree about how frequently leaders actually rely on it (P. Schroeder, 1994a). Balancing involves efforts to prevent another state from upsetting the status quo—from increasing its share of power at the "defending" state's expense (Waltz, 1979; Walt, 1987; Jervis and Snyder, 1991). One form of balancing involves a leader's efforts to build up his state's military capabilities. International relations scholars call this "internal balancing" because a leader is relying on the state's own resources to deter a potential aggressor or to defend against the foreign aggressor should deterrence fail. A leader can also try to check a threatening state by pooling resources with other states through the formation of alliances.[2] This is called "external balancing." Balancing against foreign threats frequently involves some combination of internal mobilization and alliance formation, though typically, leaders do attach greater weight to one strategy or the other. Unlike war, which can be revisionist or status quo in nature, balancing is a defensive strategy.

Appeasement, buckpassing, and bandwagoning are also status quo strategies.[3] Appeasement refers to efforts by a leader to conciliate or "buy off" a potential aggressor by making unilateral diplomatic and economic concessions (Gilpin, 1981; Rock, 2000; Ripsman and Levy, 2008). . . . In t[he] case [of buckpassing], a leader relies on some other state to check the potential aggressor, while keeping his own country on the sidelines. . . . Bandwagoning is a strategy by which leaders willingly subordinate their states and themselves to the stronger power, seeing little hope of diffusing the threat posed by the foreign challenger, and seeing political security or profit in collaborating directly with it (Walt, 1987; Labs, 1992; Doyle, 1993).[4]

Expensive Versus Cheap Strategies

Grand strategies also differ by cost, and the differences between strategies in terms of cost can be substantial. Wars of conquest, imperialism, and internal balancing are comparatively expensive. Building an army takes time and money, which can be hard to extract from a resistant populace or legislature (Lamborn, 1983; Morrow, 1993). Military spending can also limit a state's ability to satisfy important social welfare goals. (This is the "guns versus butter" trade-off.) Other strategies, such as appeasement or buckpassing, are considerably cheaper. They require little in the way of taxation or conscription because they rely disproportionately on the use of diplomacy as a tool of foreign policy.

. . . American Balancing in Historical Perspective

Balancing is one of statecraft's oldest grand strategies. It is also one that America's leaders had little occasion to use, at least before World War II. Before the 1940s, the only president who could be classified clearly as a "balancer" is Woodrow Wilson (1913–21), and in Wilson's case, this was true for a two-year span (1917–18) of his presidency.[5]

In the American context, the classic era of balancing was the Cold War (Mearsheimer, 2001, 323)....

What would eventually become known as the strategy of containment directed against the Soviet Union (and, for a time, China) was an axiom of U.S. planning by 1945 (Trachtenberg, 1999, 34–35).

It was the depth and durability of the commitment to containment, or internal balancing, that distinguished the country's foreign policy in this era from what had come before. All of America's Cold War presidents can be described as opting for the grand strategy [of balancing]. Internal balancing for all of them involved costly efforts to defend the post-World War II status quo by checking and containing Soviet power. Yet as John Lewis Gaddis (2005) points out, the Cold War consensus was not a consensus over how much of the state's resources to invest in national security. On this, there was variation across administrations. Harry Truman (from 1950 on), John Kennedy, and Ronald Reagan presided over large increases in U.S. military spending and constitute the starkest cases of internal balancing during the Cold War. Others, including Dwight Eisenhower, Richard Nixon, and (initially) Jimmy Carter, were internal balancers who looked for ways to dampen down arms spending.[6]

The theory of executive choice of grand strategy that we have developed in the preceding chapters offers considerable leverage in accounting for both the similarity and the differences across the grand strategies of America's Cold War presidents. For leaders who presided over parties that strongly favored investing in "guns," geopolitical imperatives and party politics provided mutually reinforcing incentives to make heavy investments in internal balancing. In the late 1940s and early 1950s, the combination of deteriorating geopolitical conditions in Europe and East Asia and the growing support inside the Democratic Party for military Keynesianism (Fordham, 1998) gave Truman strong incentive to actively balance against Soviet power.[7] A decade later, Soviet technological breakthroughs and penetration into the Third World, and the Democratic Party's strong (if ultimately unsustainable) support for both guns and butter, gave Kennedy and his successor, Lyndon Johnson, every reason to double down on Soviet containment. Twenty years later, a widely held view that geopolitical events were trending against the United States, and the wholesale shift of powerful pro-defense constituencies and voting blocs to the Republican Party, led Ronald Reagan to do much the same thing (Trubowitz, 1998, 225–32). Reagan invested in expensive military strategies aimed at containing Soviet power in Europe and checking nationalist challenges to U.S. interests in the Third World (Zakaria, 1990). Truman, Kennedy, and Reagan could invest heavily in internal balancing against Soviet power at little political cost to themselves. Military buildup even generated domestic political advantages. What was considered good statecraft (containing Moscow) also made good party politics.

This could not be as easily said of Eisenhower, Nixon, or Carter. Each presided at a time when his party was reluctant to spend vast sums of money on military build-up (or, in the cases of Eisenhower and Nixon, on social welfare). All three cut the Pentagon's budget. For these Cold War presidents, allies were partly a substitute for arms: Eisenhower via his "New Look" network of cheaper security pacts (e.g., SEATO [Southeast Asia Treaty Organization] in Southeast Asia; CENTO [Central Eastern Treaty Organization] in the Middle East); Nixon through his "tacit alliance" with Communist China (Mann, 2000, 56) and his American-centered system of "regional policemen" in the Middle East, sub-Saharan Africa, and Latin America; and Carter, more indirectly, through his efforts to align America's interests with the UN General Assembly.

Throughout the Cold War, America's presidents as day-to-day reelection seekers thought as much about what geopolitics could do to them as they did about what it could do for them. The risk of strategic failure (e.g., the possibility of a technological breakthrough that would tip the nuclear balance to the Soviets, the fall of a country to communism) led them to look for ways to hedge and limit their political exposure. Because Truman's, Kennedy's, and Reagan's parties stood to benefit disproportionately from investing in guns, actively balancing against Soviet power had the virtues of being both desirable and possible. By contrast, Eisenhower, Nixon, and Carter had powerful incentive to find less expensive ways to balance against Soviet power.

Geopolitics and Partisan Politics: Managing Cross-Pressure

...This book is based on the premise that this international-domestic distinction is counterproductive and unnecessary. In making grand strategy, leaders take both geopolitics and domestic politics seriously because it is in their political self-interest to do so. By going to the microfoundational level of the individual leader, it is possible to take into account both Realpolitik's concern with security and power and Innenpolitik's emphasis on domestic interests and coalitions ...

...Core ideas in Realpolitik and Innenpolitik can be brought together in a parsimonious model to explain when we can expect leaders to favor ambitious and expensive grand strategies, and when they are likely to define the nation's interests more narrowly and to rely on less costly means. Indeed, this approach makes it easier to understand why some states overreach in foreign affairs while others are remembered for failing to do enough. Leaders most susceptible to strategic overcommitment are those who lead domestic coalitions that strongly prefer investing the state's resources in guns rather than butter. These leaders have powerful incentives to invest in ambitious, expensive foreign policies. They are the most susceptible to overshooting the mark, or what international relations scholars refer to as overbalancing and overexpansion. By contrast, leaders who preside over domestic coalitions that strongly prefer butter to guns are the statesmen most apt to underreach or underbalance in foreign policy. Because these leaders' coalitions favor security on the cheap, the practical realities of holding on to power make satisficing strategies and isolationism more politically attractive.

Realpolitik leads us to expect that leaders facing similar international circumstances will choose similar grand strategies. As we have seen, sometimes leaders do. However, frequently they do not. Monroe and Van Buren, for example, held office when security was plentiful; they had geopolitical slack. Yet they chose radically different strategies: Monroe favored expansionism and spheres-of-influence; Van Buren saw advantage in retrenchment. McKinley and Hoover also chose strategies that differed sharply in ambition and cost, even though both had geopolitical slack. Relative international power also does not account for these differences.[8]

...Our model...illuminates the circumstances under which leaders will invoke some strategic narratives and not others. Leaders like Monroe, McKinley, and Bush who hold power when security is plentiful and expansionism pays well domestically are the ones who are most likely to invoke grandiose arguments about national greatness, "manifest destiny," and spreading civilization. There is little geopolitical risk, and substantial partisan advantage, in doing so. By contrast, leaders who need security on the cheap (presidents like Washington, Lincoln, and Roosevelt during the 1930s) are more likely to stress the limits of national power, the need to keep ends and means in balance, and the dangers of foreign adventurism. . . .

In each of the cases examined in this book, presidential choice had a great deal to do with presidents' international and domestic political circumstances—their place in "political time," to borrow Stephen Skowronek's (1997) apt phrase. It had very little to do with presidents' personality traits, governing styles, or foreign policy backgrounds. Classic "first image" distinctions between pragmatists and crusaders, "extroverts" and "introverts," and experience and inexperience are poor predictors of the type of grand strategy (the mix of ambition and cost) leaders prefer. Historians generally consider Washington, McKinley, and Clinton to be pragmatists. Yet their foreign policies differed markedly, both in ambition and in cost. . . . Similarly, Lincoln, Truman, and Bush all came to the presidency with no diplomatic experience to speak of. This had little bearing on their choice of foreign policy approach. The same can be said of presidents who were well versed in foreign affairs: Monroe, Van Buren, and Roosevelt are examples. Their experience made them no more likely to favor ambitious grand strategy than others. What we have seen is that political leaders who are placed in similar strategic situations (on both the domestic and international fronts) behave in broadly similar ways: they chose the same type of grand strategy.[9]

Presidents' choices are also much less sensitive to "time in office" than popular wisdom holds. Second-term presidents are often thought to be uniquely autonomous from domestic political pressures because they do not face the demands of reelection yet. When viewed together, the cases examined in this book indicate that two-term presidents are no more likely to buck their partisans and "play to the history books" than first-termers. . . . . . .

Barack Obama and Grand Strategy

The arrival of the Obama administration has produced a shift in U.S. grand strategy that is in line with our model's expectations. In contrast to George W. Bush, who had strong incentives to exploit American primacy for partisan gain, Obama is choosing a strategy of retrenchment . . . This is apparent from Obama's rhetoric and the actions he has already taken. In contrast to Bush, Obama has emphasized the centrality of international cooperation and acknowledged the emergence of a more level global playing field, while at the same time seeking to rein in the country's military commitments (Kupchan and Trubowitz, 2010). While offering hope and inspiration to a world bereft of international leadership, Obama has spoken plainly at home about the limits of American power and the importance of keeping the U.S. effort proportional to the interests at stake in any particular situation. As he noted in a much-anticipated speech at West Point in December 2009, "I refuse to set goals that go beyond our responsibility, our means, or our interests. And I must weigh all of the challenges that our nation faces. . . . That's why our troop commitment in Afghanistan cannot be open-ended— because the nation that I'm most interested in building is our own" (Obama, 2009b). This is the rhetoric of retrenchment.

We see signs of retrenchment in Obama's commitment to bring down U.S. force levels in Iraq and in the decision to set a withdrawal date for Afghanistan.[10] It is evident in his efforts to generate cost savings in the Pentagon's budget (Wirls, 2010, 194–95) and to pressure Europe, China, and others to shoulder a greater share of the international security burden (e.g., in containing Iran's nuclear ambitions).[11] Signs of retrenchment are also evident in Obama's decision to pull back from the Bush administration's efforts to negotiate free trade agreements. Obama wants to focus more attention on enforcing U.S. trade laws and World Trade Organization rights and less attention on an activist negotiating agenda (Schott, 2009). The same is true of the administration's efforts to "reset" (improve) the strategic relationship with Russia, revive America's commitment to international institutions and multilateralism, and look to diplomacy rather than coercion to resolve disputes with unfriendly regimes.[12] These diplomatic initiatives have boosted America's standing in the world (American Political Science Association, 2010) in no small part because they contrast so sharply with Bush's combative approach to international institutions.[13] Yet Obama's heavy reliance on cheaper diplomatic means serves his domestic purposes too.

Obama has strong incentives to prioritize domestic needs. He came into office facing the worst economic crisis since the Great Depression. Many of his party's core constituencies (e.g., labor) were hit especially hard. Meanwhile, popular frustration over Bush's $700 billion bailout of Wall Street strengthened the Democrats' resolve to do something for Main Street. The economic crisis solidified the Democrats' long-standing preference for butter over guns, and as table 1 indicates, this has meant strong support on Capitol Hill for Obama's efforts to bring commitments and costs back into line.[14] While many Democrats disapproved of Obama's decision to send more troops to Afghanistan, they have nevertheless backed his plan for stabilizing Afghanistan and neighboring Pakistan, rejecting more costly Republican schemes for combating the Taliban and terrorism in the region. Democratic support for Obama's efforts to scale back defense spending and rely more heavily on diplomacy and foreign aid is also solid. The differences between Democrats and Republicans in each of these areas could not be starker.[15]

None of this predicts that Obama will slavishly follow a linear path toward retrenchment: tactical adjustments are to be expected. This is because retrenchment is not without risk. Foreign leaders may find it in their interest to act more assertively to fill any resulting geopolitical vacuums. Meanwhile, skittish allies in Asia and elsewhere could find it prudent to realign their interests. Republicans could seize setbacks on either front to make political hay. We should not be surprised to see Obama maneuver geopolitically in one theater to offset likely losses from retrenchment in another; to tighten relations in one region of the world (e.g., Southeast Asia) while downsizing the nation's presence

Table 1 Democratic and Republican Support for Barack Obama's Foreign Policies, 2009

	Stabilize Afghanistan		Cut Defense		Support Diplomacy	
	Party Support	Party Cohesion	Party Support	Party Cohesion	Party Support	Party Cohesion
Democrats	90%	80%	91%	83%	94%	89%
Republicans	2%	96%	25%	89%	15%	85%

Roll call voting in the U.S. House of Representatives from the first session of the 111th Congress: Number of roll call votes: stabilize Afghanistan (9); cut defense (19); support diplomacy (13).

in another (Central Asia). What seems unlikely (and would be evidence against the argument advanced here) is that Obama will assume major new strategic commitments or ratchet up Pentagon spending. If domestic renewal, rather than foreign ambition, is driving U.S. statecraft today, then we should expect the nation's interests to be defined more narrowly and its commitments and capabilities adjusted accordingly. Although Obama often evokes comparisons with Lincoln, his international circumstances more closely resemble those of Martin Van Buren or Herbert Hoover. Like Van Buren and Hoover, Obama has geopolitical slack. The threat of terrorism remains, but today the United States does not face a geopolitical challenger, and the risk of a sudden shift in the distribution of international power is low. This is reflected in Obama's National Security Strategy (NSS), one-quarter of which is devoted to domestic policies and goals such as strengthening the economy and rebuilding the nation's infrastructure (M. Taylor, 2010). "Our national security," cautions Obama, "begins at home" (2010, 9). The party has taken advantage of the slack in the international system to invest resources at home. While some Democrats worry about Republican accusations that they are too soft on defense (a holdover from Cold War era politics), Democrats have strongly backed Secretary of Defense Robert Gates's efforts to close what he calls the "spigot of defense funding opened by 9/ 11" (Wirls, 2010, 194). More recently, they backed his plan to trim an additional $ 100 billion from the Pentagon's budget (Shanker and Drew, 2010).[16] The party has rallied behind Obama's ambitious and expensive plan to overhaul the nation's health care system and the $ 800 billion economic stimulus package, seeing it as a way to shift the guns-versus-butter balance. At a time when Obama and the Democrats have strong incentives to prioritize domestic needs, a grand strategy aimed at scaling back commitments and reducing costs is what we would expect of this president, given the model of grand strategy determinants developed in this book.

• • •

Five hundred years ago, Niccolò Machiavelli captured the essence of statecraft. He wrote of leaders caught in a vortex of competing and often conflicting pressures: some external, the others internal. Good statecraft, Machiavelli advised, requires an understanding of both geopolitics and domestic politics, and how they interact. Machiavelli's analysis of statecraft remains fresh today. Leaders who make grand strategy are cross-pressured by international and domestic imperatives. They must manage these competing pressures if they are to succeed and survive in office. Choices about grand strategy are not as scripted or straightforwardly determined by geopolitical circumstance as much analysis in the Realpolitik school would have us believe. Nor are leaders always as free internationally to respond as they please to domestic contingency, as many who subscribe to Innenpolitik seem to suggest. If we are to develop useful—parsimonious yet valid—models about how grand strategy is made, we need to move beyond these polar opposites in the study of statecraft. The way forward lies in finding ways to combine the insights of these two traditions of analysis.

Doing so helps us better understand what is happening in American statecraft today. In an era of unipolarity, America enjoys preponderant power and its leaders have a level of "geopolitical slack" that was inconceivable a few short decades ago. The challenge facing leaders who have geopolitical slack is to decide what to do with the room for maneuver they enjoy. Should they seize the moment and look for ways to strengthen their state's power and, at the risk of antagonizing other states, seek to widen their power advantages? Or should these leaders be content to maintain the international status quo and focus more attention on solving problems at home? I have argued that under international conditions like those the United States is experiencing today, when leaders have geopolitical slack, the answer will turn heavily on domestic politics: on whether a leader's party prefers guns over butter, or vice versa. What distinguishes our era in American statecraft from the Cold War is the wide scope of choice leaders have in defining the general thrust of grand strategy. How they make that choice will depend, as in earlier eras, on their calculations about how to respond to domestic political incentives and geopolitical constraints (opportunities) in a way that is most likely to guarantee their own political success and that of the domestic coalitions they lead.

NOTES

1. A third, more recent approach, sometimes referred to as Ideapolitik, focuses on the influence of national policy ideas (e.g., strategic culture). It shares some common features with Innenpolitik. However, Ideapolitik is sufficiently different to warrant treatment as a separate tradition of analysis. . . .

2. Offensive alliances such as the 1939 Molotov–von Ribbentrop Pact between the Soviet Union and Germany are rare and short-lived. On the infrequency and instability of offensive alliances, see Walt (1997, 159).

3. Most international relations scholars view bandwagoning as a defensive strategy. However, as Schweller (1997) notes, leaders sometimes bandwagon with other states to exploit opportunities to acquire additional territory, markets, or resources— that is, they can bandwagon for offensive or revisionist purposes. Schweller calls this "bandwagoning for profit." I follow standard usage here.

4. Bandwagoning is similar to appeasement in that it involves unilateral concessions to the threatening state. However, bandwagoning differs in one important respect. Leaders that bandwagon with a foreign power do so because they see no hope of diffusing the threat and possible profit in conceding sovereignty to it. Appeasers believe that the threat can be diffused or checked by making diplomatic concessions that preserve their own sovereignty and that usually come (at least in part) at some other state's expense.

5. In 1916 Wilson responds militarily to German sabotage and submarine attacks by commissioning "a navy second to none" and in 1917, by sending a substantial force of ground soldiers to France to stave off a German breakthrough and seal Germany's defeat. Having entered office with geopolitical slack and facing strong domestic pressure to invest in domestic policy. . ., Wilson responded to the outbreak of war in Europe initially by satisficing (neutrality) and ultimately by balancing against Germany. For a good concise account of Wilson's strategic adjustment, see Quester (2004).

6. After initially slowing defense spending, Carter increased it sharply in 1979 in response to a series of international setbacks and mounting criticism by the Republican right.

7. In the late 1940s, Truman's early post-World War II effort to bind other nations into a new American-led international order was transformed by the rise of Soviet power and deteriorating geopolitical conditions in Europe and East Asia. Truman responded with a hybrid strategy, actively balancing against Soviet power, on the one hand, while continuing to bind Western Europe and Japan into a Pax Americana, on the other. On Truman's efforts at binding, see Ikenberry (2001, 163–214).

8. Neoclassical realist domestic variables such as state strength are also underdetermining. Monroe and Van Buren both held office when the American state was very much "one of courts and parties" (Skowronek, 1982). The federal government was relatively weak and decentralized.

McKinley and Hoover held office during an era when the federal government's powers were expanding—when its capacity to extract national resources was growing (and its ability to respond more directly to international pressures and opportunities was increasing) (Zakaria, 1998).

9. This does not mean that leaders are completely interchangeable, or that political skill does not matter. George Washington, Abraham Lincoln, and Franklin Roosevelt held office when the pressures and cross-pressures of geopolitics and party politics were acute . . .

10. To be sure, as a wartime president, Obama has substantially expanded the size of the U.S. operation in Afghanistan. Nonetheless, he is committed to the steady withdrawal of U.S. forces from Iraq. When he unfurled his new strategy for Afghanistan, which included dispatching an additional 30,000 U.S. troops, he made clear that the mission would be of limited duration, announcing that the coalition would begin handing over operations to Afghan forces during the summer of 2011. On the political significance of Obama's West Point speech, see also Mandelbaum (2010, 1–3).

11. In both areas, so far, Obama's record has fallen short of expectations. Though the Pentagon budget that Obama approved was well below amounts requested by the military services, the budget still allowed for more than 3 percent growth over George Bush's last defense budget (Congressional Budget Office, 2010). Current forecasts do suggest that defense spending is likely to taper off in the years ahead. Because the Pentagon's budget is heavily driven by changes in personnel "end strength," the depth of future cuts will depend greatly on whether U.S. troops return on schedule from Iraq and Afghanistan (and on how strongly the Republican majority in the 112th House of Representatives pushes to maintain current defense spending levels). Obama's record in fostering international partnership is also mixed. For an early assessment of Obama's diplomatic initiatives, see T. Wright (2010).

12. Whereas the Bush administration shunned engagement with belligerent regimes, Obama has reached out to Iran, North Korea, Cuba, Syria, and Burma. Coercion is still an option in dealing with these countries, but U.S. policy is now predicated on the assumption that engagement is the preferred course (Kupchan and Trubowitz, 2010).

13. Obama has sought an international agreement to limit greenhouse gas emissions; he signed a new START [Strategic Arms Reduction Treaty] with Russia; he issued a Nuclear Posture Review that narrows the conditions under which the United States might use nuclear weapons, committed his administration to push for Senate ratification of the Comprehensive Nuclear-Test-Ban Treaty, and outlined a vision of a world free of nuclear weapons; and he approved U.S. participation as an observer in meetings at the ICC [International Criminal Court]. Obama (2009b) is committed to transforming the Group of Eight (G8) into the G-20 and told the United Nations General Assembly last September that, "The United States stands ready to begin a new chapter of international cooperation."

14. Stabilizing Afghanistan includes votes on Obama's increased troop deployment and proposed withdrawal date, as well as votes on related issues of military and economic aid to Pakistan. Votes for Obama's strategy were coded as support for the U.S. war in Afghanistan. Cutting defense includes roll call votes on the Pentagon's budget, as well as votes to cut (or increase) funding for specific programs such as missile defense. Votes to reduce spending were coded as votes to slow defense spending. Support for diplomacy includes votes on the Department of State's budget as well as Republican efforts to reduce funding for specific aid and development programs (e.g., Peace Corps). I have included only votes where the Obama administration's policy preferences were known or where the proposed amendment was clearly unfriendly to the administration.

15. Deep partisan divisions over foreign policy are also evident in public opinion polls. See Kupchan and Trubowitz (2010).

16. In sharp contrast to George W. Bush's NSS [National Security Strategy] of 2002 and 2006, Obama's NSS views the "threat" of terrorism as less consequential than other longer-term international challenges (e.g., nuclear proliferation, dependence on fossil fuels) and the more immediate challenge of "rebuilding the economy." The Obama's NSS also defines the threat of

terrorism more narrowly than Bush's, focusing on "al-Qa'ida and its affiliates" (Obama, 2010, 4) as opposed to state-sponsored terrorism at large. Obama's NSS makes no mention of Bush's doctrine of "preemptive war" and attaches comparatively little weight to "democracy promotion," a key feature of Bush's ambitious foreign policy agenda.

REFERENCES

American Political Science Association. *U.S. Standing in the World: Causes, Consequences, and the Future.* Washington, D.C.: American Political Science Association, 2010.

Congressional Budget Office. *Long-Term Implications of the Fiscal Year 2010 Defense Budget.* Washington, D.C.: CBO, January 2010.

Doyle, Michael W. "Politics and Grand Strategy." In *The Domestic Bases of Grand Strategy,* edited by Richard Rosecrance and Arthur Stein, 22–47. Ithaca, N.Y.: Cornell University Press, 1993.

Fordham, Benjamin O. *Building the Cold War Consensus: The Political Economy U.S. National Security Policy, 1949–1951.* Ann Arbor: University of Michigan, 1998.

Gaddis, John Lewis. *Strategies of Containment: A Critical Appraisal of American National Security Policy during the Cold War.* 2nd ed. New York: Oxford University Press, 2005.

Gilpin, Robert. *War and Change in World Politics.* Princeton: Princeton University Press, 1981.

Ikenberry, G. John. *After Victory: Institutions, Strategic Restraint, and the Rebuilding of Order after Major Wars.* Princeton: Princeton University Press, 2001.

Jervis, Robert, and Jack Snyder, editors. *Dominoes and Bandwagons: Strategic Beliefs and Great Power Competition in the Eurasian Rimland.* New York: Oxford University Press, 1991.

Kupchan, Charles A., and Peter L. Trubowitz. "The Illusion of Liberal Internationalism's Revival." *International Security* 35, no. 1 (2010): 95–109.

Labs, Eric J. "Do Weak States Bandwagon?" *Security Studies* 1, no. 3 (1992): 383–416.

Lamborn, Alan C. "Power and the Politics of Extraction." *International Studies Quarterly* 27 (1983): 125–46.

Mandelbaum, Michael. *The Frugal Superpower: America's Global Leadership in a Cash-Strapped Era.* New York: Public Affairs, 2010.

Mann, James. *About Face: A History of America's Curious Relationship with China, from Nixon to Clinton.* New York: Vintage, 2000.

Mearsheimer, John J. *The Tragedy of Great Power Politics.* New York: Norton, 2001.

Morrow, James D. "Arms versus Allies: Trade-Offs in the Search of Stability." *International Organization* 47, no. 2 (1993): 208–33.

Obama, Barack. "Speech to the United Nations' General Assembly." *www.nytimes.com.* September 23, 2009b. http://www.nytimes.com/2009/09/24/us/politics/24prexy.text.html.

Obama, Barack. "National Security Strategy." *White House.* May 2010. http://www.whitehouse.gov/sites/default/files/rss_viewer/national_security_strategy.pdf.

Quester, George H. "The Wilson Presidency, the U.S. Navy, and Homeland Defense." *White House Studies* 4, no. 2 (2004): 137–48.

Ripsman, Norrin M., and Jack S. Levy. "Wishful Thinking or Buying Time? The Logic of British Appeasement in the 1930s." *International Security* 33, no. 2 (2008): 148–81.

Rock, Stephen R. *Appeasement in International Politics.* Lexington: University Press of Kentucky, 2000.

Schott, Jeffrey J. "Trade Policy and the Obama Administration." *Business Economics* 44, no. 3 (2009): 150–53.

Schroeder, Paul W. "Historical Reality vs. Neo-Realist Theory." *International Security* 19, no. 1 (1994a): 108–48.

Schweller, Randall L. *Deadly Imbalances: Tripolarity and Hiller's Strategy of Global Conquest.* New York: Columbia University Press, 1997.

Shanker, Thorn, and Christopher Drew. "Pentagon Faces Growing Pressure to Trim Budget." *New York Times,* July 22, 2010. http://www.nytimes.com/2010/07/23/us/politics/23budget.html?pagewanted=all.

Skowronek, Stephen. *Building a New American State: The Expansion of National Administrative Capacities, 1877–1920.* Cambridge: Cambridge University Press, 1982.

——. *The Politics Presidents Make: Leadership from John Adams to Bill Clinton.* Cambridge, Mass.: Harvard University Press, 1997.

Taylor, Miles E. "Obama's National Security Strategy under the Microscope." *World Politics Review,* June 1, 2010. http://www.worldpoliticsreview.com/artlcles/5656/obamas-national-security-strategy-under-the-microscope.

Trachtenberg, Marc. "Making Grand Strategy: The Early Cold War Experience in Retrospect." *SAIS Review* 19, no. 1 (1999): 33–40.

Trubowitz, Peter. *Defining the National Interest: Conflict and Change in American Foreign Policy*. Chicago: University of Chicago Press, 1998.

Walt, Stephen M. *The Origin of Alliances*. Ithaca, N.Y.: Cornell University Press, 1987.

Waltz, Kenneth N. *Theory of International Politics*. New York: Random House, 1979.

Wirls, Daniel. *Irrational Security: The Politics of Defense from Reagan to Obama*. Baltimore: Johns Hopkins University Press, 2010.

Wright, Thomas. "Strategic Engagement's Record." *Washington Quarterly* 33, no. 3 (2010): 35–60.

Zakaria, Fareed. "The Reagan Strategy of Containment." *Political Science Quarterly* 105 (1990): 373–95.

—— *From Wealth to Power: The Unusual Origins of America's World Role*. Princeton: Princeton University Press, 1998.

Discussion Questions

1. Why were some of the authors of the Constitution Convention concerned about a standing army in peacetime? Are any of these concerns still important today?

2. What are George Washington's concerns about the United States becoming entangled in foreign affairs? Is the nation now so strong that his advice is no longer relevant?

3. Alexis de Tocqueville argues that citizens in democracies have reasons to favor peace, while the military in a democracy favors war. Has history proven Tocqueville right or wrong? Give both sides.

4. Has political polarization in recent years destroyed the traditional American supports for establishing global peace and prosperity under the rule of law?

5. Peter Trubowitz argues that many presidents have to limit American intervention abroad because they lack domestic political support for increased, aggressive action. How does domestic politics affect American foreign policy today, and how is it likely to affect that policy over the next decade? Consider military, trade, and other foreign policies.

Suggested Additional Reading

Chris Alden and Amnon Aran, *Foreign Policy Analysis: New Approaches* (New York: Routledge, 2011).

Graham T. Allison and Philip Zelikow, *Essence of Decision: Explaining the Cuban Missile Crisis*, 2nd ed. (New York: Longman, 1999).

Stephen E. Ambrose and Douglas G. Brinkley, *Rise to Globalism: American Foreign Policy Since 1938*, 9th ed. (New York: Penguin, 2010).

George C. Herring, *From Colony to Superpower: U.S. Foreign Relations since 1776* (Oxford and New York: Oxford University Press, 2011).

Ira Katznelson and Martin Shefter, *Shaped by War and Trade: International Influences on American Political Development* (Princeton, NJ: Princeton University Press, 2002).

James Lutz and Brenda Lutz, *Terrorism: The Basics* (New York: Routledge, 2011).

Andrew Polsky, *Elusive Victories: The American President at War* (Oxford and New York: Oxford University Press, 2012).

James T. Sparrow, *Warfare State: World War II and the Age of Big Government* (Oxford and New York: Oxford University Press, 2011).

Source Information

Adams, John and Abigail. "Women in the New Nation" from *The Letters of John and Abigail Adams*, ed. Frank Shuffleton, (New York: Penguin Books, 2004), pp. 147–149, 153–155.

Aldrich, John H. *Why Parties? A Second Look* (Chicago: University of Chicago Press, 2011), pp. 3–24. Reprinted with permission of University of Chicago Press.

Amar, Akhil Reed. "America's Constitution," from *America's Constitution: A Biography* (New York: Random House, 2005), 5–8, 10–19. Copyright © 2005 by Akhil Reed Amar. Used by permission of Random House, Inc.

——. *America's Unwritten Constitution: The Precedents and Principles We Live By* (New York: Basic Books, 2012). 204–211. Copyright © 2012 by Basic Books, Inc. Reprinted by permission of Basic Books, a member of Perseus Books Group.

Binder, Sarah, "Through the Looking Glass, Darkly: What Has Become of the Senate?," *The Forum: A Journal of Applied Research in Contemporary Politics* 9:4 (De Gruyter, 2011), Article 2, pp. 1–7, 12–14. Reprinted with permission of De Gruyter.

Bryce, Lord James. *The American Commonwealth, vol. 2* (New York: Macmillan and Co., 1891), pp 3–19.

Burke, Edmund. "Letter to the Electors of Bristol," from *The Portable Edmund Burke*, ed. Isaac Kramnick, (New York: Penguin Books, 1999), 155–157.

Bush, George W., Remarks at the Ribbon-Cutting Ceremony for the Air Force One Pavilion [at the Reagan Library] (2005), Public Papers of the Presidents: George W. Bush, U.S. National Archives, Public Papers of the Presidents: George W. Bush, 2005, http://www.gpo.gov/fdsys/pkg/PPP-2005-book2/pdf/PPP-2005-book2-doc-pg1572-2.pdf (accessed June 8, 2013)

Carpenter, Daniel. "The Evolution of the National Bureaucracy," from *The Executive Branch*, Joel D. Aberbach and Mark A. Peterson, ed. (New York: Oxford University Press, 2005), pp. 41–66. Reprinted with permission of Oxford University Press.

Clemens, Elisabeth. "Politics Without Party: The Organizational Accomplishments of Disenfranchised Women," from *The People's Lobby: Organizational Innovation and the Rise of Interest Group Politics in the United States, 1890–1925* (Chicago: University of Chicago Press, 1997), pp. 184–234. © 1997 by The University of Chicago. Reprinted with permission.

Cohen, Jeffrey E. "The Size of the President's Agenda, 1789–2002" from *The President's Legislative Policy Agenda, 1789–2002* (Cambridge and New York: Cambridge University Press, 2012), pp. 97–108. Reprinted with permission of Cambridge University Press.

Corwin, Edwin S. "The Passing of Dual Federalism," *Virginia Law Review*, vol. 36, no. 1, February 1950, pp. 2, 4, 15–17, 19–23. Reprinted with permission of Virginia Law Review.

Debates at the Constitutional Convention, "Benjamin Franklin on Signing the Constitution," "Gouverneur Morris speeches at the Constitutional Convention, July 19, 20, and 24," "Interest Groups and Democratic Politics," "Should Common Citizens be Allowed to Vote?," "Limits on Executive Power," "The Constitutional Convention Debates the Military," from *The Records of the Federal Convention of 1787*, ed. Max Farrand (New Haven: Yale University Press, 1911), Vol. II, pp. 52–53, 68–69, 103–105, 318–319, 329–330, 405, 641–643, 665–666, and *Supplement to Max Farrand's The Records of the Federal Convention of 1787*, ed. James H. Hutson (New Haven: Yale University Press, 1987), p. 229.

de Tocqueville, Alexis. *Democracy in America* (New York: Alfred A. Knopf, 1945), pp. 191–193, 195–198, 254–256, 260–261, 263–267.

Downs, Anthony. "Why Bureaus Are Necessary," from *Inside Bureaucracy* (Boston, Little, Brown 1967), pp. 32–35, 37–39. Reprinted with permission of the author.

The Federalist, edited by Jacob E. Cooke, (Middletown, CT: Wesleyan University Press, 1961), pp. 3–13, 323–327, 332–334, 253–257, 317–319, 418–422, 471–474, 476–478, 487, 541–546.

Gillman, Howard. "The Courts and the 2000 Election," from *The Votes That Counted: How the Court Decided the 2000 Presidential Election* (Chicago: University of Chicago Press, 2001), pp. 1–15. © 2001 by The University of Chicago. Reprinted with permission.

Hamilton, Alexander. "Report on Manufactures," December 5, 1791 in *Annals of Congress,* 2nd Cong., Appendix, pp. 971–1034.

Harris, Richard and Daniel Tichenor. "Organized Interests and American Political Development," *Political Science Quarterly,* 117: 4 (Winter 2002–2003), pp. 587–612. Reprinted by permission from Political Science Quarterly.

Hendrickson, David C. *Union, Nation, or Empire: The American Debate over International Relations, 1789–1941* (Lawrence, KS: University of Kansas Press, 2009), pp. 6–12. Reprinted with permission of University Press of Kansas.

Jefferson, Thomas. "Newspapers and Democracy," from Letter from Thomas Jefferson to Colonel Edward Carrington, January 16, 1787, in *The Life and Selected Writings of Thomas Jefferson,* ed. Adrienne Cook and William Peden, (New York: Modern Library, 1944), pp. 411–412.

Johnson, Dennis W. "Political Consultants at Work," from *No Place for Amateurs* (New York: Routledge, 2007), 6–13. Copyright © 2008 by Taylor and Francis Group. Reprinted with permission.

Katznelson, Ira, *Fear Itself: The New Deal and the Origins of Our Time* (New York: Liveright, 2013), pp. 20–25, 149–152. Copyright © 2013 by Ira Katznelson. Used by permission of W.W. Norton and Company, Inc.

Keck, Thomas M. "Modern Conservatism and Judicial Power," from *The Most Activist Supreme Court in History: The Road to Modern Judicial Conservatism* (Chicago: University of Chicago Press, 2004), pp. 284–296. © 2000 by Thomas Keck. Reprinted with permission.

Kernell, Samuel. "The Early Nationalization of Political News in America," in *Studies in American Political Development* (Cambridge University Press, 1986), 1: 255–276. Copyright © 1986 Cambridge University Press. Reprinted by permission of Cambridge University Press.

Kersch, Ken I. "The Right to Privacy," David J. Bodenhamer and James V. Ely, Jr., eds. *The Bill of Rights in Modern America, Revised and Expanded* (Bloomington, IN: Indiana University Press, 2008), pp. 215–221. Courtesy of Indiana University Press. All rights reserved.

Key, V.O. "The Voice of the People: An Echo," from *The Responsible Electorate* (New York: Harvard University Press, 1966), Chapter 1, pp. 1–8. Reprinted by permission of Harvard University Press.

Keyssar, Alexander. "The Right to Vote," from *The Right to Vote* (New York: Basic Books, 2000), pp. 26–33, 42–43, 52. Copyright © 2000 by Alexander Keyssar. Reprinted by permission of Basic Books, a member of Perseus Books Group.

King, Anthony, "Running Scared," *The Atlantic* 279: 1 (January 1997), pp. 41–61. Reprinted by permission of the author.

King, Desmond and Rogers Smith. "Racial Orders in American Political Development," *American Political Science Review,* vol. 99, no. 1, February 2005, pp. 75–92. Reprinted with the permission of Cambridge University Press.

Kingdon, John W. "American Public Policy in Comparative Perspective," from *America the Unusual* (St. Martin's/Worth, 1999), pp. 15–22. © 1999 Wadsworth, a part of Cengage Learning, Inc. Reproduced by permission.

Lincoln, Abraham. "Gettysburg Address," November 19, 1863. Accessed from http:// www.teaching americanhistory.org/library/index.asp&documentprint=34 on January 31, 2009.

——. "On Suspension of Habeas Corpus," from Letter to Erastus Corning and Others, June 12, 1863. http://www.abrahamlincolnonline.org/lincoln/speeches/corning.htm (accessed June 11, 2013)

——. "Second Inaugural Address," March 4, 1865. Accessed from http://www.teachingamerican history.org/library/index.asp?documentprint=35 on January 31, 2009.

——. "Speech on the Dred Scott Decision," June 26, 1857. Accessed from http:// www.teaching american history.org/library/index.asp?documentprint=52 on November 1, 2008.

Lindblom, Charles E. *Politics and Markets* (New York: Basic Books, 1977), pp. 170–175, 178–179. Reprinted with permission from the author.

Locke, John. "Of the Beginnings of Political Societies" from *Two Treatises of Government and A Letter Concerning Toleration*, ed. Ian Shapiro, (New Haven, CT: Yale University Press, 2003), pp. 141–142, 152–157.

——. "Of Prerogative," from *Two Treatises of Government*, ed. Peter Laslett (Cambridge and New York: Cambridge University Press, 1988), pp. 374–377, 379–380.

Lynn, Laurence E., Jr, "Theodore Roosevelt Redux: Barack Obama Confronts American Bureaucracy," *International Journal of Public Administration*, 32 (2009), pp. 773–780.

Madison, James. "A Candid State of Parties." Accessed from http://oll.libertyfund.org/title/1941/124404 on January 2, 2009.

——. "Memorial and Remonstrance Against Religious Assessments." Accessed from http://religious freedom.lib.virginia.edu/sacred/madison_m&r_1785.html on January 29, 2009.

Mayhew, David. "The Electoral Incentive," from *Congress: The Electoral Connection* (Yale University Press, 1974), pp. 13–15, 32–33, 49–55, 61–65. Copyright © 1974 Yale University Press. Reprinted by permission of Yale University Press.

Mencken, H.L. "Newspaper Morals," *The Atlantic Monthly*, March 1914. Accessed from http://www.theatlantic.com/doc/print/191403/mencken?x=39&y=5 on December 24, 2008.

Mettler, Suzanne. *Dividing Citizens: Gender and Federalism in New Deal Public Policy* (Ithaca, NY: Cornell University Press, 1998), pp. 1, 11–21. Reprinted with permisson of Cornell University Press.

——. "Reconstituting the Submerged State: The Challenges of Social Policy Reform in the Obama Era," *Perspectives on Politics* 8:3 (September 2010), pp. 803–809, 812–816, 818–824. Reprinted with permission of Cambridge University Press.

Milkis, Sidney M. "The President and the Parties," from *The President and the Parties* (New York: Oxford University Press, 1993), pp. 3–17. Reprinted with permission.

Mill, John Stuart. "On Liberty" (Harvard Classics, Volume 25), 1860.

Montesquieu, Baron de, Charles de Secondat. "The Spirit of the Laws" (1740). http://www.constitution.org/cm/sol-02.htm (Accessed June 11, 2013).

Morone, James. "The Democratic Wish," from *The Democratic Wish: Popular Participation and the Limits of American Government*, revised edition (New Haven: Yale University Press, 1998), pp. 1, 15–17, 19–23. Copyright © Yale University Press. Reprinted by permission of Yale University Press.

Murray, Judith Sargent. "On the Equality of the Sexes" (Boston: The Massachusetts Magazine, Vol. II, 1790).

Myrdal, Gunnar. *An American Dilemma: The Negro Problem and Modern Democracy* (New York: Harper and Brothers, 1944), pp. 3–5, xli–xlix. Reprinted with permission of HarperCollins.

Nelson, Michael. "A Short, Ironic History of American National Bureaucracy," *The Journal of Politics*, 44:3 (August 1982), pp. 748–751, 754–755, 757, 759–762, 764–768, 770–772, 774–776. Reprinted with permission of Cambridge University Press.

Obama, Barack. "Remarks at the National Defense University," May 23, 2013. http://www.whitehouse.gov/the-press-office/2013/05/23/remarks-president-national-defense-university (accessed June 8, 2013).

Owen, Diana. "Media: The Complex Interplay of Old and New Forms," from Stephen Medvic, ed. *New Directions in Campaigns and Elections* (Routledge, 2011), pp. 145–153. Reprinted with permission.

Page, Benjamin I. and James R. Simmons. *What Government Can Do: Dealing with Poverty and Inequality* (Chicago: University of Chicago Press, 2000), pp. 288–293. Reprinted with permission of University of Chicago Press.

Paine, Thomas. "Common Sense," from *Political Writings/Thomas Paine*, ed. Bruce Kuklick, (Cambridge and New York: Cambridge University Press, 1989), pp. 2–3, 16–17, 28, 30, 34–35, 37–38.

Popkin, Samuel L. "The Reasoning Voter," from *The Reasoning Voter* (Chicago: University of Chicago Press, 1991), pp. 7–21. © 1991 by The University of Chicago. Reprinted with permission.

Reichley, James. "Intention of the Founders: Polity without Parties," from *The Life of the Parties: A History of American Political Parties* (Rowman and Littlefield, 2000), pp. 17–18, 23–27. Reproduced with permission of Simon and Schuster.

Robertson, David Brian. "Madison's Opponents and Constitutional Design," *American Political Science Review* 99:2 (May 2005), 226–228, 231–232, 234–235, 240–242. Copyright © 2005 Cambridge University Press. Reprinted with the permission of Cambridge University Press.

——. *Federalism and the Making of America* (New York: Routledge, 2011), pp. 1, 8–13, 150–156.

Roosevelt, Franklin Delano. "Message to Congress on Social Security," January 17, 1935. http://www.presidency.ucsb.edu/ws/print.php?pid=15051 (accessed June 11, 2013).

Roosevelt, Theodore, "Immediate and Vigorous Executive Action," from *Autobiography* (New York: Scribner's, 1958), pp. 197–200.

——. "The New Nationalism" (August 31, 1910), at TeachingAmericanHistory.org, http://teachingamericanhistory.org/library/document/new-nationalism-speech/ (accessed June 8, 2013).

Rosen, Jeffrey. "The Most Democratic Branch," from *The Most Democratic Branch: How the Courts Serve America* (New York: Oxford University Press, 2005), pp. 19–44. Reprinted with permission.

Schattschneider, E. E. "The Scope and Bias of the Pressure System," from *The Semi-Sovereign People Re-Issue*, (Holt, Rinehart and Winston, 1960), pp. 20–24, 27–32, 34–35, 38–39. © 1975 Wadsworth, a part of Cengage learning, Inc. Reproduced by permission. www.cengage.com/permissions

Schickler, Eric. "Institutional Development of Congress," from *The Legislative Branch*, ed. Paul J. Quirk and Sarah Binder, (Oxford and New York: Oxford University Press, 2004), 35–37, 45–49, 51–59. Reprinted with permission.

Skocpol, Theda and Vanessa Williamson. *The Tea Party and the Remaking of Republican Conservatism* (New York: Oxford University Press, 2012), pp. 155–156, 169–171, 185–188. Reprinted with permission of Oxford University Press.

Skowronek, Stephen. "The Conservative Insurgency and Presidential Power: A Developmental Perspective on the Unitary Executive," *Harvard Law Review*, 122:8 (June 2009), pp. 2072–2073, 2075–2080, 2083, 2087, 2092–2100, 2102–2103. Reprinted with permission.

Smith, Rogers M. "The Multiple Traditions in America," from "Beyond Tocqueville, Myrdal, and Hartz: The Multiple Traditions in America," *American Political Science Review*, September 1993, 87: 549–566. Copyright © Cambridge University Press. Reprinted with the permission of Cambridge University Press.

Storing, Herbert, ed., "What the Anti-Federalists Were For," from *The Complete Anti-Federalist*, vol. 1 (Chicago: University of Chicago Press, 1981), pp. 8–11, 15–16, 28–30, 56–57, 65, 67–69. © 1981 by The University of Chicago. Reprinted with permission.

Sunstein, Cass. "Polarization and Cybercascades," from *Republic.com 2.0* (Princeton, N.J.: Princeton University Press, 2007), pp. 46–96. © 2007 Princeton University Press. Reprinted by permission of Princeton University Press.

Trubowitz, Peter. *Politics and Strategy: Partisan Ambition and American Statecraft* (Princeton, N.J.: Princeton University Press, 2011), pp. 2–3, 8, 12–14, 130–136, 145–149. Reprinted with permission of Princeton University Press.

Truman, Harry S. "Annual Message to the Congress on the State of the Union," January 9, 1952. Online by Gerhard Peters and John T. Woolley, *The American Presidency Project*. http://www.presidency.ucsb.edu/ws/?pid=14418 (accessed June 8, 2013).

United States Supreme Court. *Brown v. Board of Education*, 347 U.S. 483. Accessed from http://www.nationalcenter.org/brown.html on November 11, 2008.

——. *Marbury* v. *Madison* 5 U.S. 137 (1803). Accessed from http://www.lectlaw.com/files/case14.htm on January 24, 2009.

——. *New York Times v. Sullivan*, 376 U.S. 254 (1964).

——. *New York Times v. United States*, 403 U.S. 713 (1971). Accessed from http://www.bc.edu/bc_org/avp/cas/comm/free_speech/nytvus.html on December 30, 2008.

——. *Plessy v. Ferguson*, 163 U.S. 537. Accessed from http://www.bgsu.edu/departments/acs/1890s/plessy/majority.html on November 11, 2008.

Valelly, Richard M. "Institutions and Enfranchisement," from *The Two Reconstructions: The Struggle for Black Enfranchisement* (Chicago: University of Chicago Press, 2004), pp. 225–250. © 2004 by The University of Chicago. Reprinted with permission.

Verba, Sidney. "The Citizen as Respondent: Sample Surveys and American Democracy" (1995). *The American Political Science Review*, Vol. 90, No. 1 (March, 1996), pp. 1–7. Reprinted with permission of Cambridge University Press.

Washington, George. "Farewell Address to the People of the United States," September 19, 1796. http://avalon.law.yale.edu/18th_century/washing.asp (accessed June 11, 2013).

The Webster-Hayne Debates. January 19–27, 1830. http://www.constitution.org/hwdebate/hwdebate.htm (accessed June 11, 2013).

Weir, Margaret. "States, Race, and the Decline of New Deal Liberalism," *Studies in American Political Development*, 19:2 (Fall, 2005), 157, 163–166, 169–172. Copyright © Cambridge University Press. Reprinted with the permission of Cambridge University Press.

Wilson, James Q. "Constraints," from *Bureaucracy: What Government Agencies Do and Why They Do It* (Basic Books, 1989), pp. 113–115, 120–121, 129, 131–133. Copyright © 1989 by Basic Books, Inc. Reprinted by permission of Basic Books, a member of Perseus Books Group.

Wilson, Woodrow. "The Study of Administration," *Political Science Quarterly*, vol. 2, no. 2, June 1887, pp. 197–222.

Winthrop, John. "A Model of Christian Charity" (1630). http://religiousfreedom.lib.virginia.edu/sacred/charity.html (Accessed June 11, 2013).

——. "Little Speech on Liberty" (1645).

Wolfsfeld, Gadi. *Making Sense of Media and Politics* (Routledge, 2011), pp. 9–12, 17–21. Reprinted with permission.

Wood, Gordon S. "The Founders and the Creation of Modern Public Opinion," in *Revolutionary Characters: What Made the Founders Different* (New York: Penguin, 2006), pp. 243–248, 267–274.